Macroeconomic Volatility, Institutions and Financial Architectures

Other books by José María Fanelli

José María Fanelli and Rohinton Medhora (*editors*)
FINANCIAL REFORM IN DEVELOPING COUNTRIES

José María Fanelli and Gary McMahon (*editors*)
UNDERSTANDING MARKET REFORMS
Volume 1: Philosophy, Politics and Stakeholders

José María Fanelli and Gary McMahon (*editors*)
UNDERSTANDING MARKET REFORMS
Volume 2: Motivation, Implementation and Sustainability

José María Fanelli (*editor*)
UNDERSTANDING MARKET REFORMS IN LATIN AMERICA
Similar Reforms, Diverse Constituencies, Varied Results

José María Fanelli and Rohinton Medhora (*editors*)
FINANCE AND COMPETITIVENESS IN DEVELOPING COUNTRIES

Macroeconomic Volatility, Institutions and Financial Architectures

The Developing World Experience

Edited by José María Fanelli

palgrave macmillan

First published 2008 by
PALGRAVE MACMILLAN
Houndmills, Basingstoke, Hampshire RG21 6XS and
175 Fifth Avenue, New York, N.Y. 10010
Companies and representatives throughout the world

PALGRAVE MACMILLAN is the global academic imprint of the Palgrave Macmillan division of St. Martin's Press, LLC and of Palgrave Macmillan Ltd. Macmillan® is a registered trademark in the United States, United Kingdom and other countries. Palgrave is a registered trademark in the European Union and other countries.

ISBN 13: 978–0–230–54280–8 hardback
ISBN 10: 0–230–54280–8 hardback

This book is printed on paper suitable for recycling and made from fully managed and sustained forest sources. Logging, pulping and manufacturing processes are expected to conform to the environmental regulations of the country of origin.

A catalogue record for this book is available from the British Library.

Library of Congress Cataloging-in-Publication Data

Macroeconomic volatility, institutions and financial architectures : the developing world experience / edited by José María Fanelli.
p. cm.
Includes bibliographical references and index.
ISBN 0–230–54280–8 (alk. paper)
1. Macroeconomics. 2. Financial institutions–Developing countries 3. Developing countries–Economic policy. I. Fanelli, José María.

HB172.5.M3334 2007
339–dc22 2007022511

10 9 8 7 6 5 4 3 2 1
17 16 15 14 13 12 11 10 09 08

Printed and bound in Great Britain by
CPI Antony Rowe, Chippenham and Eastbourne

Contents

List of Figures

List of Tables

Acknowledgements

I am grateful to the following individuals for serving as referees for the papers in the volume and for their valuable comments on them: Ramiro Albrieu, Gustavo Cañonero, Rodrigo Cárcamo, Eduardo Corso, Jane D'Arista, Brent Herbert-Copley, Daniel Heymann, Alejandro Jara, Martín Gonzalez Rozada, Brian Kahn, Ari Kuncoro, Leong Liew, Leonardo Martínez Díaz, Rohinton Medhora, Ejeviome Eloho Otobo, Benu Schneider, Shari Spiegel, Rogerio Studart, Jomo Kwame Sundaram and Rob Vos. I would like to express my gratitude to IDRC for their financial support and to the editorial staff at Palgrave. Finally, I wish to thank Laura Pakter for her invaluable assistance.

Notes on Contributors

Adeola Adenikinju is a Reader in the Department of Economics, University of Ibadan, Ibadan, Nigeria. His research interests include growth, energy and petroleum economics, trade and industrial economics. He has published extensively in reputable national and international journals. He was a Visiting Scholar to the Research Department of the International Monetary Fund, Washington, DC in 1996 and 2005.

S. Ibi Ajayi is a Professor of Economics at the University of Ibadan, Ibadan, Nigeria. His areas of specialization are macroeconomics and monetary economics. He has published widely in reputable national and international journals on different aspects of these areas. He has consulted for a number of international organizations over the years including the World Bank, World Health Organization and the Economic Commission for Africa. He has been Visiting Scholar at various times to the Research Department of the International Monetary Fund.

Melvin Ayogu is Dean of Commerce and Professor of Economics at the University of Cape Town. An Associate of the Chartered Institute of Bankers in London, he has held positions at James Madison University, Harrisonburg, Virginia, and the University of Jos in Nigeria, and has published widely in the areas of banking, international finance, governance (civil and corporate), and economic development. His current research focus is political economy and infrastructure.

Getúlio Borges da Silveira Filho holds a PhD in statistics from the London School of Economics and Political Sciences. He is professor and researcher at the Universidade Federal do Rio de Janeiro.

Fernando J. Cardim de Carvalho is consultant at the Instituto Brasileiro de Análises Sociais e Econômicas and professor at the Universidade Federal do Rio de Janeiro. He specializes in economic theory in asset choice, indexation, and post-Keynesian economics. He holds a PhD from Rutgers-State University of New Jersey.

Hashem Dezhbakhsh is Professor of Economics at Emory University and currently at the American University of Sharjah. He is also a regular visiting faculty at the University of Cape Town. Dr Dezhbakhsh's articles have appeared in the *Journal of Econometrics*, the *Review of Economics and Statistics*, the *Journal of Financial and Quantitative Analysis*, and the *American Economic Review*. Dr Dezhbakhsh is the recipient of several teaching awards including Emory University's Williams Distinguished Teaching Award and the Ohio State University's Outstanding

Teaching Award. He has served as Department Chair and Director of Undergraduate Studies at Emory University.

José María Fanelli is Senior Researcher at CEDES, Argentina. He holds a PhD in economics from the University of Buenos Aires. He specializes in the analysis of macroeconomic and financial problems in developing countries and has published numerous academic articles and several books on these topics. He has been actively involved in the establishment of permanent research networks in the Latin American region.

Stephany Griffith-Jones is a Professor of Economics at the Institute of Development Studies, University of Sussex. She holds a PhD from Cambridge University. Her work focuses on global capital flows with special reference to flows to emerging markets; macroeconomic management of capital flows in Latin America, Eastern Europe and sub-Saharan Africa; proposals for international measures to diminish volatility of capital flows and reduce the likelihood of currency crises; analysis of national and international capital markets.

Igal Magendzo is the Manager of the Macroeconomic Analysis Unit of the Central Bank of Chile. He obtained his BA from the Hebrew University of Jerusalem and his PhD in economics at UCLA. He has published in specialized international journals, such as the *International Journal of Finance and Economics* and the *Journal of Money Credit and Banking*. Dr Magendzo also teaches macroeconomics at the Universidad de Chile.

José Antonio Ocampo has a BA degree in economics and sociology from the University of Notre Dame, and a PhD in economics from Yale University. Former Executive Secretary of the UN Economic Commission for Latin America and the Caribbean (ECLAC), he became the United Nations Under-Secretary-General for Economic and Social Affairs on 1 September 2003. As such, he heads the UN Department of Economic and Social Affairs (DESA), which is responsible for the follow-up to the major United Nations Summits and Conferences, and services the UN Economic and Social Council (ECOSOC) and the Second and Third Committees of the General Assembly. He also chairs the UN Executive Committee on Economic and Social Affairs.

Yung Chul Park is Research Professor and Director of the Center of International Commerce and Finance Graduate School of International Studies, Seoul National University. He is Co-Chairman of the Korean Public Fund Oversight Committee. He has published several academic articles and books on monetary theory and international finance. He holds a PhD in economics from the University of Minnesota.

Anatoliy Peresetsky is a professor at New Economic School and Central Economics and Mathematics Institute of Russian Academy of Science. Among his publications are *Econometrics. First Course* (with J. Magnus and P. Katyshev) (2005, 7th edition, in Russian); 'Probability of Default Models of Russian Banks' (with A.M. Karminsky and S.V. Golovan), BOFIT Discussion Papers No 21/2004 (2004); 'An Analysis of Ratings of Russian Banks' (with A.H.O. van Soest and A.M. Karminsky), Tilburg University Center Discussion Paper Series no. 85 (2003); 'The Development of the GKO Futures Market in Russia' (with G. Turmuhambetova and G. Urga), *Emerging Markets Review*, 2(1) (2001).

Piriya Pholphirul is Assistant Professor of Economics at the School of Development Economics of the National Institute of Development Administration (NIDA). He attended Chulalongkorn University, Thailand, where he received a BA in economics, focusing on international economics and development. He worked at Siam Cement Group in Bangkok, and then received an MS in policy economics from the University of Illinois at Urbana-Champaign, US. He holds a PhD in economics from Georgia State University, US. Before joining NIDA, Piriya was a research specialist under the International Economic Relations Program in TDRI. His research interests cover a range of topics in international economics, macroeconomic development, behavioral economics, and economics of the service sector.

Francisco Eduardo Pires de Souza is Professor of Economics at the Universidade Federal do Rio de Janeiro and the Universidade Federal Fluminense. He is a researcher at the Instituto Brasileiro de Geografia e Estadística and of the Financiadora de Estudos e Projetos. He specializes in monetary and fiscal economics and holds a PhD from the London School of Economics and Political Sciences.

Vladimir Popov (www.nes.ru/~vpopov) is a professor at the New Economic School in Moscow and a visiting professor at Carleton University in Ottawa. He is the author of many books and articles, including 'The Turning Point: Revitalizing the Soviet Economy' (1990), also published in Russian and Korean, co-authored with Nikolai Shmelev; 'The Asian Crisis Turns Global' (1999), also published in Russian, co-authored with Manuel Montes; 'Transition and Institutions: the Experience of Late Reformers' (2001), co-edited with G. A. Cornia; and 'Three Drops of Water: Notes on China by a Non-Sinologist' (2002)

Andrés Rius is Team Leader of the Globalization, Growth and Poverty PI. He is based at IDRC's Regional Office for Latin America and the Caribbean (Montevideo). He holds MA and PhD degrees in economics from the University of Notre Dame. His interests include political-economic analysis of economic policies, processes of institutional reform in less developed countries, macroeconomic policy, and public sector economics. He has published on those subjects and taught at the Universidad de la República (Uruguay) and the Universidad Católica del Uruguay

Liliana Rojas-Suarez is a Senior Fellow at the Center for Global Development. She is also the Chair of the Latin American Shadow Financial Regulatory Committee. She has served as Managing Director and Chief Economist for Latin America at Deutsche Bank. She has also held high-level positions at the International Monetary Fund and the Inter-American Development Bank. Dr Rojas-Suarez has also been a professor at Anahuac University in Mexico and testified before the US Senate on the issue of dollarization in Latin America. Dr Rojas-Suarez has published widely in the areas of finance and macroeconomics. She holds a PhD from the University of Western Ontario.

Dr Esther Y.P. Shea is a Lecturer in Economics at the School of Accounting and Finance, the Hong Kong Polytechnic University. Her major areas of research are the political economy of policymaking in transition economies and China's agricultural and trade policies.

Daniel Titelman is the Chief of the Development Studies Unit of the Economic Commission for Latin America and the Caribbean. He holds a PhD from the University of California San Diego UCSD, and has a Masters degree from the Latin American Faculty of Social Science. He has published a variety of articles in specialized journals on issues related to macroeconomics, financial issues, and social policies. He has also contributed chapters in various books

Pakorn Vichyanond is Research Director of the Macroeconomic Policy Program at the Thailand Development Research Institute (TDRI). Following his high school graduation, he won a King of Thailand's Scholarship to attend undergraduate studies at Williams College, Massachusetts, US, where he majored in economics and mathematics. His subsequent PhD in economics from Harvard University was sponsored by fellowships from the Bank of Thailand and the Ford Foundation. Before joining TDRI, he worked with research teams at the Bank of Thailand, the World Bank, and private consulting firms.

Yunjong Wang is currently the Vice-President of the Sk Research Institute. He has been a consultant and adviser for numerous projects and committees of the Korean government. He has been a visiting scholar to the IMF. He has served as a consultant to various international organizations including ADB, ADBI and the United Nations. He has published many books and articles in various professional journals, mainly focusing on regional financial arrangements and integration, new international financial architecture, and international finance. He has recently been involved with the ASEM (Asia-Europe Meeting) Kobe Research Project, China-Japan-South Korea Financial Cooperation Symposium, and various ASEAN+3 financial and monetary cooperation projects.

Dr Harry X. Wu is an Associate Professor of Economics at the School of Accounting and Finance, the Hong Kong Polytechnic University and a Research Associate at the Groningen Growth and Development Centre, University of Groningen, the

Netherlands. His publications cover diverse areas of the Chinese economy, especially regarding the measurement of China's growth and productivity.

Doo Yong Yang is the head of the International Finance Department of the Korea Institute for International Economic Policy. He holds a PhD from the University of Colorado at Boulder. His main publications include 'Exchange Rate Arrangements in East Asia', coauthored with Eiji Ogawa; 'Time-varying Risk Premium in the Foreign Exchange Markets: ARCH-in-mean Approach', *Korean Journal of International Economics* (1996); 'Real Exchange Rates and the Terms of Trade: the Korean Capital Market Liberalization', AEA meeting proceedings paper (1994); and 'Is it a Peso Problem or a Risk Premium?' the Research of Korean Economy, 1999.

List of Abbreviations

ABF	Asian Bond Fund
ABF2	Second Asian Bond Fund
ABI	Asian Bond Initiative
ABMI	Asian Bond Market Initiative
AC	Advisory Committees
ACFB	Almanac of China's Finance and Banking
ADB	Asian Development Bank
AFI	Asian Financial Institute
AFPs	Administradoras de Fondos de Pensiones
AFTA	ASEAN free trade area
AMCs	Asset Management Corporations
AMF	Arab Monetary Fund
APEC	Asia-Pacific Economic Cooperation
ASA	ASEAN Swap Arrangement
ASEAN	Association of Southeast Asian Nations
BASIC	Bonds-Auditing-Supervision-Information-Credit rating
BCB	Brazilian Central Bank
BFS	Brazilian Financial System
BIBF	Bangkok International Banking Facility
BIS	Bank of International Settlements
BOFIA	Banks and Other Financial Institutions Act
BOFID	Bank and Other Financial Institutions Decree
BSA	Bilateral swap agreements
CBN	Central Bank of Nigeria
CBO	Collateralized bond obligations
CBR	Central Bank of Russia
CCL	Contingent credit line
CFF	Compensatory financial facility
CMI	Chiang Mai Initiative
CNI	Confederação Nacional da Indústria (Brazil)
CODELCO	Corporación Nacional del Cobre
CPE	Centrally planned economy
CPSS	Committee on Payment and Settlement System
CSF	Copper Stabilization Fund
CSI	Contractual savings institutions
CVM	Brazilian Securities Exchange Commission
DFA	Domestic financial architecture
DTI	Department of Trade and Industry
ECAs	Export credit agencies
ECB	European Central Bank

EMBI	Emerging Markets Bond Index
EMEAP	Executives Meeting of East Asia-Pacific Central Banks
EMI	EU Commission and European Monetary Institute
EMS	European monetary system
EMU	European Economic and Monetary Union
EPU	European Payments Union
ERM	European Exchange Rate Mechanism
ESF	Exogenous Shocks Facility
ETF	Exchange Traded Fund
EWMA	Exponentially weighted moving average
FATF	Financial Action Task Force
FCF	Fixed capital formation
FDI	Foreign direct investment
FFR	Federal Reserve Funds Rate
FIDF	Financial Institutions Development Fund
FLAR	Latin American Reserve Fund
FoBF	Fund of Bond Funds
FOREX	Foreign exchange reserves
FRA	Financial Sector Restructuring Authority
FS	Financial Sector
FS&R	Financial Services and Regulation
FSB	Financial Services Board
FSF	Financial Stability Forum
FSMP	Financial sector master plan
FSU	Former Soviet Union
FSU	Financial Stability Unit
FTA	Free trade area
GARCH	Generalized autoregressive conditional heteroskedasticity
GATS	General Agreement on Trade in Services
GCE	Government consumption expenditure
GCF	Gross capital formation
GDDS	General Data Dissemination System
GDP	Gross domestic product
HCE	Household consumption expenditure
HHI	Herfindahl-Hirschman Index
H-P	Hodrick-Prescott
IAS	International Accounting Standards
IBGE	Instituto Brasileiro de Geografia e Estadística (Brazil)
IDB	Inter-American Development Bank
IFA	International financial architecture
IFIs	International financial institutions
IIT	Intra-industry trade
IMF	International Monetary Fund
IOSCO	International Organization of Securities Commissions
IPO	Initial public offering

IRB	Internal ratings-based
ISA	International Standards on Auditing
LFT	Letras Financeiras do Tesouro (Brazil)
MDBs	Multilateral development banks
MDG	Millennium Development Goals
MDIC	Ministério do Desenvolvimento, Indústria e Comércio (Brazil)
MERCOSUR	Mercado Común del Sur
MOF	Ministry of Finance (China)
MOU	Memorandum of understanding
MPR	Monetary Policy Rate
MPS	Material Product System (China)
NBFI	Non-Bank Financial Intermediaries
NBS	National Bureau of Statistics (China)
NDIC	National Deposit Insurance Company (Nigeria)
NDIC	Nigeria Deposit Insurance Corporation
NESDB	National Economic and Social Development Board (Thailand)
NFGS	Non-financial public sector
NFPS	Non-financial private sector
NIDA	National Institute of Development Administration (Thailand)
NIEs	Newly industrializing economy
NPB	Net borrowing by the public authorities
NPLs	Non-performing loans
OECD	Organization for Economic Co-operation and Development
OMO	Open market operations (Nigeria)
OPEC	Organization of the Petroleum Exporting Countries
OTC	Over-the-counter
PAIF	Pan-Asian Bond Index Fund
PBC	People's Bank of China
PCF	Net private capital flows
PPPs	Purchasing power parities
PRGF	Poverty Reduction and Growth Facility
PROER	Programa de Estímulo à Reestruturacão e ao Fortalecimento do Sistema Financeiro Nacional (Brazil)
PROES	Programa de Incentivo ã Redução do Setor Público Estadual na Atividade Bancária (Brazil)
QFII	Qualified foreign institutional investors
RAL	Reserve Augmentation Line
RB	Registrar of Banks (South Africa)
RER	Real exchange rate
RFAs	Regional Financial Arrangements
RFF	Registrar of Financial Institutions (South Africa)
RMB	Renminbi (China)
ROC	Registrar of Companies (South Africa)
ROSCs	Reports on the Observance of Standards and Codes
SAP	Structural adjustment program

SARB	South African Reserve Bank
SCO	Shanghai Cooperation Organization
SDSS	Special Data Dissemination Standard
SEC	Nigeria Securities and Exchange Commission
SELIC	Central bank target basic interest rate (Brazil)
SET	Stock Exchange of Thailand
SF	Stabilization Fund
SMEs	Small- and medium-sized enterprises
SNA	System of National Accounts (China)
SOE	State-owned enterprise
SPC	State Planning Commission (China)
SPSE	Sao Paulo Stock Exchange (Brazil)
SRF	Supplemental Reserve Facility
TB	Trade balance
TDRI	Thailand Development Research Institute
TOT	Terms of trade
UF	Unidad de Fomento
UNDP	United Nations Development Programme
VaR	Value at risk models
VAT	Value added tax
WB	World Bank
WTO	World Trade Organization

1
Macro Volatility and Financial Institutions

José María Fanelli

1.1 Introduction

In the 1980s and 1990s many developing countries enthusiastically opened their capital accounts and implemented programs to deregulate their domestic financial markets. This enthusiasm, however, is currently waning. One important reason is that the deregulation of domestic financial markets was frequently associated with financial turmoil and increased exposure to changes in market sentiment. Neither the rules of the game designed for the domestic financial architecture (DFA) nor the institutions of the international financial architecture (IFA) could effectively cope with certain financial disequilibria.

It is now accepted that building DFA institutions can be much more difficult than had been envisaged and that this is no isolated exercise; the DFA must be consistent with the existing IFA. The complexity and scale of the institution-building tasks involved can be illustrated on the basis of Figure 1.1.

Figure 1.1 represents the DFA as the union of two rectangles: one containing the elements of the financial infrastructure and the other showing the components of the macroeconomic regime that are relevant for a broadly defined DFA. The third rectangle at the top represents the IFA institutions. The rectangle on the left-hand side lists the elements of the financial structure that constitute the DFA. They are the legal and judiciary infrastructure, the regulatory framework, and the host of practices and policies affecting the structure, conduct, and performance of financial institutions and corporate governance. The components of the macroeconomic regime (right-hand rectangle) refer to those elements that impinge on the management of non-diversifiable national risk, which are associated with the country's election concerning the trilemma (Frankel, 1999) and the nominal anchor for financial contracts: the regimes for the exchange rate, monetary policy, and the capital account. The figure places the IFA/DFA linkages at center stage to underscore that in building the institutions of the DFA, the authorities cannot overlook IFA influence. The IFA institutions influence the DFA institutions through three channels: (1) the adoption of standards and codes (for example, the Basel Committee recommendations as a guideline to reform

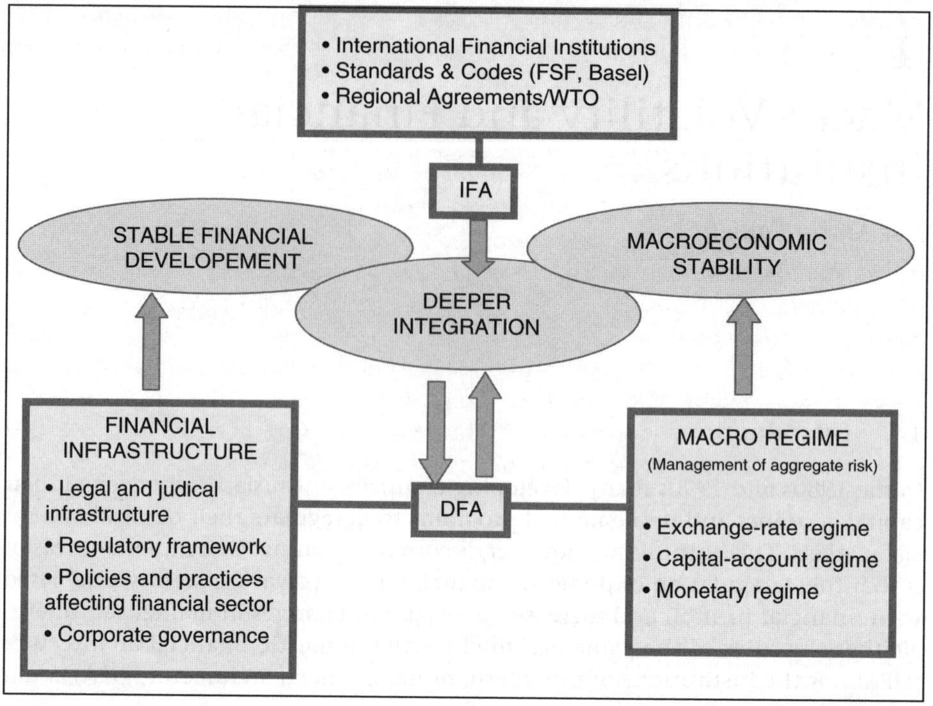

Figure 1.1 DFA and IFA
Source: Fanelli and Medhora (2001).

banking regulations and supervision); (2) the negotiations associated with trade (such as, regional agreements comprising monetary/financial regulations or GATS negotiations on financial services); and (3) the pressure of international institutions like the IMF and the WB favoring liberalization or specific elections concerning the trilemma.

The three ovals show the policy goals associated with the building of the DFA: achieving deeper integration with the global economy, developing financial intermediation in a stable environment, and preserving macroeconomic stability. Although many developing countries have made substantial progress, they have not been able, as a rule, to achieve these goals. The institutional literature has rightly identified inherited institutions as a central obstacle to developing financial institutions that are friendly to these goals (Acemoglu et al., 2004). This literature, however, has overlooked the role of a key feature of developing countries: high aggregate volatility. When financial institutions are weak *and* volatility is high, reformers face a somewhat paradoxical challenge: how to manage volatility while building the very rules of the game that are key to mitigating and managing the consequences of aggregate risk. Indeed, under these conditions, volatility and institutions can interact in a highly non-linear way, which frequently results in vicious circles and crises.

More specifically, the arguments that led us to conclude that the interactions between volatility and financial institutions matter to the building and functioning of the DFA can be summarized as follows:

- Financial reforms and opening are institution-building exercises.
- To understand these exercises it is critical to take into account that developing countries' initial conditions typically include:
  - Marked aggregate volatility with crisis events;
  - Weak overall institutional infrastructure;
  - Deficient integration with international financial markets and institutions.
- Under these initial conditions, the structures of governance of financial transactions tend to be weak and, in turn, reduce the level of financial deepening.
- When financial deepening is low, the available means (that is, market instruments, policies) for coping with uncertainty are rudimentary.
- Building the institutions of the DFA and strengthening the linkages with the IFA under these circumstances is difficult because the ability to manage shocks and policy errors during the institution-building process is limited.

These hypotheses imply that:

- There is a bi-directional causality between volatility and institutions: high volatility and crises contribute to deteriorating the rules of the financial game; weak institutions reduce financial deepening and the ability to manage risks; and this feeds aggregate volatility.

What should the strategies of domestic financial institution-building be in light of this bi-directional linkage between volatility and institutions? What contribution could the institutions of the IFA make? The project 'International Financial Architecture, Macro Volatility, and Institutions: the Developing World Experience' – which was sponsored by the International Development Research Centre – addressed a number of issues that are closely associated with these questions. Its main purpose was to understand the process of building the institutions of the DFA and the linkages with the IFA under volatile conditions. The project produced eight country studies that analyzed the DFA-building experiences of Argentina, Brazil, Chile, China, Nigeria, Russia, South Africa, and Thailand; and four thematic papers, which drew implications for building a development friendly IFA. This volume presents the thematic papers (Chapters 2–5) and the country studies (Chapters 6–13). In the rest of this introduction we will present the analytical arguments that sustain the hypothesis that volatility matters to financial institution-building and provide an overview of the research results and policy implications.

In the remainder of this chapter, we have decomposed the bi-directional causal path connecting aggregate volatility with the DFA institutions into four steps (see Figure 1.2).

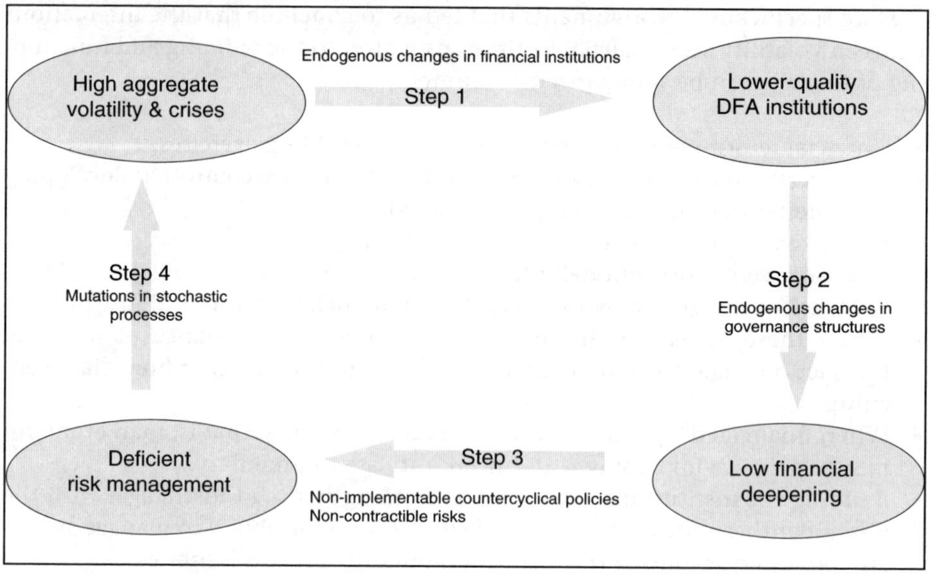

Figure 1.2 Financial institutions and aggregate volatility

- *Step 1:* Aggregate volatility and a crisis-prone environment induce instability in the rules of the financial game, which worsens the quality of the DFA institutions.
- *Step 2:* Agents adapt contracts and financial organizations (hierarchies) to operate under weak DFA and excess volatility and this results in financial underdevelopment.
- *Step 3:* Under low financial deepening, some risks are non-contractible and key countercyclical policies become non-implementable; this poses strong constraints on risk management.
- *Step 4:* Deficient risk management affects the 'deep' parameters that define the shock-generating stochastic process; this typically results in higher aggregate volatility and crises.

Sections 1.2–1.5 analyze the four steps of the bi-directional causal path connecting volatility and financial institutions; Section 1.6 summarizes the research findings on the basis of five propositions and the final section discusses the implications for the goal of achieving a more development-friendly IFA.

1.2 Step 1: Aggregate volatility has a bearing on the quality of the DFA institutions

One obstacle to operationalizing the hypotheses of the project was the ambiguity in the common usage of the terms 'volatility' and 'crisis'. Should we identify volatility with total variability or only with the portion of variability that is unanticipated? What do agents know about the probability distribution of the uncertain portion of variability? And what is the relationship between volatility and crises? We will first address these questions and then elaborate on the implications for the (in)stability of the rules of the game that make up the DFA.

The overwhelming majority of the studies on aggregate volatility in developing countries utilize the standard deviation of output growth as the proxy for volatility. This is particularly true of panel data studies (Mobarak, 2005). Another commonly used measure of volatility is the standard deviation of the fluctuations of a given magnitude around its central trend.[1] The standard deviation measures the total variability of a given variable. So, the authors who use standard deviations identify volatility – implicitly or explicitly – with total variability, as is the case with panel data studies or a good part of the macroeconomic literature on cyclical movements (for example, Easterly et al., 2000). Some authors, however, identify volatility with the unanticipated part of the stochastic process (for example, Servén, 1998; Stock and Watson, 2003). In this regard, Servén (1998) emphasizes that what matters to risk is the innovation in the variable under analysis. He argues that the conditional variance of the innovations in the process is a more accurate measure and proposes using a GARCH model to approximate this concept.

It is undeniable that it is the innovation in the process that matters when evaluating risk. For example, a risk-averse individual who is trying to smooth the future consumption path will consider unanticipated fluctuations in income and will use insurance or financial markets to stabilize it across states of nature. If transaction costs were zero, it would be wrong to identify the entire variability of a given process with uncertainty, overlooking the distinction between predictable and non-predictable movements of the variable. This point is not that clear, however, when transaction costs and 'true' uncertainty enter the picture.

If transaction costs were not zero and some market imperfections existed, even if we were prepared to assume that individuals base their predictions on the best available model of the stochastic process, we would see non-optimal plans implemented. Since individuals use markets to smooth all kinds of fluctuations, non-optimality will characterize transactions involving both uncertain *and* anticipated fluctuations; for example, agents could face difficulties in reallocating fully-anticipated income flows across time. Under these circumstances, if we were to calculate the economic costs of volatility taking into account only those uncertain fluctuations reflected in, say, the conditional variance of innovations, we would be underestimating the economic costs associated with aggregate fluctuations; we would be overlooking the fact that market imperfections preclude the agent from smoothing perfectly anticipated fluctuations. Optimal allocation calls for both the knowledge of the parameters of the stochastic process (be it either the parameters defining the 'deterministic' portion or the parameters governing the innovations) *and* a reasonably complete market structure. When this latter condition does not hold because of financial underdevelopment, agents are *market-constrained* and both anticipated and unanticipated fluctuations can impose economic costs on the agent; it follows that we cannot say a priori that total variability is a worse approximation to the economic costs of volatility than a measure of pure innovations.

In developing countries, agents frequently face situations of uncertainty rather than risk.[2] In particular, one important reason why developing countries are more volatile is that structural changes occur frequently. Permanent innovations can be thought of as drawings from a new distribution in the sense that each drawing signals a permanent change in the parameters of the process while transitory disturbances can be thought of as drawings from a known distribution (Dehn, 2000). In reality, under conditions of high volatility, it is extremely difficult for the decision-maker to decide whether the specific event that she has observed represents a drawing from a given or a new probability distribution. The traditional view of risk assumes that all disturbances are transitory and, hence, pertain to the same unconditional distribution, although predictable events may be governed by a transitory conditional distribution. Risk is a stationary concept. Under these circumstances, although ex post the agents may modify their expectations on the basis of the new conditional distribution, there is no ex ante role for unexpected 'structural' breaks, that is, for shocks that permanently change the parameters of the model. In this regard, structural changes in the unconditional parameters of the stochastic process and uncertainty in the sense of Knight are closely associated.[3] By definition, structural changes in the deep (unconditional) parameters cannot be anticipated. The agents will thus be uninsured against such a specific contingency because they cannot contract insurance against a contingency about which they know nothing.

If the uninsured contingency has no important effects on the agents' net worth, this means that the costs of wrong economic decisions induced by wrong beliefs about the stochastic structure of the economy are minor. But if errors are large and irreversible, and the agents are market-constrained, the effects are likely to be long lasting. For one thing, it will take time for individuals to learn what the new conditions are and to rearrange those contractual obligations that have not been honored. Likewise, when agents are uninsured against some contingencies because they are market constrained, an innovation – especially a sizable one – drawn from a known distribution could also induce irreversible effects on the agent's net worth. For an uninsured agent, a transitory shock can have permanent effects. According to Wolf (2004b), the shock size matters because coping mechanisms may fail once shocks have exceeded some critical threshold. In sum, these consequences of uncertainty and market imperfections suggest that under certain circumstances not only unanticipated but also a good part of anticipated variability matters in assessing the effects of volatility.

The country studies in this volume provide evidence that volatility and crises are intimately associated. This is in line with Wolf (2004b); using cross-country data he shows that a positive association exists between output growth volatility (and terms of trade volatility) and the number of crisis episodes a country experiences. Given that developing countries are more volatile than industrialized ones, it follows that the former are more crisis-prone than the latter. Notwithstanding, one important flaw in the literature on crises in developing countries is that 'crisis' and the relationship between different 'crises' have rarely been explicitly defined. Some authors define the concept of crisis empirically. Wolf (2004a), for example, distinguishes between normal volatility and extreme volatility or crisis. The latter corresponds to observations that might have been drawn from either the tails of the distribution or from a different source. He argues that determining which case it is can be a rather subjective matter. He defines as extreme those observations that go beyond an absolute threshold (say, changes of more than 10 per cent) or a distributional threshold (5 per cent largest declines) or a deviation criterion (2 standard deviations above the mean). More specifically, in the case of aggregate fluctuations, crisis is defined as two sequential years of negative output growth and normal volatility as the difference between the 25th and the 75th percentile of growth rate distribution.

Given that no theoretically sound definition of the term exists, our project adopted a pragmatic approach based on Wolf's empirical and quantitative criteria. However, the country studies also identified a number of qualitative dimensions of crises that are central to comprehending the institutional disarrays that high volatility can create; the most relevant features pinpointed in the studies and presented in this volume can be summarized as follows: (a) crises induce non-anticipated and irreversible changes; (b) agents are typically un-hedged with respect to this kind of innovation; (c) crises usually call for across-the-board changes in the governance structures that rule financial transactions; and (d) crises are likely to lead ultimately to significant changes in the DFA institutions and their linkages with the IFA. We will now discuss some analytical issues that are relevant to accounting for these facts and the reasons why high volatility and crises can give rise to institutional instability.

Financial governance structures have to do with the means of infusing order and mitigating conflict in a financial transaction, embracing both the upper-level rules of the game (laws, regulations, informal rules) and more specific governance structures (contracts and organizations). We call the rules of the financial game 'financial institutions' and identify them with the rules that make up the DFA and the linkages connecting the DFA with the IFA; we make a distinction between these upper rules and the micro-level governance structures, which make up the financial structure. We will now argue that volatility and, a fortiori, crises, can affect not only the micro-level governance structures but also the upper-level institutional hierarchy and can, therefore, generate 'large-scale' disorder in financial transactions, fueling conflict and institutional instability.

Structural shocks typically call for adaptations in governance structures. According to Williamson (2005), it is precisely unprogrammed disturbances that call for unprogrammed adaptations that make the governance issue interesting. More generally, note that it is because of the existence of non-insured contingencies that governance structures are deployed in the first place: for in the ex post contract implementation interval a shock can call for adaptations of the ex ante terms of the financial transaction relationship between the parties. This places transaction costs at center stage and is in line with Merton and Bodie (2004: 8), who state:

> The particular institutions and organization forms that arise within the financial system are an endogenous response to minimize the costs of transactions frictions and behavioral distortions in executing the financial functions common to every economy. As a consequence, in well-functioning financial systems, high transaction costs and dysfunctional cognitive dissonance among individuals may not have a material influence on equilibrium asset prices and risk allocations.

If institutions governing financial transactions are endogenous, why are they so weak in developing countries? What are the factors that impede these structures from becoming endogenously stronger? The literature on the growth–institution linkages has emphasized the role of the polity and historical inheritance, but this implies that financial institutions are exogenous to the characteristics of the macroeconomy (Acemoglu et al., 2004). The country studies in this book explore a different view: the quality of the rules of the game embedded in the DFA is bad because, firstly, high volatility and crises induce rule instability and, second, the authorities have frequently failed in reform attempts because of the extreme difficulty of building institutions under highly volatile and crisis-prone conditions.

The fact that excess volatility and crises are caused by non-contractible events (Caballero, 2003) plays a central role in this regard. Indeed, it is precisely because crises are non-contractible that 'a country's bankruptcy law can be thought of as an ex ante insurance arrangement for these ill-specified non-contractible shocks' (Caballero, 2003: 9). Bankruptcy laws and financial regulations especially tailored to deal with 'emergency situations' in the financial system are part and parcel of the DFA because after the occurrence of a sizable aggregate shock, a large number of adaptations of governance structures will be occurring at the same time, which will simultaneously affect different sectors of the economy and will eventually give rise to spillover effects. Of course, if the redefinition of the governance structures followed the guidelines established ex ante by the DFA 'emergency rules', this would not affect the stability of the upper-level rules. However, the country studies in this volume show that, when a large number of agents are uninsured against the consequences of the aggregate shocks, an aggregate shock can give rise to sizable disequilibria and conflicting claims that have to be dealt with on an ad hoc basis, as was the case with devaluation in Argentina. The ultimate effect of a sizable shock will be, in this way, the appearance of 'broken promises' and a situation in which agents anticipate that the probability of changes in the rules of the game is high, which will deter the agents' willingness to draw up contracts, especially if they are long term. In this way, shock-induced 'broken promises' at the micro level result in 'broken rules' at the upper level. It is no wonder, therefore, that the country studies repeatedly document the occurrence of across-the-board redefinitions of governance structures involving not only private contracts but also upper rules in the hierarchy, which pertain to the DFA and can even involve the linkages with the IFA.

In sum, if developing countries are more volatile, there is a positive correlation between volatility and crises, and these phenomena create institutional instability, a clear implication follows: developing countries must have more unstable institutions and governance structures and, therefore, there must be an inverse relationship between volatility and the quality of the DFA institutions. Of course, one central task in improving this situation is to strengthen the DFA, but this means that the authorities must learn to build institutions under volatile conditions, which are typically associated with distributional conflict. This suggests that to design institution-building under high volatility we need to develop 'the political economy of broken promises', as Leijonhufvud (2003) stated.

1.3 Step 2: The effects of volatility and weak DFA on the financial structure

When true uncertainty related with structural changes is present and the rules that make up the DFA are unstable, market-constrained agents (including policymakers) adapt to operating under such conditions. Step 2 in Figure 1.2 indicates that the agents' adaptive responses result in the perpetuation of low financial deepening. Most of the studies describe a financial context in which low deepening induces severe liquidity constraints, strong financial accelerator effects, weak arbitrage and market segmentation, partial dollarization, shallow markets for long-term instruments, and missing markets for risks transaction. In what follows we discuss some reasons why agents' adaptive responses to volatility can give rise to these financial imperfections.

The country studies portray situations in which, after the occurrence of a sizable shock, agents seem to experience true model uncertainty. This is suggested by the fact that they incur costs in disentangling what is going on (that is, trying to find out what the 'deep parameters' will be once the 'crisis' is gone). For example, it is observed that a good number of agents postpone their investment decisions even if this implies forgoing the opportunities opened in the post-shock situation. Two critical sources of uncertainty are whether the consequences of the shocks will be transitory or permanent and what the reaction of other agents (including the government) will be. Given that a good number of agents will be uninsured, the shock will probably call for a process of recontracting while those who perceive that they are likely to find themselves in an irreversible worse-off situation may push for ex post government assistance. The learning-cum-recontracting process following a sizable shock can be extremely costly for the economy because it can give rise to a lengthy period of disequilibrium in which conflicts of interest will be exacerbated while investment is falling. The studies corresponding to Russia, Nigeria, Argentina, and Thailand provide evidence on this. The authors of the Chilean study, in turn, show that the effects of negative external shocks are not independent of financial deepening. In Chile, the costs were higher in the 1970s and 1980s than in the 1990s and they attribute the difference to the improvement in financial intermediation.

If structural changes and sizable shocks occurred in the past, rational agents will be aware that the conditional and unconditional parameters of the data-generating process can change after the occurrence of a shock[4] and, consequently, it seems reasonable to assume that agents will ex ante adapt governance structures accordingly.

One characteristic adaptive response to excess volatility is the shortening of contracts and the higher preference for liquid assets. In addition, since uncertainty usually erodes the capacity of the domestic currency to anchor nominal values, agents tend to use dollars or other hard currencies to denominate contracts and increase the share of dollarized instruments in their portfolios. Under these conditions, the markets for domestic currency denominated long-term debt disappear or are very thin. Likewise, derivative markets are very rare because of the simultaneous presence of wide price volatility, difficulties in diversifying idiosyncratic risks, and high counter-party risk. When markets for hedging are missing, and key risks may not be hedged, a sizable shock may induce irreversible changes in the agent's net worth and place her in a Ponzi situation.

The country studies document that when volatility is high, a shock can cause the creditors' perception of the debtors' 'true' financial position to change substantially and, as a consequence, liquidity constraints can become much tighter during periods of financial distress. This is in line with the findings of Easterly et al. (2000). They emphasize the role of firms' wealth effects and cash-flow constraints. As a consequence of the negative effects of aggregate shocks on firms' net worth, a good number of firms can go into distress and financial institutions may be less willing to bear risk. Likewise, the cash-flow constraint may be a primary source of concern for a firm facing credit and equity rationing. The likelihood of bankruptcy may become a systemic concern and, under such conditions, a liquidity squeeze can become a problem of solvency, causing viable firms and banks to go bankrupt. Under these circumstances, there may be a fire sale of domestic assets and the costly termination of distressed high net present value projects. This situation is likely to lead to costly negotiations between banks and investors and the termination of customer relations that entail the destruction of informational capital.

Indeed, the adaptive responses of banks to increases in uncertainty in conjunction with dollarization and missing markets for hedging can cause irreversible financial damage to the economy. One example, relevant to the Argentine case, is risk migration.[5] In Argentina in the late 1990s, when the level of perceived systemic risk increased, banks hedged against currency risk and sought a better matching of the duration of assets and liabilities. The counterpart of this was that the firms' liquidity fell and the duration of their liabilities shortened. This augmented the firms' vulnerability, increasing counter-party risk. The ultimate effect of the banks' attempt to hedge was that risk migrated from currency risk to credit risk. This case indicates that when markets are incomplete, a greater amount of risk mitigation by banks can cause the unforeseen losses to migrate quickly from one market to another and, as risk migrates through the system it tends to emerge in its most basic form, as credit risk (Kimbal, 2000). When one takes into account the phenomenon of risk migration and its effects on banks' solvency, the argument about market discipline weakens. According to the market discipline view, a tight credit supply during a downturn is a sign of the financial system's strength because tight credit supply in the face of a recession and high-loan losses are precisely what one would expect from a banking system that is subject to market discipline. The existence of risk migration, however, calls attention to the fact that in a downturn, a financial sector will not necessarily be healthier if it simply transfers its risk to debtors. This behavior by banks can contribute to explaining the high level of sectoral co-movements and procyclicality of aggregate expenditure that is usually observed in developing countries.

When volatility – particularly idiosyncratic volatility – is high, arbitrageurs may find it hard to do their job and their adaptive responses may hinder financial intermediation. Arbitrageurs trade to exploit the mispricing of individual stocks. It is typically assumed that excess returns are eliminated by the action of a large number of investors, each with only a limited exposure to any one set of securities. But Shleifer and Vishny (1995) call attention to the fact that it is highly implausible that there are many diversified arbitrageurs. Arbitrage resources are heavily concentrated in the hands of a few investors that are highly specialized in trading few assets, and far from diversified. In addition, over a short horizon, arbitrage returns are volatile and this risk cannot be hedged. In extreme situations, arbitrageurs trying to eliminate mispricing might lose enough of their money to have to liquidate their positions. This means that they become the least effective at reducing mispricing precisely when the size of mispricing can be the greatest.[6] Arbitrage may become ineffective under extreme circumstances when prices diverge far from fundamental values. Arbitrageurs face risks that are related to idiosyncratic return volatility, not aggregate volatility, and larger pricing errors are possible when idiosyncratic firm-level volatility is high. If we take into account that volatility increases during recessionary periods and it is difficult to diversify in shallow financial markets, it follows that the risks arbitrageurs face will increase substantially in shallow markets experiencing a recessionary period. The power of arbitrage is likely to be minimal under such circumstances because the activity would be extremely risky. The consequences of mispricing could hardly be exaggerated. A reasonable level of arbitrage activity is essential for the market economy to convey reliable information to decision-makers. One way to assess the core role that arbitrage plays in financial markets is to consider the many fundamental conditions that depend on it – from the interest rate parity relation to the Modigliani-Miller and the Fisher separation theorems. If arbitrage does not work well under volatile conditions, it is no wonder that market segmentation and wide price fluctuations detached from fundamentals were routinely documented as part and parcel of the financial experiences studied in the project.

The country studies provide strong evidence that stochastic processes are not stable throughout the cycle and this seems also to be the case in developed countries. Campbell et al. (2000) show that all the components of volatility (aggregate, sectoral- and firm-level) display countercyclical behavior in the United States. They tend to lead to variations in GDP and tend to be higher during recessions. This has important implications for the diversification of risk at different stages of the business cycle: even well-diversified portfolios are exposed to more volatility when the economy turns down and this effect should be stronger for an undiversified portfolio since industry and firm-level volatility increase in economic downturns. It is only natural to hypothesize that the lack of development of the stock-exchange market in the countries under analysis has to do with the adaptive response of risk-averse investors to high and fluctuating levels of volatility.

In sum, our arguments indicate that high volatility can induce significant endogenous changes in both upper-level institutions and micro-governance structures and that this contributes to shaping the structural characteristics of financial markets in developing countries. Figure 1.3 summarizes the arguments concerning Steps 1 and 2 and shows that different combinations of specific stochastic processes with specific market structures will result in dissimilar institutional frameworks and financial governance structures. Policy design should take this fact into account. For example, the figure suggests that it is central to know what the causes are for some specific risks to be non-contractible. When the contingency is non-contractible but the parameters of the process generating the data are known (a 'risk situation'), the risks are insurable from the point of view of society as a whole but uninsurable for individuals because of governance failures. When there is 'true' Knightian uncertainty, in contrast, the stochastic

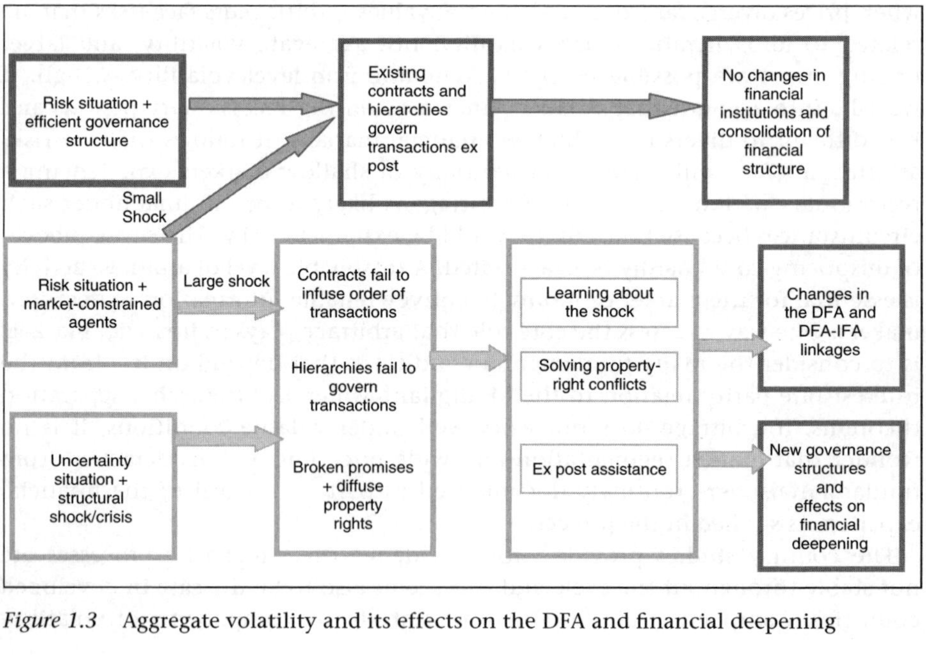

Figure 1.3 Aggregate volatility and its effects on the DFA and financial deepening

process generating the events is unknown either to the individual or to society and, consequently, the risks are not insurable even in a non-market constrained situation. This indicates that reforms aimed at facilitating private risk transaction are likely to be more successful under the first set of conditions than under the second.

1.4 Step 3: Deficient risk management

Risk management has to do with assessing risk and developing strategies to deal with the expected consequences of uncertain outcomes. In the process of managing risks, the agent can choose to bear some or all of the consequences of a particular risk; the risks can be transferred to another party; or other actions can be taken to avoid or reduce the effects of unfavorable outcomes. Transaction costs will largely determine whether risk transactions are organized via markets or hierarchies and the extent to which those opportunities for exchanging risk that are mutually profitable are effectively carried out. The findings of the case studies suggest that when financial deepening is lacking, the efficiency of the risk management outcome is, indeed, low. This is an indication that many risk transactions are non-contractible and that government policies to amend this failure are weak or absent.

We can use the very well-known features of complete-market representative-agent macroeconomic models to identify a number of risk management pitfalls that can give rise to excess aggregate volatility of the kind documented in this volume. Complete-market models assume no market imperfections and, hence, zero transaction costs. As a consequence, the costs of volatility are strictly associated with unpredictable movements in the relevant variables; within the context of an open economy, domestic consumption volatility will be correlated with aggregate world output volatility and domestic consumption volatility will be lower than domestic output volatility.[7] The key point is that aggregate fluctuations do impose costs on the economy but these costs are unavoidable to the extent that mutually advantageous risk trades are exhausted; if all risk trades are *contractible*, rational agents will manage risk optimally.

If we introduce transaction costs and uncertainty, the markets for transacting certain risks will likely be missing and some mutually advantageous trades will not be carried out; some risks will become non-contractible. If, additionally, the institutional structure is weak, countercyclical policies will be difficult to implement or will even be non-implementable. The country studies provide evidence that fiscal policies tend to be pro-cyclical in countries like Nigeria, where government revenues are highly correlated with the terms of trade. Under these conditions, some insurable contingencies will go uninsured, and agents will bear excessive volatility costs.[8]

One important constraint on efficient risk management is that risk unbundling is difficult when financial intermediation is weak. Firms and financial intermediates may not be able to manage specific risks separately by means of hedging each risk in the corresponding market because of the shallowness of derivative markets. For example, exchange rate risks are typically difficult to hedge in developing countries. This contributes to exacerbating the effects of changes in the exchange rate. The literature on financial crisis and twin crises has called attention to balance sheet mismatchings that result in excessive currency risk bearing.

The existence of non-tradable producing sectors has important financial implications within this context. In imperfect markets, appropriate collateral is the key to credit access. But, as Caballero (2000a, 2003) emphasizes, non-tradable producers will not be able to use their non-tradable assets as collateral to access international credit markets.[9] When, say, adverse terms of trade shocks occur, the value of traded goods declines and the quality of the economy's international collateral deteriorates. This reduces the country's borrowing capacity and may also reduce the country's international liquidity. Caballero argues that this factor has a key role as an amplification mechanism of external shocks (such as terms of trade shocks) because domestic agents will not be able to use credit to smooth cash flow fluctuations, be they either anticipated or unanticipated fluctuations. This will affect the stochastic properties of the investment function to the extent that producers will face a tighter liquidity constraint during recessionary periods, when their cash flow falls and they have no fluent access to credit. A consequence repeatedly mentioned in the studies is the abrupt fall in investment, including the interruption of ongoing investment projects.

Another important factor harming the quality of risk management is the difficulty in separating the decisions concerning risk and finance from the decisions about production plans. When the shares of firms are not traded or are listed in thin and illiquid markets, the firm owner typically has to decide whether to bear a higher proportion of the firm's idiosyncratic risks or reduce the exposure through other non-market transactions. If investors are unable to hold well-diversified portfolios, it will not be possible to diversify some portion of those idiosyncratic risks that would be diversifiable in complete markets. This poses strict limits on firms' ability to raise capital in stock markets and, consequently, it is not surprising that firms' leverage tends to be higher in developing countries.

Excessive leverage may compound the pitfalls in risk management. When leverage increases, stockholders bear a greater share of the total cash flow risk of the firm. According to Campbell et al. (2000), this effect was important during the Great Depression. Hence, *ceteris paribus*, investors will bear more risk when holding shares of a given firm in developing countries, precisely in a context in which the diversification of idiosyncratic risk is more difficult because stock markets are thinner. This makes the interdependency between real and financial decisions stronger.

When diversification via capital markets is difficult, we often observe that the firm's governance structure (the hierarchy) experiences endogenous transformations aimed at improving the management of risks. This is the case of the 'groups' that participate in different activities in order to diversify productive risks in developing countries. It is frequently observed that owners choose a more diversified productive structure in order to increase the firm's value. They typically opt to establish conglomerates that diversify risk by investing in different sectors (Bebczuk et al., 2003). In fact, this strategy is complementary to the use of internal finance and cross-holdings and cross-subsidization by firms with weak legal protection. Of course, this strategy is costly because a manager's first-best option is to fully exploit productive specialization while shareholders use financial markets to diversify the increment in idiosyncratic risk that a higher degree of specialization implies. Idiosyncratic-risk mitigation can also take the form of low investment and reduction in the duration of projects and contracts. When idiosyncratic risks are difficult to trade, entrepreneurs may try to avoid risks by reducing investment in those projects that show high volatility. The point is that the obstacles to managing risk have a bearing on the real side.

The government can help the private sector to manage risks by building institutions and implementing policies such as countercyclical macroeconomic policies, social safety nets, risk-related financial subsidies, and lender of last resort activities. Likewise, countercyclical policies can contribute to mitigating aggregate fluctuations in consumption; a correct election of the exchange rate regime can greatly help to isolate the economy from external shocks; firmly anchoring nominal values can lower transaction costs substantially, and so on. However, the same factors that make some risk transactions non-contractible – namely, institutional instability and low financial deepening – make government intervention non-implementable. The country studies provide ample empirical evidence concerning the difficulties of implementing and sustaining countercyclical fiscal and monetary policies, as well as sound financial policies.

These features of risk management in developing countries suggest that neither markets nor hierarchies or policies can induce an allocation of risks that can approximately replicate the allocation that would be achieved under the zero-transaction costs paradigm. And by 'approximately replicate' we mean the kind of risk allocation observed in those developed countries in which markets for trading risks are more sophisticated – even though the density of these market structures are far from the complete markets assumed in zero-transaction-cost models.

1.5 Step 4: The effects of risk misallocation on aggregate volatility

Step 4 of the volatility–institutions causal path relates risk management with aggregate fluctuations. When risk management is deficient and, therefore, resources are inefficiently allocated across states of nature, it is only natural to hypothesize that this must have a bearing on the properties of the stochastic processes that govern aggregate fluctuations, including both shocks and propagation mechanisms. The cases collected in this volume provide ample evidence that fluctuations in developing countries present substantial differences with respect to fluctuations in industrial countries. In particular, in these countries, consumption tends to be more volatile than income; consumption fluctuations tend to be independent of the world's consumption fluctuations; national income does not fluctuate less than output; and investment is markedly more volatile than in developed countries.

In terms of Step 4, the most relevant consequence of deficient risk management is that idiosyncratic national risk is not well diversified. The findings on the aggregate idiosyncratic-risk relationships presented by Imbs (2002) will help us to clarify this assertion. Imbs shows a fact that, a priori, is striking: volatile countries grow slowly but volatile sectors within countries grow fast. This seems contradictory. If country A is growing fast and country B is a slow grower, it must be because country A's sectors tend to be fast-growing and highly volatile as compared to B's sectors. In this case, aggregate volatility in country A should be higher. The author shows, however, that there are conditions under which aggregation can reverse the measured link between growth and volatility at the sectoral level in A and B. This occurs because aggregate volatility has two components: (i) a weighted average of sectoral or idiosyncratic volatilities; and (ii) a covariance term between activities, which captures shocks that tend to affect all sectors in the economy alike, thus 'macroeconomic' in nature. He shows that for country B (with the slow-growing low-volatility sectors) to show high aggregate volatility, the growth rates of the different sectors must be highly correlated. In short, cyclical co-movements are more synchronized across sectors in low-growth and volatile economies. This suggests that firms in volatile countries must bear a sizable portion of aggregate risks and that sectoral risks are difficult to manage when financial markets are underdeveloped.

Imbs highlights a second important fact. Although investment is unresponsive to volatility in the aggregate, volatile activities attract high investment rates. This means that the availability of cheap financial instruments for risk diversification may foster productivity growth and that financial market completeness does matter to productivity. The greater availability of financial instruments facilitates a 'safe' growth-enhancing diversification of resources from safe low-yield activities to risky high-yield ones without simultaneously increasing aggregate fluctuations.

Some stylized facts collected by the business cycle literature also point to the relevance of the financial development/risk management/aggregate fluctuation linkages. More specifically, the literature about business cycles in developed countries provides evidence of a reduction in the volatility of the cycle in recent decades. In the case of the US, Blanchard and Simon (2001) detect a 'long and large decline in output volatility over the last half-century'.[10] This seems also to have been the case in other developed countries. The reasons for this decline are being discussed in the literature,[11] but we would like to highlight another aspect. For the same period, Campbell et al. (2000) detected the presence of a positive deterministic trend in idiosyncratic firm-level volatility with the correlation between individual stock returns declining over the past few decades while market and industry volatility shows no trend. This clearly suggests greater diversification opportunities for the firm and is consistent with the hypothesis that financial deepening helps in this regard, given that the financial sophistication of developed countries has increased during the period. Note, on the other hand, that these stylized facts are also consistent with the Imbs hypothesis. The increase in idiosyncratic risks does not necessarily result in larger aggregate volatility to the extent that lower aggregate co-movement compensates for the increase in idiosyncratic risk.

In light of the potential benefits of financial deepening in terms of risk management, it is not surprising that the countries analyzed in this volume and developing countries in general had opened their capital account in an attempt to overcome existing financial market failures. If an investor faced difficulties in diversifying idiosyncratic risks within the country and this resulted in higher levels of sectoral co-movements, financial openness would provide domestic investors with the opportunity to achieve higher diversification through international markets. With the outstanding exception of Chile, the findings reported in the country studies indicate that the results have not been as beneficial as was anticipated. This is in line with Kose et al.'s (2003) findings; after analyzing a cross-section of countries, they conclude that 'it has proven difficult to find robust evidence in support of the proposition that financial integration helps developing countries to improve growth and to reduce macroeconomic volatility' (p. 11).[12] These authors also highlight the fact that the volatility of consumption growth relative to that of income growth on average increased for emerging market economies in the 1990s.

Prasad et al. (2005) relate these findings with pro-cyclical access to international capital markets. Indeed, pro-cyclical access to external credit can give rise to perverse interactions with undiversified idiosyncratic risks related with trade specialization. In principle, in theoretical models the direct effects of global integration on output volatility are ambiguous. Financial integration provides access to capital that can help capital-poor developing countries to diversify their production base. On the other hand, rising financial and trade integration could also lead to increased specialization in production as a result of comparative advantage considerations, thereby making economies more vulnerable to shocks that are specific to industries (Kose et al., 2003). If the risks of increased specialization cannot be diversified away, the volatility effect will be stronger. If capital movements are, in fact procyclical, the situation will be worse.

Indeed, the idea that structural factors associated with trade are important in explaining aggregate fluctuations when market imperfections exist has a long tradition in the literature. In particular, in the literature on optimum currency areas, factors such as the characteristics of the tradable sector and the degree of openness and diversification of exports have received a good deal of attention as part of the efforts to characterize the symmetry of the cycle in the analysis of optimum currency areas (Bayoumi and Eichengreen, 1992). Likewise, structural factors play a prominent role in the current research on the changes in the dynamic of business cycles in G7 countries (Blanchard and Simon, 2001; Stock and Watson, 2003). Furthermore, many authors have observed that certain features of the economic structure may be a source of excessive volatility. In his work on the US regional cycle, Kouparitsas (2002) found that, in those US regions that devote a disproportionate share of their industrial activity to the production of commodities, region-specific cycles are dominated by fluctuations in commodity prices that are largely exogenous to the region. In contrast, economy region-specific shocks account for an insignificant share of income's business cycle variation in those states where industrial composition is virtually identical to that of the aggregate US. If countries specialize in distinct goods, they will be affected very differently by a given disturbance. In the case of Mercosur, Fanelli and Gonzalez-Rozada (2003) found that the bulk of cyclical movements depend on idiosyncratic country risk, which suggests an inability to diversify risk. Likewise, changes in the country risk premia are highly correlated with cyclical co-movement within the bloc, which indicates an important influence of imperfect access to international capital markets.[13]

Overall, we believe that this empirical evidence points to the relevance of the linkages between the deficient risk management and aggregate stochastic processes that Step 4 highlights.

1.6 Concluding remarks on the research findings and the implications for the IFA

The findings of the country studies can be summarized on the basis of the five propositions that we list below. Figure 1.4 illustrates the relationship between these five propositions, as well as the way in which they contribute to generating a bi-directional relationship between volatility and institutions.

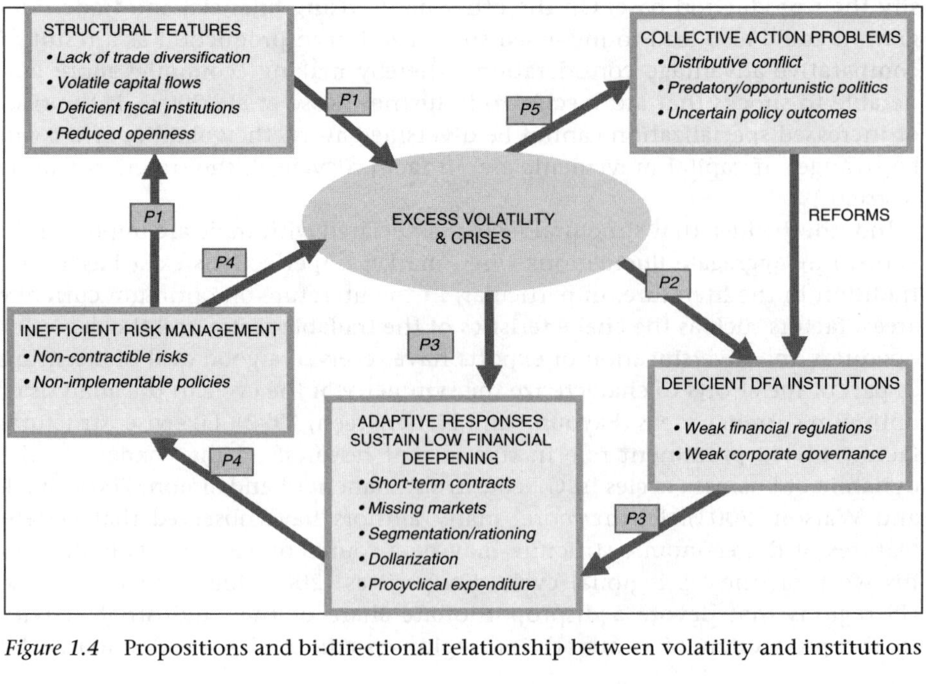

Figure 1.4 Propositions and bi-directional relationship between volatility and institutions

P1. Some shocks associated with structural features that are typical of developing economies contribute to generating excess aggregate volatility and crises because risks cannot be appropriately managed under conditions of low financial deepening.

The country studies pinpoint the following structural features as sources of aggregate shocks: the lack of export diversification and volatile terms of trade (Russia, Nigeria, South Africa); reduced openness (Argentina, Brazil); bad-quality fiscal institutions (competition between regions in China; extreme dependence on oil revenues in Nigeria; excessive debt burden in Brazil); procyclical capital movements and sudden stops (important in all countries, but less so in China). The shocks associated with these features generate excess volatility because low financial deepening makes some risks non-contractible and countercyclical fiscal and monetary policies non-implementable. The Thailand, Argentine, Nigerian, and Russian studies analyze the difficulties in implementing countercyclical policies to offset external shocks. The Brazilian study shows that a good part of excessive state indebtedness stems from the actions of the government as 'hedger of last resort'. The Chinese and Chilean studies illustrate the role of the fiscal structure; the Chinese study shows that competition between provinces affects financial development while the authors of the Chilean study pinpoint the fact that well-designed countercyclical fiscal policies can significantly contribute to improving aggregate risk management and financial development.

P2. Uncertainty associated with excess aggregate volatility and – especially – crisis episodes weaken the quality of the governance structures and institutions that rule financial transactions.

The cases of Argentina, Nigeria, Thailand, Russia, and Chile (in the early 1980s) illustrate that macro volatility and financial crises induce modifications in regulations and violations of property rights that make the building of a strong DFA extremely difficult. Additionally, the country studies show that inflation and large swings in the nominal exchange rate jeopardize the goal of securing a nominal anchor, which is key to strengthening the contractual structure. The studies also document, nonetheless, cases of institutional improvement, especially in Chile and to a certain extent in Brazil. Furthermore, most countries have made efforts to improve the quality of the DFA and to adopt international standards. Rojas-Suarez (Chapter 4) however, calls attention to the fact that in designing prudential regulations, it is critical to take into account the level of development.

P3. Agents' adaptive responses to weak DFA institutions and volatility shape the financial structure; these responses can worsen market imperfections and debilitate governance.

The studies provide ample evidence that agents adapt their behavior to the institutional and macro environment in which they live, and that some adaptations preclude the mutual advantages of financial trades from being fully exploited. The most common responses registered in the case studies are the shortening of contracts, market segmentation and rationing, dollarization, instability in the level of risk-aversion, and procyclical expenditures.

P4. When some key risks are non-contractible and some countercyclical policies are non-implementable, risk management is inefficient and a source of excess volatility and crises.

The most relevant indicators of excess volatility generated by deficient risk management that were detected in the country studies are:

(1) Consumption is more volatile than income. This is generalized and particularly marked in the cases of Argentina and Nigeria. Interestingly, in Chile there was a substantial fall in consumption volatility *pari passu* with financial development; in China the volatility of consumption also fell after reforms.
(2) Output, consumption, and investment volatility are high as compared to international standards.
(3) The frequency of downturns tends to be high, although this is not the case with China and Chile.
(4) Heteroskedasticity and volatility clusters in the neighborhood of sizable shocks and crises are common features characterizing the stochastic processes.
(5) The occurrence of crises is frequent. Several countries in our sample experienced at least one important crisis in the last quarter of a century, but the frequency of crisis occurrence differs. Argentina, Russia, and Nigeria are crisis-prone. Chile has been more resilient to crisis since the mid-1980s. China did not undergo a 'true' crisis period.
(6) Imports tend to be more volatile than exports (generalized), reflecting that external liquidity constraints matter in determining output expansion and contraction.

P5. Distributional conflicts originating in broken promises and conflicts over property rights deteriorate society's institution-building ability.

The studies document several instances in which exacerbated distributive conflicts resulted in increasing uncertainty about the relationship between policies and outcomes, and often paved the way to regulatory capture and predatory politics. This is particularly so concerning the experiences of Russia, Argentina, and Nigeria. Of course, a crisis can also open a window of opportunity for reform in general, but this does not imply that crises are not institutionally costly from the financial point of view.

Andrés Rius (Chapter 5) elaborates on the political economy implications of the case studies.[14] Rius highlights the fact that volatility alters the political economy of initiating, implementing, sustaining, and systematically upgrading the institutional foundations of financial markets. He emphasizes that policies and coordination mechanisms that mitigate aggregate volatility can yield a double dividend: they will produce the direct economic gains associated with greater stability and growth and at the same time will create favorable conditions to tackle the institution-building challenges. He advocates a new approach to conditionality in which private consumption would be a more relevant target variable. The IFIs should actively collaborate in designing forms of technical assistance and/or funding oriented to reducing consumption volatility. He notes, nonetheless, that IFIs might face a conflict of interests. The counterpart of stabilizing consumption could be a more volatile trajectory of national savings and this puts IFIs, which are often a lead creditor, in the difficult situation of deciding between doing what could be best for their borrowing client and doing what is best for themselves and other influential creditors.

In the view of financial development that follows from the project results, volatility-reducing policies and the initiatives affecting the linkages with the IFA are integral components of financial development strategies. By stabilizing the cycle, the authorities help the agents to reproduce the decisions that they would have made in a low-transaction-cost market setting.[15] In light of this, what are the developing countries' demands for designing a financial development-friendly IFA? Griffith-Jones and Ocampo (Chapter 2) argue that volatility and contagion in international financial markets increased the incidence of financial crises and growth volatility in the developing world, and reduced 'policy space' to adopt countercyclical macroeconomic policies. Therefore, they consider that a major task of a development-friendly IFA is to mitigate procyclical effects of financial markets and open 'policy space' for countercyclical macroeconomic policies in the developing world. In Chapter 2 they explore a series of policy instruments to achieve these objectives: the explicit introduction of countercyclical criteria in the design of prudential regulatory and supervisory frameworks; designing market mechanisms that better distribute the risk faced by developing countries throughout the business cycle (GDP-indexed and local currency bonds); multilateral instruments that encourage more stable private flows, such as countercyclical guarantees; and the better provision of countercyclical official liquidity to deal with external shocks.

Drawing on the Asian experience, in Chapter 3 Yung Chul Park et al. argue that despite many misgivings about the role of regional economic arrangements, the experience of the past decade suggests that they have served as building blocks rather than stumbling blocks for a more financially integrated world economy. Furthermore, policy dialogue could serve as a vehicle for promoting coherent policy formation at the regional level and, at the same time, for ensuring the effective implementation of high-quality banking and financial standards.

The three pillars for regional financial and monetary cooperation are liquidity assistance, monitoring and surveillance, and exchange rate coordination. The building of the institutions corresponding to these pillars is no simple task and, consequently, its development will likely be evolutionary. Yung Chul Park et al. stress that despite some progress, East Asia has a long way to go before it can formalize and put into effect the Chiang Mai Initiative (CMI) and launch other types of institutionalized arrangements. Creating a regional financial institute with a permanent secretariat would help to cultivate support for deeper cooperation on the various issues of financial institution and infrastructure-building. Such a regional institute, made up of a body of experts with agenda-setting power, could promote the process of regional cooperation. Rigorous multilateral surveillance on a regional basis, consistently applied and with associated peer pressure, can help build the domestic financial architecture and ultimately mitigate excessive macroeconomic volatility. Furthermore, such an institute could be a venue for building a consensus and reflecting regional views in the negotiation process of setting the global financial standards.

The international architects should not overlook the fact that the changes in the rules of the financial game have the potential to become an independent source of instability if 'perverse' interactions with non-insured sources of shocks occur. The view that governance structures and institutions are endogenously determined in the process of financial development calls for a thorough scrutiny of the one-size-fits-all standards and codes. Rojas-Suarez addresses this issue in Chapter 4 and concludes that the convergence of financial regulatory practices should be a long-term objective. In the medium term, the direct adoption of industrial country regulations might cause more harm than benefits. It is important to ensure consistency between macro policies and the state of financial development. If Basel I is in place, expansionary fiscal policies need to be avoided. The choice of prudential regulation should depend on the degree of financial development, which, in turn, is influenced by the degree of macro/financial volatility and the strength of institutions. The challenge for the least financially developed countries is to identify and develop indicators that reveal the true riskiness of banks. For the more financially developed countries it is to design a 'transitional' capital standard that appropriately reflects the risks of banks' assets; in this regard, it is necessary to manage the development of ex ante risk-based regulations in loan loss provisions; the correct risk assessment of government bonds; and the introduction of distinct capital charges for borrowers in the tradable and non-tradable sectors.

In sum, reforming the DFA and strengthening the linkages with the IFA are exercises in institution-building; a collective endeavor performed by strategic agents, which can give rise to both virtuous (Chile) and vicious (Russia) circles. The key challenge for both domestic and international architects is to design policies that can control volatility while building the rules of the financial game that will ultimately contribute to mitigating the sources of aggregate risk.

Notes

I gratefully acknowledge the excellent research assistance of Eduardo Ariel Corso. I am also grateful to Ramiro Albrieu and Martín González Rozada for their insightful comments.

1. The following articles are representative of the empirical treatment of volatility: Wolf (2004a) and Ferranti et al. (2000).
2. According to Knight (1921), when an agent faces a situation of risk, she can assign probabilities to outcomes. When the agent cannot make such an assignment, she faces

a situation of uncertainty. An agent facing a risk situation must know, at the very least, the unconditional parameters of the distribution. Of course, if this variable is 'predictable', in the sense of Clements and Hendry (1998), she can also use the information set available to improve her prediction on the basis of the conditional distribution.

3. The inability of agents to identify precisely the characteristics of the data-generating stochastic process has always been a problem for the traditional approach to risk. The usual way to circumvent the difficulties posed by Knight's distinction between risk and uncertainty is to assume that the individual can always define a subjective probability distribution that will help her to decide under uncertainty. This assumption is a useful shortcut that enables us to use the theory of utility under uncertainty. However, it does not solve the key problem: if the subjective probability distribution does not coincide with the 'objective' one, the individual will be de facto uninsured against some contingencies and will likely have to renegotiate contracts if the unexpected contingency occurs. This is true even if the agent is a Bayesian individual capable of learning because the individual will be uninsured during the learning process.
4. The difficulties that this learning process poses is well illustrated by the efforts of the business cycle literature to determine whether the reduction in the volatility of the business cycle in various developed countries is transitory or permanent and whether it was due to policy or good luck. The battery of tools used to test this is sophisticated but inconclusive (see Ahmed et al., 2004; Fritsche and Kuzin, 2004; McConnell and Perez-Quiros, 2000; Stock and Watson, 2003).
5. Risk tends to migrate in the financial system because hedging does not reduce systemic risk. It only transfers the exposure elsewhere or transforms the type of the exposure. Because of risk migration, activities such as hedging do not reduce the amount of systemic risk, especially if the access to hedging instruments is markedly segmented (see Kimbal, 2000).
6. Therefore, arbitrageurs are concerned with total risk, and not just systematic risk. Systematic risk is not the only potential determinant of pricing and high idiosyncratic risk deters arbitrageurs. The Shleifer and Vishny (1995) hypothesis claims that volatile securities will exhibit greater mispricing and a higher average return to arbitrage in equilibrium.
7. Obstfeld and Rogoff (1996: Chapter 5), present the standard model and summarize the main results.
8. Indeed, the problem of 'excess volatility' due to market failures is routinely researched in the finance literature. According to Shiller's (1981) seminal work, stock markets display 'excess volatility' because the variation in dividends alone cannot fully account for the variation in stock-market prices. It seems that asset prices tend to make long-lived swings away from their fundamental values.
9. Other risks that cannot usually be traded are the risks of a person's future labor income or the risk of future housing prices (Athanasoulis et al., 1999; Olivei, 2000). Although this is also the case in developed countries, the incidence is much stronger in emerging countries. In fact, uninsurable labor income and the existence of non-tradables give rise to many phenomena that are crucial to understanding how non-contractible risks and fluctuations contribute to macroeconomic instability in developing countries.
10. The proximate causes of this decline are the decline in inflation volatility; a steady decrease in investment volatility, and even more so in consumption volatility; a decline in the volatility of government spending; and a change from procyclical to countercyclical investment in the 1990s.
11. In passing, it is interesting to note that the bulk of the panel data work comparing developed and developing countries coincides with this period and this raises doubts concerning the interpretation of the estimated coefficients to the extent that volatility was changing within countries.

12. On the financial openness/volatility nexus see also Caballero (2000a, 2000b), Calvo and Reinhart (1999), Claessens (2004), and Easterly et al. (2000), Ferranti et al. (2000), and Mobarak (2005).
13. It is important to take into account, in this regard, that the bulk of aggregate market volatility arises from changing discount rates rather than changing aggregate cash flow (because of the diversification effect on cash flow). Discount rates are much more volatile in emerging countries, especially because of changing country-risk premia. This is consistent with the fact that market fluctuations have much greater explanatory power in less-developed markets (Campbell et al., 2000).
14. We have analyzed the political economy of reforms in Fanelli and McMahon (2006).
15. In addition, a successful reduction in the level of volatility could foster growth via the effects on investment. Servén (1998) shows that there is a negative association between macroeconomic uncertainty and private investment.

2

A Countercyclical Framework for a Development-Friendly IFA

José Antonio Ocampo and Stephany Griffith-Jones

2.1 Introduction

The last three decades have seen developing countries, and particularly those more integrated into world financial markets, swing to the rhythm of highly procyclical external financing. Financial volatility has a direct effect on the balance of payments and domestic financial markets, and through them, on domestic economic activity and other macroeconomic variables. In the face of strong swings of private capital markets, developing countries lost 'policy space' to adopt autonomous countercyclical macroeconomic policies, and faced difficult challenges in creating deep financial markets. A vicious circle involving procyclical financing, incomplete financial markets and institutions, and constraints on macroeconomic policy emerged. Imperfect financial markets have been a source of volatility, but deep financial markets, improved financial governance structures and countercyclical macroeconomic policies have been difficult to develop in a highly volatile financial environment (Fanelli, 2006). The unfortunate outcome of this dynamic is that 'twin' external and domestic financial crises have become far more frequent since the breakdown of Bretton Woods exchange rate arrangements (IMF, 1998; Bordo et al., 2001).

This chapter thus argues forcefully that the major task of a development-friendly international financial architecture is to mitigate the procyclical effects of financial markets and to open 'policy space' for countercyclical macroeconomic policies in the developing world. We look first at features and costs of capital account volatility and the underlying international asymmetries, then at different ways to reduce such volatility and to open space for countercyclical macroeconomic policies.

2.2 Capital account volatility in the developing world

Trade and terms of trade fluctuations play a major role in the determination of business cycles in developing countries, particularly in commodity-dependent economies. Domestic macroeconomic policies and political factors also play a role in determining business cycles. Since the 1970s, however, business cycles in developing countries have been characterized by the leading role played by *capital* account fluctuations. This has been particularly true for economies more integrated into world financial markets, the 'emerging economies'.

Boom–bust cycles reflect investor herding and associated contagion – of both optimism and pessimism. Volatility is associated with significant changes in risk evaluation, which involve the alternation of periods of 'appetite for risk' (more precisely, underestimation of risks) with periods of a 'flight to quality' (risk-aversion). Market-sensitive risk management practices as well as other features of financial markets (for example, the evaluation of managers against competitors) increase herding (Persaud, 2000). Furthermore, due to information asymmetries, different assets tend to be pooled together in risk categories that are viewed by market agents as being strongly correlated. This practice turns such correlations into self-fulfilling prophecies.

Boom–bust cycles have given a renewed relevance to the endogenous unstable dynamics of financial markets analyzed by Minsky (1982), who emphasizes how financial booms generate excessive risk-taking by market agents, which eventually leads economies into crises. From a different theoretical perspective, a similar explanation has been recently suggested by White (2006), who underscores how the 'search for yield' that is characteristic of low interest rate environments generates incentives for credit creation, carry trade and leverage that can easily build up asset bubbles. 'The main risks to the financial sector could stem from financial excesses linked to a generalized complacency towards risk reinforced by a benign short-term outlook' (BIS, 2005: 120). A low inflation environment may actually encourage such behavior, as monetary policy tends to be accommodative and may even (according to influential views, such as those of Alan Greenspan) be powerless in the face of asset price bubbles, although it can later mitigate the effects of asset price busting. This was evident in Japan in the 1990s as well as the US in the 2000s.

In developing countries, fluctuations in capital markets are reflected in the procyclical pattern of spreads, variations in the availability of financing (the absence or presence of credit rationing) and in maturities. This involves short-term volatility, such as very intense upward movement of spreads and the short periods of interruption (rationing) of financing observed during the Mexican, Asian, and Russian crises. More importantly, they also involve *medium-term* cycles, as the experience of the past three decades indicates (see Figure 2.1 in relation to spreads since 1994). During this period, two full medium-term cycles were experienced: a boom of external financing in the 1970s, followed by a major debt crisis in the 1980s; a new boom in the 1990s, followed by a sharp reduction in net flows after the Asian and Russian crises of 1997–98. Since 2002–03 a new such cycle has been in place, which has already undergone a phase of turbulence, in May/June 2006.

Interestingly, as Figure 2.1 also indicates, fluctuations in risk premia for emerging markets tend to correlate with spreads of US high-yield bonds. Thus, the procyclicality of financial markets affects all types of assets considered risky by market agents. The correlation is imperfect, though, reflecting specific factors that determine different asset classes.

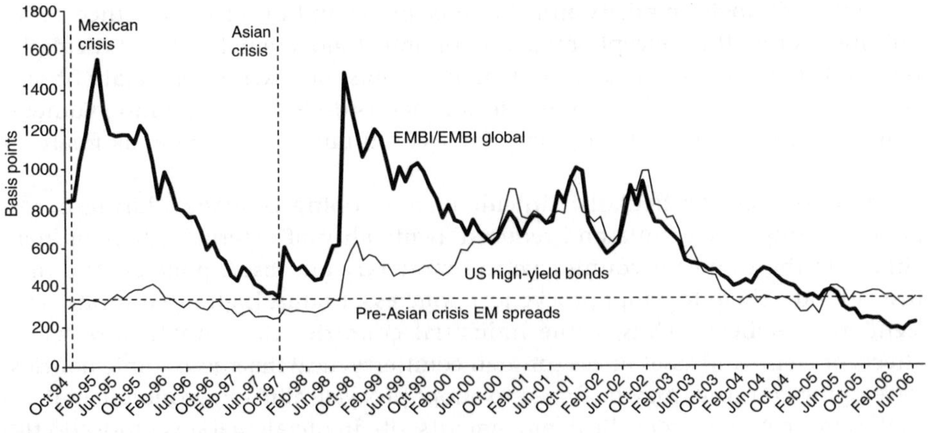

Figure 2.1 Emerging markets spreads
Source: ECLAC, on the basis of data from Merrill Lynch's US High-Yield Master II Index (H0A0), JP Morgan Chase's EMBI and EMBI Global.

Different types of capital flows show different volatility patterns. The higher volatility of short-term capital indicates reliance on such financing is highly risky (Rodrik and Velasco, 2000), whereas the smaller volatility of FDI vis-à-vis all forms of financial flows is considered a source of strength. However, 'financial engineering' may be making different flows increasingly similar. Particularly, the use of risk management techniques by multinationals, via derivatives, may make FDI in critical moments as volatile as traditional financial flows.

Volatility in financial markets is partly transmitted to developing countries through public sector accounts, especially through effects of the availability of financing on government spending, and of interest rates on public sector debt service payments. In commodity-dependent developing countries, links between the availability of financing and commodity prices reinforce the effects on public sector accounts. However, the most important effects of capital account fluctuations are on *private* spending and balance sheets. Capital account cycles, their domestic financial multipliers and their reflection in asset prices have thus become the major determinant of growth volatility in the developing world, whereas price and wage rigidities emphasized in the 'neoclassical synthesis' have played a rather secondary or even insignificant role (Easterly et al., 2000).

During booms, developing countries viewed by markets as 'success' stories are almost inevitably drawn into the capital account boom, inducing private sector deficits and risky balance sheets (Ffrench-Davis, 2001; Marfán, 2005). However, even countries with weak 'fundamentals' may be drawn into the boom (see, for example, Calvo et al., 1993) and all countries, again with some independence from their 'fundamentals', will be drawn into 'sudden stops' of external financing (Calvo and Talvi, 2004). What markets judge as 'success stories' during booms and as 'pariahs' during crises may also be subject to cyclical variations. Note, for example, the transformation of Argentina from 'success story' to 'pariah' of financial markets and the opposite evolution of Russia since 1998. This means that the concept of 'macroeconomic fundamentals' and, particularly, the market evaluation of such fundamentals must be taken with a grain of salt. However, some objective macroeconomic factors do help to determine vulnerability to crises, particularly large current account imbalances and weak financial sectors.

Conditions are particularly difficult in developing countries during crises, because rising risk premia and reduced availability of external financing may eliminate the room for countercyclical monetary and fiscal policies, and may instead force them to adopt procyclical policies – that is, high interest rates and tight fiscal policies. Thus, while industrial countries can smooth procyclical effects of credit and asset prices through countercyclical macroeconomic policies, developing countries may be forced to adopt procyclical macroeconomic policies that reinforce the procyclical movements of financial markets. Indeed, the 'credibility' of authorities to financial market agents during crises will be judged according to their capacity to adopt austerity policies. Interaction between increases in country risk premia and reduced availability of financing during crises can be particularly destabilizing in economies with high debt ratios (Frenkel, 2005).

There is also widespread evidence that ample private sector financing encourages procyclical macroeconomic policies during booms. Austerity policies during crises may generate a political economy bias toward expansion when financing again becomes available. In turn, ample private sector financing encourages procyclical responses from markets and macroeconomic authorities. Thus, unstable external financing distorts incentives that both private agents and authorities face *throughout* the business cycle, inducing procyclical behavior of economic agents *and* macroeconomic policies (Kamisky et al., 2004; United Nations, 2006). In the words of Stiglitz (2003), increased exposure to financial market risks replaced Keynesian automatic stabilizers with automatic *de*-stabilizers. Contrary to the view that, with liberalization, financial markets would play a disciplining role, dependence on financial swings encouraged adoption of procyclical monetary and fiscal policies that increased both *real* macroeconomic instability and the alternation of financial euphoria and crises.

Crises are deleterious for financial development and institution-building as they destroy the 'rules of the game' for financial transactions and it takes time to build new rules. They also generate endogenous responses in financial structures that contribute to volatility: shallow markets for long-term instruments, missing markets for risk transactions, market segmentation, liquidity constraints for many market agents and, in some cases, dollar/euroization (Fanelli, 2006). One of the most important effects is the endemic maturity and currency mismatches that characterize the balance sheets of economic agents in developing countries. Maturity and currency risks are accumulated during periods of financial euphoria; thus, the sharp reduction in liquidity, increased domestic interest rates, and exchange rate depreciations during crises have strong balance sheet effects.

Although procyclicality is inherent in financial markets, domestic financial and capital account liberalization in the developing world have accentuated its effects. A lag in developing adequate prudential regulation and supervision frameworks increases the risks of financial liberalization. The development of appropriate financial governance structures is itself made difficult in volatile financial environments, and they only help to mitigate (that is, they do not eliminate) the increased volatility that financial liberalization generates.

The costs of such financial volatility in the developing world in terms of economic growth are high. There is now overwhelming evidence that procyclical financial markets and macroeconomic policies have increased growth volatility and have not encouraged growth in the developing world (Kose et al., 2003). Whatever the efficiency gains from financial market integration, they are swamped by the negative effects of growth volatility.

Eichengreen (2004) estimated that over the past 25 years, the income of developing countries had been reduced by 25 per cent due to currency and banking crises. Others have estimated even higher average annual costs of crises. Indonesia experienced larger falls in output and incomes during the Asian crisis than the United States during the Great Depression. In the presence of increasing returns, such strong recessions generate cumulative effects (Easterly, 2001: Chapter 10). In the most adverse cases, it will lead to a displacement in the long-term growth *trajectory* (for example, most Latin American countries in the 1980s, or Indonesia since the Asian crisis).

Each medium-term financial cycle may have specific features. The current one has been characterized by an unprecedented accumulation of international reserves and reduced debt ratios – 'self-insurance' against the financial instability experienced during previous crises. Such 'self-insurance', together with booming exports and the rapid development of local currency bond markets (see below) may have changed conditions surrounding developing country financing in recent years.

However, new risks have emerged or become more prominent. First, increased dependence of developing countries on export-led strategies and on high commodity prices have made them more vulnerable to trade cycles. The interaction between trade and capital account fluctuations has been a traditional source of vulnerability, but may be assuming new dimensions given the greater openness of most developing countries.

Second, new sources of potential procyclicality have emerged, particularly related to the explosive growth of derivatives worldwide. In developing economies, derivative contracts are being used both as instruments to hedge risk and for speculation by international hedge funds and investment banks, for example via the 'carry trade'. Large parts of these derivative markets are not regulated (as they operate in the OTC market and off-shore). Nor have existing regulations fully incorporated the risks that derivatives pose in situations of stress, when they can add to systemic risk.

Third, uncertainties associated with the risk of a disorderly unraveling of global imbalances may drastically change the prospect for developing economies. A major paradox is that measures of 'self-insurance' of developing countries (large current account surpluses, increased international reserves and reduced indebtedness) are also part of global imbalances. The new sources of strength of developing countries, when viewed on a country-by-country basis, turn out to be one of the elements of vulnerability for developing countries as a whole. A global cooperative approach to provision of 'collective insurance' and management of global imbalances would thus be a more desirable solution (Ocampo et al., 2006: Chapter 4).

2.3 Implications of financial volatility for international cooperation

The underlying financial and macroeconomic asymmetries

The dynamics of boom–bust cycles is deeply rooted in the operation of financial markets, and in basic asymmetries that characterize the world economy (Ocampo and Martin, 2003). In the financial area, such asymmetries are reflected in: (i) the incapacity of most developing countries to issue liabilities in international markets in their own currencies, a phenomenon referred to as 'original sin' (Eichengreen et al., 2003; Hausmann and Panizza, 2003), partly mitigated by recent growth in local currency debt markets; (ii) differences in the degree of domestic financial and capital market development, which lead to an undersupply of long-term financial instruments; and (iii) the small size of developing countries' domestic financial markets vis-à-vis the magnitude of speculative pressures they may face. This implies that domestic financial markets in the developing world are significantly more 'incomplete' than in the industrial world and thus that some financial intermediation must be conducted through international markets. Developing countries are plagued with a myriad of financial market imperfections, particularly by variable mixes of currency and maturity mismatches. Financial asymmetries generate, in turn, important macroeconomic asymmetries, particularly in the capacity of developing countries to undertake countercyclical macroeconomic policies.

The risks associated with financial instability can be partly corrected by domestic policy actions, involving variable mixes of foreign exchange reserve accumulation during booms, countercyclical fiscal policies, strengthened prudential regulation and supervision, and variable mixes of exchange rate intervention, the management of the capital account (including through incentives to reduce debt or improve its term structure during booms) and the use of the margins for countercyclical monetary policy that those policies generate (Ocampo, 2005).

However, such actions are not costless. Thus, the accumulation of international reserves to cover risks associated with short-term capital is usually expensive. The risks faced by the domestic financial sector can be counterbalanced by stricter prudential regulations but this raises the cost of financial intermediation and may restrict the development of new financial services. Furthermore, many regulatory actions that emerging economies can adopt to manage risks merely shift rather than correct the underlying risks.

The public sector (including the central bank) can also act as the 'insurer of last resort' of private sector risks, through the issue of foreign currency denominated bonds that the private sector can use to cover its currency mismatches. Although this may help the private sector to absorb shocks, it implies additional public sector liabilities and, possibly, a larger tax burden to service them. The Brazilian experience provides the best example of the potential costs of such a risk absorption strategy (Pires de Souza et al., 2006).

There is a profound sense in which financial and macroeconomic asymmetries that affect developing countries are inescapable. The search for shortcuts and 'silver bullets' (hard pegs or the adoption of international currencies) does not eliminate the difficult trade-offs that such asymmetries generate.

Implications for the design of the international financial architecture

The wave of crises in the developing world has underscored the need for a broad framework for macroeconomic stability. In the recent debate, this has been reflected in the focus on *sustainability*, including external, fiscal and financial sector sustainability (IMF, 2004). But given the procyclical bias of financial markets and the strong incentives to adopt procyclical macroeconomic policies, an equally important emphasis should be given to the *countercyclical* dimensions of macroeconomic and financial policies.

The countercyclical dimensions have received much less attention in recent debates. This is reflected in the absence of this concept in the new IMF medium-term framework (IMF, 2005a). This contrasts with the importance this concept played in past macroeconomic debates and the explicitly countercyclical focus of macroeconomic policies in some industrial economies, particularly the United States. It is also in contrast with the call by the major grouping in developing countries in financial issues, the Group of 24 (2005), to include explicit countercyclical objectives in the IMF's support to developing countries. In this area, there is an increasing consensus on the need to use expansionary periods to strengthen fiscal positions, and a more limited recognition of the need to avoid explicitly procyclical fiscal policies during crises (such as targeting the current deficit in a context in which tax revenues are declining). However, this represents only a very limited recognition of the need to fully mainstream countercyclical concerns in designing macroeconomic frameworks.

It has also become increasingly recognized that liberalized capital accounts and financial markets generate excessively risky private sector balance sheets, and that excessive reliance on short-term external financing enhances the risk of currency crises. Preventive (prudential) macroeconomic and financial policies, which aim at avoiding the accumulation of unsustainable public and private sector debts and balance sheets during periods of financial euphoria, have thus become part of the standard recipe. However, even well-established countercyclical prudential practices, such as the Spanish system of forward-looking provisions, have received limited attention, and the need to reduce procyclicality was not given adequate attention in the revision of Basel standards. Rather, Basel II may increase the procyclicality of both international and domestic bank lending.

Managing countercyclical policies for developing countries in the current globalized financial world is, of course, no easy task, as financial markets generate strong incentives to adopt procyclical policies and reduce the room for maneuver to undertake countercyclical macroeconomic policies. It is thus essential that international cooperation in the macroeconomic policy area be designed to overcome such incentives and constraints.

This means that the first role of international financial institutions, from the point of view of developing countries, is to mitigate the procyclical effects of financial markets and open 'policy space' for countercyclical macroeconomic policies. This can be achieved by: (i) smoothing out boom–bust cycles at the source through regulation; (ii) helping partially to cover or diversify the risks (especially of a cyclical nature) that developing countries face in international capital markets; and (iii) increasing incentives and degrees of freedom that developing countries have to adopt countercyclical policies.

A number of measures can be suggested. They include: (i) explicit introduction of countercyclical criteria in the design of prudential regulatory and supervisory frameworks, in capital source and developing countries; (ii) designing market mechanisms that better distribute the risk faced by developing countries throughout the business cycle (GDP-indexed and local currency bonds); (iii) instruments that encourage more stable private flows, such as countercyclical guarantees; and (iv) countercyclical official liquidity to deal with external shocks. Since the design of a development-friendly international financial architecture should include not only global but also a complete network of regional institutions, we examine cooperation between developing countries.

2.4 Countercyclical prudential regulation and supervision

The origins of problems that erupt during financial crises are associated with both excessive risk-taking during booms and the inevitable mix of maturity and currency mismatches that characterize balance sheets in developing countries. Inadequate risk analysis by financial agents and weak prudential regulation of domestic financial systems exacerbate this. However, even well-regulated systems in industrial countries are subject to periodic episodes when risks are underestimated. In Argentina a system of prudential regulations considered to be one of the best in the developing world – and with a large-scale presence of multinational banks – failed to avert the effects of major macroeconomic shocks on the domestic financial system.

One of the major problems seems to be the focus of prudential regulation on microeconomic risks, and the tendency to underestimate risks that have a clear *macroeconomic* origin.[1] Whereas microeconomic risk management can reduce risks that depend on the individual characteristics of each borrower through diversification, they cannot reduce systematic risks, associated, for example, with business cycles. The basic problem in this regard is the inability of individual financial intermediaries to internalize collective risks assumed during boom periods.

Moreover, traditional regulatory tools, including both Basel I and Basel II standards, have a procyclical bias. The basic problem is the highly procyclical nature of a system in which loan-loss provisions are tied to loan delinquency or to short-term expectations of future loan losses. Such a system may be ineffective in hampering excessive risk-taking during booms, when expectations of loan losses are low, thus effectively underestimating risks and the counterpart provisions for loan losses. The sharp increase in loan delinquency during crises reduces financial institutions' capital and, hence, their lending capacity, potentially triggering a 'credit squeeze'; this would reinforce the downswing in economic activity and asset prices and, thus, the quality of the portfolios of financial intermediaries. Since credit ratings are also procyclical, basing risk on such ratings is also procyclical.

Given the central role all these processes play in the business cycles of developing countries, and the important influence of banking regulation on credit availability in the modern economy, the crucial issue is to introduce a countercyclical element into prudential regulation and supervision. The major innovation is the Spanish system of forward-looking provisions, introduced in 2000 and modified in 2005, and later adopted by Portugal. According to this system, provisions are made when loans are disbursed based on the expected losses ('latent risks'), estimated on the basis of a full business cycle (Fernández de Lis et al., 2001). This system implies that provisioning follows the criteria traditionally used by the insurance industry, where provisions are made when the insurance policy is issued.

Under this system, provisions build up during economic expansions and are drawn upon during downturns. They are accumulated in a fund that is used to cover loan losses. Although the accumulation and drawing down of the fund has a countercyclical dynamic, this only reflects the cyclical pattern of bank lending. Thus, the system is, strictly speaking, 'cycle-neutral'. It can be complemented by strictly countercyclical prudential provisions, which can be decreed by the regulatory authority for the financial system as a whole or for some financial agents on the basis of the excessive growth of credit (relative to some benchmark), the bias in lending to sectors characterized by systematic risks and the growth of foreign currency denominated loans to non-tradable sectors.

The explicit analysis of the countercyclical elements of prudential regulation and supervision should thus become a central concern of the Basel Committee. The benefits to developing countries would accrue through both a less procyclical supply of credit and more resilient domestic financial systems.

Ensuring a more precise measurement of risk in bank portfolios should also be the subject of attention in drafting international accounting standards. Indeed, existing standards give no room for concepts such as the 'latent risks' in bank portfolios, leading to both an overestimation of their 'fair value' during periods of euphoria and an underestimation during phases of excessive pessimism. The tax system should also accept such transparent provisions as fiscal costs.

In developing countries these provisions should be supplemented by more specific regulations aimed at controlling currency and maturity mismatches (including those associated with derivative operations), and at avoiding the overvaluation of collateral generated by asset price bubbles. The strict prohibition of currency mismatches in the portfolios of financial intermediaries is the best rule, but authorities should also closely monitor the currency risk of non-financial firms operating in non-tradable sectors, which may become credit risks for banks. Regulations can be used to establish higher provisions and/or risk weighting for these operations, or a strict prohibition on lending in foreign currencies to non-financial firms without revenues in those currencies.

Moreover, many regulatory practices aimed at correcting risky practices shift underlying risks to non-financial agents. Thus, for example, lower risk ratings for short-term credit and strong liquidity requirements reduce direct banking risks, but also reinforce the short-term bias in lending. Maturity mismatches are thus displaced to non-financial agents and may result in reduced fixed capital investment. Also, prudential regulations forbidding banks from holding currency mismatches in their portfolios may encourage non-financial agents to borrow directly from abroad. Reduced direct vulnerability of the domestic financial sector will have, as a corollary, the currency and, possibly, maturity mismatches of non-financial agents. This is why capital account regulations aimed at avoiding an inadequate maturity structure of borrowing in external markets by all domestic agents, and at avoiding currency mismatches in the portfolios of those agents operating in non-tradable sectors, may be the best available option (Ocampo, 2003). Also, as long as there is no international lender of last resort, international rules should continue to provide room for the use of capital account regulation by developing countries.

The evaluation of the vulnerability of the domestic financial system and the development of regulatory and supervisory frameworks have become essential elements of financial sector assessments undertaken by the IMF and the World Bank. It is essential that the macroeconomic and, particularly, the countercyclical dimensions of prudential regulation and supervision be equally and routinely incorporated into such assessments and advice.

In addition, Basel II has a number of problems that require attention: it is complex where it should be simple; it is implicitly procyclical when it should be explicitly countercyclical; and although it is supposed to more accurately align regulatory capital to the risks that banks face, in the case of lending to developing countries it ignores the proved benefits of diversification. In particular, by failing to take account of the benefits of international diversification of portfolios, capital requirements for loans to developing countries will be significantly higher than is justified on the basis of the actual risks attached to such lending. There are therefore fears that Basel II creates the risk of a sharp reduction in bank lending to developing countries, particularly during crises (thus enhancing the procyclicality of such lending), and of an increase in the cost of a significant part of the remaining lending, particularly for low-rated borrowing countries.

One clear way in which Basel II could be improved to reduce these problems would be to introduce the benefits of diversification into the internal ratings-based approach. One of the major benefits of investing in developing and emerging economies is their relatively low correlation with mature markets. This has been tested empirically using a wide variety of financial, market and macro variables. Different simulations that compared estimated losses of portfolios that were diversified across both developed and developing countries with the losses of portfolios in developed countries only indicate that the former were from 19 to 23 per cent lower (Griffith-Jones et al., 2003). If risks are measured precisely, this should be reflected in lower capital requirements.

An additional positive effect of taking account of the benefits of diversification is that this makes capital requirements far less procyclical than otherwise. Indeed, if the benefits of diversification are incorporated, simulations show that the variance over time of capital requirements will be significantly smaller than if they are not.

2.5 Market instruments

GDP-linked bonds

GDP-linked bonds could be particularly beneficial to smooth debt service payments by linking part of the annual debt servicing of the bond to the growth of the debtor country's GDP growth (Griffith-Jones and Sharma, 2006). The interest coupon would be totally or partially tied to the issuing country's rate of growth. Given the requirement for many institutional investors to hold assets that pay a positive interest rate, a floor can be determined beyond which the coupon rate cannot fall.

GDP-indexed bonds could be beneficial for all countries, but especially for developing ones. They would provide two major benefits. First, they stabilize government spending and limit the procyclicality of fiscal pressures by requiring smaller interest payments at times of slower growth – thus providing space for higher spending or lower taxes during crises. They also curb an excessively expansionary policy in times of rapid growth. The issuance of such bonds would make it easier for governments to follow countercyclical fiscal policies. Second, by allowing debt service ratios to fall in times of slow or negative growth, they reduce the likelihood of defaults and debt crisis.

Simulations indicate that gains for emerging-economy borrowers can be substantial. Research by Borensztein and Mauro (2004) shows that if half of Mexico's government debt consisted of GDP-indexed bonds, it would have saved about 1.6 per cent of GDP in interest payments during the Tequila crisis of 1995.

To help create a market for these instruments, it might be better if they were issued first by countries with greater credibility. Two such groups of countries can be identified. The first are developed countries. The second are developing countries, like Mexico or Chile, that are attractive to markets. The precedent of introducing collective action clauses into bonds, done first by developed countries and later followed by developing ones, shows that demonstration effects can be very effective for introducing financial innovations. Positive precedents – for example, by investors with Argentine warrants that provide an upside to debt servicing if growth is above a fixed level – also create a propitious climate for them.

GDP-indexed bonds may also provide benefits for issuer industrialized countries, especially in Europe. They may be particularly attractive for EMU countries, given that the Stability and Growth Pact tends to render their fiscal policies procyclical if their structural fiscal position is not too distant from the maximum allowed deficit. They are also particularly relevant for European countries where pensions are indexed against GDP growth, such as Italy.

Investors are likely to receive two main benefits from the introduction of GDP-linked bonds. First, they would provide an opportunity to take a position on countries' future growth prospects. Though this is possible to some degree through stock markets, these are often not representative of the economy as a whole. Since growth rates across emerging markets tend to be fairly uncorrelated, a portfolio including GDP-indexed bonds for several of these economies would have the benefits of diversification, thus increasing the return/risk ratio. Second, investors would benefit from a lower frequency of defaults and financial crises, which often results in costly litigations/renegotiation and sometimes in outright losses.

On a broader level, GDP-indexed bonds can be viewed as desirable vehicles for international risk-sharing, as a way of avoiding the disruptions from formal defaults and as a mechanism to help smooth growth. They have the characteristic of a public good as they generate systemic benefits above those going to individual investors and issuing countries.

These externalities provide a justification for some public action to help create such a market. Thus, the World Bank and regional development banks could play the role of 'market makers' for GDP-linked bonds (Ocampo et al., 2006: Chapter 2). These institutions could begin by developing a portfolio of loans, the repayments of which could be indexed to the growth rate of the debtor country. Once they have a portfolio of such loans to different developing countries, they could securitize them and sell them in the international capital markets. Such a portfolio could be particularly attractive for private investors as it would offer them the opportunity to take a position on the growth prospects of a number of emerging economies simultaneously. As correlations among growth rates of developing countries tend to be lower at the global level, the World Bank may be best placed to do such securitization. One disadvantage of GDP-linked bonds is that developing countries' ability to pay is not only associated with GDP growth but also with the ability to generate a sufficient supply of foreign exchange, and thus with the evolution of the real exchange rate. To the extent that fluctuations of this variable are procyclical, real exchange rate volatility will compound GDP fluctuations. These instruments could be eventually indexed to GDP measured in the currency of issuance of the bonds, but this may reduce their attractiveness.

But perhaps the main concern for developing a GDP-linked bond market is uncertainty about their future liquidity. This has been a problem for issuing other new instruments such as inflation-indexed bonds. However, such problems have been overcome once such paper was issued on a significant scale.

Local currency bonds

Another alternative for better managing the risks faced by developing countries throughout the business cycle consists of the introduction of local currency denominated bonds. These bonds offer a cure against the currency mismatches that characterize the debt structure of developing countries. At the domestic level, the development of domestic capital markets, especially bond markets, also creates a more stable source of local funding for both the public and private sectors, mitigating difficulties created by sudden stops in cross-border capital flows.

The recognition of their virtues has been reflected in a boom of domestic bond markets in developing countries since the Asian crisis (see Figure 2.2). The financial infrastructure required to provide adequate liquidity involves adequate regulation, well-structured stock and bond markets – with bonds usually providing a larger market in most countries – and investment banks that play the role of 'market makers' to help provide liquidity. There is also growing attention to issuing local currency denominated bonds in international markets, although these instruments still represent only a small, if expanding, share of the market. As the experience of those countries that have been more successful in issuing these bonds indicates (for example, South Africa), they are largely used to cover the currency risks of long-term investors.

Domestic markets for these instruments also tend to be less liquid than similar markets in industrial countries, and the reduction of currency mismatches comes

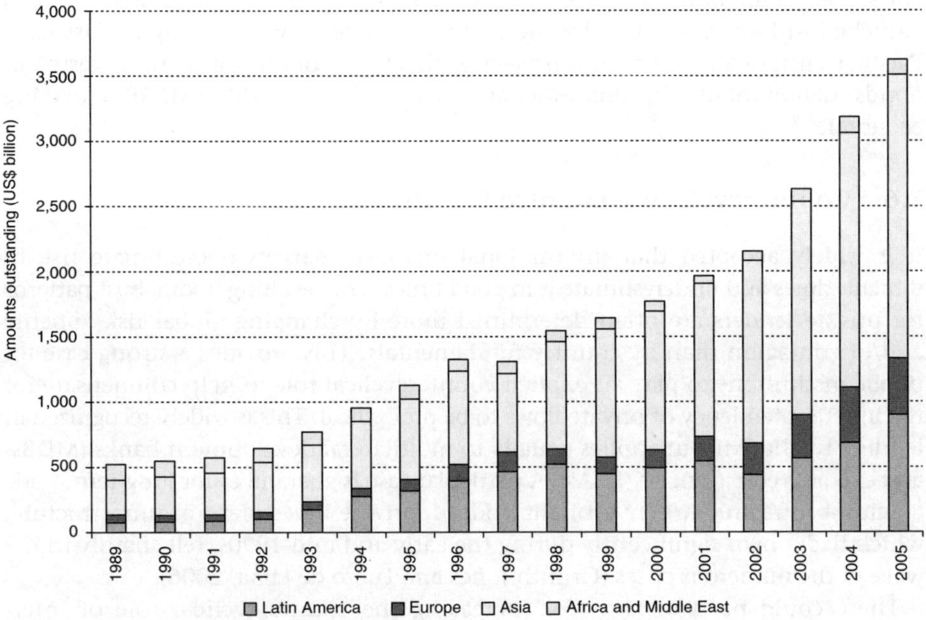

Figure 2.2 Domestic bonds issued by developing countries
Source: Bank for International Settlements, http://www.bis.org/statistics/secstats.htm.

at the cost of additional maturity mismatches (Jeanneau and Tovar, 2006). For international investors, the attractiveness of these instruments depends on expectations of exchange rate appreciation, and their demand may thus be subject to strong procyclical swings. The advantages in terms of reduced currency mismatches for developing country issuers may thus not be accompanied by reduced volatility of external capital flows. This may lead, in turn, to a stronger link between exchange rate expectations and domestic interest rates. Minimum holding periods for the associated funds or exit taxes may thus be useful to get the full benefits of diversifying the currency risks but may reduce their appeal for international investors and the liquidity of these instruments.

Innovative proposals have been advanced to make local currency investments more attractive on a stable basis by international investors. Dodd and Spiegel (2005) have suggested raising capital in international markets by forming diversified portfolios of emerging market local currency debt issued by sovereign governments. These portfolios would – by using risk management techniques of diversification – generate a return-to-risk that competed favorably with other major capital market security indices. A portfolio of emerging market local currency debt can raise rates of return relative to risk that compete with those of major US and European securities indices in international capital markets.

A similar effect could be achieved by multilateral development banks raising funds in the local markets of developing countries. The World Bank and the regional development banks could also design pilot projects of diversified bond issues that would provide information on returns, risk, and prices that could encourage emulation by private agents. The second Asian Bond Fund (ABF2) launched in December 2004 by the 11 EMEAP (Executives Meeting of East Asia-Pacific Central Banks) is a pilot project of this type. All central banks invested in bonds denominated in domestic currencies of the eight EMEAP emerging economies.[2]

2.6 Countercyclical guarantee facilities

It is widely accepted that international financial markets overestimate risk in difficult times and underestimate it in good times. The resulting boom–bust patterns for private lenders are often determined more by changing global risk appetite and/or contagion than by country fundamentals. This provides a strong case for public institutions to play an explicit countercyclical role to help compensate for the inherent tendency of private flows to be procyclical. This is widely recognized in lending by the IMF but applies equally to multilateral development banks (MDBs) and export credit agencies (ECAs). A particular case is guarantees for long-term trade credit for infrastructure investment. Indeed, private investment in infrastructure, which had grown significantly during the early and mid-1990s, fell sharply in the wake of the numerous crises (Griffith-Jones and Fuzzo de Lima, 2006).

There could be two paths for increasing the countercyclical role of international financial institutions in this area. One would be for MDBs to provide more countercyclical lending than already occurs (for example, in infrastructure).

Another path, which could provide more leverage of the public resources they manage, would be for MDBs and ECAs to be more active in issuing guarantees to private sector lenders with an explicit countercyclical element in the associated risk evaluations. This requires MDBs and ECAs to assess risk for issuing guarantees with a longer-term perspective than is typically done by commercial banks; when banks or other lenders lowered their exposure to a country, MDBs or ECAs would increase their level of guarantees if they considered that the country's long-term fundamentals were basically sound. When market risk evaluations improve and the willingness to lend increases, MDBs or ECAs could decrease their exposure.

To the extent that MDBs and ECAs increasingly use models to assess risks, taking a longer-term view would require the use of models with a longer-term perspective than those used by private lenders. These models would presumably be better at 'seeing through the cycle', using more measures of risk focused on long-term factors.

It is important that guarantees should be tailor-made to correct market imperfections and avoid moral hazard. Otherwise, they might undermine the initiatives to enhance private capital flows to developing countries. First, they must maintain the private investors' incentives to choose only good projects – to avoid adverse selection – and run them efficiently. Second, guarantees can impose excessive costs on taxpayers or consumers and expose them to too much risk. To overcome this, it is crucial that contingent liabilities of guarantees be carefully monitored and their risks assessed. Furthermore, in the case of infrastructure projects, the risks to be guaranteed have to be carefully defined in such a way that private agents assume normal market risks (which can be subject, however, to some countercyclical evaluation), whereas non-market risks (such as regulatory risk or force majeure) should be subject to greater attention by authorities granting guarantees.

An alternative way to mitigate risks is to push forward regional efforts to create guarantee agencies that enable risk-sharing among countries that have common interests, including infrastructure development in neighboring economies. This could enhance the creditworthiness of single country members and therefore of their government guarantees, especially in difficult times.

This innovation could work with the technical assistance of regional or subregional development banks. A sovereign guarantee pool could be developed as a contractual mechanism for risk-sharing among governments that benefit from the same infrastructure project but have different credit ratings. The country with the higher rating could have an interest in having the project funded via this mechanism, due to positive externalities derived from the project. The lower-rated country could compensate the guarantee coverage provided by its higher-rated partner.

2.7 The provision of countercyclical official liquidity

For capital account-led crises

At the country level, central banks have acted for many decades as lenders of last resort to prevent financial crises and their deepening when they occur.

Equivalent international mechanisms are still at an embryonic stage, with the current IMF arrangements operating more under the principle of the 'emergency financier', since there is no automaticity in the availability of financing during crises (Griffith-Jones and Ocampo, 2003). The enhanced provision of emergency financing at the international level in response to external shocks is essential to lowering unnecessary burdens of adjustment and to avoid the spread of crises. Appropriate facilities should include a liquidity provision to cover large capital flow reversals and volatility in real export earnings.

In recent decades, capital account liberalization and large capital account volatility has greatly increased the need for official liquidity to deal with large reversals in capital flows. There is increasing consensus that many of the recent crises in emerging markets have been triggered by self-fulfilling liquidity runs (see, for instance, Hausmann and Velasco, 2004; see also the case studies in this project). Indeed, capital outflows could be provoked by many factors not related to countries' policies.

The enhanced provision of emergency financing in the face of capital account crises is thus important not only to manage crises when they occur, but to prevent such crises and to avert contagion (Cordella and Yeyati, 2005; Griffith-Jones and Ocampo, 2003).

To address this obvious need, the IMF has made efforts in recent years to improve its lending policy during capital account crises. In 1997, the Supplemental Reserve Facility (SRF) was established. The evidence that even countries with good macroeconomic fundamentals might be subject to sudden stops of external financing also gave broad support to the idea that a precautionary financial arrangement, closer to the lender-of-last-resort functions of central banks, had to be added to existing IMF facilities. In 1999 the IMF introduced the Contingent Credit Line (CCL). The facility was never used and was discontinued in November 2003. Among the factors that may have contributed to the fact that countries failed to use it, observers have emphasized 'entry' and 'exit' problems (Buira, 2005). Contrary to what was desired, the potential use of the CCL was seen as an announcement of vulnerability that could harm confidence. Another problem was that the country had to go to the IMF Executive Board to secure a loan.

Since the expiration of the CCL, the IMF has been exploring other ways to achieve its basic objectives. As the IMF has recognized, the instant liquidity provided by a well-designed contingency line 'would place a ceiling on rollover costs – thus avoiding debt crises triggered by unsustainable refinancing rates, much in the same way as central banks operate in their role of lenders of last resort' (IMF, 2005b). The medium-term strategy of the IMF (2005a) thus includes a provision for a continued dialogue on a mechanism of contingency financing. Based on proposals by the managing director of the IMF and approved by the International Monetary and Financial Committee in April 2006, a first proposal on a Reserve Augmentation Line (RAL) was put forward in August 2006. This line would be 300 per cent of quota for one year, the full amount being available from the outset. It would require pre-qualification, made at the country's request, which would allow the country to use the resources automatically when needed (IMF, 2006). Automaticity is, of course, essential for pre-empting liquidity runs. Some developing countries have stated that the RAL is a step forward but that its design must be improved. The pre-qualification process and the amount of resources available under this line are likely to provoke considerable debate.

The additional demand for IMF lending facilities that was evident during the succession of crises in the late 1990s implied that a significant strengthening of the resource base of the IMF might be necessary, and that the potential loss to the global economy of failing to act was much higher than the opportunity costs of a larger fund size (Kelkar et al., 2005). Even though the IMF has recently sharply reduced its lending to emerging economies, in the absence of capital account crises, it is very important to maintain or expand its lending capacity to help prevent future crises.

For compensating terms of trade shocks

The provision of appropriate official liquidity to avoid costly and unnecessary adjustment to temporary terms of trade shocks is also important, particularly for low-income countries, where these shocks have larger negative effects on growth and poverty (Collier and Dehn, 2001). Furthermore, low-income countries have limited room to build foreign exchange reserves as a buffer against such shocks.

The IMF has facilities to compensate for terms of trade shocks, but they are far too limited and in some cases have become more so in recent years. The major IMF facility designed in the 1960s to compensate countries for terms of trade shocks, the Compensatory Financial Facility (CFF), has been used less and less, especially as its conditionality has been tightened. Indeed, since the modification of the CFF in 2000, when upper-tranche conditionality was introduced as a condition for its use, the CFF has not been used at all, in spite of relevant shocks.

As regards low-income countries with access to the high conditional Poverty Reduction and Growth Facility (PRGF), the augmentation of such programs has been the main vehicle used for countries hit by shocks. This has the advantage of concessionality. However, it is linked to a highly conditional fund arrangement, inappropriate for shocks caused by external events. Secondly, as the IMF recognizes, PRGF augmentation was very small compared to the impact of the shock and granted to only half the PRGF countries experiencing shocks (IMF, 2005c).

In 2005 the IMF established a second concessional PRGF 'window', called the Exogenous Shocks Facility (ESF), for countries without a PRGF program that experience shocks (which also include natural disasters). It is also, however, a high conditionality arrangement and its scale is again limited.

It seems, therefore, important that IMF facilities in these areas be modified following two criteria. First, far lower conditionality should be attached to lending for externally caused shocks, whether for middle- or low-income countries. Indeed, the original CFF and the Oil Facilities had such low conditionality and were amply as well as efficiently used. This recognized the principle that countries should not adjust policies (if these are reasonable) when faced with purely exogenous and temporary shocks. Second, the scale of existing facilities, including the concessional component in the case of low-income countries, should be significantly expanded to compensate for a far larger proportion of temporary shocks. This would reduce negative unnecessary effects on growth and poverty reduction.

A reason given for the small scale of PRGF augmentation and the ESF is the lack of concessional resources in the IMF. However, in a context of fairly rapid scaling up of aid flows, higher resources should be allocated to the IMF for financing the subsidy element of such compensatory lending.

2.8 Macroeconomic cooperation between developing countries

Contrary to the rich historical experience in the area of development financing, there is a dearth of experiences in the area of macroeconomic cooperation in the developing world.[3] However, several initiatives have been launched in recent years, often aiming to replicate European arrangements. European macroeconomic cooperation emphasized building strong institutions and subordinated capital mobility to other objectives of regional macroeconomic cooperation, particularly real exchange rate stability to facilitate regional trade integration (Wyplosz, 2006). In the developing world, although intraregional trade links are weaker (though growing rapidly in some regions, particularly in East Asia), two additional rationales are present: building defenses against global financial shocks, and avoiding distorting competition between export-oriented economies (Sakakibara, 2003).

More than monetary unions – which in the developing world have been neither abundant nor successful – the European experience has encouraged looser forms of macroeconomic dialogue among developing countries. Different initiatives break up macroeconomic cooperation into its three basic components: macroeconomic policy dialogue and eventual policy consultation and surveillance; liquidity support during crises; and exchange rate coordination (Ocampo, 2006). The frequency of shocks faced by developing countries eliminates (or significantly postpones) the desirability of the third component – which was the major objective of European macroeconomic cooperation.

The first of these components of cooperation has been reflected in the adoption of Maastricht-type criteria in the context of several integration processes in sub-Saharan Africa and in Latin America and the Caribbean. However, unless these criteria lead to regular surveillance and consultation processes that help internalize the effects of macroeconomic policies on regional partners, their credibility and rationale may be totally lost. In the developing world, it is also necessary to strike a balance between targets and policy flexibility, essential for economies subject to large shocks.

The experience of Latin America in this regard (Machinea and Rozenwurcel, 2005) indicates that the exchange of information and periodic technical meetings help build knowledge and mutual trust, and the transition to more explicit coordination mechanisms is difficult. Furthermore, a major incentive for policy coordination that was important in Europe, the ability to 'borrow credibility' from neighbors, has been absent.

The ASEAN Surveillance Process, adopted in 1998, is probably the most advanced of its kind. However, neither this mechanism nor the less structured ASEAN+3 (now integrated into the Chiang Mai Initiative) qualifies as an effective surveillance process due to the overemphasis on consensus and non-interference in the peer review process.

The second component of cooperation – liquidity support during crises – could provide an important incentive for macroeconomic coordination between developing countries but has been widely underutilized in the developing world. The experience of the Latin American Reserve Fund demonstrates that even a modest fund can make essential contributions to the balance of payments financing of developing countries (Titelman, 2006). Since 1978, this fund has provided financing to member states equivalent to 60 per cent of that of the IMF, benefiting in particular its smallest members. Its financing was clearly countercyclical, and its 'preferred-creditor status' has been reflected in its healthy portfolio, even in the face of two major crises. Furthermore, Agosin (2001) estimated that, during recent decades, even a relatively modest fund, equivalent to 15 per cent of Latin America's international reserves, could have provided financing to cope with capital outflows equivalent to the entire short-term debts of all countries, except Mexico.

The most ambitious project of this kind is the Chiang Mai Initiative agreed upon in 2000 by ASEAN+3 (Park, 2006). The agreed mechanism is the negotiation of bilateral swap arrangements between the central banks of the member countries, which added up to US$71.5 billion in February 2006. Aside from liquidity financing, the mechanism has provided an instrument of policy dialogue and a surveillance mechanism (which is deemed essential by net contributors, particularly Japan). The mechanism entitles countries to an automatic disbursement of up to 20 per cent of the maximum amount of drawings, but beyond that a formal IMF program is required. A modest step towards the multilateralization of bilateral swaps was taken in May 2005, when it was decided that the swap-activation process would be based on a collective decision-making process. The mechanism has not yet been utilized and, indeed, the buoyant conditions of the member countries in recent years may have slowed down the pace of action.

The recent decision to multilateralize the swap arrangement could lead to reserve pooling and even serve to back a common reserve currency. If a strong surveillance mechanism is put in place, financing could be detached from an IMF program. In addition, the policy dialogue could also eventually evolve into a more formal system of policy coordination. Moreover, if the membership of the initiative is expanded to include other countries (particularly India), the system could eventually evolve into a fully-fledged Asian monetary system (Rana, 2005). This is more likely if the issue of Asian countries' voice and participation in the IMF is not solved in an acceptable manner.

2.9 Conclusions

Volatility and contagion in international financial markets has increased the incidence of financial crises and growth volatility in the developing world, and reduced 'policy space' to adopt countercyclical macroeconomic policies. Therefore, this chapter argues that the major task of a development-friendly international financial architecture is to mitigate procyclical effects of financial markets and open 'policy space' for countercyclical macroeconomic policies in the developing world.

To achieve these objectives, the chapter explores a series of useful policy instruments: the explicit introduction of countercyclical criteria in the design of prudential regulatory and supervisory frameworks; designing market mechanisms that better distribute the risk faced by developing countries throughout the business cycle (GDP-indexed and local currency bonds); multilateral instruments that encourage more stable private flows, such as countercyclical guarantees; and better provision of countercyclical official liquidity to deal with external shocks. It also suggests that some forms of macroeconomic cooperation between developing countries can play a role, particularly regional macroeconomic consultation, and common reserve funds or swap arrangements.

Notes

This chapter began as a paper for the CEDES/IDRC Project on 'International Financial Architecture, Macro Volatility and Institutions: the Developing Country Experience'. The authors are grateful to José María Fanelli and Jan Kregel for comments.

1. For recent analyses of these issues and policy options for managing them, see BIS (2001: ch. 7) and Ocampo (2003).
2. China, Hong Kong SAR, Indonesia, the Republic of Korea, the Philippines, Malaysia, Singapore, and Thailand.
3. See United Nations (1999), Culpeper (2006), Mistry (1999) and Ocampo (2006).

3
Regional and Multilateral Efforts: Institution-Building

Yung Chul Park, Yunjong Wang and Doo Yong Yang

3.1 Introduction

Developing countries are vulnerable to external economic volatilities. To accelerate economic growth, most developing countries have opened their economies to the world. Trade contributes to fostering domestic industry, and increases national income. Financial openness, on the other hand, provides better opportunities for reducing volatility by diversifying risk. The benefits from economic openness are even greater for developing countries that are intrinsically subject to higher volatility on account of having less diversified production structures than industrial economies. However, in reality, developing countries have shown macroeconomic volatilities associated with the boom–bust cycle and, moreover, they are prone to crises in extreme cases. In order to reduce these vulnerabilities, there have been tremendous efforts at the national, regional and global levels. However, as witnessed by the Asian crisis and other emerging market crises since the 1990s, current international institutions are not enough to mitigate their risks and volatilities when global economic turmoil is spreading.

Against this background, this chapter aims to address the following issues: (1) opportunities for cooperation on mitigating macro volatility at the regional level; (2) scope for regional financial arrangements (RFAs) to facilitate the management of risks and a reduction in the instability of capital movements; (3) evaluation of the institutional constraints on regional cooperation in light of the findings of country studies concerning the DFA (domestic financial architecture) and linkages of the DFA with regional and multilateral institutions; and (4) identification of demands for the coordination of national, regional, and multilateral initiatives for financial institution-building from the point of view of developing countries.

The chapter is organized as follows. First, it examines the sources of excess aggregate volatility in emerging market economies. Second, it assesses forceful reasons explaining why regional economic cooperation is crucial to mitigating macroeconomic volatility in developing economies. Third, it suggests necessary regional financial arrangements to facilitate the management of risks and a reduction in the instability of capital movements. In this process, we presumed some institutional constraints on regional cooperation based on ASEAN+3 experiences, followed by a solution of financial institution-building, with national, regional, and multilateral initiatives.

3.2 Sources of excess aggregate volatility in emerging market economies

The country studies in the CEDES/IDRC Project on 'International Financial Architecture, Macro Volatility and Institutions: the Developing Country Experience' have shown that aggregate volatility in developing countries is substantially higher than in developed countries. Two important elements explain the presence of this excess volatility: structural factors and financial imperfections associated with the adaptive responses of private and public agents to an institutionally weak and volatile environment. Despite varying degrees of each country's integration with the global economy, the studies commonly identify two kinds of structural features associated with the external sector. First, on the trade front, developing countries tend to exhibit high export volatility, mainly due to the lack of export diversification and a continuous stream of terms of trade shocks. Second, on the financial front, developing countries are not able to finance significant current account deficits for relatively extended periods. Such deficient integration with international capital markets (the so-called external finance constraints) generates procyclicality of capital flows in developing countries.

Let us first review trade-related structural factors from the country studies. In the case of Argentina, trade diversification is still low and revealed comparative advantages that concentrate mainly on primary products. Thus, terms of trade shocks (commodity price shocks) are still relevant not only in driving business cycles, but also in determining trade account results, while changes in the real exchange rate can substantially affect the absolute value of deficits and surpluses in the short run. However, terms of trade shocks do not seem to be a major determinant of recent balance of payments problems in the case of Brazil. Brazil's export products are now highly diversified, and thus, terms of trade movements have become much less important for the trade balance and current account results than in the past.

Among the eight sample countries in this project, Chile, Russia, South Africa and Nigeria can be grouped with Argentina. The countries in this group share the characteristic of a relatively high export share of primary goods vis-à-vis manufactured goods. For example, since the mid-1970s, crude oil has dominated Nigeria's export basket. Currently, fuel accounts for over 98 per cent of the country's total exports. On the other hand, China and Thailand can be grouped with Brazil. For instance, China's accelerated growth since implementing reforms has been accompanied by labor-intensive, export-oriented industrial growth. Consequently, China has emerged as an important trading power in the world, with almost one-third of its GDP attributable to exports by 2003. Meanwhile, the share of primary goods in total exports dropped significantly, from roughly

70 per cent in the pre-reform era to only 9 per cent in 2003. The product composition and destinations for China's exports became so diversified that China has been able to maintain a stable growth of exports since the mid-1980s. However, as oil and other raw material prices increased sharply from 2003, China's terms of trade deteriorated significantly. In China, imports became more volatile than exports.

To summarize, the country with a more diversified structure of export products tends to be much less affected by terms of trade shocks. Along with the composition of trade structure, trade openness also determines the relative magnitude of external vis-à-vis domestic shocks on excess aggregate volatility. A higher value of exports to GDP (or higher value of trade volume to GDP) is more likely to strengthen trade linkages so that the changes in external conditions (global business cycles or business cycles of major trading partners) have a significant impact on economic fluctuations.

Let us now turn to external financial linkages as a source of excess macroeconomic volatility. In theory, financial linkages may allow countries to share domestic shocks with foreign countries through cross-border transactions of state-contingent assets. By trading financial assets internationally, a country can diversify its income sources and reduce country-specific risks. Such trade is a typical example of risk-sharing through financial markets. However, as is documented in Obstfeld and Taylor (2004), such financial transactions are primarily confined to rich countries, enabling the wealthy not to put all their eggs in one basket by holding assets from other rich countries. On the other hand, most developing countries, despite varying degrees of market access to international capital markets, face external liquidity constraints. When a developing country hit by a negative shock (such as a bad harvest or low prices for its commodity exports) is able to borrow and then repay out of the proceeds of a positive shock at some later time, this countercyclical pattern of capital flows could be a strong stabilizing force. However, a procyclical pattern observed in the cases of Argentina and Brazil made capital flows a potential source of excess volatility. When capital inflows were actually needed, they suddenly stopped and capital outflows began. Another example can be found in the case of Chile. Chile's decade-long capital inflows dried up in 1998 when the price of its copper exports slumped as a result of the Asian crisis. Such procyclicality of capital flows exerted an adverse influence of negative terms of trade shocks on macroeconomic fluctuations.

A key message from the country studies is that developing countries are different from developed countries in financial matters. While developed countries may be rocked by serious financial disturbances, their financial markets remain resilient and their governments and central banks have many tools available to cushion any blow. In contrast, in developing countries, even minor disturbances can have large effects. Institutional deficiencies and policy mistakes certainly matter in explaining why capital flows as a source of excess aggregate volatility can often be disruptive in developing countries. As highlighted by the country studies, inefficient risk management (deficient institutions and bad policies) is a source of excess aggregate volatility and crises.

Financial markets can only be built up gradually along with financial liberalization (both domestic and international) and they must be resilient enough to meet the risks associated with such liberalization. History tells us that this gradual process is a matter of decades, not months or years. Nevertheless, many economists imbued by the 'Washington Consensus' occasionally propose rapid liberalization under the premise of free market merits. In particular, when emerging market economies were hit by deep financial crises, the IMF program included financial sector reform measures composed of short-term operational restructuring and medium-term institutional reforms. Although a well-conceived plan for capital market development could complement the bank-dominated financial system in emerging market economies, it can only be a long-term priority because the bank-based emerging market system cannot simply be replaced by a market-based system overnight. Rapid dismantling of the existing system (even a flawed system) could create an institutional void.

Financial market liberalization per se does not necessarily raise the odds of a crisis. Nevertheless, financial liberalization in both developed and developing countries has led to hazardous outcomes, such as exchange rate instability, possibly culminating in full-blown currency and banking crises when the accompanying institutional measures have not been adequately put in place. In other words, the adverse effects of financial liberalization occur mainly in countries with poor institutions, characterized by the absence of proper banking regulation and supervision, widespread corruption and, more generally, poor law and order.

Furthermore, there exists a bi-directional causal relationship between the quality of institutions and aggregate volatility. Deficient risk management is likely to generate high aggregate volatility and financial instability. In the worst cases, such volatile boom–bust cycles and increasing financial instability can lead to crises. In an environment of macroeconomic volatility and frequent crises, governments in emerging markets cannot develop social and financial institutions sufficiently to support efficient risk management in the private sector.

Given that the road to strong financial markets and sound financial institutions is bumpy enough to deter embarkation on the trip, what would the process of safe liberalization be that could reap the benefits without incurring the costs? Answers may be easy, even though implementation is not. Most countries will eventually liberalize, but if they want to avoid the adverse effects that come with financial liberalization, it may be advisable for them to wait until they have the proper economic and financial infrastructure in place. With the necessary institutions in place, a gradual but progressive sequencing strategy can be a safe bet. However, the view favoring very gradual liberalization cannot clearly answer the question of how developing countries can catch up or converge with advanced financial systems.

In charting a new development strategy, most developing countries have adopted a market-oriented approach in which control over asset and liability management and ownership of financial institutions has been eased and financial markets and financial services industries are also deregulated and opened to foreign competition. At the same time, developing countries have taken measures to improve and increase the scale of capital markets, which have led to institutional reform of accounting, disclosure and the governance of financial institutions and other corporations. Improving the quality of legal and regulatory systems also complemented this institutional reform. However, this liberal strategy does not shed light on how long it is going to take to develop an advanced financial system. The answer depends on the ability of these countries to develop efficient market-supporting institutions, which will take a long period of time if the experiences of developed countries are any guide.

3.3 Why is regional cooperation necessary to mitigate macroeconomic volatility?

In assessing the emerging market crises of the last decade, traditional macroeconomic fundamentals were of secondary significance. If countries had put in place sound institutions to prevent investor herding, contagion, and speculative attacks, they would have been able to thwart the crisis even while going through cyclically unfavorable macroeconomic conditions. During the Asian crisis period, Taiwan and Singapore managed the contagion by floating their currencies and insulating their financial markets through a gradual and orderly sequence of capital account opening. China, another of the less affected economies, was saved by a very restricted capital account during the financial turmoil of its neighbors.

In contrast, the four crisis-hit countries in East Asia – Indonesia, Malaysia, South Korea, and Thailand – had structural deficiencies exposed to the vagaries of international capital. Pressured by Western governments and international financial institutions, these four countries rather involuntarily followed the Washington Consensus and liberalized their financial markets prematurely. As a result, they did not consider the possibility that pell-mell liberalization could invite speculative attacks and financial crises. Singapore and Hong Kong had financially sound and economically healthy fundamentals as well as mature institutions vis-à-vis the four crisis-affected East Asian countries. However, Hong Kong also became a victim of the crisis because of its firm commitment to the pegged exchange rate system that invited speculative attacks. Hong Kong weathered a series of attacks at the expense of its overall macroeconomic difficulties.

As developing countries take time to build competent institutions, selective globalization would be preferable. This entails an approach that steers an economy away from excessive short-term capital movements, but maintains trust in free trade and the virtues of foreign direct investment. Certainly, globalization is part of the solution, not a part of the problem. But, institutional changes and support mechanisms are required to cope with adverse outcomes if and when financial globalization materializes (Bhagwati, 2004). In developing countries, institutional distortions and market failures complicate credible inflation targeting, render large exchange rate movements more dangerous, make fixed exchange rates acutely crisis-prone, and apparently reduce the beneficial effects of financial globalization (Obstfeld, 2004).

The findings of the project suggest that the Brazilian and Chilean examples are highly relevant concerning inflation targeting and institution-building. In Brazil, the regime was imposed after the crisis and resulted in systematically high real interest rates while Chile introduced inflation targeting after a lengthy period of patiently implementing anti-inflationary policies and an extended process of building sound financial regulations. It seems that the Chilean approach is more akin to the selective globalization approach. The evidence in the Argentine case study, in turn, illustrates that even a currency board can be crisis-prone. The Chinese gradual approach to reform is also akin to selective globalization, although the case study shows that a lagging financial reform can give rise to important obstacles.

In the wake of financial crises, most emerging market economies have gone far into Western-style reform based on Anglo-American capitalism. While crisis-hit countries were subject to a heavy dose of domestic structural reforms, supply-side problems concerning international finance have been by and large ignored. As long as the inherent problems of international capital on the supply side are not effectively addressed, many emerging market economies will remain as vulnerable to future crises as they were beforehand. As East Asia, Russia, Brazil, Turkey, and Argentina climbed out of the danger zone and the fear of contagion receded, the G7 and international financial community appear to have lost their zeal in garnering the support they need for reform. The ongoing debate on the future direction of an international financial architecture suggests that most of the problems are likely to remain unchanged (Park and Wang, 2002). The lack of global governance, including a global lender of last resort and global financial regulator, is not likely to be remedied any time soon.[1]

This pessimistic outlook arouses a deep concern in developing countries that they will continue to be vulnerable to future financial crises, even if they faithfully carry out the kinds of reform recommended by the IMF and World Bank. The national strategy of having a very large stock of foreign reserves to deal with significant capital flight may work, but it is an extremely expensive strategy. Naturally, it has occurred to many astute economists in East Asia that a regional pooling of foreign exchange reserves may be a cost-effective response to the problem of large but infrequent capital flight. Building on this insight and from the monetary integration experience of Western Europe, a growing number of East Asian economists are realizing that a regional initiative could be an alternative solution to the deficient international financial architecture. These efforts have resulted in a number of regional cooperative arrangements, including the Chiang Mai Initiative (CMI) in 2000. For this initiative, the ten members of the Association of South-East Asian Nations (ASEAN), along with China, Japan and South Korea (known as ASEAN+3), agreed to establish a system of bilateral swaps, a facility for liquidity support for participating countries suffering from short-run balance of payments problems.

A large body of literature on contagion also argues that capital flows in different countries, particularly developing countries in the same region, are synchronized through various channels of financial contagion including herding behavior, information asymmetry, and so on (Calvo and Mendoza, 2000; Mendoza, 2001). International investors may classify different countries in a single group and make region-based investment decisions. In addition, capital flows can be highly synchronized if shocks that determine capital flows are positively correlated or spill over across countries, or if developing countries go through financial liberalization processes at the same time.

A regional grouping for support is logical given contagion's geographical concentration. Neighbors have an interest in helping extinguish a financial crisis before it spreads (Ito et al., 1999). As long as a crisis remains country-specific or regional, there is no urgent political need for unaffected countries to pay the significant costs associated with playing the role of fire-fighter. In addition to providing financial assistance in tandem with international support, a regional financial cooperation mechanism may conduct policy reviews and initiate a dialogue process.

Policy dialogue, including monitoring and surveillance, is the bedrock on which rests a coherent policy formation for regional financial arrangements. A monitoring and surveillance process would provide prompt and relevant information for assessing the situation of countries in trouble and the potential contagious effects of a crisis to neighboring countries. Furthermore, a joint exercise based on a region-wide early warning system would facilitate closer examination of financial vulnerabilities. In addition, the regional policy dialogue process would contribute to ensuring effective implementation of high-quality banking and financial standards, and promoting financial market development.

3.4 What kind of regional financial arrangements are needed to facilitate the management of risks and a reduction in the instability of capital movements?

If a scheme for regional financial cooperation is effective in facilitating the management of risks and a reduction in the instability of capital movements, no one can deny the desirability of regional financial arrangements. However, various institutions have different memberships and goals for regional financial cooperation. In this regard, regional financial arrangements and institutions should set out blueprints for clear objectives and missions, operational efficiency and effectiveness, and capable financial and human resources.

The three pillars of liquidity assistance, monitoring and surveillance, and exchange rate coordination are essential elements for regional financial and monetary cooperation. However, its development and related institutions will be evolutionary as shown in the case of European monetary integration. A shallow form of financial cooperation may comprise no more than a common foreign reserve pooling or mutual credit arrangement such as bilateral swaps. In other words, some kinds of shallow financial cooperation are conceivable without any commitment to exchange rate coordination under which exchange rates of the participating countries are pegged to each other or vanish through the adoption of a common currency.

In order to cope effectively with the instability of capital movements and manage the excess macroeconomic volatility, we can envision three kinds of regional financial initiatives: (1) institutionalizing regional financial arrangements (RFAs) as a defensive mechanism for crisis prevention and management; (2) exchange rate coordination for mitigating the adverse impact of global imbalances; (3) promoting a regional bond market.

Regional financial arrangements (RFAs)

Let us briefly review the current status of Asian financial cooperation as a candidate regional cooperative scheme for other developing countries or regions. The Chiang Mai Initiative (CMI) is the first significant effort at Asian financial cooperation meant to enable member countries to cope with disruptive capital flows and maintain exchange rate stability.[2] Substantial progress has been made in implementing the CMI. The ASEAN Swap Arrangement (ASA), one of the main components of the CMI, has increased to US$1 billion, effective as of 17 November 2000, and encompasses all ASEAN member countries. Substantial bilateral agreements have been reached regarding the network of bilateral swap agreements (BSAs) under the CMI. As of 24 February 2006, the 16 BSAs amounted to US$71.5 billion in total. Japan has been playing a leading role in terms of

Table 3.1 Progress on the Chiang Mai Initiative

BSA	Currencies	Conclusion dates	Amount (US$ billion)
Japan–Korea[a]	USD/won	24 February 2006	10
	USD/yen		5
Japan–Korea	Won/yen	27 May 2005	3 (two-way)
Japan–Thailand	USD/baht	30 July 2001	3 (two-way)
Japan–Philippines	USD/peso	27 August 2001	3 (one-way)
Japan–Malaysia	USD/ringgit	5 October 2001	1 (one-way)
Japan–Indonesia	USD/rupiah	31 August 2005	6 (one-way)
Japan–Singapore	USD/SD	8 November 2005	3
	USD/yen		1
Japan–PRC	Yen/rmb	28 March 2002	3 (two way)
PRC–Thailand	USD/baht	6 December 2001	2 (one-way)
PRC–Korea	Won/RMB	24 June 2002	4 (two-way)
PRC–Malaysia	USD/ringgit	9 October 2002	1.5 (one-way)
PRC–Philippines	RMB/peso	29 August 2003	1 (one-way)
PRC–Indonesia	USD/rupiah	30 December 2003	2 (one-way)
Korea–Thailand	USD/baht	25 June 2002	1 (two-way)
Korea–Malaysia	USD/ringgit	26 July 2002	1.5 (two-way)
Korea–Philippines	USD/peso	9 August 2002	1.5 (two-way)
Korea–Indonesia	USD/rupiah	24 December 2003	1 (two-way)

Notes: Under the New Miyazawa Initiative, a BSA exists between Japan and Korea (US$5 billion) and between Japan and Malaysia (US$2.5 billion). a. Japan and Korea concluded a one-way BSA between the US dollar and won up to US$2 billion on 4 July 2001. Following the ASEAN+3 finance ministers' agreement in May 2005 to enhance the CMI's effectiveness, Japan and Korea replaced the existing BSA with a new two-way BSA.

both numbers and amounts, and has concluded seven agreements – with Korea, China, Indonesia, Malaysia, the Philippines, Thailand, and Singapore. China concluded five agreements – Korea, Indonesia, Malaysia, the Philippines and Thailand – in addition to the China–Japan BSA. Similarly, Korea concluded five agreements – with China, Indonesia, Malaysia, the Philippines and Thailand – in addition to the Japan–Korea BSA (see Table 3.1).

At the 8th ASEAN+3 finance ministers' meeting held on 4 May 2005, some developments were taken to strengthen the CMI mechanism. First, the ministers agreed that countries holding BSAs with a country in difficulty would make a collective decision in lending money to that country. This agreement can be seen as a first step toward multilateralizing the CMI. Since the CMI swap network has not yet been tested, it would only be workable when one or two countries come under pressure. If a number of countries are simultaneously experiencing pressure from capital markets, it would be only natural to expect a degree of reluctance to take on any additional obligations in defense of their neighbors. Thus, such joint decisions and action will be required to prevent a free-rider problem. Second, the size of the swaps increased. The ASA doubled to US$2 billion. At the same time, the current swap amount of any BSA can be expanded by up to 100 per cent if both sides agree to increase the amount. Consequently, Japan and Korea replaced the existing BSA with a new two-way BSA on 24 February 2006. Third, the CMI's autonomy was strengthened in that the autonomous disbursement without IMF involvement increased from 10 to 20 per cent. These developments reflect a growing sense of regional financial cooperation.

Despite these recent developments, the CMI still has several limitations. One important issue remaining is linkage of the CMI to the IMF. As long as the CMI is a source of financial resources supplementary to the IMF, the size of the swap borrowing does not necessarily need to be large enough to meet potential needs because there exists another deep pocket of financial resources provided by the IMF. In fact, the swap amount a country can draw on without IMF involvement is still insignificant. For instance, Thailand currently maintains three credit lines, with China, Japan and Korea, through the BSAs, the total amount of which is US$6 billion. Since 20 per cent of the swap arrangements can be disbursed without IMF involvement, the available amount is US$1.2 billion, which is insignificant compared to the size of the IMF package for Thailand (US$17.2 billion). Thus, at present, the CMI cannot be a meaningful regional defense mechanism independent of the IMF.

Although the CMI is not allowed to design its own conditionality at this point, it does need to establish its own surveillance mechanism. Under the revised CMI framework, 20 per cent of the swap arrangements can be disbursed without IMF involvement. But because this 20 per cent can be disbursed only with the consent of swap-providing countries, they need to formulate their own assessments about the swap-requesting country. At present, the current practices under the ASEAN+3 process cannot effectively capture emerging problems. The real value-added contribution of the regional financial arrangements is not the additional financial resources along with the IMF, but better expertise in monitoring and surveillance of the realities and constraints facing countries in the region so that recovery packages can be tailored to fit both the recovery requirements and realities in the region (Sussangkarn and Vichyanond, 2006).

Most participating countries agree in principle that the CMI needs to be supported by an independent monitoring and surveillance system. This system would monitor economic developments in the region, serve as an institutional framework for policy dialogue and coordination between members, and impose structural and policy reform on countries drawing from the BSAs. To do so, ASEAN+3 finance ministers agreed to organize a study group to produce a blueprint for an effective mechanism of policy dialogues and economic reviews for CMI operations at the ADB annual meeting in Honolulu on 9 May 2001. The study group met in Kuala Lumpur on 22 November 2001 to discuss a report on possible surveillance modalities prepared by Bank Negara Malaysia and Japan's Ministry of Finance. However, member countries were unable to reach an agreement on the surveillance issues by the end of the first round of the CMI's implementation, agreeing only to institutionalize the ASEAN+3 meetings of deputies for informal policy reviews and dialogue. At this stage of the CMI's development, many countries feel uncomfortable about creating an independent regional monitoring and surveillance unit as part of the CMI. At the ASEAN+3 finance ministers' meeting in May 2005 it was finally agreed to integrate and enhance the current economic surveillance process with the CMI framework. However, it remains to be seen if further meaningful progress can be achieved.

In the long run, however, participating countries are likely to wean themselves from their reliance on the IMF. If the CMI develops into a more or less independent financial arrangement, then the regional financial arrangement should be designed to discipline borrowers to adhere to sound macroeconomic and financial policies by imposing conditionalities. However, ASEAN+3 countries at the current stage do not seem well prepared for establishing a policy coordination mechanism in the surveillance process.[3]

Finally, the CMI has nothing to do with exchange rate coordination. In comparison with Europe, the CMI is motivated by completely different reasons. The European facilities were created with the purpose of limiting bilateral exchange rate fluctuations among regional currencies. The CMI started with high capital mobility and flexible exchange rates, although some members of ASEAN+3 have maintained a relatively fixed exchange rate regime. So far, ASEAN+3 countries have not presumed any manifest exchange rate coordination. In the absence of such coordination, incentives for mutual surveillance will be limited because a member country facing a speculative currency attack may be free to float its exchange rate vis-à-vis those of neighboring countries (Wang and Woo, 2004). Under the current ASEAN+3 policy dialogue framework, the purpose of the CMI and mutual surveillance system is to prevent the occurrence of financial crises and contagion in the region.

What kinds of regional financial arrangements are needed to facilitate the management of risks and reduce the instability of capital movements? We can draw on the implications from the role of the (IMF) in a world of private capital markets. The IMF provides public monitoring services and negotiates programs that enable borrowers to reveal their commitment to sound macroeconomic policies. In addition, its own lending may stabilize capital flows by providing bridge financing for creditworthy countries experiencing liquidity crises, the resolution of which may be difficult to coordinate for atomistic lenders (Eichengreen et al., 2005). Regional financial arrangements (or regional financial funds) may be able to take on similar roles. However, as was mentioned above, the exact form is a function of the degree of integration. The more institutionally integrated the region is, the more comprehensive and binding the nature of policy coordination would be.

With regard to regional monitoring and surveillance services, at the most elementary stage of zero institutional integration, when governments simply take the policies of other governments as given, the existence of policy spillovers means that it would still be useful for governments to exchange information and consult each other in a setting free of any formal pressure. When regional cooperation moves to the level of mutual liquidity provisions (such as the CMI swap arrangements), moral hazard then creates a strong case for monitoring and surveillance, along with a clear need for specific enforcement mechanisms. An appropriate reference point for such regional activities would be IMF consultations and conditionality. Finally, when the regional grouping agrees to deepen integration through exchange rate coordination, monetary policy coordination then becomes as crucial as mutual economic surveillance. The appropriate reference point in this case would be the process through which Europe progressed from the Common Market to the European Union. Between non-interference and full integration lies coordination – joint problem identification and pursuit of mutually beneficial policy objectives. Various forms, such as informal consultation, peer pressure, and rule-based penalties, may be used for encouraging and enforcing certain common policies.

A regional monitoring and surveillance system should be constructed to stabilize and strengthen domestic financial systems as a supporting instrument and mechanism for regional financial arrangements. Most crisis-prone developing countries, as shown in the case studies of the project, suffer from inadequate economic and legal infrastructure resulting in an inefficient allocation of high savings, inordinately large short-term debt markets, and a general absence of arm's-length transactions. The regional policy dialogue process should therefore pay particular attention to the root problems of such countries' weak domestic financial systems. Besides strengthening prudential supervision, risk management, and corporate governance, financial authorities in the region must also actively promote long-term capital markets. This is a situation whereby financial cooperation can deepen and enhance regional financial markets.

Improved monitoring and surveillance are also useful in identifying emerging issues and potential problems, thus enabling countries to take corrective action at the national or jointly at the regional level. As often observed in the IMF surveillance process, symptoms of a crisis and economic vulnerabilities have not been captured effectively. Regional initiatives could complement the IMF surveillance process in that regional economies have become much more interdependent through trade and financial channels over the last decade. There is a pressing need to engage in regional monitoring and surveillance precisely because spillover effects in the region are insidious.[4]

The above discussion points to the need for establishing an independent monitoring and surveillance unit for the purpose of providing prompt and relevant information to any regional cooperative group. Its monitoring activities in general should cover: (1) macroeconomic trends and policy changes in the region; (2) financial market developments; and (3) structural and institutional changes. This unit would also be required to develop a policy dialogue and surveillance mechanism to enforce: (1) the implementation of common standards agreed among members; (2) policy changes and reforms required of those countries in need; and (3) economic policy coordination agreed between the members. Such a unit would evolve over time as the participating countries build trust and accumulate experience in policy dialogue.

Although structured regional surveillance initiatives provide a potentially meaningful and substantive valued-added contribution to the current ASEAN+3 policy dialogue, East Asian countries have not yet specified common policy objectives. Crisis prevention and management is rather ambiguous as a policy objective for surveillance. Surveillance mechanisms should come along with other pillars of monetary and financial cooperation. In the case of European integration, a more effective and structured surveillance process started only when the European countries sought monetary integration in the 1990s (see Table 3.2). Thus, it will take more time for ASEAN+3 countries to agree on establishing more comprehensive and structured surveillance systems such as the European Economic and Monetary Union (EMU).

In our view, an independent surveillance unit must be established to serve as a standing secretariat that leads the policy dialogue mechanism in the region. This unit may start on a modest scale. Given limited financial and human resources inside the unit, a network of government research institutions could be established and the unit could serve as a coordinating agency.

This independent surveillance unit is expected to serve as a warehouse of information and a provider of warning signals for both individual countries and the group as a whole. By conducting extensive early warning exercises at the national and regional levels, this unit will identify problems and prepare independent surveillance reports for the group. In preparing for the surveillance report, the unit may need a fact-finding mission similar to the IMF surveillance. To avoid duplication of the IMF's Article IV consultation, the unit may participate in IMF surveillance jointly with IMF staff. Combined with country reports submitted by all member countries, this unit's surveillance report will be a compendium report based on its own assessment.

The unit may also be entitled to conduct preparatory research on future cooperative issues such as exchange rate policy coordination and financial market integration. As shown in the case studies, macroeconomic volatilities are closely related to inappropriate exchange rate management and fragile financial systems. It therefore cannot be overemphasized that the regional surveillance unit must

Table 3.2 Historical development of monitoring and surveillance mechanisms in Europe

System	Period	Objects	Monitoring and surveillance institutions	Characteristics
EPU	1950–58	Trade expansion by securing payment system	Managing Board	Bilateral payment system → multilateral payment system; the board monitors and gives directives
Bretton Woods System & Treaty of Rome	1958–72	Supporting economic integration by securing fixed exchange-rate system	Monetary Committee Committee of Governors	IMF was more active than regional institutions
Snake System	1972–78	Maintaining common market and common agricultural policy by bilateral fluctuations and joint floating against dollar	European Monetary Cooperation Fund Monetary Committee Committee of Governors	National interests were greater than regional interests
EMS	1978–92	Securing internal stability of exchange rates	Same institutions, but more active	Countries with a strong currency shared the burden of intervention
EMU	1993–present	Introducing single common currency	EMI in the transition period; ECB after introduction of the euro	National competences are transferred to the community; binding rules introduced

not only be a watchdog of national macroeconomic and exchange rate policies, but also an overseer of the national financial markets, and the linkages between them and the rest of the world (Wang and Woo, 2004).

A proper design of conditionality would be a point of debate. It would be useful to distinguish between technical assistance and financial assistance. There is no reason to discourage competition in the market for technical assistance. Governments should be free to choose the source of technical assistance with the best track record. However, if multiple monetary funds were available, governments facing the imminent crisis would have an incentive to shop around for the most generous assistance and the least onerous conditionality. If the regional monetary fund (or financial arrangement) does not attach IMF-like conditionality, the international financial community might raise the issue of moral hazard. In this regard, relevant but binding policy recommendations should be imposed on borrowing countries. Without an appropriate lending discipline in place, regional financial arrangements would likely be dysfunctional due to the lax supervision of financial assistance.

East Asians presently appear to be pursuing financial cooperation in the absence of exchange rate coordination. It is not yet clear whether East Asia will emulate the European experience by adopting some form of monetary integration. However, if East Asia started monetary integration in the future, the regional surveillance mechanism would have to be structured and managed in order to support the coordinated exchange rate mechanism.

As the EU Commission and European Monetary Institute (EMI) served as facilitators to promote economic and monetary integration, East Asia should establish politically independent institutions along with an official policy dialogue process. The professionals working at this independent institution should be able to follow up on the decisions of politicians on integration, and advance common policy objectives and related modalities more adequately by adding their own creative ideas to the policy dialogue group.

Global imbalances and exchange rate policy coordination

In 2005, the United States was running its largest ever external current account deficit, in the order of 6.5 per cent of GDP, which exceeded US$800 billion. This US deficit absorbed about three-quarters of the net foreign savings of the rest of the world. A major counterpart of the US deficit has been the external surpluses of East Asian countries. About 46 per cent of East Asia's total current account surplus came from the region's trade with the US in 2004 and not surprisingly, much of it was converted into holdings of short-term US treasury securities, which have been the source of transpacific imbalances (see Table 3.3). The reserve accumulation in most East Asian economies, with the possible exception

Table 3.3 Current account balance of selected economies (US$ billion)

Country/region	2000	2001	2002	2003	2004	2005
Euro area	–66.0	–3.1	61.9	23.5	58.7	–35.9
US	–416.0	–389.5	–475.2	–519.7	–668.1	–804.9
Japan	119.7	87.8	112.5	136.2	172.1	163.8
China	20.5	17.4	35.4	45.9	68.7	n/a
Hong Kong	7.0	9.8	12.4	16.5	16.4	n/a
India	–2.7	3.4	6.3	10.6	–6.4	n/a
Korea	12.3	7.3	5.5	11.9	28.2	16.6
Malaysia	8.5	7.3	7.2	13.4	14.9	n/a
Singapore	11.9	14.4	15.7	27.0	27.9	34.9
Taiwan	8.9	18.3	25.6	29.3	18.5	16.4
Mexico	–18.6	–17.7	–13.5	–8.6	–7.2	–5.7

Source: IMF, International Financial Statistics.

Table 3.4 External reserves of selected economies (US$ billion)

Country/region	2000	2001	2002	2003	2004	2005
Euro area	242.3	235.0	247.0	222.7	211.3	184.7
US	56.6	57.6	68.0	74.9	75.9	54.1
Japan	354.9	395.2	461.2	663.3	833.9	846.9
China	168.3	215.6	291.1	408.2	614.5	818.9
Hong Kong	107.5	111.2	111.9	118.4	123.5	124.3
India	37.9	45.9	67.7	98.9	126.6	137.2
Korea	96.1	102.8	121.3	155.3	199.0	210.3
Malaysia	29.5	30.5	34.2	44.5	66.4	72.0
Singapore	80.1	75.4	82.0	95.7	112.2	115.8
Taiwan	107.1	122.2	161.7	206.6	241.7	253.3
Mexico	35.5	44.7	50.6	59.0	64.1	74.1

Source: IMF, International Financial Statistics.

of Japan, has been the result of sterilized intervention for stabilizing either the nominal or real effective exchange rate with the objective of maintaining their export competitiveness.

As shown in Table 3.4, the notable increase of external reserves in 2005 was observed in China, from US$614.5 billion in 2004 to US$818.9 billion in 2005. Although Japan was massively accumulating external reserves in most of 2002 through early 2004, it has not done so since March 2004, and the European Central Bank has largely refrained from intervening to limit the rise of the euro. Most emerging East Asian countries other than China felt less pressure for currency appreciation during the course of 2005, mainly because the US Federal Reserve's interest hike reversed the dollar's path and consequently delayed the global adjustment process. Following Japan, in 2005 only mild reserve accumulation has taken place in the four NIEs of East Asia – South Korea, Taiwan, Hong Kong and Singapore. However, as long as underlying causes of the global imbalances remain unchanged, delayed adjustment is likely to invoke large exchange rate alignments of East Asian currencies and a potentially global recession after the Federal Reserve funds rate (FFR) peaks.

Another mirror image of global imbalances can be found in the perverse pattern of international capital flows. Lucas (1990) examined the question of why capital flows from rich to poor countries have been at much lower levels than predicted by standard neoclassical models, and it is fundamentally perverse for capital to be flowing from developing countries to the United States, as is now occurring, instead of the other way around (Cline, 2005). Consequently, the excessive reserve accumulation in East Asia has incurred a relatively high cost.[5] By any measure of adequacy, East Asia's external reserves have been excessive. In realizing the high cost of reserve holdings, some East Asian economies have loosened up the control over capital outflows.

There have been various policy suggestions for resolving global imbalances. In particular, it is widely argued that the dollar needs to depreciate substantially to make US exports more attractive to foreign buyers and imports less attractive to American consumers.[6] The consequences of a sharp dollar depreciation will not be comfortable for East Asian countries with already extensive dollar-denominated assets. Furthermore, dollar depreciation alone, without any accompanying fiscal consolidation of the US, would not be successful for curbing the US external deficit. According to an IMF report (2005d), a further appreciation of East Asian currencies 'will only have limited effect on current account position' (p. 5). However, the report goes on to focus on expansion in East Asia's domestic demand rather than the US fiscal deficit adjustment.

As for a correction in the dollar, there is little disagreement that an across the board appreciation of East Asian currencies constitutes an important component of the resolution of global imbalances. However, if China insists on maintaining its limited flexibility, other East Asian countries are not likely to allow their currencies to be less competitive vis-à-vis the renminbi, as China has emerged as their export competitor in regional as well as global markets. Thus, there is clearly a need for a collective exchange rate policy for East Asia in the sense that only collective action can resolve the prisoner's dilemma problem. And there is an institutional arrangement, such as the ASEAN+3 meetings of finance ministers or their deputies, which could serve as an agency for coordination of exchange rate policy among ASEAN plus China, Japan and Korea.

One form of collective and coordinated action would be for all participating countries in the ASEAN+3 meeting to agree to allow their currencies to appreciate more or less jointly against the dollar. However, a uniform appreciation would not take sufficient account of differences in national circumstances. Less-developed ASEAN members would not necessarily be forced to join the exchange rate policy coordination, because they are not well prepared for moving to a more flexible exchange rate regime. In conjunction with its 2.1 per cent revaluation against the dollar in July 2005, China adopted as the reference point for its exchange rate policy a basket that includes a number of Asian currencies. As a tug of war between the US and China is developing, further appreciation of the Chinese renminbi vis-à-vis the dollar is anticipated. However, the reform process of China's exchange rate regime will be more or less gradual. While acknowledging the need to increase the flexibility of the renminbi, Chinese policy-makers have shown strong reservations about making a swift move. At present, a diverse exchange rate regime and operation in East Asia will be an obstacle for exchange rate coordination.

Nevertheless, developing countries are sensitive to exchange rate fluctuations because the cost of exchange rate volatility is greater than the benefit when compared to developed countries. Many developing countries are reluctant to allow the nominal exchange rate to appreciate when circumstances are favorable (that is, capital surge, positive terms of trade shocks, and so on). This probably stems from fear of 'Dutch Disease' type problems as shown in the case studies of Brazil, Russia, and Thailand during the periods of capital surge. Loss of competitiveness and serious setbacks to export promotion are major concerns for export-led developing countries. On the other hand, developing countries with large external liabilities (denominated in foreign currencies) are also required to watch for drastic exchange rate depreciations (or devaluations) that may increase the debt burden on financial institutions and heighten the likelihood of a currency and financial crisis. If a developing country's financial sector vulnerability deepens because of drastic exchange rate depreciation, the sovereign credit rating of the developing country will deteriorate; and limited access to international financial markets could lead to a sudden stop situation (Calvo and Reinhart, 2000).

In addition, exchange rate fluctuations may have a substantial impact on prices in developing countries. Abrupt exchange rate depreciation with low credibility of monetary policy may lead to heightened inflationary pressures on domestic prices through exchange rate pass-through. To cope with inflationary pressure, monetary authorities may raise the domestic interest rate, as is evident from the high variability of interest rates in developing countries. Although interest rate hikes would contribute to mitigating inflationary pressures and defending the currency, negative side effects in the real and financial sector could also be envisaged.

As also noted by the IMF (2000), large exchange rate fluctuations in small or medium-sized open developing economies may have significant economic costs. Although it is important that exchange rates be allowed to adjust in response to market pressures, it may also be appropriate to use domestic monetary policy, or intervention, to limit severe fluctuations, to the extent that they affect inflation and inflationary expectations. Thus, the IMF acknowledges that emerging market economies and developing countries can manage exchange rate fluctuations through an alternative nominal anchor, such as inflation targeting. However, it is still uncertain that this nominal anchor could effectively relieve the exchange rate misalignment caused by the constant pressure of capital flows.

Kwan (2001) and Ueda (1998), among many others, assert that one of the key determinants of the boom–bust cycle in East Asia was the sharp appreciation of the yen against the dollar between the mid-1980s and the mid-1990s, and its subsequent depreciation. They also find that real investment and flows of speculative capital within and into East Asia were overly sensitive to the movements of the yen–dollar exchange rate. Every time the yen appreciated against the dollar, the economic growth of non-Japanese Asia picked up, as happened between 1986 and 1988 and again between 1991 and 1995. The converse was also true when economic growth decelerated and the asset-price bubble burst on the back of a weaker yen in 1989–90 and again in 1996–98 (Kwan, 2001). However, this phenomenon is mainly attributable to the pre-crisis de facto dollar peg that had been maintained in East Asia. As the East Asian currency crisis vividly shows, soft-peg currencies are extremely sensitive to sharp movements in the yen–dollar exchange rate.

Since the Asian currency crisis, most East Asian countries have moved to a more flexible exchange rate regime, with the exception of China and Malaysia. At the same time, most East Asian countries have further liberalized their capital markets to foreign investors. Before the crisis, most East Asian emerging economies were net importers of international capital. Since the crisis, however, they have become net providers of international capital due to their current account surpluses. To find a less painful method for correcting global imbalances on the one hand, and effectively managing the excess macroeconomic volatility due to exchange rate fluctuations on the other, it is high time that East Asian monetary authorities considered what kind of exchange rate regime is desirable for each country and what kind of collective action is required for resolving any failure in coordination. To do so, the ASEAN+3 policy dialogue should carry out surveillance over exchange rate policies of member countries.

Regional bond market development

One of the lessons from the Asian currency crisis was that too much borrowing in US dollars increased the vulnerability of a country. When the direction of capital flows reverses, even a solvent country may find itself in a dollar-liquidity crisis. At the time of the crisis, massive capital outflows were possible, particularly when foreign capital that had come in earlier was composed of short-term flows. 'Double mismatches' – a currency and maturity mismatch – characterized the problem of financial institutions and corporations in East Asia. In order to avoid another crisis in the future, Asian financial institutions and corporations have to develop a long-term funding source denominated in local currency to match their investment needs. Thus, local currency denominated bond financing solves the double mismatch problem. There is little doubt that deep and liquid domestic bond markets will help reduce the severity of the double mismatch in the future (Ito and Park, 2004).

Since the crisis, the development of regional bond markets has been highlighted as one of the major objectives of financial reforms proposed by the IMF, the World Bank and the Asian Development Bank (ADB) for East Asian economies. Parallel to reform efforts, there have been repeated calls for the establishment of regional bond markets in East Asia (Bergsten and Park, 2002). Responding to these calls, and as the part of regional efforts towards financial cooperation and integration through the Chiang Mai Initiative, the ASEAN+3 have taken steps to explore possibilities and modalities for creating Asian bonds and market infrastructure.

The member countries agreed on the Asian Bond Initiative (ABI) to conduct detailed studies on various aspects of bond market development. Given the low degree of regional financial integration in East Asia, this initiative would be welcome if it were a means to facilitate financial market development in East Asia. Despite the strong enthusiasm of the ASEAN+3 countries for constructing bond market infrastructure and increasing the supply of as well as demand for these bonds, the creation of deep and liquid bond markets in the region will take a long time. It will require more extensive domestic financial reform, institutional harmonization and substantial investment for building the infrastructure by the ASEAN+3 (Park and Park, 2004). Eichengreen and Luengnaruemitchai (2004) also find that the slow development of local bond markets is a phenomenon with multiple dimensions. They conclude that the only solution is to work harder at strengthening market regulation, market infrastructure and other domestic conditions for the development of local bond markets before giving that process a further push by finally opening the capital account.

Many proponents of the ABI may counter this pessimistic view. Ito (2003, 2004) argues that there may be regional bias next to home bias in that investors find bonds issued in Asia attractive compared to bonds from other regions.[7] However, at this stage of development, there is no guarantee that regional efforts, even if they can be organized, could succeed in fostering regional capital markets that are competitive vis-à-vis global capital markets in the US and Europe. Furthermore, continuing globalization of financial markets and advances in information technology allow financial companies in international financial centers to dominate the international banking and investment businesses. In reality, there would be no home bias at the regional level, unlike at the country level. For example, a regional portfolio is not necessarily easy to hedge. Having better information at the regional level does not seem to be enormously more advantageous than having better information at the global level.

Another important point is that the development of a regional bond market could facilitate recycling of some of the surplus savings in the region for long-term financing within the region. Due to the huge current account surplus since the Asian crisis, external reserves in the region have increased significantly. In other words, East Asia exports risky assets while importing safe assets such as US treasury and government agency bonds. This perverse pattern of capital flows in East Asia implies that at the regional level, financial centers have not properly played their intermediary role. Furthermore, there is no strong region-wide network to connect various financial centers in East Asia such as Tokyo, Hong Kong, Singapore and many others. East Asian financial centers are basically linked to financial hubs such as London and New York. There is no clear mechanism to recycle East Asian savings through the hub and spoke network in East Asia. The construction of a region-wide network interconnecting financial hubs and spokes in East Asia will create more stable capital flows for countries in the region and largely contribute to upgrading the financial system across the region.

To develop bond markets in East Asia, more areas of market development should be considered to ensure a balanced development of financial infrastructures across the region. The first is to supply high quality financial personnel to serve Asian financial markets. This is related to invigorating the role of existing Asian financial institutions in cross-border transactions or businesses within the Asian market. In the long run, it is important to establish a regional finance institute aimed at training and developing financial personnel for the Asian market. The second is to harmonize and streamline existing rules and regulations. The third issue related to the ABMI is the choice of currency denominated bonds. It was originally agreed that bonds issued under the ABMI be denominated in local currency. It would be an interesting point to note which of the member country currencies would dominate the regional bond market.[8]

At the regional level, it is widely expected that the Asian Bond Market Initiative (ABMI) launched by the ASEAN+3 group will spearhead the development of both domestic and regional bond markets in East Asia. Regional working groups were quickly established under the umbrella of the ABMI. However, at present, the requisite infrastructure for regional bond markets hardly exists and it may take years to establish.

A related initiative by the Executives Meeting of East Asia-Pacific Central Banks (EMEAP) was the creation of the Asian Bond Fund (ABF).[9] The ABF was designed to catalyze the growth of Asian bond markets by allocating a portion of the external reserves held by regional central banks to purchases of government and quasi-government securities. The initial US$1 billion in investments, known as the ABF-1, was launched in June 2003. The ABF-1 is restricted to dollar-denominated bonds, so it cannot deal with the currency mismatch problem. ABF-2, launched in December 2004, is twice as large and includes bonds denominated in regional currencies. It has two components: a Pan-Asian Bond Index Fund (PAIF) and a Fund of Bond Funds (FoBF). The PAIF is a single bond fund investing in sovereign and quasi-sovereign domestic currency denominated bonds issued in the eight sub-funds, each of which will invest in sovereign and quasi-sovereign domestic currency denominated bonds issued in the respective markets of the eight EMEAP economies (excluding Australia, Japan, and New Zealand). The PAIF and eight sub-funds will be passively managed by private sector fund managers against a pan-Asian bond index and relevant domestic bond indices for the eight EMEAP markets.

ABF-2 can be seen as an improved step in the sense that the PAIF offers investors access to a fund backed by a basket of local currency sovereign and quasi-sovereign bonds. The PAIF is now listed on the Hong Kong Stock Exchange and can be traded by investors. Each sub-fund of the Fund of Bond Funds is also designed to be an Exchange Traded Fund (ETF) to be eventually listed in each domestic stock market. Fund managers of each of the eight sub-funds have been appointed. However, the ABF-2 is still limited to sovereign and quasi-sovereign bonds. So it again does not directly serve to channel long-term funds to the private sector (Sussangkarn and Vichyanond, 2006).

Another interesting advance arises from the cooperation between Japan and Korea to promote the development of asset-backed securities markets in East Asia. Korean Collateralized Bond Obligations (Korean CBO) are designed to provide long-term financing to small and medium-sized enterprises (SMEs) in Korea that issue yen-denominated notes with guarantees and credit facilities through the involvement of the Small Business Corporation of Korea, the Industrial Bank of Korea and the Japan Bank for International Cooperation. Unlike ABF-1 and ABF-2, this initiative is directly targeted at the private sector, particularly the SMEs who may find it difficult to obtain bond financing without government assistance.

To date, issuance on Asian bond markets has risen only modestly. Turnover rates and market liquidity remain low by international standards. There is no lack of initiatives to develop Asian bond markets, but there is still a lack of progress.

3.5 Institutional constraints on regional cooperation

Institutions are a set of rules constraining human behavior (North, 1995). If developing countries had put in place sound and competent domestic financial institutions, they would be able to cope with the negative effects of excess macroeconomic volatility. Market freedom requires vigilance through supporting institutions.

Although the 1997–98 crisis exposed a number of structural problems, East Asia's experience with the crisis by no means proves that the Anglo-American model surpasses the East Asian system. The major challenge facing East Asian economies in the coming decades is to nurture the evolution of their own specific models of economic development. In this evolutionary process, East Asian policymakers will come to realize that democratization has imposed a different participatory mechanism for consensus building.[10] Economic liberalization has reduced the scope of industrial policies and other types of market intervention. It has also required the creation of a new set of institutions for financial regulation and supervision, corporate governance and the management of industrial relations for the efficiency and stability of the market.

Evidently, emerging market economies may not have to embrace Anglo-American capitalism. However, the global realities leave them with no choice but to conform to international standards of transparency, disclosure, corporate governance and banking – all established by advanced countries in Europe and North America. Cultivating compatibility between the new domestic financial systems and global standards and codes will be important because most developing countries will continue to rely on North American and European markets for their exports and will integrate themselves with a new global economy, which is likely to be dominated by the United States and the European Union.

These two economies will dictate the rules governing international trade, foreign direct investment and international financial transactions. At the same time, viability of the new development model would require consistency with the rules of the World Trade Organization and the capacity to accommodate the global activities of multinational companies. It would also require flexibility to adjust to the ongoing revolution in information technology. The scope and speed of the overall economic reform will have to be adjusted to the quality of government, institutional capacity to reform, and the other political and societal constraints to which emerging and developing economies are subject.

Small developing countries have found it increasingly difficult to provide important public goods such as social protection, combating corruption, securing financial stability, and resolving the conflict between domestic politics and global economics. These public goods may be more efficiently produced at a regional level, because regional arrangements are more likely to focus on bringing together groups with common interests and ensuring that they are linked in useful ways. Commonality of interest is the most important criterion for useful interaction. It does not mean that all participants must be at the same stage of development, but it probably does mean that they should be traveling along much the same path, albeit at different distances and speeds (de Brouwer and Wang, 2004). Recognizing this reality, and combined with the need for solidifying regional defenses against future crises, regional initiatives may start serious discussions on the need and modality for regional integration through trade liberalization and financial cooperation at various intergovernmental forums. There is certainly no lack of initiatives for regional cooperation. But there is a lack of real progress.

As for institutional and political constraints on further progress of regional financial cooperation, the most serious problem in the case of East Asia has been that the thirteen ASEAN+3 countries have failed to articulate the ultimate objectives of the Chiang Mai Initiative (CMI). The participating countries themselves are still unclear about whether the CMI is going to be fostered as a regional liquidity support program or as a building block for a full-fledged regional monetary system in East Asia. If bilateral swap arrangements are activated collectively and supported by a surveillance system, they constitute a de facto regional monetary fund. The CMI could then be used as the base on which an elaborate system of financial cooperation and policy coordination is built by following in the footsteps of the European monetary integration. At this stage of development, many countries in East Asia are not prepared to accept the idea of – or may feel uncomfortable about – restructuring the CMI into a forerunner of an Asian Monetary Fund.

A second institutional constraint is related to the need to coordinate the activities of the CMI with other regional arrangements such as the Manila Framework supported by the US, Australia, and New Zealand. Most CMI countries also participate in the Manila Framework and APEC. At some point in the future, the leaders of ASEAN+3 countries may have to decide on the mode of cooperation and division of labor in promoting regional growth and stability between these institutions and the CMI. All thirteen countries have been engaged in policy reviews and dialogue through various APEC meetings and the Manila Framework. Unless the CMI is developed into a credible financial arrangement by increasing swap amounts, it will take on a role similar to other regional economic forums. The coherence of the group will then be weakened, as questions are raised as to whether the 13 countries constitute an appropriate grouping for a regional financial arrangement in East Asia.

A third hindering factor is that the fear of another round of financial crises has receded with the recovery that has been faster than predicted on the basis of previous crisis episodes. ASEAN+3 countries have become less interested in institutionalizing the CMI's operations. Instead, their focus has recently shifted to creating free trade areas in East Asia. The ASEAN free trade area (AFTA) now includes the whole of Southeast Asia, and AFTA continues to expand. In November 2001, China and the ASEAN countries agreed to form a free trade area within ten years, allowing for some preferential treatment for less developed ASEAN countries. Japan has concluded a free trade agreement with Singapore and started negotiations on a similar agreement with Korea and several ASEAN states on an individual basis.

The free trade movement is undoubtedly a desirable development, and the CMI could facilitate further trade liberalization by stabilizing bilateral exchange rates of regional currencies and minimizing the disruptive effects of financial market turbulence. This advantage suggests that ASEAN+3 countries may have an incentive to broaden the scope of the CMI in parallel with negotiations about establishing free trade areas in the region. In reality, however, it appears that free trade discussions have distracted many East Asian countries from their CMI negotiations. However, the prospect of a region-wide East Asian FTA, covering all 13 ASEAN+3 countries, is slow to materialize because China and Japan are seeking bilateral trade agreements rather than multilateral ones. In particular, the current pattern of regional trade agreements in East Asia is confusing. It essentially consists of a web of bilateral arrangements, many of which are still on the drawing board. There has apparently been no formal attempt to build a region-wide agreement like that of the European Common Market. Bilateral agreements are unlikely to foster a collective framework.

Finally, there is the issue of leadership, which defies an easy solution. If the 13 countries have a more ambitious goal of developing a collective exchange rate mechanism similar to the ERM in Europe with the long-term objective of adopting a common currency, they will have to increase the number and amount of BSAs. As the European experience shows, such an extension requires political leadership that can foster coherence among the 13 countries by mediating between the divergent interests of its members.

In East Asia, China and Japan would naturally be expected to provide leadership in the future developments of financial cooperation along with a region-wide free trade agreement. Despite differences in their strategies, the combination of China and Japan together is the key to developing a common political will in East Asia. Sakakibara (2003) and Murase (2004) argue that the role of China and Japan in East Asia's integration process is synonymous with that of France and Germany in Europe. Nonetheless, East Asia's lukewarm attitude toward the creation of a regional bloc on both trade and finance fronts is basically due to the lack of political capital in the region.

As far as China is concerned, economic integration with the ten ASEAN members, South Asian and central Asian countries may be more important geo-politically than financial cooperation or free trade with either Japan or South Korea. While China is a military superpower, it is still a developing economy with a huge gap to narrow in terms of technological and industrial sophistication vis-à-vis Japan. These differences in the economic and military status of the two countries suggest that, even if they manage to reconcile their troubled memories of the past, China and Japan may find it difficult to work together as equal partners for regional integration in East Asia.

Despite slow progress in reconciliation between China and Japan, China seems to emerge as an active player in both the international and regional arena. Since the mid-1990s, China has expanded the number and depth of its bilateral relationships, joined various trade and security accords, deepened its participation in key multilateral organizations, and helped address global security issues. The pinnacle of this process was the Treaty of Good-Neighborliness and Friendly Cooperation that China signed with Russia in 2001 (Medeiros and Fravel, 2003).

China borders Russia and many of the South Asian and Central Asian countries in addition to several ASEAN members. Therefore, it is natural for China to seek expansion and deepening of its trade and financial relations with those neighboring countries. In fact, for this reason, China has been courting ASEAN for a free trade agreement and joined the Bangkok agreement on a free trade area that includes Korea and the South Asian countries (Bangladesh, India, Laos, and Sri Lanka) in November 2001. In Central Asia, China has also taken a leading role in establishing the region's first multilateral group, the Shanghai Cooperation Organization. Founded to settle longstanding territorial disputes and to demilitarize borders, the organization now stresses counter-terrorism cooperation and regional trade between Russia, Kazakhstan, Kyrgyzstan, Tajikistan, and Uzbekistan and China.[11]

In contrast, Japan has not been able to articulate its strategic interests in East Asia. There is some suspicion that Japan is not interested in free trade and financial arrangements per se in East Asia for purely economic reasons. Instead, Japan is engaged in a discussion of those regional arrangements with other East Asian countries to maintain its leadership role as the region's largest economy by checking and balancing China's expansion. Many analysts believe that Japan's active involvement in regional economic integration is therefore motivated by its desire to maintain its traditional pole position in East Asia. On top of this suspicion, Japan is perceived to be a stubborn country, insensitive to and unwilling to resolve wartime legacies and disputes on historical and territorial claims. Japan's lack of a leadership in East Asian development seems to undermine its ability to pull East Asian countries together for regional cooperation and integration (Park and Wang, 2005).

3.6 Financial institution-building: national, regional, and multilateral initiatives

Since the crisis, East Asian countries have introduced and enforced new rules for accounting and auditing that conform to international standards. Along with these institutional reforms, most East Asian countries have made impressive progress in deregulating and opening financial markets. As a result, financial institutions, markets, and government policies have been evolving to a competitive and market-oriented financial system. These developments are expected to overcome the inflexibility of the existing bank-based financial systems of East Asia. However, this market-led strategy does not mean that East Asian governments lack an important role to play and must blindly move towards becoming minimalist states. Rather, the challenge facing East Asia is to develop strong governments able both to resist political pressures from domestic financial establishments and to push forward market-led financial developments along with necessary institutional reforms (Rajan and Zingales, 2003). Within such a framework, East Asian countries may have a better chance of converging with advanced financial systems in the future.

At the same time, regional initiatives can promote the DFA through specialized technical cooperation. This suggestion starts from the idea that technical exchanges were important in the process of European integration. When specialists from different countries get together to discuss fairly technical issues – not the arm-waving issues of foreign relations – they find that they have a lot in common (de Brouwer and Wang, 2004). Thus, the next stage of regional cooperation should aim at building a variety of specialized, technically-oriented forums of cooperation with enough common interest and common objectives to support a permanent secretariat. Rigorous multilateral surveillance on a regional basis, consistently applied and with associated peer pressure, can help build the DFA and ultimately mitigate the excessive macroeconomic volatility.

As regards financial institution-building, Eichengreen (2003) proposes the establishment of an Asian Financial Institute (AFI) on the platform of ASEAN+3. He admits that this idea is not his own: for example, in 1995 Bernie Fraser, the Governor of the Reserve Bank of Australia, suggested establishing an Asian version of the Bank for International Settlements (BIS) to carry out some of these functions; and subsequently Bergsten (2000) proposed the creation of an APEC Financial Institute. Thus, this institute based on a particular region or a regional group would provide technical assistance to national agencies seeking to strengthen prudential supervision and regulation. It would also deal with other financial issues related to financial institution-building. For instance, it would provide special expertise and knowledge for reserve management, clearing and settlement services, and other financial market development issues (such as the securitization of financial markets).

In addition, such a regional institute could be a venue for building a consensus and reflecting regional views in the negotiation process of setting global financial standards. In most of the forums or agencies drawing up international standards, emerging market economies and developing countries either are not represented or are underrepresented. Thus, a regional financial institute could establish a special task force to organize negotiations on the design of a separate set of regional financial standards appropriate to the region's special circumstances (Eichengreen, 2003). The one-size-fits-all approach is particularly likely to ignore the institutional constraints of emerging market economies and developing countries. If enforcement of common standards does not permit a degree of variation and flexibility at the individual country level, then standardization efforts could result in enormous adjustment costs in the emerging market economies (Rodrik, 1999).

A universal adoption of common standards on accounting, disclosure, and banking, for example, is likely to promote deeper financial integration at the global level. From the perspectives of emerging market economies, deeper integration could mean considerable erosion in their policy autonomy and hence the necessity to coordinate their macroeconomic and other policies with those of developed countries. Although the advocates of common standards claim that the universal acceptance of common standards will help stabilize the international financial market and reduce the frequency of financial crises, there is no evidence to support such an argument.

Creating a regional financial institute with a permanent secretariat would in principle help to cultivate support for deeper cooperation on the various issues of financial development. The creation of such an institute, made up of a body of experts with agenda-setting power, could push the process of regional cooperation forward, as in the case of European integration (Eichengreen, 2003).

Finally, but most importantly, regional initiatives for financial institution-building will contribute to the stability of the international financial system, as the regional development bank has done for global development finance for over 30 years. A first requirement for achieving cooperative evolution with the rest of the world is for insiders and outsiders to consult actively and candidly, in particular with the United States and the European Union.

3.7 Conclusion

Any argument for regional cooperation must begin by answering the most fundamental question of whether regional groupings, whatever forms they may take, are conducive to, or likely to interfere with, multilateral free trade and the orderly globalization of financial markets. Despite many misgivings about the role of regional economic arrangements, the experiences of the past decade suggest that they have complemented multilateral trade and financial liberalization. They have served as building blocks rather than stumbling blocks for a more integrated world economy. There is no evidence to suggest that any regional arrangement will be oriented toward a withdrawal from the global economy and hence be an obstacle to global financial integration.

There have been several developments that have encouraged the formation of a regional financial arrangement in East Asia. One development has been the slow progress of reform of the international financial architecture. The urgency of reform felt by the G7 countries has receded considerably with the rapid recovery of East Asia and other emerging market economies. The slow progress has been further complicated by the perception that a new architecture, as it is designed, may not be effective in sustaining global financial stability, nor would it safeguard financial stability in the emerging market economies and developing countries. Thus, it would be in the interest of East Asia and other regions to work together to set up their own systems of mitigating macroeconomic volatility. In particular, policy dialogue could serve as a vehicle for promoting coherent policy formation at the regional level and at the same time ensuring effective implementation of high-quality banking and financial standards.

The three pillars of liquidity assistance, monitoring and surveillance, and exchange rate coordination are essential elements for regional financial and monetary cooperation. However, its development and related institutions will be evolutionary. There has been an emerging consensus in East Asia that East Asians must join forces to establish regional financial arrangements that will help them fend off speculative attacks and, in so doing, stabilize the East Asian financial markets. Despite some progress, East Asia has a long way to go before formalizing and putting into effect the Chiang Mai Initiative (CMI) and launching other types of institutionalized arrangements. In order to cope effectively with the instability of capital movements and manage the excess macroeconomic volatility, further efforts are required. At the same time, exchange rate coordination would be required for mitigating the adverse impact of global imbalances. In addition, other initiatives for promoting financial market infrastructure will contribute to financial market development and integration.

As for institutional constraints on further progress of regional financial arrangements, the most serious problem would be the failure to articulate the ultimate objectives of the regional cooperation. As we have already observed, at this stage of development, many countries in East Asia are not prepared to accept the idea of restructuring the CMI into a forerunner of an Asian Monetary Fund. In particular, there is the issue of leadership, which defies an easy solution. As the European experience vividly shows, political leadership is essential for fostering coherence among the member countries by mediating between the divergent interests of its members.

Creating a regional financial institute with a permanent secretariat would help to cultivate support for deeper cooperation on the various issues of financial institution and infrastructure-building. Such a regional institute, made up of a body of experts with agenda-setting power, could promote the process of regional cooperation. Rigorous multilateral surveillance on a regional basis, consistently applied and with associated peer pressure, can help build the domestic financial architecture and ultimately mitigate the excessive macroeconomic volatility. Furthermore, such an institute could be a venue for building a consensus and reflecting regional views in the negotiation process of setting global financial standards.

Notes

1. The findings of the project clearly illustrate why the 'lack of global governance' is an obstacle to improving risk management.
2. There is nothing new in setting up a regional financial organization. In addition to several institutional inventions observed during the European monetary integration process, there already exists the Arab Monetary Fund (AMF) and the Latin American Reserve Fund (FLAR) established in 1976 and 1991, respectively. However, such regional funds have not been effectively used for risk management at the regional level, mainly due to lack of the members' strong commitment and operational transparency.
3. For instance, the ASEAN surveillance process is built on the basis of consensus and informality in keeping with the tradition of non-interference (Manzano, 2001). East Asia, in contrast to Europe, lacks the tradition of integrationist thinking and the web of interlocking agreements that encourage monetary and financial cooperation (Eichengreen and Bayoumi, 1999). Eichengreen and Bayoumi (1999) stress that East Asia does not meet the necessary intellectual preconditions for regional integration. For this reason they conclude that it is unrealistic to speak of pooling national sovereignties. However, while there is considerable work to be done in promoting policy coordination in the region, it is wrong to say that it cannot be done in East Asia.
4. The IMF is expected to play the role of an insurance firm that has its own monitoring and surveillance device. However, the presence of a regional fund as a cooperative partnership fund will complicate the welfare consequences, depending on whether the regional fund is in a better position to monitor the effort than the IMF. If the regional fund cannot effectively harness its monitoring capabilities to reduce the moral hazard problem, countries may become less cautious; the IMF will tend to provide less

insurance. The regional fund may crowd out the more effective insurance provided by the IMF, thus becoming completely dysfunctional. In this regard, peer monitoring is essential for controlling the moral hazards involved in the partnership fund, and may even improve welfare by enhancing the countries' risk-sharing. For a similar logic, see Kandel and Lazear (1992).

5. The cost arises from the interest rate differential between domestic and foreign interest rates. As the Federal Reserve started to raise short-term interest rates from 2004, the cost of reserve holdings became relatively much lower. However, a prospective dollar depreciation vis-à-vis Asian currencies is likely to inflict substantial capital losses on their holdings of dollar-denominated assets in East Asia.
6. A variety of different models points to the same conclusion that a 30 per cent real effective depreciation of the dollar is required for resolving the problem of global imbalances. See, for example, Blanchard et al. (2005), Caballero et al. (2005b), Cline (2005), and Obstfeld and Rogoff (2005).
7. Ito argues that there is a natural preference among investors to purchase familiar products with less perceived risk. However, he also acknowledges that regional bias is still a product of theoretical deduction rather than a widely observed phenomenon, such as home bias, supported by hard evidence.
8. US dollar denominated or euro denominated bonds were also considered, and it is interesting to note less enthusiasm for euro denominated bonds.
9. EMEAP members are all regional central banks, including the Bank of Japan, Bank of Korea, Bank Indonesia, Malaysian State Bank, Central Bank of the Philippines, Monetary Authority of Singapore, Bank of Thailand, People's Bank of China, Hong Kong Monetary Authority, Reserve Bank of Australia, and Reserve Bank of New Zealand.
10. The Chilean case study also shows that the ability to build a consensus on financial and other reforms is a key factor explaining the Chilean success.
11. In June 2001, the presidents of six countries signed the Declaration of the Shanghai Cooperation Organization (SCO). The SCO aims at strengthening mutual trust and friendly relations between member states, encouraging their further effective cooperation in politics, economy, science and technology, culture, education, energy, transportation, environmental protection and other fields, jointly ensuring regional peace, security and stability, and creating a new international political and economic order.

4
Volatility: Prudential Regulation, Standards and Codes

Liliana Rojas-Suarez

4.1 Introduction

Since the early 1990s, policymakers' decisions and concerns on the appropriate design for financial regulation in developing countries have been guided by two related findings. The first is that empirical analysis has joined theoretical research in establishing an important correlation between financial deepening and economic growth.[1] The second is the mounting evidence that the costs, in terms of output losses, of dealing with systemic financial crises are huge.[2] Taking these two results together it is not surprising to observe important efforts made by financial regulators in developing countries, and their international advisers from multilateral organizations, to develop policies and regulations aimed at both preventing the eruption of financial crises and contributing to the depth of financial markets.

Undoubtedly, the set of measures needed to achieve such an ambitious goal is large and complex, ranging from macroeconomic policies and financial reforms to institutional improvements and efforts for social development. Moreover, a lesson learned from recent episodes of 'crisis by contagion' is that the intricate workings of global markets need a new and better coordinated global regulatory and supervisory framework. While essential, effective domestic regulatory frameworks cannot be sufficient to ensure financial stability because they do not take into account the new interrelationships across countries created by globalization in a world of imperfect information. Efforts to ensure financial stability, therefore, need to focus simultaneously on strengthening domestic financial markets and improving the international financial architecture.

This chapter deals with the appropriate design of financial prudential regulations in developing countries. Should prudential regulations in developing countries be the same as those in industrial countries? Is it adequate for developing countries to adopt the set of standards and codes prioritized by multilateral organizations in their efforts to upgrade the international financial architecture? Arguments can be made in either direction. On the one hand, globalization and leveling the playing field for market participants argue for similar norms and regulations across countries, especially to avoid regulatory arbitrage. On the other hand, important economic, financial, and institutional differences between developing and industrial countries call for differences in approach. The view taken in this chapter is that the convergence of financial regulatory practices across countries needs to be taken as a long-term objective. As the discussion in the chapter will show, in the short and medium term, direct adoption by most developing countries of regulations that work in industrial countries can actually cause more harm than benefits to the stability of domestic financial systems.

The chapter claims that the degree of financial development needs to be a major determinant in the choice of prudential regulation. As countries differ substantially in their degree of financial development, so should the regulatory framework governing the activities of financial institutions. It is also argued that a close look at the particular features of developing countries can guide the design of effective prudential regulation. The chapter advances some suggestions for regulatory practices for countries at different stages of financial development.

To substantiate these claims, the rest of the chapter is organized as follows. Section 4.2 argues that high macro/financial volatility and weak institutions in most developing countries translate into particular financial features that distinguish this group of countries from the most developed economies in the world (and a sub-set of more advanced developing countries). In particular, financial intermediation in developing countries is shallow; capital markets are very small; assets and liabilities are predominantly of short maturity; and, reflecting very low depositor confidence, the deposit base is not very stable. While the discussion is oriented to developing countries as a whole, particular attention is given to the eight countries that form part of the overall project: Argentina, Brazil, Chile, China, Nigeria, Russia, South Africa, and Thailand.

Section 4.2 also shows how the particular features of developing countries generate important difficulties for the definition and measurement of financial risks faced by financial institutions. These difficulties complicate prudential regulation aiming at controlling specific risks. They also limit the effectiveness of risk assessment techniques commonly used in industrial countries.

Section 4.3 deals with central issues related to the supply of and demand for international standards and codes for financial stability. The supply of standards and codes, as determined by the international financial organizations, constitutes the basis for the menu of prudential regulations that countries can incorporate into their legislations. To assess what developing countries need and want (the demand side) in terms of prudential regulation, the section also reviews a variety of concerns raised by analysts and policymakers regarding standards and codes, both in terms of their appropriateness and of the process for setting them. The section shows that many of the concerns are founded in the particular features of financial systems in developing countries identified in Section 4.2.

Section 4.4 discusses in greater detail important problems associated with a core international standard for effective prudential regulation: the banking capital adequacy standard as recommended by the Basel Committee on Banking Supervision. Once again, the combination of high macro/financial volatility and weak institutions severely limits the effectiveness of the Basel capital standards in most developing countries. In addition, it is argued that the particular characteristics of Basel I might weaken rather than strengthen financial systems in developing countries. Moreover, the section argues that neither does the newly proposed Basel II fit the bill for most developing countries. As such, the supply of standards (Basel Committee's capital adequacy) does not meet the demand for effective prudential regulation by developing countries.

Finally, Section 4.5 addresses these problems and concerns by advancing policy recommendations. In addition to suggesting prudential regulatory practices that could be more appropriate for developing countries, the section also emphasizes the need for consistency between financial and macroeconomic policies.

4.2 Macroeconomic and financial volatility as constraints for understanding financial risks in developing countries

Addressing the issue of appropriate prudential financial regulations in developing countries requires an assessment of particular features that make these countries different to industrial countries. This section briefly discusses important differences in the behavior of key economic variables, institutions, and financial deepening. The discussion then shows how these differences affect the overall understanding of financial risks in developing countries and the limitations of standard techniques of risk assessment.

Macroeconomic volatility, institutional weaknesses and financial shallowness: a developing-country trio

Three major features of developing countries that distinguish them from industrial countries are: (i) highly volatile key macroeconomic and financial variables; (ii) weak institutions, especially those determining the rules of the game for the activities of the financial system; and (iii) shallow financial markets.

Macro/financial volatility, as represented by the standard deviation of real GDP growth and real interest rates, is presented in Table 4.1 for a group of industrial countries and for the eight core developing countries in this study.[3, 4] Statistics are calculated over the period 1990–2004. The table shows the striking difference in behavior in macro/financial variables between developing countries and industrial countries and also highlights some important differences among developing countries. Measured by the standard deviation, average volatility of real GDP growth for the group of developing countries is much higher than volatility in industrial countries. This indicator is particularly high in Russia, Thailand, and Argentina, all of which experienced dramatic financial crises in the last decade.

The negative relationship between macro/financial volatility and financial depth is presented in Figure 4.1, which displays the relationship between real interest rate volatility and the ratio of deposits to GDP for 135 countries around the world for the period 1990–2004.[5] There are two major results that derive from the figure. The first is that, as expected, most industrial countries appear in the upper left-hand side of the graph, indicating a combination of low real interest rate volatility and large financial intermediation. Likewise, the higher

Table 4.1 Real GDP growth and real interest rate in selected countries, 1990–2004

Country	Real GDP growth		Real interest rate	
	Mean	Standard deviation	Mean	Standard deviation
Australia	3.28	1.55	2.66	2.61
Canada	2.63	2.14	1.26	1.98
France	1.79	1.24	1.72	0.87
Norway	3.13	1.48	2.09	1.97
Spain	2.71	1.47	1.97	2.22
Switzerland	1.08	1.46	1.22	1.45
United States	2.91	1.44	1.72	1.68
Nigeria	3.59	2.83	–3.32	14.09
South Africa	1.82	1.90	4.53	3.31
Russian Federation	–1.57	7.58	–5.47	13.41
Thailand	5.13	5.54	3.50	2.78
China	9.30	2.74	1.31	4.94
Argentina	2.71	6.92	4.16	7.45
Brazil	1.84	2.67	18.87	10.53
Chile	5.54	3.53	4.93	2.96

Sources: IMF, International Financial Statistics (2005) and Central Bank of Chile.

volatility of most developing countries is associated with lower degrees of financial intermediation. The second result is that there is a significant variation in the behavior of developing countries. This is best illustrated by considering the countries highlighted in this study. Argentina, Brazil, Russia, and Nigeria can be typified as very high volatility/very low financial intermediation countries.[6] Chile and South Africa appear as countries with moderately high volatility/moderately low financial intermediation. Thailand (and other East Asian countries not named in the figure, but that can be identified as the squares in the upper left-hand part of the figure) resemble the behavior of industrial countries in their combination of low interest rate volatility and high financial intermediation. Finally, China stands on its own: consistent with the discussion above, factors other than the degree of real interest rate volatility lie behind the high level of financial intermediation in China.

The large differences in financial features not only between industrial and developing countries but also among developing countries observed in Figure 4.1 provide a first indication that, in order to be effective, prudential regulations might need to differ across the spectrum of countries. At least, one has to doubt that prudential regulations needed in Thailand should be the same as those needed in Nigeria.

Let us now turn to the role of institutions. The recent literature has emphasized the central role that institutional quality has on financial market development. For example, it is argued that access to bank finance is greater in countries with high respect for the rule of law and low degrees of corruption (see, for

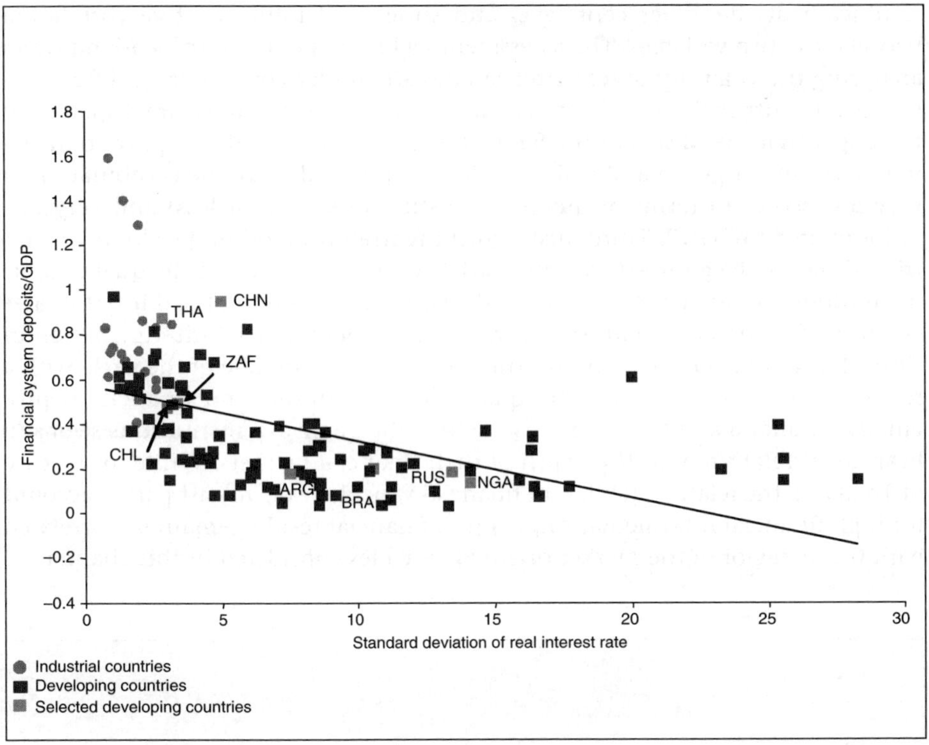

Figure 4.1 Deposits and volatility, 1990–2004
Sources: IMF, International Financial Statistics (2005) and Central Bank of Chile.

example, Beck et al., 2003). Weak institutions also have an adverse effect on investors' confidence in the quality of the banking system, and, therefore, on the depth of the system. The reason is that even good regulations have little meaning in countries where those regulations are not enforced because of weaknesses in the judiciary system and the spread of corruption. As in the case of high interest rate volatility, low confidence among investors encourages a concentration of financial investment in short-term assets.

As has become common practice in recent years, the quality of institutions can be assessed through a number of well-known indices. In this chapter, we use the Index of Governance constructed by Kaufmann et al. (2005), where governance is defined as: 'the traditions and institutions by which authority in a country is exercised for the common good'. This index is chosen because it includes sub-indices that specifically measure regulatory quality, respect for the rule of law and perceived degree of corruption, all variables associated with financial sector deepening. The index takes values ranging from –2.5 to 2.5, with higher values denoting better performance.

Figure 4.2 shows the relationship between the ratio of bank credit to GDP and the quality of institutions.[7] The regression line in Figure 4.2 is statistically significant at the 1 per cent level and shows a definite positive correlation between the two variables. The assessment yields are similar to those found when analyzing the volatility of real interest rates and underscore the large differences between countries. First, industrial countries, denoted with dots, are displayed in the upper right-hand side of the figure. Second, among the developing countries in our sample, Argentina, Brazil, Nigeria, and Russia display the combination of very low scores in terms of quality of institutions (zero or less) and very low ratios of credit to GDP. Third, distinguishing itself from other developing countries, Chile can be grouped with industrial countries in terms of the quality of its institutions. Other factors, including the still high volatility of real interest rates can be understood as remaining obstacles to deeper financial intermediation in Chile. Just as in Figure 4.1, South Africa appears in the middle of the pack, with a relatively low score in both the quality of institutions and financial depth. Finally, Thailand and China are cases where the quality of institutions seems to bear no correlation with the depth of their financial markets. While in the case of Thailand, the relative stability of financial variables can, at least partly, account for high financial intermediation, China's financial results remain uncorrelated with the behavior of the market-oriented variables considered in this chapter.

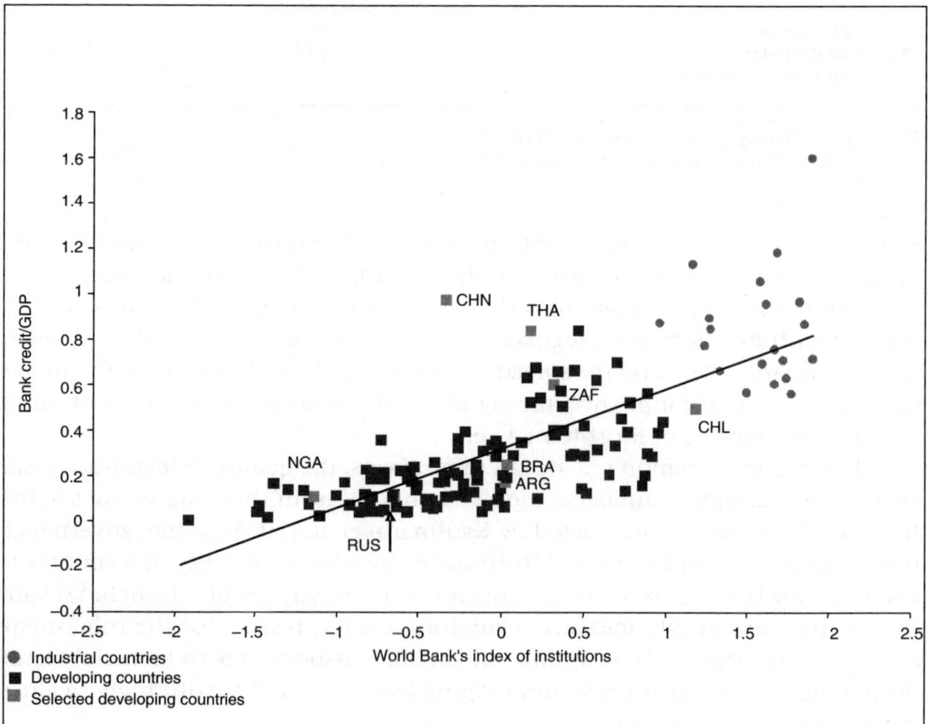

Figure 4.2 Credit and institutions, 1990–2004
Sources: IMF, International Financial Statistics (2005) and Central Bank of Chile.

Without underestimating the importance of large differences between developing countries, an important feature of this group of countries as a whole is that the large majority of them can be classified as high interest rate volatility (77 per cent of the developing countries in Figure 4.1 display a volatility greater than 3.2 – the average volatility in industrial countries plus two standard deviations), weak institutions (over 90 per cent of the countries in Figure 4.2 have a score lower than the average score for industrial countries minus two standard deviations) and low financial deepening (60 per cent of developing countries in Figure 4.1 have a deposit to GDP ratio less than 30 per cent). In other words, Argentina, Brazil, Nigeria, and Russia are more *representative* of developing countries' behavior than Chile and Thailand.

The problems for regulators and bankers in assessing risks in developing countries

The above discussion highlights the fact that high volatility and weak institutions in most developing countries translate into particular financial features that distinguish this group of countries from the most developed economies in the world (and a sub-set of more advanced developing countries).[8] In particular, financial intermediation in developing countries is shallow; capital markets are very small; assets and liabilities are predominantly short term; and, reflecting very little depositor confidence, the deposit base is not very stable. An additional feature, not discussed above, but highly related to the existence of weak institutions, is that ownership of financial and real assets is highly concentrated.

These particular features of financial markets in developing countries impinge on the effectiveness of key regulations aiming at controlling excessive risk-taking by financial institutions and at increasing the financial system's resilience to external shocks. Section 4.4 will discuss the problems associated with a central prudential regulation: capital requirements, as recommended by the Basel Committee on Banking Supervision. In this sub-section, we discuss how the specific characteristics of developing countries pose difficulties on the definition and measurement of financial risks faced by their financial institutions. These difficulties complicate prudential regulation aiming at controlling specific risks. They also limit the effectiveness of risk assessment techniques commonly used in industrial countries.

Let us start with the definition of risks. In assessing the strength of financial institutions, and especially banks, risks are usually classified into a number of categories: credit risk, interest rate risk, exchange rate risk, country risk, liquidity risk, operational risk, legal risk, transfer risk, and reputational risk.[9] Prudential regulation is designed to ensure that financial institutions adequately understand and manage these risks. In addition to the risk-based capital requirements – which deal with the overall quality of the bank portfolio and will be discussed in Section 4.4 – there are a number of additional prudential regulations aimed at avoiding excessive risk-taking in each of the individual categories listed above. It is obvious that for an effective management of specific risks it is necessary that each category of risk be adequately measured. The argument in this chapter is that the combination of high volatility and weak institutions in most developing countries often prevents this from being achieved.

To exemplify this statement, consider first the definition of credit risk. Credit risk refers to the increased probability of bank borrowers' default. A mechanism to assess this risk, endorsed by regulators, is the classification of loans according to the borrower's capacity to pay. In industrial countries, for example, banks typically attach higher credit risk to companies (or sectors) showing reduced profits or the materialization of losses. While this practice is followed in some developing countries, many of them assess credit risk only according to the payment history of the loan; that is, a loan is assessed as a higher credit risk as the number of months of payments in arrears increase. Whatever the method used to assess credit risk, regulators demand that banks increase their loan-loss reserves (or provisioning) as credit risk increases.

While this method of assessing credit risk and provisioning is appropriate for industrial countries, high macro and financial volatility severely hinders the adequacy of credit risk evaluation in most developing countries. The fundamental reason is that high volatility in developing countries is associated with sharp and sudden movements of macro and financial variables. This means that a company assessed as having a low credit risk because of a history of no arrears, can suddenly fall into trouble because of a large and sudden change in economic conditions. Moreover, in contrast to industrial countries where companies take advantage of a broad spectrum of alternative forms of finance, weak institutions and large economic/financial volatility mean that the large majority of companies in developing countries finance their operations either with retained earnings or with bank loans that, as discussed above, are mostly of short maturity. This implies that adverse conditions affect a large segment of firms simultaneously, turning loans previously assessed as in 'good standing' into 'bad' loans. The large volatility of real GDP growth and real interest rates for developing countries shown in Table 4.1 provides evidence of the difficulties of adequately assessing credit risk in developing countries. Ex post provisioning, namely, the practice of increasing loan-loss reserves *after* problems arise can, therefore, not effectively protect banks in a highly volatile financial system.

For all practical purposes, the particular features of developing countries imply that assessing borrowers' credit risk needs to go beyond the evaluation of past and current profits and the history of loan repayment. In a highly volatile environment, the best proof of solvency and creditworthiness is proof of liquidity. Borrowers with significant access to liquid assets are the ones with the greater capacity to meet payments in adverse economic circumstances.[10]

But, what assets can be considered 'liquid' in highly volatile economies? This question opens the door for the discussion on another form of risk: exchange rate risk. In many developing countries, high macro/financial volatility translates into large uncertainties regarding the real value of local currencies. This has resulted in the use of a foreign currency – mostly the US dollar – as a store of value.[11] In those countries where deposits in foreign currency are allowed, they have reached a significant proportion of total bank deposits.[12] However, prohibition against holding foreign currency denominated bank deposits in highly volatile economies does not mean that savings in local currency will increase. Instead, these prohibitions usually result in capital flight or in large holdings of foreign currency outside the formal financial system.[13]

'Protecting' the real value of financial wealth through holdings of foreign exchange is equivalent in developing countries to 'remaining liquid' in the presence of adverse shocks. This is because under adverse circumstances, the demand for foreign exchange increases. Thus, bank borrowers with significant access to foreign exchange – either through their own savings domestically or abroad or through access to foreign currency denominated funds – also become the most creditworthy borrowers in the presence of adverse shocks.

Prudential regulation calls for rules to avoid excessive exchange rate risk in banks' portfolios. In industrial countries, banks take exchange rate risk in their role of 'market makers' in foreign exchange by quoting rates and by taking open positions in currencies. Foreign exchange business rather than credit business is the banks' operational area that is more susceptible to exchange rate risk. In contrast, in many developing countries, 'liability dollarization', that is, investors' preference for holding a significant amount of their deposits in dollar accounts, implies that banks need to extend dollar-denominated loans to avoid currency mismatches. Thus, banks' credit business in many developing countries is vulnerable to exchange rate risk. Since lack of deep capital markets prevents most banks in developing countries from arranging adequate hedges on net foreign currency denominated bank liabilities, prudential rules in these countries typically imply setting limits on these exposures.

However, as has been amply discussed elsewhere, common prudential rules cannot truly isolate banks from exchange rate risk in developing countries where the use of foreign currency coexists with the use of local currency. The reason is that a significant proportion of bank loans denominated in foreign currency often go to borrowers with revenues denominated in the domestic currency. Sudden and large exchange rate depreciations of the local currency significantly hinder borrowers' capacity to service their foreign currency obligations. Thus, in many developing countries – but especially in those with large macro/financial volatility – the exchange rate risk faced by banks quickly transforms into credit risk, rendering the distinction between these two types of risks irrelevant. This, of course, complicates the efforts of bankers and supervisors to measure and control risks.

Finally, consider the standard methodology for risk assessment used by many banks in industrial countries, namely, the value at risk models, or VaR. These models are constructed to estimate potential losses on given portfolios through fluctuations in asset prices, including exchange rates, interest rates and equity prices. VaR can be defined as 'the expected maximum loss over a target horizon within a given confidence interval' (Jorion, 1997). VaR can be derived from the frequency distribution of a bank's portfolio returns. To apply these models, therefore, bankers need to choose both the holding period (target horizon) and the confidence interval.[14] In addition, the application of VaR models requires the determination of the 'data window', namely, the period for which the historical distribution of returns is sampled. In theory, data windows of several years have the advantage that a larger number of observations allow a more precise coverage of the actual return distribution.[15] However, while this might hold for industrial countries, in many highly volatile developing countries, longer data windows simply increase the probability that the return distribution has changed over the sample period. This leads to biases in VaR estimates and, therefore, reduces the usefulness of this risk assessment technique.

Thus, unlike industrial countries, the identification, measurement and management of bank risks tend to be more complicated in developing countries, given the particular features of their financial markets. In these countries, therefore, prudential regulatory practices that just mimic the rules of industrial countries significantly lose their efficacy and appropriateness.

4.3 The cans and cannots of international standards and codes for the effectiveness of financial prudential regulation in developing countries

As stated in the introduction, in the face of the large number of severe financial crises in developing countries during the 1990s, it is not difficult to understand the search for new international initiatives aimed at preventing these occurrences. Agreement that coordination between multilateral organizations and private standard-setting bodies was necessary led to the establishment in April 1999 of the Financial Stability Forum (FSF). The FSF was established for the specific purpose of promoting international financial stability by engaging the cooperation of governments, markets, and international organizations in improving financial supervision and surveillance. A major component of the activities of the FSF has been to coordinate a comprehensive set of international standards and codes to strengthen financial systems.

This section first reviews the state of the supply of standards and codes as determined by the international financial organizations. These large sets of standards are the basis for the menu of prudential regulations that countries can incorporate into their legislation. The section then examines the appropriateness and effectiveness of these standards for the purpose of strengthening financial systems in developing countries. To do so, the section reviews a variety of concerns raised by analysts and policymakers in order to grasp what developing countries need and want (the demand side) in terms of prudential regulation.

Understanding the supply of international standards and codes for strengthening financial sectors[16]

Common standards and codes have two main objectives. First, because they are common, the standards aim at facilitating international comparisons and, hence, avoid the negative externalities created by confusing and incomplete information about a country's economic policies. Second, by setting the common standards at high levels, it is expected that they could enhance the role of market discipline; that is, it is expected that countries that want to improve their access to international capital markets will have an incentive to enforce the standards, which can then act as benchmarks to guide policymakers' reform efforts.

Identifying appropriate codes and standards and prioritizing between them, however, is not an easy task. To the question of what guarantees the stability of financial systems there are a multitude of answers. They range from the attainment of macroeconomic consistency and sound domestic regulatory financial frameworks, to reforms in a number of economic and institutional sectors, to the full dissemination of a wide variety of information.

Setting priorities thus becomes a key issue when establishing and implementing standards and codes. The FSF identified 73 standards, but it has highlighted a smaller set of 12, grouped in three areas, that it deems essential for sound financial systems. These standards have been set by a number of international institutions and are understood to be minimum requirements for good practice. Each standard, in turn, contains a number of guidelines. Some are very specific, such as the standards on data dissemination, but others, including those governing certain aspects of the transparency of monetary policy, are quite general and allow for variation from country to country. Table 4.2 summarizes the supply of standards and codes as agreed by the FSF and the multilateral organizations involved.

Given the importance that the multilateral organizations attach to the observance of standards and codes, in 1999 the International Monetary Fund (IMF) initiated the preparation of Reports on the Observance of Standards and Codes (ROSCs). Assessments of the status and progress of countries on one or more standards are conducted on a voluntary basis. Sometimes these assessments take place in the context of the IMF surveillance process (Article IV consultations). It is the intention of the IMF to maintain a standardized format for all ROSCs and to continue publishing them on the institution's website.

Policymakers' responses to the establishment, implementation, and assessment of international standards and codes have been mixed. We now turn to that discussion.

What do countries need in terms of prudential financial regulation?

There is general agreement about the long-term benefits of establishing international standards to guide individual countries' policies, in general, and financial prudential regulation, in particular. However, many argue that the pressing issue for developing countries is how to handle the transition period when the preconditions needed for the effective implementation of international standards may not yet be in place. This sub-section outlines developing countries' desires and needs in terms of prudential regulation by briefly summarizing the general concerns raised regarding the setting and implementation of international standards. Discussion on the adequacy for developing countries of a central standard, the capital adequacy requirement recommended by the Basel Committee on Banking Supervision, will be the focus of the next subsection.

Table 4.2 Key standards for sound financial systems

Subject area	Key standard	Issuing body
Macroeconomic policy and data transparency		
Monetary and financial policy transparency	Code of Good Practices on Transparency in Monetary and Financial Policies	International Monetary Fund
Fiscal policy transparency	Code of Good Practices on Fiscal Transparency	International Monetary Fund
Data dissemination	Special Data Dissemination Standard (SDSS)/ General Data Dissemination System (GDDS)[a]	International Monetary Fund
Institutional and market infrastructure		
Insolvency	Principles and guidelines on effective insolvency and creditor rights systems[b]	World Bank
Corporate governance	Principles of Corporate Governance	Organization for Economic Cooperation and Development
Accounting	International Accounting Standards (IAS)[c]	International Accounting Standards Board[d]
Auditing	International Standards on Auditing (ISA)	International Federation of Accountants (International Auditing and Assurance Standards Board)[d]
Payment and settlement	Core Principles for Systemically Important Payment Systems Recommendations for Securities Settlement Systems	Committee on Payment and Settlement Systems/ CPSS-IOSCO Task Force on Securities Settlements Systems
Market integrity	The Forty Recommendations of the Financial Action Task Force/ 8 Special Recommendations Against Terrorist Financing	Financial Action Task Force on Money Laundering
Financial regulation and supervision		
Banking supervision	Core Principles for Effective Banking Supervision	Basel Committee on Banking Supervision
Securities regulation	Objectives and Principles of Securities Regulation	International Organization of Securities Commissions
Insurance supervision	Insurance Core Principles	International Association of Insurance Supervisors

Notes:

a. Economies with access to international capital markets are encouraged to subscribe to the more stringent SDDS and all other economies are encouraged to adopt the GDDS.

b. The World Bank is coordinating a broad-based effort to develop a set of principles and guidelines on insolvency regimes. The United Nations Commission on International Trade Law (UNCITRAL), which adopted the Model Law on Cross-Border Insolvency In 1997, will help facilitate implementation

c. Relevant IAS are currently being reviewed by the IAIS and 1OSCO

d. The International Accounting Standards Board (IASB) and the International Federation of Accountants (IFAC) are distinct from other standard-setting bodies in that they are private sector bodies.

Source: Financial Stability Forum: http//www.fsforum.org/compendium/key_standards_for_sound_financial_system.html.

The general concerns about standards related to prudential regulation are all interrelated. However, for expositional purposes they can be classified into four categories: perceptions of and discontent with a one-size-fits-all approach; problems with the sequencing of and countries' capacity to implement the standards; the 'ownership' problem arising from lack of sufficient participation by developing countries in setting the standards; and, most importantly, questions about the effectiveness of the standards.[17]

The one-size-fits-all approach

From the analysis in Section 4.2 it is clear that financial systems in developing countries not only differ significantly from those in industrial countries, but also display dramatic differences within the group. Because countries face different constraints at different stages of development, prudential regulations based on standards that are found to work for industrial countries may not be appropriate for the large majority of developing countries. For a number of years now, China has been one of the most vocal countries regarding this concern. An example can be found in a statement by Mr Dai Xianglong, former Governor of the People's Bank of China:

> When setting (standards and codes) not only should we draw upon the general patterns observed in global economic developments, but also pay due regard to the specific issues facing countries in their different stages of development. We should take account of the specific circumstances and needs of the developing countries. Their voices should be adequately heard.[18]

High-level officials from some of the industrial countries have raised similar concerns. For example, Gordon Brown, UK Prime Minister and formerly Chancellor of the Exchequer, has written that 'there exists a danger of pushing inappropriate measures for a given country's state of financial and institutional development, and any order of priority for implementation of the codes and standards must be carefully established on an individual basis to ensure positive net benefits' (Brown, 1998: 8). As will be argued below, this concern is fully relevant for the banks' capital adequacy standard as recommended by the Basel Committee.

Sequencing and issues of implementation capacity

Concerns about sequencing and implementation capacity are closely related to those about uniformity of standards. A main issue is that without appropriate institutions, such as adequate judicial systems and institutions enforcing the rule of law, compliance with the so-called key standards may not produce the desired results. For example, a government may fully comply with standards for disclosure yet actually disclose very little because ineffective control within the government results in a lack of accurate data.[19]

As Section 4.2 shows, with the exception of Chile, all countries in the sample display low scores in the quality of their institutions. It is, therefore, not surprising that most of the case studies stress institutional problems as constraints for adequate implementation of prudential regulation. For example, the Russian study indicates that the problems faced by supervisors in enforcing prudential regulations are rooted in deeply entrenched bad practices that have been followed for a very long period of time. Likewise, the study on Thailand points to excessive space allowed for judgment and interpretation of the norms, signaling a weak institutional framework. The case study on China bluntly describes the very low progress achieved in improving transparency, judicial systems and corruption. In the dramatic case of Argentina, the 'rules of the game' were identified as being 'endogenous' during the most recent financial crisis in that country. Nothing points more clearly towards weak institutions than a regulatory framework that accommodates to financial activities rather than guiding them.

Concern about inappropriate sequencing when applying policy recommendations largely designed in and for industrial countries to developing countries is based on past disastrous experiences. For example, the liberalization of domestic financial markets, a prescription whose long-run benefits are widely accepted, became a popular policy in Latin America in the late 1970s and early 1980s. The banking crisis that followed, which resulted in the worst economic episode in the region's recent history – the 'lost decade' – is well known. Was financial liberalization the culprit? Not really. Rather, it was a sequencing problem. Successful financial liberalization requires the adoption of sound regulatory and supervisory frameworks which must be appropriate for the individual countries, and those preconditions were not in place in the region. This was a lesson that has been learned – but only partially. The issue of what institutional reforms are needed before incorporating international standards into domestic prudential regulation remains to be properly addressed.

Moreover, even if the timing of the implementation of a particular financial standard is right, a number of countries are concerned about their capacity to pursue the task effectively. Indeed, concerns about supervisory skills and/or the technical capacity of banks' board members were raised in the case studies on Brazil, Nigeria, and Thailand.

The ownership problem

Another concern often voiced by representatives of developing countries is that their countries do not participate fully in the design and prioritization of the standards that they are then asked to adopt as prudential regulations. The argument is that under-representation of developing countries in standards-setting institutions and forums contributes to the problems of sequencing and implementation already discussed, and, most importantly, to the effectiveness when applied to domestic regulation. The importance of this issue has been documented in a number of recent reports.[20]

The number of countries participating in the different standards-setting bodies varies considerably. For example, standards set by the IMF and the World Bank, such as those on transparency and dissemination, enjoy the participation of the entire membership of those institutions (183 countries). In contrast, the Basel Committee on Banking Supervision has a membership of only 13 countries, all from the industrial world. It is true that the Basel Committee consults intensively with a large number of developing countries, especially through the Core Principles Liaison Group, but the strong perception in developing countries is that the last word remains within the membership.

Perhaps the most frequently voiced concern about developing-country involvement is the limited membership of the FSF, the main institution in charge of coordinating financial standards and codes. The FSF's membership consists of the Group of Seven major industrial countries plus four that represent important financial centers: Australia, Hong Kong, Singapore, and the Netherlands. The response of the FSF to this concern has not been to broaden its membership, but rather to establish a number of working groups with significant participation by developing countries. However, in spite of these efforts by the FSF, the perception of lack of ownership of the standards remains strong among developing countries.

The effectiveness of the standards

The institutions engaged in setting and assessing international standards recognize that adoption of these standards is an additional instrument in the policy-maker's toolbox for crisis prevention, not a magic wand that can ensure financial stability. However, a number of analysts have recently questioned the effectiveness of international standards when applied to prudential regulations in developing countries. The Argentinian crisis of early 2002 – which combined severe banking disruptions with defaults on domestic and international obligations – has heightened this concern, which can be summarized in the following two questions. First, why did Argentina, one of the developing countries most involved in the ROSC process (with five official ROSCs and two self-assessments published on the IMF website), suffer what appears to be one of the deepest and lengthiest financial crises in recent history? Second, why did a positive assessment by the IMF and the World Bank of Argentina's progress in the implementation of four standards not help shield the country against this crisis? The case study on Argentina in this project goes a long way in providing answers, and they all go in the direction of recognizing the crucial importance of identifying particular characteristics of developing countries when assessing the adequacy of regulatory practices and economic policies in general. In this regard, weak institutions and a shallow, highly volatile, short-term-oriented banking system played a central role in preventing the effectiveness of financial reforms in Argentina.

Thus, from the discussion above, and consistent with the data presented in Section 4.2, it can be inferred that what many developing countries want in terms of prudential regulation is a case-by-case approach where recognition of the degree of financial development becomes a crucial factor in deciding what regulatory practices should be adopted. The next section assesses the effectiveness of what is perhaps the core international standard for prudential financial regulation: capital adequacy requirements as recommended by the Basel Committee on Banking Supervision.

4.4 When supply does not meet demand: Basel I and II

Capital requirements are considered a key prudential tool in strengthening banking systems. The aim of this regulation is to contain the expansion of excessive risk-taking by banks. This is done by requiring banks to comply with a risk-weighted capital-to-assets ratio determined by the regulators. At least at the conceptual level, riskier assets are assigned higher capital charges.

If capital requirements were, indeed, estimated to reflect the 'true' risk features of banks' portfolios and could be effectively enforced, this would undoubtedly be a powerful tool for policymakers. In particular, country authorities could deal more effectively with the large capital flow volatility that most developing countries have been facing since the 1990s in the context of more liberalized financial systems. The tool would allow supervisors to focus on weaker banks since capital ratios would decline in those banks that increase their risk-taking activities, hence providing an early-warning signal for supervisors. In a period of large capital inflows, this policy would limit the risk-taking of banks that intermediate the inflows.

During the 1990s many developing countries directed their financial reform efforts towards implementing the recommendations of the Basel Accord on capital requirements. However, albeit with quite diverse outcomes, the recent experience of banking problems in developing countries, especially in emerging markets, indicates that capital requirements as suggested by industrial country standards (Basel) often have not performed their expected role as an effective supervisory tool: the accumulation of capital in banks' balance sheets has not acted as a 'buffer' to deal with unexpected adverse shocks to banks.

Evidence that capital ratios have been largely meaningless in signaling banking problems in many developing countries is presented in Table 4.3. The table shows the performance of 'traditional indicators' used by bank supervisors to assess the strength of individual banks in six episodes of banking crises: Mexico, Colombia, Venezuela, Thailand, Korea, and Malaysia.[21] To determine the appropriateness of these indicators in providing early warning signals of banking problems, the 'signal approach' popularized by Kaminsky and Reinhart (1999) was used. The main idea of the approach is that an indicator that exceeds a prespecified threshold provides a 'signal' that should alert supervisors and market participants to the weakening of a bank's performance. The precise definition of the threshold used for the calculations as well as a detailed explanation of the methodology behind Table 4.3 is contained in Rojas-Suarez (2001). For the purpose of this chapter, it is sufficient to explain the meaning of the data in the table. Every column in the table shows the number of banks in trouble accurately signaled in advance by each indicator, as a percentage of total banks in trouble. For example, a ratio of 10 next to an indicator tells us that the indicator correctly identified only 10 per cent of all banks that failed (closed or intervened) during the crisis episode in the corresponding country.

The results in the table are very clear. While the traditional indicators did not perform well (with the possible exception of the net profits to income), the

Table 4.3 Accuracy of traditional indicators in predicting bank problems in Mexico (1993–94), Venezuela (1993–94), Colombia (1981–88), Thailand, Korea and Malaysia (1996–97) (Predicted number of troubled banks as a percentage of total troubled banks)

	Mexico	**Venezuela**	**Colombia**	**Thailand**	**Korea**	**Malaysia**
Traditional indicators						
Capitalization	7	31	14	30	Meaningless (100)	37
Change in equity prices	37	n.a.	25	n.a.	n.a.	n.a.
Net profits to income	60	13	43	60	60	50
Operating costs to assets	40	13	29	20	20	25
Liquidity ratio	7	13	29	50	56	60
Memo item						
Interest rate on deposits	80	69	71	66	80	62

Source: Rojas-Suarez (2001).

capital to asset ratio performed the worst. For example, in Mexico, a country that claimed to have adopted the capital standards recommendations of Basel just before the eruption of the 1994–95 banking crisis, the behavior of the risk-weighted capital-to-asset ratio was useful in predicting problems accurately in only 7 per cent of the banks that experienced severe crises. Indeed, according to the data provided by the Mexican Supervisory Authority, most banks in Mexico were in full compliance with capital requirements and held a ratio well above 8 per cent!

The conclusion that can be derived from the above evidence is *not* that capital requirements can never be of use for supervisors in developing countries. As the discussion below demonstrates, the conclusion is that for the capital standards to be effective the standards need to take into account the specific risk features of developing countries. Simply adopting standards that are based on the risk characteristics of industrial countries does not work.

Why haven't capital adequacy ratios been effective prudential tools in developing countries? The reasons for the disappointing performance of this instrument can be broadly organized into two groups and have been previously discussed in Rojas-Suarez (2001, 2005). The first group relates to the specific structural features of financial markets in developing countries, including those discussed in Section 4.2 and those related to the concentration of ownership of financial and real assets. The second group relates to the particular characteristics of the Basel capital standard (Basel I), the standard chosen by most developing countries. It is argued here and elsewhere (see Rojas-Suarez, 2001) that Basel II, the more recently proposed capital standard finalized by the Basel Committee on Banking Supervision for implementation beginning by the end of 2006 in some countries, also suffers from important problems that limit its usefulness as a prudential regulation tool in most developing countries.

Turning to the first set of reasons, we raise the following question: Assuming that banks' risks were appropriately estimated in the capital standards, what features in developing countries could prevent the standards from working properly? The answer is weak institutions. Perhaps the best example is a deficient judicial framework that is unable to enforce supervisory actions when a bank's performance is deemed faulty. Lack of enforcement of the rule of law seriously undermines the efficiency of bank ratios.

However, this is not all. As discussed in Section 4.2, in most developing countries the highly volatile macro and financial environment makes it very difficult to assess and measure the different classes of bank risks, a condition that is necessary to estimate risk-weighted capital standards. This constraint is particularly binding in the most volatile/least developed financial systems. Moreover, a fundamental problem with the capital standards in developing countries, also associated with their high volatility/weak institutions features, is the lack of deep and liquid capital markets. This implies that, even when accounting, reporting and legal frameworks are adequate, capitalization ratios will be less effective if liquid *markets* for bank shares, subordinated debt, and other bank liabilities and assets are not available to validate the 'real' value of bank capital (as distinct from its accounting value). Therefore, since these markets are typically either not available or not liquid in developing countries, changes in the market value of bank capital, which provide supervisors in industrial countries with information regarding the quality of reported capital, are not an effective instrument in developing countries.

In contrast to industrial countries, asset ownership, both financial and real, is still highly concentrated in many developing countries, making the potential market for equity capital small and uncompetitive. In such an environment, the intent of the capital standard – to increase the proportion of uninsured funding (equity and subordinated debt) to insured funding (deposits) in order to reduce bank stockholders' incentives to take risks at the expense of existing public safety nets – can be easily subverted.[22] Shareholders' wealth may not really be at risk when they supply equity capital to a bank because shareholders can finance their stake with a loan from a related party, which could even be a non-financial corporation and hence outside the regulators' purview. Thus, concentration of wealth provides incentives for bank owners to supply low-quality bank capital and, therefore, to undertake higher risks than bank shareholders in industrial countries would allow. Lacking a market that assesses the quality of bank capital, capitalization ratios cannot serve as an effective supervisory tool.

Clearly, the severity of this problem varies widely across developing countries. For many countries, the constraints limiting the usefulness of capital requirements – any capital requirement, not just those proposed by the Basel Committee – are extremely binding, and therefore beg the question: Are there alternative policies to the use of capital standards for assessing and ensuring the strengths of banks now, in the immediate future, when preconditions for the effectiveness of the capital standard are not in place? This question will be dealt with in Section 4.5.

In some other developing countries, however, a continuous increase in the participation of foreign banks from industrial countries is de facto reducing the degree of connected lending among financial institutions and between financial institutions and the real sector. Furthermore, in this (still small) group of countries, institutional quality has improved and macro/financial volatility has decreased. In very few developing countries are sufficiently deep and liquid capital markets forming. Chile stands out as the country, among the case studies in this project, with the deepest capital market.[23]

For this group of countries, the relevant question becomes whether adopting the internationally accepted capital standards recommended by the Basel Committee is appropriate (both the current Accord and the newly published Basel II). Indeed, this is deeply related to the second set of factors explaining the observed inefficacies of capital requirements, and, to identify them, we ask the following question: Assuming that developing countries are structurally and institutionally 'ready' to effectively implement capital standards, are the Basel Committee's standards adequate for developing countries? To answer this question we first assess whether the classification of assets according to risk in the current Basel Accord 'matches' the risk features of bank assets in developing countries. Then, we quickly question whether a move towards Basel II could be the solution.

The argument in this chapter and in Rojas-Suarez (2001, 2005) is that there is a poor match between the assessments of risks contained in the current Accord recommendations and the actual risks in developing countries. Indeed, I argue that a straightforward application of the Basel I standard can actually weaken banking systems in developing markets as the standards create incentives for banks to increase the risk characteristics of their portfolios. Among others, there are two features of the standards that have contributed to weakening rather than strengthening banks' balance sheets: the treatment of government claims held by banks and the treatment of inter-bank lending.

Regarding the treatment of bank credit to the government, under the current Basel Accord, loans to the public sector carry a zero per cent risk weight if the country belongs to the OECD and 100 per cent if the loan is to a non-OECD government. The idea, of course, is that claims on OECD governments can be considered 'safe assets'. However, when applying the Basel recommendations to their domestic economies, most non-OECD countries attach a zero per cent risk weight to their own government paper. That is, banks in developing countries treat paper issued by their own governments as a 'safe asset', an assumption far from reality if one takes into account the default history of emerging market governments, highlighted by the recent defaults of Argentina, Russia, and Ecuador.[24] The problem with this practice is that by economizing on capital requirements, banks have a strong incentive to concentrate a significant portion of their asset holdings in government paper rather than in loans to the private sector. This incentive not only gives a false impression of 'bank safety'; even more importantly, it also contributes to reducing further the already problematic capacity of banks to assess credit risk.

While a thorough understanding of banks' decisions to hold public instead of private assets would require the specification of a complete model, it is fair to argue that the regulatory treatment of government paper has played an important role in banks' decisions. Indeed, as depicted in Figure 4.3, government paper as a share of total bank assets has increased in many countries in the 1990s relative to the 1980s (many countries are located to the right of the 45 degree line). This coincides with the adoption of the Basel capital adequacy recommendations in developing countries. As Figure 4.3 shows, the ratio of claims on government as a percentage of total bank assets not only has increased for many countries, but is also very high. Among the countries studied in this project, Argentina, Brazil, and Nigeria (the countries with the least developed financial systems in the sample) display very high ratios. It is interesting to note that the authors of these three case studies have also noted the impact of Basel I on the holdings of government paper by banks. In contrast, Chile, Thailand, and South Africa have been able to reduce this ratio to low levels.[25]

This regulatory incentive also has important consequences during recessions, as banks tend to magnify the downward trend in economic activity by shifting

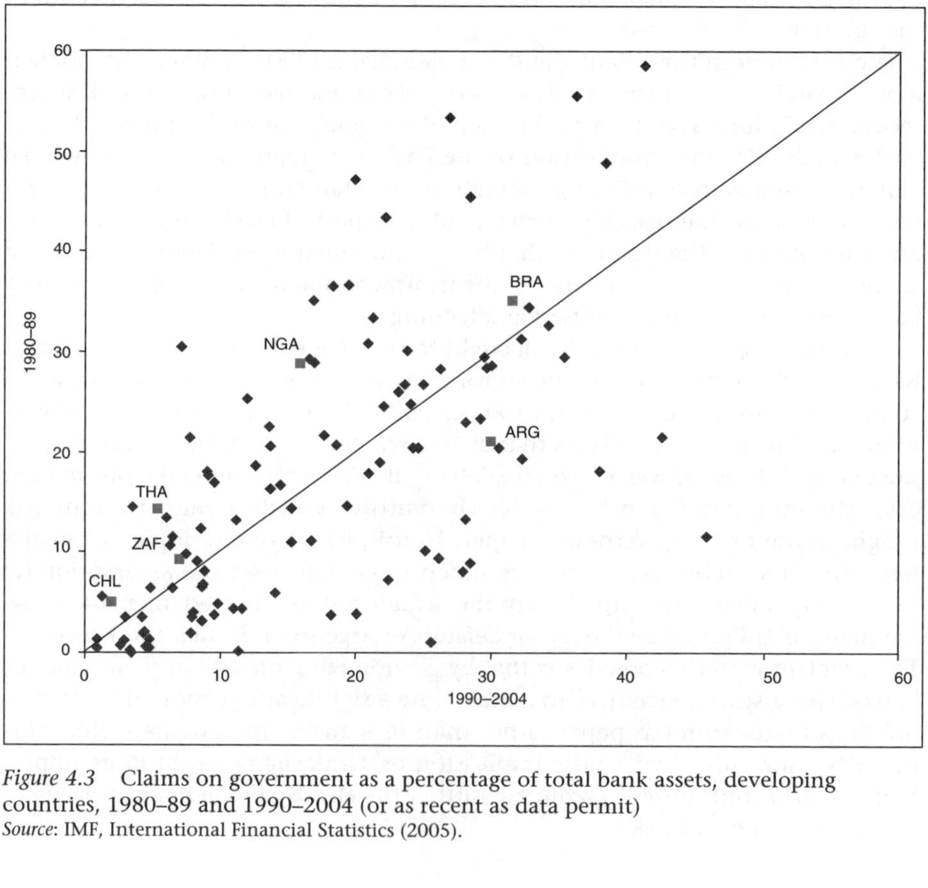

Figure 4.3 Claims on government as a percentage of total bank assets, developing countries, 1980–89 and 1990–2004 (or as recent as data permit)
Source: IMF, International Financial Statistics (2005).

their portfolio further away from credit to the private sector and towards government paper as they seek to reduce capital costs.

The evidence above suggests that the regulatory treatment of banks' claims on government tends to reduce the soundness of banking systems in developing countries.[26] This concern, as obvious as it may look, is, however, not taken into account when International Financial Institutions (IFIs) assess country progress in strengthening financial systems. Indeed, developing countries attaching zero risk weight to domestic government liabilities will not receive a 'warning signal' from IFIs even if the government is highly indebted as such a practice is not perceived as a conflict with the international standards!

Will the adoption of Basel II correct the above-mentioned problem? This seems unlikely. The consensus among analysts is that the few developing countries that might incorporate Basel II into their regulations will choose the so-called 'standardized approach'. Under this approach, risk weights are to be refined by referring to ratings provided by an external credit assessment institution. While at first sight this gives the impression that banks' risks associated with holding government paper will be determined by market forces, Basel II contains an 'opt-out' clause to be applied at the discretion of individual countries. According to this clause, banks can attach zero or low-risk weight to claims on the government where the bank is incorporated under the condition that the claim is denominated in local currency. This provides an incentive for governments to continue their practice of attaching zero risk weight to their liabilities.

Regarding the treatment of inter-bank lending, the Basel Accord attaches a risk weight of 100 per cent to bank lending to non-OECD banks with a maturity of over a year, while lending to this group of banks with a maturity of a year or less carries a risk weight of only 20 per cent. The obvious result has been a bias towards short-term cross-border lending towards developing countries' banks. This, of course, exacerbates the volatility of flows to developing countries as any adverse news from developing countries quickly translates into a sharp reduction of cross-border lending.[27] The new Basel Accord aggravates this problem as the definition of short-term has been reduced from 'one year maximum' to 'three months maximum'. Further discussion of the problems for Latin American countries associated with the plausible implementation of the Basel II Accord is contained in Latin American Shadow Financial Regulatory Committee (2001).

But problems for developing countries associated with the Basel Accord treatment of inter-bank lending go beyond increased volatility of capital flows as this regulatory provision also creates incentives to decrease the maturity of loans extended by domestic banks to the local economy. The reason is that in their efforts to strengthen their banking systems, a number of developing countries have introduced regulations that reduce the maturity mismatch between banks' assets and liabilities. The shorter the maturity of international loans to banks in developing countries, the shorter the marginal maturity of loans extended by banks in developing countries to their local customers in order to prevent a maturity mismatch between banks' assets and liabilities. This, of course, adversely affects the vulnerability of economic activity to sources of funding.

Thus, a lesson from capital standards as a prudential tool to deal with capital flow volatility is that even if adequate accounting, supervisory and judicial frameworks are in place, the current Basel Accord is not the appropriate capital standard for developing countries. One of its major shortcomings is that by incorrectly assessing the risk features of developing countries, it creates incentives for excessive risk-taking by banks in these countries.

As discussed above, Basel II worsens some of the problems associated with Basel I. It is important to note, however, that the 'spirit' of the new Accord, namely, an attempt to align 'regulatory' capital with the 'true' risk of banks' portfolios, would help, but not the actual prescriptions. This is not the place to fully discuss the problems for developing countries associated with Basel II. It is sufficient to point out here that the only approach within Basel II that allows for an adequate measurement of risk is the 'advanced internal rating-based approach' (the IRB approach). The problem, however, is that the large majority of banks and supervisors in developing countries are simply not ready to implement this approach.[28] Unfortunately, the other two approaches available under Basel II for calculating minimum capital requirements create a whole set of new problems that would have undesirable consequences for the stability of the financial systems of developing countries. See Rojas-Suarez (2001) for a comprehensive discussion of these issues.[29]

In a nutshell, the supply of capital standards by the Basel Committee does not meet the demand for effective prudential regulation by developing countries.

4.5 Making prudential regulations work in developing countries: the challenge of policy consistency and adequate design

The discussion in this chapter makes it clear that special efforts, beyond those currently undertaken by the international standard-setting bodies, are needed to design and implement adequate prudential regulation for developing countries. This section advances some recommendations in that direction.

The first recommendation is the crucial need for consistency between macroeconomic policies and the state of development of the financial system. This is because the predominance of short-term financial instruments in most developing countries implies that changes in macro policies will have an immediate and profound effect on the value of banks' balance sheets. The lower the degree of financial development, the greater the effect of macro policies on financial institutions. Take, for example, an increase in the policy interest rate by the central bank as a reaction to a sudden reversal of capital inflows. Because financial instruments are concentrated in short-term maturities and capital markets are practically nonexistent, the increase in the policy rate affects the entire maturity spectrum of interest rates (there is not a well-developed yield curve). This, in turn, adversely affects the capacity of banks' borrowers to repay their loans.

Consistency is also needed between fiscal policies and the prudential regulatory framework. As discussed in Section 4.4, the risk weights in capital requirements under Basel I give an incentive for banks to increase their holdings of government paper relative to claims on the private sector. In countries with weak fiscal institutions, Basel I might contribute to perpetuating excessively expansionary fiscal policies since local banking systems have an incentive to keep large holdings of government liabilities. While there is no incentive for governments with weak fiscal institutions to change this regulatory framework, the good news is that, in many developing countries, central banks are in charge of designing financial regulatory frameworks. To the extent that the central bank enjoys independence – a feature that has slowly gained ground in a number of developing countries – the regulatory practice of attaching zero or low risk weight to government liabilities will possibly be avoided.

What does the need for consistency tell us about the choice of exchange rate regimes? In a number of developing countries, high macro volatility and weak institutions have resulted in a large stock of domestic debt and/or a fragile banking system. Those circumstances impose important constraints on the choice of exchange rate regimes.[30] Under a fixed or managed peg, speculators would perceive a 'one-sided bet' if pressures on the exchange rate were to develop. The bet is that governments will eventually choose to abandon the announced parity (its being fixed or managed) rather than defend it by keeping interest rates very high for a prolonged period of time. This is because the defense would aggravate existing fragilities in the banking sector or increase the fiscal cost of servicing the existing large stock of domestic debt (or both).[31] As a result, speculators exacerbate the attack on the exchange rate when governments attempt to defend the parity. Thus, in developing countries with fragile banking systems, exchange rate flexibility is not a choice; it is a necessity.

Let us now turn to specific recommendations on prudential regulation. As has been argued throughout this chapter, the wide range of financial depth among developing countries implies that a uniform set of rules and regulations may not be appropriate for all countries. Because the degree of development matters, policy recommendations for the least developed countries need to differ from those for the most financially advanced developing countries. For simplicity, and following Rojas-Suarez (2005), countries can be divided into two groups according to their degree of financial development: the least financially developed countries and those countries with relatively deeper financial markets. The set of recommendations that follows is by no means complete or fully inclusive. They are simply examples of policies that are consistent with the objective of making prudential regulatory tools work.

For the first group, the financially least developed group, where traditional regulations and any capital standard would be largely ineffective, it is obvious that sustainable policies consist of removing the constraints on the effectiveness of prudential regulations. That implies strengthening institutions and developing capital markets that validate the accounting capital ratios.

Those policy reforms, however, often take a significant amount of time to implement.[32] In the transition to a more comprehensive reform, it is still possible to identify and develop some indicators of banking problems that help to reveal the true riskiness of banks. For example, deposit markets have often been identified as markets that work in many developing countries in the sense that they have been able to provide effective early-warning signals about the relative strength of banks (see Rojas-Suarez 2001). Indeed, as the memo item in Table 4.3 shows, among all the indicators presented in the table, interest rate on deposits was clearly the best performer. In all the countries in the sample, this variable by far showed the highest degree of accuracy in predicting bank problems. Thus, these countries should encourage the public offering of uninsured certificates of deposits. The central idea is that, if encouraged to do so, depositors and other holders of banks' liabilities can discriminate between sound and weak banks, for example, charging higher interest rates on deposits or withdrawing deposits from financial institutions perceived to be unsound (which entails 'pricing risk' adequately).

Thus, a central message for countries with underdeveloped financial systems is that policymakers should focus on strengthening the role of market discipline. In other words, regulators should focus on designing tools that utilize information from markets that already work or that can be developed in a relatively short period of time. An additional example is the promotion and development of inter-bank markets: if banks publish their inter-bank bids and offer rates, the flow of information on bank quality would improve.

As already discussed, the lack of an effective judicial system can be a serious obstacle for the development of financial systems because banks cannot rely on the enforcement of creditors' rights in case of default. In these circumstances, it is advisable to develop 'credit bureaus' that provide timely and relevant information about debtors' creditworthiness. As suggested in IDB (2004), the collection of debtors' information can contribute to the creation of 'reputation collateral' that might, at least partially, compensate for the lack of sound judiciary institutions.

The key for market discipline to work, however, is the elimination of distortions that encourage bank liability holders not to discriminate between banks. A typical obstacle for market discipline is a deposit insurance scheme that promises unlimited coverage to all depositors. It is important, therefore, to strengthen regulatory efforts on improving deposit insurance schemes to credibly limit the insurance, while ensuring that the scheme is sufficiently funded to finance the closing or selling of financial institutions in severe difficulties.

Another obstacle to the functioning of market discipline is a central bank that provides banks with excessive access to liquidity. This is because this practice creates a moral hazard problem that eliminates the incentive of bank liability holders to discriminate among banks by quality. Limiting access to central bank liquidity is, therefore, another important recommendation.

Finally, the process of financial internationalization – through the promotion of foreign banking – needs to be encouraged. Although foreign banks are by no means a panacea, and some recent crisis experiences have even demonstrated some shortcomings, my view is that the benefits of an internationalized financial system outweigh the costs. The reason is that adequate market depth can only be achieved if a diverse group of investors and users of capital enter the market; that is, if the market becomes less concentrated.

Policy recommendations are quite different for the second group of developing countries, which we characterize as having a sufficient degree of financial development to allow traditional prudential regulatory policies to be meaningful, but where their particular features, such as limited access to international capital markets, imply that the strict application of industrial-country regulation, such as the Basel Accord, may be of limited effectiveness. In this group of countries, the recommendations advanced for less financially developed countries have to a large extent already been implemented.

The main recommendation for this group of countries, advanced in Rojas-Suarez (2005) is to design a transitional capital standard that appropriately reflects the risk of banks' assets because Basel (I or II) does not fit the bill in the short run. The recommendation is that the standard should have two basic components. The first is the development of ex ante risk-based regulations in loan-loss provisions. While this is widely recognized by the Basel Committee to be an essential complement to any capital standard, the proposal in this chapter is one based on prioritization. Given the high frequency of adverse shocks in developing countries, especially the sudden reversal of capital inflows, the expected probability of occurrence of these adverse outcomes is very high compared to industrial countries. In this environment, provisioning, at times, takes a more important role than capitalization. As can be inferred from the discussion in Section 4.2, ex ante risk-based provisioning would be a significant departure from current practices in almost all developing countries.[33]

The second recommendation is the establishment of a reduced number of risk categories to classify assets, with the central qualification that the categories of risk should reflect the particular features of banks' assets in developing countries. If loan-loss reserves are designed to reflect the *expected* losses in banks' assets, minimum capital requirements need to reflect *unexpected* losses. Issues that need to be considered in the design of appropriate risk categories include an adequate risk assessment of government paper and the introduction of distinct capital charges for loans to agents in the tradable and non-tradable sectors.[34]

The problems associated with attaching risk weights to government paper that severely understates the risk features of those assets have already been discussed in the chapter. However, it is important to stress that as long as governments do not make the political decision to correctly price the risk of their own liabilities, banks will have an incentive to discriminate against credit to the private sector and will favor the public sector.

Additional recommendations to allow these countries to deepen their financial systems and, hence, improve the effectiveness of accepted international prudential regulation include: (a) further enhancing the mechanisms of market discipline beyond the recommendations advanced for the least developed group of countries, and (b) deepening the process of financial internationalization through the increased participation of foreign institutional investors, especially pension funds and insurance companies.

As a parting note, it is worth recalling the three basic messages of this chapter. The first is that the particular macro/institutional features of countries matter not only for the degree of development of their financial systems but for the adequacy of financial prudential regulations: as in most other economic and financial matters, one size does not fit all. The second message is that the lack of efficacy of traditional prudential regulations in developing countries does not mean that appropriate regulatory practices cannot be designed. The third and final message is that the key for successful prudential regulation in developing countries lies in focusing on the role of market discipline and on the design of transitional policies when necessary.

Notes

This chapter has greatly benefited from the excellent research assistance support of Sebastian Sotelo and from the comments and suggestions of Benu Schneider and other participants at the United Nations Conference on 'International Financial Architecture, Macro Volatility and Institutions: the Developing World Experience' held in New York, 17–18 April 2006.

1. See, for example, Beck et al. (2000) and Rajan and Zingales (1998).
2. See, for instance, Caprio and Klingebiel (1996), and Hutchison and Neuberger (2002) and the references therein.
3. Real GDP growth is presented here as a 'summary statistic' of macroeconomic behavior. It is not in the scope of this chapter to analyze the behavior of more detailed macro variables, such as those representing fiscal, monetary, and balance of payments conditions.
4. See Fanelli (2006) for a very good discussion on the pros and cons of using the standard deviation as a measurement of real GDP growth volatility. The author argues in favor of analyzing the variance of both the anticipated and unanticipated components of an economic series in developing countries in order to better grasp the cost of volatility. This is because the absence of markets prevents agents from protecting themselves against the costs of volatility even if a change in the variable studied is expected. Also, as explained in Fanelli's paper, economic series in developing countries are usually subject to statistical structural breaks, often as a result of crises. From this discussion it follows that comparisons of volatility – as measured by the standard deviation – between industrial and developing countries might suffer from important problems. In this regard, the statistics in Table 4.1, and the accompanying discussion, should be taken only as first approximations.
5. In some countries, data only go until 2003.
6. Just for the purpose of the discussion here, 'low' volatility is defined as the range observed in industrial countries in the sample, namely between 0 and 2.7.
7. Although the average of deposits to GDP for every country covers the period 1990–2004 (sometimes only 2003), the relatively new data on governance allow us to show an average that only includes the period 1996–2004.
8. Fanelli (2006) establishes a two-way relationship between these variables. He argues that high macro volatility induces endogenous changes in both institutions and the financial structure, which in turn contribute to the particular features of financial markets in developing countries, discussed above. At the same time, deficient risk management at the micro level (a characteristic of shallow financial intermediation) has an adverse effect on macro volatility. This is because the resulting sub-optimal allocation of resources at the firm level makes the economy more prone to crisis and procyclical international capital flows relative to the situation in industrial countries where more complete financial markets allow for a better allocation and pricing of risks.
9. See Basel Committee on Banking Supervision (1997).

10. Fanelli (2006) discusses situations under which a liquidity problem turns into a solvency problem for otherwise viable firms and banks.
11. In some countries, the US dollar is also being used as a means of payments and as the unit of denomination for asset prices, especially real estate. A handful of countries have also fully 'dollarized' their economies.
12. Indeed, among the countries in the sample two of the countries with the highest real interest rate volatility, Argentina and Russia, kept extremely high ratios of US dollar deposits to total deposits during the 1990s. This ratio increased significantly in the period surrounding the respective financial crises in each country, reaching 74 per cent in Argentina in 2001 and 44 per cent in Russia in 1998.
13. See, De Nicoló et al. (2003) for an analysis of the interrelationship between macroeconomic volatility and portfolio currency diversification.
14. While the first variable is related to the most common frequency of portfolio adjustments (a day, a week, and so on), the second reflects the bank's attitude toward risk (a wider confidence interval would tend to produce a larger VaR).
15. For a full discussion of VaR techniques, including their benefits and limitations, see Goodhart et al. (1998).
16. This sub-section and the next draw from Rojas-Suarez (2004).
17. See Schneider (2003) for a comprehensive discussion and concerns related to the effectiveness of the standards and codes to prevent financial crises.
18. Excerpt taken from a speech given by Mr Dai Xianglong at a meeting of the International Monetary and Financial Committee, Washington, DC, 28 September 2002, www.imf.org/external/am/2002/imfc/state/eng/chn.htm.
19. This was the result in the Uganda case study on transparency practices as reported by Brown (1998).
20. See, for example, Schneider and Silva (2002).
21. The memo item in the table includes an additional indicator: interest rate on deposits. This indicator will be discussed in Section 4.5.
22. This point has been advanced by Rojas-Suarez and Weisbrod (1997) and Rojas-Suarez (2001).
23. Chile, Hong Kong, and Singapore may be the countries, among emerging markets, with the deepest financial sectors.
24. Argentina does not attach zero risk weight to government paper, but the risk weights still favor this kind of instrument.
25. China and Russia are not included in the graph because of insufficient data.
26. A counter case may be made by arguing that domestic government debt is safer than public external debt. However, given the long history of government-induced domestic defaults, either in the form of straight confiscation of deposits or sharp devaluations and inflations that drastically reduced the real value of government paper held by residents, I find this argument simply unconvincing.
27. This effect has also been discussed in Reisen (2001) and Griffith-Jones and Spratt (2001).
28. The case studies by Brazil and Nigeria stress the capacity constraints associated with the potential implementation of Basel II.
29. For example, a major issue in the so-called 'standardized approach' relates to the reliance on credit rating agencies for the determination of 'risk weights' attached to loans in the calculation of minimum capital requirements.
30. Mexico (both in the 1982 and 1994 crises) is a good example of the restrictions imposed by a weak banking system on the conduct of exchange rate policies.
31. This is also true if most of the debt is external. Increasing the interest rate to defend the parity would lead to reduced economic activity, aggravating the risk of default. Aware of the dilemma, speculators exacerbate the attack on the exchange rate, betting that the country would prefer to abandon the parity than be forced into default.

32. Moreover, reducing the concentration of financial and real assets could be a difficult task, especially in countries where some political powers are 'captive' to the agenda of economically powerful groups.
33. This point has been raised by Cavallo and Majnoni (2001). The use of ex ante provisioning as an effective countercyclical prudential regulation tool is discussed in Ocampo (2003).
34. For a more comprehensive analysis of this proposal, see Rojas-Suarez (2001).

5
The Political Economy of Reforming Domestic Financial Architectures

Andrés Rius

5.1 Introduction

This chapter examines the political economy dimensions of building domestic financial architectures in developing countries which are more immune to recurrent crises and which contribute to high-quality and lower-volatility growth. One way of appreciating the importance of the issues is to note the effects of macroeconomic and financial crises on the incidence of poverty.[1] Between 1993 and 1995, Nigeria went through an economic downturn associated with a banking crisis (see the study by Ajayi and Adenikinju, Chapter 13 in this volume). Per capita GDP declined every year by an average 1.3 per cent. In 1992, just before the crisis, the incidence of poverty had been estimated at 43 per cent, using a nationally defined consumption threshold. This level represented a reduction of three percentage points with respect to the previous available measure (1985). After the 1993–95 downturn the comparable headcount ratio was 66 per cent (UNDP, 2004). Taking the 1992 level as the benchmark, Nigeria would need to bring such ratio to less than 22 per cent by 2015 to meet the respective Millennium Development Goal; that is, poverty would have to fall by approximately 0.9 percentage points per year. In contrast, from the 1996 level, the required yearly reduction to achieve the same target would be 2.3 percentage points (two and a half times the pre-crisis speed of reduction). Or, put differently, at the pre-crisis speed, the MDG poverty incidence level would not be achieved until 2040.[2]

This chapter aims to illuminate the extent to which aggregate economic volatility and its structural correlates affect the capacity of developing countries to build development-friendly domestic financial architectures (DFAs). The issues as just posed reverse the logic of the biggest part of the literature on institutions and economic outcomes: rather than analyzing institutions primarily as an exogenous factor that contributes to determining economic performance, this chapter – without minimizing the influence of institutions on economic outcomes – looks more in depth at the opposite hypothesis that macroeconomic volatility affects a society's capacity to build institutions for high-quality growth. If the hypothesis is supported by the evidence, it may open new windows on the debates about national and international responses to that challenge. In fact, the predominant views of the requirements for financial and macroeconomic stability rest on the assumption that dysfunctional institutions and inadequate public policies existing in developing countries explain the weaknesses of their financial systems, which in turn make their economies more volatile, more prone to crises, and less able to grow consistently. The challenge for these countries, therefore, is to build the 'right' institutions and adopt 'correct' macro policies – and designing and implementing these would be primarily a technical problem.[3] This approach, however, suffers from at least three major shortcomings.

First, the conventional causal framework tends to neglect the political-economic underpinnings of institutions and policies. The literature on economic policy reform shows that technically sound – even Pareto-improving – policy and institutional changes may not be pursued because they would destabilize a political-economy equilibrium that has allowed powerful groups to thrive.[4] This would apply in particular to the basic institutional infrastructure that supports a financial system as well as to the policies that define the broader environment for financial transactions. In this light, technically sound innovations may not be adopted not because policymakers do not know about them or cannot see their direct benefits, but because they may rightly perceive them as having broader or other indirect distributional impacts and the potential to create 'dysfunctional' instability in other realms of the political-economic process (Fanelli and McMahon, 2006, provide historical examples and a conceptual discussion).[5]

The second shortcoming of the prevailing approach to financial systems, crises and growth is the narrow definition of the relevant set of institutions and policies. In this regard, the literature could be roughly split in two. On the one hand, there is the more conventional, open-economy macroeconomics literature, focusing on the choice of policy regime and the management of specific policy levers as key drivers of growth, stability and financial depth – Frankel (1999) could be a typical example. On the other hand, there is the literature that looks at the institutional determinants of financial development and its growth implications, or at the role of some relevant sub-sets of institutions – for example, the debates surveyed in Levine (2005), and Beck et al. (2000) on the finance-growth links. There is little dialogue, in fact, between these two relevant literatures, and this often yields prescriptions that are incomplete or inadequate.

The experience of developing countries, having to address simultaneously various institutional and policy challenges, and also the political economy approach favored in this chapter, make it advisable to define 'domestic financial architectures' more broadly. With Fanelli (2006), this chapter includes in the definition both the institutional infrastructure for financial transactions (the legal and judicial institutions, regulatory frameworks, and other policies and practices affecting the financial sector, in addition to the determinants of corporate governance) as well as the macroeconomic regime (that is, the three constituents of the policy trilemma in open economies: exchange rate, capital account, and monetary policies). The two are interconnected not only by how the conditions in one directly influence the performance of the other but also by more indirect political-economy effects. In fact, the distributional implications of the choices available to policymakers in one realm (for example, the choice of exchange rate regime) are often mediated by circumstances in the other (for example, the legal and broader institutional underpinnings of the degree of dollarization).

The DFA so defined would comprise the constellation of institutions and policies that have the capacity to mitigate or amplify volatility. However, the discussion above already suggests that the institutions and policies that make up the DFA can also be affected by volatility itself. This in fact is the third shortcoming of the prevailing approaches to financial and macroeconomic stability, which is that they typically neglect the effects of volatility on a society's ability to adopt different institutions and policies. In this chapter we follow the analytical framework proposed by Fanelli (2006), which explicitly recognizes the negative effects of aggregate volatility and crises on the quality of institutions and policies, and on the conditions for collective action to improve them. In such a framework, volatility and crises have a *direct* adverse effect on collective action by intensifying distributive conflict or inviting opportunistic behaviors. One of the stylized facts from the growing empirical literature on the political economy of reforms is that there is a negative relationship between instability (economic and political) and a society's capacity to make inter-temporal political compromises associated with reaching superior cooperative equilibria (Fanelli and McMahon, 2006). For example, unreliable access to international capital markets, and a history of costly crises with sizable wealth and income redistribution, may lead a government to defend a currency (and exchange rate regime) beyond what would seem reasonable.[6] Distributional conflicts, and the experienced or latent aggregate instability, thus postpone necessary adjustments, an expression of the inability for superior collective action.

Moreover, crises and volatility also undermine the institution-building efforts *indirectly* by making some risks non-contractible and certain policies unfeasible. This could be a result of dysfunctional policies adopted to cope with a previous crisis, or due to the adaptive responses by private sector agents to high volatility and excessive risks of capital losses (Fanelli, 2006, highlights these as institutional 'mutations' that create path-dependence). When all this is taken into account, the reforms required to build functional DFAs appear as complex exercises in social innovation, requiring sustained efforts over several years and various rounds of upgrading. In such conditions, there tends to be a multiplicity of opportunities for organized interests to sabotage institutional reforms during their implementation, either by openly challenging formal rules or by developing informal rules that run counter to the aims of the formal innovations (Rius and Van de Walle, 2005). The empirical political economy of economic reforms has shown that aggregate volatility only exacerbates these difficulties. In turn, derailment of reforms during implementation can further contribute to excess volatility. These political economy dynamics and constraints acquire more significance if the excess volatility faced by developing countries is at least in part originated in structural features of their economies, or in the functioning of global markets under prevailing governance regimes – for example, if excess volatility can be shown to result from developing economies' productive and trade specialization. Then, building more solid financial architectures may require more than recognizing and correcting narrowly defined domestic 'policy mistakes'.

This chapter's methodological approach was determined by the design of the larger initiative reflected in this volume. The chapter was expected to build on the country studies, highlighting and zooming in on the relevant evidence, and drawing a number of plausible theses and implications.[7] This provides the main source of the chapter's strengths and limitations: while it has been possible to draw from fresh empirical analyses of the volatility–institutions nexus for eight significant developing and transition economies, it was not possible to dictate the contents of those country studies to provide the type of evidence that would have been required to test some of the attempted generalizations more rigorously. Because of this design constraint, the chapter's conclusions must be taken as indicative and subject to further investigation.

Four sections follow this introduction. The next three sections use selectively the evidence and narratives from the country studies to unpack and analyze elements of the hypothesis that volatility and crises undermine society's capacity for collective action and institution-building, therefore having deleterious effects on DFAs. Each of the sections highlights a set of interrelated complications arising from the 'excess' volatility that characterizes developing economies: Section 5.2 focuses on issues of timing and the sequence of institutional innovation; Section 5.3 discusses the scale of the institution-building challenges and the speed of economic processes; and Section 5.4 examines the links between the volatility of consumption and the socio-political conditions for architectural reform. Section 5.5 summarizes the main policy implications.

5.2 Timing and sequence

The country studies provide ample evidence that policy and institutional innovations affecting the DFAs follow patterns of reactive policymaking. Indeed, the narratives on the evolution of the DFAs in those countries show that (a) there tend to be more innovations during and immediately after downturns and crises, and (b) there is a tendency to modify multiple policy instruments and institutions to meet macroeconomic policy goals during those periods. These patterns influence the timing and the sequence of innovations to the institutions that form the DFA, and have the potential to generate economically dysfunctional configurations over time.

Nigeria, for instance, introduced a large number of reforms into its DFA between 1986 and 1993, altering the functioning of currency markets, removing and later reintroducing barriers to entry to financial intermediation, reducing government controls over interest rates and relaxing bank portfolio restrictions, introducing new mechanisms into the market for public securities, and – later in the period – tightening financial supervision and introducing prudential regulation. These followed four years of declining GDP resulting from a negative shock to the terms of trade, with average losses above 5 per cent per annum (1980–83) that had not been offset by the modest growth in 1984 and 1985. The post-1986 reforms reflect the conditionality associated with financial assistance by the international financial institutions (IFIs) but, as has been the case in other developing countries, the preceding crisis doubtless created local appetite and the conditions for comprehensive reforms. Twin balance of payments and financial crises – and structural adjustment programs agreed with the IFIs in exchange for assistance – also characterize the context in which comprehensive reforms were undertaken in many Latin American countries in the mid-1980s, including saliently the case of Chile discussed below.

In China, where no direct influence from IFIs occurred, the build-up of inflationary pressures in 1989 and in 1991–92 also provided the stimulus for economic reforms (Guo et al., 2004). Some of the innovations of the ensuing reformist 'leaps forward' contributed to re-shaping the DFA as discussed in Wu and Shea (2006) and below. In Argentina, the currency board regime, and the associated reforms to the charter of the central bank, the deposit insurance scheme, and the systems of financial regulation and oversight, all occurred in the brief period of two years immediately after the hyperinflation of 1989–90. Additional important alterations to the DFA took place in 1994–96, as a response to the slowdown in economic activity and other adverse domestic repercussions of the Mexican financial crisis. The Real Plan in Brazil since 1994 – a comprehensive stabilization and structural reform program – was a response to uncontrollable inflation and a stagnant or declining economy in the previous years. Capital requirements were later increased in 1997 as a response to the crisis in Southeast Asia, and other consequential innovations affecting credit markets were introduced in the aftermath of the 1999 devaluation that sought to address external imbalances and a declining economy.

These patterns of reactive policymaking have not been missed by scholars, nor are they exclusive to developing countries or to the reform of financial policies and institutions. In the 1960s, Albert Hirschman had examined the policy processes in developing countries and noted the difference between 'pressing' and 'chosen' problems. While the latter would be picked by policymakers as a result of their preferences and perceptions, the former would be those keeping them busy most of the time and 'forced (on them) through pressure from injured or interested outside parties' (Hirschman, 1963; see also Meier, 1990). These are typically problems associated with a perception of crisis. More specifically, Hirschman observed that in the presence of balance of payments crises and severe foreign exchange constraints 'the state loses its august character of sovereign pursuing its own objectives and initiating politics to this end; rather, it is seen as coping, as best it can, with a variety of emergencies, as constantly plugging holes, and stopping a wheel from creaking by applying a bit of grease in a hurry' (Hirschman, 1975: 389).[8]

Empirical studies such as those by Paul Mosley (1976, 1984) suggest that reactive patterns of policymaking are not exclusive to developing countries or to contexts of extreme volatility. He finds that a model of 'satisfycing' behavior could account for the decisions of British and American administrations with regards to macroeconomic policy over extended periods in the twentieth century. In his analysis, the authorities (i) acted in response to target variables surpassing 'satisfactory' threshold levels (or entering a 'crisis' range), and (ii) focused on one target at a time and used all available policy levers to restore that target to satisfactory levels (rather than following Tinbergen's one-objective-one-instrument rule).[9]

A similar reactive pattern had been pointed out by analysts of the structural reform processes of the 1980s and 1990s. In an early study of the responses to the 'debt crises' of the early 1980s, Joan Nelson noted the widespread clustering and conflation of short-run macroeconomic stabilization measures and longer-term structural economic reforms in the aftermath of the crises, notwithstanding country-specificities with regard to pace, sequencing and broad policy orientation (Nelson, 1990; see also Stallings, 1990, on the longer-term recurrence of the reactive pattern, and Bresser-Pereira et al., 1993). These analysts also observed that IFIs have greatest leverage in post-crisis contexts, and that also shapes the nature of the responses.

That crises beget comprehensive reforms is also one of the most robust lessons from the most recent attempts to illuminate the political economy of policy change in developing and transition economies (Fanelli and McMahon, 2006). From a large number of analytical narratives, it comes up strongly that crises upset pre-existing political-economic equilibria and thus make it harder for the authorities to preserve economic and institutional structures unchanged. The comprehensiveness of reforms, and the inclusion in reform 'packages' of innovations that appear to have little bearing on the causes or manifestation of the triggering crisis, is found by the authors to reflect the multi-layered nature of the policymaking games, and the need to articulate new political economy equilibria.

Theory has not been oblivious to these empirical regularities. Some of the main attempts to develop models linking crises and reforms in a neoclassical, 'New Political Economy' framework are contained in Sturzenegger and Tommasi (1998). In these, a set of policies or institutions are abandoned or modified when the costs associated with maintaining them are greater than the costs of their change. Crises, by increasing the former, make reforms the rational response of policymakers and other agents whose acquiescence or support is required. The need to build credibility and signal commitment to the reforms is credited in some of these analyses with explaining the bundling of diverse innovations in reform 'packages'.[10]

Alternative conceptual accounts of the reactive pattern of policymaking are provided by the literature on the policy process and the behavior of government bureaucracies. Rather than seeking to pin down costs and benefits that would be altered by crises, authors within these scholarly traditions tend to view policymakers as facing significant constraints on their time, resources, knowledge, and cognitive abilities, and as operating in environments where they must negotiate policy responses with a number of players. Under such conditions, they make 'good enough' decisions by using rules of thumb and other heuristics that reduce the need to collect and process information (Simon, 1976, 1987). Decision-making also entails 'muddling through' an interactive social process where different cognitive and political threads are intertwined (Lindblom, 1959; Lindblom and Woodhouse, 1993). Because policies develop out of ongoing interactions between groups of people and organizations concerned with a given issue (Kingdon, 1984; Sabatier and Jenkins-Smith, 1999), incremental change and trial-and-error not only become the norm but also appear as the best available alternative to impractical 'analytical' approaches to decision-making. Most importantly, even though many of these authors partake in a view of individuals as capable of 'boundedly rational' choices, the reactive and satisfycing behavior of complex organizations or whole governments can be sustained while remaining agnostic about the cognitive and decision-making powers of individuals (Conlisk, 1996).[11]

Regardless of their theoretical foundations and degree of sophistication, the 'crisis theories' of institutional innovation could be seen as having an element of tautology (Rodrik, 1996). In fact, given the uncertainties about lags and effectiveness of policy measures, why would *any* policymaker want to undertake ambitious policy change or attempt to reform prevailing institutions when things seem to be going well? On the other hand, it only seems logical that governments and other actors will try various institutional and policy innovations as a response to poor economic performance. The interesting conceptual complication comes, however, from the observation that the response to crises often involves the *bundling* of innovations with varying degrees of relevance to the problem at hand, or which may be thus adopted at the wrong time.

'Inappropriate bundling' may come as a surprise if policy changes are analyzed from a strictly economic angle.[12] However, it is hardly surprising when political economy considerations enter into the analysis. As suggested by Fanelli and McMahon (2006), specific institutional innovations that might appear 'dysfunctional' from a narrow economic perspective on the needs of the time, could be 'functionally' bundled with others in order to build winning coalitions or circumvent the power of veto players. If the objective function guiding policy choice places a premium on smooth trajectories, an externally-induced recession may not appear as the ideal time to tighten prudential regulation. However, this might be the 'functional' response to a pre-crisis liberalization of the banking system that led to excessive and careless lending, or to the need to make public securities more appealing to financial intermediaries in the face of stubborn public deficits. Conversely, good aggregate outcomes such as high growth or healthy current account balances would not necessarily reflect the strength of a financial system, but reforms that could make it stronger are often shunned during good times, in a similar apparent confusion about indicators, economic processes, and policies. On top of their own internal dynamics, 'inappropriate bundling' could result from the interaction with the IFIs, which in recent decades have tended to use post-crisis interventions as opportunities to promote comprehensive reforms that go beyond the immediate needs of stabilization. In any case, the reactive bundling of reforms – a possibly 'functional' response to policymaking under uncertainty and to political economy constraints – is likely to produce at least some innovations that are 'dysfunctional' or inopportune from a pure efficiency and stability point of view.

The country studies do show a number of instances of such apparently wrong timing and sequencing of institutional and policy changes. In 1996 the Central Bank of Nigeria responded to a recession and impending fears of devaluation by moving all public sector deposits from commercial banks to the central bank. While this may have worked to delay a devaluation, it also had the predictable short-term effect of further weakening the commercial banks' financial position, and the longer-term effect of undermining agents' confidence in the stability of the rules of the game. Many of the countries analyzed (in particular, Argentina and Brazil) increased capital requirements and/or tightened prudential regulations in other respects as a response to the East Asian financial crisis of 1997 and the Russian crisis of 1998. Thailand also tightened asset classification rules in the aftermath of its own currency crisis of 1997. These may seem to be sensible conservative responses, but among their unintended (but also predictable) consequences was a rush to public debt that usually receives a more favorable treatment in such regulation, and therefore a crowding out of private borrowers under already deteriorating macroeconomic prospects. These measures were also taken in the presence of declining or negative net capital inflows, which amplified their contractionary effects. In all these cases, sound conservative measures had been typically eschewed during good times (that is, under high growth, generous capital inflows, and expanding private lending); and even existing regulations were often weakly enforced in those periods. Other examples of 'coping' policies with undesirable longer-term effects include the introduction of exchange rate indexed bonds in Brazil after the 1999 devaluation and the *Corralito* in Argentina during the 2001 breakdown of the convertibility plan.[13] The former is behind a process of 'risk migration' (Pires de Souza et al., 2006) that forces the Brazilian government to choose between promoting financial and macroeconomic stability and stimulating growth; the latter is likely to have had durable effects on the confidence of Argentinian depositors in the banking system and the rule of law.

Problems of timing and sequencing are also evident when looking at some necessary changes to the DFAs that were *not* undertaken during apparently favorable periods. Typically, inadequate corporate governance, facilitated by incomplete or imperfect legislation (in particular with regard to disclosure and minority rights), as well as weak enforcement of contracts due to nonexistent, ill-prepared or ineffective courts, all become apparent when countries are trying to find their way out of major financial crises or attempting to strengthen their financial systems. These problems are discussed in almost all the country studies in this volume, and are often present in public discourse in the countries in the aftermath of crises, but they are typically absent from policy agendas during booms.[14] While it is easy to appreciate the wasted opportunities with the benefit of hindsight, this type of 'mistake' is not unusual or illogical when an economy is enjoying capital inflows and conditions seem to be improving significantly compared to the past. This type of dynamic can be seen, for example, when considering Thailand's establishment of a stock exchange in the late 1970s and the financial liberalization of the 1990s. In the first case, there was a deliberate and careful gradual upgrading of transparency rules to allow market disciplines to operate, while in the latter there seemed to have been no appetite for a gradual improvement of prudential regulations and supervision when capital inflows were abundant and investors were asking few questions in the face of generous margins.

Section 5.3 below discusses some of the possible socio-political dynamics behind the reactive patterns. What is worth keeping in mind from the analysis so far is that institutional innovations and policy changes seem to intensify their pace during downturns and crises and that, under stress and through 'bundling', there is a tendency to cope with extreme macroeconomic outcomes by means of innovations that often diminish the quality of the financial architecture (that is, innovations that make it harder for the financial system to play the role of buffer of shocks and channel of funding for high-quality growth). If, as shown by the country studies, adaptive responses of various agents cause many of the 'bad' innovations to become entrenched, countries that experience greater volatility and go through crises more often will tend to have poorer and harder-to-upgrade architectures. The success stories in the analyzed sample of countries also lend credence to the view that simple reactive adjustment to the DFAs constitutes a trap that needs to be avoided: the countries that have escaped the stop-and-go cycles and have built more resilient financial architectures appear to have done so by learning to maintain the reformist momentum during favorable times (or to use effectively the scarce and narrow windows of opportunity to build economically functional architectures).

That is what the study on Chile in this volume shows, in line with other literature on that country (for example, Stallings, 1990). In particular, the severe crisis of 1982 was followed by a 'messy' and costly clean-up process similar to that in other Latin American countries. However, in the second half of the 1980s, when some of the main costs had started to be absorbed and terms of trade were improving, several consequential reforms to the DFA were adopted: a banking law in 1986 introduced transparency, prudential regulation and measures to attack related lending; a Copper Stabilization Fund was set up in 1987; the central bank proactively pushed the substitution of the US dollar with an inflation-indexed unit of account in a deliberate attempt to curb dollarization; and public debt was kept under control (Magendzo and Titelman, 2006). Moreover, other important DFA-improving reforms not called for by prevailing macroeconomic conditions were introduced in the 1990s and 2000s, in the face of high growth, favorable international capital markets, and some occasional improvements in the terms of trade. Those included measures to regulate capital inflows (the *encaje* and reserve requirements on short-term flows) and the adoption of a cyclically-adjusted target for fiscal policy. All these demonstrate a capacity to break with the reactive mode of policymaking, introducing forward looking innovations that seem to have enabled the Chilean economy to cope better with external shocks in more recent times.

In brief, highly volatile countries are likely to have economically dysfunctional elements in their DFAs and to find it harder to reform them. These may not necessarily reflect lower levels of technical competence among their policymakers, but the specific conditions for collective action in high volatility environments. There are two important implications. On the one hand, these countries need to 'learn' how to improve their institutional architectures under high volatility. This is likely to require the creation of conditions for enhancing cooperation and the management of social and political conflict (Fanelli and McMahon, 2006), something that transcends economic and financial institutions and involves the rules of the political game. On the other hand, measures to mitigate aggregate volatility – which might involve forms of international collective action – would not only be welfare-improving but would also have the added pay-off of enhancing conditions for institutional upgrading. That is, there would be a double dividend from innovations allowing developing countries to smooth out their macroeconomic trajectories.

5.3 Scale and speed

Several of the country studies in this volume demonstrate how human resource and other capacity constraints of public and private agents have contributed to the financial fragility in the recent past. In Nigeria, the authors blame the low quality of the banks' portfolio, during and after the liberalization of the late 1980s and early 1990s, on the inadequate expertise of bank personnel used to managing a limited range of financial instruments under stringent financial regulation. The attempt to bring the financial system to compliance with Basel standards since 1999 is also seen to have been hindered by the low human resource capacity in commercial banks as well as in the central bank and other oversight bodies. Similar observations are contained in the Thailand study, another example of rapid liberalization in subsequent waves, under less than optimal institutional and organizational conditions. The inability of the Brazilian banks and supervisory entities to fully implement Basel II standards, despite the size of the country's human resource pool and the revealed national technological capabilities, speaks once again of the complexities of the institution upgrading involved in approaching internationally-sanctioned good practice.

The human resource constraints do not affect all agents in the same way, nor are they the only bottlenecks to be confronted. A new regulatory and supervisory framework demands new information systems and technologies, and is likely to lead to a necessary redesign of services, pricing policies and competitive strategies by financial intermediaries. Some country study authors also mention that certain services such as those provided by risk rating agencies are a precondition for market disciplines to work and these may take time to be domestically or externally supplied in developing or transition economies. Moreover, the studies show that the introduction or upgrading of prudential regulation imposes uneven costs on different financial agents. State vs. privately owned, domestic vs. foreign, large vs. small, or diversified vs. specialized intermediaries would be affected differently by more sophisticated or stringent regulation, requiring of them different types of investments and testing their ability to adapt quickly. This could affect their competitive positions and destabilize a prevailing market structure with far-reaching and partly unpredictable effects. The Nigerian study, for instance, draws attention to the fact that the pace at which new regulations are enforced would affect the capacity of locally-owned banks to compete with foreign ones, threatening the former with their possible disappearance. Those changes, in turn, could affect the access to financial services of various categories of non-financial agents. These processes would explain why, in already financially challenged environments, and particularly during economic downturns – when, as we saw, the institutional upgrading is often undertaken – the enforcement of sounder prudential and oversight regulation often advances slowly and selectively, or becomes itself a cause of undesirable upheaval. The multiplicity of direct and indirect impacts of DFA upgrading also creates opportunities for sabotage of the reforms at the implementation stage (more on this below).

The difficulties in aligning domestic legislation, regulation, and the capacity of various government branches and agencies may vary depending on the initial conditions but are found to be significant everywhere. The Argentinian, Thai, and Nigerian studies exemplify the implications of the inability to strengthen various pillars of the financial architecture coherently and simultaneously. Argentina, for example, emerged from ten years of relative macroeconomic stability with modest or no improvements in the investor protection legislation and the effectiveness of legal institutions (that is, the extent of the 'rule of law'), which would account for the shallowness of equity and private bond markets and the short maturity of contracts. This is not to say that the reformers were unable to see the perverse effects of, for example, legal loopholes and judicial practices that hindered the ability of lenders to recover their capital. Rather, the Argentinian experience shows how it might be possible to advance at very different speeds in formal and effective introduction of the enabling institutions, and how certain reforms (for example, commercial law, the judicial system) may take many years to come onto the political agenda of countries coping with wild macroeconomic swings, and even more to be pushed forward by willing and capable coalitions.

Similar institutional deficits seem to be responsible for the shallowness of the stock and corporate bond markets in Nigeria (or South Africa), and the disproportionate preference for government bonds and real estate as reserves of value. The thwarted experience of the creation of a stock exchange in Thailand in the early 1980s is also telling about how much easier it is to remove prohibitions or authorize new financial instruments versus establishing the necessary legal, judicial, organizational, and administrative supports for the sustainable expansion of a key pillar of a modern financial system. As suggested before, many of the imperfections of a process like this can easily be obscured by the apparent success of the newly created markets under unusually favorable external conditions and generous capital inflows.

Important as they are in these countries with a relatively long history of market-based capitalism, the protection of investors, the enforcement of contracts, and the establishment of institutional frameworks to promote good corporate governance are among the most fundamental challenges confronted by the transition economies of China and Russia. Popov and Peresetsky (2006) give priority to macroeconomic policies in accounting for crises and volatility in the post-Soviet era but cannot deny that inadequate corporate governance and legal flaws associated with the transition to a market economy made it possible for some perverse and costly schemes (that is, 'financial pyramids') to prosper in the weakly regulated and supervised Russian financial system. The greater reliance of firms on bank lending vis-à-vis capital market financing, the excessive number of banks, and the more general shallowness of financial markets, all seem to follow from the institutional incompleteness of an economy in transition from state-led communism to a market-based organization. Wu and Shea (2006) include Marxist ideology and lack of market knowledge and experience as key factors explaining the piecemeal approach to reform in China, implying that gradual movement towards a market-based economy is often interrupted or reversed by various forms of administrative intervention. The result is a *sui generis* form of capitalism (or socialism) where 'corporate governance' involves the ad hoc administration of state-owned enterprises by politically-appointed managers, and the financial 'market' is made up mostly of transactions between those firms and a few large banks that are similarly owned and managed. Excessive lending, borrowers that confront soft budget constraints, non-performing loans, the emergence of informal banking, and politically-motivated bail-outs are all observed (and predictable) outcomes of a DFA that could potentially become a destabilizing factor.[15]

The literature on law, politics and finance has established that flaws in legal frameworks, judicial processes, and enforcement mechanisms lead to uncertainty about property rights and to fears of expropriation with a deleterious effect on the development of sound and functional financial markets (Beck et al., 2001; Levine, 2005). The chapter providing the analytical framework for this volume (Fanelli, 2006) discusses the interrelationships and mutual causation between the legal infrastructure and other components of a more broadly defined DFA that are typically neglected by that literature. In particular, it correctly emphasizes the path-dependence created by perverse 'mutations' in institutional configurations, and by the agents' adaptation of their strategies to the existing architectures. If those arguments were not enough to appreciate the scale and complexity of the reform challenge in volatile economies, a relevant branch of the law and finance literature has demonstrated empirically that economic outcomes are most decisively affected by the effectiveness of the law, as opposed to primarily the contents of legal texts. This highlights the role of non-codified or informal aspects of the legal infrastructure. Moreover, the evidence suggests persuasively that the process of legal development and the compatibility of the new laws with pre-existing conditions is a more important determinant of such effectiveness than the particular legal tradition from which a country borrows or inherits its institutions (Berkowitz et al., 2003).[16] This is so because the law is a 'cognitive institution' – only a few rules can be fully understood and enforced without reference to other legal terms and concepts, and the application and enforcement of rules is determined by the perception of new rules by users and enforcers in the receiving country – and because effective law enforcement is a function of the extent of voluntary compliance as much as of the resources available in a given country (Pistor, 2002). Altogether, these results point in the same direction of the more encompassing view of the DFA espoused in this volume, and in particular highlight the role of informal institutions that result from the public and private agents' adaptation to changes in legal texts or administrative measures.[17] This further suggests that there are no easy fixes for 'inadequate' DFAs, and that their reform is bound to be a protracted process alternating incomplete advances and regressions in various interdependent domains.

The fiscal imbalances in large federal countries present additional complex and crucial sets of issues to the improvement of DFAs. Brazil, Nigeria and Argentina (and China in a different way) are shown to have struggled with such problems for many years. The studies clearly demonstrate that their capacity to manage them (or the lack thereof) has impacted directly on their ability to contain the crowding-out of private borrowers by fiscally-challenged governments, and to eventually promote financial deepening. To appreciate the scale of the difficulties confronted by these countries it should suffice to consider that much more stable and prosperous countries, such as Canada, that have devised complex fiscal arrangements for the management of federal relations and can rely on stable political institutions to work out the ever emerging interregional controversies, still cannot say that they have put the problems behind them. Extreme regional inequalities and the complex political dynamics associated with federal rule in weakly consolidated democracies are likely to continue to exert destabilizing pressures on countries like the ones examined here.[18]

Table 5.1 lists the components of the DFA, according to the definition adopted in this study, and some of the major challenges in upgrading them as identified by the country studies, with the aim of providing a sense of the *scale* of the DFA-upgrading efforts.

Addressing these institution-building and institution-upgrading challenges would take any modern and complex society substantial time. Moreover, the reformers may be able to introduce far-reaching innovations in a short period of time (for example, in legal and regulatory frameworks) but it may take much longer for their full benefits to materialize (for instance, if there exist severe capacity deficits or if complementary informal institutions evolve more slowly). This chapter argues, however, that highly volatile developing and transition economies confront two additional sets of complications.

First, new shocks and crises are likely to hit these economies at the same time as they are working on some of those institution-building challenges and before they have had time to correct the dysfunctional institutions inherited from the

Table 5.1 The scale of challenges in upgrading the DFA in developing and transition economies

Component of the DFA	Selected major challenges
Financial infrastructure	
Legal and judicial infrastructure	Legal appropriation, adaptation, customization Consistency with broader legal framework Establishing 'legality' (effectiveness of the law)
Regulatory capacity	Regulatory capacity (to formulate and enforce regulation) Trade-off between competition and stability objectives
Policies and practices affecting financial sector	Direct and indirect effects on market structure and access to financial services Human resource and technological capacity deficits in central bank (or superintendent agency) and in private sector
Corporate governance	Disincentives for disclosure Nonexistence of rating agencies Incipient corporate/commercial law regimes
Macro regime	
Exchange rate regime	Fiscal dominance (associated with fiscal federalism) and inability to borrow in domestic currency Currency mismatches in private sector
Capital account regime	Need to finance current-account deficits as disincentive to 'regulate' flows
Monetary regime	Fiscal dominance (fiscal federalism) Loss of instruments

previous cycle. Such a complication would still be of a society's own creation if the destabilizing shocks were all domestic in origin, but the country studies show a number of instances of the analyzed economies being hit by an externally generated shock before they could complete necessary reforms. That was the case of the Thai economy in 1983: pushed into a recession by an external shock while working on the institutional supports of a diversifying financial system, it could not cope with the loss of investor confidence and fell into a mini-financial crisis. In 1994, Brazil was hit by the Tequila effect when credit was starting to recover, stimulated by the monetary reform and newly-acquired price stability; something similar happened again in 1997. The conditions were no better for Nigeria in 1993, when the structural reforms were starting to show their effect and it received a negative terms of trade shock that drove it into another recession and banking crisis. The reform of DFAs seems thus to resemble the dismantling of a complex explosive device, both in its difficulty and in the risks confronted by the 'fixer'. The complications added by high aggregate volatility could be compared to trying to carry out the exercise on a boat, in the middle of a storm, while an unstoppable timing mechanism is ticking.

Second, the broader definition of the DFA that takes into account the interdependence of various institutional features and policies entails reform agendas that inevitably touch on various domains and affect a range of agents and sectors of the economy. Large-scale reforms, such as those required to upgrade complex DFAs, are bound to generate intricate, multi-layered, real-time distributive games, and will open numerous opportunities for the emergence of coalitions or powerful actors capable of sabotaging the reforms at the implementation stage, or capturing the relevant bureaucratic bodies.[19] The weaknesses of oversight and regulatory agencies, for example, make it possible for segments of the private sector to circumvent formal rules through related lending and other perverse schemes (Nigeria, Thailand, and Russia). The fiscal dominance associated with distributive conflicts within federal states creates tensions between fiscal policy objectives (Argentina), or exchange rate management (Brazil), and the need to strengthen the banking system.

The resolution of conflicts and concentration of political activity at the implementation stage may in some cases result from the fact that policy choice in these countries tends to be less 'pluralistic' (Meier, 1990), either as a result of the specific evolution of their political systems (O'Donnell, 1994) or because the 'choice' of reform priorities has been forced on the country by external conditionality and the imperative of foreign financial assistance. In any case, sabotage in implementation makes the outcomes of the reforms less predictable, thus contributing to the disappearance of markets that would enable more appropriate risk management, and undermining financial development. The success stories in the analyzed countries (Chile) also demonstrate the value of protecting oversight and regulatory bodies from capture, as a necessary complement to having the right configuration of laws and administrative codes in place. In brief, the studies in this volume expose institutional development challenges that volatility and crises only make less tractable by reducing the windows of opportunity for the resolution of complex collective action problems.

5.4 Economic and socio-political volatility

When reading the country studies and related literature on the volatility of developing economies, it would be appropriate to keep in mind the socio-political implications of their two better-established stylized facts: namely, the extreme volatility of income and the even greater volatility of consumption. What these statistical regularities in fact imply is that a disproportionate part of the adjustment in these economies occurs through (or is directly reflected in) changes in the material well-being of their populations. Admittedly, many of the absolutely poor may benefit little from these economies' ups and therefore perceive not much change when their trajectories turn downwards. Also, the richest in these societies may have the capacity to shelter their assets from the instability, and some may even be capable of profiting from crises. However, the significant ups and downs mean large portions of the population see their fortunes directly affected, including many who may even experience dramatic losses of relative social status.[20] The volatility figures in the country studies mean that such changes of fortune occur frequently and are sizable.

One could start to appreciate the political ramifications of such circumstances by linking them to findings from the extensive quantitative research on the association between economic conditions and political behavior. For much more stable societies, one of the classic studies (Erikson, 1989) had estimated that in the US, *ceteris paribus*, each 1 per cent change in the annual growth of per capita disposable income would translate into a variation of the same sign of 2.8 per cent in the incumbent's share of the vote.[21] Ray C. Fair, in turn, has been updating econometric presidential vote equations that are alleged to have high predictive power, and shows in his latest estimate (Fair, 2004) a 'growth' coefficient of approximately 0.7; that is, a 1 per cent drop in real per capita GDP in the election year would reduce the vote for the incumbent by about two-thirds of a percentage point. These could be seen as upper and lower bounds for the effect of macroeconomic performance on electoral behavior in a consolidated democracy whose economy is taken as a benchmark in the country studies.[22]

For developing economies, Pacek and Radcliff (1995) estimated a significant effect of economic growth on vote for the incumbent. In fact, they find that positive growth has a statistically insignificant effect on vote shares, but negative rates of GDP growth translate by slightly more than one-to-one into vote losses for the incumbent.[23] Karen Remmer (1991, 1993) had also shown previously that the crises in Latin American economies during the 1980s provoked electoral instability and turnover, with variations in exchange rates, GDP and inflation highly correlated with various indicators of electoral outcomes. Others (for example, Villarreal, 1999; Posner and Simon, 2002) have found similar patterns when analyzing support for incumbent presidents using opinion polls. Some of the results could suggest that, having grown accustomed to living in unstable environments, developing country citizens would be prepared to discount a certain greater degree of economic instability as a fact of life. Yet, all the evidence would confirm that high economic volatility is likely to be associated with high political instability. The patterns would not be substantially different in post-communist countries, although they appear to be qualified by dynamics of ideological realignment and expectations about the impact of reforms on the political agenda (Przeworski, 1991; Doyle and Fidrmuc, 2003).

A recent resurgence of the economics of 'happiness' (for example, Frey and Stutzer, 2000) is providing complementary insights on the underpinnings of these political expressions, and qualifies the role of income vis-à-vis other economic variates such as employment or inflation (Berry, 2006).[24] With these results in mind, it is worth going back to the stylized facts about highly volatile developing economies. In particular, the country studies show that aggregate investment is also more volatile than income. While this regularity is shared with more developed economies, the same pattern in economies with extreme income volatility must reflect not only the adjustment of desired investment levels to the business cycle by established firms, but also the interruption of whole investment projects and the collapse of large numbers of firms.[25] Visitors to some developing country capitals often get a sense of this through the number of unfinished construction projects that are in plain sight and with no visible activity. This is most apparent in the aftermath of a crisis but in some places it is still observable many years afterwards.[26] What is worth highlighting is that the rocky pathway of investment is paralleled by a similar trajectory of employment. In a world where global competition has workers already worried about their job stability regardless of national average income or short-term fluctuations, high volatility economies are going to be the scenario of dramatic manifestations of the political consequences of the massive loss of jobs.[27]

Considering those economic-political interactions, which are doubtlessly understood by developing country policymakers, it is not entirely surprising how those authorities approach policy change and the reform of financial architectures. Wu and Shea, for example, argue that in China the concern with maintaining steady high growth to minimize political unrest often overrides the reform agenda and strengthens the hand of those favoring a centrally-controlled status quo. Those concerns are behind the manipulation of the exchange rate policy, the bail-out of troubled state-owned enterprises and banks, and the delays to reforms that would strengthen corporate governance and subject firms to market disciplines. Nigeria's central bank decision in 1996 to deprive commercial banks of government deposits to reduce liquidity and avoid an impending devaluation, as well as the weak enforcement of prudential standards in more recent times, would be similar manifestations of concerns about a looming crisis. A similarly casual approach to enforcement is mentioned in the Argentinian case during periods under convertibility when banks' non-performing assets, liquidity, and solvency indicators were already worsening. In economies where all landings are rough, and where they hit populations that are definitely not wealthy by contemporary global standards, authorities are unlikely to be too enthusiastic about taking 'slowly maturing' measures that could reduce growth or trigger adverse chain reactions, even if the seeds of the next crisis are being sown.

A logically similar but apparently opposite pattern is manifest in countries that have recently come out of a crisis. There is little doubt, for example, that the left-of-center administration of President Lula da Silva in Brazil would have favored a more expansionary monetary stance had it not been persuaded of the risks of destabilizing an economy in which price, exchange rate, and interest rate hikes directly impinge on fiscal indicators and on the capacity to roll over debt. While its conservative, high interest rate policies are to be thanked for consolidating price stability, which, to a great extent, has also benefited the poor, the country has not been fully isolated from political shocks or contagion effects (as argued by Pires de Souza et al.), and the monetary stance has stalled a much needed growth revitalization and employment creation. South Africa is another example of conservative policymaking by administrations that would have been expected to prioritize growth and employment generation. The study by Ayogu and Dezhbakhsh (Chapter12) shows that, in the face of recurrent shocks and permanent fears of macroeconomic instability, the financial system remains under tight constraints (for example, barriers to entry in retail banking preventing competition from stimulating financial deepening), and banks and funds are over-invested in government debt and in state-owned companies.

Thus, a dual pattern of 'fear of crises' (even fear of mild slowdowns, as in China) seems to reveal itself in the country studies, which determines sub-optimal responses by policymakers to impending perils. It would lead to either myopic policymaking to avoid fueling short-term instability in pre-crisis contexts (Nigeria, Argentina, China), or over-reaction by bulletproofing financial systems that contribute little to the countries' growth objectives (Brazil, South Africa). In other words, the high volatility of income and consumption (and investment), and the resulting fear of crises, reinforce the reactive pattern of policy and institutional innovation that was characterized in Section 5.2, and yield financially dysfunctional and harder to upgrade financial architectures.

The fear of crises is not unrelated to two other 'fears' that have been identified in the literature, but the analysis here may suggest complementary explanations of observed policy responses. In fact, the original story about the 'fear of floating' (Calvo and Reinhart, 2002) refers specifically to the management of exchange rates and emphasized – as a general analytical case – awareness by the monetary authorities of their policies' lack of credibility. It also highlighted the fact that devaluations in emerging markets tend to be associated with recessions, due to pervasive liability dollarization and to the predictable financial system repercussions of large swings in the exchange rate. Other reasons for the 'fear of floating' are the high pass-through from devaluation to inflation and the adverse trade effects of exchange rate variability. Here, in turn, we do not unpack those relevant economic interactions but emphasize authorities' concern about the known social repercussions of wild macroeconomic fluctuations, and in particular of employment and private consumption volatility. These would also suggest a low tolerance for exchange rate fluctuations and an interventionist reaction, but could perhaps account for a broader set of policy choices vis-à-vis the upgrading of DFAs. The 'fear of crisis' hypothesis would seem to be more encompassing as it would account for the response pattern of, for example, the Chinese authorities, for whom the lack of credibility or some of the mentioned emerging-market dynamics might still seem to be more distant concerns.

The more recent arguments about a 'fear of sudden stops' (Caballero et al., 2005a) do not neglect but de-emphasize domestic economic processes and bring to the forefront the policymakers' concern about external sources of volatility. Specifically, comparing countries such as Australia and Chile, it is argued that those lacking in 'currency trust' and 'country trust' (that is, Chile, in the comparison) would react more conservatively to terms of trade and financial shocks because of the worse domestic consequences of similar shocks under poorer access to international financial markets. In conjunction with the 'fear of floating' analyses, the two would be broadly consistent and supportive of the approach to DFAs that is espoused in this volume. They, however, pay less attention to the political repercussions of volatility, adopt a narrower definition of DFA, and therefore miss the volatility-collective action nexus (or the feedback effects).

The episodes of escapes (complete or partial) from the boom–bust cycle also reinforce the importance of mitigating consumption volatility to enable necessary reforms to DFAs. The experience of Chile after the 1982 crisis is one of a drastic fall in consumption volatility after the crisis, as much as one of a window of relative stability that was efficiently used to introduce forward-looking, creative and functional institutional innovations. In fact, the country study shows a steep decline in the volatility indicator for private consumption in the five to seven years after 1982. This appears associated with a more gradual and balanced revitalization of financial markets in the following years, at a pace that would have given institutional and policy adjustments time to mature.

Yet, it must be remembered that Chile's macroeconomic achievements in the 1980s were possible at an extraordinary social cost that has led some qualified observers to doubt that the experience could have been replicated in more open political environments. Meller (1991) recalls that unemployment was kept above 24 per cent of the labor force for four years, real wages fell by 20 per cent and were kept depressed for five years, and per capita social public expenditure was reduced by 10 per cent over a period of six years. By comparison, it is worth noting that the volatility of consumption in Argentina actually increased in the five years after the parallel 1982 crisis, but in this case the political environment was of a transition to democracy in which popular demands were much harder to ignore by the newly elected government.

The Brazilian experience around the 1999 devaluation of the real (and to some extent that of the Argentinian and Uruguayan mega-devaluations of 2001 and 2002) would show another instance of somewhat repressed consumption playing a role in the resolution of a macroeconomic crisis. In this instance, it was the unexpectedly low pass-through from the devaluation to inflation, and the sluggish recovery of wages, that made it possible for the economy to rebound more quickly than in the past from the exchange rate hike, even without having introduced some of the institutional innovations that Chile managed in the 1980s. While completed fully under democratically elected administrations, the aftermath of the 1999 Brazilian devaluation may reveal underlying changes in the structure of labor markets and in the bargaining power of unions, which had made salaried workers less able to protect their real income during and after a crisis.[28] The episode illustrates another type of dynamic that, despite some apparent benefits, could not be easily reproduced elsewhere.[29] Chile in the 1980s and Brazil in the late 1990s, in turn, suggest that less painful stabilizations could have been feasible with appropriate supports from a different international financial architecture.

This leads to a reflection about democratization. Many, if not all the analyzed countries, are trying to upgrade DFAs under high volatility while simultaneously attempting to build or strengthen fragile democracies. If the significant social repercussions of volatility reinforce reactive patterns of policymaking, superimposing the reform calendars that would be compatible with the economic cycles on the electoral calendars to which these polities are starting to adapt should produce windows of opportunity for reformist policymakers that would be extremely narrow. While the economically-driven reform calendar would be determined by short-lived booms, the electoral calendar is known also to yield short-lived honeymoons of high support for the incumbent and cooperative play by key political actors.[30] An appreciation of these complications should further increase the value of international collective action to address the volatility problem. Those concerted efforts could be seen as helping developing countries to avoid the perverse choice between consistent and sustained reformist campaigns and upholding political democracy (see O'Donnell, 1994, 1995).

5.5 Some policy implications

The analysis so far should provide persuasive support for the thesis that extreme volatility, such as that experienced by the analyzed developing and transition economies, complicates the institutional reform challenges they confront. In other words, not only may institutional failures be responsible for high volatility, but such volatility also alters the political economy of initiating, implementing, sustaining, and systematically upgrading the institutional foundations of financial markets. That being the case, the menu of options for national and international collective action is expanded. In fact, developing countries would not only benefit from analysis, recommendations, conditionality and support to 'get their institutions right' but they could also use support – and should devise their own mechanisms – to make it through turbulent times with less aggregate fluctuations. Policies and coordination mechanisms that mitigate the volatility that these countries experience would yield a double dividend: they will produce the known direct economic gains associated with greater stability and growth (including welfare gains as well as the development of more sophisticated and deeper financial markets), and they will at the same time create the favorable conditions to tackle their enormous institutional challenges.

It is possible to be more specific about the policy and coordination mechanisms that could assist countries afflicted by excess aggregate volatility. First, the countries could benefit from all measures, national and international, that allow them to smooth aggregate income/output. For example, the cases analyzed clearly demonstrate – with success stories as much as with failures – the benefits of the diversification of exports by products and markets. The viability of such diversification obviously depends both on appropriate domestic policies and on progress in global and regional trade negotiations. It would seem that finance ministries in developed countries and particularly the IFIs would have an interest in seeing progress in the latter, and some of the IFIs' analytical work points indeed in that direction. In a world in which financial markets have still not provided efficient mechanisms for managing idiosyncratic risk, allowing developing countries to diversify trade by products and currency should be a desirable second-best strategy. The logical connection between more open trade regimes and diminished financial instability should perhaps be emphasized more strongly in the IFIs and the advocacy work of others.

At the same time, there would seem to be ample scope for improving the mechanisms for highly-specialized commodity-exporting countries to cope with inevitable terms of trade variability. While it may be harder to think of international coordination that could get rid of price volatility, these countries could use technical assistance in setting up appropriate fiscal and financial institutions, and there is – in this volume and chapter – a renewed argument for IFIs resuming more vigorously their traditional role of providing assistance to countries affected by adverse temporary shocks. To the extent that regional neighbors are specialized in goods or commodities with negatively correlated prices, there could also be scope for innovative regional stabilization mechanisms that the IFIs could also facilitate.

The above measures by themselves could contribute to mitigating consumption volatility by reducing income volatility. Yet, there may be other policy changes that could assist in this regard. One in particular seems to have potentially high pay-offs in light of the analyzed evidence, and it is the recovery of the capacity to manage international capital flows. Since these are shown to follow procyclically the fluctuations in terms of trade, and they have often been seen to be associated with consumption sprees facilitated by weakly regulated financial systems, national and international measures to throw some sand in the wheels of the international mobility of capitals might yield the double dividends mentioned before.

More generally, transitory and more long-term measures that contribute to smoothing consumption will have to be given high priority, in light of the sizable dual benefits associated with them. It is interesting to note that IFIs have here a potentially key role to play but also a conflict of interest.[31] In fact, the analytical case could be made, based on the evidence of the country studies and the analysis above, that private consumption would be a more relevant target variable for macroeconomic (stabilization) policy than, say, GDP. This would be so due to the direct social consequences of volatile consumption, but also to the indirect impacts on the quality of institutions. The fixation with GDP as the key target variable could be blamed on the uncritical extrapolation of models used in advanced industrialized economies, where functional financial systems already make it possible for the private sector to smooth the temporal trajectory of consumption. For economies such as those studied here, however, the prevailing approach to macroeconomic stabilization would neglect a key complicating feature of their aggregate performance. But the implication of focusing on stabilizing consumption would be a more volatile trajectory for national *savings*. This puts IFIs, which are often a lead creditor and are largely responsive to creditor country interests, in the difficult situation of balancing what could be best for its borrowing client against what is best for themselves. In other words, the peculiar political economy of developing country consumers and developed country lenders, in a world of imperfect global financial markets, may be one of the key factors making IFIs also 'fearful of crises' and inclined to follow reactive patterns of policymaking.

Finally, the analysis in this chapter also shows the potential value of a renovated approach to development assistance and 'conditionality'. Rather than looking at these countries as middle-income giants that are too slow to learn but that will hopefully get their act together and 'graduate' soon, international development players could find ways to play a positive role in breaking the political economy traps into which they so often seem to fall. One way of doing this would be by becoming a positive force for policy change, with various forms of technical assistance and/or financing, during the boom periods of the business cycle. Those are the windows of opportunity for a more systematic upgrading of the DFA, and ones that are too easy (and too costly) to miss under typical domestic political circumstances. Fortunately, locals and foreigners seem to be appreciating this: Nigeria's recent attempts to introduce fiscal responsibility legislation, establish an oil stabilization fund, and improve financial supervision during relatively good times, or the story of Brazil's own fiscal policy reforms in the late 1990s show that the joint efforts of various actors can start to break the cycles of wrong timing, perverse political economy, and incomplete reforms. More of these efforts may help reduce the need for crisis assistance packages in the future.

Notes

The views expressed are those of the author and do not reflect the official position or policies of the International Development Research Centre. The excellent research assistance of Carolina Robino is gratefully acknowledged.

1. Caprio and Klingebiel (1996) provide estimates of other economic costs of recent financial crises. Leijonhufvud (2003) discusses the much broader social implications of crises.
2. Specific estimates are different with the international poverty definitions used by Chen and Ravallion (2004), but the direction of changes and the substantive conclusion are the same (see http://iresearch.worldbank.org/PovcalNet/).
3. See, for example, Krueger (2003).
4. Sturzenegger and Tommasi (1998) include some of the seminal theoretical contributions and applications of this concept to macroeconomic policy analysis.
5. This is in stark contrast with the expectations of Krueger (2003), who asserts, 'As the lessons of crisis prevention and management become more widely accepted and understood, it is to be hoped that the political pressures on governments to undertake sustainable policies will reduce the instances where crises do occur.'
6. See Fanelli (2005b), on Argentina's currency board; but also, strikingly, Caballero et al. (2005a) on Chile's response to the Asian/Russian crises.
7. For this reason, unless indicated, all the evidence on Argentina, Brazil, Chile, China, Nigeria, Russia, South Africa and Thailand comes from the studies that form part of the project. These are, respectively: Fanelli (2005b); Pires de Souza et al. (2006); Magendzo and Titelman (2006); Wu and Shea (2006); Ajayi and Adenikinju (2006); Popov and Peresetsky (2006); Ayogu and Dezhbakhsh (2006); Vichyanond and Pholphirul (2006).
8. Hirschman goes on to say immediately: 'Note that this conception of the coping state goes farther than the interest-group or bureaucratic-politics approaches; these are still concerned with improving our understanding of the state's action, rather than with affirming that most of the time the state does not act, but reacts.'
9. Mosley draws inspiration from theories of bureaucratic organizations such as those by Cyert and March (1963), following the seminal work of Herbert Simon (1952).
10. Sturzenegger and Tommasi (1998) recognize that some of the models appear as ad hoc attempts to fit theory to data, and that they are frequently not robust to slight changes in key parameters, or result in multiple equilibria and ambiguous predictions.

11. Mosley (1976, 1984), for instance, attributes the determination and revision of threshold levels of satisfaction to negotiations within governments, and not to the inherent cognitive constraints of individuals.
12. Such was the logic under which the inclusion of trade liberalization in the response to the twin macroeconomic and financial crises of the 1980s could be said to represent a puzzle (Rodrik, 1996).
13. *Corralito* was the popular name for the freezing of bank deposits, and the compulsory conversion to Argentinian pesos of US$-denominated deposits.
14. Some analyses of the Argentinian experience in the 1990s, for example, highlight the neglect of reforms to critical legal, regulatory, administrative, and judicial infrastructures, all these with a bearing on the functioning of markets and the determination and protection of property rights (see, for example, Tommasi, 2002).
15. 'Without well functioning legal and bankruptcy systems or well established property rights and contracts that effectively support the rights of shareholders and creditors, "traditional corporate governance mechanisms" have nowhere to take root in the Chinese economy' (Wu and Shea, 2006).
16. These latter results apply in particular to the economies in transition, many of which have undergone large-scale experiments in legal transplantation, guided by the goal of influencing economic outcomes and, in particular, of attaining financial deepening (Pistor et al., 2000).
17. A sensible definition of informal institutions characterizes them as 'socially shared rules, usually unwritten, that are created, communicated, and enforced outside of officially sanctioned channels' (Helmke and Levitsky, 2003).
18. Not all is dark and hopeless: the recent Brazilian experience, for example, shows that it is possible to find workable compromises between the center and the states; Nigeria is considering a fiscal responsibility bill in a time of terms of trade bonanza; and Argentina was able to revert many of the irrationalities that emerged as provincial responses to the 2001 financial, currency and fiscal crisis.
19. Rius and Van de Walle (2005), Fanelli and McMahon (2006).
20. In an extreme manifestation of this, as a direct consequence of the recession and the financial crisis, 7 per cent of the Argentinian active population became jobless between 1998 and 2002, almost 10 million people fell below the national poverty line and 6.5 million became indigent (cited in Kosacoff, 2005). The history of poverty reduction in China in the last three decades, in turn, demonstrates by the opposite argument the social relevance of the macroeconomic trajectory (see, for example, Chen and Ravallion, 2004).
21. Erikson used a discounted formula to average changes in disposable income over a presidential term, in which performance closest to the election time counts most heavily.
22. The controversies on the size and significance of the effects, as well as on their theoretical foundations, comprise a massive literature. Nannestad and Paldam (1994) provide a dated but analytically useful overview, including an attempt to establish the conceptual links between *vote* and *government popularity* equations. See also MacKuen et al. (2002). MacKuen et al. (1992) and Norpoth, H. (1996) illustrate some of the main conceptual debates on the microfoundations of the established empirical regularities.
23. The robustness of these 'asymmetric' effects has been a permanent source of controversy in the literature (Nannestad and Paldam, 1994).
24. Employment (or unemployment) had revealed itself as a key concern and driver of voters' attitudes and behaviors in post-socialist economies (Fidrmuc, 2000).
25. Leijonhufvud (2003) reminds us that financial crises normally lump the financially illiquid firms with the ones that were actually bankrupt.
26. Flaws in the legal and judicial infrastructure that contribute to the shallowness of financial markets, are often to blame – directly and indirectly – for both the construction bubbles and the post-crisis delays in clarifying property rights and allowing projects to resume.

27. The fact that formal employment is a minority condition in poorer developing countries should not make these dynamics less relevant, as formally employed or modern sector workers often tend to be over-represented in the political process.
28. Without neglecting possible political and ideological realignments, a greater openness of the economy to trade flows and the global emergence of low-wage giants (that is, China) could help explain labor's loss of bargaining power.
29. On the other hand, the 1999 episode also shows the benefits of appropriate innovations that were opportunely introduced. In fact, the Brazilian government's resolute action against currency substitution (that is, dollarization) in the financial system can be thanked for avoiding a banking crisis associated with currency mismatches, which was very much the story of the Southern Cone crises of the 1980s and the more recent ones in Argentina and Uruguay.
30. Almost all the empirical analyses of economic voting cited above also confirm that support for incumbents erodes gradually over time, even controlling for other relevant economic and political factors, and for both developing as well as developed economies.
31. I thank José M. Fanelli for raising this point.

6
China

Harry X. Wu and Esther Y.P. Shea

6.1 Introduction and conceptual framework

Judged by the established link in the literature between growth and institutions, which make up the domestic financial architecture (DFA), China's post-reform rapid growth and low volatility in the absence of healthy institutions or efficient financial markets may present researchers with a serious puzzle. One may tackle this by arguing that Chinese official statistics could have exaggerated China's growth performance while at the same time smoothing out its aggregate volatility. But an equally plausible argument is that an imminent outburst of crisis is veiled by the government's attempts to play down the true extent of the state banks' non-performing loans and the misconduct of agents in the stock market, other financial sectors and the regulatory authorities. What we are trying to argue here is that even if the official statistics are accurate, they may not reveal a true picture that is necessary to uncover all these hidden issues. The China puzzle has to be solved with a deeper understanding of the channels through which growth, aggregate volatility, and institutions are linked, which requires more than the proper measure of aggregate volatility using the available official data. This is the task of the current research.

In Figure 6.1, we introduce a flow chart to illustrate the Chinese approach to the building of China's DFA, linking China's financial reform with its major constraints, the role of the IFA, and the impacts of internal and external shocks. To focus on the main issues in this study, we have made two assumptions. First, we assume that all the external factors are exogenous to the system and that they only affect the policy constraints and the reform approach to the building of DFA. Second, excluding the influences of the IFA and the WTO, the domestic factors that form the policy constraints are also exogenous, with the sole exception of 'market experience', which is endogenous to the market-oriented reform. However, we argue that its effect would be overwhelmed by ideological and political constraints under the totalitarian regime.

Regarding the style of China's financial reform, we argue that 'piecemeal' is a more appropriate description than 'gradualist'. The Chinese reform is 'piecemeal' because it has to compromise with the ideology of the Marxist orthodoxy and

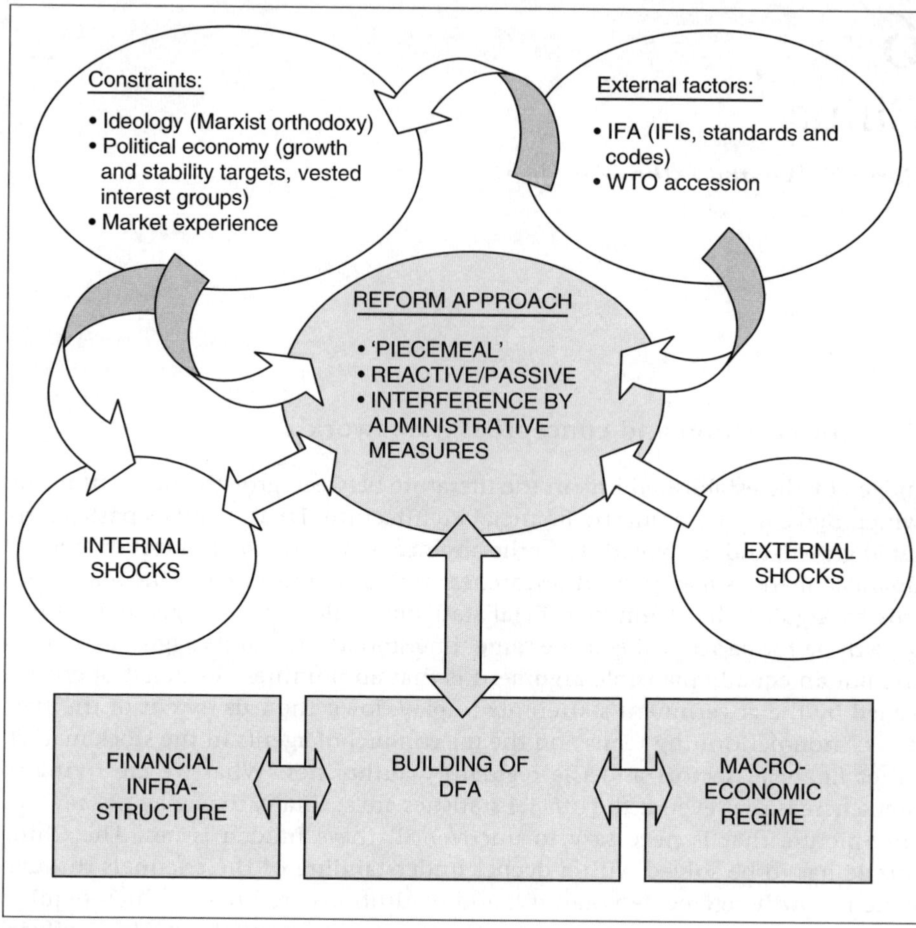

Figure 6.1 China's reform, volatility and the building of DFA

safeguard the vested interests nurtured under the old system. Besides, it lacks a clear vision of the reform outcomes due to inadequate knowledge about the market system. The market liberalization process could be disrupted by administrative interventions, or even policy retrenchments if it openly challenges the communist doctrine, threatens any of the vested interests, or induces too drastic a change. In fact, many earlier reforms in China began spontaneously from the lower level of the economic hierarchy and were only sanctioned by the central government when their 'costs' were considered justified by their 'benefits'. This approach shows that the government's reform policy tends to be 'reactive' rather than 'proactive'.

In order to stay 'legitimate' or to maintain 'political correctness', the Chinese government has to compromise with the old orthodoxy and vested-interest groups that oppose the reform. The making of reform policy sets stable economic growth as the top priority because the decline and instability of income may create a good opportunity for the old orthodoxy to fight back, tightening the ideological and political economy constraints on the policymakers. Therefore, a reform measure will have to be revised, postponed, or abandoned if it is likely to jeopardize growth or stability. The central government also tends to tolerate local governments' interference with business decisions in investment for the sake of promoting growth and maintaining stability.

Figure 6.1 also includes a counterforce to the ideological and political constraints, that is, external factors, such as the IFA and WTO accession. These factors will encourage the government to strengthen the financial institutions in order to facilitate a smooth integration with the global economy. However, uncertainty about the consequences of further opening up to global competition may increase the government's preoccupation with growth and stability, which may water down the positive effect of the external factors on the DFA reform. Furthermore, the potentially destabilizing effects of portfolio capital movements in the IFA may have discouraged China from liberalizing its capital account lest excess aggregate volatility stem from such external shocks.

Based on the above discussion, we postulate the following central hypotheses on the relationship between aggregate volatility and institutions in China:

- *Under the prevailing ideological and political constraints, the central government tends to interfere with business decisions in order to maintain growth and stability and hence tolerate local governments' heavy involvement in local investment projects.*
- *The government's administrative interventions in business decisions help maintain stable growth but at the same time impede the building of the DFA and the development of efficient markets.*
- *Weak institutions tend to invite more interventions from the government because they cause misallocation of financial resources and mismanagement of risks and, therefore, threaten stability.*
- *Given the potentially destabilizing effects on the exchange rate of portfolio capital movements in the prevailing IFA, China's adherence to a closed capital account and a pegged exchange rate tends to effectively reduce excess volatility caused by external shocks. Yet, it causes price distortions and compromises independent monetary policy and, hence, obstructs the building of the DFA.*

The rest of this chapter is organized into four sections. In Section 6.2 we focus on the measuring of aggregate volatility in the Chinese economy over both the central planning and the reform periods. We present some key indicators to identify shocks and crises over the periods when there were important shifts in policy regimes. We also compare the case of China with those of the former Soviet Union and the Eastern bloc countries to highlight some key features that differentiate China from other transition economies.

In Section 6.3 we examine the idiosyncratic structural factors of the Chinese economy as the likely sources of excess volatility with an emphasis on the effect of government interventions aiming at growth and stability. We will emphasize the role of government authorities, at both central and local levels, in promoting growth and maintaining stability and their implications for institution-building.

Finally, in Section 6.4 we conclude with the political economy analysis to investigate firstly how the government's constraints and policy targets have impeded the building of healthy financial institutions and delayed the reform of the foreign exchange regime, thereby compromising the independence of monetary policy; and secondly how a closer DFA-IFA linkage has helped loosen the political constraints on policymakers and, hence, strengthen the DFA.

6.2 Measuring aggregate volatility and identifying shocks

This section deals with the basic measurement issues in examining aggregate volatility and identifying shocks in the Chinese economy. Our investigation will be made from both historical and international perspectives. From a historical perspective, China's aggregate volatility will be examined against major shifts in policy regimes over the past half century. Excess volatilities will be identified as those volatilities that cannot be explained by the fundamentals defined by the underlying trend. To gain an international perspective, the dynamics of China's aggregate volatility will be compared with other former centrally planned economies during both the central planning and the transition periods. This is to ascertain to what extent the case of China does or does not conform to the 'norm' of the transition of centrally planned economies.

The biggest obstacle we face in measuring aggregate volatility is the problem of China's national accounts data (Maddison, 1998; Wu, 2000, 2002). Firstly, there are no high-frequency data covering the period under our investigation. Second, all the pre-1985 historical data were compiled within the framework of the Soviet-style Material Product System (MPS) and have only been roughly converted by NBS to the framework of the System of National Accounts (SNA).[1] Thirdly, NBS does not publish any constant-price GDP estimates. Lastly, there are significant discrepancies between output and expenditure accounts and between national and regional accounts.

Undoubtedly, all these data problems will have some effects on the measured aggregate volatility. However, while this study makes an effort to fill some data gaps, it does not attempt to adjust the published official statistics.[2]

Volatility, shocks, and crises in a historical perspective

An examination from a historical perspective could start with Table 6.1. The entire period under investigation in this study is from 1952 to 2004 (or the latest available year). To capture the significant shifts in policy regimes and the subsequent institutional changes in China, we divide the entire period into the central planning period and the market-oriented transition period, beginning with 1978.

As shown in Table 6.1, compared with the pre-reform period, China's per capita GDP growth in the post-reform period was 165 per cent faster per annum.

Table 6.1 China's long-run key indicators: growth and openness

	Average per capita GDP growth rate[a] (% p.a.)	Average population growth rate (% p.a.)	Average degree of openness[b] (%)	Average exports (annual 1990US$) (100 m)	Average trade balance (annual 1990US$) (100 m)	Average capital account balance/ exports[c] (%)	Average capital account balance/GDP[c] (%)
Pre-reform							
1952–57	5.7	2.2	5.0	22	9	16.8	0.7
1958–65	1.8	1.5	4.0	34	0	–10.2	–0.4
1966–77	2.9	2.3	3.7	50	–21	–5.0	–0.1
Post-reform							
1978–93	8.2	1.4	10.4	383	–58	7.9	0.8
1994–2004	8.4	0.9	24.1	5135	236	12.3	3.1
Pre-reform	3.1	2.0	4.1	39	–8	–1.6	0.0
Post-reform	8.2	1.2	16.0	2319	62	9.6	1.8
Overall	5.8	1.6	10.1	1200	28	4.2	0.9

Notes:
a. GDP estimates are based on expenditure accounts with net exports adjusted by annual balance of payments, measured in 1990 constant yuan (see text for explanation).
b. Measured as semi-sum of exports and imports over GDP, i.e. ((*EX*+*IM*)/2)/*GDP*.
c. Capital account balance for the pre-1982 period is estimated (see Wu and Shea, 2006, for the estimation).

Sources: Basic data are from DNEA (1997) and DNA (2004), updated using national accounts and price indices from recent issues of the *China Statistical Yearbook* (NBS, 2003, 2004, 2005).

Such a distinct growth performance was accompanied by an unprecedented pace of integration with the world economy through international trade and direct investment. The current Chinese economy is three times more open than it was before the reform. And the volume that China exports today is almost sixtyfold that in the central planning period.

Note that the pre-reform and post-reform periods are fundamentally different and, hence, largely incomparable, especially considering the theme of the current study. During the central planning period, there was virtually no financial market, but only a simple, state-controlled, administratively manipulated financial system. All resources were allocated and controlled by the State Planning Commission (SPC). The state banking system functioned merely as the cashier for the Ministry of Finance (MOF) which mainly played an accounting role in financing state firms or projects according to the national plans set by SPC. No private investment was allowed. Since the wage rate was purposely kept at near-subsistence levels, though supplemented by various subsidies in kind, household savings were also low. Money was simply inactive under such a system (Liew, 1997).

China began to separate its banking institutions from the MOF in 1979 in an attempt to plug the increasing leakage of financial resources out of state control as a result of decollectivization in farming and the deregulation of industrial activities in rural areas. By the mid-1980s, the establishment of the first central bank of the People's Republic, the People's Bank of China (PBC), as well as the 'big four' state banks specializing in different financial activities, marked the beginning of China's transition towards a modern financial system.[3]

To examine major policy changes we further divide the central planning period into three sub-periods: 1952–57, in which China implemented its first Soviet-style five-year plan and began an ambitious program of heavy industrialization unprecedented in Chinese history; 1958–65, in which the economy was deeply shocked by the Maoist Great Leap Forward campaign and the disasters following the collapse of the campaign; and 1966–77, in which the economy suffered from shocks caused by political struggles during the Cultural Revolution. We also divide the reform period into two sub-periods, that is, the preliminary transition period focusing on decentralization in various sectors in 1978–93 and the marketization period from 1994 to the present. We use 1994 as the cut-off point because it marks the building of some important market-supporting institutions implementing Deng Xiaoping's decree of bolder reform and the opening up in 1992–93, which ended the retrenchment in 1989–91 after the Tiananmen square massacre and successfully made Deng's 'socialist market economy' the Communist Party's new economic framework of development.

Examining the sub-periods that reflect major shifts in policy regimes, one could see a distinct feature in the dynamics of China's GDP, that is, the policy shifts during the reform period had a more significant impact on the growth performance than those in the central planning period. Notably, the degree of openness has greatly accelerated since 1994. All key indicators clearly suggest that this is the period when exports and capital inflows began to play an increasingly important role in maintaining China's impressive pace of growth and when China found itself labeled as the 'world factory', an issue whose implications for volatility will be investigated in the following sections.

In Table 6.2 we provide measures of average aggregate volatility and indicators for recessions. These indicators, supplemented by Figure 6.2, help identify shocks or crises in each period. The shocks brought by the Great Leap Forward and its disastrous aftermath in 1958–62 were exceptional even by the standard of other developing countries, for example, Argentina (see Fanelli in Chapter 1 of this book). The sub-period 1958–65 was the most volatile of all periods under investigation, indicating the extent of the policy-induced crisis that was afflicting the economy. Unquestionably, as far as these indicators are concerned, China has experienced a significant decline in aggregate volatility since the mid-1960s.

To help identify excess volatility mostly due to policy shocks in the pre- and post-reform periods, in Figure 6.2 we introduce one standard deviation from the mean growth rate of each period to assess the cyclical pattern of per capita GDP

Table 6.2 China's long-run key indicators: volatility and crises (based on per capita real GDP)

	Average rolling standard deviation[a] (%)	Frequency of recessions[b] (%)	Average duration of recessions[c] (years)	Average depth of recessions[d] (%)	Frequency of abnormal falls[e] (%)	Frequency of exceptional growth[f] (%)
Pre-reform						
1952–57	3.8	0.0	0.0	0.0	0.0	0.0
1958–65	12.7	37.5	3.0	39.4	25.0	25.0
1966–77	5.6	25.0	1.5	17.6	8.3	8.3
Post-reform						
1978–93	3.6	6.3	1.0	8.0	6.3	18.8
1994–2004	2.4	0.0	0.0	0.0	9.1	9.1
Pre-reform	8.0	23.1	2.0	28.5	11.5	11.5
Post-reform	3.2	3.7	1.0	8.0	7.4	14.8
Overall	5.5	13.2	1.6	21.7	9.4	13.2

Notes:
a. Calculated as 7-year centered window rolling s.d. However, due to data limitation, the average of 1956–57 is used for 1952–57 and the average of 1994–2001 for 1994–2004.
b. Proportion of years in which the per capita GDP growth rate was negative.
c. The average number of years in each recession.
d. The average accumulated fall in the per capita GDP growth rate from the pre-recession level in each recession.
e. Proportion of years in which per capital GDP growth rate was negative or lower than the mean (μ) growth rate (as given by the HP trend) minus one standard deviation (σ) ($\mu = 3.76$ and 8.19, $\sigma = 7.87$ and 2.94 for the pre-reform and post-reform periods, respectively).
f. Similar to (e) but changed to per capita GDP growth rate higher than the mean growth rate plus one standard deviation.

Sources: See Table 6.1.

growth obtained by the Hodrick-Prescott filter (1997). The distinct difference in growth and volatility over the two periods as seen in Tables 6.1 and 6.2 implies that the measure of 'normality' is very strict for the post-reform period ($\sigma = 2.94$ per cent), but very lenient for the pre-reform period ($\sigma = 7.87$ per cent).

The nature of the shocks that caused excess volatilities was both exogenous and endogenous. On the one hand, they were exogenous because they were caused by changes in the development policy through state plans that could only be justified by political motives. And the shocks of such nature would be the major source of volatility during the central planning period. On the other hand, they were endogenous because resource constraints could stop an ambitious expansion and force the economy into a recession, and, hence, affect the next round of policy and planning adjustments.

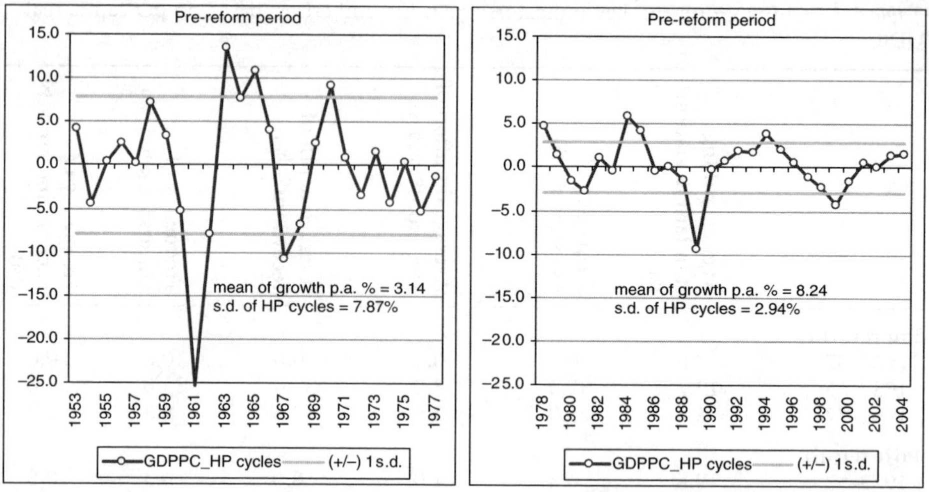

Figure 6.2 Abnormal falls and exceptional growth in China measured by the HP-filter derived cycles and one s.d. from the mean growth rate of the period
Sources: See Table 6.1.

Volatility, shocks, and crises in an international perspective

To put China's initial condition for its post-war development in an international perspective, it is best to compare it with the former centrally planned economies despite their substantial differences in history, culture, politics, and income level. Such a comparison is valid not only for the period of central planning but also for the period of transition due to the influential legacy of the Soviet model.

The fact that the aggregate volatility in China and other former centrally planned economies evolved very differently during their transition could be attributed to several factors. First, during the central planning period, China pursued self-sufficiency and was basically closed to international trade, but the Eastern bloc countries remained open to commodity trade with one another, which could to some extent help absorb the output volatility of individual member countries. Second, in the transition to the market system, China has adopted a 'piecemeal' approach to experiment with market liberalization, whereas its Eastern bloc counterparts implemented market reform measures in a 'big-bang' fashion. Third, as was discussed earlier, China's reform has not yet extended to the totalitarian political regime that began in 1949. Therefore, compared with other transition economies, the government authorities and officials in China are more capable of influencing business decisions to promote growth while maintaining stability.

Changes in national territories following the collapse of the communist regime in the Eastern bloc in the early 1990s have created serious inconsistencies in the coverage of national account estimates in many of these countries. The only consistent data available are constructed by Maddison (2001 and 2003). However, his data do not cover major items of expenditure accounts. We could only focus

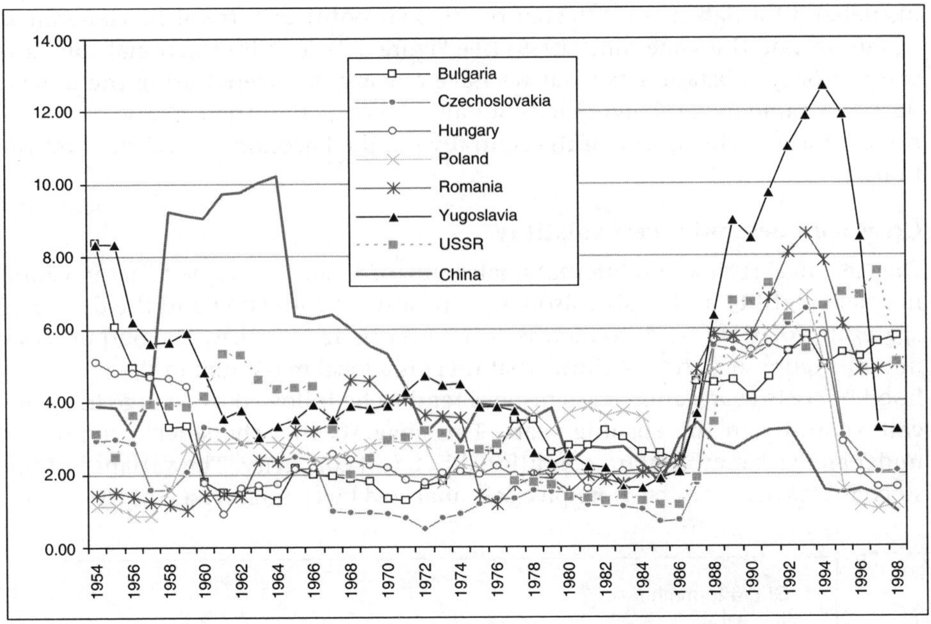

Figure 6.3 Volatility of per capita GDP: China versus the former Eastern bloc countries (7-year window rolling standard deviation of annual growth rate in percent)
Note: GDP estimates are in the 1990 PPPs or international (Geary-Khamis) dollars, which are different from the GDP series constructed in this study and hence incompatible with the measure in Figure 6.6.
Sources: The basic data used are from 1951 to 2001, constructed by Maddison (2001 and 2003).

on per capita GDP in the comparison. For the Chinese data, it should be noted that Maddison has adjusted the official estimates, and converted his results to the 1990 purchasing power parities (PPPs) as he does with all other countries. Therefore, it should be noted that the measure of aggregate volatility in Figure 6.3 is not fully compatible with other measures in this study using the official data.

Figure 6.3 reveals a very interesting picture of the dynamics of aggregate volatility in eight of the former centrally planned economies. The Maddison data cover the period 1951–2001, that is, for the whole post-World War II period. Therefore, we could calculate the rolling standard deviation on the basis of a seven-year centered window for the period 1954–99. Firstly, we find that the pre-reform Chinese economy was generally much more volatile than its Eastern bloc counterparts, especially during the Great Leap Forward and the early period of the Cultural Revolution. Although all former communist countries were not short of radical political and economic campaigns, what China experienced certainly went to extremes and deeply shocked the economy and society. Besides, since China was closed to international trade, there was no effective mechanism to help the economy absorb the shocks. Second, the collapse of the communist regime in Eastern Europe at the beginning of the 1990s was an unprecedented shock to the Eastern bloc countries, but an event from which China was insulated although it was affected by its own political turmoil in Tiananmen Square around the same time (1989) (see Figure 6.2). This international comparison not only substantiates what we have already discovered using the official data (see Table 6.2 and Figure 6.2) but also suggests that the Chinese case does not conform to the 'norm' of the centrally planned economies and their transitions.

Crisis episodes and excess volatility

Our historical review and international comparison already suggest that in China normal volatility and crisis episodes are positively correlated and the degree of aggregate volatility tends to increase whenever there is a crisis. The output series in both Figures 6.3 and 6.4 shows that there is a local maximum in the neighborhood of crisis years, and crisis episodes tend to be followed by a surge in aggregate volatility in the ensuing years. This suggests that the stochastic process under analysis may contain conditional heteroskedasticity. The variance of the stochastic process can be more precisely analyzed by estimating a GARCH model.

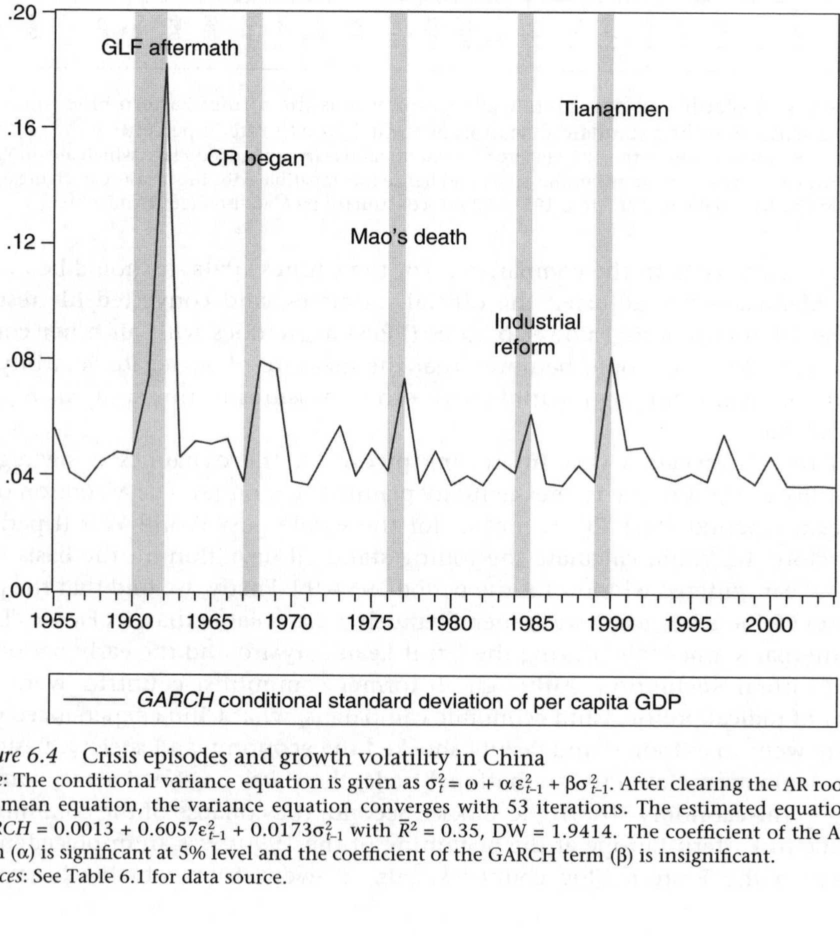

Figure 6.4 Crisis episodes and growth volatility in China
Note: The conditional variance equation is given as $\sigma_t^2 = \omega + \alpha\varepsilon_{t-1}^2 + \beta\sigma_{t-1}^2$. After clearing the AR roots in the mean equation, the variance equation converges with 53 iterations. The estimated equation is: $GARCH = 0.0013 + 0.6057\varepsilon_{t-1}^2 + 0.0173\sigma_{t-1}^2$ with $\bar{R}^2 = 0.35$, DW = 1.9414. The coefficient of the ARCH term (α) is significant at 5% level and the coefficient of the GARCH term (β) is insignificant.
Sources: See Table 6.1 for data source.

The estimation results strongly support our hypothesis of the presence of conditional heteroskedasticity.

Using the estimated GARCH conditional variance series we obtain an annual series of conditional standard deviation for the whole period under study and depict it in Figure 6.4. The shaded areas are the periods in which there were absolute falls in China's per capita real GDP that were triggered by policy shocks or drastic political events. It shows that, compared with the 'normal years' (given the regime conditions), the conditional variance indeed became larger during crises (or policy shocks) and tended to remain large in subsequent years.

This finding helps substantiate the average measures of the rolling windows standard deviation for different periods in Table 6.2. With the empirical support, it is now clear that China's high aggregate volatility under central planning was associated with more frequent crises during the 1960s and 1970s when China was closed to international trade and pursuing import-substituting development. And the decline in aggregate volatility since the reform was accompanied by a decline in the frequency of crises or extreme volatility when the government adopted market-oriented reform policies in the 1980s and deepened China's international integration in the 1990s. Such a GARCH exercise also helps distinguish excess volatility from those 'normal cycles' that may be justified by the fundamentals under prevailing regime settings. It is interesting to note that if those abnormal spikes in Figure 6.4 were removed from the GARCH conditional standard deviation series, one could easily imagine that the rest would be 'normal cycles' with a similar (or slightly declining) degree of aggregate volatility over time.

Volatility, growth, and persistence of shocks

Cross-country empirical studies on growth volatility have found that there is an evident negative relationship between volatility and growth (Ramey and Ramey, 1995) and that developing countries have a limited ability to cope with shocks (Aizenman and Pinto, 2004). That is, there is a higher persistence of shocks in these countries than in developed countries. In the Chinese case, compared with market economies, we argue that growth may be less sensitive to volatility and the economy may exhibit stronger persistence. The reason is straightforward: there is a high degree of government involvement in business decisions, especially in investment decisions, aiming to promote growth and maintain stability as was already explained in our conceptual framework (Figure 6.1). It is important to understand that such government involvement is usually not constrained by market forces and, hence, tends to make business decisions less risk-averse. Consequently, compared with private investment, government-involved projects tend to take longer to revise. It is more so for projects initiated by national plans (note that five-year plans are still used as an important guidance after the reform), where the authorities may take a long time to recognize the problems and make adjustments. Therefore, it should not be a surprise to see strong inertia in the Chinese economy.

In what follows we propose an ARCH-M model to test the above hypotheses.[4] The advantage of using such a model is that, in addition to assuming conditional heteroskedasticity, it also assumes that the growth rate depends on the standard deviation of the process. Following Aizenman and Pinto (2004), we assume that there is a concave relationship between growth and shocks due to the authorities' inability to implement effective countercyclical policies and the constraints imposed by financial market imperfections on private agents' decisions. The ARCH-M model is specified as follows.

$$y_t = \alpha_0 + \alpha_1 y_{t-1} + \alpha_2 \sigma_t + \varepsilon_t,\ \varepsilon_t \equiv h_t \sigma_t;\ \mathrm{var}(h_t) = 1;\ E(h_t) = 0 \quad (6.1)$$

$$\sigma_t^2 = \gamma_0 + \gamma_1 \varepsilon_{t-1}^2 + \gamma_1 \varepsilon_{t-2}^2 \quad (6.2)$$

where y_t is the output (GDP) growth rate measured as log difference, σ_t is the conditional standard deviation to capture shocks, and ε_t is the innovation to the stochastic process. Of the parameters α_i and γ_i to be estimated, α_2 captures the effect of volatility on growth, and α_1 and γ_i represent the degree of persistence of shocks. Based on the above discussion, we expect that in the Chinese

Table 6.3 ARCH-M model results for GDP

Dependent variable (y_t):	**Dlog(GDP)**
	Mean equation
C	0.0954***
	(0.0198)
Conditional S.D. (GARCH)	–0.5637*
	(0.3865)
AR(1) (y_{t-1})	0.4695*
	(0.2829)
	Variance equation
C	0.0008***
	(0.0002)
RESID(-1)^2 (ARCH1)	0.5512***
	(0.1968)
RESID(-2)^2 (ARCH2)	0.3826
	(0.3011)
Mean of dependent variable	0.0707
S.D. of dependent variable	0.0702
Durbin-Watson statistic	1.6227
Sample period (adjusted)	1954–2004
No. of iterations to converge	58
Inverted AR roots	0.47

Notes: Standard errors are in parentheses. Level of significance used in the hypothesis testing is based on z-statistic and indicated by *** for 1%, ** for 5% and * for 10–15% level of significance, respectively. Note that we have lowered the threshold for the last criterion in order to include marginal cases. The result of R-squared is not reported as it is irrelevant in the absence of regressors in the mean equation.

Source: Authors' estimation.

case, α_2 should still be negative but may not be to the degree found in the typical (market-based) developing-country cases. As for α_1 and γ_i, we expect stronger positive results compared with the typical developing country cases. The estimated results are reported in Table 6.3.

The results of the ARCH-M model are consistent with our hypotheses that past shocks do not have strong negative effects on growth and there is relatively strong inertia built into the system. Relative to the Argentine case (Chapter 9), the value of α_1 appears to be quite large, which reflects the higher degree of persistence that the economy exhibits following shocks. The value of α_2 is small and negative as expected but only at a significance level of 15 per cent. This reflects that the Chinese economy is indeed less sensitive to volatility, which is consistent with our postulation made on heavy government involvement in investment.

Before we come back to this issue in the next section, we would like to refer to the findings by Aizenman and Marion (1999) that volatility is negatively related to private investment and positively related to public investment, as opposed to Ramey and Ramey's (1995) conclusion that there is a lack of clear correlation between volatility and investment. We may infer that the small value of α_2 is likely a result of the dominance of public investment in total investment, as well as local governments' influence on private investment. All these make investment less risk-averse. The investors' expectation of passing on to the state any risk resulting from bad decision-making will lower the risk-consciousness of investment decisions. However, despite inefficient investment, its growth is highly correlated with that of GDP. If volatility does not dampen investment growth, it will not dampen output growth, which may well explain the relatively small negative value of α_2.

Based on the ARCH-M model results we could measure the magnitude of the average shocks in China and decompose the long-run effect of shock sensitivity and the persistence of shocks on China's long-run growth rate. Now, from Equation (6.1), we can derive the following long-run equilibrium growth equation.

$$\bar{y} = \alpha_0 /(1 - \alpha_1) + [\alpha_2 /(1 - \alpha_1)]\bar{\sigma} \tag{6.3}$$

Using the estimated coefficients in Table 6.3, we can estimate China's long-run equilibrium growth rate as follows.

$$\bar{y} = 0.1799 - 1.0625\bar{\sigma} \tag{6.4}$$

This means that each percentage-point increase in the standard deviation will reduce the growth rate by 1.1 percentage points. If $\bar{\sigma}$ is estimated as the average value of the square root of the conditional variance of the GARCH process, that is, $\bar{\sigma} = 0.0633$ (note that this is much greater than that of Argentina's $\bar{\sigma}$ of 0.0267; see Chapter 9), China's long-run equilibrium growth rate will be 11.3 per cent per annum. Not surprisingly, compared with countries like Argentina, China's growth is much more stable and less affected by shocks. However, one would expect that government-involved inefficient investment cannot continue forever and further market-oriented reforms to tackle inefficiency will force the government to withdraw from business decisions. Therefore, it is likely that the economy will become more sensitive to shocks (that is, increase in α_2). Thus, not only structural policies, but more importantly, reforms to target political economy problems also matter to China's long-run growth. These issues are investigated in the following sections.

6.3 Structural factors as sources of excess volatility

Our investigation has so far focused on measuring aggregate output volatility and identifying excess volatility in China. Two unique features of the Chinese economy have been revealed. First, despite more volatile output performance under central planning compared with other centrally planned economies, its transition to a market system has been associated with much more rapid growth and lower volatility relative to other transition economies. Second, despite huge policy-induced shocks and a strong persistence of shocks, China's output growth is less sensitive to volatility. We argue that the Chinese phenomenon could be explained by heavy government involvement in business decisions aiming to achieve fast and stable growth. In this section, from the expenditure perspective we attempt to identify idiosyncratic structural factors as the possible sources of China's excess volatility.

From the end of the 1970s, when China began its market-oriented transition, up to the early 1990s, the reform mainly concentrated on fiscal decentralization and a gradual opening up to foreign trade and direct investment. During that period a modern financial system also began to emerge from the mono-bank system that was highly integrated with and controlled by the public finance system developed under central planning. China's pace of financial reform and integration with the world economy only began to accelerate in the mid-1990s, which coincided with the second globalization period as defined in this project.

In general, as shown in Table 6.4,[5] compared with the central planning period, all indicators in the reform period exhibit much faster growth, except for investment, and less volatility, except for exports. In fact, the growth of investment, measured by gross capital formation (GCF) or fixed capital formation (FCF) remains high, much higher than comparable international experience.[6] Both exports and imports remain most volatile over time among all the expenditure indicators. As for the indicators of domestic absorption, GCF and FCF are most volatile but have also experienced the most remarkable decline since the reform. Besides, government consumption expenditure (GCE) had been more volatile than output until the mid-1990s. Lastly, prior to the mid-1960s, volatility in China's household consumption expenditure (HCE) stayed at a rather high level in comparison to international experience, but at only half the level of output volatility. Since then it has substantially declined, but increased relative to output volatility in the reform period.

Table 6.4 China's long-run key indicators: expenditure perspective (annual average growth rate and the period mean of rolling standard deviation in percentage)

Period/ regime	GDE (GDP)	Consumption			Investment		Trade	
		FCE	HCE	GCE	GCF	FCF	Exports	Imports
Pre-reform								
1952–57	8.1	6.5	6.9	4.3	14.7	23.0	13.5	5.8
	(4.2)	(5.3)	(5.8)	(10.6)	(21.4)	(31.3)	(12.4)	(18.6)
1958–65	4.4	3.1	2.8	6.0	14.2	14.1	2.2	2.8
	(14.1)	(7.8)	(7.1)	(18.7)	(39.6)	(37.4)	(18.7)	(23.7)
1966–77	5.5	4.7	4.4	5.9	9.1	9.7	7.4	9.3
	(5.7)	(3.0)	(2.7)	(8.7)	(18.2)	(14.4)	(14.0)	(23.2)
Post-reform								
1978–93	9.7	8.9	8.8	9.4	12.2	11.0	19.0	21.1
	(3.6)	(3.3)	(3.5)	(6.4)	(9.7)	(10.2)	(17.2)	(22.3)
1994–2004	9.3	7.4	7.3	7.5	11.0	12.4	20.7	18.0
	(2.4)	(1.9)	(2.1)	(2.3)	(6.1)	(5.2)	(17.6)	(13.4)
Pre-reform	5.6	4.5	4.4	5.6	11.8	13.8	7.0	6.5
	(8.6)	(4.9)	(4.6)	(12.5)	(26.3)	(24.3)	(15.6)	(23.0)
Post-reform	9.6	8.3	8.2	8.6	11.7	11.6	19.7	19.8
	(3.2)	(2.8)	(3.0)	(5.0)	(8.5)	(8.5)	(17.4)	(19.3)
Overall	7.7	6.5	6.4	7.2	11.8	12.6	13.6	13.4
	(5.8)	(3.8)	(3.8)	(8.6)	(17.0)	(16.1)	(16.5)	(21.1)

Notes:
Real growth rates are estimated using 1990 based deflators constructed by the authors.
Trade data have been reconciled with China's balance of payment and deflated to the 1990 yuan.
Figures in parentheses are the mean 7-year centered window rolling standard deviations in percentage for specified periods. Thus, we have lost three observations each at the beginning and the end of the series when calculating the period mean.

Sources: See Table 6.1.

Consumption volatility versus income volatility

Following the life-cycle/permanent-income hypothesis of Modigliani and Brumberg (1954) and Friedman (1957), households will use savings and borrowing to smooth the path of consumption. Thus, if there exists a perfect financial system that can efficiently facilitate consumption smoothing, domestic consumption will be less volatile than and uncorrelated with domestic income. This is certainly not the case in China. In what follows we examine some distinct features of China's consumption volatility.

With Figure 6.5 we can trace the dynamics of China's per capita output and consumption growth (in the first panel) and volatility (in the second panel) in the past half-century. In the absence of financial markets under central planning, as shown in the first panel, consumption in China was highly procyclical and there was a clear co-movement between per capita consumption growth and per capita income growth. This only began to change in the 1980s. Entering the 1990s when China became more engaged in international trade and direct investment, such a co-movement almost disappeared, that is, per capita consumption tended to be somewhat countercyclical.

In the second panel of Figure 6.5, prior to the 1990s, the pattern of China's per capita consumption volatility in general reflected the supply shocks brought by the early Soviet-style industrialization drive, the feverish Maoist Great Leap Forward campaign and its disastrous failure, the persistent crisis during the Cultural Revolution, decollectivization in agriculture and decentralization in industry. In comparison to international experience, prior to the mid-1960s, China's consumption volatility remained very high (7.3 per cent if estimated for 1952–65 based on data used in Table 6.4), though not as high as income volatility (to be discussed later). Subsequently, it declined before rising again during the economic reform. China's consumption volatility declined further during the globalization period in the 1990s.

A closer examination of the relative volatility between consumption and income reveals another important structural feature of the Chinese economy. As was already mentioned, in absolute terms China's consumption volatility was high under central planning, but it was very low relative to income volatility. How could this observation be explained in the absence of a financial market? A related and even more interesting observation is that following the economic reform and the preliminary development of DFA, China's consumption volatility increased rather than decreased, not only on its own but more importantly relative to income volatility. In fact, the second panel of Figure 6.5 shows that there were several periods in the reform period when consumption became more volatile than income, including the periods 1984–85 when the industrial reform

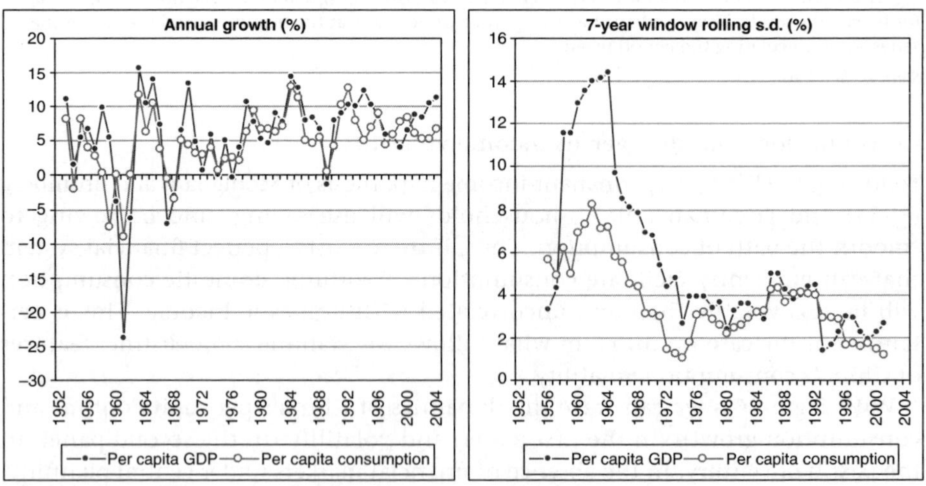

Figure 6.5 Per capita output and consumption growth and volatility in China, 1952–2004
Source: See Table 6.1.

began, 1989–90 when society was shocked by the Tiananmen square massacre, and 1993–95 when a deeper SOE reform was implemented along with reform policies that were more conducive to foreign trade and direct investment.

Together with the observed change in the annual growth pattern of consumption relative to that of income, that is, from procyclical to countercyclical, the fact that the reform policies have been more effective at reducing income volatility than at smoothing consumption volatility clearly indicates important changes in the policy regime of the Chinese economy.

Under central planning, labor compensation was minimized so that more resources could be used to support heavy industrialization. There was also a state rationing system to ensure that basic necessities were allocated equally among consumers. State firms, government units and neighborhood committees were all integral parts of the rationing system to ensure consumption stability. It was not the market but the planning authorities that decided when wage rates should be adjusted to secure production. Since the compensation level was already very low, only to meet subsistence needs, there was little room to adjust it downward. But there were occasions when it was necessary to raise it to maintain an effective labor supply and thereby achieve the higher output targets. So, the change in consumption could be as erratic as the change in production plans, albeit with a smaller magnitude.

During the economic transition to a market system, the state has gradually cast off its responsibility to finance and protect the state firms. The SOE reform has been enhanced by the increasing competition with non-state and foreign firms. Consequently, the state firms cannot afford to play the role of 'consumption stabilizer' as in the central planning era through the provision of 'from-cradle-to-grave' care to their employees. In the absence of developed financial markets which enable consumers to hedge their income risks, the risks initiated by the regime shift are largely non-contractible. Without efficient DFA, neither can the macroeconomic policies be effectively implemented to manage aggregate risks. However, consumers have to use whatever means are available to hedge their risks even though these may be inefficient. That is why consumption has exhibited some countercyclical patterns since the mid-1980s. Subsequently a good part of the costs of the reform has fallen on consumers in the form of increasing consumption volatility. Therefore, consumption volatility has been rising both on its own and relative to income volatility.

How different is the China case compared with international experience? In Table 6.5 we present per capita GDP and consumption growth and volatility for Hungary, India, Malaysia, and Thailand. Instead of pooling together all developing countries with distinct policy regimes and levels of DFA development and international integration, we believe these country examples are more relevant to our discussion as they are more compatible with China.[7] The whole period covers the mid-1960s up to 2004, with 1990 used to divide it into pre- and post-reform or the (second) globalization period.

In absolute terms, based on the estimates in Table 6.5 and those of China in Table 6.4, China's income and consumption grew more rapidly than its counter-

Table 6.5 Output and consumption growth and volatility in selected countries: effect of change in policy regime (annual average growth rate and the period mean standard deviation in percent)

	Hungary		India		Malaysia		Thailand	
Period/ regime	Per capita GDP	Per capita FCE	Per capita GDP	Per capita FCE	Per capita GDP	Per capita FCE	Per capita GDP	Per capita FCE
Pre-globalization or/and -reform								
1965–1989	3.7 (2.8)	3.1 (2.3)	1.9 (3.4)	1.5 (2.4)	4.0 (3.0)	2.9 (4.5)	5.1 (2.6)	3.9 (2.3)
Globalization or/and reform								
1990–2004	1.6 (4.9)	1.8 (4.9)	3.8 (1.9)	3.1 (2.1)	3.9 (4.5)	3.7 (5.0)	3.8 (5.3)	3.6 (4.8)

Note: Annual average growth rates are calculated based on constant local currency data. Figures in parentheses are the mean standard deviations for the specified periods.

Source: Output (GDP) and final consumption expenditure (FCE) data are from the World Bank, *World Development Indicators* (2005).

parts in the Eastern bloc or in Asia. However, China experienced more volatility than those countries before the 1990s. Table 6.5 suggests that the globalization in the 1990s tended to reduce income and consumption growth but to enhance their volatility, except for India, whose income and consumption growth doubled while volatility declined (Malaysia experienced faster income growth in this period as well). Note also that during this period, China's income and consumption growth also slowed down, while becoming less volatile.

In relative terms, under central planning both Hungary and India had lower consumption volatility relative to income volatility (with a ratio of 0.71 and 0.82, respectively, based on Table 6.5; note that the ratio = 1 when no difference exists between the two volatilities) but not as low as what China experienced (0.57, based on Table 6.4). It is obvious that the market-oriented reform and the engagement in globalization since the 1990s have had more positive impacts on India than on Hungary. However, in both cases consumption is no longer less volatile than income (with the ratio being 1.00 and 1.10, respectively), indicating that market imperfections within the context of globalization may have left a significant part of consumption unhedged. But this is not the case of China whose ratio was still below 1.00 (0.88) during the 1990s.

Excess investment volatility and the role of government

To 'measure' the influence of government policy on growth and volatility, we should first distinguish government consumption expenditure (GCE) from household consumption expenditure (HCE) for the major policy regimes as we do in Table 6.4. The dynamics of these two consumption indicators is examined together with fixed capital formation (FCF) over the entire period under study in Figure 6.6.

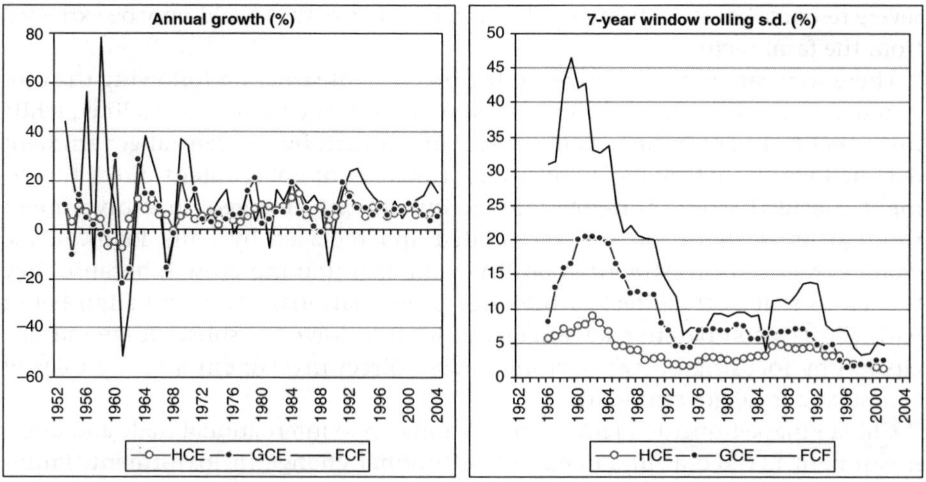

Figure 6.6 Growth and volatility of investment and government and household consumption expenditure in China, 1952–2004

If government spending policy aims to smooth consumption as in typical market economies, we expect the behavior of GCE to be countercyclical and the degree of its volatility to be close to HCE. This was not the case in China under central planning or until the mid-1980s.

Intuitively, as shown in the first panel of Figure 6.6, GCE and FCF exhibited strong co-movement up to the mid-1980s, and GCE remained more volatile than HCE until the mid-1990s as demonstrated in the second panel of the figure. This clearly suggests that the government only began to change the role inherited from the central planning system as a player in the economy to one as the regulator of the economy.

Under central planning, government consumption spending tends to facilitate the expansion of the bureaucracy designed to support the government's ambitious heavy industrialization. Therefore, government consumption spending is not likely to be countercyclical, as one would expect of a market economy. Instead, its movement would be associated with that of fixed capital investment. This, in essence, will aggravate output volatility, especially industrial output, rather than smooth consumption volatility. Indeed, China's extremely high industrial output volatility to a large extent 'duplicates' its investment volatility (see the second panel of Figure 6.6).

Under central planning, investment was completely controlled by the state and experienced radical fluctuations as illustrated in Figure 6.6. High investment was pursued to achieve high growth because it was politically justified. But it was not sustainable. As shown in Table 6.4, after the mid-1960s China's investment growth substantially slowed down before it speeded up again following the reform. However, the state investment plans were often erratically adjusted because of politically motivated production campaigns and their disastrous aftermaths and severe resource constraints imposed by limited savings that could only be extracted from the farm sector.

There were significant changes in the investment structure following the economic reform. Most importantly, investment in heavy industries declined while investment in light industries increased; investment by the central government declined while that by local government increased; government direct investment subsided while non-government investment emerged; and investment through fiscal allocation was terminated and replaced by bank loans. These changes reduced investment volatility while maintaining growth because they tended to reduce the effect of the error-prone national plans and align better with China's comparative advantage. In what follows, we substantiate our discussion by focusing on two factors: foreign direct investment and the roles of central and local governments.

China's market-oriented reform and opening up to international trade and direct investment marked a fundamental institutional change in investment. Profit-seeking private and foreign investment could not only serve as an increasingly important source of capital in addition to the state investment, but could also function as a buffer to the shocks brought on by government policies. Besides, international experience has shown that foreign direct investment is generally less volatile than portfolio investment (Prasad and Wei, 2005). In the case of China, on the one hand, foreign investors were granted preferential treatment that to a large extent insulated them from government intervention; on the other hand, compared with the state investment initiated by the politically motivated state planning authorities, foreign investment tends to engage in industries where China has a strong comparative advantage and, hence, is more competitive in the international market and more resilient to shocks. We would also postulate that such a buffer effect tends to become stronger as FDI accumulates to a certain level so that FDI-invested industries become less affected by the annual flows of FDI.

In Figure 6.7, we present both annual inflows and accumulated FDI in the past 20 years under Deng's open-door policy. Clearly, China has steadily built up its FDI stock since the early 1990s when China hastened its pace of international integration. From then on, annual inflows of FDI have fluctuated less and the FDI actually used has become more 'predictable' with reference to the contracted FDI. Note that this was exactly the time when both China's investment and output became less volatile.

The roles of government have always had an important bearing on growth and stability in China. Since central and local governments have different objective functions, our investigation should distinguish between the different roles played by the central and local governments in promoting growth and maintaining stability. This is not easy due to data problems. In the national accounts, GCE is an aggregate measure of government consumption expenditure at both the central and local administrative levels, while FCF is an aggregate measure of both private and public investment in fixed assets, including investment by both the central and local governments. In other words, GCE and FCF only capture the

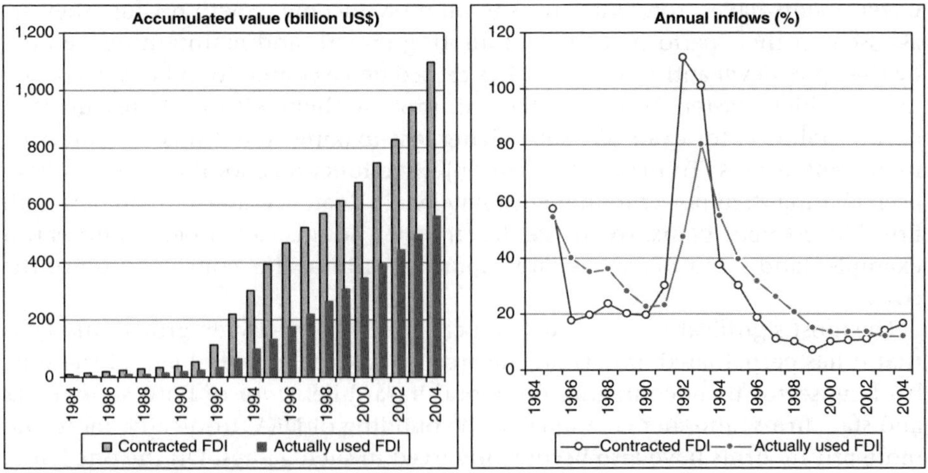

Figure 6.7 Annual inflows and accumulated FDI in China, 1984–2004
Source: NBS (2005).

'net effects' of components that may move in opposite directions over time. In the absence of the measure of these individual components, we have to rely on logical deduction to postulate their individual effects, *ceteris paribus*.

In essence, China's regional development under central planning was not in line with local comparative advantage and did not encourage specialization. Rather, it tended to mimic the structure of the national economy, that is, a heavy-industry-oriented, self-sufficient economy. We argue that the lack of the cushioning effect of local specialization would strengthen the co-movement of regional economies, thus amplifying the effect of policy shocks. The destabilizing effect of erratic changes in the central policies would be aggravated when localities with strong political incentives competed to implement the central plans and carry out these policies.

It is important to understand that the new post-reform fiscal arrangement was introduced in very different policy settings. More precisely, it took place together with the decollectivization of agriculture, the shift from a mandatory planning to a guided plan-market double-track system in industry, and the opening up to foreign trade and direct investment. This has nurtured strong local fiscal incentives in developing local economies – what is known as 'fiscal federalism' (Qian and Roland, 1998). Nevertheless, the effect of such federalism is growth-promoting but at the expense of national stability.

This fiscal reform has promoted regional growth because local governments have a better understanding of local resource endowment and, hence, local comparative advantages. Local governments also know better how to develop their local economies in an increasingly market-oriented setting subject to an exogenously given policy regime. In other words, if there had to be government intervention in business decision-making, local governments would make fewer mistakes than the central authorities. It should also be noted that local governments have strong incentives to promote income growth because they are assessed on their performance in promoting growth and maintaining stability by the upper-level authorities. This has caused fierce competition between localities to achieve faster growth as that will provide them with more resources to ensure stability, for example, subsidizing loss-making state firms or protecting inefficient sectors. To maximize their objective functions, local authorities have been abusing their power to influence state banks' loan decisions, to interfere with firms' investment plans, to charge illegal levies, to misuse public resources (for example, land), and to over-rebate exporters without due consideration of the costs.

The most significant cost of such a local-government-driven growth model is that it has perpetuated or even aggravated the governance problem of the state banking sector by encouraging the moral-hazard behavior of both state banks and state firms, and, hence, impeded the building of DFA. Ironically, more and more private firms have also become involved in such games. On the one hand, they are either tempted by easy bank loans or eager to break the tight constraint on obtaining permits from the authorities to expand their operations. On the other hand, the government is attracted by the better 'returns' that can be generated by offering the same scale of 'help' to these more efficient firms than to the state firms. This has added one more source of potential non-performing loans (NPLs) that weaken China's DFA. Subsequently, a high growth rate is perceived as the means to prevent further increase in NPLs. The real danger is that this may have driven the Chinese economy into a vicious circle.

The central authorities, then, face a big dilemma: if the game ends, everyone will lose but the central government will bear most of the costs; if the game is allowed to continue, then it will unduly delay the building of an efficient DFA. Nonetheless, the goal of income growth seems always to outweigh the concern for real financial risk arising from institutional problems. It appears that the Chinese government is betting on a race against an impending financial crisis with the belief that China is large enough to sustain a rapid, albeit inefficient growth, until such time when the institutional problems eventually dissipate. This mindset fuels the local governments' drive for 'excessive' growth that generates external costs of volatility for the whole nation. In such a game, there is no mechanism for automatic adjustment at the localities. As long as the central authorities did not apply the brakes, nothing could decelerate the growth unless there were big external shocks. Indeed, China's impressive accumulation of foreign exchange reserves indicates the government's fear of external shocks.

Trade volatility, changes in trade structure and terms of trade

Under central planning, the Chinese economy was basically closed. Trade policy merely served the needs of the heavy industrialization strategy that pursued import substitution. The limited trade transactions were highly controlled by a handful of state trading corporations according to the state trade plans as part of the national plan.[8] Therefore, China's pre-reform trade performance inevitably fluctuated whenever the national plans underwent erratic adjustments. As shown

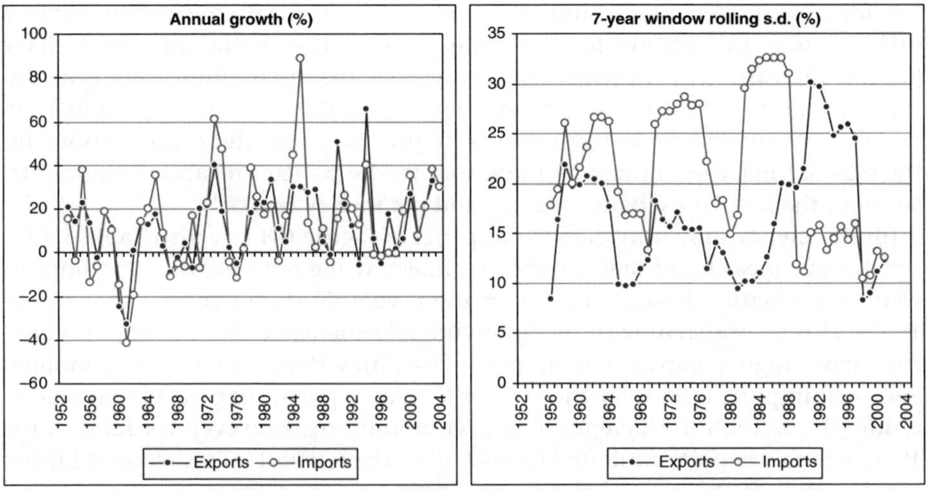

Figure 6.8 China's trade growth and volatility, 1952–2004
Source: See Table 6.1.

in the first panel of Figure 6.8, China experienced very frequent absolute falls in trade, that is, seven years in exports and 12 years in imports within 25 years. Coupled with limited primary products available for export and, hence, limited foreign exchange income to pay for imports, such a trade policy resulted in a small and declining share of trade in GDP. By the eve of economic reform, China's degree of openness (measured as the semi-sum of exports and imports over GDP) was only about 4 per cent, down from over 5 per cent in the early 1950s (Table 6.1).

China's post-reform rapid output growth has been accompanied by an even more rapid growth in exports of labor-intensive manufacturing products. Since the reform, the number of absolute falls in exports was only three and in imports it was six, all related to macroeconomic adjustment policies, with a much smaller magnitude compared with those in the central planning period. By 2004, China's degree of openness rose to 37 per cent. After 25 years of economic reform, China has emerged as a major trading power in the world. It appears that this achievement should be solely attributed to Deng's 'open-door' policy which has gradually deregulated and liberalized foreign trade and direct investment in China.

However, one should not ignore the role of government interventions in trade. Since exporting labor-intensive manufacturing products is the cheapest way for China to achieve growth and create jobs – another pressing problem facing the government – and to help maintain stability, various policy instruments have been adopted at all administrative levels to promote exports, including tax rebates, subsidies and preferential treatment for export-oriented foreign investors. There are differences in the behavior of the central and local governments. Local governments are only concerned about promoting exports even if it may cause negative externalities, such as over-rebating or various subsidies that may harm the financial system (Liew and Wu, 2007).[9] The central government plays a different role. In addition to supporting exports, the central authorities have become increasingly concerned, especially since the millennium, about the distortions that the continuously strong export growth and hence the rapid accumulation of foreign exchange reserves might cause and their implications for the existing macroeconomic regimes, that is, the policies regarding the capital account, the foreign exchange regime, and the money market.

Intuitively, as shown in the second panel of Figure 6.8 (see also Table 6.4 for the average measure of major policy regimes), while both exports and imports were very volatile, imports had been more volatile than exports prior to the 1990s. This is consistent with the international experience that developing countries have higher export and import volatilities than developed economies and their imports tend to be more volatile than exports, suggesting that macroeconomic fluctuations have more impact on imports. However, for most of the 1990s China's imports exhibited less volatility than exports. This requires further examination of the role of the central government in the context of foreign exchange policy.

During the central planning period, the RMB exchange rate was fixed and overvalued to tax exports and subsidize imports. Following the reform, a plan-market dual-exchange regime was adopted to promote exports. As the RMB market rate depreciated rapidly, making its gap with the official rate too large to manage, the government had to abandon the dual-track regime and unify the two rates at the market price at the beginning of 1994, which depreciated the RMB by 33 per cent.[10]

With a fear of further depreciation, the authorities tightened up the control over import growth (see the first panel of Figure 6.8) to reduce further depreciation pressure on the RMB, but promoted exports by every politically justifiable means. This is described officially as the principle of 'easy to get in, tough to get out' '*kuan jin yan chu*' for foreign exchange transactions (ACFB, 1995: 380–1). We argue that the tight control over imports was also due to the central authorities' being unprepared for large fluctuations in foreign exchange reserves in the absence of a healthy financial system. The Chinese government had good reason to anticipate the adverse impact on output volatility of 'sudden stops' of capital inflows, as found in empirical studies on international experiences (see Calvo and Reinhart, 1999).

Note that the authorities had only begun to consider adjusting this policy when China's foreign exchange reserves became too large to manage in the 2000s. In essence, it is not the US pressure that blamed China for deliberately undervaluing the RMB to support exports, but the huge foreign exchange reserves that had steadily accumulated in the past decade that made the Chinese government consider relaxing the control over imports in 2003 and allowing the RMB to be depegged from the US dollar with more flexibility in 2005.

Our next questions regarding China's increasing engagement in international trade and direct investment are about its impacts on China's trade structure and terms of trade (TOT) and their implications for China's macro volatility. Note that the literature on openness and volatility combines theoretical ambiguity with differing empirical findings (Wolf, 2004a). A higher degree of integration with the global economy will lead to greater sectoral specialization, as well as greater diversification across demand sources (Razin and Rose, 1994; Kose et al., 2006). International experiences suggest that developing countries tend to have greater output volatility because they focus mainly on the exports of primary products. In the case of China, in addition to government intervention, what also matters is the sheer size of the country, especially when it becomes one of the major players in international trade and direct investment.

Realizing its comparative advantage, China's increasing participation in international trade will suppress world prices of manufactured products. Meanwhile, its subsequent growth will increase its demand for and drive up the world prices of input materials, such as minerals and energy. This means that once China becomes one of the major players in international trade, it will no longer face an exogenous TOT. Rather, it may drive itself into a self-inflicted, deteriorating TOT trap. This is inevitable because it is almost impossible for China to quickly shift to capital-intensive, high value-added exports. Since a deteriorating TOT will have important implications for the welfare of Chinese workers, it will invite more government intervention.

As depicted in the first panel of Figure 6.9, the share of primary exports, including minerals and farm output, in China's total exports experienced a dramatic drop from about 60 per cent on the eve of the reform to below 10 per cent in the 2000s. This occurred when the economy underwent significant restructuring in alignment with China's comparative advantage. Supported by continuous inflows of FDI, China's exports experienced a quick shift to labor-intensive manufacturing goods including processing export. However, as we have postulated,

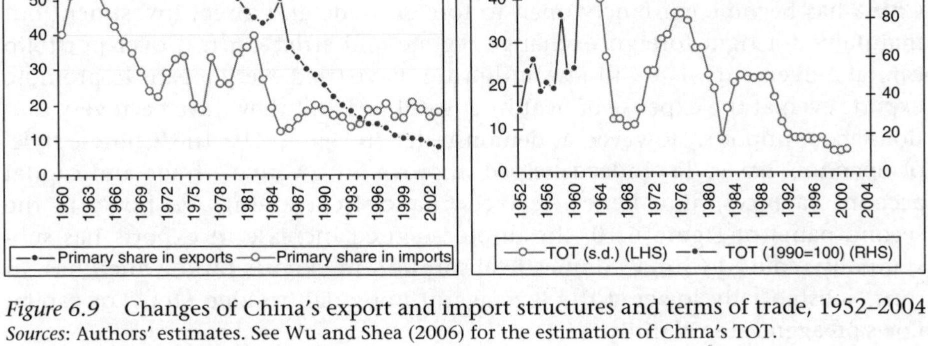

Figure 6.9 Changes of China's export and import structures and terms of trade, 1952–2004
Sources: Authors' estimates. See Wu and Shea (2006) for the estimation of China's TOT.

this was generally accompanied by a deteriorating TOT. As shown in the second panel of Figure 6.9, the oil crisis in the early 1970s marked a 'turning point' in China's TOT. Before the crisis China's TOT had generally followed a rising path. China benefited from the rising prices of primary exports, which apparently supported China's imports. However, in most of the post-reform period, China's TOT worked against the country's interests, except for a short period between 1994–97. Considering that the primary share in China's imports began to rise again from the 1990s, the decline of its TOT since the late 1990s may to a large extent reflect the influence of China as a major trading power on the world prices of both manufacturing and primary goods.

Following our argument, if China's export performance is crucial to GDP growth, the government will promote exports regardless of their costs, including those incurred due to deteriorating TOT. This is particularly true of politically motivated local governments because, as was discussed, they could externalize some of the costs of the inefficient promotion of exports. It follows logically that changes in exports would not be sensitive to changes in TOT in China. However, China's imports would still be positively related to changes in TOT because importers would eventually face a hard budget constraint imposed by export revenues. Our simple regression exercise strongly supports our argument. In the exercise, we regress the percentage change in China's real exports and imports on the percentage change in the TOT. We find that China's imports are very sensitive to the change in TOT. But we cannot reject the null hypothesis that the TOT have no effect on China's exports.[11]

We have noted that exports remained highly volatile until the 2000s despite the fall in TOT volatility from the early 1990s, followed by the decline in import volatility (Figure 6.8). It may be argued that China's high export volatility was largely due to the sectoral specialization effect of international integration. Although China has now become much less dependent on primary exports, it has relied increasingly on labor-intensive manufacturing exports that are highly competitive and, hence, subject to volatile price fluctuations. This may be another important reason for local governments to provide strong support to exports.

It is obvious that the effect of China's openness on aggregate volatility should be understood with China's unique way of integrating with the world market. China has become extremely open to foreign trade and direct investment but maintained a rigid foreign exchange regime and strict control over portfolio capital movements. The Chinese authorities have tried every means to promote exports even at the expense of healthy institutions, but they have been very cautious about imports. However, as demonstrated in Figure 6.10, the 'Chinese style' of openness has so far indeed helped improve both China's trade and capital account balances, and, hence, relaxed financial constraint. As shown in the second panel of Figure 6.10, the unprecedented increase in exports has substantially reduced China's domestic absorption to exports ratio, which has, in turn, substantially lowered the leverage of potential 'sudden stops' of capital flows on aggregate volatility.

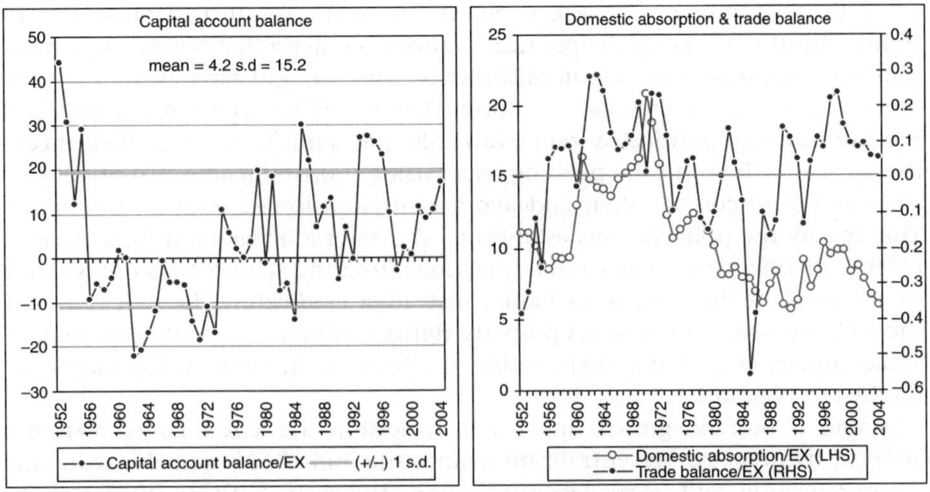

Figure 6.10 China's domestic absorption versus capital and trade account balances, 1952–2004
Source: See Tables 6.1.

In sum, it is clear that the key factor behind China's idiosyncratic structural problems is the role of government, including both central and local authorities, which often play different roles in achieving growth and maintaining stability, but are both politically and economically vital. After all, the 'China miracle' is not an archetypal market fairytale but a story of how the government has successfully manipulated various policy instruments to make the market serve its best interests, though it sometimes abuses its administrative power and, apparently, never abides by 'reform instructions' from the West.

6.4 The political economy of China's DFA-building and concluding remarks

Our discussions in Section 6.3 show that the government intervention through administrative measures has so far successfully kept China's macro volatility under control in its economic transition. However, we believe that such measures to contain macro volatility are the very obstacles to building healthy institutions because they perpetuate the problems of soft budget constraint and poor corporate governance of the state firms and state banks, which are the fundamental weaknesses of China's DFA. Three major problems found in China's reform model might have amplified the macro volatility had there not been constant interventions to suppress this symptom of the weak DFA.

First, the building of institutions to facilitate market creation has not kept pace with market liberalization. One reason is that private property is not something to be promoted under the socialist ideology. Therefore, the creation and strengthening of institutions for safeguarding the security of private property and contract-based market transactions had received little attention until the late 1990s, when the impending WTO accession weakened the socialist ideological constraint. Another reason is the political evaluation criteria that reward short-term results in administrative accomplishments, which might have made the time horizon of China's policymakers shorter than would be expected of officials in the authoritarian political system (Shih, 2004). It tends to enhance their incentive to deal with politically pressing issues using short-term administrative measures and to discourage their endeavors to attempt longer-term DFA-building. That is why the policymakers established the Asset Management Corporations (AMCs) in 1999 with huge capital injections from the state coffers to take over the NPLs of the 'big four' state banks, instead of eradicating the root causes of the NPL problem – ambiguous property rights and poor corporate governance. Some studies (Ma, 2006) suggest that the bail-out through AMCs may have resulted in even more new NPLs.

Second, to promote growth under state ownership, the central government has adopted two types of decentralization since the mid-1980s, namely, economic decentralization and fiscal decentralization. However, both of them tend to amplify macro volatility under weak DFA. The economic decentralization adopted in the SOE reform, which aimed to improve the incentives of managers by granting them more autonomy in decision-making and allowing them to share the profits, ended up enabling the state firms to 'privatize their profits' and 'socialize their losses' (Zhang, 1999: 235; Yi, 2004: 184; Liew et al., 2005). Without hardening the budget constraint and increasing managers' accountability for the losses of mismanagement, this decentralization measure encouraged them to pursue higher rates of return by taking more risks and passing them on to the state.

The fiscal decentralization aimed to reduce the administrative and fiscal burden on the central government and to encourage local governments to promote growth in their localities. The emergence of China's modern banking system in the mid-1980s was to facilitate the fiscal decentralization. Since then, the responsibility of providing investment funds and working capital for state firms has been transferred from the MOF to the 'big four' state banks. This decentralization has resulted in the interlocked interests of local governments and state firms and state banks in their jurisdiction, which has become a major source of volatility in the reform period.[12] As was discussed in Section 6.3, fierce competition between localities to promote growth has impeded the building of DFA. In particular, the interlocked interests of local governments, state firms and state banks have turned the state banks into a channel for transmitting risks created in the state sector to the rest of the economy.[13]

Third, to promote growth and safeguard its increasingly open economy from external shocks, as was mentioned in Section 6.3, China has adopted fiscal policies to promote exports and attract FDI, and maintained a closed capital account and a rigid exchange rate of RMB. Although these interventionist policies appear to have achieved the intended outcome of stable growth, we argue that they have distorted resource allocation and hindered the strengthening of China's financial institutions. While the closed capital account shielded China from potentially catastrophic portfolio capital movements during the 1997 Asian financial crisis, the pegged exchange rate adopted since 1994 has compromised the independence of China's monetary policy. The accumulation of foreign exchange reserves in the 2000s due to continuous trade surpluses and FDI inflows has led to a substantial expansion in the money supply. The subsequent sterilization policy to halt overheating the economy distorts resource allocation in favor of the exporting firms, which have an ample supply of foreign exchange and are beneficiaries of other trade-stabilizing interventions.[14] The increasingly export-oriented economy of China may lead to greater exposure to sectoral shocks.

As long as the Chinese government can maintain growth and stability by means of administrative interventions, DFA-building may not appear to be a pressing issue. In China's path-dependent incremental reform, the turning of the existing direction would need external force (Wu, 2005). This external force emerged in the late 1990s when a closer IFA-DFA linkage was forged in China's preparation for its accession to the WTO.

The potential benefits that China would reap from WTO accession made the political leaders willing to bear the costs of subjecting their policymaking to the constraints imposed by the IFA. For the development of China's DFA, the closer link with the IFA may be a mixed blessing. On the one hand, the various agreements made in the WTO protocol have altered the political power of various interest groups within the government and loosened the constraints on further DFA reform. The closer IFA-DFA link may constitute a strong enough counterforce to eventually break the vicious cycle of 'government intervention–weak DFA–government intervention' as described by our first three central hypotheses. While the time horizon of China's policymakers may not have lengthened, the greater influence of international institutions has made the structural reforms of the banking sector and capital markets possible. On the other hand, the flaws in the current IFA that allows disruptive capital flows in and out of emerging markets may be a hindrance to a smooth integration of the Chinese economy with that of the world.

A closer IFA-DFA linkage has created positive impacts on China's DFA in two ways. First, the threat posted by the scheduled opening up of China's financial sector according to the WTO protocol has speeded up the building of institutions to facilitate market creation. Since its establishment in 2003, the China Banking Regulatory Commission has been pushing for the stringent enforcement of international standards and codes regarding the accounting system, the budget system, internal controls, and so on, to facilitate specific risk controls and overcome the problem of asymmetric information.[15] Since the mid-2000s, the China Securities Regulatory Commission has taken steps to resolve the deficient supervision over listed companies and brokerages to protect creditors and minority shareholders from excessive risks. The legal and judicial systems have also been rectified to better monitor these regulatory authorities. All these changes are necessary for strengthening the prudential supervision to contain the risks created in the state sector and transmitted to the rest of the economy.

Second, the looming threat of increasing foreign competition in the domestic financial market, especially upon expiry of the five-year grace period after WTO accession in December 2001, has weakened the socialist ideological constraint that obstructed the eradication of ambiguous property rights. This constraint, which caused incomplete flotation of listed SOEs, was one of the major reasons for the sluggish development of China's stock market until around 2005.[16] The resulting split-share system, whereby two-thirds of the shares are non-tradable and held by holding companies on behalf of the state, has not only allowed ambiguous property rights to persist but also bred the problem of unchecked insider control (OECD, 2002; Wu, 2005). To eradicate these root causes of poor corporate governance, the government made its third and final attempt to float the non-tradable state shares in mid-2005 with complementary measures to prevent undue volatility in the share prices experienced previously.

In the banking sector, the weakened ideological constraint has enabled China's policymakers to improve the corporate governance of state banks through diversified ownership. Since around 2005 the state banks have been encouraged to pair up with foreign financial institutions as strategic shareholders to improve their efficiency and management accountability. In 2005 and 2006, three of the 'big four' state banks were listed on overseas stock exchanges, subjecting them to the stringent disclosure requirements for IPO. Coupled with greater participation of domestic and foreign institutional investors in the stock market following the development of an insurance industry and the launch of the qualified foreign institutional investors (QFII) scheme, these changes will help improve the corporate governance of the shareholding companies in China.

While the closer IFA-DFA linkage has benefited the institution-building of China's financial markets, the potentially destabilizing portfolio capital movements found in the IFA may have impeded the evolution of China's exchange rate system, as indicated in the last of our central hypotheses. The traumatic experience of neighboring countries in the Asian financial crisis has prompted the Chinese government to prevent at all costs disruptive capital flows that might come with convertibility on the capital account (Peng, 2003: 398). Given the prevailing weaknesses in its DFA, especially the infancy of its forward markets, the Chinese economy is too vulnerable to the financial contagion associated with investor behavior known as 'herding' or 'momentum trading', despite its admirable foreign exchange reserves position.

Despite the pressure exerted by China's trade partners for adopting a more flexible exchange rate system, the government has been extremely cautious about liberalizing the exchange rate of RMB, which may prolong the problem with its passive monetary policy. Some researchers allege that allowing more flexibility in the exchange rate while maintaining capital controls is a feasible way to overcome the 'fear of floating' and prepare the Chinese economy for eventual full convertibility (Prasad et al., 2005). That may explain the incremental approach which China utilized in replacing the pegged exchange rate system with a managed floating system for RMB on 21 July 2005.

The uniqueness of China's incremental reform model makes it inappropriate to evaluate its economic performance using the criteria adopted for other countries. While its impressive economic growth may be beyond doubt, the apparent absence of excessive volatility in most of the post-reform period might be misleading. We believe our findings in Section 6.3 show a disguised picture of China's macro volatility after the government has suppressed it with administrative interventions. Nevertheless, our investigation of the China case substantiates the main hypothesis of the project. That is, there is a bi-directional relationship between institutions and volatility. In the process of building DFA from scratch in China, an increase in volatility leads to tighter government control, which, in turn, impedes institution-building. The resulting persistence of weak DFA and poor risk management causes higher volatility, which then invites more government intervention. Although the closer IFA-DFA linkage forged by China's accession to WTO may have weakened the government's influence on DFA-building, it is still too early to accurately assess the implications for the bi-directional relationship between institutions and volatility.

Notes

1. See comments on this problem by Maddison and his alternative approach (Maddison, 1998).
2. See Wu and Shea (2006) for details of the data work behind Tables 6.1 and 6.2.
3. The 'big four' specialized state banks include the Agricultural Bank of China, specializing in the agricultural and rural sector; the Industrial and Commercial Bank of China, specializing in the industrial and urban sector; the People's Construction Bank of China, specializing in public projects; and the Bank of China, specializing in the external trade sector.
4. This follows the exercise conducted in the Argentine case (see Chapter 9).
5. Figures on gross domestic expenditure growth and volatility in Table 6.4 differ from those of Tables 6.1 and 6.2, which are estimated on per capita bases.
6. For example, the average annual growth rate of GCF in eight former Eastern bloc transition economies in 1991–2004 was 6.6 per cent (*World Development Indicators*, 2005), compared with 12.4 per cent in China (Table 6.4).
7. Hungary was one of the Eastern bloc countries, while India also practiced the Soviet-style central planning system prior to the 1990s. As for Malaysia and Thailand, they are in the same region as China and currently compete with China in the world manufacturing market.
8. See Liew and Wu (2007: Chapter 3) for details of trade policy under central planning.
9. By estimating an export function for China for the period 1986–2004, Liew and Wu (2007) found that export subsidies, using official measures of tax rebate as a proxy with one-period lag, played the most important role in explaining China's export performance. They also found that China's exports do not really respond to the change in the world demand for exports using the world GDP as a proxy.
10. See Liew and Wu (2007) for details of the making of the Chinese foreign exchange policy.
11. We use annual percentage change of the 1990 constant-price value of exports (dEX) and imports (dIM) over the period 1953–2004. In both the export and import models we also include a policy dummy variable (D) that distinguishes the period from 1984 from the rest to capture the effect of China's industrial reform that encouraged local governments to influence local industrial development in the best of their fiscal interests. The estimated export model is $dEX = 8.9998 - 0.0599dToT + 15.3365D$, with $t = -1.133$ for $dToT$, $t = 4.197$ for D, the adjusted R-squared = 0.264, DW = 1.722; and the estimated import model is $dIM = 10.2695 + 0.4956dToT + 12.8829D$, with $t = 4.876$ for $dToT$, $t = 1.834$ for D, the adjusted R-squared = 0.314 and DW = 1.759.

12. The fiscal decentralization and the resulting accommodative credit policy have been widely acknowledged by Chinese and Western scholars as the cause of the boom–bust cycles in post-reform China (Lou, 1997; Yu, 1997; Brandt and Zhu, 2000; Feltenstein and Iwata, 2005).
13. See Wu and Shea (2006) for details of the transmission mechanism.
14. See Liew and Wu (2007) for details of trade-stabilizing interventions; see Ba (1999), Tao (1998) and Yi and Min (1997) for details of the sterilization process.
15. The problem of asymmetric information is identified by Mishkin (2000: 515) as the reason for securities markets to play a much smaller role than banks in developing and transition economies.
16. See Wu and Shea (2006) for a more detailed discussion of China's stock market problems.

7
Thailand

Piriya Pholphirul and Pakorn Vichyanond

7.1 Introduction

Over the course of several decades, the Thai economy grew at a very satisfactory rate. Between 1960 and 1995, the average real GDP growth rate was about 7.7 per cent per annum. This led to substantial improvements in the welfare of the Thai population. Especially in the early 1990s, the country's economic performance was regarded as an example of the so-called 'East Asian Economic Miracle' (World Bank, 1993). Yet, just a few years after this categorization, the country experienced a severe financial and economic crisis. Key elements of the 1997 crisis reflected Thailand's cumulative balance of payments problems, particularly persistently large current account deficits. Since public debts surged significantly, the country became effectively insolvent in that there were not enough usable foreign reserves left to meet foreign obligations. Assistance from the International Monetary Fund (IMF) was therefore needed, and a painful adjustment process to recover from the crisis had to be carried out.

This chapter examines Thailand's experience based on the hypothesis motivating this project: '*There is a bi-directional causality between volatility and institutions: high volatility and crises contribute to deteriorating the rules of the financial game; weak institutions reduce financial deepening and the ability to manage risks and this feeds aggregate volatility.*' We will explain the causes of various financial crises in Thailand by examining situations that comply with the hypothesis. The deficiencies and weaknesses of financial institutions indicate that the financial market failures in Thailand between 1979 and 1997 were largely due to imprudent regulation, poor corporate governance, immature domestic financial architecture (DFA), and inconsistent macroeconomic policy. Exogenous shocks and macroeconomic volatility also played a role in sparking the crises. These crisis events then caused the country's performance to deteriorate overall.

This chapter is organized into four sections. Section 7.2 analyzes the structural patterns and aggregate volatility of the Thai economy, particularly shocks to output, consumption, and investment over the periods since 1970. It shows that Thailand could successfully maintain economic stability under stabilization policies in the periods before the 1990s. However, it clearly finds that the 1997 financial crisis increased the country's aggregate volatility. Section 7.3 identifies the main sources of shocks, both domestic and external, but with emphasis on external sources, such as the volatility of trade and capital flows. We also explain the positive correlation between the Thai economy and the global economy and analyze the country's diversified economic structure. Section 7.4 characterizes Thailand's domestic financial architecture and shows that financial crises in the periods prior to the 1990s came mainly from a deficiently-designed and weak financial structure. Section 7.5 examines the 1997 financial crisis and illustrates the bi-directional causal relationship between volatility and financial institutions. The changes in the rules of the game regarding the implementation of financial liberalization in the early 1990s show the existence of the linkages between the international financial architecture (IFA) and domestic financial architecture (DFA). It also examines the evidence that the 1997 crisis originated in deficient institution-building, imprudent regulation, and an inconsistent currency exchange rate regime, all of which could cause economic turmoil. Section 7.6 concludes and emphasizes the implications of DFA in the future.

7.2 Structural patterns and aggregate volatility

Notwithstanding the 1997 crisis, we can observe how well the Thai economy performed in the past if focus is given to various macroeconomic indicators, for example, the real growth of national income, inflation or changes in price levels, and rates of employment. Nonetheless, despite a history of high and steady growth, periods of instability did occur, as in other countries, and Thailand experienced several economic shocks. Since macroeconomic variables show how well the country could adjust itself to those shocks, a number of questions might be addressed: first, how could the Thai economy perform adequately during the period 1970–89 even though a number of external shocks affected the country's current account? Second, what were the main causes of the shocks from 1990 that finally led to such turbulence in financial markets and the severe crises toward the end of the 1990s?

Long-run patterns of the Thai economy

The main goal of this section is to analyze the aspects of the Thai experience of macroeconomic volatility. First of all, we can divide Thailand's economic experience during a period of three decades (1970–present) into four sub-periods as follows.

Sub-period I: 1970–85

The decade of high growth and satisfactory stability in both the global and the Thai economies from 1960 to 1969 came to an end in the early 1970s, starting with the changes in the international monetary system after the collapse of the Bretton Woods system. Thailand chose to peg its currency to the US dollar, which thereafter proved to be a costly decision when the US dollar appreciated against other major currencies during the period 1978–85. The Thai baht therefore appreciated, which caused the country to lose its competitiveness.

Other serious economic problems during this sub-period were two oil crises. In 1973, the Organization of the Petroleum Exporting Countries (OPEC) triggered the first oil crisis, which resulted in a fourfold increase in the price of oil internationally. The first oil price shock did not damage Thailand's current account position immediately because the export price of the country's primary products rose during that period, which mitigated the adverse effects of the oil shock.[1] After three years of recovery during the period 1976–78, the global economy was ensnared by a second oil shock. This time, Thailand faced real difficulties when that oil crisis hit in the period 1979–80, that is, with mounting budget deficits and government debts.

Sub-period II: 1986–90

After more than half a decade of economic difficulties and strenuous management of macroeconomic policy, Thailand had from 1986 entered an era of historic economic prosperity. Several factors underlay the impressive economic performance during the second half of the 1980s. First, a global economic change took place that had a tremendous impact on Thailand's economic structure. Based on the Plaza Accord of 1985, Japan, Hong Kong, Taiwan, and Singapore adjusted the value of their currencies upward. With cost-effective production, large inflows of foreign direct investment from those countries flooded into Thailand at an unprecedented rate from 1987, facilitating a boom, especially in the manufacturing sector. Second, along with the major currency realignments from 1986 there had been a sharp decline in oil prices, which also greatly benefited Thai exports. Third, the political system was relatively stable during the period 1980–88, which encouraged steady economic growth. The stable system further enhanced the positive atmosphere, thus facilitating private investment. The second half of the 1980s into the 1990s was therefore a prosperous time for the Thai economy; the average growth rate during this period was 10 per cent annually.

Sub-period III: 1991–96

Consequent to the rapid growth of the economy, speculation in real estate and financial securities, especially in the stock market, took place at an alarming rate. Both domestic and international investors rushed in without proper risk analysis; they were supported by overly optimistic views of the financial institutions that provided credits to financially-constrained firms. During this period, several drastic changes occurred in Thailand's financial arena. One of the major factors affecting the Thai economy was the financial liberalization that took place during the first half of the 1990s. In the early 1990s, total private inflows were about 20 times the level of the mid-1980s. We can conclusively identify the first half of the 1990s as a period of capital shock, when an excessive amount of capital inflow nullified the effectiveness of monetary and exchange rate policies.

Sub-period IV: 1997-present

In mid-1997, Thailand experienced a crisis that included insufficient international reserves, the instability of the Thai baht, weakness in the financial system, high levels of non-performing loans (NPLs), high inflation, liquidity shortage, large capital outflows, a dramatic contraction of GDP, and a very high unemployment rate. The financial crisis brought an abrupt halt to Thailand's decade of rapid economic growth. The economic growth rate became negative for the first time ever (the GDP growth rate was –1.4 per cent in 1997 and –10.5 per cent in 1998).

Aggregate volatility, growth, and persistence

In terms of output growth volatility, measured by the standard deviation of variable growth rates, Thailand is considered a relatively stable economy among the emerging economies, with a growth volatility of about 0.044, which is, however, higher than that of some developed countries: for example, Japan (0.027), Australia (0.018), and the United States (0.022).[2] Nevertheless, if we focus on the period 1970–80, Thailand's output is less volatile that that of Japan and about the same level as that of the US. Table 7.1 offers an international comparison of mean output volatility.

The standard deviation of total consumption growth, investment growth, and income growth determines the aggregate volatility of each variable. The definition of a complete-market approach is imposed here to predict the relationship between consumption and income volatility. The model assesses excess volatility in terms of the agents' hedge to mitigate consumption risk. Household consumption should be lower than income volatility in order to interpret the financial market's ability to generate consumption-smoothing behavior. Accordingly, non-smoothing consumption is the result of imperfections in market structures and institutions. From the computation, since consumption was less volatile than output, this shows that Thailand could successfully maintain its consumption-smoothing behavior indicating no signal of failure in the financial market.

Table 7.1 International comparison of mean output volatility

Countries	1970–2002	1970–80	1981–90	1991–2002
Thailand	0.044	0.029	0.033	0.057
Selected OECD countries				
Japan	0.027	0.032	0.013	0.014
Australia	0.018	0.015	0.026	0.013
United States	0.022	0.027	0.024	0.016
Selected ASEAN countries and China				
Malaysia	0.040	0.030	0.035	0.052
Singapore	0.040	0.031	0.040	0.045
Indonesia	0.041	0.012	0.026	0.060
Philippines	0.035	0.017	0.050	0.024

Source: Authors' calculation. Data collected from World Development Indicators, various years.

However, the conclusion might be changed if the standard deviation of investment is measured; it is found to be much more volatile than that of output growth. The investment share was found to be quite stable at about 0.293 (29.3 per cent of GDP) during the period 1980–85. In the boom decade (1986–96), the ratio increased substantially from 0.264 (26.4 per cent of GDP) in 1986 to a high of 0.425 (42.5 per cent) in 1996. As was mentioned previously, the early stages of the post-1985 boom were driven by the relocation of manufacturers from Japan, Hong Kong, and Taiwan to Thailand. At the beginning of 1990, the increase in investment share was followed mainly by the aforementioned asset price bubble and speculation. When the bubble burst, banks faced difficulties as borrowers began to default. NPLs rose rapidly as a result of a sharp decline in investment to 0.213 (21.3 per cent of GDP) in 1998, reaching the low of 0.197 (19.7 per cent of GDP) in 1999.[3] (See Table 7.2 for an international comparison of aggregate volatility.)

Table 7.2 International comparison of aggregate volatility

		Selected OECD countries			**Selected ASEAN countries**			
Periods	**Thailand**	**Japan**	**Australia**	**US**	**Malaysia**	**Singapore**	**Indonesia**	**Philippines**
Consumption								
1970–80	0.020	0.029	0.014	0.023	0.039	0.029	0.062	0.009
1981–90	0.041	0.013	0.016	0.016	0.069	0.039	0.126	0.024
1991–2002	0.056	0.010	0.011	0.013	0.060	0.050	0.051	0.008
1970–2002	0.042	0.024	0.014	0.017	0.056	0.040	0.082	0.016
Investment								
1970–80	0.141	0.077	0.242	0.104	0.162	0.131	0.069	0.091
1981–90	0.139	0.046	0.195	0.104	0.156	0.103	0.075	0.192
1991–2002	0.189	0.039	0.111	0.069	0.202	0.144	0.169	0.110
1970–2002	0.161	0.060	0.178	0.090	0.174	0.130	0.138	0.134
Government expenditure								
1970–80	0.062	0.032	0.024	0.015	0.066	0.069	0.111	0.047
1981–90	0.046	0.013	0.018	0.014	0.052	0.083	0.042	0.067
1991–2002	0.036	0.011	0.012	0.018	0.073	0.063	0.069	0.041
1970–2002	0.052	0.023	0.019	0.017	0.068	0.070	0.092	0.056
National income								
1970–80	0.029	0.032	0.015	0.027	0.030	0.031	0.012	0.017
1981–90	0.033	0.013	0.026	0.024	0.035	0.040	0.026	0.050
1991–2002	0.057	0.014	0.013	0.016	0.052	0.045	0.060	0.024
1970–2002	0.044	0.027	0.018	0.022	0.040	0.040	0.041	0.035

Source: Authors' calculation. Data collected from World Development Indicators, various years.

Figure 7.1 illustrates the evolution of the nine-year rolling variance of GDP growth, variance of consumption growth, variance of investment growth, and variance in saving (GDP minus consumption) growth. It predicts a clear consumption-smoothing pattern of the Thai economy during the pre-1997 crisis period. However, there was a substantial increase in the variance of all aggregate variables during the crisis events. Output volatility surged as well as consumption volatility, while the volatility of investment growth increased remarkably due to the collapse of investment share. Even though we explain consumption smoothing in the pre-crisis period, the quality of the countercyclical policies attributed to smoothing consumption deteriorated during the crisis, thus consumption became more volatile.

Since the variance of saving did not change much after the crisis, it therefore implied that the smoothing of saving rather than the smoothing of consumption was privileged in the post-crisis period. Given that saving equals investment plus the trade account (exports minus imports) and investment volatility was much higher after the crisis, the smoothing of saving reflects a negative correlation between investment and the trade account. In other words, the role of shock absorber played by consumption was replaced by net exports. This fact might indicate that the fall in the availability of foreign funds constrained investment and forced the country to run trade surpluses during the crisis periods.[4]

To confirm the above conclusions about excessive investment volumes, aggregate variables can be extracted to identify the degree of persistence. The simplest model posits the generalized autoregressive conditional heteroskedastic (GARCH)

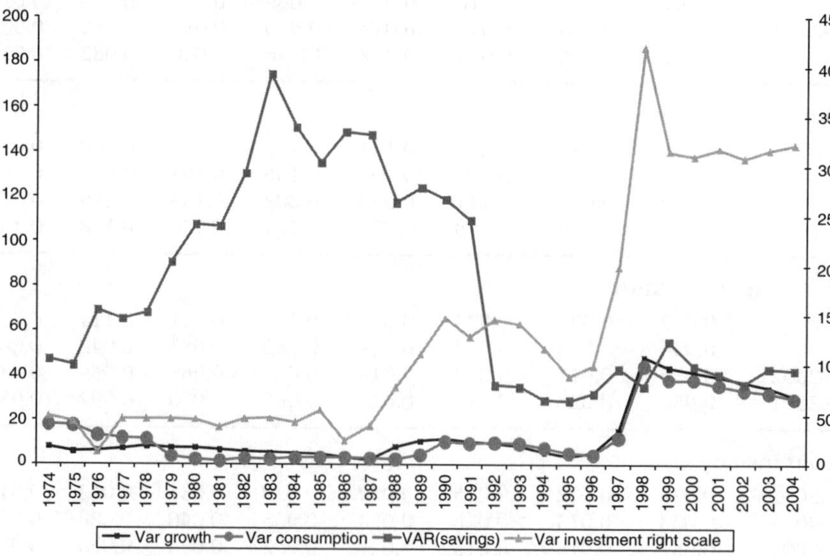

Figure 7.1 Nine-year rolling variance of GDP growth, consumption growth, investment growth, and saving
Source: International Financial Statistics, IMF.

model for examining a number of variants in the basic model for conditional volatility (see Table 7.3). Excess volatility can be measured if the aggregate variables, displaying a high degree of persistence when the model would define the changes in volatility, are caused by time-varying values of the standard deviation of the term of shocks. Using quarterly data from the second half of 1993 to the first half of 2005, we estimate the GARCH-M process to allow the mean of a variable to depend on its own conditional variance. The estimated results confirm that volatilities are found to negatively affect the growth of the following aggregate variables: output, consumption, and investment. The estimated equations of output growth, consumption growth, and investment growth are significant at conventional levels, and the estimated values of the autoregressive coefficients imply stationary condition and convergence. By observing the estimated coefficients that are all significant, the coefficient of conditional variance of investment growth is –1.327, while those of output and investment are –0.454 and –0.881, respectively. Intuitively, Thailand's investment growth is determined more significantly by its volatility than by the other aggregate variables: consumption and output.[5]

Since the crisis induced permanent changes in domestic absorption (as a ratio of GDP), the level of trade openness, the country's ability to run trade surpluses, and limited access to foreign funds caused the capital account/exports ratio to fall substantially from 1997, and it has never recovered its pre-financial liberalization level. This result is paradoxical in that Thailand opened its capital account to improve access to external finance, but the ultimate result was just the opposite, and this occurred despite the fact that the economy is currently more open to trade. This suggests that failures in institution-building and the crisis can have long-lasting effects on financial development (see Figure 7.2).

Table 7.3 Generalized autoregressive conditional heteroskedasticity (GARCH) process of aggregate volatility

Variables	**Output**	**Consumption**	**Investment**
Constant	0.015***	0.024***	0.118***
(*t-statistic*)	*–5.09*	*–3.78*	*–4.49*
Conditional variance	–0.454**	–0.881*	–1.327***
(*t-statistic*)	(*–1.99*)	*–1.72*	(*–2.73*)
AR(1)	0.356**	0.361***	0.323**
(*t-statistic*)	(*–2.15*)	(*–3.09*)	(*–2.51*)
MA(4)	0.363**	0.341***	0.28**
(*t-statistic*)	(*–2.33*)	*–4.59*	*–2.37*
Prob. F-statistics	0.10	0.12	0.19
Observations	48	48	48

Note: *** 0.01; ** 0.05; * 0.1 significance levels.
Source: Authors' calculation.

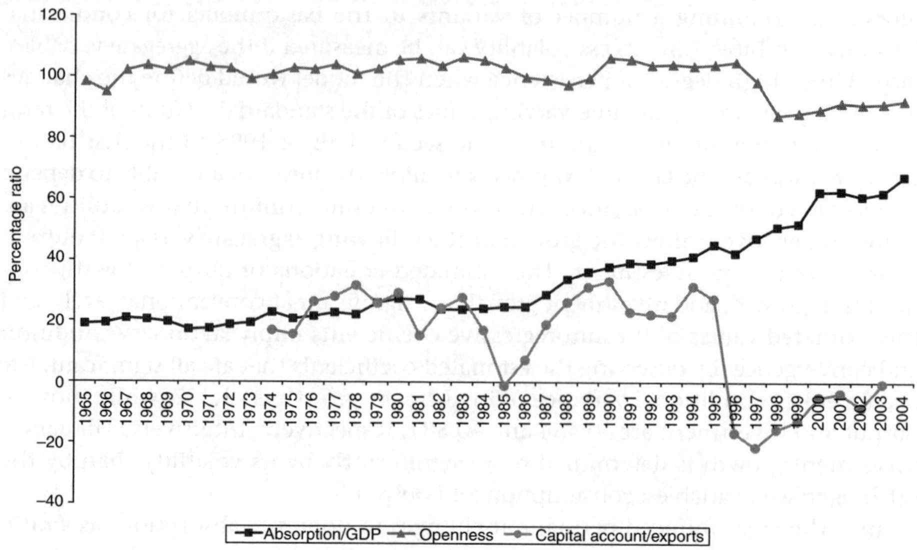

Figure 7.2 Domestic absorption, openness ratio, and capital account/exports
Source: International Financial Statistics, IMF.

In conclusion, Thailand had to cope with a number of international scenarios, for example, the Plaza Accord in 1985 that benefited the country's economic well-being with a tremendous change in its economic structure. The consequent influx of foreign investment and new technology into Thailand helped the country to achieve a double-digit economic growth rate during the late 1980s. However, until the beginning of the 1990s, a series of liberalization measures were taken, resulting in much less control over the flow of foreign currencies into the country, which caused asset speculation and excessive investment in Thailand. During that period prior to 1997, investment volatility surged remarkably. Nonetheless, there have been substantial changes in volatility since the crisis. Investment fell substantially due to firms' financial constraints. Both output volatility and consumption volatility increased; the explosion of aggregate volatility during the crisis therefore indicates the presence of a severe economic crisis.

7.3 Shocks, external volatility, and diversified structure

Thailand is considered a small open economy in which economic fluctuation came mainly from external factors such as oil-price shocks, global recession, a boom in agricultural prices, and so on. Among other factors explained in Section 7.2, even though there were a number of external shocks, the country could successfully maintain its stability during the period 1970–90. The structural features of the Thai economy will be discussed, as they form an understanding of shocks, macroeconomic policies, and the country's diversified structure. The linkages between these variables help to answer the questions addressed previously. Two factors explain why the country could maintain its economic stability from 1970 to 1990, which were (i) its stabilization and adjustment policies, and (ii) its diversified economic structure.

Relationship between Thailand and the global economy

First of all, to observe the relationship between Thailand and the global economy, the correlation coefficients of macroeconomic variables between those of Thailand and those of some industrial countries, for example, Japan, Australia, and the United States, can be estimated.[6] The results indicate a positive correlation of output growth during the period 1970–90. Even though Thailand's GDP growth rate is negatively correlated with that of Australia and the United States after 1990, the positive correlation of Thailand's output growth to those countries for the past three decades might be sufficient to indicate a strong relationship between Thailand and the global economy. As with the comparison of output growth, the positive correlation of the inflation rate and that of the industrial countries indicates a positive relationship of the price levels between Thailand and the global economy (see Table 7.4).

By comparison with other countries, we can identify Thailand as a very small open economy in which the country's economic structure is determined largely from international trade (Figure 7.3). The degree of trade openness (defined by the equation (exports + imports)/GDP multiplied by 100) increased almost four times from 32.7 in 1960 to 122.2 in 2002. Prior to 1985, the ratio of trade openness was less than 50. After the Plaza Accord, excessive inflows of foreign direct investment changed the role of Thailand; the country became more involved in the international context. Export shares increased from 20.4 per cent of GDP during the period 1970–85 to 35.3 per cent during the period 1986–96, and to 60.5 per cent during the crisis period.[7]

Table 7.4 Correlation of GDP growth and inflation between Thailand and industrial countries

Industrial countries	1970–90	1991–2002	1970–2002
Correlation of GDP growth			
Japan	0.508	0.489	0.436
Australia	0.201	–0.463	0.078
United States	0.225	–0.336	0.519
Correlation of inflation			
Japan	0.633	0.550	0.191
Australia	0.694	–0.537	0.236
United States	0.499	0.249	0.717

Source: Authors' calculation; data collected from International Financial Statistics, various years.

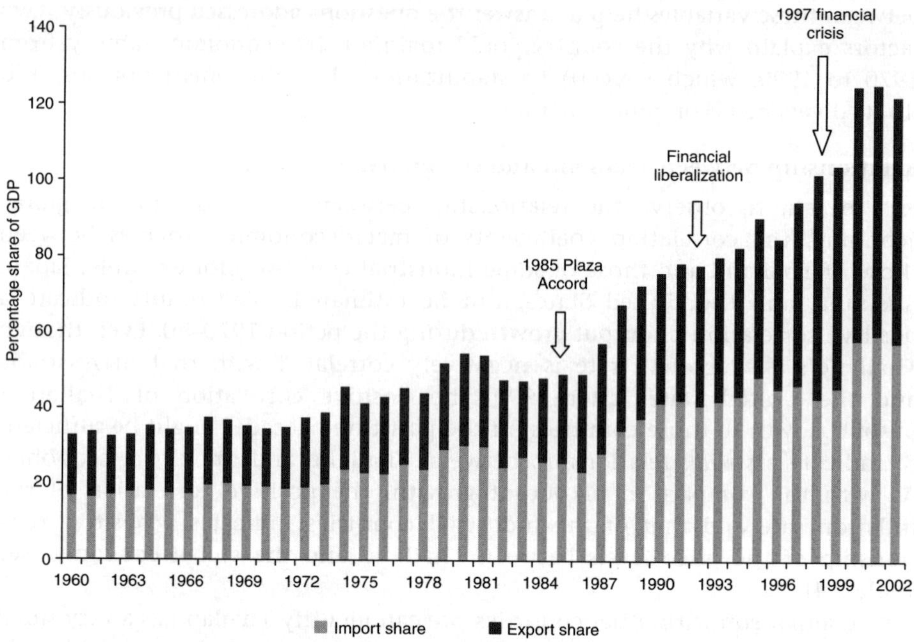

Figure 7.3 Export share, import share, and degree of trade openness
Source: Authors' calculation; data collected from World Development Indicators, various years.

Stabilization and adjustment policies

Concentrating on stabilization policies was the main reason why the country could maintain economic stability even in times of financial crisis. However, since Thailand's economic structure is generally linked to the international arena, as was discussed previously, one of the most important strategies was maintaining exchange rate stability. In 1984, Thailand utilized the currency-basket system, pegging the baht to the value of a number of currencies, specifically those of its trading partners, particularly the US dollar. This strategy was very important; it kept the value of the baht tied to a basket of major currencies rather than to the US dollar alone. In addition, the currency-basket system also enabled the Bank of Thailand to manage the value of the baht by changing the weight structure of the currencies in the basket.[8] The second stabilization strategy was the country's effective controls on public spending and the installation of discipline with regard to external debt creation. A 'zero growth' fiscal policy was adopted in 1986–87, freezing the government's overall real spending not to exceed the previous year's level. The newly created external debt within the public sector was controlled by setting up an upper limit each year.

Undoubtedly, financial stability and macroeconomic stability are intricately related. A sense of prosperity during expansion gives rise to overoptimism, complacency, and overconfidence. Bold and risky projects, propelled by excessive credit expansion, are undertaken unnecessarily. Part of the reason for the crisis may be related to the very success that Thailand had experienced with regard to the good economic performance it had experienced over many decades, and particularly the very rapid growth after 1995; this probably led to a sense of economic overconfidence. As soon as overvaluation of asset prices had been realized, a loss of confidence, pessimism, and overreaction set in, increasing the number of bankruptcies, non-performing assets, and bank runs, all of which are the order of the day in a debt-deflation economy. The greater the amount of debt accumulated over the expansion phase of the cycle, the deeper the trough and the longer the duration of the recession. Even though financial stability and macroeconomic stability are related to each other, financial instability leads to macroeconomic instability and vice versa.

Diversified economic structure

Besides the stabilization and adjustment policies implemented during the 1980s, the diversified structure of the Thai economy was an important factor that helped to mitigate its aggregate volatility. Diversification distinguishes between 'market diversification' and 'product diversification'. Market diversification is explained by analyzing the diversification of the country's export and import markets. Risks from a given shock from a country's trading partner are lower if market diversification exists. So far, observed in 2004, the country has had quite a number of export markets, which can be distinguished in terms of export shares as follows: ASEAN members (20.6 per cent), United States (17 per cent), Japan (14.2 per cent), and European Union countries (14 per cent). Other important export markets include China (7 per cent in 2003), Hong Kong (5 per cent), Taiwan (3 per cent) and South Korea (2 per cent).

Besides market diversification, product diversification of a country's export structure indicates low dependence on primary export groups, the prices of which are volatile. Based on the traditional theory of international trade, product diversification in exported items might imply a comparative advantage for domestic production. Thailand's top five major export items are computers and components (around 10 per cent of total exports), car assemblies and spare parts (6.9 per cent), electronics and circuits (4.7 per cent), petrochemical products (3.8 per cent), and para rubber (3.2 per cent), respectively. Export diversification is considered important in explaining why Thailand could maintain economic stability despite the occurrence of the crisis. The country is slightly dependent on relatively few primary commodities for export earnings. Unstable prices for these commodities have less adverse impacts for the country when facing serious terms of trade shocks. The Herfindahl-Hirschman Index (HHI) is computed to measure the extent of Thailand's export diversification (Figure 7.4).[9] HHI is found to vary around 0.25–0.3, which implies a high degree of export diversification (or low extent of export concentration). The point concerning the diversification of the Thai economy is very important here in suggesting why aggregate volatility did not diminish because of the volatility of capital flows under terms of trade stability.[10]

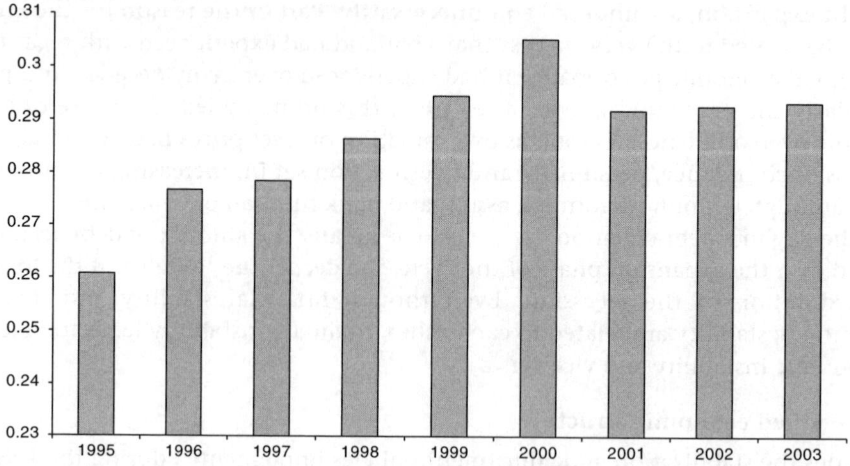

Figure 7.4 Herfindahl-Hirschman index of export diversification
Source: Authors' calculation; data collected from PC-TAS, United Nations.

The volatility of trade and capital flows

Even though the evidence indicates that economic diversification is a special pattern for mitigating the terms of trade volatility, which is linked to lower aggregate volatility, Thailand still experiences some degree of volatility in trade specialization. A comparison of the volatility of the export side and the volatility of the import side demonstrates that the volatility of the percentage of import growth during the period 1985–2005 was higher than that of export growth during the sample periods. This evidence implies that external liquidity constraints might exert downward pressure on import demand via changes in real exchange rates. The changes in imports are correlated with fluctuations in absorption stemming from changes in the availability of foreign funds, as Figure 7.4 suggests.

Figure 7.5 presents additional evidence by using quarterly data. There are simultaneous structural breaks in the import/export ratios (M/X) and capital account/export ratios (CK/X) after the 1997 crisis. In 1997, these ratios fell below the one standard deviation limit as a consequence of the sudden stop in growth. Since exports were relatively stable, the fall is explained by the co-movement between imports and the availability of external funds. Given this co-movement, it would be odd to attribute the fall in imports to a productivity shock. Since the mean of the annual import growth rate increased to 23.5 per cent during the period 1985–90 and the mean of the annual export growth rate reached a high level of 19.9 per cent during that period, exports and imports offset each other, and did not show evidence of the country's severe current account shock. During this period, Thailand exercised the ability to run trade deficits that proved to be particularly limited. Therefore, export volatility is likely to have a bearing on import volatility.

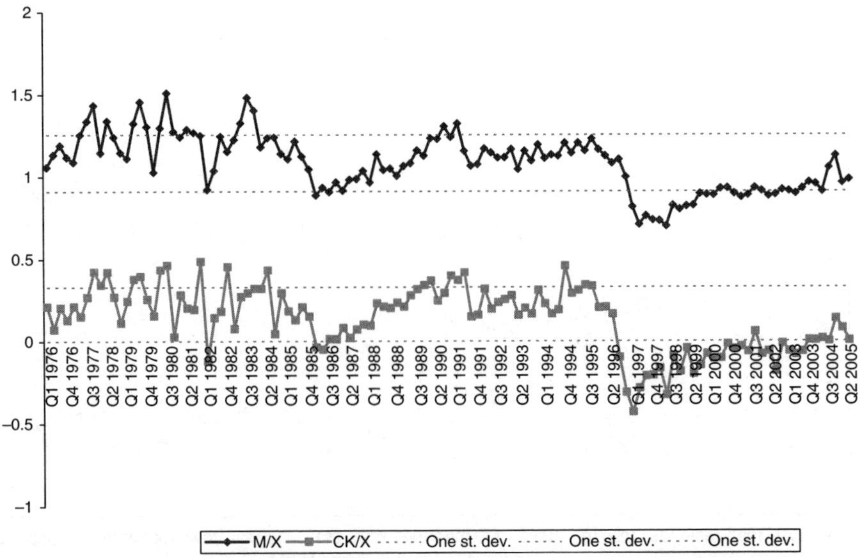

Figure 7.5 Import/export ratio (M/X) and capital account/export ratio (CK/X)
Source: International Financial Statistics, IMF.

Figure 7.6 shows the evolution of openness and the evolution of the rolling variance of the growth rate of exports (X) and imports (Y). The variance of the growth of imports is higher than the variance of the growth rate of exports. Since volatility of imports increased as a consequence of the 1997 crisis, while the variance of the exports did not change substantially, this evidence is consistent with the arguments that:

- Imports were affected by financial constraints. The depreciation of the domestic currency and the tightening of credit during the crisis period reduced investment by lowering the demand for imported capital goods.
- Increasing the diversification of exports induces a long-run fall in the variance of exports. In this situation, the failures in the credit market, both the international side and the domestic side, create a link between import volatility, which affects capital goods, and aggregate volatility.

The Thai experience highlights the fact that capital flows in emerging markets are often more volatile than in other developed economies, and are driven by sentiment rather than fundamentals. Such volatility can impose substantial risks on market agents, which they may not be able to sustain or manage. The authorities began to liberalize international capital flows in the 1980s with the relaxation of restriction on foreign direct investment (FDI). Since they focused on liberalizing portfolio investment in the stock market and bank loans, the liberalization of portfolio and banking flows was accompanied by the relaxation of foreign exchange controls.[11] Starting in 1991, the authorities began to relax foreign exchange restrictions on capital account related transactions, promoting

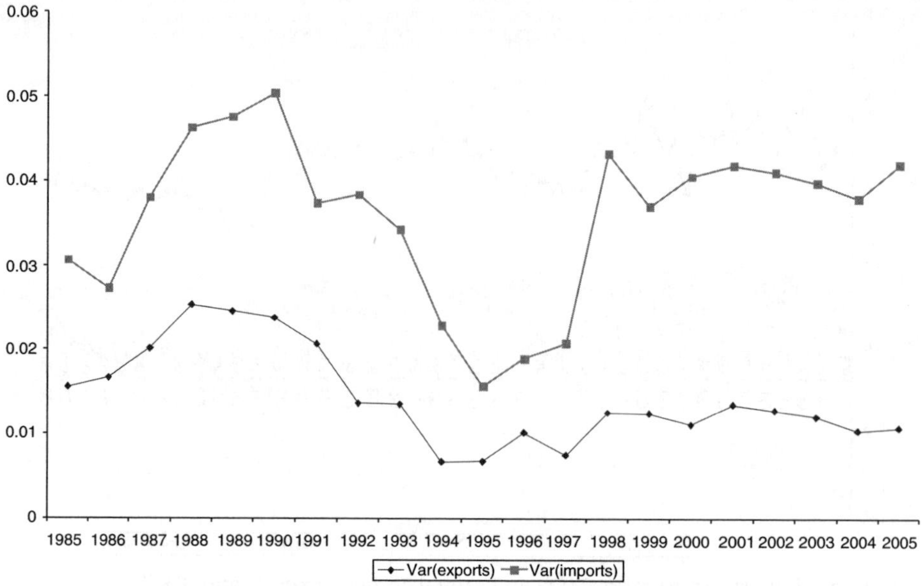

Figure 7.6 Evolution of the rolling variance of the growth rates of exports and imports
Source: International Financial Statistics, IMF.

cross-border capital flows by financial institutions. One important strategy for capital account liberalization was the establishment of the Bangkok International Banking Facility (BIBF), an offshore banking center, in 1993. Thailand saw growing inflows of foreign capital. While they were mainly in the form of FDI until the early 1990s, they recently shifted to short-term inflows. The increased openness of the capital account, together with financial market deregulation, led to a higher degree of capital mobility, largely reflected in the growing importance of short-term banking flows, portfolio investment, and non-resident baht accounts. In addition, the removal of interest rate ceilings allowed funds from overseas to become an increasingly important source of financing domestic investment, fueling speculation, and current account deficits.

Figure 7.7 provides evidence of financial liberalization and capital movements. First, the relationship between credit (CR) and money supply (M1) can be observed. The credit/money supply ratio (CR/M1) shows a marked upward trend in the pre-crisis period, but it fell substantially after 1997. This phenomenon implies that the source of credit was not the 'traditional' financial system, but the newly created BIBF segment. Credit creation was then associated with capital inflows via BIBF. Second, the figure shows the rolling correlation between the credit/GDP ratio and capital account/export (CK/X) ratio. This nine-year rolling correlation has always been positive (with the exception of the crisis period). This implies that both expansions and contractions in domestic credit were closely correlated with capital flows. Third, the rolling correlation between import/export ratio (M/X) and capital account/export ratio (CK/X) is also highly

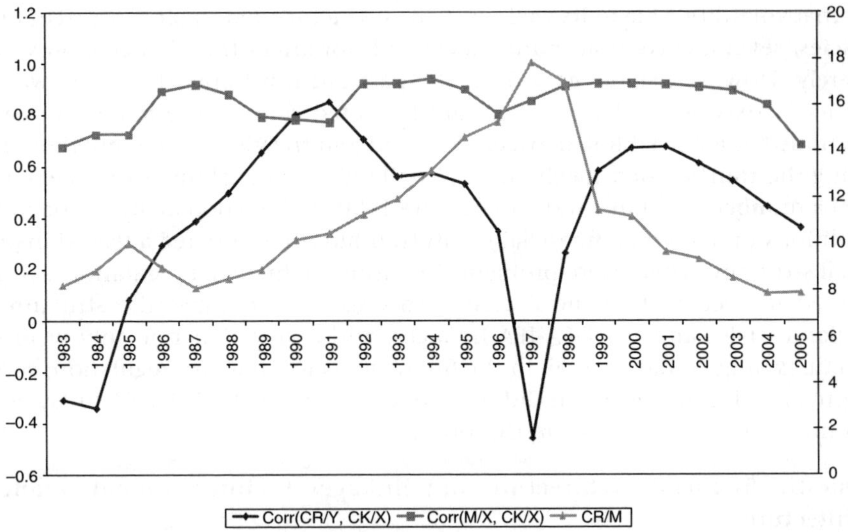

Figure 7.7 Correlation between credit/output ratio (CR/Y) and capital account/export ratio (CK/X), correlation between import/export ratio (M/X) and capital account/export ratio (CK/X), and credit/money ratio (CR/M1)
Source: International Financial Statistics, IMF.

positive. This is evidence showing a consistency in credit and capital flows, which have a substantial bearing on imports and domestic absorption.

In sum, Thailand's economy attained strong and stable growth throughout the three decades between 1960 and 1990, even though the country was slightly disturbed by external volatility (for example, oil price shocks) in some years. The fundamental reasons why Thailand was able to handle external volatility better than various other developing countries were that the Thai economy had a well-diversified structure and stable macroeconomic policies. Consequently, several current account shocks (for example, price rises for oil and other commodities) did not affect the Thai economy very severely. In the early 1990s, the transmission mechanism that established the linkage between capital account shocks (that is, liberalization) and domestic aggregate demand worked through the credit channel generated by the newly created BIBF system. Changes in the rules of the game created by the BIBF matter to aggregate fluctuations and thereby matter to aggregate volatility. The origins of the weaknesses of the financial sector fall into two broad categories: (i) excessive lending without prudent management of assets and liabilities, and (ii) inadequate regulatory and supervisory frameworks. Both of these will be discussed later.

7.4 Domestic financial architecture, financial market failures, and aggregate fluctuation

Thailand's economy attained strong and stable growth throughout the three decades from 1960 to 1990 even though the country was disturbed mainly by external volatility. Due to its well-diversified structure and stable macroeconomic policies, several current account shocks did not affect the Thai economy very severely. However, stable growth in the past did not imply that there was no financial crisis. Nevertheless, it should be noted that, as the financial system functioned as a crucial link between Thailand and the global economy thus facilitating the transmission mechanisms, Thailand's financial institutions encountered a number of failures and crises before 1990. This section analyzes the initial conditions under which financial institution-building initiated a flawed institutional structure. There were problems in enforcing financial regulations, which resulted in recurrent financial crises. This section describes the structure of Thailand's DFA and the DFA-IFA linkages, and shows that not only were the structures of governance weak in the financial sector, but also regulation, supervision, and risk management did not work well under the IFA-DFA linkages, so that financial crises occurred in the 1970s.

Domestic financial architecture and linkages to international financial architecture

Thailand's financial architecture system is considered to be a 'bank-based system', in which financial institutions are large and private commercial banks predominate with respect to, say, asset size, geographical coverage, savings mobilization, and credit extension. Second to commercial banks, especially before the crisis, were finance companies. Between 1990 and 1997, commercial banks and finance companies captured 88 per cent of the household savings placed with all financial institutions. Meanwhile, their extended credits added up to 92 per cent of the grand total offered by all financial institutions.[12]

The IFA-DFA linkages started from the relaxation of the upper limit imposed on the interest rate in 1980, which was aimed at deregulating the financial market. However, it was interrupted in the first half of the 1980s when the economy faced serious macroeconomic difficulties following the financial crisis in the 1970s. The Thai financial sector was also made more vulnerable as a result of the Basel Capital Accord (1988), which induced most multinational banks to prefer offering short-term over long-term lending, thus partly explaining the boom in the short-term portion of Thailand's external debts. IFA-DFA linkages were prominent in the comprehensive liberalization of the financial system implemented according to schedules laid out in two three-year plans in the 1990s. The plans were intended to enhance the efficiency of the financial system and to increase the competitiveness of Thai financial institutions. The increased openness of the capital account, together with financial market deregulation, led to a higher degree of capital mobility, which was largely reflected in the growing importance of short-term flows, portfolio investment, and non-resident baht accounts. There were a number of inconsistencies in terms of supervision, exchange rate regimes, and financial regulations. First, the Bank of Thailand decided not to allow the baht exchange rate to move freely or in accordance with market forces, mainly for the purpose of upholding price stability; thereafter, this sparked the severe financial crisis. Owing to the fixed exchange rate regime, firms and banks did not hedge currency risks. Second, stronger competition in the financial system pushed domestic financial institutions to extend credits imprudently and excessively, engendering economic bubbles and excessive risk. Third, the failure of the central bank to prudently monitor and supervise financial institutions was due to the incompetence of Bank of Thailand officers. These three factors demonstrate inconsistencies in the linkages of IFA and DFA, which finally caused the financial failure. This detailed story of policy errors and inconsistencies will be explained later in the chapter.

Finance company crises (1979–83)

When Thailand's GDP growth rate accelerated from 4.4 per cent in 1974 to 10.4 per cent in 1978, the demand for funds rose to the extent that local liquidity tightened remarkably. The credit/deposit ratio of commercial banks climbed from 75 per cent in 1972 to 94 per cent in 1975, 100 per cent in 1978, and 111 per cent in 1979.[13] Robust economic growth and the tight liquidity of the commercial banks motivated finance and securities companies to compete heavily in extending credit. Given that finance and securities firms did not possess widespread networks of branches like those of commercial banks, it is understandable that they exerted strenuous efforts in all the activities allowed. The fees and capital gains from securities trading caught the attention of finance and securities companies. However, a large number of such firms were tempted to go beyond what was allowed in order to increase their earnings. Such malpractice cases were not driven by politics; instead, they were partly due to the defects of the Bank of Thailand's supervisors and examiners. The most notable case of malpractice was a sizable finance and securities company named 'Raja Finance'. That company extended a string of credit lines to its affiliated companies without requiring ordinary collateral. Those credit lines were meant for purchasing Raja's own stock on the Stock Exchange of Thailand (SET) so that its price rose exorbitantly amid the first stock market boom during which the SET index grew more than 300 per cent in two years, from 82.70 in 1976 to 257.73 in 1978. Raja alleged that the purchased stocks backed up those credit lines. Therefore, the company's stability depended largely upon the price of its own stock.

After the second oil shock, which occurred in 1979, domestic inflation skyrocketed from 7.7 per cent in 1977–78 to 9.9 per cent in 1979 and 19.7 per cent in 1980. Tight local liquidity was exacerbated by the rapid surge in interest rates globally, from 9.5 per cent in 1978 to 12 per cent in 1979. These foreign shifts had a severe negative impact upon the Thai economy, as was evident in the sharp drop in the GDP growth rate from 10.4 per cent in 1978 to 5.3 per cent in 1979. Unsurprisingly, Raja encountered various difficulties in achieving a performance that would justify its very high stock price. Consequently, the public lost confidence in the company and the price of the firm's stock nosedived to the extent that both the company and its affiliates faced acute liquidity shortages, as well as financial losses. Eventually, the government withdrew Raja's business license and that of other finance companies that were in a similar state.[14]

This first round of crises in finance companies generated considerable adverse impacts upon both clients and SET. The Thai government attempted to provide assistance in several formats, for example, liquidity support, lower margin rates in order to rehabilitate SET, and funds established to develop capital markets. The assistance that the government provided to ailing finance companies did not create a moral hazard. However, while the damage remained shrouded, it played an active role in the disintegration of certain finance and securities companies owing to the lack of knowledge on the part of certain leaders. Overall, a huge portion of the finance business sector encountered further problems because the confidence of the general public continued to weaken to such a degree that massive volumes of promissory notes were withdrawn prematurely. As a result, the majority of finance companies steadily ran short of liquidity until another round of crises emerged in 1983.

The second round of crises was caused primarily by four factors. First, the 1979 oil crisis had engendered persistent adverse repercussions. Second, the oil price rise in the period 1979–82 sharply increased global interest rates. The tension over domestic liquidity was exacerbated by the devaluation of the baht twice in 1981 and the restrictive monetary policies that were implemented with the aim of narrowing the trade gap. Third, numerous private financial institutions did not manage their units efficiently, and they did not comply with legal requirements. For instance, such institutions extended credit to borrowers whose financial status was not stable. In addition, a considerable amount of credit was extended to executive members and affiliated companies without collateral. Fourth, some administrators themselves were guilty of malfeasance and even created bogus debtors.

The painful experience of the finance companies clearly demonstrated strong linkages between aggregate volatility and the financial system. Aggregate volatility is here represented by the pace of real GDP growth and domestic inflation, whereas the financial system is represented by liquidity tension (or the credit/deposit ratio) and the SET index. In 1979 aggregate volatility was sparked by oil price rises and sharp increases in global interest rates. These shocks had severe negative impacts on most businesses and borrowers, leading to contractions in both business volume and credit demand. Furthermore, some debts were postponed or went into default. It is thus unsurprising that some private financial firms encountered market failure (see Table 7.5).

In short, even though the central authorities tried to narrow the trade gap by devaluing the baht and implementing restrictive monetary policies, mismanagement and the shortcomings of private financial firms (for example, the extension of credit on favorable terms to affiliates or family-related clients, extending credit which required insufficient or no collateral, lacking a discreet credit-monitoring mechanism after loan extension, inappropriate portfolio diversification, excessive speculation in real estate and the stock market, lacking an early warning system concerning asset quality, maturity mismatching such as borrowing short and lending long, and leaving net foreign exchange positions uncovered) were so strong that several financial crises emerged in 1983. What should be noted is that

Table 7.5 Commercial banks' credit/deposit ratio, oil price, and SET index

Year	Commercial banks' credit/deposit ratio (%)[a]	Brent oil price (US dollars per barrel)[a]	SET index[b]
1973	87.69	4.25	–
1974	92.10	12.93	–
1975	93.93	11.50	84.08
1976	89.41	13.14	82.70
1977	92.90	14.31	181.59
1978	100.05	14.26	257.73
1979	111.07	32.11	149.40
1980	100.84	37.89	124.67
1981	97.80	36.68	106.62
1982	92.43	33.42	123.50
1983	98.54	29.78	134.47
1984	95.70	28.74	142.29
1985	93.79	27.61	134.95
1986	86.70	14.43	207.20
1987	89.41	18.44	284.94
1988	95.54	14.98	386.73
1989	97.84	18.25	879.19
1990	102.86	23.71	612.86

Notes: a. Bank of Thailand; b. Stock Exchange of Thailand (SET).
Source: Authors' calculation.

the weakening of confidence among the general public, as a result of proliferating market failures, was a crucial factor which exacerbated both subsequent aggregate volatility and its adverse impact on the financial structure of the Thai economy.

Commercial banking problems (1984–87)

While finance companies were struggling with difficulties, several commercial banks faced similar circumstances. Thai commercial banks were often inclined to extend credits to their affiliated firms or alliances. Besides, risk diversification was often inadequate. For example, Asia Trust Bank in 1984 lacked systematic organization and efficient executives. Imprudent administration thus arose. Worse, it extended excessive credits to affiliated firms, creating substantial NPL. The government tried to resolve these matters by many means. For example, it assigned new executives to run the banks, adjusted the management system, expanded the capital base by using government funds, converted bank status to that of government banks and merged banks with other government banks. For some years afterward, some commercial banks were still affected by the economic downturn to the extent that their poorer financial status could engender strong problems. Thus, the government stepped in to prevent problems in the system as a whole by urging those vulnerable banks to amend their management system and strengthen their financial status. Simultaneously, the enlargement of the capital base and bad debt provisioning were demanded until they reached adequate level. All these government efforts definitely resulted in more stability and strength in the whole banking system.

One notable aspect is that, while the government stepped in to examine, supervise, and assist some financial institutions, it met some legal obstacles. A number of laws were thus amended several times in order to raise efficiency (that is, flexibility and concision) for the government to examine, supervise, and resolve the financial institutions' problems.[15]

Underlying deficiencies in the financial system

If we examine the basic structure of Thailand's financial system, it is not surprising to learn about the recurrence of financial crises in Thailand, especially those of finance and securities companies. Finance companies, first established in 1969 (or 81 years after commercial banks), captured strong attention from local businessmen, primarily because the establishment of the Stock Exchange of Thailand in 1975 provided promising business opportunities. However, the controlling Act placed various restrictions upon the finance companies. For example, while commercial banks can take deposits from the public, finance companies could rely only on issuing promissory notes and borrowing from commercial banks. Because of these limitations, the total assets of finance companies in 1995 amounted to only one-third of those of commercial banks. Even though the number of finance companies was three times that of commercial banks, finance companies had only 66 branches while commercial banks operated 2991 branches. These statistics indicate the heavy competition between, and the risks faced by, finance companies.

One characteristic of the finance companies that placed a very heavy burden upon the Bank of Thailand was that all of these companies were separate entities, unlike the branching network of commercial banks.[16] Consequently, the central bank did not demand that the finance companies report their financial status as often as the commercial banks. Besides, the process of examining/analyzing/supervising was largely subjective, depending very much upon personal judgments. Given the infrequent data reported by many finance companies, the Bank of Thailand's pertinent officers who lacked professional experience in actual business were liable to misinterpret data and make incorrect comments or suggestions. Because of the several reasons mentioned previously, most supervisors tended to be narrow-minded. As a result, their superior officers were inclined to put off or postpone their decision-making as regards what measures should be taken against finance companies suspected of irregularities.[17] By and large, the following list summarizes the above-mentioned shortcomings of supervision by the Bank of Thailand:

- Infrequent data reporting
- Highly subjective judgments
- Lack of professional business experience
- Not forward looking
- Excessively micro-oriented (overlooking the macro picture)
- Likely to delay making important decisions.

In sum, Thailand was prone to encountering financial crises because of the extreme growth of finance companies and commercial banks, which were administered by inexperienced executives, coupled with inadequate supervision undertaken by the authorities. The lack of expertise tempted those executives to extend credits to consumers for consumption purposes rather than productive investment. Therefore, the financial failures of finance companies and commercial banks in Thailand between 1979 and 1987 were attributed largely to the inherent defects or weaknesses of not only the finance companies and commercial banks but also the examination and supervision procedures of the central authorities. These financial institutions were therefore affected by external shocks and macroeconomic volatility, such as oil price rises and interest rate fluctuations, which thereafter played important roles in sparking crises.

7.5 International financial architecture–domestic financial architecture linkages and effects of crisis

The previous section shows the structures of governance and supervision that were weak in the financial sector, which caused financial market failures during the period 1970–80. Not only was the financial sector still weakened from the crisis earlier in the decade, but the overall incentive framework in which financial institutions operated also remained deficient. Further, the regulatory and supervisory framework was not strengthened sufficiently in the aftermath of the crisis. The origins of the 1997 crisis could be traced to the early 1990s when the country accepted the IMF Article VIII, which lifted foreign exchange controls on current account transactions; this marked the beginning of a series of financial liberalization measures. However, financial liberalization was made difficult because of the deficiently-designed institution-building of financial institutions under the conditions analyzed in the previous section, particularly because of the inability to manage shocks and policy errors during the period of financial liberalization. This section is worth screening in detail for the causes, effects, and consequences of the 1997 crisis. We start by investigating a series of financial liberalization measures in the first half of the 1990s, scrutinizing the actual causes of the 1997 crisis from the viewpoint of domestic financial architecture, and summarizing valuable lessons from the institution-building process.

Financial liberalization (1989–94)

The rapid expansion of the Thai economy starting in 1988, which was led by the industrial and service sectors, engendered demands for more complicated and diversified financial services. The Bank of Thailand therefore launched a plan in 1990 to improve Thailand's financial system with the aim of reducing official interventions, increasing competition among financial institutions, and developing new accommodative instruments and services. Thailand's acceptance of IMF Article VIII in May 1990, which lifted foreign exchange controls on current account transactions, marked the beginning of a series of financial liberalization measures.

BIBF was permitted to be established by financial institutions in September 1992. To enable BIBF to compete with other centers, its transactions were granted various tax privileges (for example, the reduction of corporate income tax, and the exemption from special business tax and withholding tax on interest income). BIBF played a crucial role in expanding international bank loans. Figure 7.8 illustrates the evolution of the BIBF-generated credit/GDP ratio. It is clear that there was an explosive growth in credit from the early 1990s until the maximum point was reached in 1997. During that year, BIBF loans reached a high of about 40 per cent of GDP.

Since banks and finance companies played a key role in intermediating capital inflows in Thailand, it is also obvious that the explosion in credit came in the form of the out-in loans, which increased substantially in 1996, just before the 1997 crisis was triggered. Bank borrowing played a relatively minor role during the period 1988–92. This occurred as a result of the establishment of the BIBF and was due mainly to two factors: first, BIBF institutions were granted considerable tax advantages; and second, many Thai firms which could not directly access overseas capital markets were able to borrow from BIBF Thai banks. Thailand thereafter saw growing inflows of foreign capital. Even though those capital inflows were mainly in the form of foreign direct investment until the early 1990s, they later shifted to short-term inflows, including bank loans. The volume of financial sector credit extended to the private sector also expanded significantly.

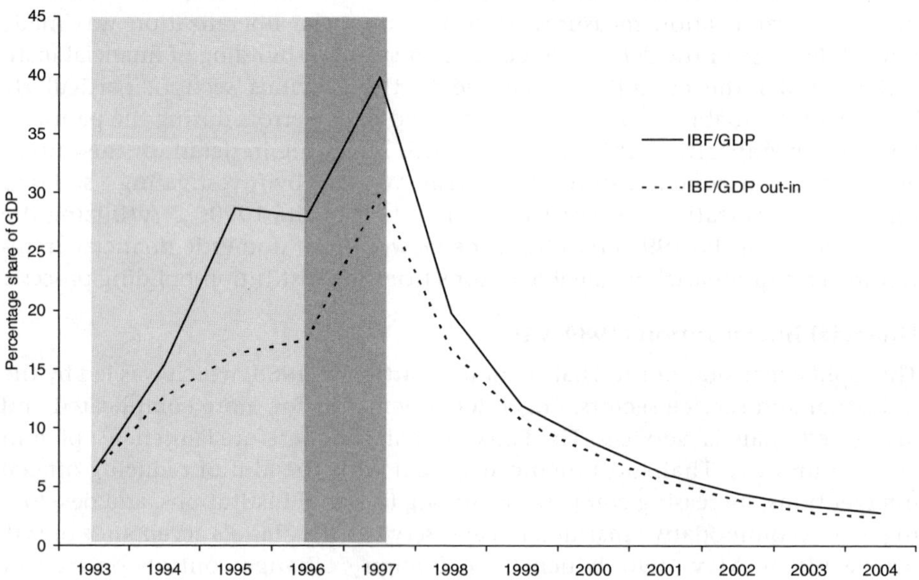

Figure 7.8 IBF/GDP
Source: Bank of Thailand.

Economic and financial crises (1997)

Financial liberalization induced a flood of capital funds into Thailand in the period 1990–96, fueling investment spending, speculation, and current account deficits. What was extremely threatening was that those liberal capital flows strongly disturbed the traditional transmission mechanisms of monetary policies. The variable that became highly vital and influential was the exchange rate. One notable point is that, though more freedom was given to cross-border capital flows, the government still pegged the value of the baht to the same basket of currencies adopted in 1984. As the US dollar commanded a predominant weight, roughly 85 per cent of the basket, the Thai baht did not move much against the US dollar. Therefore, numerous private corporations and financial institutions resorted to cheap foreign borrowings without purchasing forward cover to protect themselves against exchange risks. For the central authorities, how the exchange rate should be handled was a big puzzle because allowing it to be determined by market forces could cool down capital inflows, but price instability would emerge. As a result, maintaining exchange rate stability meant nullifying the effects of typical monetary policies.

However, the central authorities decided not to allow the exchange rate of the baht to move freely or in accordance with market forces, mainly for the purpose of upholding price stability. Meanwhile, stronger competition in the financial system pushed domestic financial institutions to extend credit imprudently and excessively, engendering economic bubbles and excessive risk (Table 7.6). Speculative and imprudent lending from BIBF inflated several 'bubble sectors', especially in the stock market and the real-estate sector.[18] Consequently, the asset quality of financial institutions deteriorated markedly.

In conclusion, Thailand's economic meltdown in mid-1997 has been attributed largely to the following three significant policy errors:

- Liberalization of foreign capital flows while keeping the exchange rate rigid
- Premature liberalization of financial institutions
- Failure to prudently monitor and supervise financial institutions

Table 7.6 Economic bubble and financial crisis

Year	Current (%)	Net capital (%)	External debt (%)
1990	–9.6	12.7	40.1
1991	–9.2	13.6	44.4
1992	–7.0	10.5	44.3
1993	–6.5	10.8	46.7
1994	–7.5	11.4	51.1
1995	–11.5	18.6	69.1
1996	–11.9	15.8	65.9
1997	–1.3	–5.3	64.8

Source: Bank of Thailand.

These three policy errors were closely linked. In the presence of healthy GDP growth and a stable exchange rate, foreign capital inflows were strongly encouraged by the measures liberalizing exchange controls. The flood of capital inflows generated vigorous competition with credit extension by local financial institutions. Even though local financial institutions were given more freedom to compete, as elaborated in the previous section, these institutions were unaccustomed to the new financial instruments. Yet, they felt that they had to try their best to compete with foreign capital; otherwise, they would lose clients rapidly. Therefore, local commercial banks as well as finance companies undertook heavy competition but misbehaved in various respects, for example, extending excessive credit without adequate collateral or capital support, and without careful forward-looking assessments or the exercise of prudence on asset quality. Such misbehavior could have been avoided if the central bank's officers had been able to closely monitor and supervise financial institutions. Unfortunately, those officers were not acquainted with new financial techniques and strategies. Consequently, local commercial banks and finance companies mishandled competition as well as their balance sheets and thereafter encountered serious problems. The situation was worsened by the Bank of Thailand's decision to step in to rescue weak local financial institutions for stability purposes, because those rescue operations aggravated the macroeconomic imbalance (that is, larger current account deficits and faster inflation) originally aroused by the foreign capital inflows. Therefore, the 1997 financial crisis in Thailand has been attributed to the following factors that caused deficient domestic financial architecture institutions.

(1) Commercial banks as well as finance companies lacked good credit appraisal systems for evaluating loan requests. Instead, they tended to depend more on collateral, and over-priced such collateral, while ignoring project feasibility.
(2) Commercial banks and finance companies gave preference to intra-affiliate credit as well as that connected with their shareholders or management directors.
(3) In the presence of financial liberalization and a booming domestic economy, commercial banks and finance companies were tempted to extend excessive credit without adequate prudence, thus engendering a financial bubble. Worse yet, some of that credit clustered around a few sectors, raising the risk of bubbles.
(4) Other related problems were the underqualified staffs of commercial banks and finance companies, maturity mismatching, too much foreign exchange risk exposure, too loose a system of asset classification, loan loss provisioning, and capital inadequacy. Most of these problems arose from allowing too much flexibility and subjective judgment to play a role in implementing rules and regulations.

The evidence relating to the 1997 financial crisis clearly demonstrates that the crisis originating in these deficiently-designed institution-building measures severely hindered the stability of the Thai economy. The major cause of the above-mentioned problems was that Thailand's financial sector had been long protected. Domestic financial institutions therefore remained rather immature in competing efficiently with international forces brought about by financial liberalization measures (for example, BIBF). Unsurprisingly, these domestic (both public and private, large and small) financial institutions misbehaved in various respects. Worse yet, the government tended to assist them when they encountered problems. Such a situation created moral hazards and encouraged further misbehavior. Consequently, floating the exchange rate became unavoidable.

Impacts of the crisis: intricacies and reforms

After the Bank of Thailand adopted the floating exchange rate system in July 1997, the value of the baht declined drastically. So did the price of stocks and real property because of the close linkage between the financial system and the real economic sectors. Numerous finance companies were near bankruptcy. The government suspended the activity of 58 of the total 91 finance companies; however, it announced guarantees for the deposits and loans of commercial banks and finance companies. Furthermore, several organizations (including the following) were established for the purpose of resolving the problems of the financial institutions.

- *Property Loan Management Organization*: This provided liquidity to financial institutions by purchasing problem loans, converting assets into securities, and retailing real estate projects.
- *Secondary Mortgage Corporation*: This supplied incremental funds to financial institutions by purchasing small installment mortgage loans, lowering the interest burden, and converting credits.
- *Financial Sector Restructuring Authority (FRA)*: This oversaw the suspended finance companies, assisting their depositors and creditors, and liquidating the irreparable finance companies.[19]
- *Asset Management Corporation*: This purchased and managed the assets of the units which were taken over by the Bank of Thailand's Financial Institutions Development Fund (FIDF).

Originally, most official resolution measures were aimed primarily at finance companies. Later on, it became apparent that some commercial banks faced severe problems as well. Their asset quality rapidly deteriorated and public confidence was shaken. Depositors made massive withdrawals of funds, while foreign creditors started to refrain from rolling over maturing debt, which compelled ailing banks to seek assistance from the FIDF. These liquidity shortage problems were so critical that 7 out of 15 commercial banks had to borrow funds from FIDF every day. In October 1997, the government utilized the following measures and explicitly intervened in three banks, the deposits of which accounted for up to 10 per cent of those of all commercial banks.

Table 7.7 New system of asset classification and loan-loss provisioning, effective July 1998

Loan classification	Months overdue	Provisioning (%)	
		Previous	New
1. Pass	< 1	–	1
2. Special mention	1–3	–	2
3. Substandard	3–6	15	20
4. Doubtful	6–12	100	50
5. Loss	> 12	100	100

Source: Authors' calculation.

(1) Commercial banks had to improve their capital funds by writing off bad debts and raising new capital.
(2) Commercial banks had to comply with new rules, which were more stringent than previously with regard to asset classification and loan loss provisioning.
(3) Commercial banks were prohibited from paying dividends on their shares in 1997 and 1998.
(4) Foreign entities were permitted to hold more than 49 per cent of bank shares for 10 years.

In March 1998, the Bank of Thailand tightened regulations on asset classification, loan-loss provisioning, and the realization of income in its efforts to upgrade financial institutions to international standards by 2000 (Table 7.7). For example, loans were classified into five levels (instead of three as had been the practice), as was loan-loss provisioning. Financial institutions were required to report their status to the Bank of Thailand on a quarterly instead of yearly basis.

The tightening of regulations on asset classification and loan-loss provisioning clearly demonstrates a valuable lesson. That is, if rules are prudently articulated in the sense that they conform to international standards and can be rapidly or effectively implemented (for example, classifying debts on their 'passed due date', the extent of required provisioning depending upon the months overdue), then all parties concerned will remain cautious. Commercial banks will screen their potential clients in greater detail, and they will closely monitor their clients' status after extending credit. On the part of customers, they will try their best to comply with the terms of borrowing since not doing so would adversely affect banks, which would be more ready to impose punishments (such as penalty fees or fewer credit lines) as a result of the required provisioning.

Valuable lessons and adjustments

The efforts exerted by the government to restructure the financial system in various formats, as was mentioned above, absorbed a stupendous amount of resources. For instance, in 1998 the IMF estimated that the Thai government

Table 7.8 Government debt as a percentage of GDP

Countries	1996	1999[a]	2000[a]
Thailand	11.0	55.4	52.7
Domestic debts	2.0	26.4	24.7
Foreign debts	9.0	29.0	28.0
Indonesia	51.1	93.0	98.3
Domestic debts	25.1	57.0	64.3
Foreign debts	26.0	36.0	34.0
Malaysia	47.7	59.5	63.3
Domestic debts	31.7	36.5	39.3
Foreign debts	16.0	23.0	24.0
South Korea	28.2	41.3	40.7
Domestic debts	19.2	25.3	24.7
Foreign debts	9.0	16.0	16.0

Note: a = approximate.
Source: World Bank.

devoted 20 per cent of GDP to support liquidity and another 8 per cent of GDP to increase capital funds. According to a World Bank estimate, the public debt of four countries in Asia, especially that of Indonesia and Thailand, surged at an unbelievable pace during the period 1996–2000 (Table 7.8).

The enormous incremental debt burden of the governments, which arose from attempts at financial restructuring, should help to provide many important lessons for both creditors and debtors if another financial crisis is to be averted in the future.

Creditors' lessons

(a) There was imprudent competition to extend credit with inadequate or no collateral.
(b) There was a lack of discreet credit monitoring after the extension of loans.
(c) Operations were mismanaged by favoring affiliated or family-related clients using various means.
(d) Frequently there was speculation in booming businesses, such as real estate and the stock market, without carefully looking forward.
(e) There was a lack of early warning systems concerning asset quality.
(f) Portfolios of assets and liabilities were inadequately diversified so that risks were clustered.
(g) There was a lack of efficient staff and units responsible for debt restructuring.

Debtors' lessons

(a) An administration format was lacking which would have yielded satisfactory efficiency, transparency, and good governance.
(b) Standard systems of accounting, especially those concerning cash flows, were lacking.

(c) There was a resort to funds from abroad without careful protection against exchange rate risks.
(d) People yielded to the temptation to pursue new or popular businesses without having the necessary experience, thus engendering too many risks.

The malpractice and the misbehavior of creditors and debtors were exacerbated by the weaknesses found among regulators (examiners and supervisors) as follows.

(a) Regulators lacked expertise and actual experience in working at commercial banks or finance companies.
(b) The number of bank branches and finance companies was very large relative to the number of regulators.
(c) Rules were spelled out and implemented subjectively, depending very much upon personal interpretation and judgment.
(d) Most results of regulators' examination and analysis were based only on past data, largely without examining current status and future projections.
(e) Regulators focused their attention only upon micro data, while the macro picture and projections were mostly neglected.
(f) Since regulators were also in charge of monetary and exchange rate policies, some cases of financial institutions' misconduct did not receive immediate attention. Thus, problems or troubles regarding financial institutions' stability or efficiency persisted and in some cases were multiplied.

The errors and weaknesses of Thai creditors, debtors, and regulators, as was mentioned above, indicate that the financial market failures in Thailand between 1979 and 1997 were largely due to domestic factors such as family lending, land and stock speculation, the inefficient role played by regulators, and bad corporate governance. Exogenous shocks or volatility including oil price rises, interest rate increases, and exchange rate fluctuations played the crucial role of providing the spark.

What happened in Thailand before the 1997 crisis was overspending fueled by superfluous and incautious lending of domestic financial institutions, together with excessive foreign borrowing. Commercial banks and finance companies offered credit to their clients too hastily in order to compete with abundant capital inflows. In any case, two distressing problems emerged: a surge in low-quality assets of domestic financial institutions, and an expansion in foreign indebtedness. Those poor-quality assets could be substantiated by the skyrocketing NPL ratio, which exceeded 50 per cent after 1997. Eventually, the central authorities were forced to float the baht in the middle of 1997.

In sum, four immediate recommendations can be made:

(1) Changes (for example, financial liberalization) should be made only when all the parties concerned are ready.
(2) Policy consistency should be continually maintained.

(3) As most financial markets around the world are closely linked, the domestic macro-financial policies of small developing countries should be steadily adjusted for the purpose of achieving harmony.
(4) In case overspending is unavoidable, strong attention should be paid in advance to the role and status of domestic financial institutions, that of foreign capital, and the country's external debt-servicing capacity.

Fortunately, the central authorities in Thailand started to realize that, in order to achieve solid progress in the development of the financial system, it is necessary to have firm roots or a firm basis. A new financial sector master plan (FSMP) was therefore drawn up in 2002 and eventually approved by the Thai government in 2004. FSMP is aimed at consolidating financial institutions to attain more professionalism, effective supervision, and the provision of more equality plus stability.

7.6 Conclusions

The main findings can explain the experiences associated with financial crises in Thailand. Given the propositions initiated previously, we can explain a bi-directional linkage between volatility and institutions. The Thai case study complies with five propositions as follows:

P1. Some structural features that are typical of developing economies contribute to generating excess aggregate volatility and crises because of the imperfections in the financial intermediation structure.

Although Thailand, like other developing countries, has undergone several economic shocks transmitted from outside the country, the fundamental reasons why Thailand was able to handle external volatility better than some other developing countries are that the Thai economy had a well-diversified structure and stable macroeconomic policies, especially with regard to the exchange rate. Nevertheless, Thailand's financial institutions encountered many failures and crises before 1990, such as the finance company crisis (1979–83) and commercial banking problems (1984–87). Even though those financial crises did not result in severe economic downturns, they still showed evidence of deficient DFA institutions. With a financial sector weakened from the crisis earlier in the decade, the deficiently-designed institution-building of financial institutions under the policy of financial liberalization led to the occurrence of the 1997 crisis.

P2. Uncertainty associated with excess aggregate volatility and especially crisis episodes weaken the quality of the governance structures and institutions that rule financial transactions.

The structures of governances were weak in the Thai financial sector. The deficiencies and weaknesses of Thai creditors, debtors, and regulators indicate that the financial market failures in Thailand between 1979 and 1997 were similar and largely due to the imprudent regulation of domestic factors: the lack of systematic risk appraisal, family or affiliated-firm lending, land and stock speculation, and the inefficient roles played by regulators. Exogenous shocks and macroeconomic volatility also played an important role in sparking the crises.

P3. Agents' adaptive responses to weak DFA institutions and volatility shape the financial structure; these responses can worsen market imperfections and debilitate governance.

Since instruments of financial liberalization were unfamiliar to the Bank of Thailand's officers, three significant policy errors causing the crisis were: (i) keeping the exchange rate rigid while liberalizing capital flows, (ii) the premature liberalization of financial institutions, and (iii) the failure of the central bank to prudently monitor and supervise financial institutions. From this point of view, these policy errors demonstrate how important coherent economic policy and improved financial institutions – including consistent IFA-DFA linkages – are to the economy.

P4. When some key risks are non-contractible and some countercyclical policies are non-implementable, risk management will be inefficient and a source of excess volatility and crises.

The 1997 crisis originating from the liberalization attempt has to do with the fact that firms were un-hedged with respect to currency risk, which caused banks to manage risk inappropriately. Meanwhile, stronger competition in the financial system pushed domestic financial institutions to extend credits imprudently and excessively, engendering economic bubbles and too much risk. This inefficient risk management also explained the case of the finance company crisis in 1979 when finance companies extended a string of credit lines to their affiliated companies without requiring ordinary collateral. Consequently, the asset quality of financial institutions deteriorated markedly, which thereafter generated financial crises.

P5. Distributional conflicts originating in broken promises and conflicts over property rights deteriorate society's institution-building ability.

This proposition slightly explains the Thai case. Since numerous finance companies were near bankruptcy, several organizations, such as Property Loan Management Organization, Secondary Mortgage Corporation, Financial Sector Restructuring Authority, and Asset Management Corporation, were established for the purpose of resolving the problems of the financial institutions. Lower asset quality rapidly deteriorated public confidence and caused depositors to withdraw the funds. These liquidity shortage problems were so critical that 7 out of 15 commercial banks had to borrow funds from FIDF every day.

In sum, the stylized facts identified in this project, which concern the discussion of bi-directional causal relationships between volatility and financial institutions, the DFA structure, and the linkages with the IFA, contribute to explaining the Thai case. Relatively good macroeconomic policies and diversified structure were able to compensate for financial imperfections and the weak structure of corporate governance in the financial sector in the period 1970–90. Under these conditions, real GDP growth was positive, inflation was relatively low, and consumption was relatively less volatile than GDP. The 1997 crisis, however, severely affected the ability of central authorities to smooth fluctuation. Investment and consumption volatility increased substantially. This implies that, when countercyclical policies are difficult to implement and incomplete markets exist, it is much more difficult to stabilize consumption. The financial crises of Thai commercial banks and finance companies did not demonstrate that the DFA lagged far behind the IFA. DFA was, however, inferior to IFA in two main respects. First, the pace of financial liberalization undertaken during the period 1990–96 was too quick for the staff of financial institutions. The resultant competitive pressure was intensified by inconsistent exchange rate rigidity, as stated above. Second, the central bank long stipulated significant regulations in the examination, monitoring, and supervision of financial institutions.

As Thailand had experienced earlier, greater liberty means more involvement with foreign markets for capital, commodities, and exchange rates. These factors make DFA increasingly vulnerable to exogenous shocks or volatility. Therefore, domestic financial institutions should be strengthened by various means; otherwise, exogenous shocks or volatility may spark another painful occurrence of distress in the DFA. Finally, the recent FSMP should be examined as a means for changing the fundamental features of Thailand's DFA in the near future. It might elucidate the significant determinants of whether a financial crisis will recur in the future and how Thailand should prepare itself to cope with any future IFA.

Notes

1. According to Warr (1993), the reason why Thailand was less adversely affected by the oil crisis as compared with many other oil-importing countries was because of the high prices and ready markets for Thai exports that tended to offset the increase in the cost of imported oil.
2. Although using a standard deviation is not a perfect measure of estimating volatility, many studies in the literature compare this variable across countries by following this practice (for example, Easterly et al. 2000; Ramey and Ramey, 1995).
3. This resulted from a deceleration of investment in real estate, especially in the construction of residential buildings, commercial buildings, condominiums and factory buildings. Purchases of machinery and equipment for the production of goods and services also slowed in accord with the reduction of capital utilization in the manufacturing sector in the crisis period.
4. It should be noted that, both in 1997 and 1998, import compression and export surges in terms of the baht also helped cushion the impact of the reduction in private spending.

5. Since the conditional variance coefficient is significant only at the 10 per cent level, this is consistent with the fact that growth volatility reflects on investment and saving rather than consumption, although post-crisis consumption becomes more volatile.
6. The industrial countries (Japan, Australia, and United States) are proxies for the global economy.
7. Corsetti et al. (1998) point out two reasons why economies that are relatively open are less likely to face sustainability problems. First, a large export sector, which generates foreign currency receipts, strengthens a country's ability to service its debt obligations. Second, the economic and political costs of a crisis are relatively large as the dependence of the economy on the rest of the world is high. This situation might be applicable to the case of Thailand in which the degree of trade openness of the country is relatively high; there might be either positive or negative effects in terms of trade shocks that might easily improve or deteriorate the country's terms of trade and economic structure.
8. For example, the Bank of Thailand decided to increase the US dollar's weight in the basket after its sharp decline in late 1985, which played an important role in boosting Thai exports from 1986.
9. The Herfindahl-Hirschman Index is a quantitative measure of export concentration (or the inverse of diversification). The more diversified the composition of exports, the lower the value of this index.
10. Besides export diversification, another positive feature of Thailand's export structure is the high degree of intra-industry trade between ASEAN countries. Intra-industry trade is not only a main driver of growth in global trade as Krugman (1995) suggested, but also serves as one of the main driving forces of intra-regional trade within ASEAN. Pholphirul (2007) estimated the Intra-Industry Trade (IIT) Index for Thailand, the ASEAN-4 (Indonesia, Singapore, Malaysia, and Philippines), and East Asian countries, such as China, South Korea, and Japan. Intra-industry trade is higher within the ASEAN countries, especially within major product groups such as textiles, machinery, auto parts, and chemicals.
11. See Sirivedhin (1997) for the implications of capital account liberalization in Thailand.
12. Specialized government banks captured 9.5 per cent of the total deposits in the financial system and 14.2 per cent of its total assets. Government-related and government-established financial institutions, for example, Government Savings Bank, Bank for Agriculture and Agricultural Cooperatives, Industrial Finance Corporation of Thailand, and Government Housing Bank, have played a more important institutional role as borrowers and lenders after periods of economic crisis. However, as the specialized banks are of minor importance for the analysis performed, this chapter will only focus on commercial banks and finance companies.
13. The Stock Exchange of Thailand (SET) had been established coincidentally in 1975, as planned by the National Economic and Social Development Board (NESDB). Some private firms with acceptable financial status could tap funds from SET.
14. However, it took a long time before the government decided to revoke Raja's license because the government was afraid to disturb domestic financial stability.
15. Examples of these laws were the Act on the Undertaking of Finance Business, Securities Business and Credit Foncier Business, B.E. 2522 B.E. 2526 B.E. 2528, Commercial Banking Act, B.E. 2505 B.E. 2528, and Bank of Thailand Act B.E. 2485 B.E. 2528.
16. From an interview with Bank of Thailand officers, monitoring and supervising 29 commercial banks, which had 2991 branches, was definitely easier than monitoring and supervising 91 finance companies, which had only 66 branches.
17. Besides, as monetary policy represented one very crucial task, the high-ranking officers of the central bank preferred not to focus their attention on supervising or restructuring finance companies.
18. According to Renaud (2000), approximately 45 per cent of domestic investment came from foreign direct investment and approximately 15 per cent of that total was from

BIBF procedures. Also, approximately 5 per cent and 15 per cent of BIBF inflows respectively were allocated to construction equipment, or financial institutions directly or indirectly related to the real estate market. The main proportions of housing credit in Thailand were from commercial banks.

19. FRA separated finance companies by using three criteria: (i) the amount of the official liquidity support needed; (ii) the depreciation of capital funds; and (iii) the size of non-performing loans. By December 1997, FRA and the Ministry of Finance permanently closed 56 of the 58 suspended finance companies.

8

Russia

Anatoliy Peresetsky and Vladimir Popov

8.1 Introduction

Would a particular country be willing to reduce volatility at the expense of lowering the long-term growth rate if there were a trade-off between volatility and growth? Fortunately, there is no such trade-off. As many studies have documented (see Aghion et al., 2004 for a recent survey of the literature) the relationship between volatility and growth is negative, that is, rapid growth is associated with lower volatility. This result holds if one compares fast- and slow-growing countries, as well as periods of fast and slow growth/recession in the same country. So, policies to promote growth, if successful, are likely to reduce volatility as well, even though the mechanism of such a spin-off is not well understood. Nevertheless, the volatility of macro variables cannot be totally explained by their growth rates: even when controlling for the average speed of change, there remain huge variations in volatility in various countries and periods.

Russia, following its 1992 transition to the market economy, was definitely one of the most volatile countries. The goal of this chapter is to identify sources of volatility in Russia in 1992–2004 and to examine the role of domestic and international financial architecture in propagating/mitigating economic instability. Following the introduction to the project (Fanelli, 2004), we organize the discussion around the five hypotheses formulated for the country studies.

In Section 8.2 we provide measures of volatility of Russian GDP, consumption, investment, external trade, capital flows, and financial markets and discuss the patterns of change of these indicators for particular periods of recent Russian economic development as compared to other countries. Import volatility, as in other countries, tends to be higher than export volatility, even though 50 per cent of Russian exports consist of oil and gas with highly volatile prices. In addition, it appears that the volatility of GDP is not very correlated with the volatility of exports, whereas the correlation of GDP growth with the volatility of imports is high due to the impact of GDP on imports, and not vice versa. These relationships signal the existence of other internal sources of volatility, which are identified later (monetary shocks).

Russia constitutes a somewhat special case in this study. It did not become a market economy until 1992, when prices were deregulated. It experienced huge supply shocks associated with the dramatic change in relative prices, institutional collapse, privatization, and so on during the transition to the market economy (from a centrally planned economy). Because of these special circumstances, aggregate Russian volatility in the first half of the 1990s was extremely high. For this reason we focus our analysis on the 1994–2004 period, that is, when the reduction of output due to the transformational recession (nearly a 40 per cent fall in 1989–94) was largely over.

In Section 8.3 we start with the investigation of the contributions of the external shocks (the change in oil and gas prices) to aggregate volatility. We show that the aggregate volatility of GDP growth rates is closely linked to the volatility of the real exchange rate (RER), whereas the volatility of the RER itself cannot be explained totally by the external (terms of trade and capital flows) shocks. A large portion of the variation of RER should be attributed to the bad quality of macroeconomic policy, not to objective circumstances like the external shocks. In particular, we argue that there are two basic flaws in Russian macroeconomic policy: (1) the inability to perform a countercyclical management of foreign exchange reserves in the Central Bank and in the Stabilization Fund (created in 2004) to stabilize the RER (accumulation of reserves in good times and running them down on 'rainy days'); (2) monetary shocks, the instability of monetary policy – the inability to ensure predictable and stable growth rates of money supply.

In Section 8.4 we examine the Russian financial system and its role in mitigating/propagating the volatility of the whole economy. The 1998 crisis resulted in the demonetization and dollarization of the Russian economy and the weakening of the banking system (which was not very strong to begin with). The security of contracts and contract rights were badly damaged when the Russian government defaulted on its bonds and Russian banks defaulted on their forward contracts and other obligations. It was not until 2000 that the ratio of bank assets and other financial indicators to GDP began to grow and it was not until 2002 that the share of long-term credits that fell sharply after the crisis began to rise again. According to our findings, in Russia we have a sort of vicious circle: crises + a volatile environment + deficiently designed institution-building and policies → low financial development → bad risk management → crisis → high volatility → worsening of policies and institutions.

In Section 8.5, we discuss the implication of our analysis for the reforms of the DFA and IFA. The general desirable direction of these reforms is quite obvious. For the DFA, better macroeconomic policy (changing FOREX in line with terms of trade, so as to keep the RER relatively stable; stable and predictable monetary policy without monetary shocks; control over the short-term capital flows) and a stronger financial system (tight prudential regulations guaranteeing financial contracts and the stability of financial institutions plus the easy access of economic agents to credits and financial contracts diminishing risks). For the IFA, greater availability of funds from foreign governments and international financial institutions to counter adverse terms of trade shocks and destabilizing private capital flows, greater control over the short-term capital flows, and price-stabilization funds for commodities with highly volatile prices. However, these measures are not easily implementable due to political economy constraints, implying the existence of vicious and virtuous circles. We discuss the most promising way to break the Russian vicious 'volatility – poor DFA – volatility' circle.

8.2 Excess volatility and crises

Analysis of aggregate volatility

Russia became a market economy in January 1992, after prices were deregulated.[1] The transition to a market economy was associated with an unprecedented transformational recession: the reduction of output continued for 9 years (1990–98), GDP at the 1998 trough was only 55 per cent of the 1989 level. The recession was partly structural (caused by a dramatic change in relative prices after deregulation); it was partly due to the collapse of the state institutions (the increase in the crime rate and a shadow economy that worsened the business climate greatly) and should be partly attributed to poor macroeconomic policies, in particular high inflation of 1992–95 (up to several thousand per cent a year).[2]

In 1995 the Russian government enacted a program of exchange rate-based stabilization. It appeared to work for three years – the nominal exchange rate was generally stable (a crawling-peg regime), high inflation subsided to single digits, and in 1997 there was even a modest increase in GDP by 1 per cent. This stabilization, however, led to the appreciation of the real exchange rate; imports increased substantially, while exports stagnated (partly due to the fall in oil prices) producing a deterioration in the Russian balance of payments and the currency crisis of August 1998.

The month after the currency crisis, in September 1998, the Russian economy started to grow and is still growing. Initially, right after the crisis, there was an outburst of inflation in the last months of 1998, which later went down. Formally, Russia has had a floating exchange rate since 1998, but in reality it is a very dirty float with a virtually stable nominal rate. The real exchange rate has appreciated considerably since then and is not causing a balance of payments crisis only because of high world market fuel prices (fuel is a major Russian export).

To assess whether the economy experiences a degree of volatility that exceeds the one justified by fundamentals we use the magnitude of the volatility in developed countries as a benchmark, considering differences in the volatility between developing and developed countries as 'excess volatility'.

The sources of this 'excess volatility' could be classified in the following way:

- Excess volatility resulting from the external sector, for instance, from more volatile changes in terms of trade (Russia is more dependent than other countries on the export of commodities – oil and gas – with very unstable prices) and unstable capital inflows/outflows.

- Greater market imperfections in developing countries that do not allow the country to digest the natural shocks and thus avoid volatility (the reasons for these imperfections are associated partly with poor institutions, partly with the poor development of the financial sector that does not allow it to spread shocks intertemporally). A high share of commodities in exports does not preclude many open economies from limiting volatility to very low levels.
- Poor government policies in developing countries that do not mitigate natural shocks in the same way that these policies do in developed countries (partly due to bad institutions, partly due to political economy considerations).
- Poor government policies (due to political economy considerations) that create shocks and volatility by themselves, even in the absence of natural internal or external shocks.

Consider the volatility in output, for instance: in few countries, if any, has volatility in the recent decade been more pronounced – growth rates ranged from –15 per cent to +10 per cent. The bulk of this volatility was directly triggered by poor government policy. The supply-side recession (adverse supply shock) occurred due to immediate rather than to the gradual deregulation of prices, which resulted in huge changes in relative prices. For fuel, energy, steel, non-ferrous metals and food industries, the terms of trade shock was positive (relative prices increased), whereas most secondary manufacturing industries experienced a deterioration in the terms of trade. The exchange proportion of fuel and non-ferrous metals to light-industry goods (clothing and footwear) changed from 1:1 in 1990–91 to 1:3 in 1992 and afterwards. It is no surprise that light industry lost 90 per cent of its output in 1990–98. Generally, the reduction in output was strongly correlated with the change in relative prices.

Components of aggregate volatility

Even incomplete data show that volatility was extremely high during the first several years of transition (standard deviation of quarterly GDP growth rates was close to 10 percentage points in Latvia and Lithuania) and decreased to levels that are typical of market economies in 'good times', that is, in the absence of recession (1–2 percentage points), only by the end of the 1990s, that is, a decade after the shock associated with the deregulation of prices.

It is noteworthy that different measures of volatility[3] give very similar results. Figure 8.1 shows seasonally adjusted quarterly growth rates: seasonal fluctuations were eliminated in the first case through X11 procedure and in the second case through a simple 4-quarter moving average. The results are very much the same, as trends calculated by applying the Hodrick-Prescott (H-P) filter are virtually identical. Similarly, the rolling 16-quarter window standard deviations (computed as explained above, with the assumption of linear trend[4]) and from the trend computed by applying H-P filter are very much the same.

Investment in Russia, as in other countries, is the most volatile component of GDP. It could be expected that the volatility of consumption is lower than that of output because it is mitigated by a countercyclical behavior of government

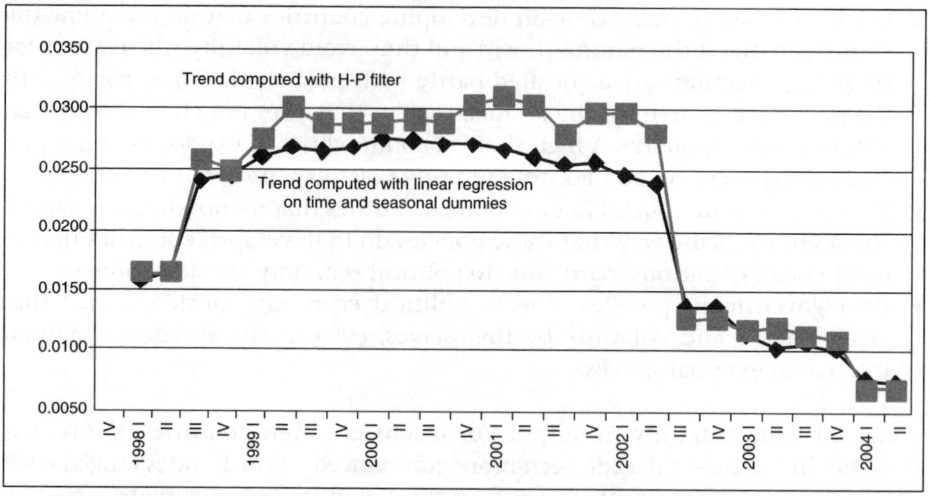

Figure 8.1 Volatility of quarterly growth rates of GDP (standard deviation from trend computed with and without H-P filter)

purchases of goods and services and, perhaps, net exports (if international capital markets help to smooth internal shocks). In Russia, however, volatility of consumption was higher in the 1990s than that of GDP suggesting that (1) external shocks probably contributed to total volatility, and (2) international financial markets did not help to lower the excess volatility of consumption (higher than the volatility of output).

This is further confirmed by looking at the volatility of exports and imports, which was way above that of GDP (Figure 8.2). Growth rates of exports and imports, unlike growth rates of GDP, are measured in current dollar prices, that

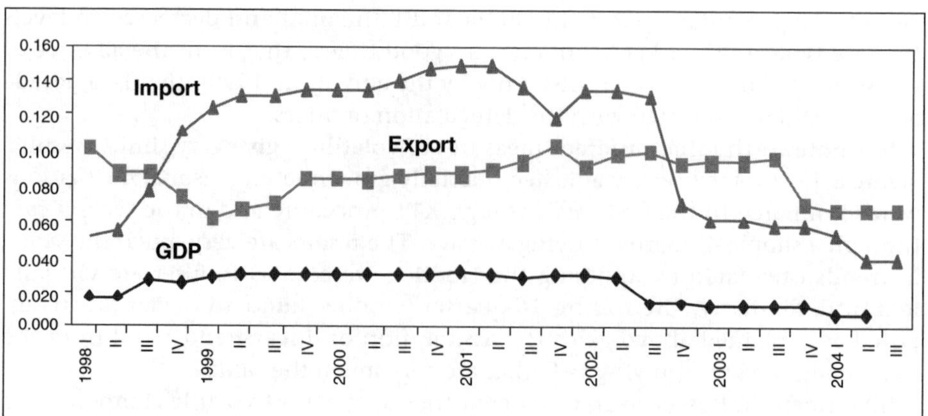

Figure 8.2 Volatility of quarterly growth rates of export, import and GDP, 1994–2004 (III)

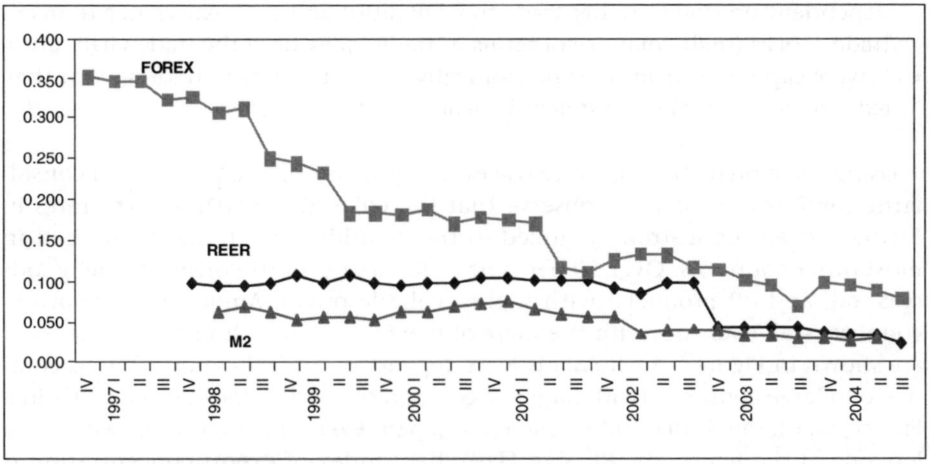

Figure 8.3 Volatility of quarterly growth rates of real effective exchange rate, foreign exchange reserves and M2 to GDP ratio, 1994–2004 (III)

is, they include not only changes in volumes, but also changes in dollar prices for exported and imported goods (there are no indices of export and import prices in Russia, unfortunately). We will later examine prices of major Russian export items (oil and gas) to see what the contribution of these factors was to the total volatility of the value of exports and imports.

It is also of interest to look at the volatility of the real exchange rate (RER), which is comparable to the volatility of exports and imports, and the volatility of foreign exchange reserves (FOREX), which was extremely high before the August 1998 currency crisis, before and during the period of exchange rate-based stabilization (1995–98), which decreased afterwards, but was still twice as high as the volatility of RER in 2000–04 (Figure 8.3).

8.3 Structural factors, shocks, and excess volatility

Sources of volatility

Given the short period of existence of the market economy in Russia and the data constraint (as we have data for only ten years, which precludes the analysis of the volatility with annual data, we have to use quarterly data), it is reasonable to use cross-country regressions for the prolonged period – 1975–99 – to develop some understanding of the role of external factors in aggregate volatility and to apply these findings to Russian quarterly data to see if the results hold.

Some important conclusions from the cross-country regressions are the following (see note 4):

- The volatility of GDP growth rates, even after controlling for GDP per capita and average GDP growth rates, is higher for countries that are more dependent on trade (higher trade to GDP ratio) and that experience terms of trade shocks (high volatility of terms of trade index or of the trade-GDP ratio).

- Private capital flows move synchronically with the terms of trade so that they exacerbate external trade shocks instead of mitigating them.

Using these predictions from cross-country regressions as a guide when considering the Russian story, we observe that the volatility of GDP growth rates in Russia is even more strongly linked to the volatility of external trade than in most other countries. Over 50 per cent of Russian exports consist of fuel goods (gas, oil, and oil products) with highly volatile prices. Among fuel exporting countries – all countries with the share of fuel in total exports of over 50 per cent are shown in Figure 8.4 – Russia is least dependent on fuel exports, but as compared to large countries (with larger or comparable GDP – Brazil, Canada, China, France, Germany, India, Indonesia, Italy, Japan, Pakistan, UK, US) shown on the left side of the figure, the Russian Herfindahl index of export concentration is rather high. We need to bear in mind that the dominant export category for these countries is 'manufacturing goods', which include many different varieties of products with less volatile prices.

Despite intuition, however, it is import, not export, volatility that is closely correlated with the volatility of GDP growth rates. Additionally, changes in import volatility sometimes lag behind changes in real GDP volatility, so it is plausible to conclude that the volatility of imports is caused by the volatility of GDP and not vice versa.

Given the dependence on oil and gas exports, we could hypothesize that the volatility of Russian growth is caused by the terms of trade shocks, that is, changes in the world prices for oil and gas. However, the volatility of exports and

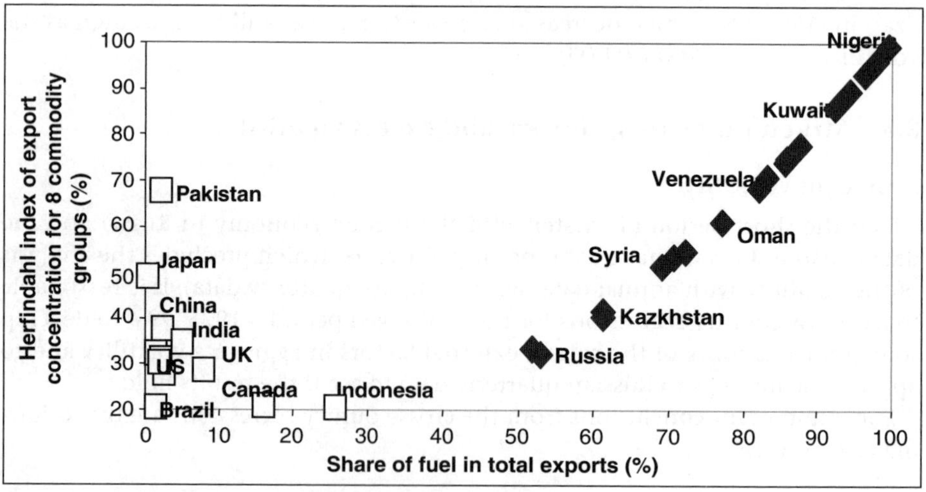

Figure 8.4 Share of fuel in total exports and Herfindahl index of export concentration for oil exporting countries (%, 2003 or latest available year)

volatility of oil and gas prices are not closely related to the volatility of GDP growth rates.

Overall, the volatility of GDP growth rates in 1994–2004 is very well explained by the volatility of external trade.[5]

$$GDPvol = -0.0015 - 0.11Ygr + 0.36TRvol$$

($N = 28$, $R^2 = 86$ per cent, all coefficients are significant at 1 per cent level, DW = 1.87), where

GDPvol – standard deviation from trend of GDP growth rates in 16 preceding quarters,

Ygr – average growth rates of GDP for 16 preceding quarters,

TRvol – volatility of nominal $ value of external trade (export + import) in 16 preceding quarters.[6]

However, this regression obviously captures the post-factum impact of GDP volatility on import volatility when import changes responded to changes in income (GDP). To analyze the mechanism of the influence of terms of trade shocks on the volatility of GDP, it is necessary to take a closer look at the changes in the real exchange rate and foreign exchange reserves.

Aggregate volatility and the current account

We compare the co-movement of output, investment, and private consumption (retail sales) in real terms and the current account in dollar terms. At face value

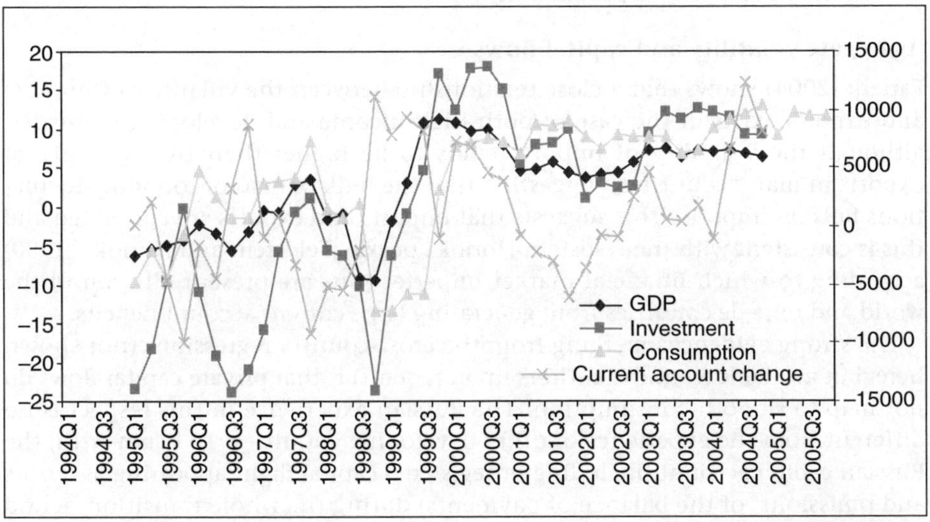

Figure 8.5 Annual (quarter to previous year quarter) change in real GDP, investment, private consumption (left scale) and quarter to previous year quarter increase in current account ($ million right scale)

(see Figure 8.5), consumption seems to fluctuate in line with the other components of GDP – less intensively than investment, but more intensively than output – which is typical of developing countries. In developed countries, the volatility of output is absorbed by the synchronical movement of savings (investment + government budget deficit + current account surplus) so that consumption is smoothed. But in developing countries, fluctuations of investment and the current account balance are not enough to reduce the volatility of consumption below the volatility of output.

Data show that the current account balance appears to change countercyclically with the gap between consumption and output growth rates. That is, when consumption grows faster than output, the current account deteriorates. It is thus plausible that there are mechanisms at work that smooth consumption – prevent it from growing faster than production (for instance: high growth of consumption → increase in imports → exchange rate depreciation → decline in imports and consumption). This was certainly the case after the August 1998 currency crisis: the dramatic devaluation of the ruble led to brisk improvement in the current account and a sizable drop in consumption (Montes and Popov, 1999).

It is quite obvious, though, that these mechanisms did not operate in the periods before and after the 1998 crisis, in 1995–97 and 1999–2006 (the exchange rate was de facto fixed and the real exchange rate was constantly appreciating, allowing consumption to grow faster than output). Under the de facto fixed exchange rate, sharp fluctuations in terms of trade (oil prices) led to unaffordable long-run increases in consumption. Additionally, periods of growing and high oil prices were often associated with a faster growth in consumption as compared to production.

Aggregate volatility and capital flows

Fanelli (2004) shows that a close relationship between the volatility of imports and exports exists in the case of both high-income and developing countries, although the volatility of imports tends to be higher than the volatility of exports in many countries, suggesting that the bulk of macroeconomic fluctuations falls on imports. This suggests that imports and exports are correlated and this is consistent with the Feldstein-Horioka puzzle (Feldstein and Horioka, 1980) according to which financial market imperfections are present all around the world and impede countries from generating large current account deficits.

The strong evidence emerging from the cross-country regressions (not shown here, but available from the authors upon request) is that private capital flows do not help to smooth consumption. The Russian experience in this respect is no different from the experience of other developing countries. To begin with, the Russian capital account (including unregistered capital flight appearing as 'errors and omissions' of the balance of payments) during the whole transition period was mostly negative, so Russia had to earn a positive current account to finance the outflow of capital. High risk, caused in part by poor DFA – macroeconomic uncertainty and weak financial infrastructure – placed Russia in a position of a net lender to the world during times when the country badly needed not only domestic, but also foreign savings. Whereas all other transition economies in Eastern Europe and the former Soviet Union were net importers of capital over the last 15 years, Russia's savings – equal to several per cent of GDP annually – were flowing abroad, which predictably had an adverse impact on consumption. In 1994–2004, current account surplus was on average \$23 billion a year; this surplus turned into deficit only once – in 1997, right before the currency crisis. By 2004, the surplus increased to \$58 billion; the cumulative surplus in 1994–2004 totaled \$250 billion.

To investigate the issue more closely, we grouped all capital flows into three categories: (1) *PCF* – net private capital flows (including sizable 'errors and omissions' in the balance of payments that are widely believed to be a euphemism for capital flight), the minus sign indicates the outflow of capital; (2) *NPB* – net borrowing by the public authorities, the minus sign indicates the outflow of capital; and (3) *dFOREX* – the increase in FOREX, the plus sign indicates the outflow of capital. The sum of these items equals the current account deficit (*CA*):

$$CA = PCF + NPB - dFOREX$$

It turns out that *PCF* moves mostly in line with oil prices (terms of trade), although the correlation is weak; *NGB* is negatively (also weakly) correlated with oil prices, whereas the increase in FOREX (*dFOREX*) exhibits quite a high positive correlation with oil prices.

Because it is known that real incomes and consumption in Russia are closely linked with terms of trade (fuel prices), the described relationships could mean that private capital flows do not help to smooth consumption, but contribute greater volatility, whereas net government borrowing and changes in foreign exchange reserves have a de facto stabilizing effect on consumption. This could be observed in figures 8.6 and 8.7 below: outflows of private capital are to an extent being balanced by the inflows of capital due to public borrowing and to a

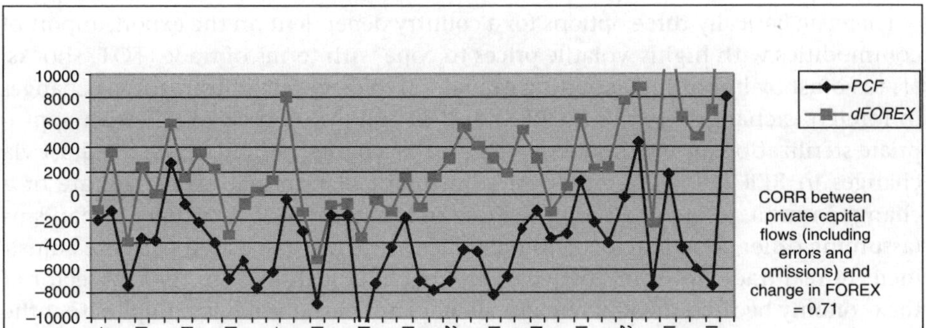

Figure 8.6 Private capital flows (including errors and omissions) and change in FOREX, 1994–2004 (\$ million)

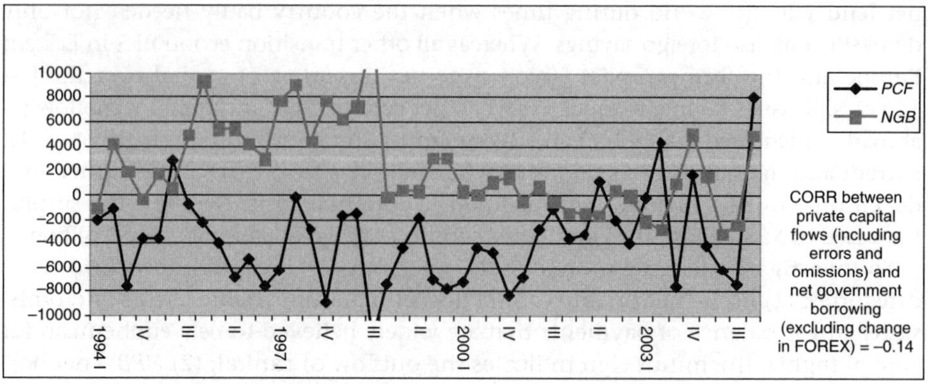

Figure 8.7 Private capital flows (including errors and omissions) and net government borrowing (excluding change in FOREX), 1994–2004 ($ million)

decrease in FOREX. To what particular extent? Does public policy – government borrowing and the management of reserves – counterweigh the negative effects of private capital flows on consumption volatility?

Options for managing terms of trade shocks

In 2005 Russia exported about 150 million tons of oil and 150 billion cubic meters of gas worth about $100 billion (all numbers have been rounded). The price of oil and gas varied greatly – only in recent decades have oil prices gone from $10 to over $60 a barrel ($60 to $360 a ton), and gas prices, which are strongly correlated with oil prices changed accordingly. In a rather bad (for Russia), but not totally unrealistic scenario oil prices would drop to $10 a barrel and would stay at this level for five years. Annual Russian revenues from exports of hydrocarbons would fall to about $20 billion instead of $100 billion, so that in five years there would be an accumulated $400 billion shortfall (Russian GDP at the official exchange rate in 2005 totaled about $600 billion). How could Russia adjust to such a negative trade shock (deterioration in terms of trade)?

There are basically three options for a country dependent on the export/import of commodities with highly volatile prices to cope with terms of trade (TOT) shocks: (1) to adjust by importing/exporting capital; (2) to carry out adjustment via changes in foreign exchange reserves (FOREX) and/or Stabilization Fund (SF) with appropriate sterilization and without changing real exchange rate (RER); (3) to adjust via changes in RER (allowing either an adjustment of nominal exchange rate or a change in money supply altering the rate of inflation). The first two mechanisms (assuming other good macroeconomic policies) are not associated with the adjustment in real trade flows and hence do not entail adjustments in the real sector of the economy because the RER remains stable. The third mechanism implies that the volumes of export and import change in response to changes in RER, hence, the real sector of the economy also responds (output changes).

Three options for managing TOT shocks under different exchange rate regimes are summarized in Table 8.1. Under a fixed exchange rate with no sterilization

Table 8.1 Options for managing the terms of trade shock for a resource exporting country

Patterns of change in variables/ Exchange rate and macro regime	FOREX	Nominal exchange rate	RER	Correlation between			
				FOR-M	TOT-FOREX	TOT-RER	FOR-RER
External shocks							
Fixed exchange rate without sterilization (currency board)	VOLAT	STABLE	VOLAT (prices)	HIGH	HIGH	HIGH	HIGH
Fixed exchange rate with sterilization	VOLAT	STABLE	STABLE	0	HIGH	0	0
Clean float	STABLE	VOLAT	VOLAT (nom. rate)	HIGH	0	HIGH	0

the nominal exchange rate is stable, but domestic inflation accelerates when FOREX expands due to a positive trade shock, so RER appreciates. Under a floating rate, a positive TOT shock causes the appreciation of the nominal exchange rate, which leads to the appreciation of RER. And only under a fixed exchange rate regime (including crawling pegs and dirty floats with nominal rate following a stable trend) with full sterilization of money supply changes resulting from FOREX fluctuations due to TOT shocks, can RER remain relatively stable – because all TOT shocks are absorbed by an increase/decrease in FOREX, which in turn are fully sterilized (Popov, 2003a; 2003b; 2005).

Empirical evidence: how Russia managed external shocks

The results from cross-country regressions suggest that good macroeconomic policies (which help to reduce volatility) are the following:

- Stable RER helps to reduce volatility of growth (in fact there is a strong correlation between volatility of GDP growth rates and volatility of RER).
- Stability of RER is achieved through policies of absorbing the TOT shocks via changes in FOREX and sterilizing the impact of FOREX fluctuations on money supply (high correlation of TOT and FOREX, low correlation between FOREX and RER and low correlation between M and FOREX).

To test this hypothesis explicitly we regressed volatility of GDP growth rates (cross-country regressions) on a variable for sterilization – correlation coefficient between FOREX to GDP ratio and M2 to GDP ratio (the higher this coefficient, the lower the sterilization of changes in the money supply resulting from the fluctuations of FOREX). The resulting equation is given below:

$$GDPvol = CONST. + CONTR.VAR. + 0.24TR/Y + 0.044TOTvol + 2.44FORvol - 1.65TOT\_FORcor + 1.23RER\_FORcor + 1.02M\_FORcor$$

($N = 58$, $R^2 = 47$, all coefficients significant at less than 8 per cent level, except for *TOTvol* coefficient, which is significant at 13 per cent level), where

Control variables – PPP GDP per capita in 1975, $, and annual average growth rates of GDP per capita in 1975–99 in per cent
M_FORcor – correlation coefficient between FOREX to GDP ratio and M2 to GDP ratio in 1975–99, and all other notations are same as before

It turns out that countries, which were carrying out sterilization policies (low *M_FOREXcor*), while responding to TOT shocks via changes in FOREX (high *TOT_FORcor*) and not allowing the RER to fluctuate together with FOREX (low *RER_FORcor*) were most successful at reducing the volatility of their economic growth.

The Russian story, however, is different from the international story that was derived from cross-country regressions. As Figure 8.8 suggests, the volatility of GDP is highly correlated with the volatility of the real exchange rate: periods of high volatility of Russian GDP growth appeared to be associated not so much with volatility of oil and gas prices, but rather originated in direct government mismanagement – the inability to keep the RER stable. Volatility of RER in time-series regressions for Russia turns out to be by far the most important and the most statistically significant variable.

As Figure 8.9 suggests, the high volatility of Russian GDP and RER are associated not so much with the volatility of oil prices, but with the absence of a sterilization policy – high correlation between changes in money supply (M2/GDP

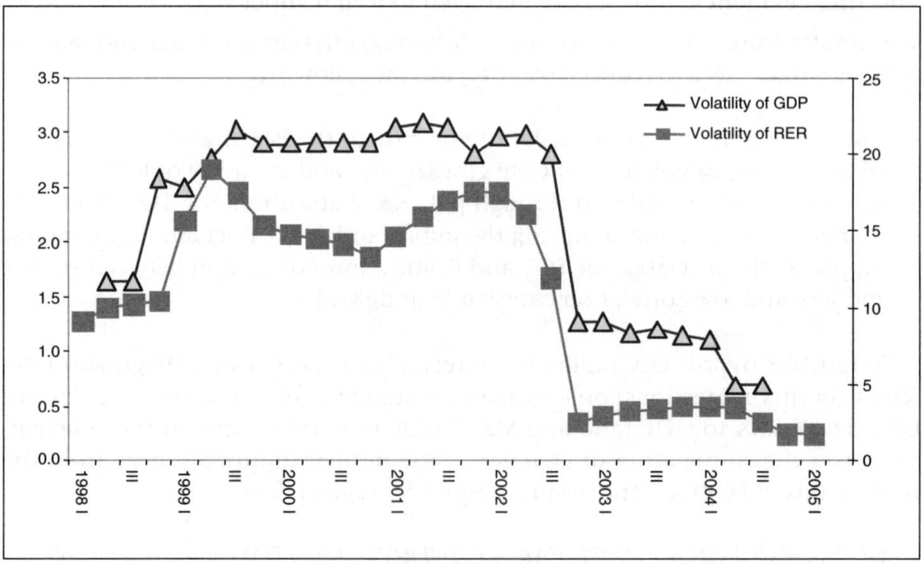

Figure 8.8 Volatility of GDP (left scale) and RER (right scale) in Russia, 1994–2005 (%)

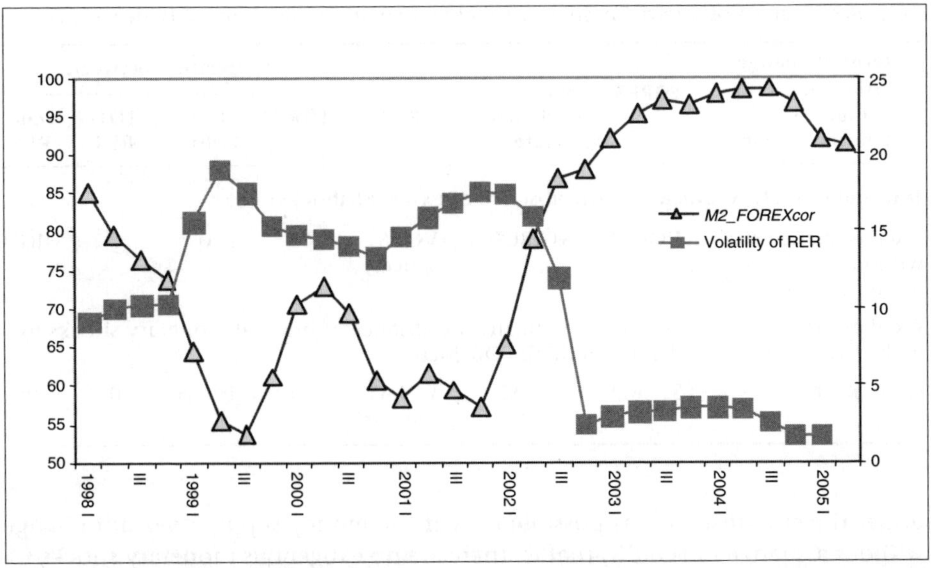

Figure 8.9 Volatility of RER (right scale) and correlation coefficient (left scale) between M2 and FOREX in Russia, 1994–2005 (%)

ratio) and foreign exchange reserves (FOREX/GDP ratio). The higher the correlation coefficient between M and FOREX was, the lower the volatility of RER and GDP – these indicators obviously move in opposite directions.

This puzzle is resolved by making the distinction between external and internal shocks. As was argued earlier (see Table 8.1), in the presence of an external shock, sterilization under a fixed nominal rate means a low correlation between FOREX and money supply, so the higher this correlation is, the less pronounced sterilization and the higher is the volatility of growth. But if shocks come from domestic sources, for instance from the central bank altering money supply without any external shocks, a high correlation between M and FOREX signifies the absence of internal shocks themselves – how can money supply change, if FOREX remains stable and all changes in money supply are sterilized? Consider, for instance, an exogenous increase in money supply by the CB in the absence of external shocks. Under a fixed nominal rate this would immediately cause an increase in prices (hence, an increase in RER and additional RER volatility) and a drop in real interest rates, and later, the balance of payments deficit (due to lower trade competitiveness and outflow of capital) and a decrease in FOREX, and finally the contraction of the money supply. Under a fully flexible rate monetary expansion would also immediately cause an increase in prices (hence, an increase in RER) and a decrease in real interest rates, and later devaluation (with no changes in FOREX). In both cases initially RER would change, which is bad for GDP volatility, while the correlation between money supply and FOREX would be low (money supply increases, but FOREX would not), so high GDP and RER volatility would be associated with a low correlation between FOREX and M. A high correlation between FOREX and M

Table 8.2 Impact of internal monetary shocks on volatility (no terms of trade shocks)

Patterns of change in variables/ Exchange rate and macro regime	**FOREX**	**Nominal exchange rate**	**RER**	**Correlation between**			
				FOR-M	**TOT-FOREX**	**TOT-RER**	**FOR-RER**
Internal monetary shocks (in the absence of external shocks)							
Fixed exchange rate without sterilization (currency board)	VOLAT	STABLE	VOLAT (prices)	0	0	0	HIGH
Fixed exchange rate with sterilization	Sterilization means the absence of internal monetary shocks by definition (high FOR_Mcor)						
Clean float	STABLE	VOLAT	VOLAT (nom. rate)	0	HIGH	0	0

under the circumstances is possible only if the money supply does not change without a change in FOREX, that is, there are no exogenous monetary shocks.[7]

Table 8.2 summarizes changes in the variables in question caused by an internal monetary shock. The bottom line is that, unlike in Table 8.1, which describes the dynamics of variables during the external shock, in this case, under the domestically generated monetary shock, lower volatilities of GDP and RER are associated with higher and not lower correlation coefficients between FOREX and M. These higher *FOR_Mcor* coefficients prove, in fact, that the exogenous monetary shocks are largely absent.

Regressions on Russian time-series data provide additional support for the existence of the described relationship. First, unlike in cross-country regressions, *TOTvol* does not have any significant explanatory power for *RERvol*, even when included on the right-hand side of the equation without any other variables. Although *TOTvol* matters for explaining the GDP growth rates volatility, the significance of coefficient of *RERvol* is much higher. Second, unlike in cross-country regressions, the correlation coefficient between *TOT* and *RER* is negative, not positive. And, third, unlike in cross-country regressions, *FOR_Mcor*, the correlation coefficient between M and FOREX, characterizing the absence of sterilization policies, enters on the right-hand side with the significant, but negative sign:

$$RERvol = 34.1 - 0.52AR(-1) - 30.7FOR\_M2cor - 4.7TOT\_RERcor + 0.01TOTvol$$

($N = 28$, $R^2 = 91$, all coefficients significant at less than 1 per cent level, except for *TOTvol*, which is insignificant (99 per cent); AR(–1) term is included because without it the Durbin-Watson (DW) statistic is bad)

and

$$RERvol = 16.5 + 0.95AR(-1) - 16.4\ RER\_FORcorr$$

($N = 28$, $R^2 = 95$, all coefficients significant at less than 1 per cent level; AR(–1) term is included because without it the DW statistic is bad), where

AR(–1) – volatility of RER in the preceding quarter
RER_FORcorr – correlation coefficient between RER and FOREX
FOR_M2cor – correlation coefficient between M2 and FOREX
TOT_RERcor – correlation coefficient between RER and FOREX
TOTvol – volatility of oil prices, $ a barrel

These equations imply that the volatility of RER is negatively, and not positively as in cross-country regressions, linked to the non-sterilization indicator (correlation between changes in FOREX and M2) and to the correlation between RER and FOREX. As was argued above, this is consistent with the assumption that the volatility of RER in Russia was primarily caused by internal monetary shocks: the expansion, for instance, of money supply without any apparent reason led to the increase in prices and appreciation of RER (higher volatility of RER); whereas TOT did not change (so the correlation between TOT and RER was low) and FOREX was stable (so the correlation between money supply and FOREX was low), the volatility of GDP was on the rise due to RER appreciation.

Hence, it may be hypothesized that the main causes of volatility in Russia were not foreign, but domestic, that is, the volatility of growth resulted not so much from the volatility of the terms of trade (even though *TOTvol* was high and Russia was very dependent on exports of oil and gas with highly volatile prices).[8] This is one of the main conclusions of this chapter: even in countries that export resources with highly volatile prices, like Russia, the volatility of economic growth could be associated not so much with objective circumstances (TOT shocks) as with poor macroeconomic policies – the inability to keep the RER stable. Poor macroeconomic policy, in turn, was largely inevitable in bad-quality institutions and a highly volatile and crisis-prone environment (see next section).

Figure 8.10 presents additional evidence of poor macroeconomic policy in Russia. First, Russia failed to respond to the TOT fluctuations by altering FOREX – only in 3 quarters out of 28, for which correlation coefficients between TOT and FOREX were computed for a 16-quarter moving window; these correlation coefficients were higher than 50 per cent. Second, for most sub-periods of 1994–2005 these correlation coefficients were moving in the direction opposite to the volatility of oil prices – when volatility of TOT increased, government policies of stabilization of RER through moving FOREX together with TOT were especially weak. Instead of mitigating the volatility from external shocks, the Russian government and monetary authorities were adding insult to injury by contributing to the economic volatility by generating their own monetary shocks.

In a regression linking RER volatility with the volatility of terms of trade (proxied by the volatility of oil prices) and the volatility of M2 growth rates, only the latter variable is significant, while the former is not:

$$RERvol = -0.02 + 0.83AR(-1) + 0.01TOTvol + 1.14Mvol$$

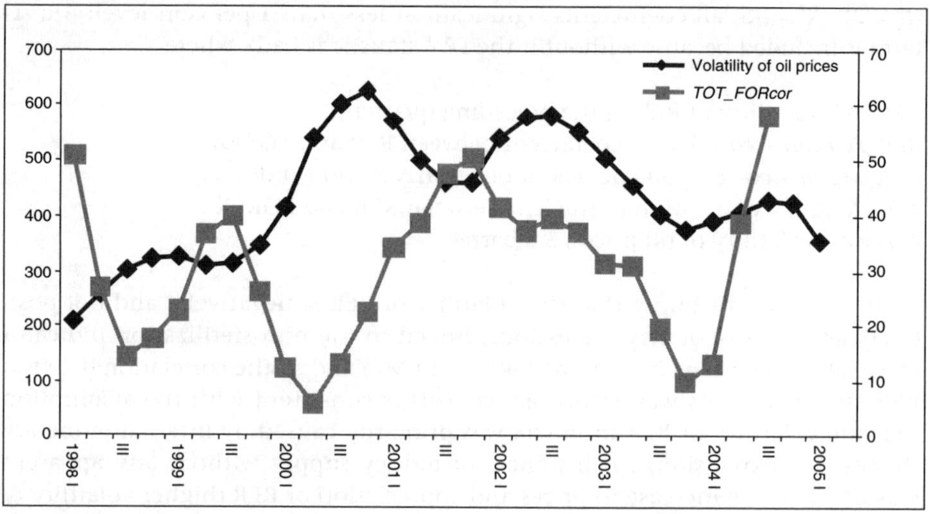

Figure 8.10 Volatility of TOT (oil prices, cents a barrel – left scale) and correlation coefficient between TOT and FOREX (right scale, %) in Russia, 1994–2005

($N = 27$, $R^2 = 85$ per cent, DW = 2.08, all coefficients significant at 6 per cent level or less, except TOT volatility coefficient, which is insignificant), where:

Mvol – standard deviation of M2 quarterly growth rates in 16 preceding quarters

That is, the instability of RER is determined mostly by the instability of the money supply, not by the instability of the terms of trade.

Similarly, in a regression linking GDP growth rates volatility to TOT volatility, RER volatility and M2 volatility, all three explanatory variables are highly statistically significant:

$$GDPvol = -0.01 + 0.003TOTvol + 0.07RERvol + 0.27Mvol$$

($N = 28$, $R^2 = 87$, DW = 1.7, all coefficients significant at less than 2 per cent level).

That is, even controlling for the volatility of the terms of trade and the volatility of RER, the volatility of output growth in 1994–2004 in Russia was dependent on the volatility of money supply caused by unstable monetary policy.

8.4 The DFA, financial market failures, and aggregate fluctuations

Cross-country comparisons (Aghion et al., 2006) suggest that a higher level of financial development allows mitigating volatility resulting from domestic and external shocks.

In this section we examine the vicious circle between aggregate volatility and financial institutions: general economic volatility undermines the banking system and the depth of financial markets, leads to demonetization and dollarization of the economy, destroys the security of financial contracts, especially long-term contracts, whereas all these negative developments in DFA preclude the diversification of risks and thus do not create an environment that is conducive to the reduction of volatility. On the basis of the evidence provided in previous sections, we show that a volatile environment with deficient rules of the financial game (flawed financial liberalization, bad corporate governance, and fiscal imbalances) induced adaptive responses that severely hindered financial developments and ultimately resulted in low financial deepening.

Monetization and volatility

In virtually all countries that experienced high inflation, monetization fell and credits as a percentage of GDP decreased markedly. Figure 8.11 shows the demonetization of the Russian economy that occurred in recent years. To make it worse, there is a ratchet effect here, so that many years of low inflation will be necessary to drive monetization back to high levels.

Many transition economies experienced a similar collapse in monetization and bank credit due to high inflation. In fact, only China and Visegrad countries managed to avoid dramatic declines in real bank credit by keeping inflation in check, whereas in FSU states and even in most Balkan countries the ratio of bank credit to GDP fell several times.

The collapse of bank credit was part of the broader process of the demonetization of the economy under high inflation: due to dollarization, barterization and the accumulation of payment arrears in inflationary transition economies,

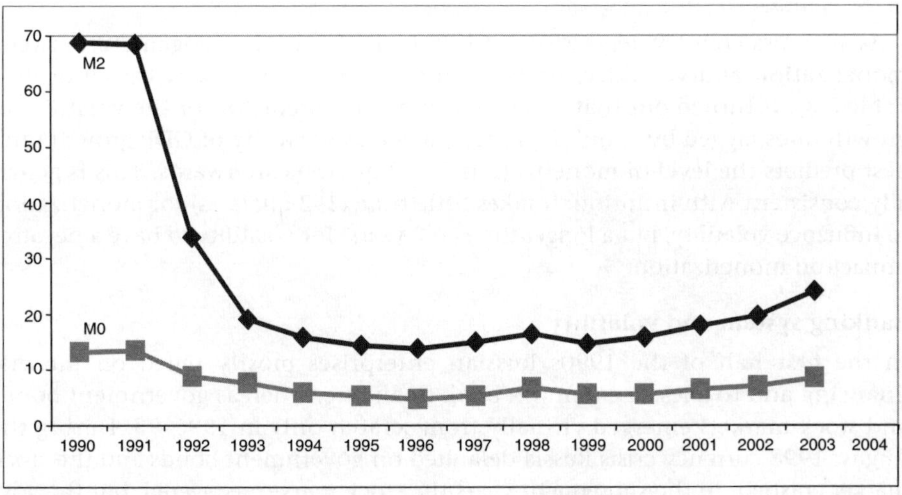

Figure 8.11 Monetary aggregates (end of year), 1990–2004 (% of GDP)

M2/GDP ratios decreased markedly, that is, money velocity jumped due to the proliferation of explicit and implicit money substitutes, such as foreign currency, barter trade, and non-payments. As the data suggest, there is a strong link between inflation and demonetization, between demonetization and total domestic bank credit, and between the latter and credit to the private sector in particular.

Under the Soviet government, total bank credit to enterprises exceeded half of GDP with long-term credits alone amounting to 12 per cent of GDP. After the deregulation of prices in 1992 the demonetization of the economy proceeded surprisingly quickly: total bank credits outstanding fell to about 10 per cent of GDP by the end of 1996, while the long-term credits shrank to less than 1 per cent of GDP.[9] When the possibility of the bank crisis was discussed in the summer of 1996 the frequently-made argument was that the total bank assets were so small as compared to the size of the economy that even the collapse of major banks would not become a disaster.

Like the cross-country regressions for the longer period of time, regressions on Russian time series prove the negative relationship between monetization and volatility of growth rates:

$$GDPvol = 0.001 + 0.002TOTvol - 0.001RERvol - 0.014M2/Y$$

($N = 28$, $R^2 = 96$, all coefficients significant at less than 1 per cent level, DW = 2.28), where

GDPvol – standard deviation from trend of GDP growth rates in 16 preceding quarters
TOTvol – volatility of world oil prices, $ a barrel, in 16 preceding quarters
RERvol – volatility of RER index in 16 preceding quarters
M2/Y – ratio of M2 to GDP in preceding 16 quarters

As in cross-country regressions, there is an issue of endogeneity between monetization and volatility, so we used Granger test for likely causation (see Table 8.3). It turned out that *M2/Y* ratio is a good predictor for the volatility of growth rates lagged by 1 and 2 quarters, whereas volatility of GDP growth rates best predicts the level of monetization 5 to 7 quarters afterwards. This is generally consistent with intuition: it takes little time (1–2 quarters) for monetization to influence volatility, but a longer time (1–2 years) for volatility to have a negative impact on monetization.

Banking system and volatility

In the first half of the 1990s Russian enterprises mostly relied on internal financing and to a lesser extent on bank financing, whereas government bonds and stock markets emerged virtually from scratch only in 1995–98. During the August 1998 currency crisis Russia defaulted on government bonds and the stock market crashed. In the subsequent years the stock market recovered, but the government bonds market remained weak.

Table 8.3 Granger test for *Yvol* and M2/Y ratio

Null hypothesis	Obs	F-Statistic	Probability
Lags: 1			
Yvol does not Granger cause M2/GDP ratio	27	2.39429	0.13487
M2/GDP ratio does not Granger cause *Yvol*		7.55532	0.01118
Lags: 2			
Yvol does not Granger cause M2/GDP ratio	26	1.15675	0.33375
M2/GDP ratio does not Granger cause *Yvol*		3.82788	0.03825
Lags: 3			
Yvol does not Granger cause M2/GDP ratio	25	0.80677	0.50645
M2/GDP ratio does not Granger cause *Yvol*		2.52268	0.09030
Lags: 4			
Yvol does not Granger cause M2/GDP ratio	24	0.96659	0.45430
M2/GDP ratio does not Granger cause *Yvol*		2.04690	0.13911
Lags: 5			
Yvol does not Granger cause M2/GDP ratio	23	3.16093	0.04752
M2/GDP ratio does not Granger cause *Yvol*		1.52748	0.25322
Lags: 6			
Yvol does not Granger cause M2/GDP ratio	22	5.60612	0.01118
M2/GDP ratio does not Granger cause *Yvol*		1.26271	0.36126
Lags: 7			
Yvol does not Granger cause M2/GDP ratio	21	11.5075	0.00421
M2/GDP ratio does not Granger cause *Yvol*		1.97461	0.21263
Lags: 8			
Yvol does not Granger cause M2/GDP ratio	20	5.73996	0.08913
M2/GDP ratio does not Granger cause *Yvol*		2.02097	0.30415

One of the strong beliefs in Russia is that the expansion of the market for government bonds in 1995–98 was counterproductive because limited savings were used for the construction of the financial pyramid rather than for investment in tangible assets. Enterprises switched to barter exchange, and non-payments mounted because investment in government bonds was so much more profitable.

Some elements of the DFA may cause more volatility than others depending on the stage of development. One of the hypotheses may be similar to that of Bolton and Freixas (2000) – they suggest that the equilibrium combination of bank credit, bond and equity financing depends on the riskiness (credit rating) of the firms. Their analysis may be applied to industries and whole economies at different stages of development and with different investment climates (that is, under a poor investment climate, equity and bond financing do not work that well). Most transition economies developed a German-Japanese institution-based financial system, whereas Russia's very low concentration in the banking sector, which is focused mostly on payment functions rather than on deposit-credit operations, may be an exception (Popov, 1999). In Russia's highly volatile high-risk environment, bond and stock markets cannot function that well, but the banking system fills the gap because of its weak and low concentration (owing to historical reasons).[10] This may be exactly the case of a 'low-institutional high-volatility trap equilibrium' described in Fanelli (2004).

After high inflation in the first half of the 1990s the credit/GDP ratios, like the M/GDP ratios, fell dramatically, to levels several times lower than in developed countries, and even several times lower than the ones that had been observed in the late 1980s in Russia itself, when the economy was centrally planned. These ratios only began to recover very slowly during the short-lived period of macroeconomic stabilization of 1995–98, falling again after the currency crisis of 1998. In 1996–98 the Central Bank of Russia introduced regulations that were very similar to those required by the Basel I Accord, although this did not save Russian banking from bankruptcy or license withdrawal after the August 1998 currency crisis. The number of commercial banks in Russia decreased from 1697 on 1 January 1998 to 1274 on 1 January 2001 and remained around this level afterwards (1249 on 1 January 2006). CBR intends to comply with Basel II Accords by 2008–09.

Credits to and deposits of non-financial enterprises as a percentage of GDP reached the bottom in 1999, one year after the crisis, whereas total assets of the banking system and deposits of individuals as a percentage of GDP continued to decline for another year and bottomed out in 2000 (see Table 8.4). From that time virtually all items of assets and liabilities of banks as a percentage of GDP

Table 8.4 Selected balance sheet indicators of the Russian banking sector (% GDP, end of period)

Indicator	**1998**	**1999**	**2000**	**2001**	**2002**	**2003**	**2004**
Number of operating credit institutions	1476	1349	1311	1319	1329	1329	1299
Assets	39.8	32.9	32.3	35.3	38.3	42.4	42.5
Capital (own funds)	2.9	3.5	3.9	5.1	5.4	6.2	5.6
Funds attracted from physical persons	7.6	6.2	6.1	7.6	9.5	11.5	11.7
Funds attracted from enterprises and organizations	10.7	9.7	9.9	10.1	10.1	10.5	11.8
Credits extended to non-financial enterprises and organizations	13.0	9.9	11.0	13.2	14.7	17.2	18.8
Credits extended to non-financial enterprises and organizations as percentage of total assets	32.7	30.1	34.1	37.4	38.4	40.6	44.2

Source: Central Bank of Russia.

increased gradually (the slowdown of growth of personal deposits to GDP ratio in 2004 was associated with the small banking crisis in the summer 2004), but only in 2003–05 did they reach pre-crisis levels (see Table 8.4). Banks are now more involved in the financing of the real sector of the economy. (Before the crisis they preferred to operate in the government securities market (GKO) which was less risky and much more profitable.) Credits extended to non-financial enterprises and organizations to GDP ratio in 2004 (42.5 per cent) are still lower than those in East European countries (67–121 per cent) and much smaller than in the EU (280 per cent).

Equity (banks' own capital) as a proportion of GDP has increased twofold since the crisis – from 2.9 per cent in 1998 to 5–6 per cent in 2003–04 (see Table 8.4), whereas the ratio of banks' own capital to total assets[11] grew from 7 per cent in 1998 to 13–14 per cent in 2003–04, which is believed to be prudent enough to ensure the stability of the banking system. This ratio stays at about 5–6 per cent for developed countries and 20 per cent for some countries in Africa and Latin America. On the one hand, it may be argued that the banking system today is more stable than before the crisis. On the other, this is a definite sign of the poor credibility of the banking sector – doubling equity to assets ratio was needed just to restore the level of development of the banking system that existed before the crisis.

The concentration in the banking sector increased after the 1998 crisis (due to the bankruptcy and closure or mergers/restructuring of many smaller banks). However, Russia still has too many banks and the process of concentration significantly slowed down after 2001. One positive sign, though, is that the determinants of successful performance of banks after the 1998 crisis do not look as extraordinary as they did before the crisis. In the post-crisis period the probability of default of banks depends negatively on their profit before taxes, negatively on loans to non-financial institutions and positively on the amount of overdue loans. Before the crisis the coefficients of these variables were insignificant and/or had the 'wrong' signs (Peresetsky et al., 2004), which could have been caused by poor accounting practices, as well as by the existence of 'pocket banks' of enterprises and large investment into government securities.

Dollarization, contract duration, and volatility

The 1998 crisis seriously impacted the credibility of the national currency: the share of total loans denominated in rubles (which was quite low to begin with) fell in the anticipation of and during the crisis from 60 to 30 per cent and could only recover the pre-crisis level by 2001. After the crisis, the share of ruble loans grew in all segments. In 2001–03 these shares were stable, but from 2004 the share of ruble loans started to increase again. Most of the short-term (less than 1 year) loans from 2000 were denominated in rubles. But the share of long-term loans (over 1 year) only reached pre-crisis levels (about 50 per cent) in 2004. The longer the term of the loan, the greater the share of dollar-denominated loans in total credits. This means that the credibility of the central bank in ensuring the stability of the ruble exchange rate is still quite low. So, when it comes to issuing loans of one year and more, banks prefer to denominate these loans in hard currency rather than rubles. The effect of the 1998 crisis on the denomination of long-term loans lasted for a full six years (1999–2004).

The impact of the 1998 crisis on the duration of loans was a bit less pronounced but much more lasting than the impact on the credibility of the national currency. The share of 'long loans' (with over 1 year duration) decreased from nearly 50 per cent right after the crisis, in the first quarter of 1999,[12] to below 30 per cent in 2001–02. From 2002, the share of 'long' loans steadily increased, but was still below the 1999 level of nearly 50 per cent even by mid-2005.

Regarding credits to non-financial enterprises and organizations by loan duration, the central bank registered an increase in the share of long-term (> 1 year) loans from the end of 2001. The largest share of ruble loans falls on credits of the duration of between 6 months and a year and 1–3 years, whereas the largest share of foreign currency loans is provided for the duration of 1–3 years, 6 months–1 year and >3 years. Banks are obviously more inclined to denominate long-term loans in foreign currency.

Effects of the 1998 crisis on the denomination and the term structure of credits

Figure 8.12 demonstrates the relationship between GDP volatility and the share of ruble and long credits in total credits. Remember that the GDP volatility is measured for the period of 16 preceding quarters, so that the volatility shown for

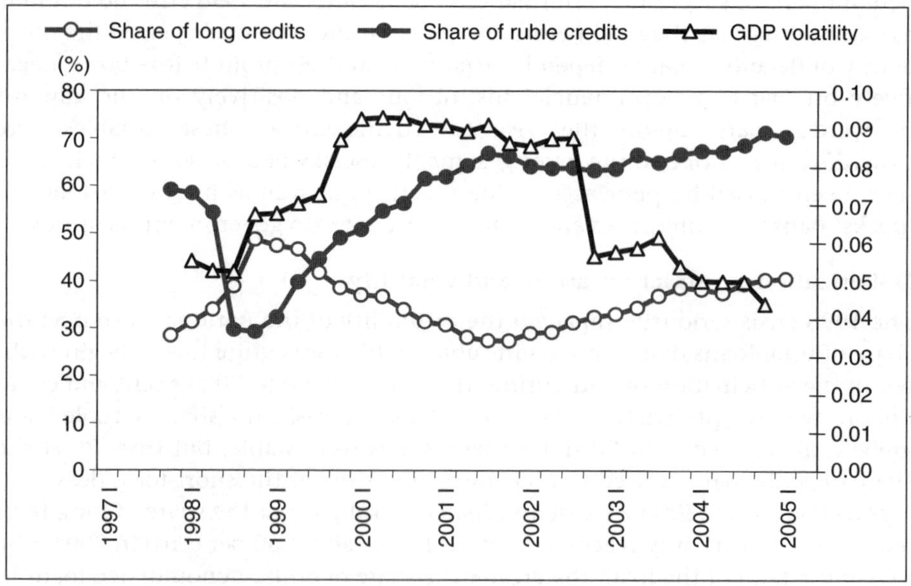

Figure 8.12 The volatility of GDP versus share of ruble credits and share of long credits, 1997–2005

the first quarter of 1998 is, in fact, the volatility of GDP for the period of 1994/1–1997/4. Taking this into account one can observe a very sharp, but short-lived dollarization impact of the 1998 crisis and a substantial and extremely lasting negative impact on long-term financial contracts. That is, the credibility of the national currency that was undermined by the 1998 crisis was restored quite quickly, reaching pre-crisis levels in just two years, whereas the credibility of financial contracts, as measured by the share of long-term credits, only approached pre-crisis levels in the 2004–06 period after the crisis. Credit markets definitely have a longer memory than currency markets. Default on government bonds in August 1998 thus seems to have done more damage than the devaluation.

Figure 8.13 is even more telling; it shows the share of long-term credits against the share of credits in rubles. It is obvious that the positive correlation between the share of long-term credits and the share of ruble credits, observed over the 1998–2004 period, was interrupted by the 1998 financial crisis (points for 1–2 quarters of 1998 are more in line with points for 2002–04 than they are with the points for the period of 3/1999 to 4/2002). The 'stable' relationship between the share of ruble credits and the share of long-term credits would have been a positive one if it had not been interrupted by the 1999–2002 period, when the relationship between these variables was negative owing to a lag in the reaction of credit markets to a crisis as compared to currency markets.

Main problems of risk management under excess and extreme volatility

It seems obvious that Russia's 1998 currency crisis badly damaged the emerging and still very weak system of financial institutions. It led to a new demonetization

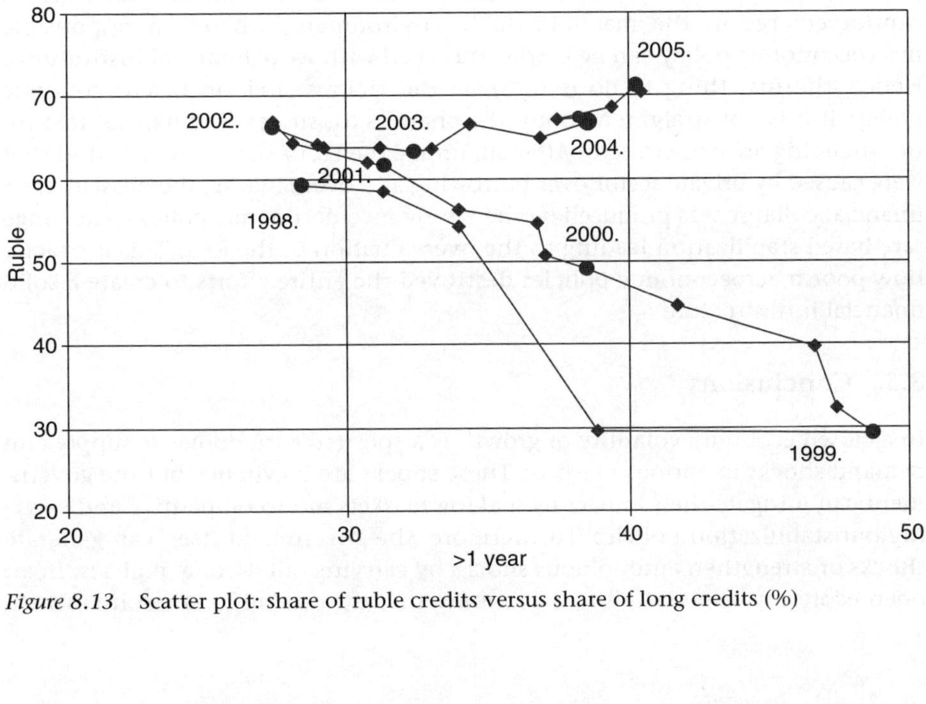

Figure 8.13 Scatter plot: share of ruble credits versus share of long credits (%)

and dollarization of the Russian economy, completely wiping out all modest positive trends that had been observed during the short-lived macrostabilization of 1995–98. It took two to six years of non-stop economic growth in a favorable external environment (high oil prices) to achieve pre-crisis levels of monetization and the credibility of the national currency. In addition, the crisis undermined the security of financial contracts – only six years after the crisis did the share of long-term credits in total loans approach the pre-crisis level. In turn, the weakness of financial institutions obviously makes another financial crisis more probable. How does one break this vicious circle?

The strength of the national banking and financial system is supposed to help reduce the volatility of growth almost by definition – because it contributes to the inter-temporal distribution of risks in the economy. It is not exactly clear, however, what particular regulations help to build a healthy banking and financial system. Prudential regulations were strengthened in Russia after the 1998 crisis, and some obvious fraud schemes (like financial pyramids) were prohibited. But prudential regulations in the East Asian countries largely conformed to the Basel guidelines, which did not insulate them from the crisis. The ratio of liquid assets of banks to their total assets does not seem to have had an impact on volatility in cross-country regressions. This indicator has a predicted (negative) sign, but is not statistically significant. Indeed, institutional memory – traditions that emerge from learning by doing, including traditions in the enforcement of regulations – probably has greater impact on the stability of the financial system than particular prudential regulations themselves.

A more promising way to break the 'volatility–institutions–volatility' vicious circle seems to be the creation of built-in stabilizers and checks and balances that preclude irresponsible macroeconomic policies. Strong financial institutions cannot emerge in the macro-unstable environment, whereas a responsible macroeconomic policy can be carried out even with weak financial institutions. Hence, the first thing to do is to break the vicious circle in macroeconomic policy. If it is not straightened out, the chances for successful financial institution-building are close to zero. After all, unlike the East Asian currency crises that were caused by private sector over-borrowing and over-lending, the Russian 1998 financial collapse was produced by the wrong macroeconomic policy – exchange rate-based stabilization leading to the overvaluation of the RER. This is exactly how poor macroeconomic policies destroyed the entire efforts to create a solid financial infrastructure.

8.5 Conclusions

In a closed economy volatility of growth is associated with domestic supply and demand shocks in various markets. These shocks are inevitable, but the government can mitigate their impact by making markets more competitive and carrying out stabilization policies. Furthermore, the government itself can generate shocks or strengthen autonomous shocks by carrying out 'wrong' policies. In an open economy, especially in an economy that exports/imports resources with highly volatile prices, there are additional sources of volatility – external shocks associated with terms of trade changes and volatile private capital flows (which, unfortunately, reinforce terms of trade shocks instead of mitigating them). Thus, in an open economy, the government should assume another responsibility – managing the external shocks in such a way as to reduce their impact on the volatility of the national economy. With new responsibilities come new dangers, however: an open economy becomes not only vulnerable to external shocks, but also to new policy mistakes in managing these shocks. Instead of mitigating external shocks the government with the 'wrong' policies can reinforce existing shocks or even create new ones.

The volatility of GDP growth rates in Russia in the first half of the 1990s was due mostly to the unique policy-generated supply shock – the immediate deregulation of prices that created the need to reallocate resources between industries. The impact of this shock, together with the collapse of state institutions (another supply shock), caused an unprecedented reduction of output (about 40 per cent in 1989–95). By 1995, however, the impact of this initial shock was largely over and subsequent development was very much comparable with that of a typical resource-exporting developing country or emerging market economy. We focus in our study on this latter period (1994–2004), when domestically generated real shocks largely exhausted themselves, and conclude that the volatility of output was caused mainly by poor macroeconomic policies – not only did the government and the central bank do a poor job in managing external shocks, but they also contributed to the instability by generating monetary shocks themselves. As a result, the volatility of the GDP quarterly growth rates in Russia in the first part of the period in question (1994–2000) was not only higher than in developed countries, but also one of the highest in the world (standard deviation of 3 p.p.). Only in the second period (2000–04) did volatility decrease to levels observed in other developing countries for quarterly GDP growth rates (1 or 2 percentage points).

In countries that export resources with highly unstable prices, like Russia, the excess volatility of economic growth is associated mostly with the volatility of RER, which, in turn, is caused mainly by the inability to accumulate enough reserves in FOREX and in a Stabilization Fund. The option of attracting foreign capital during difficult times, when the country faces a negative trade shock, seems to be unavailable for resource-based developing countries because private capital flows change procyclically with terms of trade, thus reinforcing the trade shocks, whereas official capital flows, even though they may be countercyclical, are not enough to compensate the destabilizing effect of private capital movements.

Volatility in Russia is obviously associated with the volatility in the terms of trade – in fact GDP and investment growth rates closely follow the dynamics of world oil prices. However, it is the volatility of Russian imports, not exports, that exhibits the highest correlation with the volatility of GDP and it is the result rather than the cause of the GDP volatility. The link between TOT volatility and GDP volatility is RER and the complication is that the RER can change not only in response to TOT and capital flows shocks, but also due to internal monetary shocks that have played a prominent role in Russia in the past ten years.

It turns out that volatility of RER is linked positively (although not significantly) to the volatility of terms of trade, to the correlation between FOREX and M (no sterilization indicator), positively and significantly to the correlation coefficient between FOREX and RER (suggesting that volatility of RER is higher, when, for instance, the accumulation of FOREX cannot prevent the appreciation of RER), but it is linked negatively to the correlation coefficients between TOT and FOREX (that is, when FOREX does not change in response to TOT shocks, RER changes) and between TOT and RER (suggesting that when RER changes without TOT shocks, that is, due to domestic shocks, this correlation coefficient is low and volatility of RER is high).

Whereas in cross-country regressions the volatility of output and RER was lower in countries that carry out sterilization policies (low correlation between FOREX and M), Russia's experience was exactly the opposite: periods of high volatility of output and RER were associated with a higher sterilization activity of the central bank. This means that the monetary authorities, unlike in other countries, were generating shocks themselves instead of mitigating external shocks. The pre-1998 currency crisis monetary policy is a case in point – despite the fall in oil prices in 1997–98 the central bank was tightening monetary policy in an attempt to prevent the devaluation of a grossly overvalued exchange rate of the ruble that finally led to balance of payments and currency crises.

Therefore, the main causes of volatility in Russia were not foreign, but domestic. That is, the volatility of growth resulted not so much from the volatility of terms of trade (even though TOT volatility was high and Russia was very dependent on oil and gas exports with highly volatile prices). This is one of the main conclusions of our chapter: even in countries that export resources with highly volatile prices, like Russia, the volatility of economic growth could be associated not so much with objective circumstances (TOT shocks), but with poor macroeconomic policies – the inability to keep the RER stable.

Private capital flows did not help to reduce the volatility of GDP and consumption, but rather reinforced the effects of TOT shocks on volatility. Even more surprising is the fact that fluctuations in FOREX contributed to the volatility of consumption rather than to smoothing consumption. After controlling for changes in output (which also moves largely synchronically with oil prices and consumption) it turns out that fluctuations in FOREX were contributing to the volatility of consumption (outflows of state capital in the form of FOREX accumulation were high during periods of the largest differences between consumption and production growth rates). Only net government borrowing had a stabilizing effect on consumption, but it was completely counterweighed by the destabilizing impact of private capital flows and changes in FOREX.

The role of financial infrastructure is crucial for the reduction of volatility. Theoretically, perfect financial markets spreading the costs of adjustment intertemporally can reduce volatility resulting from demand and supply shocks, no matter whether they are caused by domestic autonomous developments, external instability, or poor government policies. Financial deepening helps to reduce volatility – this is a very robust result that is observed in cross-country comparisons and in time series for Russia. It appears that causation here runs both ways: higher monetization reduces volatility very fast (in the following 1–2 quarters), whereas lower volatility helps to increase monetization after 1–2 years. But because the causation runs both ways, in a volatile environment the economy enters a vicious circle: sound financial institutions do not emerge in the unstable environment, whereas without a sound financial infrastructure it is difficult, if not impossible, to reduce volatility substantially.

There is enough evidence that the financial infrastructure was badly damaged by the transformational recession. In particular, the high inflation of 1992–95 resulted from the inability of major interest groups to take the necessary collective actions to raise government revenues. Besides, there emerged previously unheard of mutations in financial and payment contracts, such as the proliferation of non-payments, barter and monetary substitutes. There is also much evidence that Russia's 1998 crisis weakened the financial infrastructure that had just begun to emerge in the period of macroeconomic stabilization of 1995–98: monetization and the ratio of bank deposits and credits to GDP fell, dollarization increased, short-term financial contracts expanded at the expense of long-term contracts.

Figure 8.14 illustrates the vicious circle: general economic volatility deteriorates the quality of macroeconomic policy and weakens financial infrastructure, which, in turn, leads to greater volatility. The complication is that the poor quality of macroeconomic policy undermines financial infrastructure not only indirectly, via the impact on volatility, but also directly, through changes in exchange rate, inflation, interest rates, and so on. So, the surest and shortest way out of this vicious circle is to fix the macroeconomic policy first. Another argument is that it may be easier to fix macroeconomic policy than to build sound financial institutions. Prudent macroeconomic policy is by no means a sufficient

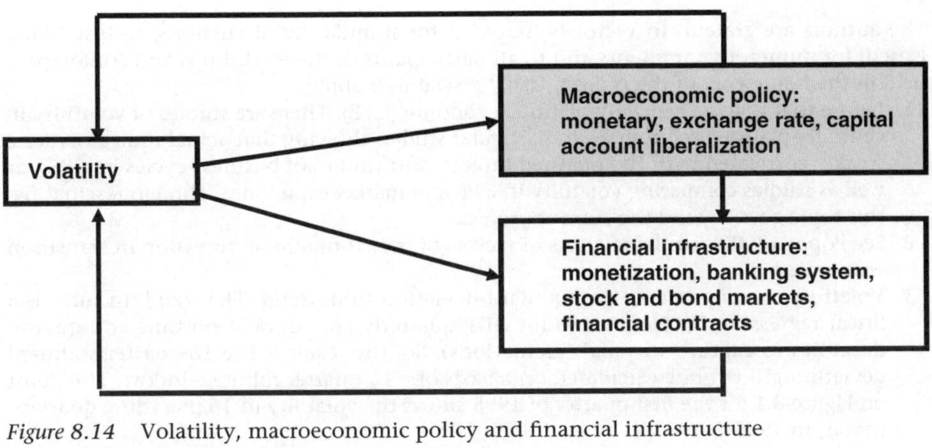

Figure 8.14 Volatility, macroeconomic policy and financial infrastructure

condition for low volatility, but it is definitely a necessary condition and a prerequisite for breaking the vicious circle.

The policy implications for the DFA are thus pretty obvious. A good macroeconomic policy for Russia would be: (1) not to generate monetary shocks and (2) to cope with inevitable external shocks via changes in FOREX and SF, while keeping the RER stable. To reach this goal, reserves in FOREX and SF should be sufficient to withstand an adverse trade shock, that is, judging by previous experience, should be roughly equal to annual GDP. Preservation of capital account controls for short-term capital flows would make it easier to cope with external shocks.

Needless to say, measures to strengthen the financial system, such as the increase in the concentration of the bank assets, tight prudential regulations, and the promotion of long-term financial contracts, even if this would require direct guarantees from the government, would contribute to diminishing volatility. But without prudent macroeconomic policy, these measures are not likely to yield impressive results. In addition, government and external indebtedness should be kept within reasonable limits. Even though the Russian time series does not allow us to prove the negative impact of debt on volatility, there is strong support for this conclusion from cross-country regressions.

Among the policy implications for the IFA are measures to limit short-term speculative capital flows (Stiglitz, 2000; Griffith-Jones et al., 2001; Singh, 2002; Kose et al., 2003), to strengthen the international organizations' lending capacity to countries affected by external shocks (TOT shocks and capital flows), as well as by domestic shocks, and to create price stabilization funds for resource commodities. It would be in Russia's interests to participate in the International Stabilization Fund which would receive contributions from resource exporters and lend this money to resource importers in periods of high prices in commodities, while in periods of low resource prices it would carry out borrowing-lending operations in the opposite direction.

Notes

The authors are grateful to Victor Polterovich for stimulating discussions, to José María Fanelli for numerous comments and to all participants of the workshops and conferences held in the framework of the project. Usual disclaimers apply.

1. Before that it was a centrally planned economy (CPE). There are studies of volatility in centrally planned economies, in particular studies showing that actual indicators were weakly correlated with the planned targets, and studies of business cycles in CPEs, as well as studies comparing volatility in CPE and market economies. Though fascinating, this topic goes beyond the current project.
2. See Popov (2000) for the analysis of factors of transformational recession in transition economies.
3. Volatility is computed as the standard deviation from trend. The trend, in turn, is a linear regression for 16 quarters (of GDP quarterly growth rates on time and quarter dummies to capture seasonal fluctuations). So, the result is the 16-quarter standard deviation growth rate calculated on a basis of a 16-quarter rolling window. The point on Figure 8.1 for the first quarter of 1998 shows the volatility in 16 preceding quarters, that is, in 1990/1–1993/4.

4. The results of this analysis are not reported here, but are available from the authors upon request.
5. All regressions in the chapter which use overlapping time series (that is, annual growth rates with quarterly frequencies) were estimated with Newey-West standard errors, which give consistent estimates of coefficients' standard errors in the presence of heteroskedasticity and autocorrelation.
6. We control for the average growth rates of GDP (because the empirical relationship between the volatility and growth is well documented, even though it is not well understood). Because there may be an endogeneity problem (not only growth affects volatility, but also vice versa), we tried a number of instruments, such as money supply growth rates and M2/GDP ratio, squared and cubed indicators of *TRvol* – the result was that coefficients did change, but their signs significance remained intact. Also, the Granger test for GDP growth rates and volatility of these growth rates did not reveal any possibility for the causation relationship.
7. This argument is consistent with the findings of Edwards and Magendzo (2003): they find that dollarized economies and currency unions have higher volatility than countries with a currency of their own. Our argument, though, is a bit different: among countries with currencies of their own external shocks are best dampened (evened out, mitigated) when FOREX completely absorb TOT shocks and fluctuations of FOREX are completely sterilized, so that RER stays stable.
8. For a discussion of theoretical issues of Russian monetary policy and the Taylor rule for the Russian central bank see Sosunov and Zamulin (2005), Vdovichenko and Voronina (2004).
9. Total assets of Russian banks may have been as much as two times lower than the official statistics suggest if international accounting standards (excluding double count) are applied (*Finansoviye Izvestiya*, 18 November 1997).
10. For the analysis of the Russian banking system as compared to other countries see Dmitriyev et al. (1996), Filatochev (1997), Frye (1997), Fan et al. (1996), Hayashi (1997), Peresetsky et al., (2004).
11. This ratio is similar to the 'capital adequacy', N1, prudential ratio set by CBR. N1 ratio is equal to: (Capital, computed according to CBR regulations)/(Risk weighted assets net of reserves).
12. The reason why the share of long-term loans peaked only 2 quarters after the August 1998 crisis is the simple balance sheet inertia: after August 1998 almost no banks issued new loans, but old 'long' loans were still alive, so the share of long-term loans increased.

9
Argentina

José María Fanelli

9.1 Introduction

In the 1990s, many qualified and influential observers considered Argentina a kind of poster child for the Washington Consensus-inspired reforms (Tommasi and Forteza, 2006). To a great extent, this reputation was due to the rapid reform of the domestic financial architecture (DFA).

DFA[1] reform and the introduction of a currency board radically eliminated the risk of hyperinflation from which the country had been continuously suffering from the late 1980s. The institutions of the international financial architecture contributed to shaping the DFA reforms through three channels: (1) the adoption of the Basel Committee recommendations as a guideline to reform banking regulations; (2) the GATS negotiations on financial services; and (3) the pressure of international institutions like the IMF and the WB favoring liberalization. The country completely liberalized foreign financial flows and allowed huge flows of foreign direct investment into the banking sector. These factors contributed to changing substantially the financial market structure.

The ultimate outcome of these policies, however, was discouraging: after a decade of reforms, in 2001, the country suffered a financial collapse. The currency board was abandoned, property rights were violated and the country defaulted on its external obligations. Why was the country unable to sustain financial and monetary rules that were designed in line with the best international practices? What went wrong with this exercise in institutional engineering?

We postulate the following hypothesis:

One essential cause of the derailing of the reforms of the domestic financial architecture in Argentina is that, in designing and implementing reforms, the authorities did not pay sufficient attention to two facts: Argentina suffers from excessive aggregate volatility and the instruments (that is, markets, policies, and institutions) to manage the consequences of shocks and their amplifications during the reform period were rather limited.

The main goal of this chapter is to explore the plausibility of this hypothesis. Section 9.2 analyzes shocks and aggregate volatility in Argentina in order to detect the presence and assess the importance of excess volatility. Section 9.3 brings the country's idiosyncratic structural features into the picture; our primary interest is to identify a set of stylized facts concerning aggregate volatility that have a bearing on aggregate volatility because financial market failures preclude the appropriate management of risks. In Sections 9.4 and 9.5, we explore the two-way causality linkages between volatility and financial institutions, using the DFA reforms of the 1990s and the ensuing crisis as a source of empirical evidence. Section 9.6 draws some lessons regarding the DFA institutions and the DFA-IFA relationships and concludes the chapter.

9.2 Aggregate volatility, shocks, and crises

The hypothesis states that it is *excess* volatility rather than volatility per se that has a bearing on the DFA institutions. Therefore, we do not intend to make an exhaustive analysis of aggregate volatility but rather to evaluate whether and to what extent Argentina shows a degree of volatility that exceeds that justified by fundamentals. In practice, this is not a simple task because all economies present a degree of market imperfection and, thus, suffer from excess volatility costs. Hence, we will try to find a relative rather than an absolute measure of the degree of excess volatility in Argentina and will utilize both empirical and analytical standards.

The analytical standards to detect signs of excess volatility will be based on the predictions of the complete-markets model (see Obstfeld and Rogoff, 1996). This model assumes that some fluctuations are socially efficient and compatible with market equilibrium. We will use the predictions about the characteristics that these efficient fluctuations should have to detect the presence of excess (or inefficient) fluctuations. The empirical standard has two dimensions: international and historical. For the international dimension, we will draw from the evidence on cross-country volatility presented in Fanelli (2005a) and the recent literature on volatility in emerging countries, particularly Aizenman and Pinto (2004). The historical dimension can help us to understand the linkages between the IFA and the DFA to the extent that these linkages showed significant variation under the successive international regimes of the last century.

Volatility, crisis, and international regimes: a long-run view

The annual average growth rate of the Argentine per capita GDP over the last 130 years has been 2 per cent. This growth process has three characteristics that are highly relevant to our study. First, the growth rate reveals pronounced short-run swings; second, it is possible to distinguish extended periods of both high and low growth; and third, the largest and more persistent downward movements in the growth rate are associated with changes in the international scenario.

Following Basu and Taylor (1999) we have divided the 130-year period under analysis into four sub-periods in accordance with the changes in the international financial architecture: First Globalization (1875–1930), Autarky

(1931–45), Bretton Woods (1946–78), and Second Globalization (1979–present).[2] As Table 9.1 indicates, the country grew during the First Globalization and Bretton Woods periods and was stagnant during the Autarky years and the most recent globalization.

The economy's degree of openness – as measured by both trade and capital flows – achieved its highest level during the First Globalization (see Table 9.1). Trade openness, defined as the semi-sum of exports plus imports over GDP, was 20.5 per cent while the capital account surplus averaged almost 20 per cent of total exports. The discouraging evolution of trade in the Bretton Woods and Second Globalization years is surprising, given the rapidly expanding world trade. Two primary factors explaining the evolution in the Bretton Woods period are the anti-trade bias of Argentina's development strategies and the growing world protectionism affecting agricultural products, which was particularly damaging for a country with Argentina's relative factor endowment. However, in spite of the aggressive trade liberalization initiatives implemented from 1989 on as part of the structural reforms, during the 1990s the trade share achieved a historic minimum of 8 per cent. The substantial currency appreciation that occurred after the implementation of the currency board has undoubtedly had a bearing on this. Trade and capital flows, however, took different directions after liberalization. In the 1990s, capital flows increased substantially. The capital account surplus/export ratio and the capital inflows/GDP ratio also showed a significant rise. These capital inflows, nonetheless, would not recover the relevance that they had had between 1875 and 1930 and would follow a strongly procyclical pattern. To provide an overall picture of the importance of capital flows across regimes, Table 9.2 describes the evolution of the capital account/export ratio (*k*) and its standard deviation.

Table 9.1 Argentine key long-run indicators (I)

International regimes	Length of period (years)	Average per capita GDP growth rate (annual, %)	Population growth (Annual, %)	Average degree of openness[a] (%)	Average exports[b] (annual, 2002 US$ m)	Average trade surplus[b] (annual, 2002,US$ m)	Capital account/GDP[b] (estimated, %)
First Globalization	55	3.1	2.7	20.5	717.1	80.6	12.0
Autarky	16	0.2	1.8	12.9	483.5	177.8	3.0
Bretton Woods	33	1.9	2.1	10.7	2,099.9	199.4	1.2
Second Globalization	26	0.4	1.3	8.0	17,578.2	340.1	2.5
Overall period	130	2.0	2.1	13.2			

Notes:
a. Semi-sum of exports plus imports over GDP.
b. Available only from 1913.

Table 9.2 Argentine key long-run indicators (II)

International regimes	Average capital account[a]/exports ratio	Average standard deviation	Coefficient of variation	Average imports/ exports ratio	Average standard deviation	Coefficient of variation	Average absorption/ exports ratio	Average standard deviation	Coefficient of variation
First Globalization	74.0	132.7	1.8	90.0	20.5	0.2	7.0	1.3	0.2
Autarky	36.7	128.6	3.5	66.5	22.3	0.3	9.3	2.6	0.3
Bretton Woods	16.7	90.2	5.4	98.1	23.6	0.2	20.5	3.7	0.2
Second Globalization	30.6	31.5	1.0	91.3	29.9	0.3	12.5	3.7	0.3
Overall period	35.1	97.0	2.8	90.0	26.4	0.3	13.7	6.3	0.5

Note: a. Available only from 1913.

The mean value and the volatility differ significantly across regimes. As expected, the lowest value of the *k* coefficient corresponds to the Bretton Woods period when capital controls were in force. Two facts are surprising. First, the average value of *k* is low during the Second Globalization. This is very discouraging if we take into account that exports followed a sluggish path in the period and that Argentina implemented aggressive capital account liberalization policies. Second, the volatility of the *k* coefficient is always high, but is higher during the Autarky and Bretton Woods periods when international capital flows faced considerable obstacles. The coefficient of variation is, in fact, lower under the two globalizations. Another striking fact is the divergent path followed by the volatility of *k* and the imports/exports ratio (*m*). Table 9.2 indicates that the coefficient of variation of the *m* ratio increases during 1979 while the volatility of capital flows fell in that period. If capital flows contributed to stabilizing domestic expenditure and, *a fortiori* to stabilizing import expenditures, we should observe the opposite evolution of these variables. In the case of Argentina, it is as if expenditures were an instrument to stabilize capital flows.

Table 9.3 shows a set of indicators that will help us to elaborate a more complete picture of output volatility under different international architectures.

The standard deviation of the growth rate during the two globalization periods is higher than during the other international regimes. Despite showing similar values for the standard deviation, however, the contrast between the First and the Second Globalization is striking: since the late 1970s, the frequency of downturns in Argentina has been roughly twice as high as it had been in the First Globalization while the proportion of years of low growth is substantially higher than during the other periods. Indeed, the frequency of occurrence of abnormally severe recessions has shown a permanent tendency to increase since the 1930s, and the negative evolution of aggregate fluctuations in Argentina over the last 30 years in terms of frequency, depth, and duration is quite striking when

Table 9.3 Argentine aggregate volatility: long-run view[a]

International regimes	Average standard deviation 9-year window[b] (%)	Frequency of downturns[c] per capita GDP (%)	Frequency of downturns[c] based on GDP (%)	Average duration of recessions (years)	Average depth of recessions[d] (%)	Frequency of abnormal falls[e] (%)	Average duration of expansions (years)	Average growth rate during expansion[f] (%)	Frequency of exceptional growth[g] (%)
First Globalization	5.9	21.8	14.5	1.8	5.0	10.9	6.1	5.3	21.8
Autarky	4.6	37.5	25.0	1.5	3.1	12.5	2.3	3.0	6.3
Bretton Woods	4.3	30.3	18.2	1.4	3.4	15.4	3.3	4.2	7.7
Second Globalization	5.1	42.3	38.5	2.2	5.4	34.6	2.5	4.7	11.5
Overall period	5.1	30.7	29.4	1.7	4.3	16.2	3.9	3.8	13.8

Notes:

a. The volatility indicators are based on per capita GDP. The indicators based on GDP show basically the same qualitative picture.
b. The standard deviation for a given year is calculated on the basis of the eight previous years in addition to the year under analysis.
c. Proportion of years in which the per capita GDP growth rate was negative.
d. Average percentage per capita GDP fall from peak to trough. This is a rough estimate because of the low frequency of the data available.
e. Proportion of years in which the per capita GDP growth rate was negative and lower than the mean growth rate minus one standard deviation.
f. Average percentage per capita GDP increase from trough to peak. This is a rough estimate because of the low frequency of the data available.
g. Proportion of years in which the per capita GDP growth rate was positive and larger than the mean growth rate plus one standard deviation.

assessed in light of the evolution of developed countries. In these countries, the frequency, volatility, and depth of recessions have shown a declining trend (see Chapter 1 in this volume).

Although the depth and duration of recessions do not differ substantially between the two globalizations, there is a marked disparity concerning the duration of the expansions. The average duration of expansions between 1875 and 1930 was more than six years and the average growth rate was very high. Indeed, in more than one-fifth of the years of this period the economy experienced exceptionally high growth. The Argentine economic performance since the late 1970s has been just the opposite; the country was unable to sustain growth over extended periods, although the growth rate during expansions tended to be relatively high. We can conclude, then, that one key factor explaining the difference between the expansionary period of 1875–1930 and the present stagnation is the former period's remarkable ability to sustain high growth over extended periods.

During the 50 years corresponding to the Autarky and Bretton Woods regimes, output was relatively less volatile. Despite the increase in the frequency of severe downturns, the occurrence of periods of both very high and very low growth rates tended to be less frequent; recessions were milder (the average depth and duration of recessions was lower); and the overall standard deviation was also lower. Note that this occurred during a period in which the economy was reducing its trade share and capital movements were extremely limited.

Taken together, these facts clearly indicate that the Argentine economy experienced the highest degree of volatility under the Second Globalization. Not only has the standard deviation of the growth rate increased but also the frequency of resilient abnormal falls has augmented dramatically. This suggests that we should pay attention not only to the variance of output growth rates but also to periods in which exceptional disequilibria occurred, which resulted in deep and lasting recessions. Following Wolf (2004a) we will define 'crisis' as periods in which we observe abnormally large and persistent falls in output. Operationally, we will identify crises with those episodes in which per capita GDP fell for at least two consecutive years and the fall in each year was higher than the mean minus one standard deviation.

Table 9.4 describes our findings concerning the identification of crises. A number of facts deserve attention. First, the output losses associated with crises are very large. Second, all crises occurred under an international scenario of globalization. Although substantial output contractions are observable in the decades

Table 9.4 Argentine economic crises

Crisis[a]	Starting year	Duration[b]	Depth[c]	Associated with international events[d]	Conditional st. deviation (a)[e]	(b)[f]	(c)[g]
Baring	1892	2	14.84	Yes	4.8	6.0	5.7
First World War	1913	5	29.84	Yes	4.8	5.9	7.0
1929 crisis	1930	3	20.11	Yes	4.8	5.7	4.9
Debt crisis	1981	2	9.52	Yes	5.0	5.8	5.2
Hyperinflation	1988	3	14.90	No	6.1	5.6	5.1
Fall of convertibility	1999	4	22.66	Yes	5.3	6.9	nd

Notes:
a. Crisis is defined as a situation in which per capita GDP fell in two or more consecutive years and in each of those years the fall was higher than the mean growth rate minus one standard deviation.
b. Number of consecutive recessionary years.
c. Accumulated fall in per capita GDP.
d. To identify international downturns we used IMF (2002).
e. Average conditional standard deviation in the four years previous to the crisis.
f. Average conditional standard deviation during the crisis.
g. Average conditional standard deviation in the four years following the crisis.

corresponding to Autarky and Bretton Woods, they are less severe and less persistent. Third, all crises were closely associated with large disturbances (shocks) in the international scenario, with the exception of the hyperinflation crisis. Fourth, the evolution of the Argentine economy under the current IFA has been by far the most volatile. While there was crisis every 18 years in the 1875–1930 period, a crisis occurred every 8 years between 1979 and 2004. Fifth, each globalization period produced its own 'big' crisis. That is, if we adopt a more stringent definition of crisis and set the cut-off level as the mean growth minus two standard deviations, we can identify two crises: one triggered by World War I and the other by the Russian default in 1998.

Since the frequency of crises is higher in those periods in which the variance of growth is also higher, the question naturally arises whether volatility and crises are positively associated.

Figure 9.1 depicts the evolution of the rolling standard deviation of the growth rate calculated on the basis of a nine-year centered window.[3] As can be seen, the series tends to show a local maximum in the neighborhood of crisis years and crisis episodes tend to be followed by an outburst in volatility in the ensuing years. This suggests that the stochastic process under analysis can display conditional heteroskedasticity. To test this hypothesis, we modeled the growth series using a GARCH model. Table 9.5 presents the estimation output.

The results are compatible with the presence of conditional heteroskedasticity. The last column of Table 9.4 presents the evolution of the estimated conditional standard deviation in the period preceding and following a crisis. In all cases, the conditional variance is much higher during crisis periods and tends to remain

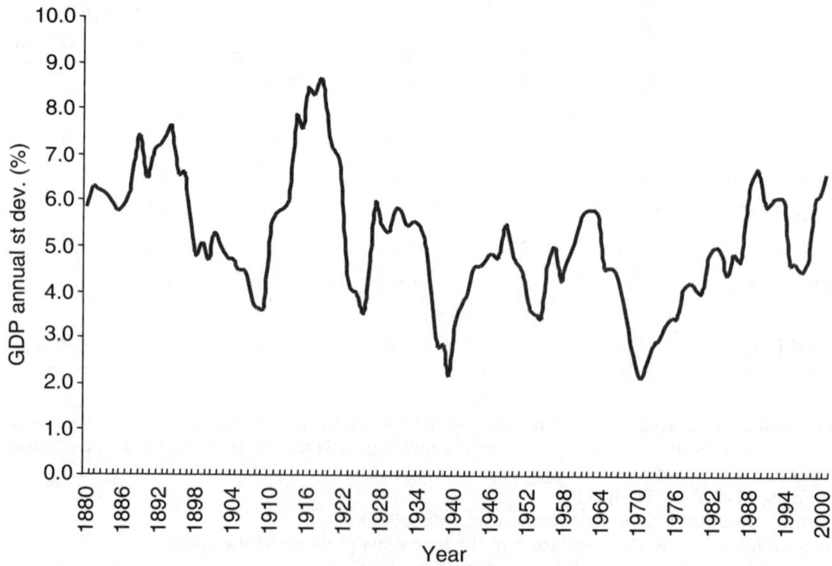

Figure 9.1 Annual growth volatility: rolling 9-year window standard deviation (%)
Sources: Central Bank of Argentina and Ministry of Economy and Production.

Table 9.5 Estimation results, annual data

	Coefficient	Std. error	z-statistic	Prob.
C	0.029668	0.002815	10.54044	0.0000
AR(1)	0.238486	0.129373	1.843400	0.0653
AR(2)	−0.166475	0.101174	−1.645430	0.0999
MA(3)	0.122667	0.071878	1.706614	0.0879
MA(8)	−0.711559	0.059151	−12.02960	0.0000
Variance equation				
C	0.000397	9.32E-05	4.258881	0.0000
RESID(−1)^2	−0.204957	0.018473	−11.09518	0.0000
GARCH(−1)	1.007685	0.051117	19.71343	0.0000
R-squared	0.231688	Mean dependent var		0.029533
Adjusted R-squared	0.165291	S.D. dependent var		0.052394
S.E. of regression	0.047868	Akaike info criterion		−3.190094
Sum squared resid	0.185603	Schwarz criterion		−2.966397
Log likelihood	149.9592	F-statistic		3.489420
Durbin-Watson stat	2.006799	Prob(F-statistic)		0.002554
Inverted AR roots	.12−.39i	.12+.39i		
Inverted MA roots	.94	.68−.69i	.68+.69i	.02−.96i
	.02+.96i	−.68+.66i	−.68−.66i	−.98

Notes:
Dependent variable: D(LNGDPARG)
Method: ML – ARCH
Sample (adjusted): 1916 2004
Included observations: 89 after adjustments
Convergence achieved after 13 iterations
MA backcast: 1908 1915, Variance backcast: ON
GARCH = C(6) + C(7)*RESID(−1)^2 + C(8)*GARCH(−1)

high in the years that follow a crisis. This conclusion is consistent with the cross-country evidence presented in Wolf (2004a).

In sum, this evidence indicates that, under a globalized international setting, Argentina's growth volatility tends to be higher: the standard deviation of the growth rate is larger; crises are more frequent; big crises originating in large foreign shocks have occurred; and volatility tends to increase when a crisis occurs, which implies that the stochastic process presents heteroskedasticity.

Short-run volatility, growth, and persistence

We will focus next on the short-run characteristics of aggregate volatility. Figure 9.2 depicts the evolution of the quarterly rolling standard deviation calculated on the basis of a 12-quarter centered window. A visual inspection reveals three high-volatility periods: the hyperinflation episode, the Tequila crisis in the mid-1990s, and the period of the Russian crisis from 1998–IV on.

To check for the presence of conditional heteroskedasticity we use an ARCH-M model. In addition to conditional heteroskedasticity, this model assumes that the growth rate depends on the standard deviation of the process, which intends to

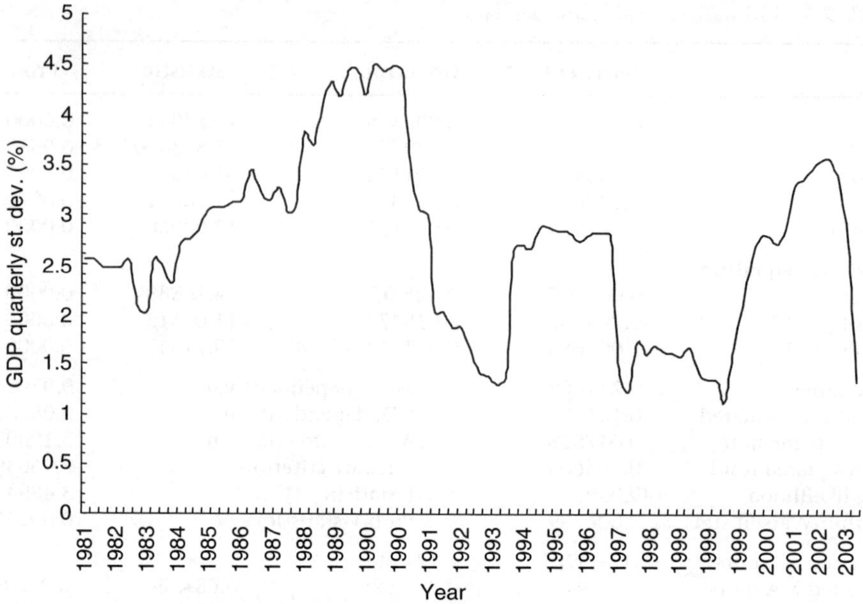

Figure 9.2 Quarterly growth volatility: rolling 12-quarter window standard deviation (%)
Sources: Central Bank of Argentina and Ministry of Economy and Production.

capture the effects of volatility on growth. Following Aizenman and Pinto (2004) we hypothesize that there is a concavity in the relationship between growth and shocks and will later make the case that this concavity is associated: (1) with the authorities' inability to implement effective countercyclical policies; and (2) with the constraints posed by incomplete financial markets on private agents' decisions. Specifically, we propose the following ARCH-M model:

$$y_t = \alpha_0 + \alpha_1 y_{t-1} + \alpha_2 \sigma_t + \varepsilon_t \tag{9.1}$$

$$\varepsilon_t \equiv h_t \sigma_t;\ Var(h_t) = 1;\ E(h_t) = 0$$

$$\sigma_t^2 = \gamma_0 + \gamma_1 \varepsilon_{t-1}{}^2 + \gamma_2 \varepsilon_{t-2}{}^2 \tag{9.2}$$

where y_t is the output growth rate, σ_t is the conditional standard deviation, ε_t is the innovation to the stochastic process and α_i and γ_i are parameters to be estimated. While α_2 represents the effects of volatility on growth, α_1 and γ_i are meant to capture the degree of persistence of shocks. The higher these parameters are, the higher the degree of persistence will be. According to the cross-country literature (Aizenman and Pinto, 2004; Fanelli, 2005a), there is an inverse relationship between persistence and per capita GDP. This means that there is less inertia in the developing world. The estimation results appear in Table 9.6.

The sign of the α_2 parameter is negative, as was expected. The ARCH terms are significant and the 'memory' of the process is not too long, to the extent that the parameters corresponding to the GARCH term are not relevant. This is consistent

Table 9.6 Estimation results, quarterly data

	Coefficient	Std. error	z-statistic	Prob.
SQR(GARCH)	–2.152872	0.620844	–3.467651	0.0005
C	0.060850	0.016163	3.764748	0.0002
AR(1)	0.222410	0.091716	2.424981	0.0153
Variance equation				
C	0.000741	0.000110	6.741632	0.0000
ARCH(1)	0.057593	0.059200	0.972864	0.3306
ARCH(2)	–0.087799	0.020333	–4.317966	0.0000
R-squared	0.075545	Mean dependent var		0.003773
Adjusted R-squared	0.025843	S.D. dependent var		0.028654
S.E. of regression	0.028281	Akaike info criterion		–4.293072
Sum squared resid	0.074384	Schwarz criterion		–4.135792
Log likelihood	218.5071	F-statistic		1.519953
Durbin-Watson stat	2.057622	Prob(F-statistic)		0.191131
Inverted AR roots	.22			

Notes:
Dependent variable: D(LNGDP)
Method: ML – ARCH (Marquardt)
Sample(adjusted): 1980:3 2005:1
Included observations: 99 after adjusting endpoints
Convergence achieved after 46 iterations
Variance backcast: OFF

with the hypothesis that past shocks matter to volatility but there is little inertia built into the system.

The long-run equilibrium solution for the growth rate is:

$$\bar{y} = \frac{\alpha_0}{1 - \alpha_1} + \frac{\alpha_2}{1 - \alpha_1}\,\bar{\sigma} \tag{9.3}$$

Since the unconditional standard deviation appears in equation (9.3), volatility matters not only in the short run but also in the long-run evolution of the growth rate. According to this expression, the higher the degree of persistence (that is, the larger the value of α_1) and the sensitivity of the economy to volatility (that is, the larger α_2), the stronger the negative effect of the standard deviation on the growth rate. We can interpret parameters α_1 and α_2 as reduced-form representations of the authorities' and the private sector's equilibrium choices. Parameter α_2 can be interpreted to reflect the influence of risk aversion in a context of pervasive financial market failures, which affect growth via the investment equation. Parameter α_1, in turn, has to do with the propagation mechanisms built into the economy. In a volatile context, contracts tend to be shorter and countercyclical policies ineffective; since this makes the economy less inertial, we expect a α_1 lower than in industrial countries. Although we do not know the structural parameters that give rise to equations (9.2) and (9.3), we will later try to shed some light on the propagation mechanism that operates via financial intermediation.

According to our estimates, the long-run equilibrium can be written as:

$$\bar{y} = 0.0782546 - 2.7686467\,\bar{\sigma} \tag{9.4}$$

If we estimate $\bar{\sigma}$ as the average value of the square root of the conditional variance of the process (0.000714^(1/2) = 0.02672077), the long-run quarterly growth rate is 0.43 per cent. Note the strong effect of volatility on growth; each percentage-point increase in the standard deviation reduces the growth rate by 2.7 percentage points.

This implies that structural policies, which are deemed to modify the long-run evolution of the economy, could have very strong effects on growth if they succeed at reducing either the size of $\bar{\sigma}$ or the value of the parameters α_1 or α_2. Reducing the size of $\bar{\sigma}$ implies reducing the magnitude of the shocks that hit the economy. Diminishing α_1 means diminishing the economy's degree of persistence while diminishing α_2 calls for the reduction of the sensitivity of the economy to the volatility of shocks. The cross-country evidence and the literature on the cycle in developed countries strongly suggest that the growth-volatility link weakens as the economy becomes richer while α_1 either remains constant (US) or declines slightly (Germany). In addition, since the empirical evidence indicates that persistence is currently low in developing countries, we cannot expect persistence to contribute substantially to the reduction of the sensitivity to shocks. The bulk of the reduction in the sensitivity of growth to volatility in a country like Argentina, consequently, should not be expected to come from a reduction in α_1 but in α_2. In sum, we can conclude that both impulses and the propagation of shocks matter to growth and that better aggregate risk-management policy could make a central positive contribution. For this reason, the reform of the DFA and the linkages with the IFA should be considered part and parcel of growth-enhancing structural reforms.

9.3 Structural factors and excess volatility

We will now examine a set of structural aspects that are relevant in accounting for excess volatility. The rationale for highlighting the role of structural 'details' in Argentina is straightforward. If financial market failures are pervasive and countercyclical policies are weak, agents will be unable to give the best response to shocks. The inability to achieve the desired allocation of resources across space, time, and states of nature will likely strengthen the short-run effects of shocks and increase the costs incurred along the adjustment path. In what follows, we discuss five structural features associated with the external sector that we deem critical to understanding excess aggregate volatility in Argentina.

The volatility of Argentine exports is high

Although there are exceptions, the international evidence indicates that in general: (1) developing countries exhibit higher export volatility; (2) in many cases this volatility is associated with the lack of export diversification and with a specialization pattern biased in favor of primary products, which strengthens the effects of the terms of trade volatility; and (3) contrary to analytic intuition, developing countries do not run large current account disequilibria for extended periods – the so-called Feldstein-Horioka puzzle.

The Argentine experience is basically in line with these stylized facts. The country experiences high export volatility. While the annual standard deviation of export growth corresponding to the G7 countries in the last three decades has been 9.7 per cent, the volatility of this variable in the case of Argentina has been 24.9 per cent (see Fanelli, 2005a).

Argentina's trade diversification is low and the revealed comparative advantages concentrate on primary products. Another negative feature of the export structure is that the participation of intra-industrial trade – as measured by the Grubel and Lloyd or Aquino indices – is small and basically involves Argentina's partners in MERCOSUR (Fanelli et al., 2001). Domestic production, in turn, cannot substitute for a large number of technologically sophisticated imports.

The country is unable to finance significant current account deficits for relatively extended periods

Argentina's ability to run trade deficits has proved to be particularly limited. In the 1913–2004 period the accumulated trade deficit was nil while the country ran a small trade surplus that averaged 0.02 per cent of GDP in the years of the Second Globalization (1979–2004). The imports/exports ratio (*m*) has hovered at 0.9 and most of the observations fall in the interval delimited by the mean plus/minus one standard deviation dotted lines. In other words, the imports/exports ratio registers a strong mean-reverting behavior and the speed of the reversion is relatively high. This prima facie indicates a reduced ability to run sizable current account deficits.

Figure 9.3 shows the evolution of domestic absorption and the trade balance over the Second Globalization period. There is a substantial negative correlation between the domestic absorption/exports ratio (*a*) and the trade balance/exports ratio (*tb*), which suggests a limited ability to run current account deficits in difficult times.

The volatility of imports is higher than the volatility of exports

The cross-country evidence shows that imports are more volatile than exports in developing countries (Fanelli, 2005a). This also occurs in Argentina. Given that the evolution of Argentine exports is much smoother than the evolution of imports, it follows that the changes in the value and the sign of the trade balance are basically explained by sudden swings in imports.

Notwithstanding, the relationship between the volatility of imports and exports has changed over time. Three facts deserve to be highlighted in this regard. First, imports have been consistently more volatile than exports since World War II, the period in which the economy became more closed and Argentina faced increasing difficulties in accessing international capital markets.

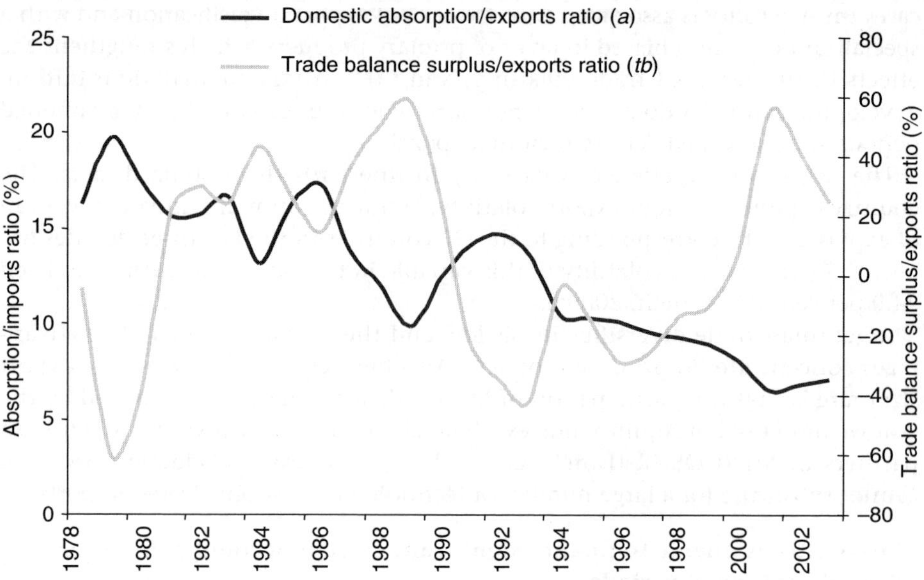

Figure 9.3 Domestic absorption, exports and the trade balance
Sources: Central Bank of Argentina and Ministry of Economy and Production.

Second, in the same period, the volatility of exports fell. Third, this process became more acute during the Second Globalization; the volatility of imports exploded, unlike the volatility of exports, which registered an overall downward trend. The fall in export volatility is consistent with the observed fall in Argentina's terms of trade standard deviation and the relative improvement in the diversification of exports.

Since the trade balance shows a marked countercyclical pattern, these facts suggest that short-run macroeconomic adjustments have had a significant influence on the volatility of imports and that this has been particularly so during the Second Globalization.

The Argentine economy is rather closed, as assessed on international standards

Over the last decades, the Argentine economy has been one of the closest in the Latin American region. Although the degree of openness has augmented since 2001 – as a consequence of the real depreciation of the currency – the economy is still rather closed and the recent increase in trade participation is likely to partially reverse if the peso appreciates as expected. One important consequence of the lack of openness is that the domestic absorption/exports ratio (*a*) is currently very high.[4] During the Second Globalization period the value of this ratio was 12, contrasting with the First Globalization when it was less than 7 (see Table 9.2).

When the ability to run current account deficits is limited, the value of the *a* ratio has a bearing on aggregate volatility because the lack of openness leverages the fluctuations in domestic expenditures. In effect, if current account deficits cannot be large, the absorptions/imports ratio cannot be substantially different from the *a* ratio. Hence, if *a* is large and the country faces a liquidity constraint (say, a sudden stop), each dollar saved in imports to gain liquidity induces, *ceteris paribus,* a large downward correction in the level of absorption, fueling aggregate volatility. In the case of Argentina, each new dollar for imports can potentially 'create' 12 dollars of domestic absorption and, obviously, each dollar that portfolio investors send abroad could destroy a similar amount.

Capital flows are procyclical

Although sudden stops can always occur, if capital movements were countercyclical in normal times, a high value of *a* would be much less relevant. This is not, however, the case of Argentina.

Figure 9.4 describes the evolution of the capital account surplus/export ratio (*k*) over the 1978–2004 period and the one standard deviation boundaries corresponding to the period. In the 1990s, *k* surpasses the boundaries many times. This was the period in which capital flows were both free and intense. We have also drawn (changing the scale) the evolution of the capital account to highlight the fact that the fluctuations in the *k* indicator are basically explained by fluctuations in net capital flows rather than in the variability of exports. Figure 9.4 also depicts the evolution of the import/export ratio (*m*) to illustrate the close comovement between imports and capital flows. Furthermore, observe the intensity of capital outflows during the crisis period in 2001–03 and the concomitant

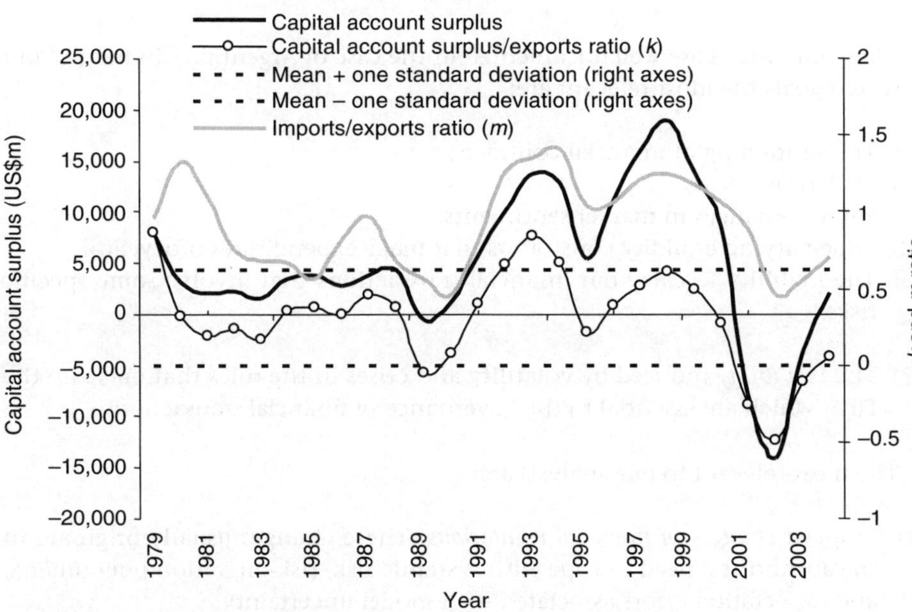

Figure 9.4 Capital flows and imports
Sources: Central Bank of Argentina and Ministry of Economy and Production.

and substantial fall in the *m* ratio. The correlation between *k* and the absorption ratio *a*, in turn, has also been systematically positive over the whole period under analysis. It is worth highlighting that both the correlation between *m* and *k* and between *a* and *k* experienced a sharp increase in the 1990s.

Overall, we interpret this evidence as a clear indication that capital movements are procyclical and, consequently, we conclude that the lack of openness in conjunction with procyclical capital flows is a source of excess volatility in Argentina. Note that in assessing excess volatility not only the size of the variance of capital flows but also the sign and size of the relevant correlations matter to aggregate volatility.

9.4 Weak DFA, financial market failures, and excess aggregate volatility

We have already made the case that excess volatility is present in Argentina and have highlighted the importance of structural factors. Our next step in the following two sections is to examine the linkages between aggregate volatility and the DFA institutions. In line with the framework concerning the bi-directional causality between aggregate volatility and institutions developed in the introductory chapter to this volume, we focus on two factors:

(1) The *adaptive responses* of both the private and public agents to *volatility*, *crises*, and *weak DFA*, which translate into permanent mutations in the financial structure.

These mutations are well documented in the case of Argentina.[5] In light of our research goals the most relevant are:

(a) The shortening of financial contracts.
(b) Dollarization.
(c) Sudden changes in market sentiments.
(d) Time-varying liquidity constraints that make expenditures procyclical.
(e) The inability to carry out financial transactions that involve some specific risks.

(2) The *instability* induced by volatility and crises in the rules that make up the DFA, which are essential to the governance of financial transactions.

The most relevant to our analysis are:

(f) *Frequent changes in financial regulations:* These changes usually originate in the authorities' need to cope with systemic risk, risk-migration phenomena, and expectation errors associated with model uncertainty.
(g) *Insecure property rights:* Property rights are difficult to define when shocks are frequent and large. In addition, in the case of Argentina, the events of

extreme volatility (that is, 'crises') have had particularly damaging effects on contracts and institutions to the extent that they resulted in the redefinition of property rights, and distributional/political conflicts.

(h) *Uncertain nominal anchor:* This relates to unexpected fluctuations in the inflation rate, associated with policy shocks and changes in the exchange rate regime, typically after the occurrence of a large external shock.

The DFA's flaws make some risks non-contractible and key countercyclical policies non-implementable (see the introductory chapter) and this in turn limits the agents' and the authorities' ability to manage risks. The misallocation of risk creates excess volatility. In this section we will try to identify the effects that pervasive financial market failures have in terms of excess consumption and investment volatility in the case of Argentina. We examine the elements associated with factor 2 in Section 9.5. We rely on the evidence concerning the implementation and crisis of the reforms of the prudential regulations and the monetary regime in the 1990s.

Financial market failures and aggregate fluctuations

When mutations (a)–(e) are present, the scarcity of market and policy instruments to cope with shocks contributes to generating excess volatility. In order to analyze the empirical evidence and the indicators of excess volatility, the following expressions will be useful (we continue to express the variables as export ratios):

$$tb = 1 - m = y - a \tag{9.5}$$

where we define: $tb = TB/X$; $m = M/X$; $y = Y/X$; $a = A/X$; and TB, X, M, Y, and A stand respectively for the trade balance surplus, exports, imports, GDP, and domestic absorption. The trade balance can also be expressed as the difference between the variation in the stock of foreign exchange reserves (f) and the net inflow of 'fresh money' (vk). We use vk as a proxy for the liquidity constraint that the country faces in a given period.[6] Both variables are expressed as ratios to exports.

$$tb = f - vk \tag{9.6}$$

The variance of the trade balance, therefore, can be expressed in the following alternative two forms:

$$Var(tb) = Var(y) + Var(a) - 2\,Cov(y;a) \tag{9.7}$$

$$Var(tb) = Var(f) + Var(vk) - 2\,Cov(vk;f) \tag{9.8}$$

These relationships have a number of implications that are extremely helpful in detecting excess volatility. To begin with, these equations tell us that, by definition, the variance of the trade balance is associated with the volatility of reserves and net capital inflows on the 'financial' side (equation (9.4)) and with the volatility of output and domestic absorption on the domestic 'real' side (equation (9.3)). Since these are not independent random variables, in both cases we have to correct for the influence of the covariance.

According to the cross-country evidence, the value of *Var(tb)* corresponding to Argentina is well above the value of countries with similar per capita GDP (see Fanelli, 2005a). This excessive volatility is consistent with the fact that the 'real side' variances – *Var(y)* and *Var(a)* – tend to be high as compared to international standards. This raises the question of whether the high volatility of the 'financial' variables (*f* and *vk*) merely reflects the real shocks affecting output and absorption or, to the contrary, is an independent source of shocks associated with financial imperfections, such as changes in market sentiment and contagion effects that are not justified by changes in fundamental variables. A second related question is what the co-movements represented by *Cov(y;a)* and *Cov(vk;f)* reveal concerning the presence of excess volatility.

In the case of a small open economy facing an infinitely elastic supply of funds at an exogenously given and stable international interest rate, causality should run from 'real' domestic volatility to 'financial' external volatility. In a world in which the Fisher separation and Modigliani-Miller conditions hold, financial conditions would only affect the real side through the international interest rate and a direct link would not exist between the quantity of funds supplied and domestic expenditures and production. Note, additionally, that if markets were perfect, money and the exchange rate regime should be basically neutral and, consequently, *Var(f)* would not matter much in explaining the aggregate volatility of real variables. If markets worked reasonably well and domestic and foreign assets were perfect substitutes, the domestic/foreign assets mix in the private sector's portfolio would be largely irrelevant to real decisions. Under these conditions, we would not have a prior about the sign and size of *Cov(vk;f)*.

The structural features analyzed in the previous section (particularly the fifth) and the occurrence of mutations (a)–(e) in financial intermediation have three implications that are worth mentioning. First, if quantitative financial constraints are relevant to production and expenditure decisions, 'autonomous' shocks affecting external financial conditions matter to real aggregate volatility. Second, policy and regime-change shocks that contribute to determining the size of *Var(f)* and the size and sign of *Cov(vk;f)* become potential sources of excess volatility. Third, if policies and regimes matter, the DFA institutions matter. We will now briefly analyze the Argentine experience in light of this argument.

In the 1991–2001 period a currency-board regime was in force in Argentina. On several occasions during this period, market sentiments proved to be very volatile. Figure 9.5 shows the quarterly evolution of the financial variables that appear in Figure 9.4. The evolution of *Var(vk)* reveals an interesting feature: volatility tends to be countercyclical. It is very elevated in the vicinity of hyperinflation, the Tequila crisis, and the 1998–2001 crises while it is much lower in 1992–93 and 1996–97, when the economy was growing fast.

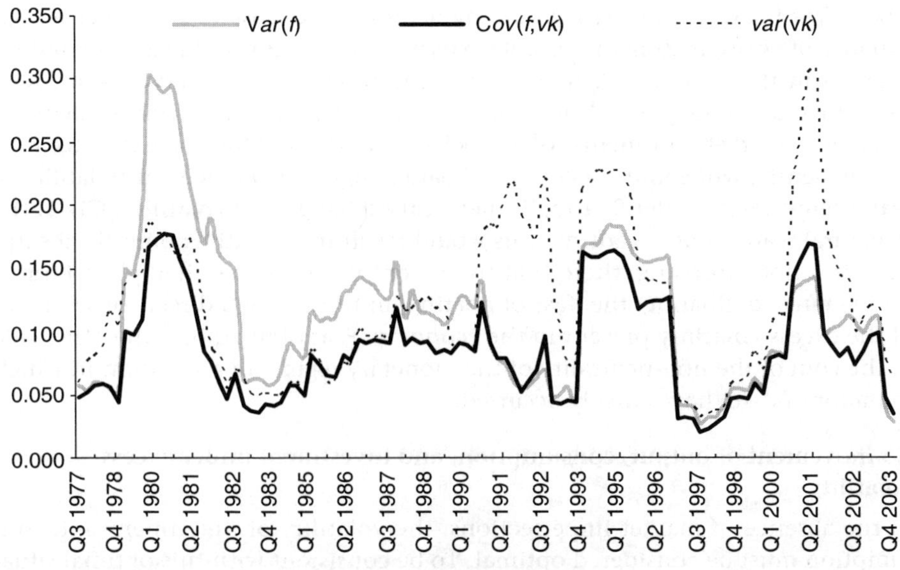

Figure 9.5 Volatility of the trade balance: the 'financial' side
Sources: Central Bank of Argentina and Ministry of Economy and Production.

Cov(vk;f) and *Var(f)* also exhibit a marked countercyclical pattern. This dynamic has implications that can help in studying the interactions between the exchange rate regime and excess volatility. Let us assume that there is a marked negative swing in market sentiments – as was the case after the Russian crisis in 1998, followed by the Brazilian devaluation in early 1999. This will induce a fall in the demand for domestic currency (and bank deposits) and *f* is likely to fall. The net supply of external funds *vk* is also likely to fall. The two may even become negative. In any case, we will observe a positive *Cov(vk;f)*. Of course, if domestic interest rates increased sufficiently, thereby contributing to closing the foreign exchange gap, the changes in *f and vk* would be lower. If the bulk of the adjustment fell on domestic interest rates, we should not observe the 'jumps' in *Var(f)* and *Var(vk)* that Figure 9.5 shows, while the value of *Cov(vk;f)* should be less significant. I interpret the occurrence of these jumps during periods of crisis as an indication that the scope for the upward adjustment in the level of the real interest rates is very narrow when the level of financial deepening is low: increasing real interest rates implies increasing government default risk, which could foster rather than stop capital outflows (see Blanchard, 2004). Likewise, in the case of Argentina, sizable increases in the interest rates harm the quality of the banks' balance sheets. This balance sheet effect has been one important factor that explains the worsening in the market's default risk perception since 1998. In sum, procyclical capital flows, coupled with countercyclical *Var(vk)*, *Var(f)* and sizable positive *Cov(vk;f)*, are the forms that excess volatility takes when financial market failures are pervasive.

After the abandonment of the currency board, Argentina adopted a floating regime and there has been a substantial reduction in volatility (see Figure 9.5).

Under free floating, *Cov(vk;f)* should by definition be close to zero since a high variance of *vk* originating in unstable external conditions should basically induce changes in the nominal exchange rate with no change in reserves. With relatively rigid domestic prices, this means that there will be a direct linkage between changes in market sentiments (or a shock to exports) and the real exchange rate. Consequently, while under a currency board a high *Var(vk)* fuels the volatility of real interest rates, under floating it fuels real exchange rate volatility. Given the structural features of Argentina, this would result in a volatile domestic absorption. It is not surprising, then, that the Argentine authorities had placed limits on the range of floating: the 'fear of floating' in this case is a direct consequence of the excess volatility present in the economy. Fear of floating is the other side of the coin of the non-neutrality of the monetary regime in a situation in which mutations (a)–(e) have already occurred.

Co-movement of output, consumption, and investment under excess volatility

In the absence of market imperfections, the volatility of investment and consumption must be considered optimal. To be consistent with this optimal situation the co-movement of output, investment, and consumption must meet some conditions at the aggregate level. Our strategy will be to specify such conditions and to check whether they hold in the case of Argentina. Should the conditions fail to hold, we interpret that excess volatility is present.

We can express consumption as: $C = Y - S$, where S stands for total savings (that is, the non-consumed part of output). The rate of growth of consumption is, then:

$$c = \omega_y g - \omega_s s \tag{9.9}$$

The weights ω_y and ω_s are given respectively by the Y/C and S/C ratios. ω_y will usually be higher than one and ω_s positive and lower than one; c, s, and g stand for the growth rate of consumption, total savings, and GDP, respectively. Expression (9.9) indicates that for the consumption growth rate to follow a smooth path, sudden changes in the output growth rates should induce changes in the rate of growth of total savings rather than jumps in consumption growth. For example, if there were an unexpected positive shock to g and domestic agents perceived this shock to be temporary, they should temporarily save more to stabilize consumption. Therefore, if consumption smoothing dominates, we expect a close degree of co-movement between g and s to exist.

Since the non-consumed portion of output is: $S = I + TB$, it follows that changes in S must necessarily be associated with changes in investment and/or the trade balance. Consequently, we can decompose the rate of growth of savings (s) into the contributions made by investment (i) and the trade balance (b):

$$s = i + b \tag{9.10}$$

where: $i = \Delta I/S$ and $b = \Delta(X-M)/S$ are the contributions of investment and the trade balance to the growth of savings. The way in which agents allocate an increase in savings has important financial implications. For one thing, for the trade balance to increase ($b>0$) domestic agents must increase the payments abroad – which in Argentina are basically financial payments – or buy financial assets abroad (of course, this includes reserve accumulation and the buying of the country's own liabilities to reduce net indebtedness).

From (9.9) we can express the consumption variance as:

$$Var(c) = \omega^2_y\ Var(g) + \omega^2_s\ Var(s) - 2\ \omega_y\ \omega_s\ Cov(g;s) \qquad (9.11)$$

On the basis of (9.10), the variance of total savings growth can be decomposed as:

$$Var(s) = Var(i) + Var(b) + 2Cov\ (i;b) \qquad (9.12)$$

It will also be useful to decompose the covariance between growth and savings as follows:

$$Cov\ (g;s) = Cov\ (g;i) + Cov\ (g;b) \qquad (9.13)$$

If consumption is less volatile than output, as predicted by the complete-market theory, we should observe that:

$$(\omega^2_y - 1)\ Var(g) + \omega^2_s\ Var(s) < 2\ \omega_y\ \omega_s\ Cov\ (g;s) \qquad (9.14)$$

If we divide this expression by ($\sqrt{Var(g)} \cdot \sqrt{Var(s)}$), we obtain:

$$\left[[(\omega^2_y - 1)\frac{\sqrt{Var(g)}}{\sqrt{Var(s)}} + \omega^2_s \frac{\sqrt{Var(s)}}{\sqrt{Var(g)}}]\ 2\ \omega_y\ \omega_s < \rho(g;s) \right] \qquad (9.15)$$

Given that the left-hand term in (9.15) is a positive number, a necessary condition for consumption to fluctuate less than output is that the correlation between the growth rate of output and total savings be positive.

We can now use this framework to detect the presence and relevance of excess volatility in the case of Argentina when mutations (a)–(e) are present. International data indicate that consumption is more volatile than output in developing countries. This means that positive shocks to g tend to induce increases in s, but the degree of positive co-movement is not large enough to stabilize consumption.

The volatility of output and the volatility of total savings tend to be very high in developing countries as compared to the covariance between them. Figure 9.6 shows that, in fact, this is the case of Argentina. The figure displays the evolution of *Var(g)*, *Var(s)*, *Var(c)*, and *Cov(g;s)*, estimated using rolling variances calculated on the basis of 12-quarter windows.

Many factors point to the presence of excess volatility. To begin with, consumption variance tends to be higher than the variance of GDP over the sample

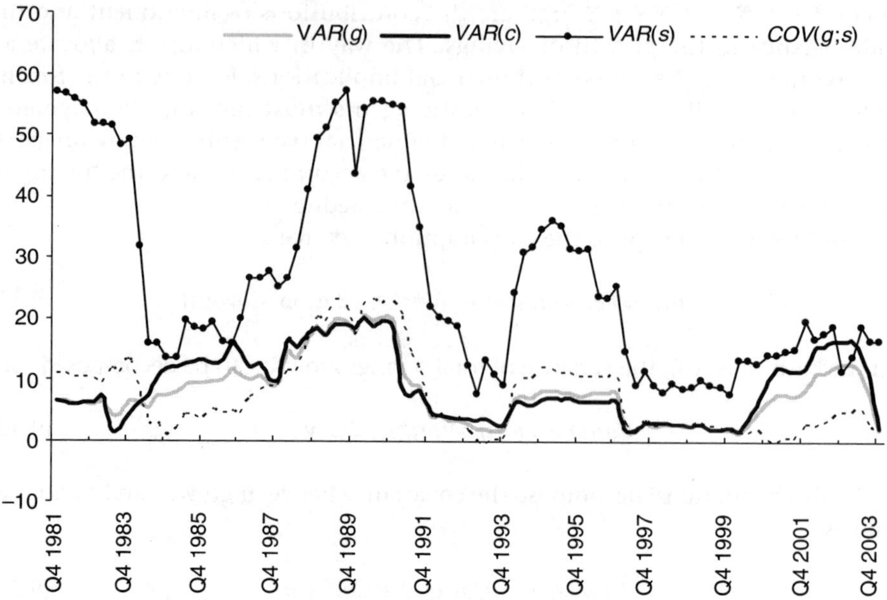

Figure 9.6 Volatility of output, consumption, and total savings (12-quarter window, %)
Sources: Central Bank of Argentina and Ministry of Economy and Production.

period. It is interesting that Argentina fails to meet condition (9.10) in spite of the fact that the average sample value of the ρ*(g;s)* coefficient is 0.5, which means that the co-movement of *g* and *s* has the right sign. One could even think that ρ is large enough to stabilize consumption. However, this does not occur.

Var(g) and *Var(s)* are very large.[7] We have already mentioned that a high *Var(g)* is a structural characteristic of developing countries. But, what are the factors behind the high variance of *s*? Equation (9.12) – which decomposes the variance of total savings into the contributions of investment and the trade balance – will help address this question. Figure 9.7 shows the evolution of the variances and covariances that appear in equation (9.12): *Var(i), Var(b)* and *Cov(i;b).*

Figure 9.7 clearly shows that investment volatility accounts for the largest part of *Var(s)*. Furthermore, the contribution of investment to the variance of the rate of growth of total savings tends to be higher during downturns. Following the literature (see Hubbard, 1998) on imperfect financial markets and investment and the evidence in Bebczuk et al. (2003) on financial constraints in Argentina, we can conjecture that it is the tightening of the financial constraints during recessions that induces over-adjustments in the investment rate and makes investment more volatile in the vicinity of recessionary periods. The contribution of the trade balance to the volatility of savings is also relevant and follows a similar cyclical pattern (that is, rising during downturns). The high *Var(b)*, of course, is consistent with the high and resilient volatility of the *m* ratio that we noted above. The contribution of the trade balance to the volatility of savings

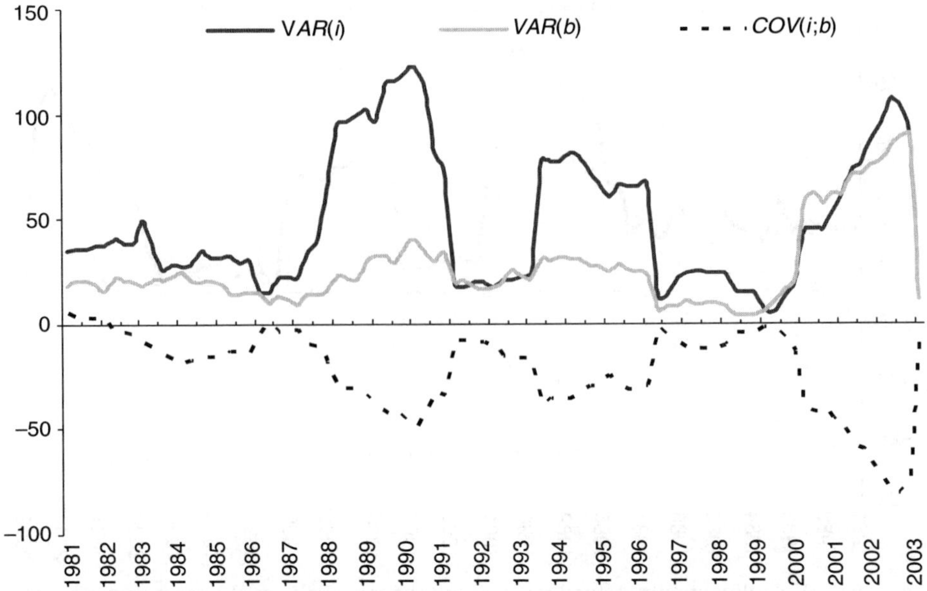

Figure 9.7 Volatility of investment and the trade balance (12-quarter window, %)
Sources: Central Bank of Argentina and Ministry of Economy and Production.

reached a maximum during the convertibility crisis, when *Var(b)* became as high as *Var(i)*.

The covariance between investment and the trade balance is also telling about excess volatility. As can be seen in Figure 9.7, in the case of Argentina, *Cov(i;b)* is negative and, consequently, the contribution of *Var(b)* and *Var(i)* to savings volatility is lower than their sum; the negative correlation between investment and the trade account dampens the volatility of savings. Figure 9.7 also shows that the absolute value of *Cov(i;b)* tends to increase substantially in the vicinity of downturns.[8] This indicates that the co-movement of the trade balance and investment over recessionary periods exerts a stabilizing effect on savings to the detriment of consumption smoothing. In effect, given output growth volatility, a smoother path for total savings growth means a more volatile consumption growth path.

The previous argument suggests that a good part of the volatility of *g* is passed through to *c* rather than to *s*. We can use equation (9.13) and Figure 9.8 – which decompose *Cov(g;s)* into *Cov(g;i)* and *Cov(g;b)* – to shed further light on this dynamic.

Figure 9.8 shows that in the case of Argentina, while output and investment growth tend to move in the same direction, *Cov(g;b)* is negative and higher in absolute value during downturns. While the positive output growth/investment growth correlation is compatible with consumption smoothing, the counter-cyclical behavior of the trade surplus is not. The negative sign of *Cov(g;b)* implies that more savings are allocated abroad during recessionary periods precisely

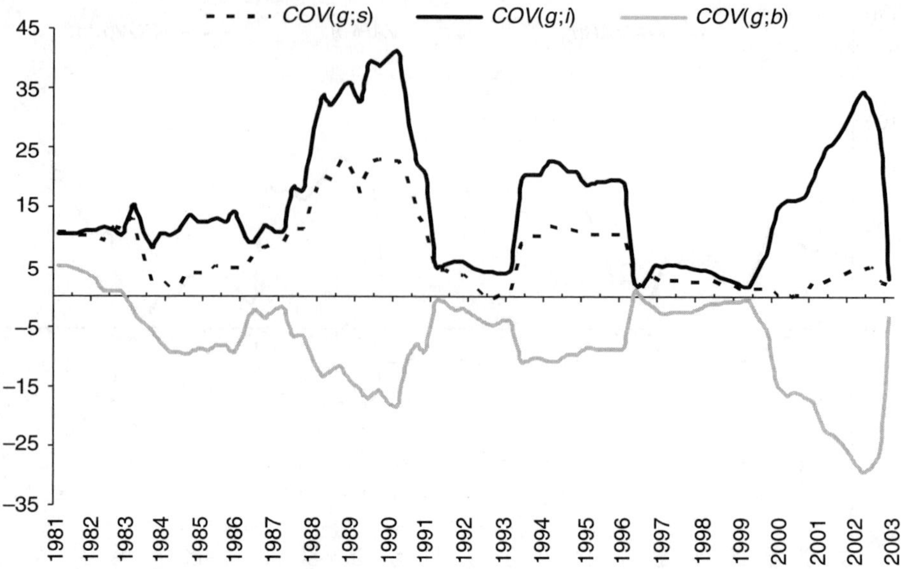

Figure 9.8 Volatility of output, total savings, and the trade balance (12-quarter window, %)
Sources: Central Bank of Argentina and Ministry of Economy and Production.

when they are needed to finance the stabilization of the consumption growth rate. This means that consumption, investment, and GDP tend to move together, while the trade surplus follows a countercyclical pattern. This co-movement would not be observed in a context in which financial constraints were not binding and consumption smoothing was privileged. In effect, if the shock that triggers the downturn induces a sudden fall in investment profitability, we would expect investors to allocate their funds abroad, but it makes no sense for them to reduce consumption as well. The hypothesis that agents face tighter liquidity constraints during downturns (for example, because the value of collateral falls, thereby worsening credit conditions), which causes both investment and consumption to fall, appears to fit the stylized facts better. It is also in line with the fluctuations in the *a* ratio that we analyzed above. We interpret this dynamic as an indicator of excess volatility, which in turn is rooted in two structural features in Argentina that we have already called attention to: procyclical capital flows and low financial deepening originating in mutations (a)–(e).

In order to check for the robustness of these results, we have used a GARCH-M framework similar to the one utilized in the case of output growth to analyze the evolution of consumption and investment. Tables 9.7a and 9.7b present the estimation results, which are consistent with our findings concerning the behavior of the rolling-standard deviation.

Increases in consumption and investment present conditional heteroskedasticity, and volatility negatively affects both these variables. The evolution of the estimated conditional variances over the sample period confirms that consumption tends to be more volatile than output, while investment presents the

Table 9.7a Consumption

	Coefficient	Std. error	z-statistic	Prob.
@SQRT(GARCH)	–0.396690	0.213386	–1.859024	0.0630
C	0.018168	0.006826	2.661693	0.0078
AR(1)	0.230425	0.090287	2.552142	0.0107
Variance equation				
C	0.000395	8.56E-05	4.611695	0.0000
RESID(–1)^2	0.756968	0.278912	2.714009	0.0066
R-squared	0.045342	Mean dependent var.		0.003801
Adjusted R-squared	0.004718	S.D. dependent var.		0.029930
S.E. of regression	0.029859	Akaike info criterion		–4.241599
Sum squared resid.	0.083807	Schwarz criterion		–4.110532
Log likelihood	214.9591	F-statistic		1.116138
Durbin-Watson stat.	2.076841	Prob.(F-statistic)		0.353626
Inverted AR roots	.23			

Notes:
Dependent variable: D(LNC)
Method: ML – ARCH (Marquardt) – Normal distribution
Sample (adjusted): 1980Q3 2005Q1
Included observations: 99 after adjustments
Convergence achieved after 26 iterations
Bollerslev-Wooldrige robust standard errors & covariance
Variance backcast: ON
GARCH = C(4) + C(5)*RESID(–1)^2

Table 9.7b Investment

	Coefficient	Std. error	z-statistic	Prob.
@SQRT(GARCH)	–0.140351	0.098954	–1.418338	0.1561
C	0.014663	0.006757	2.170093	0.0300
AR(1)	0.350207	0.079590	4.400127	0.0000
Variance equation				
C	0.003916	0.001159	3.377691	0.0007
RESID(–1)^2	0.412024	0.249169	1.653592	0.0982
RESID(–2)^2	–0.068893	0.019409	–3.549587	0.0004
R-squared	–0.015309	Mean dependent var.		0.000317
Adjusted R-squared	–0.069895	S.D. dependent var.		0.084645
S.E. of regression	0.087553	Akaike info criterion		–2.369415
Sum squared resid.	0.712894	Schwarz criterion		–2.212135
Log likelihood	123.2860	Durbin-Watson stat.		2.571461
Inverted AR roots	.35			

Notes:
Dependent variable: D(LNI)
Method: ML – ARCH (Marquardt) – Normal distribution
Sample (adjusted): 1980Q3 2005Q1
Included observations: 99 after adjustments
Failure to improve likelihood after 42 iterations
Bollerslev-Wooldrige robust standard errors & covariance
Variance backcast: ON
GARCH = C(4) + C(5)*RESID(–1)^2 + C(6)*RESID(–2)^2

highest variance. This reinforces domestic absorption's procyclical behavior; during downturns, greater volatility exerts downward pressure on consumption and investment; during the expansionary stage, in contrast, the fall in volatility strengthens the recovery of global demand.

In the last two sections we have presented evidence of the way in which the conjunction of structural factors such as the lack of openness and procyclical market sentiments, and financial market failures can magnify domestic fluctuations so as to produce excess volatility of the kind analyzed in the first section for the case of Argentina. We emphasized the fluctuations of domestic absorption. We can present further empirical evidence by decomposing the volatility of domestic absorption growth in terms of the growth contributions of its components:

$$Var(a') = Var(b') + Var(g') + 2Cov\,(a';b') \tag{9.16}$$

where: $a' = \Delta A/A$; $b' = \Delta X - M/A$; $g' = \Delta Y/A$.

Figure 9.9 shows that the evolution of these variables is compatible with the dynamics that we have suggested. The volatility of domestic absorption *(a')* is higher in recessionary years while the covariance between absorption and the trade balance *(b')* is negative and also tends to rise during recessions. Likewise, note the high volatility of domestic absorption as compared with the volatility of the growth rate *(g')*.

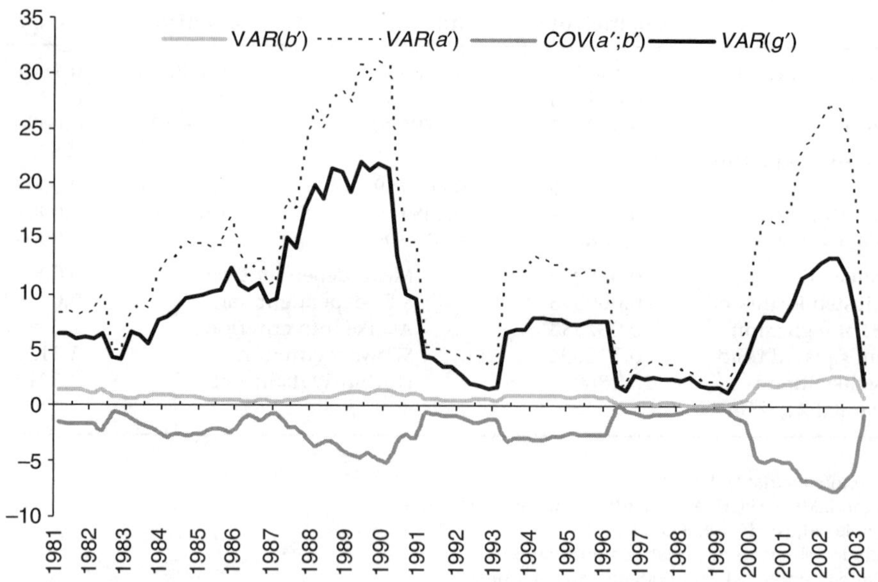

Figure 9.9 Volatility of absorption, output and the trade balance (12-quarter window, %)
Sources: Central Bank of Argentina and Ministry of Economy and Production.

In sum, from the analysis of the co-movement of investment, output, and consumption, we can conclude that there are indications that financial imperfections generate excess volatility in Argentina, because:

- The changes in the exchange rate regime are non-neutral.
- Consumption is highly volatile and its volatility is larger than output volatility.
- The volatility of the growth rate of total savings *Var(s)* is a primary factor contributing to consumption volatility.
- The negative covariance between investment and the trade balance contributes to dampening consumption volatility, but it simultaneously reveals the presence of financial constraints.
- There are clusterings of volatility in the vicinity of downturns associated with heteroskedasticity.
- Crisis and recessions in general matter to volatility to the extent that volatility increases in downturns and 'explodes' during periods of abnormal negative growth.
- Volatility negatively affects not only GDP growth but also consumption and investment growth.

9.5 The building of the DFA institutions under excess volatility

In this section we analyze the interactions between excess volatility and financial institution-building in Argentina. We focus on the reforms of the DFA that were first implemented in the early 1990s and ultimately resulted in the 2001–02 crisis.

The DFA reforms, excess volatility, and rule-instability

The most relevant modifications of the DFA institutions in the 1990s involved the monetary and exchange rate regimes and the regulatory framework of the financial system. With respect to the former, the authorities instituted a currency board (the 'convertibility' system),[9] the complete deregulation of the capital account, and a new Central Bank Charter establishing the independence of the central bank. The reforms of banking regulations followed the Basel guidelines. Notwithstanding, no progress was made in the reform of the legal and judiciary infrastructure. Neither were there improvements in corporate governance arrangements. Traditional features such as the family control of corporations, and the tendency for multinationals to fully control corporate shares went untouched by the reforms. These developments were at odds with another major reform: the establishment of a private pension fund system. The reduced stock of private bonds and of stock market capitalization obliged institutional investors to hold a disproportionate amount of public debt and bank deposits in their portfolios. This is but one example of the inconsistencies that can result from a partial approach to DFA reform.

The liberalization of the banking system in Argentina was wide. In addition to canonical deregulation measures, dollar-denominated deposits and credit operations were permitted from the beginning of the reform. In the period prior to the collapse of 2001, the process showed two distinct stages separated by the Tequila Effect of 1995. As a consequence of the Mexican shock, several banks faced severe solvency problems,[10] and to improve the reliability of the system the authorities introduced a new regulatory framework. The new framework sought to base financial stability on market discipline. The banks' capital adequacy standards were based on the 1988 Basel Capital Accord. A minimum of 11.5 per cent of assets at risk was the standard requirement. There was also a capital requirement for credit risk. The indicator of credit risk was the interest rate charged on each loan. In 1996 market risk capital requirements were introduced. Argentina implemented the Amendment to the 1988 Accord. The 'standardized' approach was used, which requires the service of a credit-rating agency to evaluate risk. Capital requirements were further augmented in 1999 to cover interest rate risk on the banking book.[11]

With the primary goal of protecting systemic liquidity, a new liquidity requirement system was implemented in 1995 to replace the existing minimum reserve requirement scheme. Liquidity requirements were set on virtually all liabilities, although the rates declined as the maturity of the liability increased. Reserves were remunerated at rates reflecting short-term dollar interest rates. The system was subsequently modified to permit bank reserves to be deposited in qualified foreign banks. The purpose was to reduce the implicit tax burden on banks that a liquidity requirement implies.

In addition to this increase in capital and liquidity requirements, other measures were implemented to improve solvency and information. In 1992, a main debtors' database was created; the provisioning requirements were substantially tightened after the Tequila crisis; and, in 1997/1998 a plan to oversee banks based on the BASIC system was implemented.[12]

The three institutional pillars of the new regime – the currency board, the capital adequacy standards, and the liquidity requirements system – however, were not resilient enough to the level of excess volatility observed in Argentina. The regime was put under extreme pressure between 1998 and 1999, after the occurrence of the Russian crisis, when a number of aggregate shocks simultaneously hit the economy (see Fanelli, 2002).

The shocks triggered a recession and a substantial increase in real interest rates. Firms' and individuals' financial positions worsened substantially and the proportion of non-performing loans increased. In addition, the new and tighter prudential regulations induced changes in lending practices that, in turn, affected the sectoral allocation of credit. One relevant effect was the increment in the proportion of loans allocated to the public sector and the high participation of larger loans in the credit supply. The political economy stance and some specific features of the capital adequacy requirements contributed to these results. First, capital requirement introduced a bias in favor of the allocation of funds to the public sector. While a minimum of 11.5 per cent of assets at risk was required in the case of the private sector, the requirements for the government component of assets were much lower (between 1 and 5 per cent). Besides, no provisioning was required for credits to the public sector. Second, the evaluation of credit risk as a function of the interest rate charged on loans created a bias against smaller firms. In the case of small-scale borrowers, higher rates may reflect higher administrative costs rather than higher risk. Third, the increase in capital requirements created a competitive edge favoring foreign banks. Many national banks were unable to raise domestic capital to increase their capitalization. A number of small retail domestic banks, with well-established customer relations with small firms, disappeared or were absorbed by larger banks, especially after the Tequila crisis. This frequently entailed the loss of the accumulated stock of information and smaller firms faced increased difficulties in accessing credit markets. This hypothesis is consistent with the elevated concentration of loans observed. According to the main debtors' database, 1 per cent of the total number of loans absorbed 60 per cent of credit. Fourth, after the tightening of prudential regulations, the banks tended to reduce the proportion of their assets at risk as a proportion of total assets. Despite this reduction, there was an increment in the participation of non-performing loans. As a consequence, solvency indicators worsened. The non-performing loans (net of provisioning) as a proportion of banks' net worth increased from around 20 per cent in 1998 to 24.5 per cent in 2000, in the period that preceded the crisis.

As banks' liquidity and solvency indicators deteriorated, they found it increasingly difficult to meet regulations. To hinder the breakdown of the credit and payment systems, the enforcement of the rules continuously weakened and the central bank was ultimately obliged to assist the banks via rediscounts. One negative consequence of this increasing softening of the regulatory framework, however, was that the authorities' behavior contributed to confirming the expectations that the banking system was experiencing severe difficulties and this was, de facto, instrumental in coordinating the run on the banks. In an attempt to stop the run, the authorities established severe constraints on deposit withdrawals in November 2001 (the so-called *corralito*). Of course, the violation of financial property rights fed capital flight and the country was soon unable to roll over its external obligations, resulting in a partial default on the foreign debt. In addition, to stop the foreign reserves drain, the authorities abandoned the currency board in favor of a dirty floating. In sum, a domino effect occurred: the negative external shocks induced the non-fulfillment of a good number of private contracts, which led to the modification of financial regulations and, in turn, resulted in the across the board violation of financial property rights and the destruction of the nominal anchor. Note the close similarity between these developments and stylized facts (f)–(h).

From our point of view, these developments are good examples of the way in which excess volatility induces endogenous changes in the rules of the game. While reforms were theoretically designed to change the rules of the game so as to eliminate market failures and thereby reduce volatility, in practice, it was extreme volatility that ultimately redefined the rules of the game. In light of our analysis, the reforms had two weaknesses: first, they were not resilient to the typical shocks associated with the Argentine economic structure; second, the changes in the rules were not effective at modifying the crystallized consequences of agents' adaptive responses to aggregate volatility. In this regard, it is worth taking a closer look at the way in which the survival of the 'wrong' financial mutations (a)–(e) interacted with the consequences of shocks to destroy the rules of the financial game.

The reform's failure to foster financial development

To shed some light on the ineffectiveness of the reforms at reversing mutations (a)–(e) induced by volatility and weak institutions, we will discuss a set of specific stylized facts corresponding to the 1990s.

The short duration of financial contracts (mutation (a)) persisted and, in fact, contributed to widening cyclical fluctuations and to increasing agents' vulnerability to aggregate shocks in the short run. Bebczuk et al. (2003) show that, under the new DFA of the 1990s, the stock of short-term debt held by firms was higher than that of long-term debt during almost the entire sample period and that their proportions were comparable to other developing countries (Booth et al., 2001). Bebczuk et al. also show that firms tended to reduce the leverage ratio in recessionary periods and to resort to short-term debt when they faced either increasing costs in the markets for long-term debt or rationing. The prominence of instruments with short maturity indicates that staged finance (Stulz, 2000) was a feature characterizing Argentina's debtor/creditor relationships after the implementation of reforms and suggests that moral hazard and informational problems continued to be important.

Dollarization (mutation (b)) did not reverse. Although the establishment of the currency board was instrumental at stopping currency substitution concerning the transaction motive, the dollarization of portfolios widened. The proportion of dollar-denominated instruments grew continuously. At the end of 2000, just before the crisis, more than 60 per cent of credits and deposits were denominated in dollars.

The banks were hedged against a devaluation of the currency. The proportion of dollarized credit was greater than the proportion of deposits. This immunization against the currency risk, however, implied that the firms had to bear the bulk of currency risk. This proved to be particularly damaging in the case of the producers of non-tradables. After the 2002 devaluation, they were unable to repay their dollar-denominated debts and incurred arrears. This revealed that a risk-migration phenomenon had occurred: risk migrated from currency to counterparty risk. The new regulatory framework did not take into account risk-migration phenomena and this probably opened the way for firms to behave opportunistically.

After devaluation, the government did bail firms out. To improve the financial position of dollarized debtors the authorities converted dollar-denominated debts into peso-denominated ones, as they did with deposits. The terms of the conversion into pesos were more favorable for deposits and this affected the banks' net worth. To offset this effect, the banks received government bonds. In this way the government and depositors paid the costs of the crisis.

Neither did mutation (c) lose importance. The economy was far from resilient to changes in market sentiments. Under the new DFA rules, the evolution of the demand for domestic assets proved to be highly dependent on external conditions. External shocks impacted rapidly on the demand for domestic assets and the credit supply. The Mexican crisis interrupted the upward trend in deposits and credit that had followed the implementation of the currency board. After the recovery in 1996–97, the Russian crisis had the same effect. External shocks also influenced the cost of domestic credit. The main link between external and domestic credit markets was the country-risk premium. The volatility of both domestic and external conditions echoed in the evolution of the country risk. Via its influence on the cost of credit, this volatility increased the variance of aggregate demand. Fanelli and Gonzalez Rozada (2003) show the close relationship between the evolution of the risk premium and aggregate fluctuations.

The evolution of liquidity constraints throughout the cycle played a central role in producing excess volatility in the 1990s, which suggests that mutation (d) continued to be a relevant factor constraining agents' expenditure decisions. We have already seen that average maturity tended to fall during downturns in the 1990s. In light of this, firms had to increase their demand for liquid assets so as to maintain their liquidity position (that is, to keep the liquid assets/short-term debt ratio constant). The available evidence, however, points against this hypothesis (Bebczuk et al., 2003). During the 1990s, firms' liquidity positions tended to worsen in periods of macroeconomic instability. That is, liquidity constraints moved procyclically. The comparison of the evolution of liquidity (liquid assets/short-term liabilities) with the evolution of country risk – interpreted as a proxy for macroeconomic disequilibrium – revealed a negative correlation: liquidity worsened when the risk premium increased. This is reflected at the macro level in the close association between the supply of credit and the activity level. Fanelli and Keifman (2002) found that credit and the activity level are cointegrated, that in the short run the availability of credit affects the activity level, and that there is a negative correlation between the country-risk premium and the evolution of the macroeconomy.

Finally, the inability to carry out financial transactions that involve some specific risks, as was mentioned in the case of mutation (e), was also resilient to the changes in the DFA. In particular, a firm's idiosyncratic risks could not be optimally allocated given that the stock exchange did not grow and the markets for hedging various market risks continued to be missing or underdeveloped. One key fact in this regard is that it was extremely difficult for Argentine firms to separate the financial decisions concerning debt duration and debt denomination. In effect, the inspection of balance sheets in the 1990s reveals that there was a close correlation between dollar-denominated and long-term liabilities because the primary source of long-term credit was external markets. Hence, every time the firms sought to hedge against devaluation, the share of long-run liabilities in the firms' balance sheets tended to fall. Under these conditions, agents' risk management was suboptimal and this, in turn, contributed to making the overall environment more uncertain.

9.6 Conclusions

We have tried to demonstrate that excess volatility is present in the case of Argentina and that the country is prone to generating periods of crisis. We highlighted two elements that account for the presence of excess volatility: structural factors and financial imperfections, associated with the adaptive responses of agents to an institutionally weak and volatile environment. In our view, all these factors contributed to generating a vicious circle involving financial institutions and aggregate volatility, which was a serious obstacle to the success of DFA reforms. In concluding the chapter, we would like to elaborate briefly on some of the policy implications of our analysis.

Our discussion suggests that when financial imperfections exist, the volatility of external financial conditions becomes an autonomous source of excess aggregate volatility and can ultimately nurture a crisis. This is an important channel through which finance can affect growth. When financial markets are poorly developed, capital flows' instability harms growth via its negative effects on aggregate volatility, institutions, and contracts. It follows that changes in policies or institutions that reduce the volatility of the external financial shocks or are instrumental at reversing mutations (a)–(e) will enhance growth even if such changes do not improve the availability of savings or credits. This means that there may be a trade-off between the speed of institution-building and the speed of financial development. Once again, this puts the old question of sequencing at center stage.

From the Argentine point of view, the most important service that the IFIs can pay is to help countries diversify national risk and manage liquidity under circumstances of financial distress. The literature on international risk-sharing tends to emphasize the analysis of the potential welfare gains of consumption smoothing. But this literature frequently assumes implicitly that domestic risk-sharing opportunities have been exhausted, that there are no liquidity problems, and that the probability distributions of returns are stable and known. When domestic financial market failures are pervasive, better access to instruments to diversify national income risk would improve the functioning of the financial market, thereby facilitating the exploitation of domestic opportunities to share risk optimally and to manage liquidity. This means that the welfare gains would be much higher than the literature suggests.

The actual rules that govern financial transactions result from the interactions between the agent's micro-behavior, volatility, and institutions. Hence, the authorities should not design the DFA rules while overlooking the fact that bi-directional causality links exist between aggregate volatility and institutions. To be sure, this does not mean that policymakers cannot induce changes in the agent's behavior by reforming the DFA. The point is, precisely, that institutional reforms should be carefully designed to be consistent with the context in which they are to be applied. The stylized facts that we examine in Section 9.5 indicate that reforms in the DFA in the case of Argentina were basically inconsistent with the adaptive transformations that had been induced by excess volatility and this was a primary cause of the demise of the institution-building exercise of the 1990s.

Of course, one key objective of financial institution-building in Argentina should be to eradicate stylized facts (f)–(h). The reform of the 1990s failed in this regard to the extent that the crisis led to the violation of property rights, frequent changes in regulations, and the deterioration of the nominal anchor as a result of the abandonment of the currency board. To establish a firmer base for nominal contracts, the authorities must enhance their ability to manage national risks and this, in turn, means eliminating the stop-and-go pattern that macroeconomic aggregates usually show in Argentina. It was precisely because the DFA reforms did not eliminate this pattern that the important advances concerning inflation under the convertibility regime could not be maintained. The inability to manage national risk resulted in an increase in volatility and the activation of the perverse feedback channel between volatility and financial sector stability.

We believe that the best institution-building strategy is to adopt a systemic view of the DFA reform. This applies to both the 'internal' consistency of the different DFA components and the 'external' consistency between the DFA and the IFA. Likewise, the approach calls for a comprehensive evaluation of the effects of the changes in the DFA that embraces financial institutions, macroeconomic stability, political economy aspects, and the country's ability to reap the benefits of trade in international assets. It does not limit the monitoring of the reform to overseeing the performance indicators of financial institutions. It also gives special consideration to the effects on firms' balance sheets; to the interactions between solvency, liquidity, national risk, and cyclical fluctuations; and to the problem of risk migration.

Notes

1. For a definition of the DFA and the linkages with the IFA see Chapter 1 of this volume.
2. This periodization shows minor changes in relation to Basu and Taylor (1999). In particular, we extend Bretton Woods until 1978 while these authors establish the demise of Bretton Woods to be 1971. In the case of Argentina, the economic regime that was developed under the aegis of Bretton Woods actually collapsed in 1975 and the first comprehensive attempt to adapt the regulatory and policy framework to the new post-Bretton Woods conditions was launched in December 1978. This is why it seems reasonable to draw the line in 1979.
3. To calculate the standard deviation corresponding to year t, we have used the growth rate corresponding to the four years preceding and following year t. This should capture the behavior of the standard deviation in the neighborhood of a crisis.
4. To highlight the role of openness, in what follows we express the variables as export ratios.
5. We will just present the stylized facts that are strictly necessary to our analysis. For detailed analysis see Bebczuk et al. (2003).
6. *vk* is defined as the algebraic sum of the result of the capital account and net payments to foreign factors of production, including unilateral transfers.
7. In addition, it seems that heteroskedasticity is present. All the variances display ample variability and tend to rise during recessionary periods – that is, they rose during hyperinflation (1988–90), the Tequilazo (1995) and the convertibility crisis (2000–01). As

was the case with *Var(vk)* and *Cov(vk;f)*, volatility increases in the vicinity of negative shocks.

8. Since the absolute value of the covariance between the trade surplus and investment tends to fall during expansions we can conjecture that during expansionary periods the negative correlation between investment and the trade surplus becomes less significant because financial constraints are looser when collateral values are high. More specifically, if the shock that gives rise to the expansionary stage produces a sufficiently strong increase in the return to capital assets, the economy is likely to run a trade deficit in order to finance greater capital expenditures and, consequently, *Cov(i;b)* will be negative. On the other hand, if profitability does not increase substantially, the agents will place their savings abroad and, therefore, the sign of the covariance will tend to become positive (or will remain negative but decrease in absolute value).
9. The peso was pegged to the US dollar and the parity was fixed at one peso per dollar. It was established that the central bank would hold an amount of international reserves that would at least be equal to the currency in circulation. The regime was abandoned in January 2002 when a substantial devaluation of the peso occurred and the authorities implemented a dirty-floating system that is still in effect.
10. During the Tequila crisis, some wholesale banks with relatively large government bond portfolios or other financial market exposures were severely affected by the fall in the price of financial assets. The solvency indicators significantly worsened. Other small banks were also affected, giving rise to a wave of mergers and absorptions.
11. See Calomiris and Powell (2000) for details on the calculation of capital requirements.
12. BASIC is an acronym: B = bonds, A = auditing, S = supervision; I= information, and C = credit rating. See Calomiris and Powell (2000) for a detailed explanation.

10
Brazil

Francisco Eduardo Pires de Souza, Getúlio Borges da Silveira Filho and Fernando J. Cardim de Carvalho

10.1 Introduction

The debt crisis of 1981–82 initiated an era of instability and crises in the Brazilian economy. It was the result of a sudden stop of capital flows combined with a strong deterioration in the terms of trade. External adjustment to that shock dramatically aggravated domestic imbalances. Inflation soared, and several stabilization plans failed until the Real Plan was eventually successful in 1994. Reforms that preceded that plan, and were intensified after its launching, had mixed results. Despite undeniable improvements in institutions and policies, sustained growth at high rates was not resumed until the first years of the new century. Moreover, although volatility was lower than in the 1980s, it remained high in several aspects. With regard to the general objective of the research project – the relationship between volatility and macroeconomic performance, exploring the way volatility affects institutions and conversely – there are three issues that seem particularly relevant to the Brazilian experience.

First of all, concerning the relationship between volatility and institutions, it should be noted that in the Brazilian case one will find a combination of continuity and rupture, construction and deconstruction, in a way that requires a careful conclusion as to the quality of institutions. Let us take, for instance, the issue of public sector finance. Since the 1980s, when macroeconomic volatility reached its peak, a process of gradual institutional improvement with the aim of recovering control over public finances began to be developed, which would proceed through several governments.[1] However, in another sense there was a concurrent loss of quality in the institutions as well. For instance, there has been a deterioration in the quality of the tax structure and in the composition of public debt, both of which are related, directly or indirectly, to macroeconomic volatility. Given the purposes of the present research, this chapter will be concerned only with those institutional changes associated with volatility.

Second, with respect to the sources of shocks that cause volatility, one of the hypotheses of the research project relates to terms of trade. In the case of Brazil, however, while terms of trade have had some importance in the distant past, their relevance after the oil shock of 1979–81 has been diminishing, for reasons that will be explored in this chapter. On the other hand, certain structural features – in particular the combination of a low level of trade openness with a high level of external debt – made the economy highly sensitive to shocks originating in the international financial markets.

Finally, with regard to the transmission mechanism of external shocks, and, in particular, those originating in swings of capital flows, it is quite remarkable that external shocks did not cause major financial distress that could amplify and propagate its effects on the rest of the economy. In the aftermath of the currency crisis of 1999 there was neither a banking crisis nor a major recession. The financial architecture erected in Brazil, although it had important flaws (as will be discussed later), had the merit of preventing dollarization and of avoiding very deep recessions as a consequence of external shocks. On the other hand, it did not avoid aggregate volatility in the form of very short business cycles, around a low average rate of growth in the last 15 years (even after high inflation was defeated). These short cycles are characterized by expansion processes that are prematurely interrupted by shocks that propagate through the financial structure, as will be discussed in detail in Section 10.4.

Before going into those questions, some background information is necessary for the analysis that will be carried out in the following sections. Therefore, the rest of this introduction will describe some stylized facts regarding the behavior of the Brazilian economy in the last 60 years or so, trying to highlight those macro changes that are relevant to the purposes of the present research project. After that, Section 10.2 will analyze the aggregate volatility, using different measures and approaches in an effort to identify the presence of excess volatility. Section 10.3 discusses the shocks and structural factors responsible for macroeconomic volatility in Brazil. Sections 10.4 and 10.5 deal with the bi-directional relationship between volatility and institutions – particularly financial institutions – and explore the specific ways in which economic agents and governments reacted to shocks and economic instability in the last 15 years in Brazil, as well as the consequences of their reactive behavior on the economic performance. Section 10.6 concludes.

A bird's eye view of the macroeconomic performance in the last 60 years

The Brazilian economy grew at very high rates from 1947–80 (7.5 per cent per year). Since 1981, however, performance has been characterized by low rates of growth and high instability (short cycles). During the so-called 'lost decade' – which lasted 12 years, up to 1992 – the average rate of growth of GDP fell to only 1.4 per cent per year and per capita income shrank by 6 per cent (in the period as a whole). The troubles began with the debt crisis and the recessive effects of the balance of payments adjustment required to meet the new restrictive conditions derived from the absence of voluntary capital inflows. From the mid-1980s on, as the external adjustment was eventually accomplished, a deep internal maladjustment followed. Chronic high inflation became extremely aggravated. In fact, the evolution of the Brazilian economy was shaped, from then on, by alternate periods of accelerating inflation and (unsuccessful) stabilization plans, leading to increasing uncertainty and a worsening in economic performance.

As a reaction to the gloomy conditions of the 1980s, a process of economic reforms was put into practice during the 1990s. It began with trade liberalization in 1990 and proceeded with capital account liberalization, privatization, and other market-oriented reforms. A turning point in the economic reforms was the launching of the Real Plan in July 1994; bringing to an end the long-lasting process of chronic high inflation dramatically reduced uncertainties and increased transparency in the economy. This was seen, at the time, as a sufficient condition (when taken in conjunction with the reforms) for the re-establishment of a process of sustained growth.

In fact, the average rate of expansion of GDP increased only slightly, to 2.6 per cent (or 1.2 per cent per capita) per year. Volatility of growth was reduced, but remained as an important phenomenon in the form of very short business cycles, especially if we compare them with those of the period 1950–80, when expansion cycles of six to eight years were common.

A distinctive feature of these short-lived cycles has been that in each and every case, much before the economy achieved a state of full employment and overheating, the growth process was reversed by shocks. So, the economy has been shock-prone. A question thus arises as to the causes of this vulnerability to shocks, which we will discuss at the end of this introduction.

The reversal of the expansion cycles could be described through the following stylized facts. An external event that was judged to affect the debt servicing capacity of the economy led to a rise in the country risk, and eventually to a halt in the flow of funds to the country. This, in turn, created a scarcity of dollars in

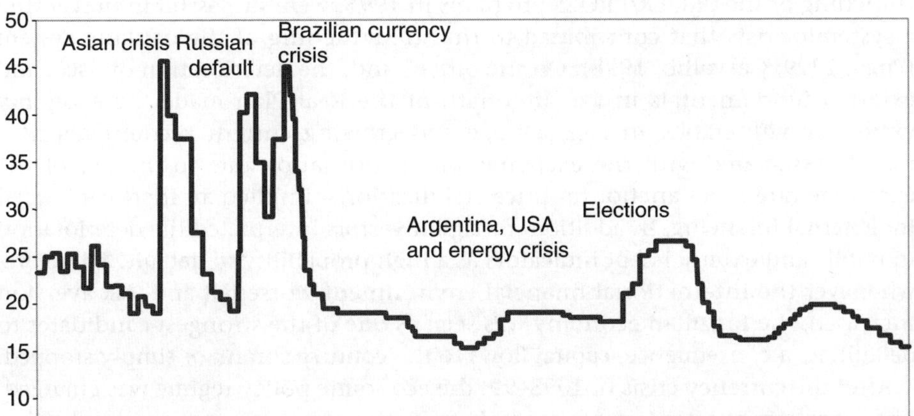

Figure 10.1 Central bank target basic interest rate (SELIC) (% per annum)
Source: Banco Central do Brasil.

the foreign exchange markets, whose consequence was either a loss of reserves or soaring exchange rates. In both cases the central bank reacted by raising the basic interest rate. Finally, such sudden increases in interest rates precipitated a recession in the economy. Figure 10.1 shows the sharp upward movements of interest rates engineered by the central bank in response to shocks that have affected the foreign exchange market in the last ten years. One should notice, however, that the intensity of the interest rate shocks diminished after the transition to the floating exchange rate regime in 1999.

Although most shocks had external sources, there were two exceptions. In 2001, an energy crisis that implied a rationing of the supply of electrical power for some months added to other external incidents that were already creating a shortage in the supply of foreign exchange and an increase in interest rates. The 2002 episode was however more important because, although the mechanism of the crisis was similar to the previous ones, the main factor that triggered the sharp movement upwards of the Brazilian country risk was internal – the presidential elections with the prospect of a victory by the Workers' Party (which eventually occurred) frightening foreign investors with the risk of a default on public and external debt.

Fundamentals and institutions

Why was the Brazilian economy so vulnerable to external shocks? On the one hand, there is no doubt that there had been a substantial improvement in the institutional framework since the beginning of the 1990s. Regarding the financial sector, the adoption of prudential rules according to the Basel principles, and the launching of the PROER/PROES programs in 1995, were successful in preventing a systemic crisis that contributed to the strengthening of the banking system (Puga, 1999; Carvalho, 1998). On the other hand, the deterioration of fiscal and external fundamentals in the aftermath of the Real Plan made the economy extremely vulnerable. In fact, a huge and growing current account deficit – mainly associated with the exchange rate appreciation due to the use of the exchange rate as an anchor for price stabilization – implied an increasing need for external financing. In addition, foreign investors interpreted the deterioration in public and external debt indicators as a high probability of default. Therefore, whenever the international financial environment worsened and risk aversion increased, the Brazilian economy was seen as one of the strongest candidates to default. As a consequence, capital flows to the country shrank or simply stopped.

After the currency crisis of 1998–99, the economic policy regime was changed. The new arrangement comprised three main elements (a tripod): floating exchange rates, inflation targeting, and a new fiscal regime aimed at stopping the exponential growth of public debt. The change in the economic policy regime produced a sharp improvement in fiscal and external fundamentals: the public sector's primary balance went from a deficit position until 1998 to a surplus of more than 4 per cent of GDP in 2003–04, while the balance of payments current account moved from a deficit of about 4.5 per cent of GDP in 1998 to a surplus slightly above 1.9 per cent of GDP in 2004.

Given the sharp improvement in fiscal and external fundamentals two questions arise. The first one, relevant to the objective of the present research work, is whether these new fundamentals are a sufficient condition to avoid the high volatility of financial variables (especially the rate of interest and the exchange rate) and therefore to create the conditions for a stronger and sustained process of growth. The second question is whether an emerging economy should not absorb foreign savings (thus having current account deficits) when the rates of growth and investment increase, and if, in such a case, an external fragility would emerge again.

Finally, despite the improvements in institutions and fundamentals that have taken place in the recent past, it is evident that markets are far from complete and there is still much to do in terms of institution-building.

10.2 Analysis of volatility and crises

In what follows, we begin by describing a set of results of different volatility measures for the main macroeconomic variables with the aim of characterizing the aggregate volatility of the Brazilian economy and checking its adherence to the main hypothesis of the research project. Whenever it is applicable, our results are compared to those reported in Fanelli (2005a), which provides a benchmark for the country studies.

Measuring volatility

To measure volatility we will follow Fanelli (2004) and use different measures to assess the variability of GDP, investment, consumption, terms of trade, capital flows, export revenues, and imports.[2] When comparing two or more data sets associated with a unique variable but with non-overlapping time intervals, we will use either standard deviations or median absolute deviations (MAD) as volatility measures. Note that for the years (or quarters) within one of the non-overlapping time intervals there will be a unique (identical for all years in the time interval) volatility measure.

When exploring the evolution of a time series it is convenient to consider dynamic versions of volatility measures. We will consider three such versions: rolling standard deviations, exponentially weighted moving average (EWMA), and a measure related to the GARCH family (see Fanelli, 2004, and the references therein).

Needless to say, the employment of the above techniques is constrained by the availability and quality of data. Regarding Brazilian statistics,[3] there are quarterly series for a sufficiently extensive set of variables only starting from 1991, while yearly series, for a slightly more restrictive set, are available from 1947. Finally, data coverage for longer time series (from 1901) comprises very few economic variables, the most relevant ones, for our purposes, being GDP, per capita GDP, and terms of trade. We will start the analysis of aggregate volatility of the Brazilian economy with a long-term overview based upon the behavior of those variables.

Empirical evidence based on secular trends

In this section and throughout this chapter, when suitable, the analyzed period is broken down into sub-periods. We take the international context into account by following, with small adjustments, the characterization adopted by Fanelli (2005b), from Basu and Taylor (1999). However, we also break down some periods according to domestic determinants. Apart from very specific contexts, the following time periods will be adopted:

1900–46 A stage characterized by a primary-exporting model. For some purposes this period could be broken down into two, with regard to the international context: the First Globalization (1900–30) and the period of Autarky (1931–46).

1947–80 A period that corresponds to the Bretton Woods era (although an extended one), marked by industrialization and very high rates of economic growth.

1981–92 A phase that has been dubbed *the lost decade*, and that coincides with the beginning of the Second Globalization period.

1993–2004 This last period starts with the launching of the first stage of the Real Plan, which put an end to the high-inflation era.

Adopting a long-term perspective, Brazilian GDP has presented a continuing tendency to less volatile growth rates. In Figure 10.2 GDP volatility is measured by exponentially weighted moving averages (EWMA). It can be seen that apart

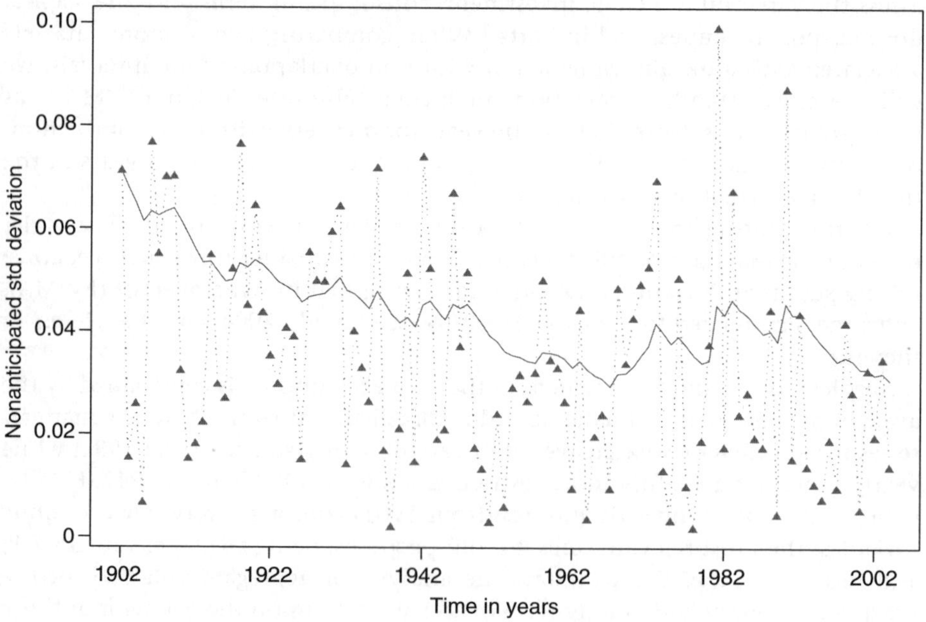

Figure 10.2 Exponentially weighted moving average estimate of GDP volatility

from a brief period in the 1970s and a more extended one in the late 1980s and early 1990s, the declining trend is sustained. The behavior of this historical series is consistent with cross-sectional studies (Fanelli, 2005a; Wolf, 2004a) that propose an inverse relationship between income *level* and GDP growth volatility.

When we try to connect the evolution of volatility to the international broad context, the links are not always very clear. It is quite interesting to note, for instance, that volatility of per capita GDP did not show any relevant change from the era of the First Globalization to the period of Autarky (Table 10.1). However, during the Bretton Woods period, when the economy achieved its best growth performance in the last century, volatility of per capita GDP falls. In the period of the new globalization, volatility shows a sharp increase in the 1980s, to be reduced in the 1990s to even lower levels than those of the Bretton Woods era – at least when we measure it by the standard deviation of the growth rates of per capita GDP. One may argue that the strong difference in the behavior shown in the two sub-periods (1981–92 and 1993–2004) was due to difficulties and resistance to adapting institutions to the new globalization rules. Anyway, at this high level of generality, one cannot find a clear relationship between the international monetary and financial arrangements and the volatility of domestic macroeconomic variables.

With respect to more specific determinants of macroeconomic volatility, the recent literature on the subject has identified a set of variables: terms of trade, international interest rates, natural catastrophes, political instability, financial crisis and capital flows (Wolf, 2004a; Fanelli, 2005a). For the 100-year time span, the variable for which reliable data are available is terms of trade. Regarding this variable, Table 10.1 also shows a systematic and significant fall in volatility.

According to our hypothesis, to be developed in Section 10.3 below, the continuing fall in the terms of trade volatility is associated with deep changes that have taken place in the profile of the Brazilian external trade. This variable (terms of trade) tends to lose its relative importance in the explanation of the product's volatility – because of the changes both in the external trade composition (leading to a lower terms of trade volatility) and in the balance of payments structure (capital flow's increasing importance at the expense of exports).

Table 10.1 Volatility of per capita GDP and terms of trade

	Standard deviation	
Period	**TOT**	**Per capita GDP**
1901–2004 (Whole period)	0.156	0.042
1901–1929 (First Globalization)	0.201	0.047
1930–1946 (Autarky)	0.155	0.047
1947–1980 ('Bretton Woods')	0.156	0.031
1981–1992 (Second Globalization I)	0.107	0.041
1993–2004 (Second Globalization II)	0.069	0.019

Source: Authors' calculations based on IBGE data.

Closing in the focus: an analysis of the period 1947–2004

For a broad impressionistic view of the Brazilian economy's behavior and its aggregate volatility in the post-World War II period, let us look at Figures 10.3 and 10.4. The first one shows the actual evolution of per capita GDP on an

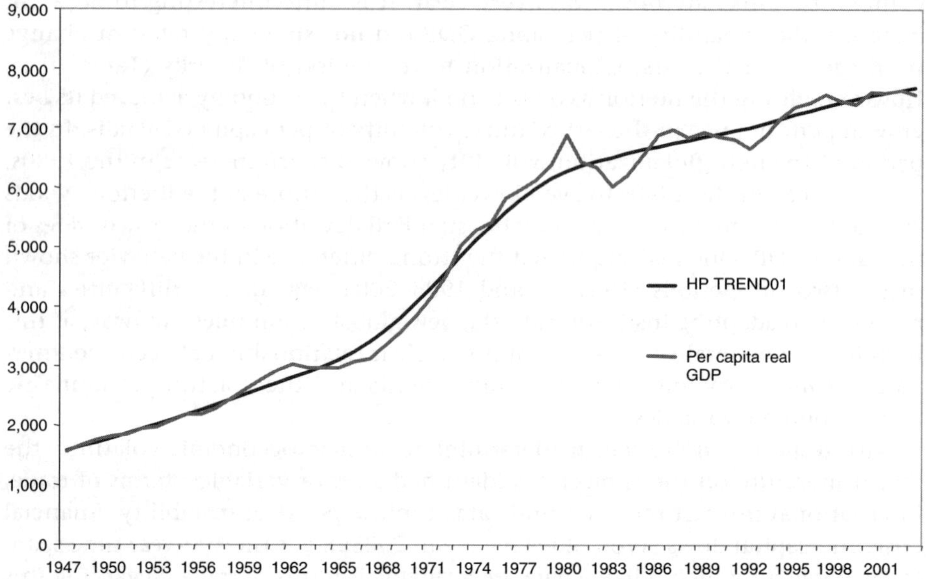

Figure 10.3 Per capita GDP in constant R$ of 2002

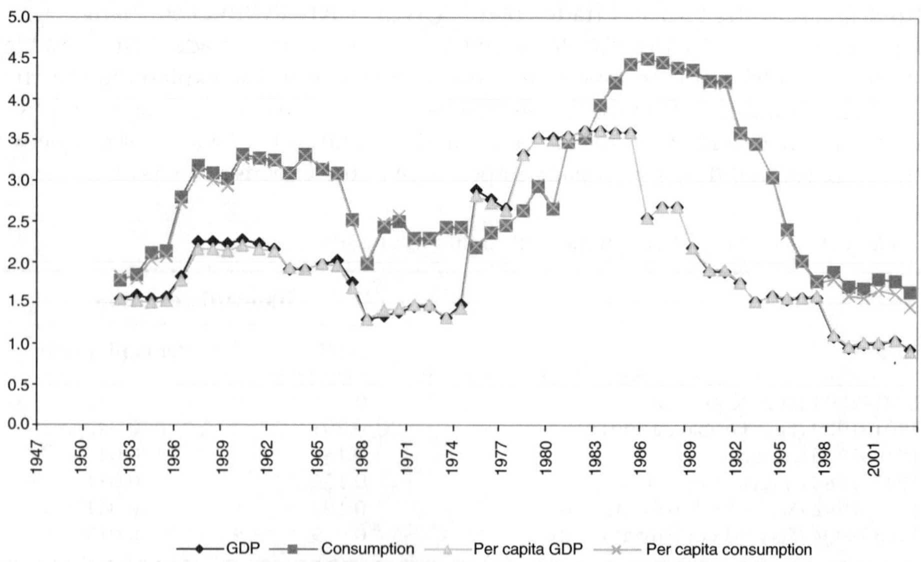

Figure 10.4 Macroeconomic variables' volatility (rolling standard deviations) (%)

annual basis from 1947 to 2004, as well as its HP trend. As one can see, the rate of growth decreases sharply after the economy was hit by the debt crisis in the early 1980s. In response, volatility increased during the 1980s, to decrease afterwards, in the 1990s, as shown in Figure 10.4.

A more accurate view emerges from Table 10.2, which shows three measures of the main volatility of macroeconomic variables for the period 1947–2004 and sub-periods: (i) standard deviation of growth rates; (ii) residual standard deviation in relation to an HP trend; and (iii) the absolute deviation in relation to the median. For the purposes of the present research project, the main conclusions to be extracted from the table are that, on the one hand, volatility of GDP is relatively low when compared to other Latin American economies; and, on the other hand, that if we take as a reference the complete-markets model, we will find evidence of excess volatility in the fact that consumption volatility is much higher than that of GDP. But that is not all. Through a broader reading of Table 10.2, the following results should be highlighted:

1. The three measures show, in a systematic fashion, a rise in the volatility of all variables in the period 1981–92 followed by a steep decline in the period 1993–2004. For all of them, volatility in this last interval is lower than in the period 1947–80. This is an intriguing outcome – for the rate of growth is incomparably higher in 1947–80 – which we will explore further.
2. Aggregate consumption volatility is larger than GDP volatility in all sub-periods analyzed, which is in accordance with the present research hypothesis – which stresses the lack of financial instruments that allow agents to diversify risk away or to cope with it – as well as with empirical evidence found in cross-country studies.
3. Aggregate investment is more volatile than all other macroeconomic variables, which is consistent with the nature of this variable.
4. Volatility of GDP, as well as of per capita GDP, is relatively low for the whole period, when compared with middle-income countries as reported by Wolf (2004a: 13) for the period 1960–2002.[4] Taking as a reference the sample analyzed in Fanelli (2005a: 8) for the periods 1960–89 and 1990–2002, GDP volatility here calculated is convergent with the reported ones for Asia and lower than the Latin American average. However, consumption volatility (deflated by CPI) comes close to those estimated for middle-income countries (Wolf, 2004a) and Latin American ones (Fanelli, 2005a).

Finally, in order to deepen the analysis of the variance of the above series and to evaluate if there is a relationship between crises and volatility, we conducted some exercises using GARCH family models. For the annual data we could not find the presence of heteroskedasticity. For the quarterly data, we did find strong evidence of (conditional) heteroskedasticity. However, contrary to the Argentine case, we found no significant relationship between (levels of) GDP growth rates and the corresponding volatility. In other words, volatility has no explanatory power as a regressor for the GDP growth rates.

Table 10.2 Volatility of main macroeconomic variables, 1947–2004 (%)

		Variables							
Period	**Volatility measures**	**GDP**	**Total consumption**[a]	**Per capita GDP**	**Per capita consumption**[a]	**GFCF**	**Total consumption**[b]	**Household consumption**[b]	**Government consumption**[b]
Whole period	Standard deviation	3.9	4.7	3.7	4.5	9.3	6.4	7.0	7.8
	Residual standard deviation	2.2	2.7	2.2	2.7	6.1	3.9	4.2	4.6
	Median absolute deviation	2.7	3.3	2.5	3.0	6.5	4.1	4.3	5.0
1947–80	Standard deviation	2.8	4.0	2.9	4.0	8.2	5.9	6.3	7.3
	Residual standard deviation	2.1	2.5	2.1	2.7	5.8	3.7	4.1	4.5
	Median absolute deviation	1.9	3.0	2.0	2.9	5.2	4.1	4.3	4.4
1981–92	Standard deviation	4.1	5.2	4.1	5.3	10.2	7.0	7.7	10.2
	Residual standard deviation	3.7	3.7	3.7	3.9	9.0	5.9	6.3	5.6
	Median absolute deviation	3.2	3.5	3.3	3.4	5.5	4.8	6.6	7.6
1993–04	Standard deviation	1.9	2.4	1.9	2.4	6.6	4.5	4.5	6.6
	Residual standard deviation	1.7	2.0	1.7	1.7	5.1	3.3	3.0	4.5
	Median absolute deviation	1.8	1.7	1.7	1.6	5.2	1.8	2.6	3.6

Notes:
a. Deflated by GDP deflator.
b. Deflated by consumer price index.
Source: Primary data from IBGE and Getúlio Vargas Foundation.

We now turn back to the question raised above concerning the evolution of volatility across the three sub-periods under consideration. It is somehow surprising that the period 1947–80, characterized by extremely high and continuous growth rates, and in which the presence of a 'growth convention' (Castro, 1994) was considered to have been established, presents an aggregate volatility higher than the one observed in the period 1993–2004, when the economy grew at a much lower average rate. In what follows we try to find an explanation for this paradox.

One possible answer lies in the fact that data aggregation in annual periods may blur the volatility of short-term movements. One feature of the period starting in 1990 is its very short economic cycles. The fact that the cycles are not synchronized with the calendar year leads to a smoothing of the series when using annual data in the analysis. Table 10.3 shows the volatility in GDP, consumption and investment growth on a quarterly basis. Even though growth rates are measured in four quarters[5] – a procedure which smoothes the series – the resulting volatilities are well above those obtained with annual data for those same periods.

An alternative way to evaluate volatility is the measurement of the length of business cycles. Table 10.4 shows the average duration of Brazilian economic cycles since 1991, using the criteria of two consecutive quarterly falls in real GDP to identify a recession period. The results suggest much more volatile behavior than annual data would show for this period. Expansion periods lasted from 4 to 10 quarters, while recessions lasted from 2 to 4 quarters.

Table 10.3 Volatility of main macroeconomic variables, 1991–2004 (quarterly data) (%)

		Variables			
Period	**Volatility measures**	**GDP**	**Household consumption**	**Government consumption**	**FBCF**
Whole period	Standard deviation	3.1	4.6	3.7	9.4
	Residual standard deviation	1.8	2.4	1.8	5.4
	Median absolute deviation	2.2	2.8	1.4	6.5
1991–94	Standard deviation	4.1	5.5	5.4	10.8
	Residual standard deviation	2.5	3.2	2.7	5.5
	Median absolute deviation	1.5	2.8	2.2	4.9
1995–98	Standard deviation	2.7	4.1	3.6	7.8
	Residual standard deviation	1.4	1.9	1.7	5.9
	Median absolute deviation	2.3	1.8	2.5	6.4
1999–04	Standard deviation	3.8	4.3	2.8	7.9
	Residual standard deviation	1.3	1.6	0.7	4.8
	Median absolute deviation	3.2	2.8	0.8	6.6

Source: Primary data from IBGE and Getúlio Vargas Foundation.

Table 10.4 Time span of Brazilian business cycles, 1991–2004

	Recessions		Recoveries	
Cycle	**Interval**	**Length in quarters**	**Interval**	**Length in quarters**
1st	IV-91–III-92	4	IV-92–I-95	10
2nd	II-95–III-95	2	IV-95–IV-97	9
3rd	I-98–IV-98 (W shaped)	4	I-99–I-01	9
4th	II-01–IV-01	3	I-02–IV-02	4
5th	I-03–II-03	2	III-03–	–

Source: Primary data from IBGE and Getúlio Vargas Foundation.

Table 10.5 Per capita GDP: rate of growth and years of recession

Period	GDP growth (% p.y.)	Population growth (% p.y.)	GDP per capita growth (% p.y.)	Number of years		
					Years with fall of per capita GDP	
				Total	Total	(%)
1901–29	4.6	2.4	2.1	29	13	45
1930–45	3.9	1.8	2.1	16	4	25
1948–80	7.5	2.8	4.6	33	1	3
1981–92	1.8	2.1	–0.3	12	7	58
1993–2004	2.7	1.5	1.2	12	4	33

Source: Based on IBGE, Estatísticas do Século XX and Quarterly National Accounts.

There is a presumption among most Brazilian economists that during the period 1947–80 such short cycles did not occur. Unfortunately, there are no quarterly data for the national accounts covering the high-growth period (1947–80) to check this presumption.

Finally, another way to evaluate volatility that may shed some light on the issue we are dealing with is to estimate the frequency of negative variations in GDP and per capita GDP. Table 10.5 shows that Brazil experienced declining per capita GDP only 3 per cent of the time from 1948 to 1980 – an excellent performance compared with the average of non-OECD countries and even with OECD countries as reported in Easterly et al. (2000). However, during the so-called 'lost decade' per capita GDP shrank 58 per cent of the time. Finally, from 1993 onwards per capita GDP fell 33 per cent of the time. We have thus arrived at an indicator which shows a greater volatility in the period 1993–2004, when compared to the high-growth period (1947–80).[6]

10.3 Structural features of the Brazilian economy, aggregate volatility, and its sources

This section deals with the main structural and institutional features of the Brazilian economy that have a bearing on the question of the determinants of aggregate volatility, followed by an exploratory analysis of the shocks which are sources of volatility.

One of our research hypotheses is that macroeconomic fluctuations in developing countries are associated 'with the structure of international trade, the external financial constraints and the characteristics of domestic contracts' (Fanelli, 2005a). In fact, in the Brazilian case economic instability seems to have been traditionally related to the external sector.[7] Although some have argued that as the industrialization process advanced, the economic dynamics proved to be endogenously determined,[8] the oil crisis in 1974 and the debt crisis in 1982 re-established the importance of factors connected to the external scenario.

Nonetheless, it is worth noting that after those events took place, the nature of the external shocks and the way they impacted the Brazilian economy had changed substantially in relation to the primary-export phase. The reasons for this were the changes in the external trade profile and the prevalence of capital flows in the balance of payments. Let us look at the details of these changes.

The role of terms of trade and its structural determinants

The pattern of Brazilian external trade has undergone two major changes in the last 40 years. The first one took place between 1965 and 1980, when Brazil began to export industrialized goods. During this period, the share of primary products fell from 81 per cent of total exports to only 30 per cent, while the share of manufactured goods increased from 10 per cent to 56 per cent. This phenomenon is confirmed through the analysis of the evolution of the structure of exports using the Herfindahl-Hirschman index of export diversification (which varies from 1 to 0, where 1 stands for complete specialization) as shown in Figure 10.5.

A contemporaneous and important phenomenon in explaining terms of trade behavior relates to import composition. The major structural change regarding imports was certainly the import substitution of oil and its derivatives, which occurred chiefly from 1980 to 1990. Such movement, together with trade liberalization in the early 1990s, produced a drastic change in import composition. This is, probably, the main reason underlying the reduction in terms of trade volatility, which was mentioned in Section 10.2.

The main consequences of these changes in trade structure were: first, terms of trade tended to fluctuate less than they used to in the past; second, reflecting less volatile terms of trade, trade flows also began to show greater stability as both exports and imports turned less volatile; finally, terms of trade movements have become much less important for trade balance and current account than in the

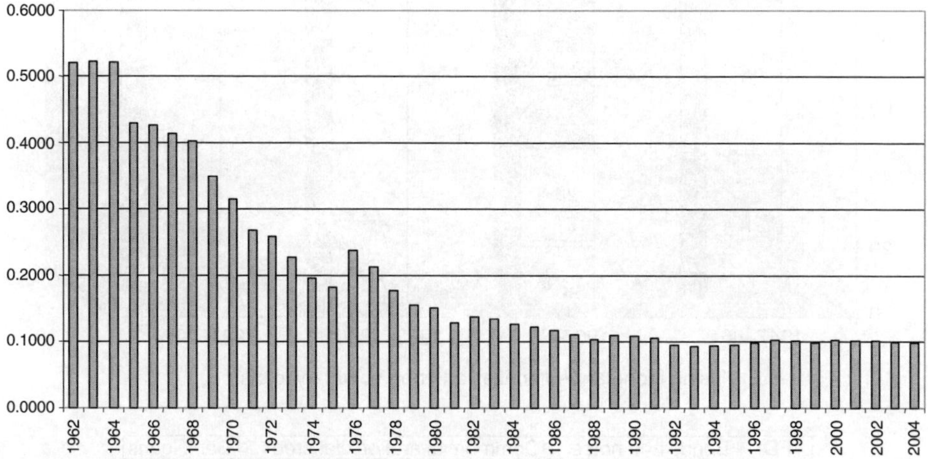

Figure 10.5 Herfindahl-Hirschman index for total Brazilian exports, 1962–2004
Source: Calculated by the authors on the basis of data from United Nations COMTRADE.

past. As a consequence, the impact on GDP and consumption volatility tended to fade.

The role of capital flows

Despite the decreasing variability of terms of trade, one key stylized fact regarding the performance of the Brazilian economy in the Second Globalization period is the increase in macro volatility – as measured, for instance, by the frequency of downturns or by the length of business cycles. Moreover, instability still seems to be strongly related to swings in balance of payments flows. This time, however, downturns have been determined basically by shortages in capital inflows. Thus, it seems that the main source of shocks in the Brazilian case is related to sharp reductions or even sudden stops in capital inflows, not to trade.

Let us then focus on the evolution and role of capital flows for Brazil. By showing the changing composition of capital flows, Figure 10.6 will help elucidate the changing role and importance of capital flows for Brazil during the period 1947–2004. It shows that from 1991 external borrowing through bonds and notes became the most important single component of net inflows. As credit flows were again increasing at a higher rate than exports, the net capital inflows/exports of goods ratio increased, making the economy more vulnerable to swings in foreign capital flows.

Thus, the period after 1990 is of special importance for our analysis of sources of shocks. In order to provide a rough view of the questions raised above, we turn to Figures 10.7 and 10.8. They show quarterly data on the current account, capital flows and the global balance of payments. A striking feature, highlighted

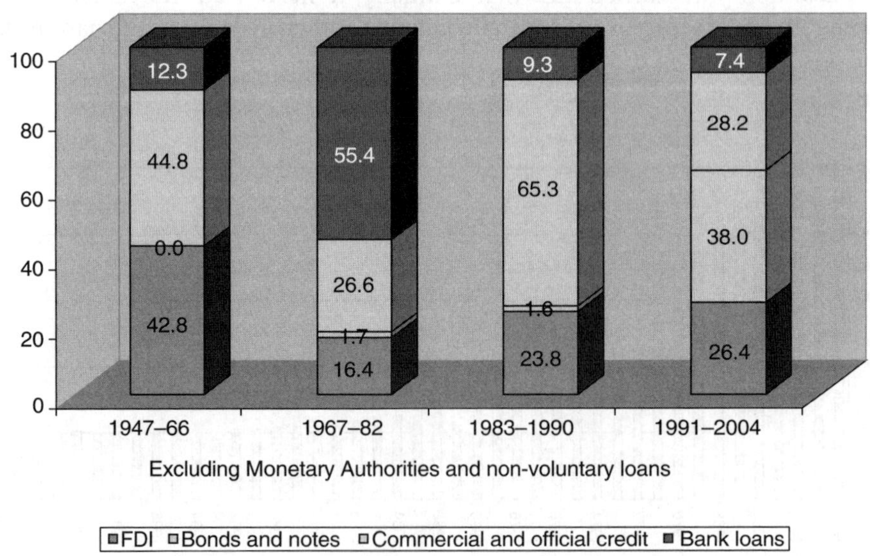

Figure 10.6 Composition of gross capital flows (%)
Source: Elaborated by the authors on the basis of the Brazilian Central Bank data.

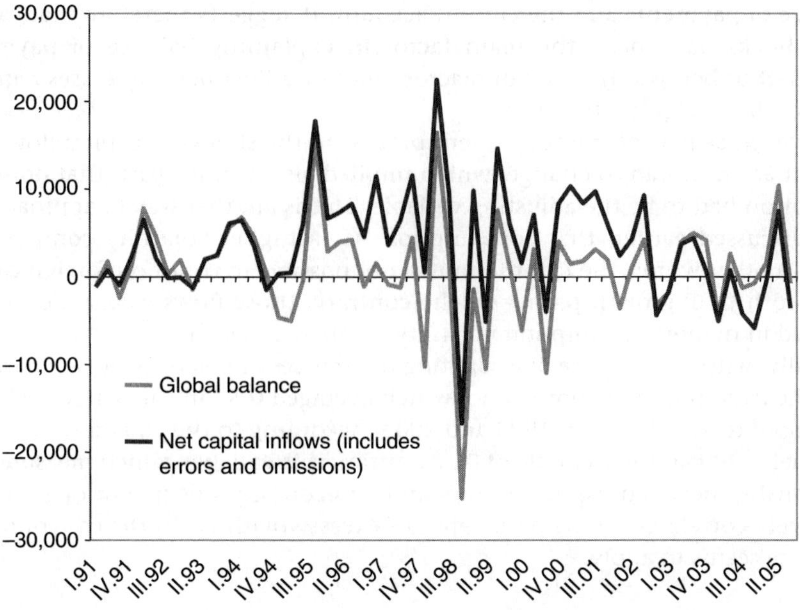

Figure 10.7 Net capital inflows and the balance of payments (US$ million)

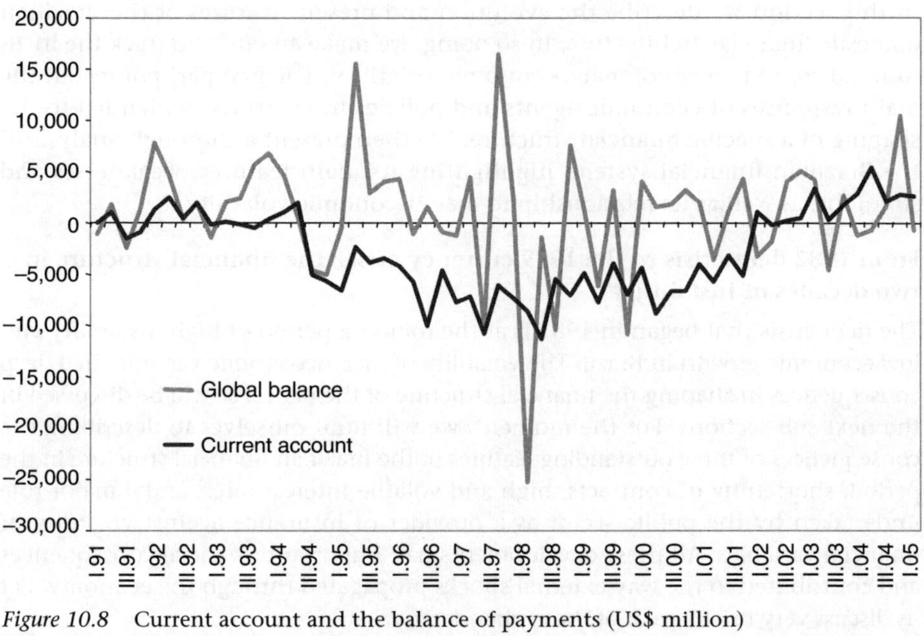

Figure 10.8 Current account and the balance of payments (US$ million)

in the figures, is that the balance of payments (and therefore the change in reserves) and capital flows (see Figure 10.7) series show strong co-movements, which can hardly be detected when one observes the joint evolution of the balance of payments and the current account. It suggests therefore that capital flow shocks have been the main factor in explaining balance of payments swings, thus being at the root of macroeconomic adjustment processes required to meet the foreign exchange crisis.

However, as part of the adjustment process to the shocks of capital flows, the current account had to change, which implied, as a counterpart, that domestic absorption had to be the adjusting variable. This is another way to approach the fact, discussed earlier, that consumption has a higher volatility compared to GDP. In other words, the fact that it was not possible to count on foreign capital to smooth GDP growth path – on the contrary, those flows were procyclical – resulted in higher consumption volatility compared to GDP.

Finally, with the purpose of evaluating the sources of volatility, it is remarkable that the fresh money/exports ratio, which averaged 0.57 in the period 1947–92, was raised to 1.45 between 1993 and 2004. According to the equation estimated by Fanelli (2005a) for a sample of 81 countries, this variable, which measures the relationship between capital inflows and an economy's degree of openness, is positively correlated to the occurrence of excess volatility. In the case of Brazil, the same seems to apply.

10.4 The Brazilian domestic financial architecture

In this section we describe the evolution and present features of the Brazilian domestic financial architecture. In so doing, we make an effort to track the institutional consequences of macroeconomic volatility. The first part points out the main responses of economic agents and policies to volatility, which led to the shaping of a specific financial structure. We then present a thorough analysis of the Brazilian financial system, highlighting its main features, weaknesses and strengths, as well as its relationship to macroeconomic volatility.

From 1982 debt crisis to the 1999 currency crisis: the financial structure in two decades of instability

The debt crisis that began in 1982 is at the root of a period of high instability and low economic growth in Brazil. The volatility of macroeconomic variables had deep consequences in shaping the financial structure of the period as will be discussed in the next sub-sections. For the moment, we will limit ourselves to describing the consequences of three outstanding features of the Brazilian financial structure in the period: shortening of contracts, high and volatile interest rates, and a major role undertaken by the public sector as a provider of insurance against volatility of financial variables. All these developments had important financial consequences and contributed to the way external shocks propagated through the economy. Let us discuss very briefly each of these phenomena.

The process of shortening contracts as a protection against uncertainties caused by very high and unstable inflation was intensified during the 1980s. By the end of that decade, not only had the maturity of most contracts shortened, but also indexation had become daily in numerous cases.

It is true that after stabilization was achieved in 1994, indexation was abolished for most contracts and, when maintained, would have to be no shorter than yearly. Nevertheless, regarding public debt, the main treasury security held by the public (Letras Financeiras do Tesouro – LFT), while having maturities that could extend for more than one year, still has its return indexed to the overnight interest rate – a feature that makes its duration very short. One important consequence of this fact is that an increase in interest rates leads to an immediate expansion of public sector interest outlays. On the one side, it enlarges public deficit and deteriorates all public sector indicators. On the other side, it renders monetary policy less efficient, since interest rate hikes promote an immediate transfer of rent from the public to the private sector (instead of having the conventional wealth effect), compensating part of the effect interest rates should have on aggregate demand.[9] Thus, the interest rate has to be raised to higher levels than otherwise in order to obtain a given effect on aggregate demand – this having, once more, a negative effect on the public sector budget.

The second important consequence of macroeconomic (excess) volatility was that high and volatile interest rates increased the costs and the risk of borrowing. This induced firms to rely mostly on internal funds to finance investment and current operations, therefore contributing to reducing and maintaining a low level of credit to the private sector. With risk increasing and firms trying to reduce the level of indebtedness, banks concentrated their assets on public debt. It should be noted that these features had a double effect on the development of the financial system: a low financial deepening when measured by the volume of credit, and the development of an interest rate derivatives market to insure against changes in the price of money. Something similar happened in what concerns exchange rate risk, as will be examined in Section 10.5. Both these developments are important to understanding the mechanisms of transmission of shocks.

The third consequence relates to the institutional response to the increasing demand for insurance against macroeconomic volatility. It was a combination of the development of specific markets for that purpose with a major intervention by the public sector to fill the gaps in those markets and, in some cases, to substitute for them, which turned out to be the main hedge against instability. Two such developments deserve to be highlighted: the guarantee of daily indexation and liquidity, either through the mechanism of '*zeragem automática*' (see below) or through the government's issue of securities indexed to overnight interest rates; and the issue of dollar-denominated securities.

The issuing of the first type of security[10] was introduced to cope with the fact that, up to 1994, both monthly inflation rates and nominal interest rates varied too much, so that real interest rates were extremely volatile. To issue daily-indexed debt instruments was a way to reduce the costs that the government had to pay for its debt in permanently turbulent times, as well as precluding the emergence of dollarization. In fact, it was a way to insure private liquid assets (denominated in national currency) against the risk of great losses that could stem from forecast errors in an environment of high uncertainty. This kind of daily-indexed instrument has remained as the main instrument of public debt even ten years after the successful defeat of high inflation and despite the reduction in the volatility of interest rates (Figure 10.3).

Another significant demand for insurance against volatility emerged from the new wave of foreign borrowing that took place in the 1990s. With the anticipation of the currency crisis of January 1999 and, after that, with the high volatility of the exchange rate that accompanied the new floating regime, the demand for exchange rate hedging grew steeply. Although the derivatives markets in general – and in foreign exchange in particular – expanded rapidly, the public sector played a very special role as a net supplier of insurance against exchange rate changes – both by its impact in terms of volume and by the fact that it entered the market in moments of crisis when private agents were refraining from offering hedging.

To sum up, short maturities of contracts and duration of securities, low levels of credit to the private sector and the role of the government as a provider of insurance against volatility were key developments in response to the high volatility of macroeconomic variables in the last two decades. Financial structure was in some way distorted by the effect of those developments. Moreover, the way external shocks affected the performance of the Brazilian economy was, at least in part, determined by this specific financial structure.

In the introduction we discussed why the Brazilian economy was so vulnerable to external shocks and how those shocks affected the economy. Concisely, when the inflow of foreign funds shrinks or even stops abruptly, as a consequence of an increase in risk aversion abroad, deep disequilibria in the foreign exchange markets follow. The central bank reacts through sharp increases in the target daily interest rate (SELIC) and the economy goes into a recession. Let us now proceed with the description, but inserting a mechanism of transmission related to the discussion above.

One immediate consequence of the interest rate hike was the increase in the public sector deficit since a large part of its debt was indexed daily. Furthermore, following the adoption of the floating exchange rate regime, currency depreciation, which also resulted from the disequilibrium in the foreign exchange market, produced an increase in the value of the dollar-denominated public debt. All this contributed to the deterioration of public sector indicators with two basic consequences: an increase in the country risk, which required still higher interest rates to calm the markets; and a further fiscal adjustment to compensate for the increase in the interest (and exchange rate) burden. The ensuing fall in consumption and investment precipitated a recession. Therefore, fiscal policy was procyclical – although more frequently through the increase of taxes than by means of expenditure reductions. To be sure, as a consequence of successive hikes in taxes in the context of those crises, the fiscal burden in Brazil was raised from an average of 25 per cent of GDP in the period 1991–93 to an average of 35 per cent of GDP in 2002–04.

The upside of those developments is that, by assuming exchange and interest rate risks, the government avoided the emergence of serious balance sheet effects related to sharp exchange rate depreciations, as well as preventing a severe banking crisis as a consequence of both the currency crisis and interest rate hikes. If this is true, we can conclude that the specific financial devices built to face volatility were able to avoid major disruptions of the financial system as well as very deep recessions, although it led to very short-lived cycles of economic activity around a low average of economic growth. Since this is an important link in the characterization of the relationship between volatility and macroeconomic behavior in the Brazilian case, we will dedicate the rest of this section to the analysis and quantitative estimation of the exchange rate hedging markets during turbulent and calm periods in the last six years,[11] highlighting the particular role the public sector played.

The current profile of the Brazilian financial system

The Brazilian financial system (BFS) is a textbook example of a bank-based financial structure. Efforts have repeatedly been made by federal authorities, since the 1960s, to develop securities markets, but these initiatives have not been sufficient so far to transform the issuance of securities into a relevant alternative to fund private debt, particularly those created to finance private investment. For a number of reasons, notably – at least until 1994 – the sustained high rates of inflation experienced by the Brazilian economy since the early 1960s,[12] securities issuance has remained a relatively marginal channel to direct financial resources to private borrowers. Securities markets survived mostly because of the growth of public debt.

The bank-based character of the BFS can be gauged by the data in Table 10.6, which compares the size of the banking sector with the securities markets as a share of GDP. The data reflect the fact that firms do not see securities markets as a viable source of funds.[13] Even as a provider of liquidity, the Sao Paulo Stock Exchange (SPSE) has performed a limited role. The value of turnover is low and highly concentrated in a small number of firms.[14] As a result, Brazilian corporations appeal to the internal generation of resources (retained profits) to a larger extent than other countries at a comparable level of development.[15]

Table 10.6 Sources of funding as percentages of GDP

	Banking sector			Equities: SP stock exchange		
	Total assets	**Private credit**	**Issuance of debentures**	**Primary issuance**	**Value of capitalization**	**Annual turnover**
1999	77.9	27.6	0.7	0.3	42.0	16.0
2000	78.4	28.0	0.6	0.1	40.0	17.3
2001	81.8	27.0	1.3	0.1	35.9	12.5
2002	83.7	27.2	1.1	0.1	32.6	10.3
2003	86.2	25.5	0.3	0.0	43.5	13.1
2004	84.9	26.4	0.5	0.3	51.2	17.2

Note: End of period balances for bank information and capitalization value at the SPSE; total annual values for debenture and equity issuance and turnover at the Stock Exchange.

Sources: Central Bank of Brazil; CVM; author's elaboration.

The BFS in the immediate aftermath of the monetary reform

In 1988, the central bank acknowledged that the segmented financial structure legislated in the 1960s no longer existed, and issued Resolution 1542/88, which allowed the creation of multiple banks, the Brazilian name for the German-type universal banks. These institutions could combine multiple lines of operation, including the deposit-taking activities of commercial banks and the purchase and sale of securities activities of investment banks. As a result of the central bank initiative, most commercial banks, as well as other financial institutions, became multiple banks. By the mid-1990s, when the real stabilization plan was adopted and developed, these banks were by far the dominant kind of institution in the Brazilian financial system.

In order to understand the performance of the BFS at the time, one must bear in mind that rapid inflation acceleration in the 1980s dramatically narrowed the range of business lines open to them. Credit risks created by very high and volatile interest rates charged on private securities and loans became overwhelming. Many segments of the domestic financial market simply disappeared, for instance, the issuance of exchange bills used to finance consumer loans.

The best business opportunities until the 1994 price stabilization plan were those offered by dealing with public debt. The increasing difficulty of funding budget deficits in the late 1980s and early 1990s led the federal government and the central bank to offer many incentives to prospective holders of public securities, including facilities that were created to guarantee that liquidity risks would be very low (near zero) by having the monetary authority serve as a buyer-of-last-resort for these securities (a practice that was known locally as *zeragem automática*).

A large proportion of banks' earnings in the period were constituted by inflationary gains.[16] The 1994 Real Plan represented a direct threat to these gains. The sudden elimination of inflation earnings, in fact, threatened the stability of the entire banking system. On the one hand, the sector operated under heavy fixed costs created by an excessive network of branches designed to maximize the capture of deposits. On the other hand, it was expected that interest rates would dive with price stabilization. Finally, it was also believed that price stabilization would make it easier for the government to balance its budget so that public securities would become a declining business line.

The banking sector was pressed to change the product mix toward serving the private demand for credit, which was in fact growing very quickly as a result of the price stabilization itself. Therefore, credit expanded fast in the first six months that followed the monetary reform in July 1994. Balance of payments imbalances, aggravated by the Mexican crisis of late 1994, however, blocked the path to the growth of the economy that would feed an increasing demand for credit. A steep rise in policy-determined interest rates in early 1995, plus the adoption of a set of measures destined to bring credit growth to a halt, completed the picture that would lead later in the year to an episode of bank distress, in which three of the ten largest private banks would go under, and many smaller institutions would be closed down or subject to central bank intervention.

In fact, the threat to systemic stability in 1995 was significant and led the government to adopt some emergency measures, notably PROER, an initiative designed to finance, at highly favorable terms, the purchase of problem banks by healthy banks. Although PROER was severely criticized because of its costs in terms of subsidies given to the banks that agreed to acquire problem banks, it was certainly effective in avoiding a systemic crisis of the type that took place in other countries.[17] A short while later, a similar program, named PROES, was created to stimulate the closing down of public banks owned by state governments.

The BFS in the post-stabilization period

Once the banking distress of 1995 was put under control, a measure of normality in the operation of the financial system was quickly restored, but the previous path toward expanding credit to private borrowers was not to be resumed. In fact, with the sharp increase in interest rates and the quantitative restrictions on bank lending imposed by the monetary authority early in the year, credit risks of private borrowers became overwhelming. On the other hand, the new macro-policy mix implemented to consolidate price stabilization ironically ended up renewing the appeal of public securities to financial institutions and investors in general in comparison with lending to the private sector.

As the Real Plan policy mix (high interest rates, appreciation of the exchange rate, and increasing fiscal deficit and public debt[18]) led to growing 'twin deficits' in the second half of the 1990s, expectations of a major exchange rate shock accompanied by an equally major interest rate shock spread throughout the economy. The realization that imbalances had reached a critical point in 1998 inevitably created a highly turbulent environment for all kinds of financial activity.

To contain financial instability and reduce the impact to financial institutions of possible adverse developments in both markets, the federal government decided to issue large amounts of public securities indexed both to the US dollar and to the short-term interest rates (SELIC, the cost of reserves in the interbank market). This was intended to direct speculative demands from those betting on either a sharp currency depreciation or a steep increase in interest rates, or both,[19] toward these securities instead of foreign currency or cash. At its peak, in June 2003, the share of public securities indexed to the US dollar and to the SELIC rate reached 70 per cent of the total of public debt outstanding.

As the federal government absorbed both the exchange risk and the interest rate risk, the 1999 currency crisis in Brazil exhibited a very peculiar trait: banks could not only protect their earnings, but they actually recorded exceptionally high profits in 1999 as a result of the sharp devaluation of the real that followed the decision to float and the increase in the short-term interest rate imposed in order to stop capital flight. The experience of other countries with twin crises, in exchange markets and the banking sector, was not reproduced in Brazil.

For the financial system, it meant that public securities continued to be the market of choice and bank lending to private borrowers maintained its subordinate place when compared to the market for public debt.

The quality of banking regulation and supervision

The Central Bank of Brazil adhered to Basel I in 1994, imposing the minimum regulatory capital at 8 per cent of risk-weighted assets. This floor was later raised to 11 per cent, where it now stands. Brazil's leading banks have, in fact, been very conservative for a long time. When Basel was adopted, most of the industry's leaders were already maintaining capital coefficients that were higher than the regulatory floor. Even when the minimum was raised to 11 per cent, these banks still maintained higher capital coefficients as a matter of internal policy.

In addition to adopting Basel I, the Central Bank of Brazil, responsible for banking supervision, has invested continually in the modernization and improvement of prudential regulation, implementing the Basel Committee's *Core Principles for Effective Banking Supervision*. In some aspects, such as demanding the periodic rotation of banking groups' auditors, the Brazilian supervisor has even gone further (and earlier) than US regulators. Another important initiative was the loan classification in risk classes that serves not only for supervisory purposes but also to guide banks' policies on provisions.

A few major limitations, however, remain. Rules dealing with connected lending are still less than satisfactory. In some cases of bank failures, such as Bamerindus in 1996, connected lending was a major reason underlying the bank's dire situation. Another important current weakness refers to accounting rules.

BCB divulged in December 2004 a calendar for the introduction of Basel II rules. If the proposed sequence is actually followed, the implementation of Basel II, including the advanced methods of dealing with credit and operational risks, will be complete by 2011. Implementation of Basel II capital coefficients to cover credit risks will begin with the Standardized Approach, where external ratings will, however, be replaced by weights set by the central bank itself. Thus, initially, the adoption of Basel II will in fact consist of improving the table of risk weights provided by Basel I. BCB will also initiate the studies necessary to implement internal ratings-based (IRB) methods. Of course, important uncertainties remain as to the ability of the Central Bank of Brazil to implement such a complex supervisory strategy as the one proposed in Basel II. The bank is proceeding cautiously, however, and plans to upgrade officials' capabilities within the time horizon advanced for the Accord implementation.

Overall, one cannot say that the poor quality of banking regulation and supervision has been a cause of financial fragility in Brazil. Generally, there was a significant measure of surprise in 1995 when major banks such as Nacional and Economico, both then listed among the ten largest private banks in the country, were revealed as having falsified their accounts extensively and for some time. The central bank was reproached by politicians and the press, in addition to the clients of those institutions who suffered losses, and those of other institutions fearful that something similar could happen to them. The central bank, however, seems to have taken the lesson of the crisis to heart and consistent effort has since been expended to improve supervision. Of course, it is necessary to wait until the next distress episode to verify the extent to which BCB's efforts were actually successful.

On the other hand, the very favorable performance of the Brazilian banking sector in the last seven years, despite a major exchange crisis in 1999 and a severe market disruption in 2002, although they are consistent with the hypothesis that the system is generally solid, should not be construed as indicating that the sector is above any threat. Banks' profitability in the period should be attributed to the fact that the federal government absorbed the relevant risks (exchange and interest rate risks) without charging for them.

10.5 Adapting to volatility and financial market failures: the reaction of economic agents and the government's role

In this section we turn to the consequences of volatility and financial market failures on the behavior of economic agents, making explicit the very special role the Brazilian state played in that process. The section focuses on the shortening of contracts and then explores the way shocks are transmitted through the foreign exchange and derivative markets, making reference to the literature on fear of floating and original sin, to show how these phenomena could be viewed in the Brazilian case.

Systemic volatility, risks, and shortening of contracts

The current structure and mode of operation of the Brazilian financial system has been deeply influenced by the ways in which the specific risks to which the Brazilian economy has been exposed were managed. New sources of uncertainty, created in the post-stabilization period, opened new business opportunities to financial institutions, but the latter were also exposed to new risks. In fact, although risks related to the behavior of inflation were dramatically reduced after 1994, uncertainty as to the behavior of exchange and interest rates grew in an equally dramatic way.

The Brazilian financial system adapted to these sources of volatility and risk by shortening maturities and/or the duration of financial contracts, particularly those related to public debt. To be sure, a split has developed between contractual maturity and duration. Formal maturities, that were very low by the time of price stabilization, increased almost monotonically after 1997, at least until the end of 2001. The increase in maturity, however, meant much less in terms of confidence in the future, since duration has increased much more slowly and to a far lesser extent. Longer maturity securities carried adjustment clauses indexing their returns to either the short-term interest rate (SELIC) or to the exchange rate in increasing volumes after 1997. As a result, longer-lived securities actually behaved like a string of much shorter-lived securities.

After the currency crisis of 1998–99, the context changed but the exchange rate and interest rate risks remained as the most important forms of risk incident on financial contracts, and particularly public securities. A floating exchange rate regime was combined with an inflation-targeting regime for monetary policy. Exchange rate risk now takes the direct form of exchange rate volatility *and* the indirect form of interest rate volatility through the policies the central bank may be induced to implement to fight the inflationary consequences of currency devaluations.

Inflationary pressures induced by currency devaluation have not been as acute a problem as the threats to the exchange rate regime before 1999. The volatility of interest rates has accordingly been diminished. A measure of normalcy was thus reached that allowed a decrease in the share of public securities indexed to the exchange rate. The duration of public securities has accordingly increased, although the divergence of behavior between maturities and duration still shows that uncertainty remains high.

In fact, uncertainty is still too pervasive and widespread to leave the entire responsibility for creating hedge instruments sufficient to overcome these limitations up to the private sector. At the end of the day, it is the state that is capable of offering protection to market agents that are permanently alert to any sign of turbulence, as we will see below.

Fear of floating, exchange rate regime, and public sector vulnerability

When describing the way external shocks are transmitted to domestic macroeconomic variables we emphasized the role of the foreign exchange market: up to January 1999, pressure on that market would lead to sharp falls in reserves and, from then on, to strong exchange rate movements – in both cases leading to interest rate hikes (although milder in the floating rate regime). The fact that very large exchange rate movements have been allowed in Brazil since 1999 is somewhat unexpected, considering the experience of most emerging economies as analyzed by the literature on the fear of floating phenomenon.[20]

Pires de Souza and Hoff (2003) have shown, by using indicators of the type built by Calvo and Reinhart (2002) and by Hausmann et al. (2000), that the Brazilian economy does not seem to demonstrate a fear of floating. Goldfajn and Olivares (2001) argued that one of the main reasons for having a fear of floating – the negative effects of devaluations for countries with currency mismatches – did not apply in the Brazilian case on account of the development of hedge markets – which resulted from flotation. The fact that in the aftermath of the currency crisis of 1999 there was neither a banking crisis nor a major recession might be considered as evidence that the economy was relatively protected against exchange rate shocks.

The argument above could be challenged. It is true that the market for exchange rate hedging has greatly developed in the last ten years, especially after 1998. Accordingly, the total stock of unliquidated contracts of exchange rate hedging grew from US$100 billion in the middle of 1998 – when expectations of a change to floating were beginning to spread – to US$193 billion (approximately 115 per cent of the net external debt) in September 2002, just before Lula was elected president of Brazil. Despite the relatively high size of this market, one can argue that since Brazil is a net debtor abroad, there is an aggregate problem of currency mismatching. In such a case, hedging operations could do no more than transfer exchange exposures between economic agents, in a kind of zero sum game.

That is not, however, our conclusion. In what follows we argue that although the internal change of exchange rate exposure between agents does not solve the aggregate problem of currency mismatching, it does make a difference in the way external shocks that propagate through the foreign exchange market affect the economy.

Government and market in the process of hedging

At the time of the Russian crisis (1998) and of the growing mistrust in the capacity of the central bank to avoid a major devaluation, the market for foreign exchange hedging gained a great impulse, which would be reinforced by the transition to floating in January 1999.

Despite the development of the private market for hedging, in those moments of crisis the upward pressure on the exchange rate was deemed unbearable by the private sector. In fact, when a bank, for instance, sells dollars in the forward or future markets to firms, it generally tries to protect itself by purchasing dollars in the spot market to avoid its own currency mismatch. It could, otherwise, sell dollars short, adopting a speculative posture, but they certainly were not keen to do that in an environment of high risk and uncertainty. As a way to avoid a very large depreciation and its consequences on inflation, the government decided to offer exchange rate hedging by issuing dollar-indexed bonds.

However, in order to have a broader picture of the role of government action in insuring against exchange rate volatility, we must go beyond the data on public sector debt and track all the processes of exchange of dollar assets and liabilities that take place in three main markets. With this aim, we have built matrices of redistribution of exchange rate risk for several points in time from June 1998 to June 2005. For that purpose, we divided domestic economic agents into three categories or institutional sectors – non-financial public sector (NFGS), financial sector (FS), non-financial private sector (NFPS) – and took a first picture of the currency mismatch for each group, based mainly on central bank statistics for the net international investment position of the country. Then we proceeded by tracking the change in dollar assets and liabilities in the future and forward markets to arrive at a final currency mismatch by economic groups. Figure 10.9 shows the primary distribution of exchange rate risk, which corresponds to the net debt position before any contract is bought or sold in the markets for hedge. All three institutional sectors have relevant currency mismatches at all moments of the sample.

Quite a different picture emerges when we look at the distribution of exchange risks after the transactions in the hedge markets take place (Figure 10.10). As one can observe, in critical moments of pressure in the foreign exchange market, as at the end of 2001 and during most of 2002, much of the exchange risk originally borne by the non-financial private sector and by the financial sector has

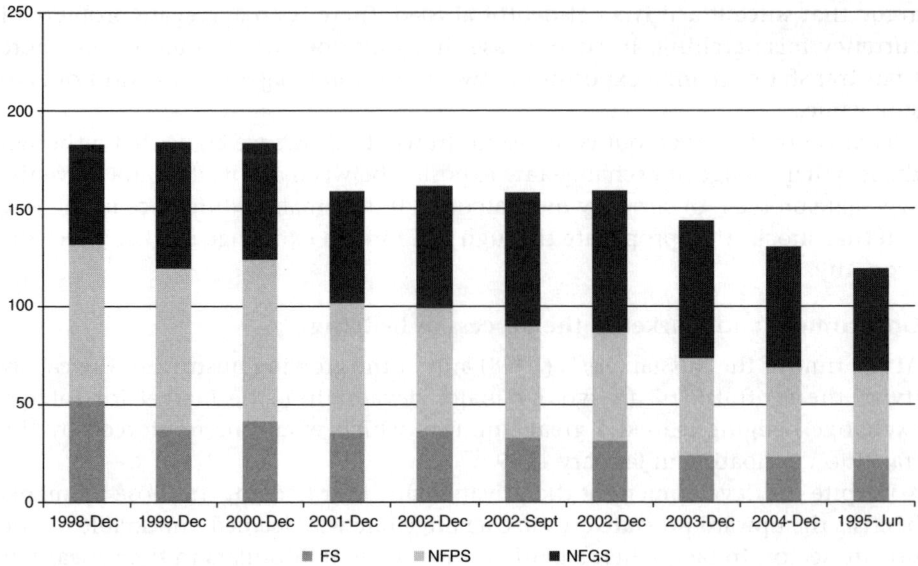

Figure 10.9 Primary distribution of exchange rate risk (US$ billion) (foreign net liabilities by institutional sector)

been transferred to the public sector. In September 2002, for instance, the latter moved from a primary situation in which it bore 43 per cent of the aggregate currency mismatch of the economy to 89 per cent after hedging operations were undertaken.

Considering the results in Figure 10.10, it is likely that the particular redistribution of exchange rate risk in Brazil is the most likely explanation for the fact that the balance sheet effect has not proven to be very important after major exchange rate depreciations in the last six years. Thus, the response of the public sector to exchange rate volatility would be a perfect solution if the story ended at this point. However, the fact that the burden of exchange rate depreciation is transferred to the public sector has had a tremendous negative effect on the evolution of public debt.

Let us take for instance the consequences of the 53 per cent depreciation of the real that took place in 2002. According to central bank estimates, the exchange rate effect was responsible for an increase in the net public debt equivalent to 9.5 per cent of GDP! Incidentally, the actual growth of the ratio of net public debt to GDP was 4 percentage points – from 52.5 per cent to 56.5 per cent – because the other determining factors contributed to a reduction in the debt. In other words, a more restrictive fiscal policy – in the form of an increase in the tax burden – had to be put into practice to compensate for the negative effects of depreciation. Moreover, as this compensation was not full, public sector debt indicators deteriorated, contributing to the increase in the country risk and in interest rates. This, of course had recessive effects.

To sum up, the problem of the original sin affects the Brazilian economy not through the balance sheet of private firms or of the financial sector, but instead

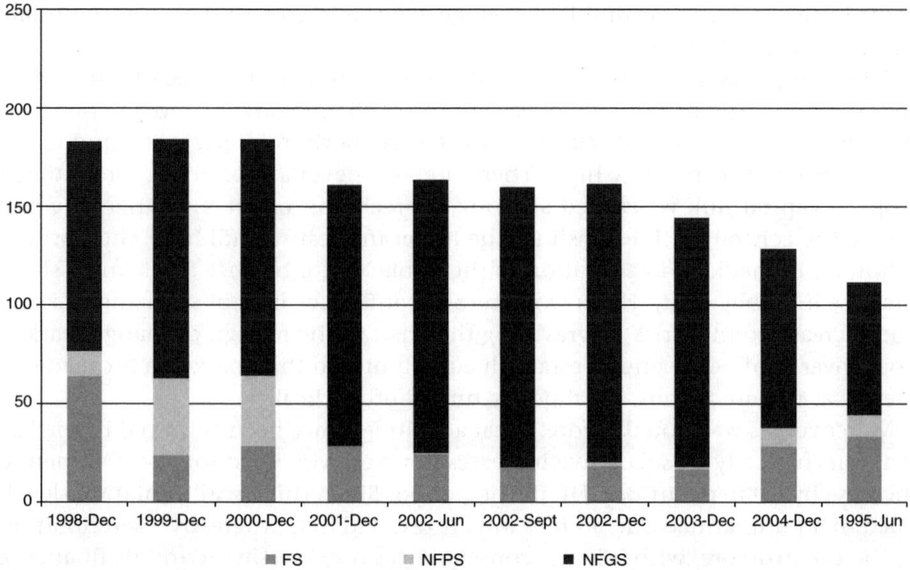

Figure 10.10 Distribution of exchange rate risk after hedging (US$ billion)

through the deterioration of fiscal indicators. If this happens – as was the case, at least, until 2002 – under circumstances in which foreign financing needs are very high, the government is forced to react through an increase in interest rates and in its primary surplus. Even if the effects of those measures may be milder than the alternative effect of a deterioration of private finances,[21] it has been one of the main factors responsible for the instability and low growth of the Brazilian economy.

10.6 Conclusion: an overall assessment

A distinguishing feature of the Brazilian case regarding the issues of the present research project is that the risk-management role of the public sector has been extremely important in mitigating the effects of institutional flaws on volatility. There was no dollarization; there were no deep crises (as compared, for instance, with Argentina). Likewise, there were no deep financial crises; the major banking distress (in 1995) did not evolve into a systemic crisis – which was good for institution-building. Further, the financial sector was less badly hit than in other countries by interest rate hikes when external shocks forced a sudden monetary policy response in the form of an interest rate shock. Firms in both financial and non-financial sectors did not suffer much from a balance sheet effect when exchange rate shocks occurred. And all these results are associated, as we have seen before, with the particular role played by the state as a risk-absorber.

However, the results above were achieved at a high cost for the public sector and implied a specific kind of macroeconomic volatility, in the form of very short business cycles around low average economic growth. Let us recapitulate this in a stylized fashion.

Absorbing risks, in the sense above described, implied the issue of public debt indexed to overnight interest rates or to the exchange rate. As most public debt proved to be so indexed, its elasticity to changes both in interest rates and in the exchange rate became very high. Therefore, whenever a shortening (or a sudden stop) of capital inflows caused a strong depreciation of the exchange rate and forced the central bank to push up the target interest rate (SELIC), there would follow an immediate deterioration in the public sector balance sheet and a sharp increase in public debt, which would erode confidence in debt servicing capacity and increase country risk, aggravating the crisis in the foreign exchange market. To recover confidence and re-establish equilibrium in that market, a fiscal adjustment was required. Thus, fiscal policy turned procyclical.

Moreover, as was noted before, fiscal adjustment has been achieved in the last ten years basically by successive increases in taxes, which led the fiscal burden to increase by 10 per cent of GDP in the period. Since this fiscal escalation developed in an unplanned and ad hoc way, it resulted in a progressive deterioration of the tax structure, with adverse consequences on investment and its financing (for instance, on account of informalization).

However, it was not only fiscal policy that was impaired. Monetary policy was rendered less efficient because interest rate increases generated a transfer of rent from the public sector to the financial wealth owners, compensating part of the effect interest rates should have had on aggregate demand. Thus, as was already argued, interest rates had to be raised more than would otherwise have been the case in order to obtain a given effect on aggregate demand.

Finally, the downside of the picture from the standpoint of the financial structure is the extreme dependence that characterizes the banking sector on the continuing willingness of the federal government to maintain a policy that is always under intense scrutiny by the public in general, as well as by other constituencies, such as non-financial firms (whose access to credit is rationed and expensive), unions (resenting the effects of high interest rates and rationed credit on employment), and even sectors of the federal government itself.

If and when the knot represented by the role of public securities is finally cut, however, there are at least three factors that may justify some measure of optimism with respect to future possibilities for the Brazilian financial system. First, financial institutions operating in Brazil have exhibited a propensity to innovate that has allowed them to survive, and actually thrive, through difficult periods. One would expect then that if the attractiveness of public securities were not changed in a cataclysmic way, banks could recycle their activities toward offering credit to the private sector on better terms. A second important promising factor is the existence of a relatively large (and growing) and sophisticated number of institutional investors and fund managers who are able and willing to deal in returns and risks and who could demand securities of a more diversified nature than public debt. Finally, regulation and supervisory authorities, such as the central bank and CVM (the Brazilian equivalent to the Securities Exchange

Commission) are actively engaged in modernizing and improving the operation of financial markets.

Regarding the high vulnerability to external shocks responsible for the short business cycles that have characterized the macroeconomic performance, there is also ground for a moderate optimism – although with an objection. Since external sector indicators and debt coefficients have been improving dramatically in the last three years or so, as a consequence of successive and high current account surpluses, the economy is heading for a situation in which it is less prone to crises related to external shocks. Once again, however, there is a downside to the picture: Brazil, as an emerging economy, in order to avoid external vulnerability and the economic volatility that results from it, is exporting capital to the advanced economies.

Notes

1. The main steps in this process of institution-building were: the creation of the Secretary of the Treasury and the end of the movement account (through which Banco do Brasil had unlimited access to central bank financing) during Sarney's administration in the 1980s; the fiscal adjustment through the DRU during Franco's administration, which created the fiscal basis for the Real Plan; the Fiscal Responsibility Law, approved during Cardoso's administration in the late 1990s; and finally, the Social Security Reform during the Lula administration.
2. For the sake of conciseness many of our results will not be presented here. The reader who is interested in a more complete description of methodology and of results may request them from the authors.
3. For all the figures and tables of Sections 10.2 and 10.3, the sources of primary data from which calculations were made are: Instituto Brasileiro de Geografia e Estatística (IBGE), *Estatísticas do Século XX* and *Contas Nacionais*; Ministério do Desenvolvimento, Indústria e Comércio (MDIC) – SECEX, www.midc.gov.br; FUNCEX, Índices de Comércio Exterior; Banco Central do Brasil, www.bcb.gov.br, *Séries Temporais*; and IPEADATA.
4. The values calculated by Wolf (2004a) for the average of middle-income economies lie in the range of 5.3 per cent to 5.9 per cent. We avoid making direct comparisons with developed economies since the costs of volatility are higher where financial markets are incomplete (see Fanelli, 2006).
5. Meaning that the variable growth rate for each quarter is equal to its variation in relation to the same quarter of the preceding year.
6. It is interesting to observe that in the Argentine case, volatility was also highest in the period of its fastest growth (the period of the First Globalization) when measured by the standard deviation of growth rates. A different picture emerges, however, when volatility is evaluated by the frequency of downturns or the number of years of marked low growth. After mentioning these facts Fanelli (2005b: 8 and 9) concludes that one major difference between the golden age (1875–1930) and the period after 1979 was 'the ability to sustain high growth over extended periods'.
7. The nature of downturns and upturns has had little to do with the canonical models of business cycles (Easterly et al., 2000).
8. See Tavares (1977).
9. See Pastore and Pinotti (2000).
10. The initial LBC (issued by the Central Bank) was later replaced by the LFT (issued by the Treasury).
11. This was the period for which we were able to collect reliable data.

12. For the characteristics of a high inflation regime, compare Frenkel (1979), and Carvalho (1991, 1993).
13. It is likely that in the coming years, one will begin to see a movement in the direction of the increase in the importance of capital markets due to the consolidation of low inflation and to decreasing interest rates.
14. See Mendonça de Barros et al. (2002).
15. See Cunha (2003) and CNI (2003).
16. See IBGE/Andima (1997).
17. On the severe banking distress of 1995/1996, see Carvalho (1998). About PROER, its structure and costs, see Ministry of Finance (1996).
18. See Giambiagi and Alem (1999).
19. Or, alternatively, to satisfy those seeking to hedge against either or both these developments.
20. See, for instance, Calvo and Reinhart (2002) and Hausman et al. (2000).
21. Because, in the absence of a financial crisis, when confidence is reestablished, capital flows resume and the rate of interest may be reduced immediately with positive effects on the public and the private sectors.

11
Chile

Igal Magendzo and Daniel Titelman

11.1 Introduction

In the last two decades, the Chilean economy has been able to strengthen institutions and economic policies oriented to smoothing economic cycles and better absorb economic shocks. These policies resulted in a relatively stable economic path with an average growth rate of 5.8 per cent during 1985–2005. Volatility of growth, consumption, and investment has dropped significantly since 1985 and has subsequently stabilized. Also, economic shocks, which were not very different in nature and magnitude, produced very different outcomes, with a fall in GDP of 13 per cent in the 1981–82 crisis and of 1 per cent in the 1997–98 crisis.

Since the mid-1980s, the country has been through a deep process of structural and policy changes. Due to the interrelations between volatility and institution-building, it is not easy to establish Granger-causality between these two factors. However, we argue that these two elements interacted in a positive way initiating a virtuous circle between volatility reduction and policy and institution-building. After the 1981–82 crisis, improved institutional design, together with better economic policies and political consensus, triggered a path of financial development, stability, and economic growth.

We analyzed two elements that significantly contributed to this virtuous cycle. First, fiscal policy exhibited a strong commitment to stability, which implied a significant public sector surplus from the 1990s. The fiscal stance greatly facilitated the changes in monetary and exchange rate policies, making room for a better management of capital inflows. Second, changes in the domestic financial architecture through a better regulatory framework and prudent regulations, together with the development of capital markets, played an important role in strengthening the financial sector.

The chapter begins by discussing the volatility of GDP, consumption, investment and domestic demand. The changes in volatility relate to changes in external conditions, and changes in the institutional and policy framework of fiscal, monetary, and exchange rates. Taking into account the effect of the different policies, the chapter examines the evolution of the financial sector and its impact on volatility.

We then compare the outcome in terms of GDP and financial turmoil of the crisis in the early 1980s and the crisis in the late 1990s. We argue that the different results are explained by the institutional and policy changes that Chile started in the 1980s.

The development of the domestic financial architecture has played an important role in helping to reduce economic volatility. After the debacle of the early 1980s, a prolonged financial institution-building process began. Recognizing the relationship between macro volatility and financial development, a key feature of this process was the consistency between the macroeconomic regime and the financial rules. Changes in macroeconomic policies, together with better supervision and prudential regulation, permitted a healthy and rational development of the financial sector. The ability to build financial institutions and improve the quality of the domestic financial architecture can explain the difference between financial deepening and financial development.

A key lesson that comes from the Chilean experience is that size and quality are not synonymous in the financial markets. Even though the banking system was relatively big in the late 1970s, financial institutions and regulations were weak. The rules of the game for the financial sector designed in the 1970s resulted in very weak governance structures for financial transactions, giving rise to related loans, the flawed allocation of risks, a distorted banking structure, and ultimately, a full-fledged financial crisis.

Despite the institutional disarrays after the 1981–82 crisis, Chile was able to overcome a situation of weak institutions and marked volatility, and to build a much sounder financial sector in the 1980s and 1990s. Under the new conditions, the adaptive responses of agents induced permanent changes in the financial structure. The most relevant were the increase in the maturity of financial contracts, the absence of dollarization, and the development of capital markets.

The early 1980s showed that weak financial markets could play an important destabilizing role, amplifying negative shocks. The late 1990s showed that a well-developed financial market that includes instruments to manage risk and cope with uncertainty can do the opposite. By comparing the performance of the economy under similar shocks but dissimilar domestic financial architecture, the chapter shows that the quality of the financial system matters a great deal to the ability to manage shocks.

International private capital markets have been an important source of financing, but their role in consumption smoothing has been less relevant. In spite of the developments in macroeconomic and domestic financial institutions, international spreads continue to be well above those of richer countries that exhibit similar volatility. Risk classifications remain slow to improve. Chile still depends on its domestic fiscal, monetary and financial institutions to smooth terms of trade shocks, while the capital account plays only a modest role.

We conclude by recognizing the importance of a broad political consensus in favor of economic stability. Many factors well beyond the scope of this chapter contributed to this consensus. Political actors in Chile strongly considered the stability of macroeconomic policies and institutions to be a fundamental asset for the democratic transition initiated in the early 1990s.

11.2 Excess volatility and crises

In this section, using descriptive statistics, we discuss the volatility of GDP, consumption, investment, and domestic demand. The characteristics of the GDP cycle and some relevant co-movements to detect excessive volatility are briefly analyzed. We conclude that Chile went through a significant change in terms of the volatility of its main macroeconomic variables. The 1970s and the first half of the 1980s showed relatively high volatility, but volatility has fallen substantially since the second half of the 1980s.

To measure the evolution of volatility we look at standard deviations of a rolling window. We use a centered window of nine observations for yearly data and a centered window of 12 observations for quarterly data. For the analysis of excess volatility of consumption, we look at the decomposition of the variance of this variable.

In order to deal with non-stationary time series we follow two strategies. The first is to use growth rates instead of levels. The other is to use rates relative to exports. This last option has the advantage that it emphasizes the role of openness as a structural element that affects volatility.

Figure 11.1 shows that from 1970 to the mid-1980s volatility of GDP and domestic demand increased considerably. On the other hand, in the mid-1980s the volatility of these two variables dropped and went back to levels similar to

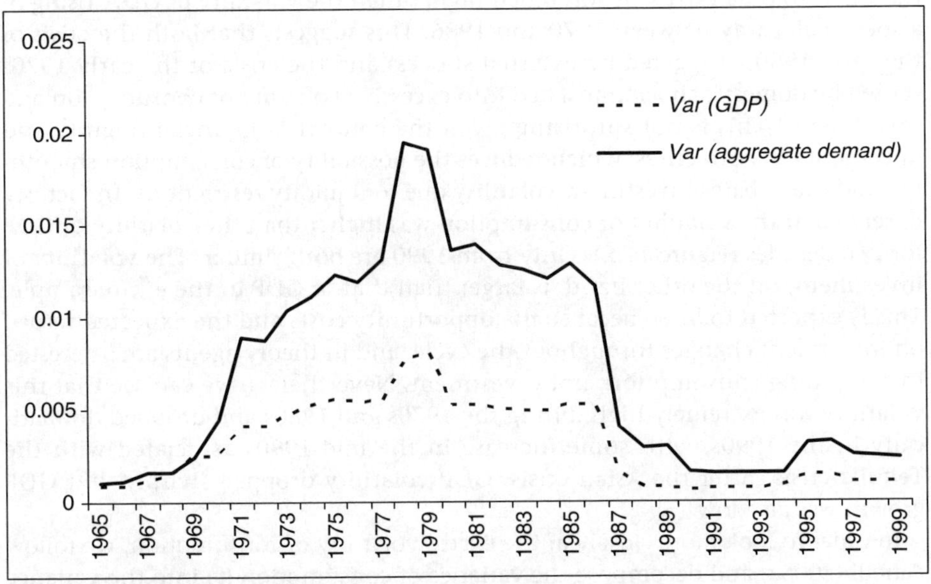

Figure 11.1 Volatility of growth and domestic absorption: annual data

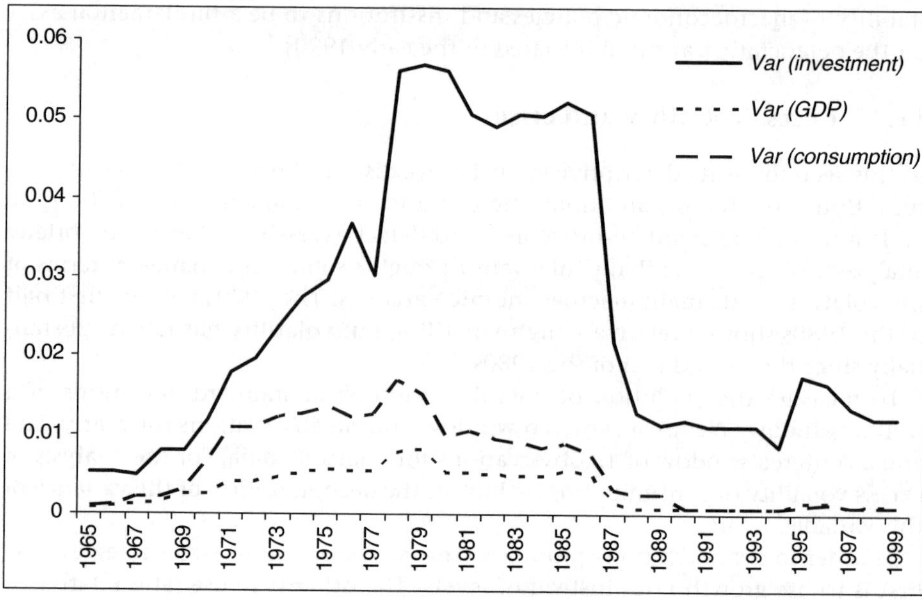

Figure 11.2 Volatility of growth, consumption and investment: quarterly data

those observed in the mid-1960s. Measured in quarterly data (Figure 11.2) GDP volatility began to fall in the late 1980s.

It should be noted that volatility of domestic demand from the beginning of the 1970s to the mid-1980s was much higher than the volatility of GDP, rising in a spectacular way between 1970 and 1986. This suggests that both the crisis of the early 1980s (triggered by external shocks) and the crisis of the early 1970s caused by domestic shock translated into excessive volatility of consumption and investment.[1] This is not surprising given the context of financial fragility and uncertainty of both crises, which reduces the possibility of consumption smoothing and exacerbates investment volatility due to liquidity restrictions. In fact, we observe that the volatility of consumption was higher than the volatility of GDP for two decades (Figure 11.2). Only from 1990 are both similar. The volatility of investment, on the other hand, is larger than that of GDP in the entire sample. This is expected to be so because the opportunity costs and the expected return on investment changes throughout the cycle, and in theory agents are interested in smoothing consumption, not investment. Nevertheless, we can see that this volatility was extremely high during the 1970s and 1980s and dropped dramatically in the 1990s, with some increase in the mid-1990s associated with the Tequila crisis. After the Asian crisis, GDP volatility dropped sharply, but GDP growth was also low.

In order to look more closely at the excess volatility of consumption, we follow Fanelli (2005a) and decompose the variance of consumption (c) into the variance of GDP (g) and the variance of total savings (s):

$$Var(c) = \omega_y^2 Var(g) + \omega_s^2 Var(s) - 2\omega_y\omega_s Cov(g;s), \qquad (11.1)$$

where $\omega_y = \dfrac{Y}{C}$ y $\omega_s = \dfrac{S}{C}$ are positive numbers.

Consumption smoothing is assumed to be welfare improving and it necessarily means that $Var(c) < Var(g)$. Replacing and reordering we obtain that there is consumption smoothing to the extent that:

$$(\omega_y^2 - 1)Var(g) + \omega_s^2 Var(s) < 2\omega_y\omega_s Cov(g;s). \qquad (11.2)$$

Dividing both sides by the product of the standard deviation of GDP and savings ($SD(g)$ and $SD(s)$, respectively) we obtain:

$$(\omega_y^2 - 1)\frac{Var(g)}{DS(g)DS(s)} + \omega_s^2 \frac{Var(s)}{DS(g)DS(s)} < 2\omega_y\omega_s \frac{Cov(g;s)}{DS(g)DS(s)} \qquad (11.3)$$

or:

$$\left[(\omega_y^2 - 1)\frac{Var(g)}{DS(g)DS(s)} + \omega_s^2 \frac{Var(s)}{DS(g)DS(s)}\right] \Big/ 2\omega_y\omega_s < \rho(g;s) \qquad (11.4)$$

The left-hand side of inequality (11.4) can be labeled 'excess volatility threshold'. Volatility of consumption is less than the volatility of GDP only if the coefficient of correlation of s and g is positive and bigger than the excess volatility threshold. In other words, for consumption to be smooth over time fluctuations in GDP have to be positively correlated with total savings: a (temporary) positive shock to GDP has to translate more into higher savings than higher consumption.

Figure 11.3 shows the excess volatility threshold and the correlation coefficient of savings and GDP. The correlation coefficient was systematically below the threshold from the mid-1970s to the end of the 1980s. In the second half of the 1980s, the coefficient started to increase and reached values close to the (relatively stable) threshold in the first years of the 1990s. The dotted line of Figure 11.3 increases to the extent that shocks to GDP translate into volatility of savings, with changes in investment and/or the current account. The development of the financial system plays a central role in facilitating the conversion of savings into investment and the flow of external assets and liabilities.

Econometric exercises (not reported) to test for heteroskedasticity, including correlograms and LM GARCH test, did not find significant evidence for the presence of heteroskedasticity in GDP, consumption, or investment. That means that for the last 20 years shocks in Chile have not been translated into persistent volatility increases.

As can be seen in Figure 11.4, during the 1990s Chile's growth volatility became much more like that of the industrialized countries. During the 1970s and 1980s the volatility coefficient of the Chilean economy was around ten times that of the industrialized countries while today it is less than double. In terms of regional comparison, Chile has outperformed other Latin American countries.

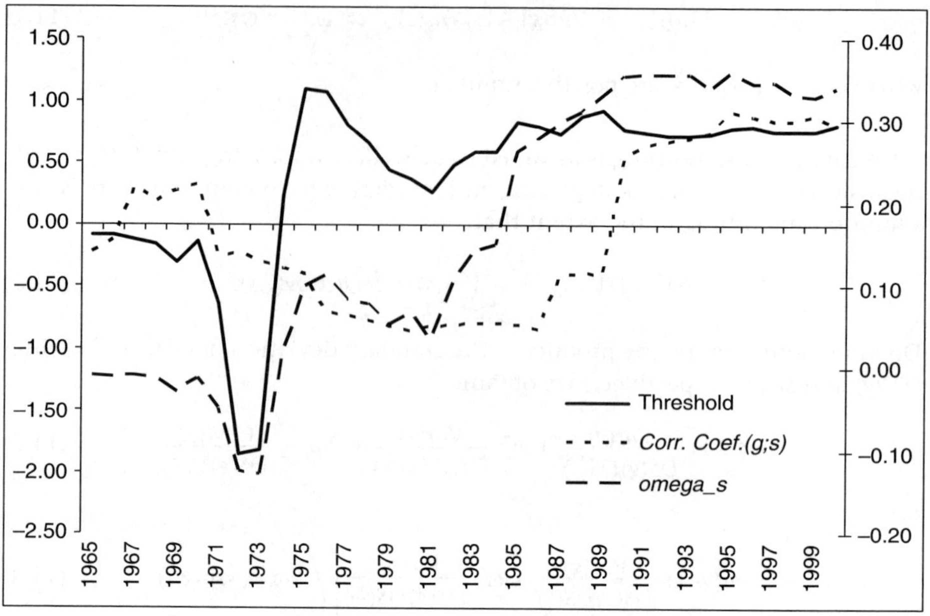

Figure 11.3 Excess volatility

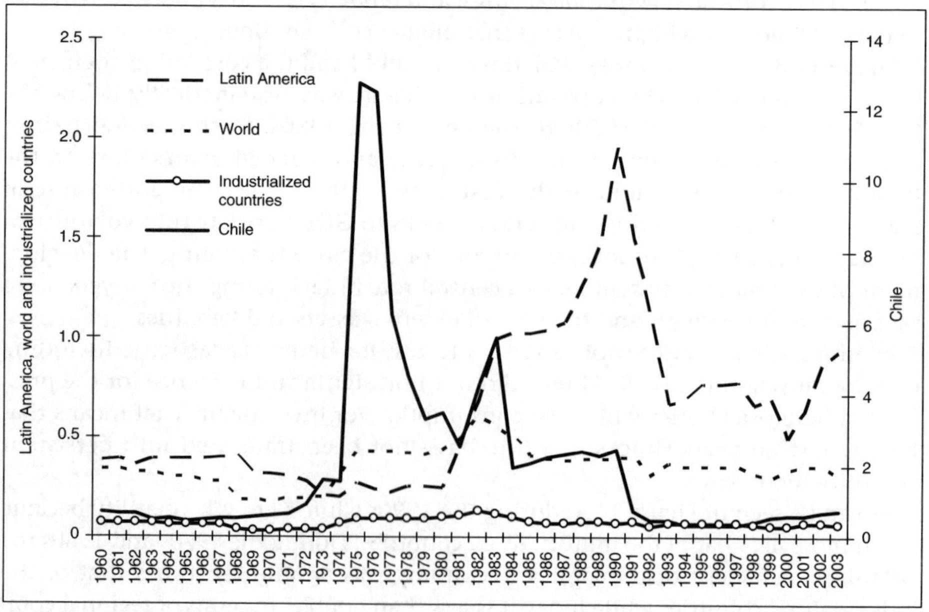

Figure 11.4 Volatility of GDP growth (coefficient of variation, 10-year-moving average)

11.3 Volatility reduction, domestic financial architecture, and macroeconomic policies

At the same time as macroeconomic volatility has fallen since the mid-1980s, the country has gone through a deep process of structural change, which has caused identification problems and made it hard to establish Granger-causality between institution development, policies, and volatility. We argued that, taking into account simultaneity issues, macroeconomic and financial policies and their interactions jointly played a causal role concerning the reduction in aggregate volatility. There are two distinctive features worth noting. First, fiscal policy has exhibited a strong commitment to stability, which has implied a significant public sector surplus since the 1990s amounting to 1 to 2 per cent of GDP. The fiscal stance greatly facilitated the changes in monetary and exchange rate policies allowing for a better management of capital inflows and preventing unwanted exchange rate appreciation during part of the 1990s. It has also allowed for countercyclical monetary policy. Second, there has been a strengthening of the institutional setting of the financial sector, particularly the financial infrastructure, which, as defined by Fanelli (2006), includes the regulatory framework, policies, and practices affecting the financial sector and corporate governance.

In what follows we provide some descriptive insights on relevant structural changes since the 1970s. We relate these structural changes to the change in volatility. We start with what we believe to be the most exogenous of these factors, that is, external conditions. Then we analyze changes in institutions that are definitely more endogenous to overall volatility, such as fiscal, monetary, and financial reforms.

External conditions

Trade, terms of trade fluctuations, and capital flows play a significant role in Chile's economic performance. This implies that a possible explanation behind the strong reduction in aggregate volatility is that in the last decades external shocks have become smaller, both for terms of trade and capital flows. Less volatile external conditions should result in a less volatile GDP and investment and possibly, to a lesser extent, in less volatile consumption.

In relation to the terms of trade, Figure 11.5 shows that in the last decade and a half they have become higher and less volatile. Extreme shocks are less frequent and smaller. This could be an important factor behind the reduction in volatility observed in Chile, except that the fall in volatility of macroeconomic aggregates seems to have occurred before the fall in volatility of terms of trade. Furthermore, it is possible to argue that the reduction in volatility of external variables is to some extent endogenous to the fact that the economy has become more stable. However, this argument is less likely to be true for the terms of trade of the Chilean economy since they are very dependent on the price of commodities.

A factor that can reduce the volatility of terms of trade for a particular economy, as well as the impact of terms of trade volatility at the aggregate level,

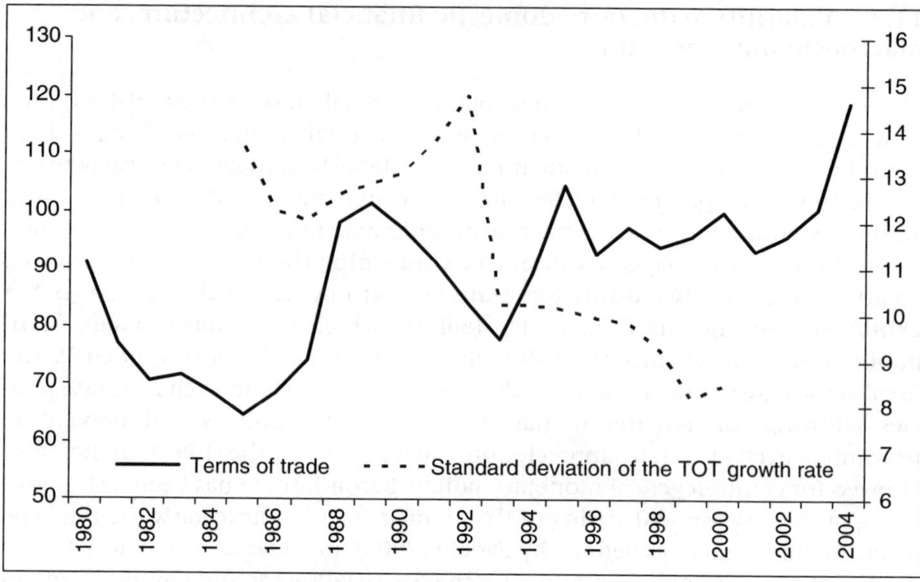

Figure 11.5 Terms of trade and their volatility

is the diversification of exports. In the Chilean case, we observed a modest export diversification during the last decades. The importance of copper in total exports has been reduced from an average of 46 per cent for the period 1978–91 to 37 per cent for the period 1992–2004. Industrial exports have increased their participation from 32 per cent in the first period to 41 per cent in the second. It is important to take into account, though, that an important part of industrial exports (at least 25 per cent) are products that are relatively intensive in natural resources, such as salmon, wine, wood derivatives, and cellulose. The prices of these goods behave very much like commodities.

Capital flow volatility has become smaller since the mid-1980s, contributing to a more stable macro-financial environment.[2] In order to show this, we look at a measure of net resource transfers to the economy (fresh money): capital inflows net of financial services and changes in reserves (*VK*). Figure 11.6 shows the volatility of this measure (normalized by exports) together with the volatility of a decomposition of this measure: the volatility of the trade balance (*TB*) (equivalent to capital flows net of financial services), the volatility of changes in reserves (*DR*) and the correlation of changes in reserves and our measure of fresh money. After the mid-1980s, the volatility of *TB/X* falls substantially and never increases again. If we take into account that *TB* reflects the difference between GDP and domestic absorption, this means that there have been no periods of large macroeconomic adjustment, as was the case in the previous period in which the high variance of *TB/X* reflected the sudden changes in domestic absorption vis-à-vis GDP. This can be interpreted as a result of better volatility management at both the micro and macro levels. The variance in *VK/X* was much higher in the 1990s,

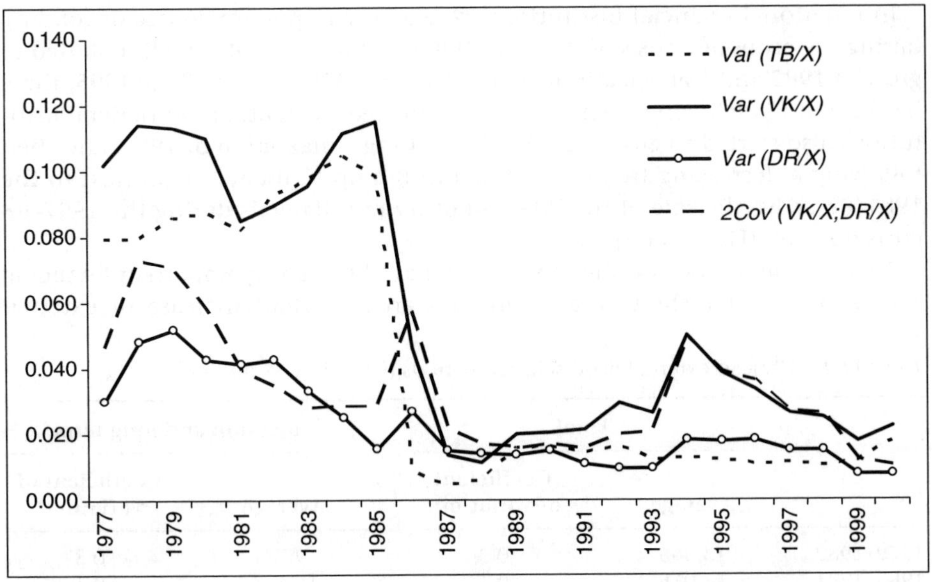

Figure 11.6 Volatility of fresh money and reserves

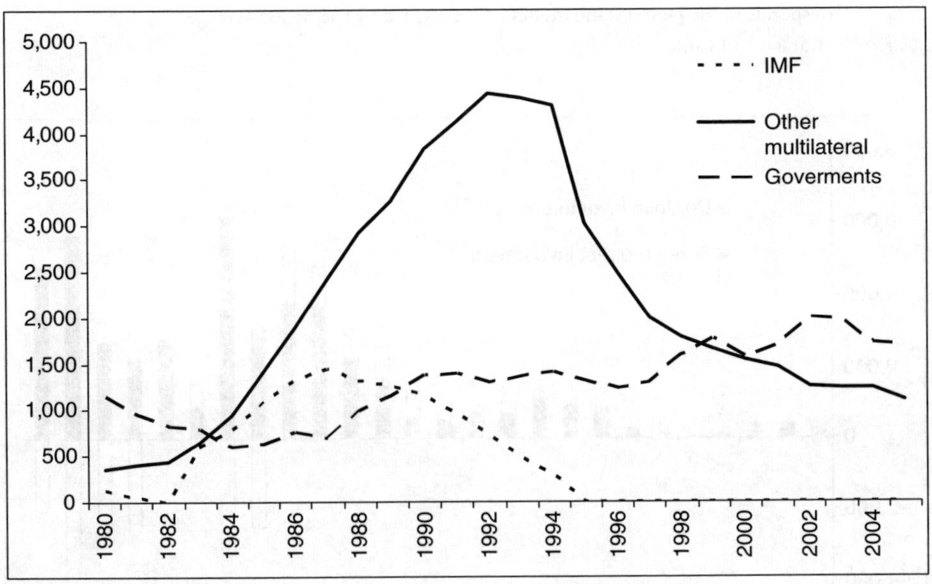

Figure 11.7 External public debt with organisms (US$ million)
Source: Central Bank of Chile.

meaning a higher volatility of capital flows. The greater variation of *VK* was compensated by changes in international reserves, which increase the covariance between *DR* and *VK*.

International financial institutions were a very important source of funding during the economic crisis of the early 1980s. Public debt with the IMF started to grow in 1982 and reached a peak in 1987 at US$1450 million. Since 1995, there has been no indebtedness with the fund. The debt with other multilateral institutions also started to grow after 1982, reaching a maximum in 1992, and then following a decreasing trend, which continues up to today. In contrast to the 1981–82 crisis, the role of the IMF and other multilaterals during the 1997–98 crisis was null (Figure 11.7).

Private capital flows, on the other hand, have been a very important financing source. Table 11.1 shows that there was an important increase in external

Table 11.1 Chilean external debt: selected periods (stock in US$ million)

	Total		**Medium and long term**	
	Average	**Coefficient of variation***	**Average**	**Coefficient of variation***
1979–1982	13,066	0.3	9,771	0.3
1983–1991	18,016	0.1	15,658	0.1
1992–2000	25,891	0.3	21,033	0.3

Note: * Corresponds to the period standard deviation divided by the period average.
Source: Central Bank of Chile.

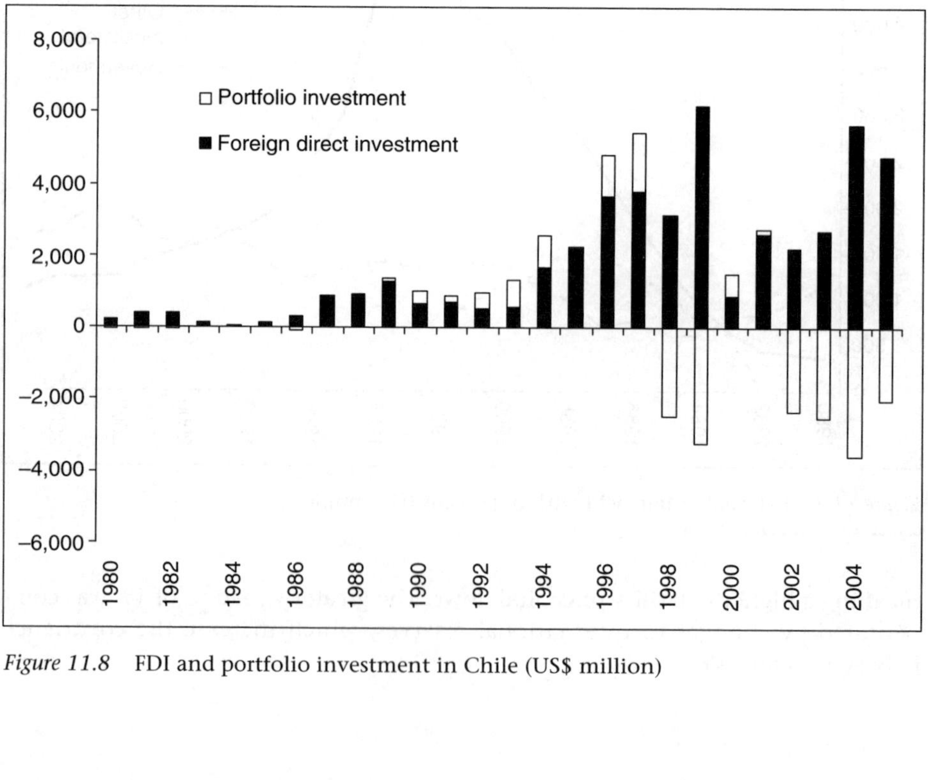

Figure 11.8 FDI and portfolio investment in Chile (US$ million)

financing after 1991. This increase was concentrated in the medium to long term. The fact that this increase was not concentrated in short-term debt is probably the consequence of the imposition of the *encaje*, a differentiated tax on short-term capital inflows (Ffrench-Davis, 2003).[3]

Foreign investment also increased during the 1990s. Because FDI comes directly to finance investment projects, it is likely to be less volatile than other forms of capital flow. As can be seen in Figure 11.8 both FDI and portfolio investment have shown an increasing trend since the late 1980s; the latter has exhibited a more volatile behavior since 1998.

Both the fall in terms of trade and capital flow volatilities seem to have been important for Chile since 1990. Even though capital flow volatility dropped after the second half of the 1980s, it was not until the 1990s that Chile became well integrated into international capital markets. In consequence, it is hard to attribute an important initial effect on the fall of macroeconomic volatility to the fall in the terms of trade and capital flow volatilities because the latter fell some years before the former. However, even though the first step in the reduction of macro volatility was due to domestic factors (better policies) the reduction in the variance of external shocks in the 1990s ('good luck') reinforced the positive effects of domestic policies, triggering a cumulative process that led to better DFA and lower aggregate volatility.

Development of fiscal and monetary institutions

Fiscal, monetary, and exchange rate policies underwent important changes during the 1990s and early 2000s. These reforms were possible largely because fiscal debt was kept relatively under control even after the crisis of 1982. When a country is not constrained by fiscal sustainability targets (fiscal dominance) and the economy is not subject to too much volatility, it has room to implement countercyclical policies. An important feature of Chile's fiscal policy during the 1990s was the reduction of public debt from 45 per cent of GDP in 1990 to 13 per cent of GDP in 1998, with a fiscal surplus in almost every year.[4]

Behind the prudent stance of fiscal policy, there has been a strong political consensus on the need to keep the fiscal budget in equilibrium. An example of this consensus on economic stability is tax policy. The military dictatorship during the second half of the 1980s made a number of tax reforms that reduced tax collection. In 1984 taxes on individuals were lowered through a reduction of the marginal rates and especially by increasing the income brackets. In 1988 VAT was reduced from the former 20 per cent to 16 per cent. In 1989 reinvested utilities were exempted from utility taxes. Overall, these changes had the effect of reducing government income in local currency from 19 per cent of GDP in 1981 to 14.5 per cent in 1990 (see Marfán, 1998). In 1990, when the first democratic government took power after the Pinochet era, the newly elected government proposed a reform that would increase government income by about 2 per cent of GDP in order to finance social expenditure. It was estimated that the success of the transition to a sustainable democracy was very much associated with a tax reform that would increase government income in order to finance the most urgent social needs (Marfán, 1998). The final proposal had generalized political support. The proposal rested on increasing broad taxes and not touching particular taxes that could bring opposition from particular sectors.[5]

The institutional framework of fiscal policy reflects a long historical process, where authority over fiscal policy has been concentrated in the executive and taken away from the legislature. Only the president can propose laws that have implications for public spending. Similarly, the executive makes the proposal of the yearly budget and the Congress can only reduce the budget, never increase it. If the Congress does not approve the budget in the time attributed by law, it is automatically approved as the executive had sent it. Public debt has to be approved by the Ministry of Finance, and local governments, such as *municipalidades*, cannot normally issue debt (unless it is expressly authorized by law). This concentration of decisions on public spending in the government makes the president accountable and responsible for the fiscal result.

Another important pillar of fiscal policy during the 1990s was the constitutional prohibition on linking the financing of a particular spending item to a specific tax.[6] This policy allows more flexibility to resource assignment and to accommodate overall spending to macroeconomic conditions. Also, the creation of the Copper Stabilization Fund (CSF) in 1987 was a policy oriented to smoothing fiscal income and expenditure. The CSF accumulated about US$528 million in 1990 with an average price of copper of 1.29 US$/lb and reached US$1.8 billion in 1997.

To strengthen the countercyclical role of fiscal policy, in 2000 the Chilean government introduced a self-imposed fiscal rule to be implemented for the first time in 2001. According to this rule, the government targets a structural balance, related to structural income variables adjusted for changes in temporary income. This type of policy has a number of purposes. First, it tends to ensure the stability of fiscal debt across time. Second, it can be used as a (predictable) countercyclical policy device. Third, it serves as an indicator of fiscal discipline. Fourth, it gives the policymaker a longer planning horizon.

According to the rule, fiscal policy is based on a yearly structural surplus of 1 per cent of GDP. The basic logic is to stabilize public expenditures over the business cycles and smooth the impact of swings in the price of copper, preventing excessive adjustments in periods of recession or unsustainable expenditure levels in periods of prosperity. Hence, the rule is designed to generate savings in times of prosperity to pay debt contracted in times of recession, thus softening the economic cycle and granting sustainability to public finances. At the same time, because it is a known and transparent rule, it reduces uncertainty for economic agents regarding the future behavior of public finances, and stabilizes public expenditure in economic and socially sensitive areas, such as investment and social spending.

In the case of emerging economies, which are inclined to suffer significant and recurrent external shocks, empirical evidence seems to corroborate the fact that from a certain threshold ratio of public debt to GDP these economies tend to have high degrees of volatility – some studies place this threshold between 25 and

30 per cent of GDP (Reinhart et al., 2003). By decreasing the dependence on foreign savings and showing sustainable fiscal accounts, the vulnerability of the economy in the face of external shocks decreased.

Moreover, net asset accumulation over time by the central government will help meet future public sector commitments that grow at a higher rate than fiscal revenues, and potential expenditures on contingent liabilities. Within the latter, the most relevant are the guarantees for minimum revenues in infrastructure concessions, the state guarantees on deposits, liabilities originated in legal demands against the government, and the minimum pension guarantee in the pension system. To this, one can add the central bank's losses due to quasi-fiscal activities undertaken in the past.[7]

Therefore, it is likely that the structural surplus of 1 per cent will allow increases in debt over time only to finance investment by public enterprises. Local or provincial governments are not relevant for this matter because they cannot contract debt.

According to the structural-balance rule, the expenditure level for the current budget is established as follows. Starting from the assumed macroeconomic scenario, an accrued level of revenues is projected. The level of expenditures is influenced by the structural factors as well as the phase of the economic cycle and the movements of the price of copper. The projected revenues also reflect expected changes in tax collections derived from legal changes, such as changes in tax laws. Using the long-term reference copper price and the gap between the projected GDP and the estimate of trend GDP, the revenue is corrected to determine the level of structural revenues. This corresponds to the level of adjusted fiscal revenues that would exist if the projected copper price were equal to the reference price and GDP were equal to trend GDP. The latter is the level of activity that theoretically would exist if the productive resources were used with normal intensity – for example, if unemployment were equal to long-term unemployment. Having established the structural level of revenues, we calculate the expenditure level that is consistent with a surplus of 1 per cent of GDP.

Therefore, the key equation to estimate the structural balance, which includes the cyclical correction of taxes revenues, and copper revenues is:[8]

$$SBt = Bobserved - T_t + \left(T * \left[\frac{Y_t potential}{Y_t} \right]^{\varepsilon} \right) - CS*(P^{FOB}_t - P^{REF}_t)*\alpha \qquad (11.5)$$

where:

SB stands for the structural balance.

Bobserved is the accrued balance of the central government.

T expresses the tax revenue plus actual pension contributions.

Potential represents the nominal trend GDP level, calculated by experts.

Y is the nominal GDP level.

ε represents the output elasticity of tax revenues, with a 1.05 value.

CS shows Codelco's sales of fine copper in metric tons.

P^{FOB} is the FOB copper price of Codelco exports.

P^{REF} is the long-term copper price, calculated by experts.

α = 2,204.62/100,000, factor used to convert price in US dollars per metric ton to cents per pound.

To maintain transparency and avoid tinkering with the assumptions of trend output and a long-term copper price, these figures are estimated by a group of independent experts employed by the government. Computation of the accrual and the structural balance are shown in Figure 11.9. It is worth noting that during 1991–98, the economy moved along the path of a 1 per cent structural surplus.

During the period 1975–82, monetary and exchange rate policies favored economic volatility under a fixed exchange rate regime and a passive monetary policy (Ffrench-Davis et al., 1998). After the 1981–82 crisis, the policy framework changed significantly, creating a better environment for volatility reduction. In the 1990s, Chilean monetary authorities used a wide range of instruments to face the surge in capital flows. A relatively stable economic environment post-1985 fostered a slow but steady increase in monetary policy activism and the flexibility of the exchange rate. Monetary policy during the 1990s was characterized by a heterodox combination of a semi-fixed exchange rate (crawling band system), inflation targeting, and capital controls. This policy combination is reflected in the positive covariance between capital flows and international reserves as shown in Figure 11.6

After the 1981–82 crisis, the fixed nominal exchange rate system was replaced by a crawling peg with a floating band of ± 2 per cent, widened to 3 in 1988, and

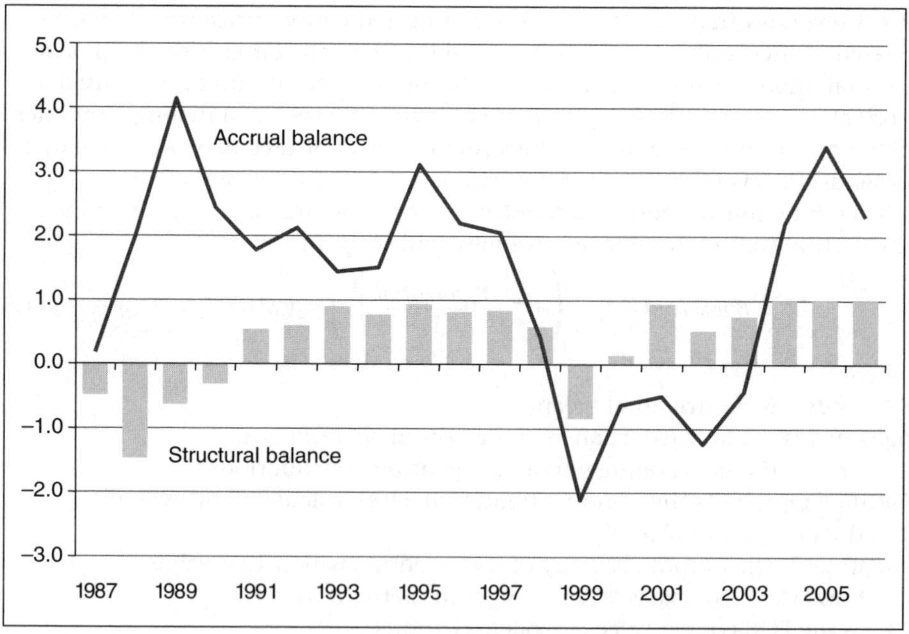

Figure 11.9 Accrual and structural balance of the central government (as percentage of GDP)

to ± 10 per cent in 1992. The exchange rate was managed to keep a competitive real exchange rate. As in the early 1980s, huge capital inflows pushed an appreciation of the exchange rate. To avoid excessive appreciation, the peso was allowed to appreciate at a real annual average of 4 per cent a year between 1991 and 1997. Central bank intervention in the foreign exchange market implied a large accumulation of international reserves. This accumulation implied that the money supply was growing faster than was consistent with the official inflation targets. To reduce domestic liquidity the central bank sterilized the monetary effects of the purchase of foreign exchange by issuing domestic debt papers. The sterilization effort was made in order to keep the money supply in line with the reduction of the inflation rate targets, which has been the main objective of the central bank since it became autonomous (granted by constitution) in 1990, and to reduce inflation slowly, rather than abruptly as in the late 1970s and early 1980s. The economic cost that sterilization implied to the central bank, together with the pressure on the domestic interest rate made the sterilization policy unsustainable in the medium and long run; also, the need for sterilization changed in the second half of the 1990s. In the year 2000 a permanent inflation target was introduced together with an (almost) free floating of the exchange rate.[9] The target consisted of a range of 2–4 per cent that was to be achieved in a horizon of 12 to 24 months.

Since 1985 the main instrument of monetary policy has been the interest rate. From 1985 to April 1995, the three-month real interest rate (indexed to headline CPI inflation) was used. From May 1995 to the beginning of August 2001, the monetary policy instrument was changed to an overnight indexed interest rate. Since August 2001, the central bank has implemented its monetary policy by defining a target level for the nominal interbank rate, known as the monetary policy rate (MPR), which is controlled through the use of several instruments: open market operations, buying and selling short-term promises and notes, and liquidity deposits and lines of credits (expanded facilities).

To cope with the surge in capital inflows in the 1990s and to discourage short-term inflows, the central bank established an unremunerated reserve requirement on foreign capital inflows (*encaje*). The *encaje* consisted of a non-interest bearing reserve requirement of 20 per cent on foreign loans. The reserves had to be kept in the central bank for a minimum of 90 days and a maximum of one year, depending on the maturity of the operation. As capital flows kept increasing, the reserve requirements tightened in 1992 to include time deposits in foreign currency and purchases of Chilean stocks by foreigners, and the reserve requirement was raised to 30 per cent. The period for which the deposit had to be maintained in the central bank was extended to a year independently of the maturity of the loan. After the Asian crisis, the reserve requirement was lowered to 10 per cent and became zero in 1998.

Development of financial institutions

One of the most striking differences between Chile in the late 1970s and in the late 1990s is in the domestic financial institutions. Two radically different institution-building experiences are observed. The changes introduced in the second half of the 1970s not only favored volatility but were also made within the context of high volatility (and responding to an effort to infuse resources into a highly repressed financial system). The changes introduced from the second half of the 1980s and during the 1990s favored stability and were made within the context of a more stable economy (and with a financial system recovering from a severe systemic crisis). These experiences favor our view of a Chilean virtuous circle between volatility and institutions. The two different outcomes of the financial reforms of the 1970s and the 1980s suggest the difficulties of developing financial markets in the context of developing economies characterized by a weak overall institutional structure, weak public policies, lack of transparency, and asymmetric integration with world financial markets.

Every review of the Chilean financial system in the late 1970s tells a similar story (see Edwards, 1991; Held and Jiménez, 1999; Cifuentes et al., 2002; Velasco, 1991). This is a story of rapid liberalization but poor supervision, a story of a financial system that grew at a fast rate but with very weak foundations.

The period between 1975 and 1981 marks the end of at least 30 years of financial repression in Chile. This was a period of rapid and drastic deregulation of the financial system. All quantitative limits on credit were abolished and the power of the central bank to rule in this respect was seriously limited. Interest rates were freed, for deposits and credits, indexed and nominal. Only a relatively lax maximum interest rate for credit remained as well as a restriction on indexed financial instruments (a minimum duration of 90 days). Reserve requirements were progressively lowered. By 1980, there was a requirement of 10 per cent on demand deposits and 4 per cent for deposits longer than 30 days. The domestic credit market was liberalized in terms of interest rates, quantitative restrictions, and type of credits.

Access to external liquidity was also liberalized. By 1979 there were almost no restrictions for banks to take external debt. All limits on financing credits payable in foreign currency, mainly related to international trade, were abolished. Additionally, banks were allowed to convert external debt into domestic currency credits indexed to the foreign currency through the central bank. These credits were subject to flow and stock restrictions that were (gradually) abolished by 1980. In other words, the banking system was given wide access to external credit.

By the year 1978 all but three banks were privately owned,[10] many of which had been effectively owned by the state before 1975. In 1978 previous (ineffective) limits on bank ownership were abolished, letting the market determine the concentration of property. In 1974 restrictions on the entrance of foreign banks were lifted and in 1977 foreign investment in national banks was allowed. Previous normative rules on bank specialization were abolished giving rise to banks that offered a wide range of instruments (multipurpose banking). In 1978 even the Banco del Estado (State Bank) was given a commercial status as opposed to its previous status as a development bank, and its monopoly on certain instruments (on demand saving accounts) was ended. In fact, normative changes introduced in the years 1980 and 1981 eliminated the differences between commercial, development and mortgage banks. The number of banks increased from 21 in 1974 to 45 in 1981, 18 of which were foreign.

However, it was not only the banking system that was liberalized. The 1974 normative changes allowed individuals to commit freely on deposit and loan transactions, without any requirement or supervision. This gave rise to a new kind of financial entity, the *financieras*. In 1978 these reached a peak of 21 in number.

The liberalization of the financial system resulted in a sharp increase in financial activity. Banks and *financieras* proliferated. Total financial assets rose from 20 per cent of GNP in 1975 to 48 per cent in 1982. This process was accompanied by an important increase in the share of financial assets issued by banks and *financieras*. Interestingly, most of this expansion came from the shift from money to interest-bearing assets with maturities of less than 90 days.

The stock of debt of the private sector rose significantly in the liberalization years. The stock of loans from the banking system to the private sector went from 5 per cent of GDP in 1974 to 62 per cent in 1982. The increase in the stock of loans was accompanied by an important increase in the stock of dollar-denominated loans. Also, the short-term domestic currency debt increased significantly.

In appearance, the banking system was not only dynamic, but relatively solid. Nevertheless, important amounts of related lending were hidden behind this apparent solvency. It was only in 1982 that binding limits on related lending were introduced. It is estimated that in 1982 almost 20 per cent of domestic private bank lending corresponded to related lending (see Held and Jiménez, 1999). Risk classification was a rather difficult task. The Superintendencia de Bancos e Instituciones Financieras only began fully to enforce risk classification in 1982.

In 1982 international conditions deteriorated and there was a capital account reversal. The financial system was unable to accommodate the shock and it collapsed. Between 1982 and 1986, 16 financial institutions were closed, others were saved by the central bank which bought the bad assets, and some were re-capitalized in different ways. Massive debt restructuring took place and debtors in foreign currency gained access to preferential exchange rates. According to some estimates the rescue of the banking system had a cost of about 35 per cent of GDP (Edwards, 1991; Held and Jiménez, 1999). GDP fell 13 per cent in 1982 and an additional 3 per cent in 1983. Inflation rose to more than 20 per cent and the unemployment rate reached 25 per cent. Volatility induced by an external shock was detrimental to the financial system, resulting in further volatility.

As opposed to what has happened in other countries where excess aggregate volatility and crisis episodes deteriorate the quality of institutions for a long period, after the crisis of the early 1980s – in spite of the high disturbance and costs that it implied – economic institutions (the financial system in particular) entered a spiral of lower volatility and strengthening. Stabilization policies gained broad support. Consensus was built around these policies. Even after 1990 with the fall of the military dictatorship and the return to democracy, the social agreement in favor of stability of policies and institutions was strengthened. Economic stability and stable rules of the games (institutions) were considered to be crucial to consolidating the new democratic regime.

In November of 1986 a new banking law was put in place. The new law was mainly aimed at increasing the levels of transparency, solvency and liquidity of the banking system. Since 1987 banks have been publicly ranked according to their expected losses on credits. The law also enforced the provision of risky assets. Credit risk diminished considerably during the 1980s and the early 1990s. This has been accompanied by healthy profits in the system.

Compared to the late 1970s and early 1980s the Chilean financial architecture of the late 1990s was characterized by what most call 'prudential regulation'. Related lending was heavily restricted. Any individual owning more than 1 per cent of the stocks of a financial institution – or with more than 5 per cent of an institution that owns more than 1 per cent of the financial institution – was defined as 'related to the property' of that institution. The same definition applied to any financial institution whose manager owned more than 5 per cent of that firm. Restrictions applied to lending to related individuals or firms. Since 1986 related lending has dropped to one-tenth of the early 1980s level.

Also, in the late 1970s some financial institutions collapsed and the de facto government bailed out the depositors. The new law made it clear that there was a limited guarantee on interest-bearing deposits.

Capital requirements were not modified until 1997. In that year there was an important move to adopt capital requirements as a function of the credit risk, as proposed by the Basel Accords. In particular, effective own capital cannot be less than 8 per cent of total assets weighted by risk. The 1986 law introduced a number of cases in which there can be presumption of financial instability or deficient management. These cases were extended in 1997. In addition, cases of presumption of severe insolvency were introduced. Corrective measures for each case were established.

Banks have been allowed to access new products, such as factoring, custody, securitization, insurance, and so on. Also, the banks have been allowed to internationalize their operations. International branches are allowed, as well as participation in the property of foreign banks abroad.

All this has resulted in a smooth but steady deepening of the financial sector. As Figure 11.10 shows, the ratio of M2A and M7 to M1A – arguably indicators of financial deepening – increased from 1985 to 1997. The figure also shows the increase in the total amount of mutual funds as a ratio of M1A, an indicator not only of the growing banking sector but also of the progressive sophistication of Chilean financial markets.

One of the main problems that emerging economies face is their massive inflow and outflow of capital in relatively short periods. The creation and development of markets for long-term bonds and share markets are fundamental to dealing with this volatility. Institutional investors play a fundamental role in the provision of long-term financing for the private and public sectors.

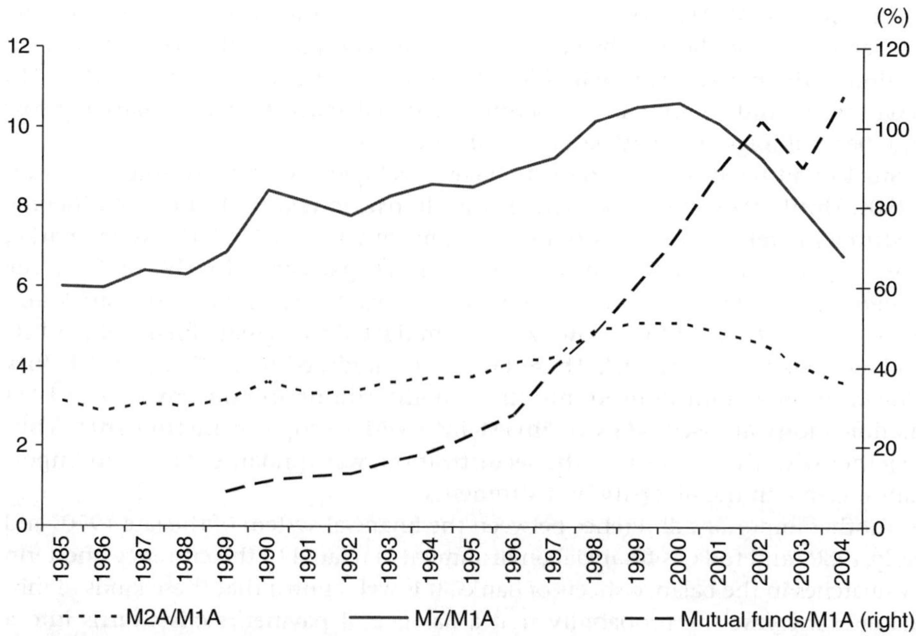

Figure 11.10 Financial aggregates and M1A in Chile
Source: Central Bank of Chile.

In May 1981 Chile introduced a deep reform in its pension system. The old pay-as-you-go system was replaced by a system of individual capitalization. The administration of most of the funds was transferred from the state to private companies, the Administradoras de Fondos de Pensiones (AFPs). Even though AFPs were not forced to invest in public debt, they did not have many relevant alternatives. Zahler (2005) argues that this allowed the government to achieve two important macroeconomic objectives: first, to finance the transition from the pay-as-you-go system to the fully-funded system; second, to issue debt to finance the recovery of the banking system after the 1982 crises. An additional important role that the AFPs have played is the development of the market for *Letras Hipotecarias* (indexed papers backed by a mortgage). This was important for the deepening of the market for long-term financial papers and also helped in the development of the construction sector. These instruments went from almost zero in 1982 to US$1200 million in 1990 and US$3800 in 1995. At the end of 2002, 76 per cent of the *Letras Hipotecarias* were in the hands of the AFPs and the stock reached US$5300, 8 per cent of GDP. This is a clear example of how financial markets develop as a result of overall economic stability.

In 1992 AFPs were allowed to invest in external assets for the first time, with a limit of 1.5 per cent of total portfolio. The limit was expanded that same year to 3 per cent, to 9 per cent in 1995, to 12 per cent in 1997, to 16 per cent in 1999 and to 20 per cent in 2002.

The impact of AFPs on the volatility of long-term interest rates and the exchange rates has been debated in Chile. This is because of the size and concentration of the market and their ability to influence prices. Even though the AFPs have been fundamental in deepening financial markets, their relatively low number and huge size may be a destabilizing factor.

Stocks and fixed income markets have developed extensively since the mid-1980s. Until 1984 the stock market was almost nonexistent and fixed-income instruments represented less than 5 per cent of GDP. In 1995 the stock market was 16 per cent of GDP and fixed income 120 per cent of GDP. In 1981 the Superintendencia de Valores y Seguros was created (to regulate the stock and insurance markets) and new laws were promulgated to regulate financial markets and 'Sociedades Anonimas'. These laws were modified in 1987 and 1994. Risk classification was introduced into these modifications and improved. The 1994 modifications allowed AFPs to invest in a wider scope of instruments. This, together with the creation of the securitization, was fundamental for an important increase in the diversity of instruments.

Another important difference between the financial system of the late 1970s and early 1980s and today's financial environment is related to the currency and term mismatches in the balance sheets of banks. It is well known that these kinds of mismatches increase the probability that a balance of payments crisis turns into a financial crisis due to exchange rate adjustments. During the second half of the 1970s around 40 per cent of bank loans were in dollars, while dollar deposits were only around 10 per cent of total deposits (falling from 20 per cent in 1977 to close to 5 per cent in 1981). In contrast, deposits, as well as loan dollarization, were around 10 per cent in 1997, isolating the financial system from the devaluation that followed the adverse international shock of 1998 (Herrera and Valdés, 2004). The reasons behind this financial mismatch of the 1970s are the usual ones. First is the progressive and aggressive liberalization of restrictions on a bank's external debt. Banks' foreign debt increased from US$660 million in 1978 to US$6.5 billion in 1981 (from 34 per cent of total private external debt to 65 per cent). Second, the fixed exchange rate provided an implicit guarantee against currency risk.

The drop in the use of foreign currency in the financial system in the last two decades relates directly to indexation measures. The *Unidad de Fomento* (UF), an indexing unit, was created in 1967. The UF was originally restated on a quarterly basis according to past inflation and later on a monthly basis, but it remained relatively unimportant until 1982. The way the 1982 banking crisis was managed is central to understanding the increasing importance of the UF and the decreasing importance of the dollar.

Herrera and Valdés (2004) provide a number of reasons why indexation to the UF became so important in the financial sector and dollarization did not. First, the UF gained much credibility because its mechanism was not altered in order to deal with the costs of the crisis. Second, the exchange rate was indexed to past inflation, so the dollar-UF exchange rate was stabilized and there was a de facto 'UFication' of dollar loans. Third, peso-denominated loans were restructured in UF. Fourth, the central bank offered UF-denominated credit lines so banks could reprogram mortgages. Fifth, the central bank bought loans from banks at par value giving back bonds in UF (Herrera and Valdés, 2004).

At the same time, the accumulation of mandatory savings in private pension funds provided a stable flow of demand for UF public debt. After 1982 monetary and foreign exchange operations by the central bank were aimed at stabilizing the UF interest rate and the UF value of the dollar. Public debt was mostly UF-denominated. Between 1982 and 1989 the value of UF operations increased by more than 100 times while peso operations declined by 30 per cent. UF loans increased to 70 per cent of total loans and UF deposits to 65 per cent of total deposits. On the other hand, the dollarization of loans stayed below 20 per cent with a moderate downward trend, and dollarization of deposits below 20 per cent with a moderate upward trend.

Financial dollarization was also prevented by the use of restrictions on capital flows. During the second half of the 1980s restrictions on foreign currency transactions were important and were eased very gradually. Also, a policy was implemented to exchange foreign debt for domestic debt, mostly UF-denominated.

As Herrera and Valdés (2004) point out, it is interesting to note that in spite of macroeconomic and inflation stability during the 1990s indexation practices remained stable. This poses the question of how persistent indexation or dollarization practices can be.

Table 11.2 shows a number of recent indicators of capital markets development for some selected countries. Chile outperforms most Latin American coun-

Table 11.2 Indicators of financial development: Chile and selected countries

Countries	Private credit/GDP	Stock market capitalization/ GDP	Turnover ratio	Private bond/GDP	Financial strength index
Argentina	12	62	6	10	0
Brazil	33	36	32	10	24
Chile	75	86	10	19	58
Mexico	18	18	21	3	42
Colombia	23	15	3	0	24
USA	174	118	121	113	77
France	88	67	85	42	73
Germany	117	37	129	43	47
Spain	111	71	157	24	77
UK	110	120	100	39	83
Italy	83	37	121	44	63
Finland	61	96	11	22	73
Japan	105	60	87	44	21
Korea	120	48	235	50	18
Malaysia	132	141	34	53	35
Philippines	35	40	90	19	–
Czech Rep.	30	18	52	7	41
Poland	28	15	27	n a	31

Source: International Monetary Fund, 2004 World Economic Outlook and Policy Issues, IMF.

tries in every indicator, but is still far from the levels of developed countries. The last column of Table 11.2 shows an index of financial strength which shows that Chile is in good shape relative to other emerging countries.

11.4 A tale of two crises

In the last 30 years, the Chilean economy has been subject to two important negative external shocks. This provides a natural setting for studying the importance of policies and institutions in times of crisis. The first of these two events is the 1982 twin crisis (the balance of payments and financial crises). The second is the 1998–99 balance of payments crisis. Even though both crises were the consequence of a severe and relatively similar deterioration in international conditions, the outcome in terms of GDP loss and financial turmoil varies significantly. As argued, these differences are explained by the changes in the domestic financial architecture, and in the macroeconomic policies discussed earlier. While during the 1970s the country looked very much like any other Latin American country in terms of volatility and institutions, by the end of the 1990s it had developed solid institutions and rules of the game.

In what follows we describe both the 1982 and the 1998 crises and emphasize the differences between the two episodes. It is clear from this experience that if a country takes advantage of low volatility periods to build countercyclical institutions, volatility can remain low even in the presence of significant adverse shocks.

External shocks in the crises of the early 1980s and the late 1990s

The price of copper, which accounts for about half of Chilean exports, fell by 35 per cent between 1980 and 1982 and by 31 per cent between 1998 and 1999.[11] Figure 11.11 shows the evolution of the terms of trade, where the years 1982 and 1999 are indicated by shaded columns. The graph also shows that in both events international interest rates went up, coinciding with a reversal in capital flows. The 3-month dollar libor went from 10 to 17 per cent between 1978 and 1981 and from 3 to 6 per cent between 1993 and 1998. During 1980–81 net capital inflows to Chile averaged more than US$3 million; in 1982 net flows were almost null; and in 1983 there were net outflows of more than US$3 million. Similarly, between 1992 and 1997 net inflows to Chile averaged more than US$3 million per year, in 1999 there were capital outflows (Figure 11.12).

Tables 11.3a and b summarize the shocks that affected Chile in 1982 and 1998–99. Table 11.3c shows shocks for the year 2001, another year of bad international fundamentals for Chile.

The macroeconomic environment

The period before the 1982 crisis followed the typical dynamics of a Latin American stabilization program: high growth rates accompanied by an expenditure boom, liability dollarization, exchange rate overvaluation, and high domestic interest rates.

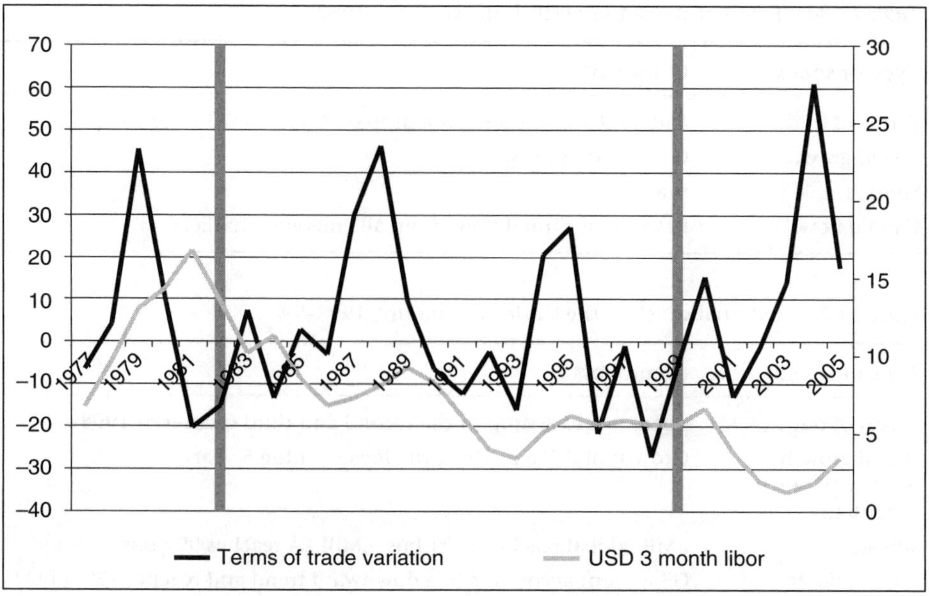

Figure 11.11 Terms of trade variation and international interest rates (%)

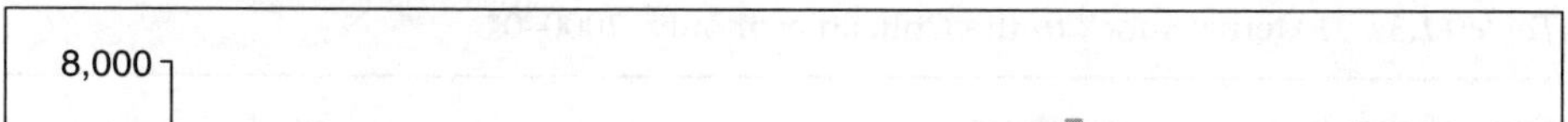

Figure 11.12 Capital flows (US$ millions)

In a long historical perspective, Chile's average GDP growth has been around 3 per cent a year (1.5 per cent in per capita terms, see Table 11.4). The 1977–81 pre-crisis period was one of relatively high economic growth. GDP grew on

Table 11.3a External shock to the Chilean economy, 1982

Type of shock	Comments
Terms of trade	Different measures show a drop of 7% to 13% during 1982
World growth	G3 countries grow –1%
Spreads	n/a
Capital flows	Reversal of capital flows from all emerging markets

Table 11.3b External shock to the Chilean economy, 1998–99

Type of shock	Comments
Terms of trade	There is a 13% drop in the second and third quarter of 1998
World growth (exchange rate weighted)	Growth of 2.2% in 1998, the lowest in the 5 years
Spreads	EMBI global reaches 1171 bps, EMBI LA reaches 997 bps
Capital flows	G3 current account is in a downward trend and reaches –2% of G3 GDP

Table 11.3c External shock to the Chilean economy, 2000–01

Type of shock	Comments
Terms of trade	In the third and fourth quarter of 2001 falls between 10% and 15% according to different measures
World growth	In 2001 world growth is 1.2%, the lowest in six years
International interest rates	Important increase of international interest rates. The 180 days libor goes above 6%
Spreads	EMBI global reaches 895 bps, EMBI LA reaches 844 bps
Capital flows	Capital flows to the region stay low

average 8 per cent a year. This growth was accompanied by booming domestic expenditure. Investment grew on average 18 per cent and consumption 10 per cent; exports grew on average 8 per cent, while imports grew 22 per cent. The current account deficit was on average 6 per cent between 1977 and 1980 rising to 14 per cent in 1981. Average wage and price inflation in 1977–81 was 45 per cent, while the exchange rate devalued on average 27 per cent a year in the same period.

Thanks to the policy changes explained in the previous sections, the macroeconomic environment was substantially different when the 1998 shock arrived. GDP growth was also high in the five-year pre-crisis period: 7.6 per cent in 1993–97. Nevertheless, it was accompanied by a much more moderate expendi-

Table 11.4 Chilean annual GDP growth in perspective

	GDP per capita	Total GDP
1811–78	0.8	2.7
1879–1929	1.5	2.6
1930–50	0.3	2.1
1950–71	2.0	4.2
1972–83	–1.1	0.4
1984–97	5.3	7.1
1998–2003	1.3	2.6
1900–99	1.5	3.2
1900–84	0.9	4.1
1985–2003	4.1	5.7

ture boom and the current account deficit averaged 4 per cent of GDP during that period.

Investment rates reached a historical minimum of 12 per cent of GDP in 1982, after which they embarked upon a steady increase, reaching more than 25 per cent of GDP in the mid-1990s. As Figure 11.13 shows, before 1989 the investment rate was above 20 per cent only in 1963. After 1989 it was above 20 per cent almost every year with the sole exception of 1991.This points to a structural break in the behavior of capital accumulation in Chile.

The 1990s was also a period of extraordinary price stability from a historical perspective. Chile has a long history of volatile inflation rates. Short-lived periods of low inflation were usually followed by extended periods with inflation

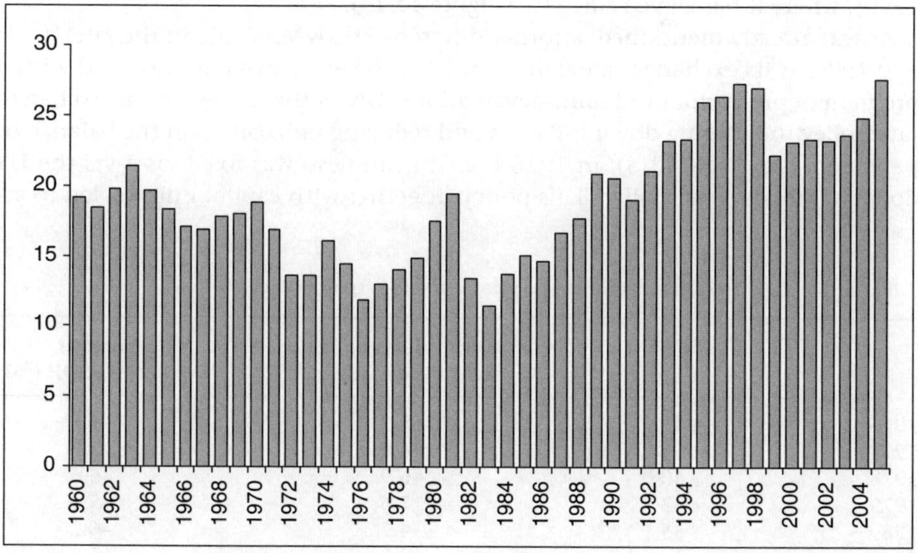

Figure 11.13 Investment to GDP ratio in Chile (%)

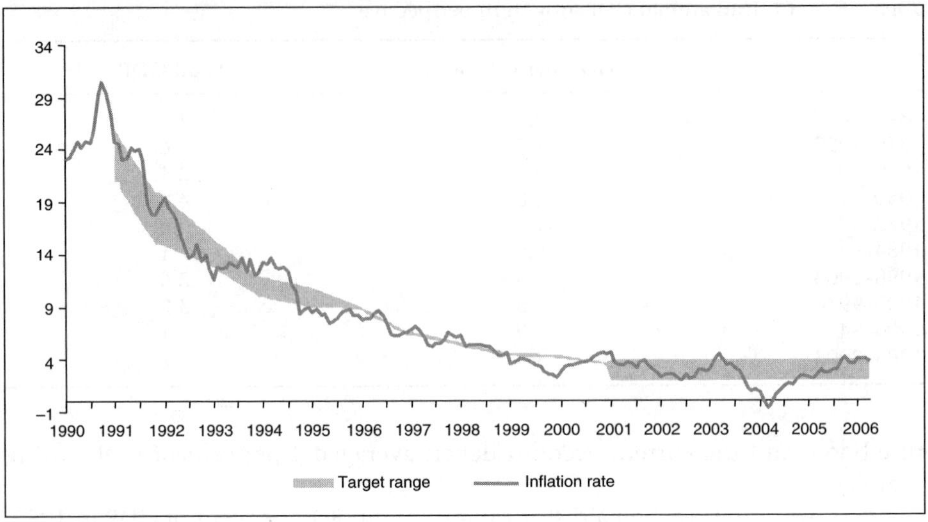

Figure 11.14 Inflation and inflation targets in Chile (%)
Source: Central Bank of Chile

rates above 20 per cent and sometimes even above 50 or 100 in the early 1970s. After 1990 Chile began a path of slow but steady reduction in inflation. In 1991 an inflation-targeting scheme was adopted, first oriented at reducing the inflation rate in conjunction with other targets for monetary policy and since 2000 in a more orthodox version with a constant target of 2–4 per cent. Inflation fell from around 30 per cent in the early 1990s to around 3 per cent in the late 1990s, where it has stayed since (see Figure 11.14).

As was already mentioned, another difference between Chile in the late 1970s and 1990s is its exchange rate policy. In 1974 the exchange rate was fixed with a program of pre-announced mini-devaluations. Given the success of the exchange rate policy in bringing down inflation and reducing imbalances in the balance of payments (see Table 11.5), in 1978 the Chilean peso was fixed vis-à-vis the US dollar at 39 pesos per dollar. This policy, together with capital inflows, led to an

Table 11.5 Late 1970s stabilization program in Chile (percentages)

	CPI (% change)	Nominal exchange rate (% change)	Current account/GDP (%)
1976	211.9	165.8	1.4
1977	91.9	64.9	–3.8
1978	40.0	46.9	–6.6
1979	33.3	17.6	–5.4
1980	35.1	4.7	–6.7
1981	19.6	0.0	–13.5

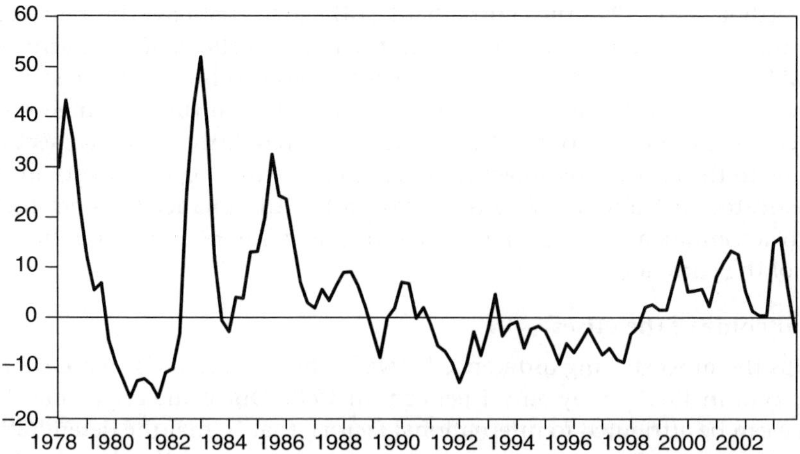

Figure 11.15 Real exchange rate (quarterly data, % change on previous year)

important overvaluation of the currency. Changes in the real exchange rate are shown in Figure 11.15. Different time series models of fundamental determinants of the real exchange rate show that by 1982 the peso was about 40 per cent overvalued. The current account deficit increased, reaching a record of 13.5 per cent of GDP in 1981. External debt was more than 50 per cent of GDP by that year. Net international reserves were equivalent to six months of imports in 1981 (US$3775 million).

Overall exposure at the macro level was also present at the micro level. The fixed exchange rate system also translated into implicit exchange rate risk insurance, with the associated moral hazard problem. This, together with poor bank supervision, led to an increasing mismatch in the financial system with the associated currency exposure, as was discussed in Section 11.3.

The sudden stop of capital inflows in 1981 required an important devaluation of the exchange rate. Monetary policy credibility was invested in the fixed exchange rate and the required devaluation was postponed. Interest rates increased and net international reserves dropped by US$1200 million during 1982. Capital kept flowing out and the central bank was unable to defend the parity any longer. In 1982 the peso was devalued with the associated loss to the real and financial sectors, as well as foreign creditors.

The intermediate exchange rate regime (an exchange rate band) of the 1990s allowed the country to be in a better shape to face an adverse external shock than in the early 1980s. Though not too high, the volatility of the exchange rate forced the real sector and the banking system to avoid excessive exposure to the exchange rate. The market for foreign exchange derivatives went from a turnover of almost zero in 1993 to US$100 billion in 1997.[12] Also, the increasing indexation to past inflation instead of the dollar helped to isolate the financial system from the exchange rate. This, together with good bank supervision resulted in a solid financial sector, well prepared for difficult years.

Nevertheless, by 1998 the central bank still feared that pass-through and currency mismatch could be too big. When the external shock of 1998 arrived, the central bank decided to defend the value of the peso and let the interest rate rise. The huge rise in interest rates was not sustainable and the exchange rate was allowed to rise. Even though the real sector suffered, the financial sector was immune to the crisis. Bank supervision, combined with deeper markets and more sophisticated instruments were the key to a healthy financial system that was able to accommodate the shock through the rise in interest rates and the devaluation of the currency.

The outcome of the crises

Perhaps the most striking difference between the two events is that GDP fell by 13 per cent in 1982 but by only 1 per cent in 1999. One could argue that the difference can be attributed to international factors, that is, that the deterioration of international conditions was more severe in the early 1980s than in the late 1990s. We test this hypothesis using simple growth regressions of annual GDP growth on international variables. The results, reported in Table 11.6, show that for four different specifications more than 40 per cent of Chilean annual GDP growth from 1976–2004 can be explained by exogenous changes in international variables, such as the price of copper, world GDP growth, international interest rates and some measure of availability of foreign capital (see the adjusted R-square). Nevertheless, about 30 per cent of the unexplained part (the sum of squared residuals) corresponds to the extraordinary fall in GDP of 1982 alone,

Table 11.6 Chilean annual GDP growth and external conditions

Dependent variable: log (GDP)	(1)	(2)	(3)	(3)	(4)
Constant	–0.01	0.02	0.03	0.06	0.03
	(–0.58)	(0.89)	(0.95)	(2.31)	(2.30)
(G3 Curr. Acc./G3 GDP) –1	0.01	0.01	–0.002	–0.003	0.001
	(1.20)	(1.21)	(–0.36)	(–0.47)	(0.13)
log(GDP) –1					0.38
					(2.09)
log(commercial partners GDP) –1	2.23		1.41		
	(3.01)		(1.64)		
log(terms of trade) –1	0.29	0.30			0.35
	(2.66)	(2.41)			(2.98)
log(world trade) –1		0.51		0.19	
		(1.48)		(0.54)	
Real libor			–0.41	–0.51	
			(–2.58)	(–3.13)	
Estimation period 1979–2004					
Adjusted R^2	0.394	0.222	0.386	0.320	0.287
Standard error of regression	0.039	0.045	0.040	0.042	0.043
Durbin-Watson	1.89	1.78	2.19	2.09	2.02

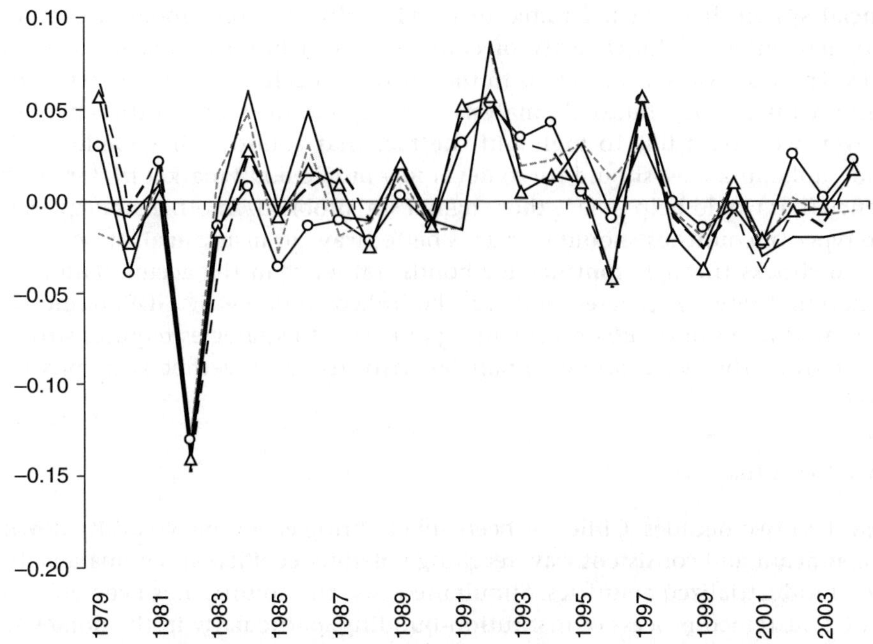

Figure 11.16 Residuals of regressions in Table 11.6

while only 10 per cent is explained by the fall in 1999. The 1999 figure is similar to the negative residual of 1983 and the positive residual of 1992 (see Figure 11.16). In other words, while the slowdown of GDP growth following the Asian crisis is explained to a great extent by the behavior of external variables, the fall in GDP in 1982 has an important unexplained component, about three times as big. The unexplained component may reflect the different policy and institutional environment as well as the volatility of the economy. In fact, one of the main differences between the 1982 and the 1999 crises was that in the former there was a massive collapse of the financial system, while in the latter not a single bank experienced trouble.

It is worth noting that the GDP drop in 1999 would have been less if the international financial system had been able to contribute to smoothing the negative external shock. As argued by Caballero et al. (2005a), Chile's imperfect access to international capital markets often exacerbates the effects of real shocks. Capital inflows and terms of trade are positively correlated, reflecting the fact that the international financial architecture has not been able to help consumption smoothing and capital flows behave in a highly procyclical way, reducing the capacity of the country to undertake countercyclical macroeconomic policies promoting 'precautionary recessions' (Caballero, 2003).

In spite of macroeconomic stability and the development of domestic financial markets, international spreads continue to be well above those observed in countries that exhibit similar economic volatility. This suggests that the international financial system has not been able to provide global public goods (Ocampo, 2006) that enhance the capacity of countries like Chile to manage external shocks. There are various proposals in the literature dealing with ways to reduce external vulnerability, but their analysis goes beyond the scope of this chapter. However, we would like to highlight the fact that countries like Chile, with sound public finances, should try to develop a public bond market in domestic currency that would help to face the 'original sin' problem. Another strategy that these types of countries should pursue is better ways to insure against negative external shocks through contingency bonds, rather than the accumulation of international reserves. These bonds can be linked to domestic GDP, domestic inflation, or terms of trade. Implementing one or both strategies requires strong support from the international financial institutions, together with private markets.

11.5 Conclusions

In less than two decades, Chile has been able to bring economic volatility down in a significant and consistent way, reaching volatility coefficients comparable to those of industrialized countries. Simultaneously, the country has been able to initiate a sustained process of institution-building, particularly in the domestic financial architecture and macroeconomic policies.

Since the mid-1980s, but particularly during the 1990s, the country has been able to achieve a relatively balanced macroeconomic situation (external debt and public debt were relatively low), and to build countercyclical policies and institutions. We argue that a mix of good policy and good luck came together to initiate a virtuous circle between volatility reduction and institutional development.

We highlight five distinctive factors that play an important role in initiating this virtuous circle. First, the volatility of capital flows and terms of trade has been reduced, contributing to a more stable macro-financial environment. Second, after the costly 1982 crisis and a short period of institutional breakdown, the country rapidly initiated a deep process of policy and institutional reform. In fact, none of the macroeconomic policies implemented before the debt crisis were in place after 1985. Third, the fiscal policy has exhibited a strong commitment to stability, which implies a significant public sector surplus since the 1990s. The fiscal stance greatly facilitated the changes in monetary and exchange rate policies giving room for a better management of capital inflows. Fourth, changes in the domestic financial architecture through a better regulatory framework and prudent regulation, together with the development of a capital market, have played an important role in the strengthening of the financial sector. Fifth, there has been a broad political consensus in favor of macroeconomic stability.

Even though the country still has a highly concentrated export structure, a feature of developing economies that tends to be associated with high volatility in the terms of trade, volatility of the latter during the last two decades has dropped and its evolution has been broadly positive. This behavior reflects positive external shocks (good luck), rather than domestic policies. Capital flows have also been less volatile and have played a positive role in financing growth. Foreign investment has been less volatile than financial flows.

Chilean fiscal and monetary institutions have contributed to dampening economic shocks in the last 16 years. Chile made important progress in reducing volatility by slowly introducing rules for monetary and fiscal policy. To strengthen the countercyclical role of fiscal policy, in 2000 the Chilean government introduced a self-imposed fiscal rule based on structural targets, a 1 per cent surplus in the Chilean case. This type of policy will help to reduce economic volatility since it tends to ensure stability of fiscal debt throughout the years, serves as an indicator of fiscal discipline, and gives the policymaker a longer planning horizon. In addition, the fiscal rule is set up in an institutional environment where the authority over fiscal policy is concentrated in the executive and not the legislature, making the president accountable and responsible for the fiscal results.

There has been a slow but steady increase in monetary policy activism and the flexibility of the exchange rate. During the 1990s, monetary policy was characterized by a heterodox combination of a semi-fixed exchange rate (crawling-band system), inflation targeting and capital controls mainly through the '*encaje*'. After 2000, a permanent inflation target was introduced together with an (almost) free floating of the exchange rate.

Even though the 1982 crisis was, among other factors, triggered by the weakness of the domestic financial institutions and the regulatory framework, since the late 1980s economic stability has allowed for a healthy and rational development of the financial system. The development of the domestic financial architecture has also played an important role in helping to reduce volatility.

Two radically different institution-building experiences in the financial markets have been observed. The changes introduced in the second half of the 1970s favored volatility and were made within the context of high volatility, while those introduced since the second half of the 1980s and 1990s favored stability and were made in the context of a more stable economy. A key lesson from this process is that size and quality are not synonymous in the financial markets. That is, even in the presence of a substantial increase in the financial assets/GDP ratio, important inefficiencies in financial intermediation can persist. The banking system was relatively large in the late 1970s but of poor quality, which was reflected in the massive breakdown of the system in the 1982 crisis. In contrast, during the 1998 crisis, the capital market and banking system remained solid and not a single bank went bankrupt. The early 1980s showed that financial markets could play an important destabilizing role, amplifying negative shocks. The late 1990s showed that a well-developed financial market, together with the right policies, could do the opposite.

Macroeconomic stability, together with a better regulatory framework and indexation measures, allowed for an increase in the length of financial contracts, an improvement in the currency and terms mismatches in the balance sheets of the banks, the development of derivative markets, and a deepening in capital markets, particularly long-term bond issues and equity markets.

Using regression analysis we considered the reasons why – when faced with negative external shocks of similar magnitudes and characteristics – the outcomes in terms of GDP loss and financial turmoil were so different. The explanation must lie in the changes observed in economic volatility, macroeconomic policies, and the development of the financial sector. As argued, this development allowed for better countercyclical institutions.

A key ingredient in building solid institutions and countercyclical policies was a broad political consensus in favor of macroeconomic stability. Many factors that go well beyond the scope of this chapter contributed to this consensus. In particular, there was a strong commitment to economic stability as a cornerstone of the sustainability of the democratic transition.

Finally, it is worth noting that even though international capital markets have been an important source of financing, their role in consumption smoothing has not been that important. Chile still depends mostly on its domestic fiscal, monetary and financial institutions to smooth terms of trade shocks and still faces problems of sudden stops. The capital account has played a modest role in helping to reduce external vulnerability. International financial institutions, as well as private markets, should be more active in pushing the creation of public bond markets denominated in domestic currency, together with the development of contingency bond markets, which seem to be a more efficient way to insure against shifts in capital flows than solely accumulating international reserves.

Notes

The authors are grateful to José María Fanelli, Alejandro Jara, Rodrigo Carcamo and Cecilia Vera for their comments. We also benefited from discussion with other participants at the conference on International Financial Architecture, Macro Volatility, and Institutions: the Developing World Experience.

1. Although during this period the country faced an oil shock, the domestic political and economic crisis of 1973 was overwhelming.
2. The ratio of the financial account surplus to exports shows an upper trend in the mid-1970s and a sharp fall after the crisis of 1982. The ratio increases slightly during the 1980s and becomes stable during the 1990s.
3. A number of papers have studied the effects of capital controls during the 1990s, see Edwards and Rigobon (2005), De Gregorio et al. (2000), Edwards (1999), Valdés-Prieto and Soto (1998).
4. Taking into account the debt of the central bank, public debt was reduced from 75 per cent of GDP in 1990 to 34 per cent in 1998. Net public debt, which takes into account public assets and in particular international reserves, went from 34 per cent of GDP in 1990 to 5 per cent of GDP in 1998.
5. In fact, a number of particular taxes that were proposed were later dropped because of pressure from the agricultural sector and from the high-income sector.
6. An exception is that part of the income from copper is assigned to the armed forces.
7. Associated with the rescue of commercial banks in the early 1980s and the sterilization of large capital inflows in the 1990s.
8. See Marcel et al. (2001) and García et al. (2005). Since 2005 the estimation of structural surplus includes an additional adjustment in the revenues coming from private mining due to the copper price cycle.

9. Since 2000 exchange rate interventions have been relatively rare and transparent, mostly associated with the contagion effects of crises in other countries.
10. The three exceptions were the Banco del Estado and two banks with legal problems.
11. Furthermore, the price in 1999 was about 46 per cent of the price in 1995.
12. See Jadresic and Selaive (2005).

12
South Africa

Melvin Ayogu and Hashem Dezhbakhsh

12.1 Introduction

Case studies can offer a new body of evidence on the exogenous sources of volatility in developing countries and, hence, allow us to examine several competing hypotheses about volatility and institutions. The premise is that volatility stresses institutions but that strong institutions can mitigate shocks. However, when institutions are weak they can amplify or induce volatility that renders institutions even less capable of mitigating shocks. Therefore, volatility and institutions plausibly embody bidirectional causality.

South Africa is an important case country because during the apartheid era, macroeconomic volatility was rooted in both political and economic forces from which financial markets could not completely be immunized. Post-apartheid, we can expect political factors to become less salient so that effects of volatility can be attributed more to deficiencies in the risk-bearing capacity of the financial system. The South African experience thus presents a natural control for political factors even though the robust correlation of politics with economics makes such a control weak.

As a brief background, South Africa became a republic and dissociated itself from the British Commonwealth in 1961. The new government inherited an entrenched regime of extreme racial segregation called apartheid. Through a series of liberation struggles with worldwide support, apartheid ended in 1994 with the election of a democratic government. The country's economic production and exports are dominated by agriculture, mining, and quarrying.

The rest of the chapter is organized thus: Section 12.2 addresses the hypothesis that aggregate volatility in developing countries is substantially higher than in developed countries. Section 12.3 identifies the main sources of shocks with a view to examining the hypothesis that certain structural features that are typical of developing countries contribute to generating excess aggregate volatility. Sections 12.4 and 12.5 characterize South Africa's domestic financial architecture and examine the main problems of risk management in the economy. Section 12.6 concludes with implications for the international financial architecture and, in particular, what South Africa would want to see in the redesign of the international financial architecture.

12.2 Excess volatility and crises

Aggregate volatility in South Africa: measures, methods, and stylized facts

The main goal of this section is to analyze aggregate volatility of output, consumption, and investment; to test for the presence of excess volatility; and to identify episodes of extreme volatility.

One measure of total variability is standard deviation, which can be easily obtained if the data are stationary. To allow comparison with other country studies in this project, as well as with studies in the growth literature that have used this measure extensively, we adopt standard deviation as our main measure of total variability rather than mean absolute deviation or interquartile range, which are more resilient to outliers.

We use both annual and quarterly data seasonally adjusted as necessary. The samples span 1960–2004 unless noted otherwise. Units of measurement are the local currency (rand) except when making cross-country comparisons where the US dollar is the unit of measurement. Although our main analysis is based on quarterly data to avoid aggregation smoothing and loss of variability information, some series are available over a long span only in annual frequency, leaving us no other choice but to use annual data in parts of our analysis. Since the stationarity of a series is crucial for our analysis, we next apply unit root tests to series used here.[1]

The unit root test results suggest that the macroeconomic series are difference stationary in level and stationary in growth rates (log difference) except for ratios of two variables that are stationary in the level. Therefore, using the growth rate series to estimate volatility is statistically justified.

Stylized facts: volatility estimates

Table 12.1 reports mean, standard deviation, and range for South Africa's key quarterly macroeconomic series. Results are reported for the full sample that covers 1960–2004, as well as two sub-samples truncated at the political regime-change date. The analysis of the two sub-samples is meant to shed some light on the volatility pattern in Figure 12.1 which, overall, exhibits an appreciable reduction in recent years. However, it should be noted that more robust inferences on the pattern of volatility await further analysis based on rolling standard deviation. That technique allows us better to see how volatility is affected by various events over time.

First consider the pooled samples (1960–2004). Investment, terms of trade, export, import, and exchange rate have a relatively large standard deviation. The range of the growth rates illustrates the magnitude of quarterly fluctuations of these key macroeconomic variables. Throughout the period 1960–2004 investment has been more volatile than consumption which, in turn, has been more volatile than output. Furthermore (as shown later), the co-movement of output and consumption worsened, meaning that these variables over time have assumed greater correlation, contrary to what one would ideally expect in an improving domestic financial environment.

Table 12.1 Statistics for South Africa's key macroeconomic time series

Series	1960–2004 sample			1960–1993 sample			1995–2004 sample		
	Mean	St. Dev.	Range	Mean	St. Dev.	Range	Mean	St. Dev.	Range
In growth rate									
GDP	0.78	1.12	(–2.11, 5.02)	0.79	1.26	(–2.1, 5.0)	0.67	0.49	(–0.2, 1.8)
Consumption	1.07	1.51	(–4.03, 5.65)	1.04	1.65	(–4.0, 5.6)	1.07	0.93	(–1.6, 2.5)
Investment	0.73	4.17	(–11.7, 16.7)	0.62	4.66	(–11.7, 16.7)	0.59	2.40	(–7.3, 4.1)
Terms of trade	0.15	5.00	(–17.9, 13.4)	0.18	5.12	(–13.2, 13.4)	–0.11	3.36	(–7.6, 6.6)
Export	1.24	6.48	(–21.7, 22.2)	1.27	6.83	(–21.7, 22.2)	1.49	6.21	(–9.6, 14.3)
Import	1.19	6.91	(–26.0, 20.4)	1.06	7.68	(–26.0, 20.4)	1.02	3.84	(–9.3, 9.0)
M2	3.63	2.74	(–3.0, 10.6)	3.69	2.86	(–3.0, 10.6)	3.25	2.52	(–1.7, 7.0)
R/$ Exch. Rate	1.35	5.59	(–18.4, 23.4)	1.28	5.08	(–18.4, 23.4)	3.36	5.45	(–6.9, 20.0)
In level									
Inflation rate	8.43	5.46	(–4.7, 24.5)	9.12	5.64	(–0.4, 24.5)	6.59	3.57	(1.1, 16.4)
Discount rate	10.10	5.02	(2.35, 21.8)	9.06	5.04	(2.35, 21.7)	15.39	2.70	(11.7, 21.8)
Money market rate	9.56	5.33	(1.7, 22.5)	8.76	5.62	(1.7, 22.5)	13.98	2.93	(9.5, 20.5)

Notes: All series are quarterly and seasonally adjusted when appropriate. GDP, consumption, investment (gross private), export, and import series are all real (inflation adjusted); the growth rates reported for these series are for one quarter and not annualized. When splitting the sample into apartheid and post-apartheid sub-periods, 1994, which is the transition year, is excluded.

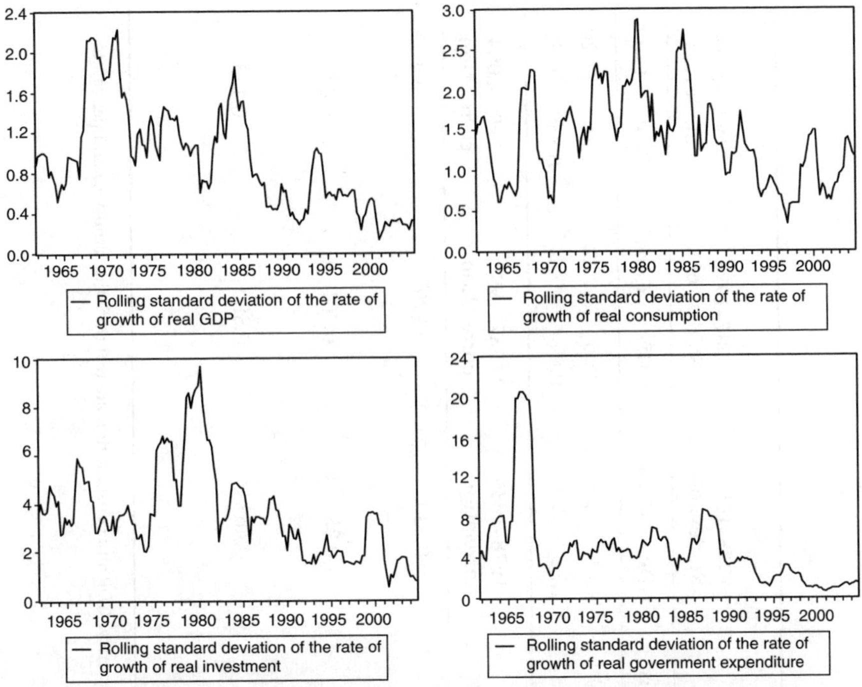

Figure 12.1 Volatility of South Africa's key macroeconomic variables

Volatility of consumption vs. GDP

Results reported here (Tables 12.1 and 12.2) show that the relative magnitude of growth volatility for consumption and GDP changes when the data frequency changes. Quarterly data suggest a more volatile consumption growth, while annual data suggest the opposite. This might seem puzzling at first, but careful examination dispels the appearance of contradiction. Obviously, the mean operator has additive property, so a higher quarterly growth rate means a higher annual growth rate, and if one of the two series has a higher growth rate at quarterly frequency, the same series must have a higher growth rate at annual frequency.

The additive property, however, does not hold for the variance (and thus standard deviation) operator. Seasonal series provide good illustrative examples, as they exhibit seasonal fluctuations, and possibly growth volatility at quarterly frequency, but such series might show steady and non-volatile growth annually (year over year). Therefore, if we compare two series when one exhibits quarterly fluctuations with an annually stable pattern of growth and the other exhibits stable growth both at quarterly and annual frequencies, then quarterly data will give a volatility ordering which is the opposite of their volatility ordering based on annual data.

Here consumption appears to have a stronger seasonal component than GDP, making the quarterly consumption growth more volatile than quarterly GDP

Table 12.2 Intertemporal volatility comparisons

	Full sample (1960–2004) St. dev. of		1960–1968 St. dev. of		1969–1977 St. dev. of		1978–1986 St. dev. of		1987–1995 St. dev. of		1998–2004 St. dev. of	
	GDP	**Cons**	**GDP**	**Cons**	**GDP**	**Cons**	**GDP**	**Cons**	**GDP**	**Cons**	**GDP**	**Cons**
South Africa	3.56	2.56	3.30	2.30	4.11	2.61	4.74	3.58	2.06	2.32	1.36	1.20
World	3.43	3.25	4.96	4.83	5.27	4.93	1.72	1.52	0.89	0.64	0.85	0.51

	Full sample correlation	1960–1968 correlation	1969–1977 correlation	1978–1986 correlation	1987–1995 correlation	1998–2004 correlation
South Africa consumption & GDP	0.799	0.566	0.824	0.830	0.879	0.894
South Africa consumption & world GDP	0.019	–0.177	–0.137	–0.251	0.701	0.032
South Africa consumption & world consumption	–0.036	0.186	0.171	0.469	0.580	–0.173

Notes: All series are annual due to unavailability of some of the series at quarterly frequency. GDP and consumption are real (inflation adjusted) and per capita. Correlation estimates are based on real (inflation adjusted) per capita growth series.

growth, while the annual growth of GDP seems to be more volatile than the annual growth of consumption.

Comparison with trading partners

With respect to the volatility of key macroeconomic growth series, we compare South Africa with her major trading partners – the US, the UK, Japan, and Zimbabwe.[2] This exercise is important because the findings of excess volatility in key macroeconomic variables do not in themselves say much about the relative magnitude of the disturbances.

The selected four major partners represent four different continents. Moreover, three of these countries are among the economic superpowers with developed economies and relatively low volatility. Therefore, they can be used as a benchmark. We compare growth rates of inflation-adjusted GDP, consumption, and investment. Given that we compare countries with different population growth rates, all measures are per capita even though all-inclusive census figures for South Africa 1971–91 are not reliable.

Results are reported in Table 12.3. South Africa has the second lowest mean GDP per capita growth rate after Zimbabwe. The volatility of this rate is less than Zimbabwe, as well as Japan, the latter having the highest GDP growth rate. South Africa's per capita consumption during this period grew on average at a rate higher than its GDP but with less volatility, as suggested by a smaller standard deviation. Nonetheless, South Africa has the lowest rate of consumption growth of these five countries. All five countries have experienced more volatility in their gross domestic investment than in their consumption or income. With the exception of Zimbabwe on both counts, South Africa's average growth rate is the lowest and its volatility the highest.

Overall, South Africa's key macroeconomic variables are considerably more volatile than those of the United Kingdom and the US, less volatile than those of Zimbabwe, and almost on a par with Japan.[3] To summarize, our results suggest that South Africa's macroeconomic series exhibit considerable volatility in

Table 12.3 Cross-country growth and growth-volatility comparisons, 1960–2003

	GDP per capita growth		**Consumption per capita growth**		**Investment per capita growth**	
Countries	**Mean**	**St. dev.**	**Mean**	**St. dev.**	**Mean**	**St. dev.**
South Africa	0.92	3.56	1.32	2.56	1.43	8.01
Japan	4.05	3.65	4.00	3.25	4.88	7.33
UK	2.11	1.80	2.54	2.41	2.41	5.06
US	2.23	1.97	2.58	1.80	2.99	5.60
Zimbabwe	0.45	5.81	1.43	12.42	–1.20	14.56

Notes: All series are annual due to the unavailability of some of the series at quarterly frequency. GDP, consumption and investment are all real (inflation adjusted). Series for UK consumption and investment and Zimbabwe consumption and investment have a few missing observations in the early sample years. Sampling period ends in 2003 rather than 2004 due to data unavailability for some countries.

comparison to major trading partners with more developed financial markets. For a developing country, the higher volatile environment importantly affects economic growth through its impact on investment. According to the real options theory, the level of uncertainty in an economic environment matters more than interest rates for investment decisions.

12.3 Structural factors, shocks, and excess volatility

Main sources of aggregate volatility

Using South African data, we address the hypothesis that certain structural features typically present in developing economies induce excess volatility. To do this, we first develop time series measures of volatility and then use them to identify sources of macroeconomic volatility. It would not have been difficult to identify factors that affect the volatility of a variable like GDP growth if we had a panel data set consisting of n time series for different countries. In such a case, we could use each of the n GDP growth series to obtain one volatility estimate (for example, standard deviation of the GDP growth of a sampled country). These n estimates could then be used in a regression analysis with n data points to identify country specific characteristics that affect volatility.

When only one country is analyzed, however, the task is more challenging because there is only one time series for a given variable such as GDP growth resulting in only one volatility estimate. No correlation or regression analysis is possible with only one data point. To overcome this challenge, we need to obtain many volatility estimates for each variable, each estimate pertaining to a sub-sample, rather than just a single estimate for the entire sampling period. These temporal measures of volatility for each key South African macroeconomic variable are obtained using rolling standard deviation of quarterly series suggested by Blanchard and Simon (2001). The resulting volatility series will assist us in identifying factors that affect such volatility.

Rolling standard deviation and volatility series

Temporal estimates of volatility for a given variable are a series of volatility estimates obtained at different points in time using a sampling window. The sampling windows overlap to allow many estimates, similar to calculating moving averages. We use a moving window of eight quarters, where the volatility estimate of a variable at each point (a given quarter) is the standard deviation of the current as well as seven preceding quarterly observations on that variable. Thus, the first observation in the resulting volatility series corresponds to the fourth quarter of 1961, because the starting sample point is the first quarter of 1960.

The overlap of the moving windows allows us to capture the dynamic characteristics of the volatility propagation mechanism, or to infer how volatility is affected by various events over time.[4] Obtaining multiple estimates of volatility for a country, rather than just one estimate for the entire sampling period, has the added advantage of reducing the temporal aggregation bias that affects panel data studies.

Figure 12.1 includes graphs of the rolling standard deviation of growth rate of real GDP, consumption, investment, and government expenditures. Figure 12.2 includes graphs of the rolling standard deviation of growth rate of real exports, real imports, and terms of trade. Figure 12.3 includes similar graphs for the monetary sector, including inflation rate, discount rate, money market rate, and growth rate of the rand/dollar exchange rate.

Comparing Figures 12.1 and 12.3, we note a remarkable difference in the progression of volatility pattern for the key real macroeconomic variables on the one

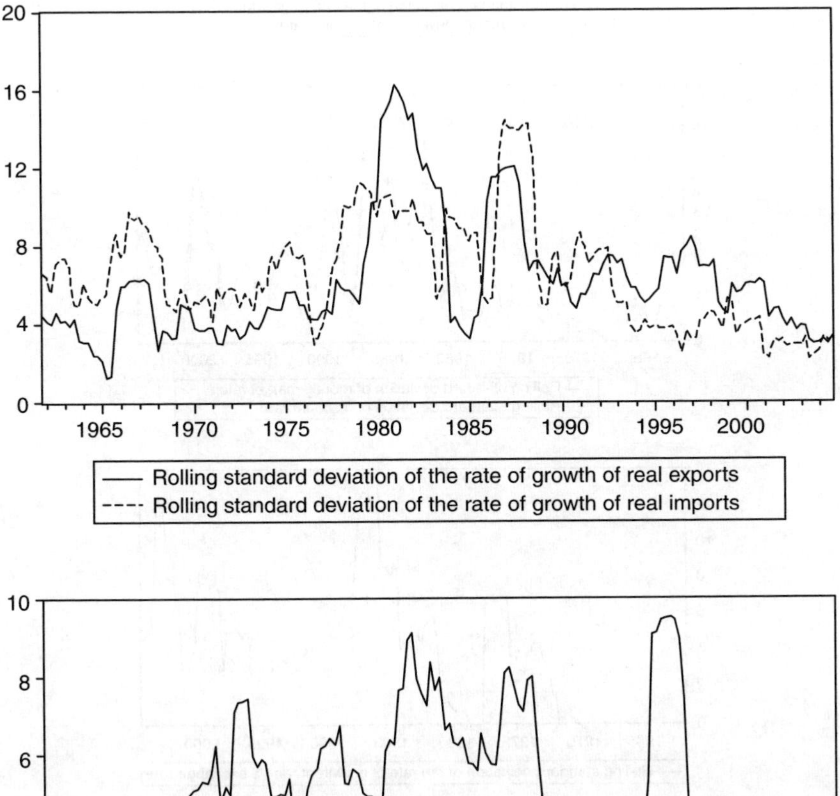

Figure 12.2 Volatility of trade sector in South Africa

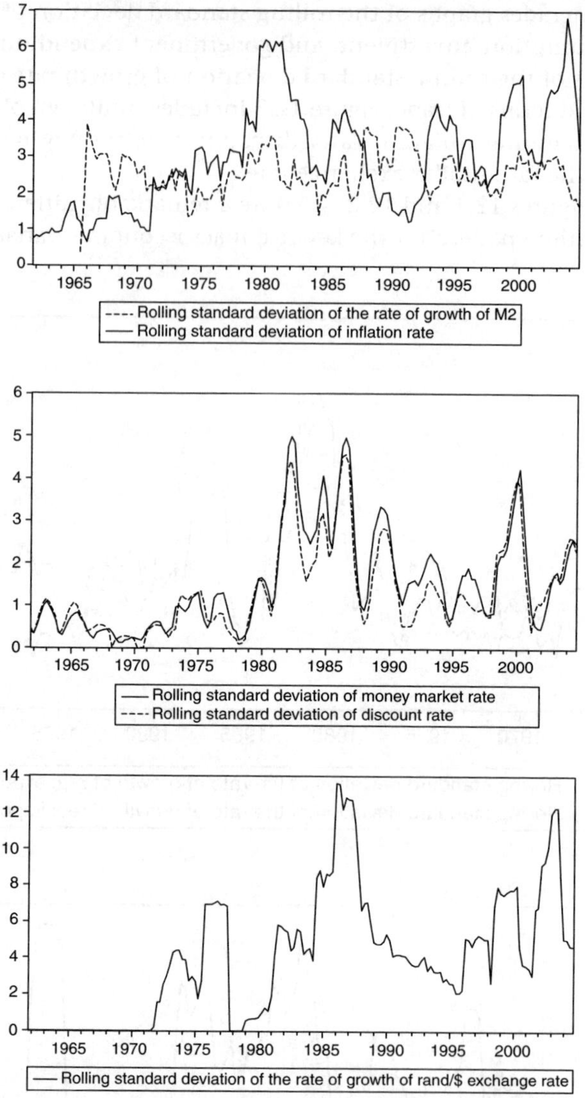

Figure 12.3 Volatility of financial sector in South Africa

hand and monetary variables on the other hand. Volatility of GDP, consumption, investment, and government expenditures appear to be on the decline, particularly during the post-apartheid period. This is consistent with the estimates presented earlier.

Variations in growth of real exports and imports are similar, as indicated by similar patterns in their rolling standard deviation. Interestingly, the four major sources of imports were the same as the four major export markets during 1961–90, bearing in mind that details of petroleum trade were not published

(Jones and Müller, 1992a). The foreign sector volatility portrayed in Figure 12.2 also suggests a decline in volatility in recent years – with one exception. The terms of trade changes appear to have acquired considerable volatility in the mid-1990s; see the graph in lower panel of Figure 12.2. This coincides with the period of political transition and increasing openness.

Role of the structure of exports and imports: insufficient diversification?

The movements in the terms of trade have become fairly volatile since the 1970s, even after controlling for the political regime change. First, it must be noted that South Africa's exports are dominated by primary exports, particularly gold and other minerals (see Table 12.4). The metals index which gives an indication of the price of the major mineral exports is also dominated by gold despite the importance of platinum, vanadium, chrome, manganese ore, and diamonds. In 1980, South Africa ranked number one in world production of these minerals, except diamonds where it ranked third even though it ranked second in the Western world (Jones and Müller, 1992a). Therefore, movements in gold prices and the exchange rate are useful in understanding terms of trade shocks and the volatility they induce on macroeconomic variables.

Imports have been just as volatile but in addition have been highly correlated with capital formation. This is understandable because capital goods, which are the dominant import, also constitute a significant part of capital formation (investment). Scholars of South African economic history (Jones and Müller, 1992a) note that the volume and composition of imports have been influenced both by the pace of industrialization and progress with import substitution. Consequently, semi-manufactures, machinery, transport equipment, and chemicals feature prominently on the import list. It is easy to understand how the sale of mechanical appliances, vehicles, and transportation equipment can be procyclical. They are part of asset-backed lending which is one of the most procyclical parts of credit; credit being generally procyclical (see Figures 12.4 and 12.5).

The role of globalization: vulnerability to global events

Before 1970, the price of gold was fixed and the exchange rate was stable – linked to gold with a fixed price. Post-Bretton Woods, gold and exchange rates became variable, with gold reacting to both political uncertainty (flight to quality) and to

Table 12.4 Distribution of exports by sector (%)

Year	Primary	Secondary
1989	45	55
1994	68	32
1999	59	41
2004	67	33
2005	67	33

Source: SARB Quarterly Bulletin.

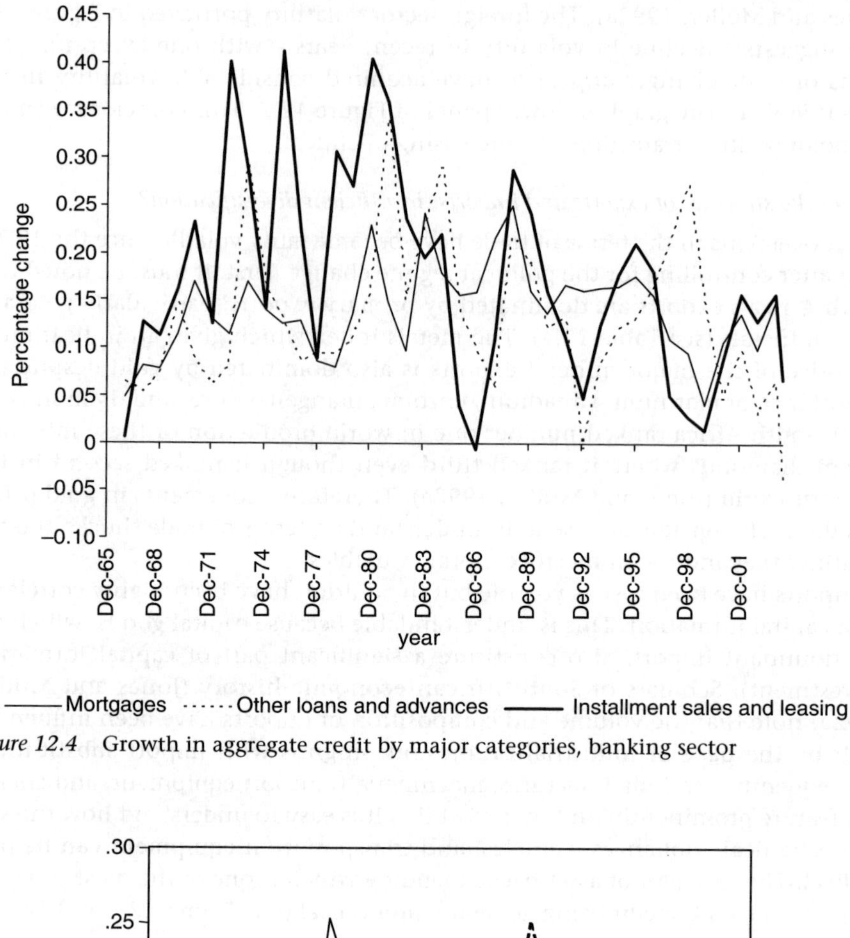

Figure 12.4 Growth in aggregate credit by major categories, banking sector

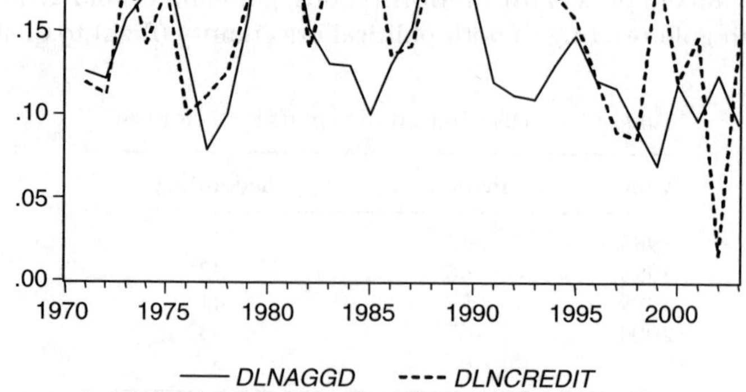

Figure 12.5 Growth in aggregate demand vs. growth in aggregate credit

economic shocks (inflation hedge). Examples of events with global consequences include the Egypt-Israel (Yom Kippur) war coincident with the beginning of the floating regime and the first oil shock (1973); the Soviet invasion of Afghanistan in 1979, the hostage crisis in Iran 1979 and the oil shock in 1980; the revaluation of gold in 1980, the Kuwait invasion in 1991, and the Iraqi crisis 2004.

All these events and their linkage to gold and other strategic minerals found in South Africa suggest that international stabilization mechanisms can have beneficial effects on South Africa. Furthermore, as long as the world's monetary system is underpinned by gold, reconfigurations of the international financial architecture will continue to hold important ramifications for the South African economy.

> Each $50 change in the gold price ... altered the value of annual gold production by about $1 billion ... not only caused fluctuations in the revenue and profitability of mines, in their dividends, and in their contribution to national income, but also in their contribution to the balance of payments and to the state's tax revenues ... also a greater volatility in the money supply.
>
> (Jones and Müller, 1992b: 265)

Determinants of volatility: domestic and external

Regression analysis is an appropriate tool for identifying factors that affect growth volatility for any of the key macroeconomic variables examined here. Since our temporal measures of volatility are based on overlapping windows, any regression that uses these volatility measures as the dependent variable is likely to exhibit significant serial correlation. Estimating such regressions without correcting for serial correlation in regression errors leads to biased standard errors and invalid inference. To deal with this problem, we use the following regression model in the analysis presented in this section:

$$Y_t = f(b, X_t) + u_t, \text{ and} \tag{12.1}$$

$$u_t = e_t + q_1 e_{t-1} + q_2 e_{t-2} + L + q_q e_{t-q}, \tag{12.2}$$

where $f(g)$ is a linear function with vectors of coefficients b and regressors X_t; regression errors follow a q'th order moving average (MA) process with parameters q's that satisfy invertibility condition, and u's are white noise normally distributed errors with mean zero and variance. The two equations are jointly estimated using the nonlinear maximum likelihood method.

Decomposition of GDP growth volatility

It is not uncommon to find that volatility of GDP components contributes to GDP volatility. For example, Blanchard and Simon (2001) have identified consumption and investment volatilities as important factors affecting GDP volatility in the US. Therefore, we examine the volatility of the components of GDP to identify their contributions to volatility in GDP growth. In particular, we estimate a regression equation with the GDP growth volatility as the dependent

Table 12.5 GDP growth volatility decomposition and consumption growth volatility/output growth volatility relationship

	Dependent variable			
	GDP volatility		Consumption volatility	
Regressors	**Full sample**	**Post-1994 sample**	**Full sample**	**Post-1994 sample**
Volatility				
Consumption	0.094*	0.076*		
	(0.050)	(0.041)		
Investment	0.016	0.042**		
	(0.019)	(0.019)		
Government expenditures	0.006	0.144**		
	(0.010)	(0.019)		
Exports	–0.016	0.029**		
	(0.012)	(0.008)		
Imports	0.037***	–0.014		
	(0.012)	(0.010)		
Constant	0.558***	–0.066	1.085***	0.728***
	(0.132)	(0.061)	(0.121)	(0.176)
GDP	–	–	0.311***	0.342
			(0.104)	(0.249)
Diagnostics				
Adjusted R^2	0.89	0.89	0.80	0.77
Durbin-Watson	1.73	2.01	1.94	1.87
Order of MA errors	4	4	4	4

Notes: All series are quarterly. Volatility series are the rolling standard deviation of growth rates for the corresponding variables. All variables are based on real (inflation adjusted) measures. Sampling period starts with fourth quarter of 1961 as this is the first year where rolling standard deviations with an eight quarter window can be estimated. When making a pre/post-apartheid distinction, the transition year 1994 is omitted. Standard errors are in parentheses. *, ** and *** indicate significance at the 10%, 5%, and 1% levels respectively.

variable, and rates of change in the volatility of consumption, investment, government expenditures, exports and imports as explanatory variables, with regression error terms that follow an MA process as described earlier. We use both the full sample and the post-apartheid samples in our estimation. Results are reported in Table 12.5.[5]

Before discussing the results, we need to address an estimation issue that is important for the results in Table 12.5 and Table 12.7 (below). The variables that serve as regressors and regressand here may give the impression of simultaneity. If the involved series were at the level, we would have had simultaneity, but the series are in volatility of growth rate. We are running regressions where each data series is growth rate volatility for the corresponding variable. For each period the volatility measure is estimated over the previous eight quarters, given the eight-quarter estimation window. Therefore any bi-directional influence that may exist when variables are measured in level is diluted by the aggregation and transformation of eight quarterly data points. That is why the volatility studies often estimate volatility regressions in cases where a similar regression of variables in level series, rather than volatility series, could have led to simultaneity (see, for example, regressions reported in Blanchard and Simon, 2001).[6]

Domestic and external factors

For the full sample covering 1961:IV through 2004, import volatility seems to be the only factor that contributes significantly to GDP volatility.[7] Consumption volatility has a significant effect but only at the 10 per cent level.[8] For the post-apartheid sample, the volatilities in consumption, investment, government expenditure, and exports all seem to contribute to growth volatility, although the consumption coefficient again is only significant at the 10 per cent level. Among these, government expenditure seems to have the most significant impact on growth volatility. Government expenditure and its influence can be understood in terms of social spending on poverty alleviation by way of transfer payments, capital expenditure relating to housing and urban integration and, of late, in response to the challenges of HIV-AIDS. We should add that although democratic South Africa is a developmental state and had inherited a low quality fiscal institution, its recent record of fiscal responsibility has been exemplary among developing countries. South Africa does not borrow from Bretton Woods institutions.

Does GDP volatility affect consumption volatility?

To examine the extent to which GDP volatility affects consumption volatility, we use an estimation method similar to the one used above, switching the GDP volatility and consumption volatility. Results are reported in the two right-hand columns of Table 12.5. The estimates suggest that while historically GDP volatility has contributed to consumption volatility in South Africa, as suggested by the significant coefficient of GDP volatility in this regression equation, the pattern has changed since the transition. GDP volatility no longer seems to drive the volatility of consumption although both exhibit a high co-movement. Increased co-movement of these variables indicates that agents are not smoothing consumption, perhaps due to 'incomplete markets' and other financial intermediation constraints.

Financial integration and outward orientation: testing the 'complete-markets' model (as a structural feature of developing countries)

The complete-markets proposition asserts the existence of incompletely diversified consumption risks due to the imperfections in the market mechanism. It embodies two joint propositions: access to credit and the correct specification of the response of economic agents to consumption risks.

The model asserts that *volatility imposes costs on economic agents only when it is unanticipated*. Anticipated fluctuations can be hedged and the associated risks diversified using both domestic and international financial markets and institutions. A key assumption of the model is the *availability of market mechanisms and institutions that facilitate hedging.* Its testable implications are that (i) domestic consumption volatility is uncorrelated with domestic output volatility and (ii) domestic consumption volatility is similar to world consumption volatility.

Empirical results

Volatility estimates for South Africa's consumption and income, and that for the world for 1960–2004, as well as for non-overlapping nine-year intervals are reported in the upper panel of Table 12.6.[9] All estimates are from per capita series to allow meaningful comparisons. Estimates suggest that the volatility of South Africa's per capita annual consumption growth is less than its annual GDP per capita. This is true for the full sample as well as most of the sub-sample, with the exception of 1987–95.

A similar pattern is also observed for world GDP and consumption volatilities although with a much smaller discrepancy. Moreover, consumption volatility is lower in South Africa than in the world when we estimate volatility over the

Table 12.6 Consumption growth-output growth relationship

Dependent variable: South Africa consumption	**1960–2003 sample Coef. estimates**	**1960–1993 sample Coef. estimates**	**1995–2003 sample Coef. estimates**
South Africa GDP	0.579**	0.577***	0.746**
	(0.071)	(0.073)	(0.242)
World consumption	0.035	0.041	–1.145
	(0.063)	(0.065)	(0.895)
Constant	0.706**	0.641	2.637
	(0.063)	(0.396)	(1.704)
Adjusted R^2	0.623	0.633	0.453
Dependent variable: South Africa consumption	**1960–2003 sample Coef. estimates**	**1960–1993 sample Coef. estimates**	**1995–2003 sample Coef. estimates**
South Africa GDP lagged one period	0.291*	0.290**	0.506
	(0.105)	(0.108)	(0.442)
World consumption	0.072	0.076	–0.410
	(0.069)	(0.070)	(1.360)
Constant	0.975**	0.920*	1.723
	(0.412)	(0.518)	(2.753)
Adjusted R^2	0.164	0.167	0.253

Notes: All variables are per capita real (inflation adjusted) growth rates. The transition year 1994 is dropped from the post-apartheid samples. Sampling period ends in 2003 rather than 2004 due to world data unavailability. Robust (heteroskedastic and autocorrelation-consistent) standard errors are in parentheses. *, ** and *** indicate significance at the 10%, 5%, and 1% levels, respectively.

entire sampling period and the first two sub-periods. But starting from 1978 (the third sub-period) South Africa's consumption volatility exceeds the world consumption volatility, which has continued to decline during the past 25 years.

To make a finer point of the matter, the growth rate of per capita consumption for South Africa is regressed on the growth rate of per capita GDP for South Africa and the growth rate of world per capita consumption. If the residents of South Africa had access to international capital markets and if domestic institutions in South Africa were sufficiently developed to allow diversification of idiosyncratic risk, then the estimated coefficient corresponding to domestic GDP should be insignificant while the estimated coefficient corresponding to world consumption should be positive and significant (world consumption is by assumption 'smoothed'). We estimate the equation using the full sample (1960–2003)[10] as well as two sub-samples corresponding to the apartheid period (1966–93) and post-apartheid period (1995–2003), with the transition year omitted as before.[11]

The top panel in Table 12.6 presents these regression results. Heteroskedasticity and autocorrelation-consistent covariance estimates proposed by West and Newey (1987) are used to obtain robust standard errors. In all three samples, the coefficient estimate for South African GDP is positive and significant rather than insignificant, and the coefficient estimate for world consumption is insignificant (negative in one case) rather than positive and significant. Coefficient estimates substantiate the correlation results that a complete-market model is not descriptive of the financial system.

Given that the above regression might be susceptible to simultaneity and absent a structural model linking country consumption to world consumption, we use the next best approach to check the findings just reported. We rerun the above regressions replacing the growth rate of real per capita GDP of South Africa with its one period lagged value. The lagged variable is predetermined and cannot be influenced by the dependent variable that leads it one period. This regression does not have simultaneity. Results, which are reported in the lower panel of Table 12.6 are markedly similar to those with contemporaneous variables. The estimated coefficient for South Africa's GDP is significant in two of the three periods. The coefficient estimate for the world consumption is statistically insignificant in all three sub-periods. This finding reaffirms that the complete-market model does not seem to be descriptive of South Africa's financial system.

Other volatility factors (including the effect of fiscal and monetary regimes)

To identify other factors that contribute to the volatility of income and consumption growth in South Africa, we estimate GDP and consumption–volatility equations with an expanded set of explanatory variables. We cannot rely on established theory in selecting these variables because such theory is not yet available (Fanelli, 2004). Instead, we rely on stylized facts, anecdotal evidence, and theories in the growth literature to identify plausible explanatory variables for the income and consumption volatility equations.

For instance, factors whose link to output or consumption volatility has been examined in the literature include terms of trade volatility (Acemoglu et al., 2003), inflation volatility (Blanchard and Simon, 2001), globalization, financial integration, outward orientation of trade (Kose et al., 2003; Buch et al., 2005), monetary and fiscal policy shocks (Ramey and Ramey, 1995; Caballero, 2000b; Buch et al., 2005), social and ethnic fragmentation and political instability (Ramey and Ramey, 1995; Easterly et al., 2000; and Acemoglu et al., 2003), strong dependency on export revenues (Caballero, 2003), government deficit (Caballero, 2000b), and financial deepening (Easterly et al., 2000; Denizer et al., 2000; Acemoglu et al., 2003; Kose et al., 2003).

Based on the above literature, our regressors include a binary variable that marks the transition from apartheid, the terms of trade, capital inflow and outflow, rand/dollar exchange rate, money market interest rate, money supply (M2), inflation rate, and three ratios that include M3/GDP, exports/GDP, and government deficit/GDP. The M3/GDP ratio measures financial deepening as reflected by the extent of financial intermediation. Exports/GDP ratio is a proxy for the domestic economy's dependency on export earnings. The deficit/GDP ratio measures potential for the crowding-out effect occasioned by deficit financing.[12] Except for ratios, interest rate, and inflation rate, all series are in terms of growth volatility of the corresponding variable (Model I). To examine the robustness of the results with the measures used here, we repeat the estimation replacing standard deviation of growth with mean of growth for variables where such substitution makes sense (Model II). Coefficient estimates for Models I and II are reported in Table 12.7. There are several interesting results.

First, the coefficient estimates for regime change are strongly significant in all four specifications, suggesting that the post-apartheid era is marked by lower volatility in output and consumption even after controlling for other contributing factors. Second, the estimated coefficient of the financial deepening variable is also strongly significant in all four specifications. An implication of this result is that domestic financial architecture matters for income and consumption volatility.

Third, volatility of inflation rate adds to consumption volatility as indicated by a positive and significant coefficient estimate for inflation. This result is not surprising given the absence, until recently, of indexed financial instruments and the lingering exchange control restrictions that constrain consumers' diversification horizon. Besides, the high co-movement of income and consumption predicts high variability in consumption when income is buffeted by inflation.

Fourth, fiscal policy appears to affect consumption volatility, presumably through changes in the financing of expenditure (such as tax policies), transfer payments, general social spending, and other appropriations. To summarize, inflation, broad money supply, fiscal policy, terms of trade and the regime dummy seem to have picked up much of the volatility in this model; hence suggesting the importance of politics, finance, and developments in the international arena.

Table 12.7 Components of GDP volatility and consumption volatility

	Dependent variable			
	GDP volatility		**Consumption volatility**	
Regressors	**Model I**	**Model II**	**Model I**	**Model II**
Constant	–1.5644	–0.2146	–2.4544	–4.6758***
	(1.0710)	(1.2760)	(1.3959)	(1.5966)
Regime switch	–0.3176***	–0.3330***	–0.5354***	–0.4600***
	(0.1104)	(0.1057)	(0.1367)	(0.1317)
Volatility (shocks)				
Terms of trade (growth)	0.0280*	0.0233	0.0259	0.0226
	(0.0169)	(1.2760)	(0.0223)	(0.0223)
Capital inflow (growth)	0.0005	–	–0.0029	–
	(0.0016)		(0.0026)	
Capital outflow (growth)	–0.0004	–	–0.0001	–
	(0.0005)		(0.0008)	
Rand/dollar exchange rate (growth)	0.0041	–	0.0120	–
	(0.0112)		(0.0175)	
Money market rate	–0.0249	–	0.0040	–
	(0.0416)		(0.0598)	
M2 (growth)	–0.0105	–0.0042	–0.0185	–0.0464
	(0.0367)	(0.0360)	(0.0594)	(0.0538)
Inflation rate	0.0247	0.0275	0.1246***	0.1460***
	(0.0248)	(0.0241)	(0.0431)	(0.0321)
Mean				
M3/GDP (financial deepening)	6.8951***	5.2367***	5.4512***	7.0250***
	(1.6567)	(1.8088)	(2.0500)	(2.2096)
Export/GDP	–5.1677***	–5.7265***	1.2179	4.2099
	(1.8393)	(1.7341)	(2.4765)	(2.1614)
Government deficit/GDP	–3.7405	0.3034	–24.6474*	–46.887***
	(11.6374)	(11.3176)	(15.0913)	(15.5274)
Capital inflow (growth)	–	–0.0022	–	0.0042
		(0.0020)		(0.0027)
Capital outflow (growth)	–	0.0004	–	0.0003
		(0.0011)		(0.0018)
Rand/dollar exchange rate (growth)	–	0.0182	–	0.0058
		(0.0129)		(0.0183)
Money market rate	–	–0.0309**	–	0.0260
		(0.0142)		(0.0171)
Diagnostics				
Adjusted R^2	0.90	0.91	0.71	0.84
Durbin-Watson	1.81	1.84	2.16	1.92
Order of MA errors	4	4	4	4
Effective sample size	158	158	158	158

Notes: All series are quarterly. Volatility series are the rolling standard deviation of growth rates for the corresponding variables. When appropriate, variables are based on real (inflation-adjusted) measures. Sampling period starts with fourth quarter of 1961 as this is the first year where rolling standard deviations with an eight-quarter window can be estimated. Due to data unavailability some series are shorter, reducing the effective sample size. Standard errors are in parentheses. *, ** and *** indicate significance at the 10%, 5%, and 1% levels, respectively.

Summary

Our findings are consistent with the literature linking volatility with certain structural features that are typical of developing countries. In particular, we have shown that the level of financial deepening and inflation matters for volatility. The level of financial deepening is one aspect of the quality of domestic financial architecture which in itself is a structural feature. We also found that imports and exports were volatile and that import volatility affects output volatility. The volatility of imports, investment, and the procyclical nature of credit suggest that either external credit was rationed, was unavailable, or that domestic credit could not fully immunize agents from the aggregate shocks. Either way, it indicates a structural flaw, namely, a constrained financial architecture.

12.4 Extreme volatility and institution-building

Identifying extreme volatility

Despite the prevalence of crisis episodes, there is no agreed upon and sound theoretical definition of crisis. So, we seek an empirical definition instead. Wolf (2004a) and Fanelli (2004) suggest basing such a definition on the empirical distribution of volatility as an economic variable because extreme volatility is crisis. We follow their suggestion and identify episodes of crisis for a variable as those corresponding to the largest quantiles of the empirical distribution of volatility measure for that variable. Continuing our practice in this study, we use standard deviation as the measure of volatility.

To identify volatility distribution for a series, we have to obtain a number of volatility estimates for the series over various sub-samples (sub-periods). We obtain two-year estimates by dividing a quarterly series into eight segments, spanning non-overlapping two-year periods. The standard deviation of the series over each sub-period is the estimate of its volatility during those two years. The sample starting point is 1964–65 to ensure that data are available for all examined series and the last sub-sample is 2002–03.[13] Overall, 20 volatility estimates are obtained for each series. Note that these estimates are different to the rolling standard deviations estimated earlier as they are based on non-overlapping sample periods, and therefore, obtained only on a biannual and not on a quarterly basis. The estimates for some of the key variables used in this study are reported in Table 12.8. The extreme values are identified by the largest quartile of the distribution of the resulting estimates and are printed in bold type.

Before discussing the estimates in Table 12.8, we present an alternative method for identifying periods of extreme volatility for the variables of interest. These estimates are based on rolling standard deviations. As discussed earlier, rolling standard deviations produce quarterly estimates of volatility where each estimate is based on the preceding eight quarters. They include many more volatility observations for each series than the biannual estimates based on non-overlapping samples.

However, successive estimates are based on common observations that are not independent, so they do not generate an empirical probability distribution to be

Table 12.8 Periods of crisis measured by key macroeconomic variables, South Africa

	Biannual volatility measures									
Years	**GDP**	**Consum.**	**Invest.**	**Govern. expend.**	**Terms of trade**	**M3 GDP**	**Export GDP**	**Deficit GDP**	**Inflation**	**MMR**
1964–65	0.95	0.79	3.27	**12.63**	4.07	0.005	0.013	0.0054	0.83	0.67
1966–67	**2.11**	**2.00**	**4.17**	**16.21**	3.14	**0.016**	0.006	0.0042	1.90	0.41
1968–69	**1.72**	0.97	2.94	2.13	5.07	0.012	0.015	0.0061	1.19	0.23
1970–71	**1.55**	1.65	3.70	4.45	4.97	0.009	0.007	0.0052	2.14	0.61
1972–73	1.23	1.38	2.01	4.33	5.79	0.012	0.011	0.0080	2.65	0.92
1974–75	0.99	**2.14**	**6.55**	5.53	4.40	**0.021**	0.009	**0.0091**	2.80	0.47
1976–77	**1.32**	1.35	3.93	4.48	**6.73**	0.010	0.013	**0.0124**	3.12	0.45
1978–79	1.02	**2.23**	**8.73**	3.94	4.22	**0.016**	**0.024**	0.0088	**5.99**	1.63
1980–81	0.69	**1.93**	**5.50**	**6.82**	**9.12**	**0.018**	**0.045**	**0.0116**	**5.13**	**3.42**
1982–83	**1.51**	1.49	**4.80**	3.77	**6.80**	0.012	0.016	**0.0090**	2.62	**2.46**
1984–85	1.29	**2.31**	2.34	**5.76**	6.04	0.007	**0.036**	0.0089	3.65	**3.10**
1986–87	0.69	1.32	3.52	**8.06**	**7.09**	0.014	**0.021**	0.0086	3.44	1.01
1988–89	0.68	1.21	2.66	3.22	3.92	0.015	0.012	0.0090	2.02	**3.15**
1990–91	0.28	1.73	1.62	3.78	2.91	0.010	0.015	0.0080	1.67	1.57
1992–93	1.03	0.78	1.94	1.32	1.94	**0.025**	0.008	0.0071	**4.02**	2.01
1994–95	0.57	0.77	2.01	2.07	**9.51**	0.006	0.010	**0.0117**	3.48	1.73
1996–97	0.62	0.58	1.56	2.30	4.21	0.013	0.013	0.0053	2.41	0.78
1998–99	0.52	1.42	3.64	0.99	2.92	0.008	0.011	0.0079	**5.05**	**3.34**
2000–01	0.27	0.66	1.00	0.87	0.76	0.014	0.016	0.0076	2.89	0.47
2002–03	0.27	1.36	1.19	1.06	2.90	0.017	**0.029**	0.0080	**6.83**	1.67

Notes: All series are quarterly. Volatility series are the standard deviation of growth rates for (or the ratio of) the corresponding variables, obtained using an eight-period window. When appropriate, variables are based on real (inflation-adjusted) measures. Sampling period is adjusted to make all samples equal to the smallest available sample. Extreme volatility estimates (corresponding to the highest quartiles) for each variable are in bold type.

used for identifying extreme values. To overcome this problem, we analyze these rolling standard errors in a regression context. Accordingly, we run each series of rolling standard errors on a set of binary variables, each denoting two consecutive years – assuming a value of one for quarters during these two years, and zero otherwise. These binary variables span 1966 to 2003. To correct for the serial correlation that rolling samples create, we use the method of maximum likelihood estimation with regression errors that follow a high order moving average scheme.

The estimated coefficient for each binary variable measures the difference between the volatility estimate for the two years corresponding to that variable and the smallest volatility measure for all other sub-samples. The largest coefficient estimate belongs to binary variables for the most volatile two-year periods. These regression results are reported in Table 12.9. Again the largest 25 per cent of the estimates are indicated in bold, showing the most volatile periods. Note that the starting point is 1966 due to data unavailability for some series. The table also reports the moving average coefficient estimates, indicating the number of MA lags used to correct for serial correlation in these regression equations.

Table 12.9 Periods of crisis measured by key macroeconomic variables, South Africa (regression based)

	T-statistic capturing size of volatility in a given year for each volatility series									
Years	**GDP**	**Consum.**	**Invest.**	**Govern. expend.**	**Terms of trade**	**M3 GDP**	**Export GDP**	**Deficit GDP**	**Inflation**	**MMR**
1966–67	9.03	6.83	6.80	**21.18**	5.31	4.46	3.59	9.72	3.43	1.77
1968–69	**11.00**	9.13	7.50	8.38	5.89	7.19	5.33	13.02	4.00	2.95
1970–71	**16.86**	7.36	7.52	8.46	5.93	6.99	5.91	10.89	4.76	2.79
1972–73	**14.86**	10.55	7.89	**9.63**	**9.46**	8.82	6.86	13.90	6.85	1.88
1974–75	9.36	**11.38**	**8.32**	9.34	8.49	**10.64**	5.51	17.32	7.46	1.09
1976–77	10.09	**11.89**	**11.39**	**10.33**	**10.06**	8.58	6.24	**23.02**	8.71	2.04
1978–79	9.73	**12.42**	**12.80**	**10.67**	**8.84**	8.14	8.80	**21.51**	**11.51**	3.01
1980–81	7.59	**13.62**	**11.61**	**10.08**	**8.74**	**14.26**	**14.34**	**21.70**	**13.95**	3.19
1982–83	**10.91**	10.18	**9.62**	8.96	7.79	9.45	**10.61**	**22.03**	**10.74**	14.62
1984–85	**10.54**	**14.00**	7.17	6.10	8.26	**9.64**	**11.06**	18.17	9.25	**18.62**
1986–87	10.40	9.95	8.09	7.39	7.30	9.38	**9.26**	17.68	10.43	**17.28**
1988–89	7.87	8.98	7.74	7.22	**8.58**	7.38	8.47	17.87	6.30	**17.81**
1990–91	5.21	6.48	4.66	4.89	7.02	7.12	6.87	19.36	5.25	**16.54**
1992–93	5.36	6.18	4.65	4.89	6.44	8.87	5.32	16.11	8.29	**16.76**
1994–95	4.50	5.89	4.00	4.49	6.97	**10.48**	4.76	**21.52**	9.41	**15.44**
1996–97	4.15	7.13	3.88	4.07	6.88	**9.97**	5.94	12.23	8.71	11.21
1998–99	4.60	8.01	4.71	3.44	4.39	7.91	5.91	13.76	10.57	14.90
2000–01	2.47	5.80	4.52	3.33	4.22	5.88	7.35	15.75	**10.58**	15.02
2002–03	1.64	3.82	2.58	3.06	3.97	7.59	**9.30**	15.85	**13.55**	12.67
MA(1)	16.61	12.99	12.38	14.73	15.39	18.57	10.89	6.21	8.65	27.29
MA(1)	8.29	5.46	7.71	8.62	10.82	10.43	5.73	3.97	3.85	15.18
MA(3)	5.19	1.93	5.12	8.43	7.31	5.86	3.54	–	1.80	19.07
MA(4)	7.17	5.83	–	2.87	6.48	7.76	–	–	–	44.95

Notes: All series are quarterly. Volatility series are the rolling standard deviation of growth rates for (or the ratio of) the corresponding variables. When appropriate, variables are based on real (inflation-adjusted) measures. Sampling period is adjusted to make all samples equal to the smallest available sample. Extreme t-values (corresponding to the highest quartiles) for each variable are in bold. The statistics corresponding to MA(i) are the t-statistics for the corresponding moving average regression error terms, where the order is determined through testing of added terms.

Although the high volatility periods for each macroeconomic series reported in Tables 12.8 and 12.9 are not identical, due perhaps to differences in methods used and sampling variations, there are many overlaps. The identified episodes of extreme volatility reported in the two tables mark 1974–76 and 1980–87 as times of unusually high volatility in key macroeconomic indicators. These periods coincide with the two global oil price shocks, South Africa's default on its foreign debt, and investment collapses. The latter is captured as a catastrophic drop in asset-backed lending circa 1974–77 and 1981–86.

Looking again at Table 12.9, we can detect shock persistence or volatility inertia, meaning that when there is a significant increase in volatility or a large shock hits the economy, it would seem that such a shock tends to persist. Therefore, a sizable shock, such as from oil, debt default, drought, or commodity prices may not go away quickly, certainly not without dramatic improvements in the risk-coping capabilities of the economy. The tables also indicate episodes of volatility-clustering which again may be indicative of feedback effects in the shock propagating mechanism.

A note on GARCH and shock propagation

Generalized autoregressive conditional heteroskedasticity (GARCH) is a stochastic process typically used to model the error component of a regression equation. In such cases, the dependent variable in the regression equation is autoregressive and the regression errors are conditionally heteroskedastic as well as autocorrelated. GARCH parameterization is useful in enhancing the accuracy of the forecasts obtained for the dependent variable using regression equation. This approach, however, has limitations in cases where one needs to identify the drivers of volatility rather than modeling volatility to improve forecasts; see also Fanelli (2004: 37) who argues that the GARCH approach has little use in cases where the volatility is driven by structural variables such as a propagation mechanism. The approach does not lend itself to identifying how the volatility pattern changes over time. Therefore, we chose not to use this approach in our analysis of volatility.

Domestic financial institutions: characterization and functioning

This section motivates subsequent analysis of the impact of extreme volatility on the domestic financial architecture. We begin by describing South Africa's domestic financial architecture and emphasizing that building institutions entails not only financial regulations but also ensuring the consistency between these regulations and the macroeconomic regime. In other words, for financial regulations to be effective, they require complementary principles and practice of fiscal and monetary policies as well as functional institutions.

Domestic financial architecture (DFA)

(i) *Banks and non-banks.* In Appendix 12.1 the hard line denotes oversight responsibilities (executive powers) whereas the soft line (dotted) denotes advisory functions.

Generally (provided it acts within its enabling legislation) the reserve bank is independent of the government in the formulation and conduct of monetary policy. Despite this independence of the bank and its strict responsibilities for the safety and soundness of the banking system, the national treasury (through the Minister of Finance) stands at the apex of the regulatory system. This preeminence is by virtue of the ministry's overarching powers through its legislative responsibilities in matters of financial regulation. It turns out that this close connection is a virtuous link in the sense that it helps establish and maintain the consistency required between the regulatory and the macroeconomic regime.

Another aspect of South Africa's financial architecture that can be considered an innovation in institution-building is the Financial Stability Committee of the Banking Supervision Department. This unit, which is charged with managing systemic risk, represents the first formal attempt in South Africa to expand the focus of central bank responsibilities beyond the traditional role of price stability and payment system integrity to recognizing the importance of systemic stability and the macroeconomic consequences of its absence.[14] Implicitly, this constitutes an effort to harness the state and the market in order to avoid banking failures, asset-price bubbles, collapse of liquidity and the consequent impairment of the payments and settlements system.

One of their risk management strategies involves coordinating across relevant regulatory agencies in order to achieve synergies in oversight and policy, essentially ensuring consistency between regulation and the macroeconomic regime. This coordination burden is considerably lessened by the presence of the Finance Ministry as part of DFA.

(ii) *Public Finance (quality of fiscal institution).* To appreciate the impact of public finance, it is necessary to recall that although there is a fall in the volatility of all real variables analyzed, the decrease is greater in the case of GDP, as can be seen from Table 12.9. This dramatic fall in the volatility of GDP is accounted for by the drop in the volatility of government expenditure (see the lower right panel of Figure 12.1). Post-apartheid, the government had to reconfigure its operations, resulting in significant savings and stability in spending, both on the basis of reduced security risk and the consolidation of the parallel but unequal government structures constructed during apartheid for the different racial groupings. Furthermore, the government had also changed its asset and liability management considerably.

In the domestic financial market, it sought to reduce the cost of borrowing, manage the maturity profiles of its liabilities, diversify funding instruments, become more transparent, and thus build its reputation. The marketing of government debt through primary dealers was introduced in 1998 and the funding instruments diversified from fixed income bonds and treasury bills to inflation-linked bonds, variable rate bonds and retail bonds. Moreover, considerable progress has been made in improving cash management through investments in interest-bearing deposits.

According to our findings, stability in government expenditure can mitigate consumption volatility. Therefore, government spending is not only a significant component of the autonomous consumption of many poor residents, but also forms part of the available risk insurance products (unemployment benefits and other social expenditures). We can claim that it has not only been responsible for the dramatic drop in GDP volatility shown in Table 12.9 but also for stabilizing consumption (by virtue of increasing its spread across society post-apartheid).

(iii) *Monetary policy and exchange control.* In sharp contrast to the real sector, the volatility of the monetary sector appears to have been increasing since 1994 as can be seen from Figure 12.3. This can be attributed partly to an inherited high inflationary financing in the 1980s and the subsequent move to solve the problem through a change to inflation targeting.

In February 2000, the South African monetary authorities introduced inflation targeting as their monetary policy, interest rates as their instrument, and the consumer price index as their target variable. The framework for inflation targeting requires an explicit forecast of inflation, announcement of benchmarks that must be reached over a specific time frame, and no pre-commitment to exchange rate parity. Under this regime, changes in the interest rate may have increasingly influenced exchange rate movements as the country gradually lowered capital controls.

Nonetheless, there are other complicating factors in the volatility equation, such as the massive open forward contracts held by the Reserve Bank of South Africa (that have now been fixed). Second, there were externalities from the adverse political developments in Zimbabwe following the implementation of a highly controversial land redistribution policy. Third are the emerging-market crises of the late 1990s that could also have influenced perceptions about South Africa. With regard to capital controls, the authorities have followed gradualism in what is perceived as an outbound bias in the net direction of capital flows.

12.5 Financial market failures, adaptive responses and problems of risk management

Synopsis of the 1985 and emerging market crises

A central hypothesis of this research project is that agents' adaptive responses can result in market failures and that market failures can cause impediments to risk management, all of which can feed a crisis. We analyze two issues that are of importance to this central hypothesis: financial crises and the effect of market imperfection.

With regard to financial crises, we identify two major contrasting episodes hereinafter referred to as the 'emerging markets crisis' and the '1985 crisis'. The latter illustrates how the absence of complementary principles elaborated in Section 12.2 impaired the ability of the economy to manage a crisis, whereas in the case of the emerging market crisis, the DFA was reasonably sound, embedded as it were in a consistent regulatory and macroeconomic regime.

The 1985 crisis

In view of the extensive analysis of volatility in this paper, it is important to note that with regard to the 1985 crisis, excessive volatilities of macroeconomic variables as per Tables 12.8 and 12.9 were a consequence of the crisis rather than its cause.

(i) *Genesis of the crisis.* Following the global energy crisis in 1979, the South African economy went into a recession that culminated in a severe financial crisis. During this pre-crisis period, output fell and thus reduced the government's revenue base. Rates on taxes surged to support continuing government expenditure. Gold prices peaked and then plummeted, the rand depreciated, inflation escalated, and nominal interest rates increased. The state responded by encouraging recourse to international financing; the Reserve Bank of South Africa subsidized the cost of external finance by lowering the premium on forward cover for loans of three months or longer.[15]

In 1982, the government approached the IMF for a standby loan of US$1.1 billion that opened up access to private international banks, which then provided South Africa with relatively large amounts of credit. Subsequently, the government abolished the dual exchange rate system introduced in 1979 and slackened exchange control regulations. With the slight relaxation of exchange controls, unsound banking practices surfaced and were largely condoned by the regulatory authorities. The large banks (Barclays, Standard, and Nedbank) accumulated large foreign currency exposures to a combined total of approximately US$6 billion (Padayachee, 1991: 98). In particular, Nedbank was borrowing short in New York where interest rates were much lower and lending long in South Africa where rates were higher, although a large proportion of the lending was to state-owned enterprises. Evidently, the role of international financing was crucial in managing the pronounced macroeconomic volatility that marked the 1980s (see Tables 12.8 and 12.9).

(ii) *The crisis.* Ultimately however, South Africa's political liability overwhelmed its short-term management apparatus. As a protest against apartheid, Chase Manhattan Bank, at the time the second largest US lender to South Africa, ceased further lending to South Africa and froze existing credit lines on 31 July 1985. This was followed by a 20 per cent drop in the value of equities at the Johannesburg stock exchange, a depreciation of the rand by 25 per cent, and continuing massive capital flight. The crisis came to a head on 1 September 1985 when South Africa defaulted on its loans by declaring a debt moratorium.

Concurrent events included international businesses and other foreign banks that began divesting from South Africa. Other US banks toed Chase Bank's line by refusing to roll over maturing debt obligations. Although the debts were mostly short term, they nonetheless represented 72 per cent of the foreign debt (Kahn, 1991). By the end of 1987, 40 per cent of foreign firms had divested, while between 1985 and 1993 net capital outflow amounted to about R45 billion or approximately 11 per cent of gross domestic fixed investment (Padayachee, 1991).

Emerging markets crisis

Several emerging market economies suffered banking and currency crises between 1994 and 1998: Mexico in 1994–95, Thailand 1997, Indonesia 1997, Korea 1997, Russia 1998, Brazil 1998, and Argentina's catastrophic crisis in 2000. We identify South Africa with these emerging market crises, but only by way of contagion effects, through higher volatility of interest rate, inflation, investment and consumption in 1998 in comparison to the adjoining years (see Table 12.8).

As we elaborate below, the South African economy proved resilient to these contagion effects principally due to the presence of two elements of DFA that have proved crucial to the way in which the EM crises have played out – capital controls and a floating exchange rate regime.

For instance, in the case of Mexico 1995, the problems of non-performing loans in the banking system surfaced only after the crisis had manifested, even though that situation pre-dated the crisis. The Asian problems were rooted in expansive credit that was short-funded with hot money (capital inflows). In Russia deficit spending was being financed with hot money under the euphoria of a notional transition to a market economy, but that expectation fizzled. On the other hand, South Africa ran a regime of a floating exchange rate and capital control which largely ensured that the country was insulated from the more extreme ravages of contagion effect and 'sunspots'.

Lessons from the crises

The causes of the crises and the ways in which they were managed differed. The 1985 crisis was rooted in politics, and the management of the macroeconomic volatilities of that decade was embedded in a highly charged political environment. The government's adaptive response was perhaps largely a survivalist strategy. The regulatory laxity and weak supervision of banks created a moral hazard problem, but that alone was not responsible for the defining event of the 1985 crisis, which was politically motivated and so would have occurred eventually. The credit crunch may not have been so severe if the country had not been overextended, but the degree to which the overextension was due to the problem of moral hazard is an open question.

With regard to the emerging markets crisis, South Africa suffered indirectly through contagion effects but appears to have weathered the contagion better than other emerging market countries. It is not simple to define what South Africa did differently from the other emerging economies, but we can say that this episode and how it played out indicates that crises can be well managed if DFA is reasonably sound. Presumably, South Africa's domestic financial architecture and macroeconomic regime in the late 1990s were a huge improvement on the situation in the 1980s. In particular, as we have identified, two elements of the DFA proved to be crucial – flexible exchange rates and 'managed' capital controls.

The main problems of risk management are structural

A key impediment to risk management is capital control, which has invariably created limited opportunities for the diversification of risks. Another key factor is the high cost of access to financial services. The high cost of access is a structural problem as well. South Africa's financial system is highly concentrated in terms of the number and size distribution of firms (market share), an arrangement that is buttressed by interlocks in the governance and pattern of ownership. Ironically, these features to a large extent account for the stability of the system.

On how these features impart stability, it is useful to consider that the partially protected and concentrated banking market ensures rents while the pattern of ownership has engendered a solid capital base that has kept institutions strong. Until 2005 the four largest banks were all owned by life assurance companies. Old Mutual controls Nedbank, which it had previously rescued from disaster; Liberty Life controls Standard Bank; Southern Life controls First National Bank; and Sanlam controlled Absa Bank (which it had rescued as well) but has now ceded to a foreign shareholder, Barclays Bank. Together with a fringe competitor, Investec Bank, these four banks account for over 80 per cent of the asset base in the industry.

12.6 Conclusions

Summary

The body of evidence presented in this chapter suggests that South Africa is subject to considerable macroeconomic volatility, much more than is experienced in industrialized countries. Some of the sources of the volatility are structural, such as high dependence on primary commodity exports which leaves the economy vulnerable to terms of trade shocks. However, at no time within the last four decades has extreme volatility generated a financial crisis either through impairing the functioning of domestic financial institutions or by inducing adaptive responses by economic agents that in turn impaired the functioning of markets or institutions.

Some of the extremely volatile periods (and in fact the two crisis episodes described) have been linked either to developments in the global economy or to political problems domestically. Reflecting on the way in which institution-building has evolved during this period, particularly after political uncertainties were resolved (post-1994), we can observe that building the DFA goes beyond financial regulations to include ensuring consistency between regulations and the macroeconomic regime.

On these bases, we have shown that inflation and the level of financial deepening matter to volatility. These two factors in turn are related to the quality of DFA. When sizable aggregate shocks occur (oil shocks, debt default) there are important increases in volatility which tend to persist; this is particularly so in the case of consumption and investment. Furthermore, consumption and investment volatility tend to be higher than GDP volatility. These facts indicate that countercyclical policies have not been successful at reducing aggregate fluctuations in domestic absorption. This in turn suggests that the country has not been successful at resorting to the international capital markets to reallocate intertemporally the effects of aggregate shocks.

We also found that import volatility matters for GDP volatility. When external credit rationing is present, there cannot be a significant trade imbalance; if exports are volatile, imports will be volatile, as is the case in Figure 12.2. If imports (raw materials and semi-manufactures) are necessary to sustain the activity level, it is natural that volatility of imports is associated with GDP volatility, as has been similarly confirmed (Table 12.5). This is another reason why credit constraints matter to aggregate volatility.

Implications for the international financial architecture

As shown in Section 12.2, South Africa is vulnerable to global events even with a still partially insular economy. Therefore, dismantling impediments to greater financial integration boils down ultimately to assessing the net benefits to policymakers from following one of several policy choices. The authorities can continue the restrictions to protect the domestic economy from the disturbances of capital surges or accept the costs of excess volatility (from an insufficiently diversified portfolio). The balance can be tipped in favor of further dismantling controls if the international financial architecture can address the dangers of cross-border capital surges, contagion effects from information problems, and the potential moral hazard from increased competitive pressures.[16] This is an area where a global solution trumps national remedies forged country by country.

International governance structures and institutions have not been influential in shaping DFA in South Africa because policymakers appreciate that standards and codes on their own are unlikely to insure against capital surges and financial crises. 'Sunspots' are an ever-present warning that a healthy financial system is not a sufficient condition for stability; mechanisms such as the IMF Contingent Credit Lines but with sensible conditionalities are important requisites at the supranational level for containing incipient problems so that catastrophes can be averted. That, for us, should be a focus.

Notes

1. See the data appendix (Appendix 12.2) for sources and descriptions.
2. See the data appendix (Appendix 12.2) for sources. Also note that we could have included Germany, but we would like to have representation from all four continents, while keeping the list short for convenience in presentation.
3. Major differences are reported between developed and developing countries in terms of the short-run, business cycle, and long-run components of macroeconomic volatility; see, for example, Cogley (1990) and Levy and Dezhbakhsh (2003).
4. Note that we can use a wider window, but that reduces the number of the volatility estimates and also makes the series too smooth – in the limit the window is the size of the entire sample and only one volatility estimate is obtained. Also, a few quarter increases or decreases in the size of the moving window do not materially affect our general findings.
5. As anticipated, the regression errors are serially correlated, but a fourth order MA adequately captures this correlation and the estimation method corrects for it, as evidenced by insignificant Durbin-Watson statistics.
6. Moreover, even if the volatility estimation window was smaller than 8, so some simultaneity was present, there would still not have been any way to identify a structural model, because structural models relating volatility in various economic variables are not available. A simple transposition of the relationships in level to volatilities is not appropriate either. In fact, this and the other country case studies are supposed to offer some basic facts about volatility linkages. So, there is still a long way to go before structural volatility models are developed.
7. See notes to Table 12.5 for related explanations.
8. Note that this regression does not produce a significant coefficient estimate for a variable that makes only a short-run contribution to GDP volatility; significance suggests a relatively persistent relationship.
9. The window for these non-overlapping sub-samples is selected such that we increase the comparison points without wasting recent data points or reducing the size of the sub-samples to the point that estimates become statistically meaningless. Findings are robust to alternative window lengths such as ten years and eight years, but data points for 2000–04 are left out when these two windows are used.

10. World data for 2004 were unavailable when we conducted this analysis (source for world data is Fanelli, 2005a).
11. These regressions are statistically valid given that the growth rate series used are all stationary.
12. This assumes that the marginal social benefits from government spending are below that of private investment.
13. Quarterly data for some of the series are available only after 1963.
14. It is not universally the case that central banks are bank regulators, particularly where there is a deposit insurance scheme. In some countries, such as the US, the central bank is not directly involved in banking supervision.
15. See Padayachee (1991) for details.
16. The Reserve Bank of South Africa considers non-negotiable certificates of deposits to be highly volatile funding instruments (Reserve Bank DI 300 Question 2; www.reservebank.co.za/internet/publication.nsf).

Appendix 12.1 Structure of South Africa's financial system

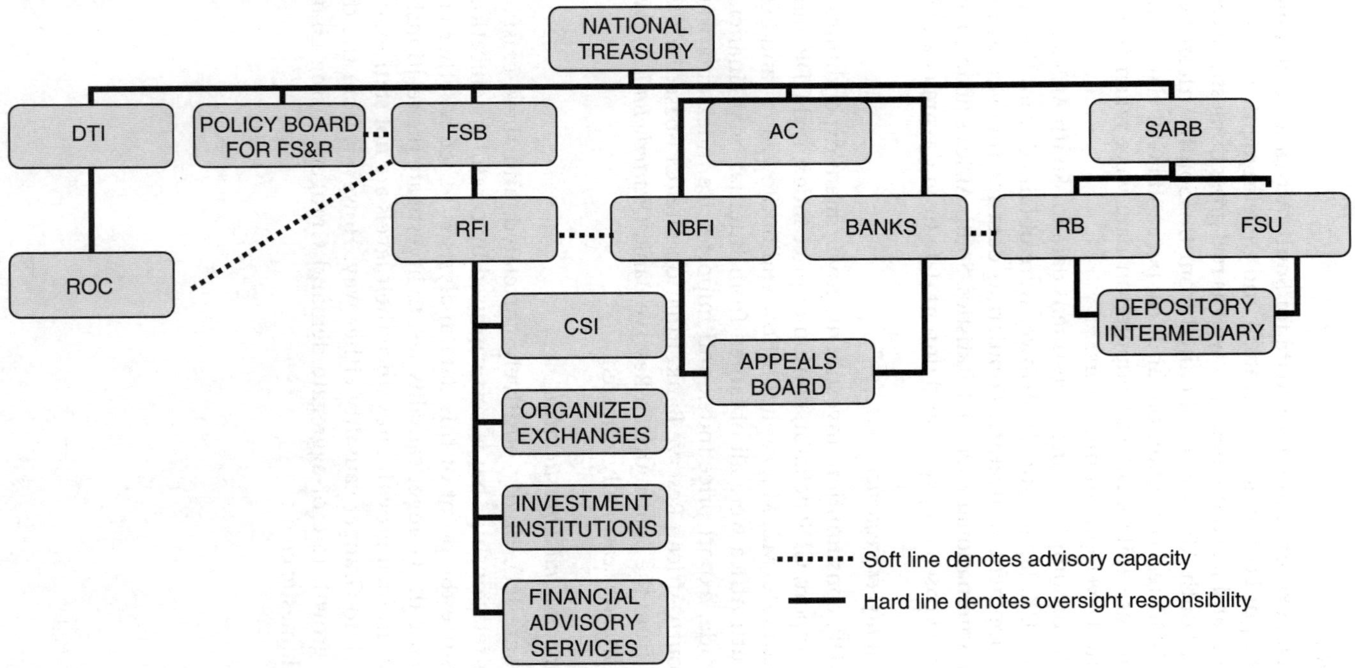

Note: Organizational structure adapted from www.finforum.co.za.

Appendix 12.2 Data appendix

Annual Data

The real GDP, export, and import data for South Africa were obtained from the Organization for Economic Cooperation and Development. Terms of trade, real consumption and its components, as well as real gross domestic investment, and M2 data for South Africa were obtained from the South African Reserve Bank. World real GDP, real consumption, and real per capita GDP data as well as South Africa's real per capita GDP and population data were taken from the World Bank's World Development Indicators.

Real GDP, consumption, and investment data for South Africa's main trading partners (US, UK, Japan, and Zimbabwe) were obtained from the World Bank's World Development Indicators. Population data for these countries were obtained from International Financial Statistics. South Africa's main trading partners were identified based on export and import data from Cassim et al. (2003).

Quarterly and higher frequency data

Nominal GDP, consumption, investment, government expenditures and deficit, export and import, GDP deflator, consumer price index, real GDP, money market rate, discount rate, M2, M3, capital inflow and outflow, and rand exchange rate data for South Africa were all obtained from International Financial Statistics. Terms of trade, export price index and import price index data were obtained from the South African Reserve Bank. Inflation rate (CPI-based) for South Africa is obtained from the South African Reserve Bank, *Quarterly Bulletin*. When appropriate the data are seasonally adjusted.

Aggregate demand and domestic credit

Both series are I(1), highly positively correlated, and there exists a valid cointegrating relationship that is best captured by careful specification of the lag structure. Since the point of this data analysis is to see whether credit is procyclical, we use the Granger-causality test to investigate the relationship between the variables in their growth rates since their levels are not stationary. With two lags, there is no Granger causality either way. However, from the third lag the test shows growth rate of aggregate demand Granger-causing changes in the growth of domestic credit.

13
Nigeria

S. Ibi Ajayi and Adeola Adenikinju

13.1 Introduction

This chapter is concerned with the Nigerian study on the link between macro volatility and institutions. Nigeria is a small, open, oil-dependent, and heavily indebted country[1] that shares most of the characteristics of countries that exhibit high volatility. Among the 79 countries included in a study by Hnatkovska and Loayza (2004), Nigeria's volatility index (measured as the standard deviation of GDP growth) of 7.556 was only surpassed by Algeria 8.285, Syria 8.204, Iran 7.718, and China 7.994. It is also higher than the mean of 4.124 for all the countries in the sample. Similarly, Fanelli (2005a) shows that among African countries, Nigeria has one of the highest income and consumption volatilities.

Since 1986, Nigeria has implemented a broad range of economic and political reforms to address the myriad of structural and economic growth problems that the country faced in the aftermath of the international oil market crisis in the early 1980s. These reforms, covering nearly every aspect of the economy, were carried out largely under the direction of the international financial institutions and in line with the so-called Washington Consensus. However, these comprehensive reforms have not delivered much success relative to the expectations that were created. Reasons adduced for the failure to meet these expectations include inconsistencies in the implementation of the reforms and the faulty design and sequencing of the reform program. Indeed, there were intermittent reversals of policies, especially with respect to tariffs, interest rates, and privatization, especially between 1986 and 1998, leading to a lack of confidence in government reforms.[2]

However, the absence or weakness of relevant institutions has also compromised the success of the structural adjustment program (SAP) in overcoming the development challenges posed by the country's external economic conditions and structural features. Reform policies had largely ignored the weakness of domestic institutions and have sometimes led to amplifications of the impact of external shocks on the economy. The reform program also largely ignored the initial conditions of the country, including significant aggregate volatility stemming largely from oil-dependence and oil revenues fiscal account linkages and weak international financial linkages. Other problems arising from complex fiscal federalism arrangements and loose financial regulations resulted in recurrent financial crises and an unstable debt path. These issues are discussed in Section 13.2.

Under these initial conditions, the ability to manage shocks and policy errors during the period of financial liberalization is limited, as we show in Section 13.3. The structures of governance of financial transactions tend to be weak, which, in turn, reduces the level of financial deepening. The implementation of countercyclical policies is difficult with a government that is heavily dependent on oil revenues and that has limited policy instruments at its disposal. Thus, building the institutions of the DFA under these circumstances is difficult because the ability to manage shocks and policy errors during the institution-building process is limited. The consequence of the low level of financial development is that the means available to economic agents for coping with uncertainty are rudimentary. Risks are not allocated efficiently because of the existence of pervasive regulatory and financial market failures. Economic agents' decisions under these conditions become sub-optimal. These issues are addressed in Section 13.4. Section 13.5 shows that a volatile environment plus deficiently designed institution-building in Nigeria resulted in low financial deepening and induces adaptive responses that severely hinder financial development. The summary of findings and conclusion of the study are presented in Section 13.6.

13.2 Excess volatility and crisis

Nigeria can be said to have experienced one major and two relatively minor economic crises since 1970. Here we define crisis loosely as a period when the country experienced consecutive declines in per capita income for three years. Between 1981 and 1983, per capita income declined by an average of –9.1 per cent per annum. This corresponded to a period of significant decline in Nigeria's terms of trade (TOT) as a result of reversals in the international price of oil, the main export commodity. The second crisis, though of a lower magnitude can be set between 1993 and 1995 when per capita income declined by a mean of –1.3 per cent. Again, as was the case with the first crisis, the second crisis was preceded by a persistent decline in TOT. This period also coincided with a major banking crisis in Nigeria. The third crisis period occurred between 1997 and 1999 when per capita income declined by a cumulative –2.3 per cent. Again, a major feature of this period was a decline in Nigeria's terms of trade (see Figure 13.1).

The introduction of a structural adjustment program (SAP) in 1986 also brought about a major shock in the economy as most macroeconomic aggregates declined sharply. Between 1986 and 1987, per capita GDP declined by –4.2 per cent cumulatively. Government and private consumption declined by –34 and –6 per cent, respectively, in 1987. Real GDP and investment also recorded negative growth rates.

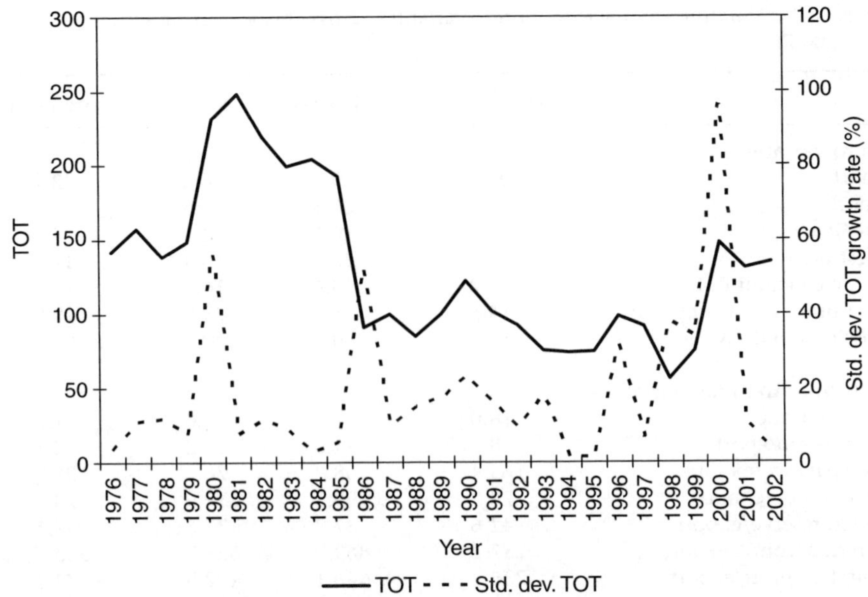

Figure 13.1 Terms of trade (1987 = 100)
Source: Computed from World Bank (2004), World Development Indicators.

Macro volatility trend

Nigeria's macroeconomic variables have experienced significant volatility since 1970.[3] We measure volatility using the standard deviation of growth of the macroeconomic variables. However, to make the analysis more interesting we examine the differences in volatility of variables across different episodes. We identify two main episodes, namely, the pre-SAP period (1970–85) and the SAP (1986–2003). The former is, in turn, sub-divided into two periods – the oil boom era (1970–80) and the oil crisis period (1981–85). Table 13.1 confirms the existence of high volatility for nearly all the macroeconomic variables across the various episodes. It shows that volatility was lowest for nearly all the variables during the oil boom and paradoxically highest during the period of the structural adjustment program, the only exceptions are real GDP and investment, which recorded the least volatility during the SAP period.

Table 13.1 shows that, on average, private consumption exhibits higher volatility than income volatility. Interestingly, however, during the oil boom and the oil crisis periods, consumption recorded lower volatility when compared with income. However, SAP reversed this trend as consumption had to bear the greater brunt of the economic crisis.

Apart from gross national savings, Table 13.1 shows that export and import recorded the highest volatility among all the macroeconomic variables in the upper segment of the table. The high external dependence of the economy suggests a high transmission mechanism of volatility between the external markets

Table 13. 1 Volatility of macroeconomic variables across episodes using series, 1979–2003 (%)

	Oil boom	Oil crisis	SAP	Entire period
Macro variable				
Export	21.1	29.4	36.8	32.7
Import	14.6	25.5	31.5	27.4
Real GDP	5.6	10.7	2.1	4.3
Investment	17.5	22.2	15.4	17.0
Private consumption	5.2	8.6	16.7	13.2
Government consumption	14.5	8.3	23.2	19.0
Gross national savings	19.5	30.4	90.5	67.1
Trade and financial variables				
Terms of trade	18.0	7.2	27.0	21.8
Absorption/export	8.1	21.6	26.2	22.1
Trade balance/export	165.4	108.8	76.7	98.3
Fresh money/export	78.2	99.7	219.9	173.2
Foreign reserve/export	42.6	37.7	77.5	64.1
Current account/export	237.2	869.9	522.7	533.7
Capital account/export	236.2	646.1	492.9	474.4

Source: Computed from data from Central Bank of Nigeria, Statistical Bulletin.

and the domestic economy. The high volatility of exports is symptomatic of the low diversification index of exports and the overwhelming dominance of oil – a primary commodity – in the country's export structure. The high volatility in imports is a reflection of the inability of the economy to manage risks efficiently because of financial market failures.[4] The trade and financial indicators in the lower part of the table show that this group of variables, which all relate to the external sector, display significant volatilities that are much higher than the macroeconomic variables in the upper part of the table.

Table 13.1 also shows that volatility of investment is quite significant. This is due to the role of the government as the largest source of domestic investment. The Nigerian government is the repository of oil revenues. Oil accounts for over 80 per cent of government revenue as well as over 97 per cent of foreign exchange earnings. Fluctuations in oil revenue often result in a major contraction in public investments and by extension aggregate domestic investment.

We also test for structural changes in the volatilities of macroeconomic variables across different periods, in particular between pre-adjustment and adjustment periods. The results, presented in Table 13.2, show that except for few variables, volatility was consistently high over the different episodes. However, for real GDP, volatility was higher during the oil crisis relative to the period of the SAP, lower during the oil boom relative to the period of the oil crisis, and lower during the SAP relative to the pre-SAP period. However, private consumption experienced higher volatility during the SAP period than during the pre-SAP period.

Figure 13.2 presents a rolling five-year standard deviation for real GDP. A visual inspection of the figure confirms three peaks of volatility, each corresponding to

Table 13.2 Tests of structural shifts in volatilities of macroeconomic variables across episodes, 1970–2003

	Real GDP	Private consumption	Investment	Export	Import	Saving
SAP vs. pre-SAP	−6.06*	9.81*	−4.49	11.53	11.46	65.58
	−3.3	−2.09	(−0.74)	−1.07	−1.15	−0.96
Oil boom vs. oil crisis	−5.14	−3.4	−4.65	−8.34	10.94	6.23
	(−1.03)	(−0.69)	(−0.47)	(−0.69)	−(−1.32)	−0.91
Oil crisis vs. adjustment	8.62*	−8.11	6.82	−7.36	5.99	−14.84
	−2.49	(−1.23)	−0.86	(−0.50)	−(−0.43)	(−1.00)

Notes: Values in parentheses are the associated t-value. * implies significance at 5%.
Source: Authors' calculations.

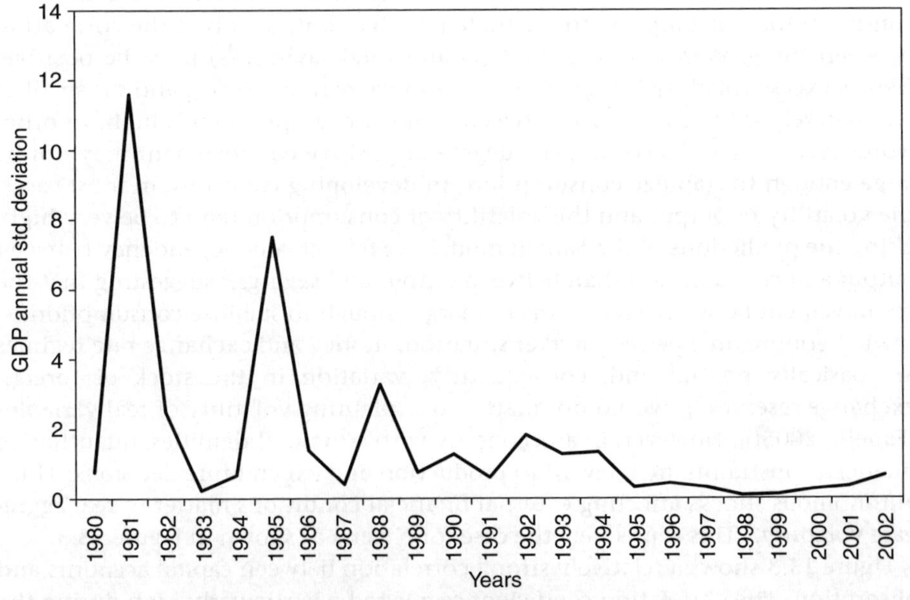

Figure 13.2 GDP, rolling 5-year window standard deviation
Source: Computed from Central Bank of Nigeria (2004), Statistical Bulletin.

particular episodes of crisis in the international oil market. Economic reforms, resulting in improved macroeconomic management, coupled with more sanguine developments in the international oil market, have contributed to the lower volatility in real output since 1995.

Excess volatility

While volatility is a normal part of the modern capitalist economy, the presence of market failures affects the ability of an economy to cope with excess volatility.

In this sub-section, we try to establish whether there is excess volatility in Nigeria relative to benchmark countries. An implication that emerged from the results presented in Table 13.1 is that macroeconomic volatility in Nigeria is very high. However, to establish the presence of excess volatility relative to developed economies, we adopt the complete-market hypothesis approach. This approach has two straightforward predictions regarding the relationship between consumption and income volatility (Fanelli, 2005a). First, private consumption volatility should be lower than income volatility because private agents can use the financial markets to smooth consumption. A necessary condition for consumption to fluctuate less than output is that the correlation between the growth rate of output and total savings must be positive. The second is that the evolution of domestic consumption should be more closely correlated with the evolution of world consumption than with national income.

Evidence of excess volatility can be gleaned from the relationship between the growth rate of output and that of savings. Fanelli (2005b) proves that a necessary condition for consumption to fluctuate less than output is that the correlation between the growth rate of output (g) and total savings (s) must be positive. Hence, excess volatility is present if the co-movement between g and s is small or alternatively if the covariance between g and consumption (c) is high. In other words, even if g and s covary, the degree of positive co-movement may not be large enough to stabilize consumption. In developing countries, in most cases, the volatility of output and the volatility of consumption tend to be very high. Using the predictions of the Fanelli model, we find greater dependency between output and consumption than between output and savings,[5] suggesting that the co-movement between g and s was not large enough to stabilize consumption.

Furthermore, in a perfect market situation, money and exchange rate regimes are basically neutral and, consequently, variation in the stock of foreign exchange reserves (f) would not matter in explaining volatility of real variables (Fanelli, 2005b). However, in an economy with structural rigidities, quantitative financial constraints are relevant to production and expenditure decisions. Thus, autonomous shocks affecting external financial conditions matter to real aggregate volatility.[6] This is precisely the case for Nigeria as shown in Figure 13.3.

Figure 13.3 shows a relatively strong correlation between capital accounts and absorption. The correlation coefficient seems to be particularly high during the crisis periods. This would not have been the case if the market worked perfectly: 'domestic agents will diversify their portfolio internationally, thereby divorcing the fluctuations in local demand from fluctuations in domestic income' (Fanelli, 2005b). However, higher oil export earnings, liberalization of the exchange rate, and higher macroeconomic management have reduced the covariability between capital accounts and absorption since the late 1990s.

We also estimated a regression model between consumption growth in Nigeria as the dependent variable and Nigeria's GDP growth and world consumption growth[7] as explanatory variables. The logic is that if Nigerian residents were to have fluent access to international capital markets, the coefficient on world consumption should be positive and significant, while the coefficient on Nigeria's

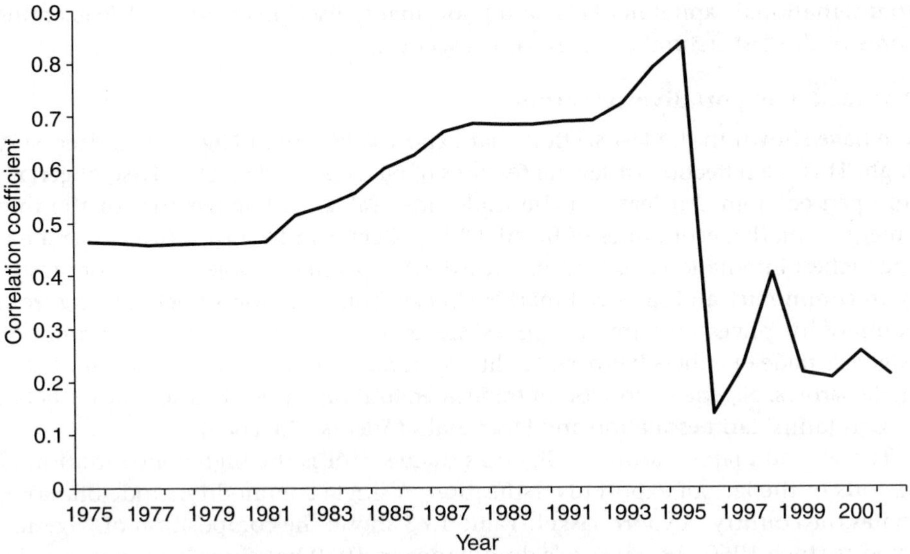

Figure 13.3 Volatility of capital accounts and absorption
Source: Computed from Central Bank of Nigeria (2004), Statistical Bulletin.

Table 13.3 Dependent variable: Nigeria's consumption growth

Variable	**Coefficient**	**t-value**
Constant	9.98	2.32
OECD consumption growth	–2.57	–2.2
Nigeria's GDP growth	0.38	1.73

Source: Authors' calculation.

GDP growth should not be significant (Fanelli, 2005a). Our result is presented in Table 13.3. The results are, basically, opposed to the complete integration hypothesis. This confirms the presence of excess volatility in Nigeria as a result of weak institutions.

In concluding this section, we can reiterate from the available empirical evidence that, like other developing countries, aggregate volatility in Nigeria is substantially higher than in developed countries, and that, indeed, excess volatility is present.

13.3 Structural factors, shocks, and excess volatility

The excess volatility in Nigeria is a reflection of the structural features of the economy. These features, which are common to most developing countries, include an underdeveloped and weakly integrative structure of the economy, a lack of export diversification, high export and import volatilities, limited access to international capital markets, and poor-quality fiscal institutions. We examine some of these structural features in this section.

The lack of export diversification

We have shown in the last section that export volatility in Nigeria is indeed very high. This is a reflection of several features of Nigeria's trade sector. First, Nigeria is an open economy, at least on the trade side. Table 13.4 shows that of the four emerging market economies of Brazil, Chile, Nigeria and South Africa, Nigeria has the highest international exposure. The extent of openness subjects the economy to both commodity and financial market shocks. Thus, external shocks arising from commodity prices and import prices are easily passed on into the economy. Nigeria's trade openness has been facilitated in recent times by the significant fall in trade barriers. Nigeria's adoption of trade liberalization has led to a significant fall in import tariffs, tariff escalation and tariff peaks (Adenikinju, 2003).

The second major feature of Nigeria's trade sector is the high concentration of exports or the lack of export diversification. A single commodity, crude oil, dominates the country's export basket. Table 13.5 shows the composition of Nigeria's exports since 1960. Agriculture's dominance in 1960 has since been replaced by

Table 13.4 Total trade-to-GDP ratios, selected emerging market economies

	Brazil	Chile	Nigeria	South Africa
Average past 5 years	0.24	0.21	0.69	0.55
Average past 10 years	0.2	0.15	0.63	0.49
Memo: 1997–2002	0.23	0.2	0.7	0.54

Source: Batini (2004).

Table 13.5 Composition of Nigeria's exports

		Percentage share in total merchandise exports		
Year	Total exports US$ billion	Agriculture	Oil and mining	Manufactures
1960	2.3	84.48	2.43	13.09
1965	2.7	59.01	32.4	2.29
1970	4.5	36.45	62.35	1.2
1975	7.99	5.75	93.77	0.48
1980	26.1	2.45	97.27	0.28
1985	15.63	2.1	96.0	1.9
1990	13.49	2.21	97.03	0.76
1995	12.65	1.8	97.54	0.66
2001	16.67	1.0	98.4	0.6
2004	34.61	1.2	97.5	1.3
2005	47.93	0.7	98.5	0.8

Source: Central Bank of Nigeria, Annual Reports and Statement of Accounts, various issues.

oil. Currently, oil accounts for over 98 per cent of the country's total exports, while manufactured exports account for less than 1 per cent.

The high concentration of exports also implies that the economy is open to shocks from a single commodity that cannot be diversified away because of weak/ineffective domestic institutions. Given the role of oil earnings as the major source of government revenue, it then implies that volatility in exports directly feeds volatilities in domestic macroeconomic variables.

Volatility of exports affects volatility of imports

Another feature of the trade sector is that the volatility of exports transmits to import volatility. The Nigerian economy is largely import-dependent and, therefore, potentially vulnerable to external shocks arising from the increase in the prices of imports, the fall in the prices and volume of oil exports, and movements in the exchange rate. This is especially true because of the country's weak financial system, poor linkages with the international financial system and the lack of export diversification. The import-dependency of the real sector of the economy places tremendous demand pressure on the limited supply of foreign exchange. The high correlation between volatility in exports and volatility of imports has been reduced or even reversed in recent years by a number of factors. First is the liberalization of the exchange rate that has made imports relatively more expensive; second is the favorable movement in international oil prices; and third is the establishment of stabilization funds by the government.

Deficient integration with international capital markets

However, while Nigeria can be said to be open on the trade side, it cannot be said to be open on the financial side. The ability of a country to smooth the effects of the volatility of exports on the economy is limited by external financial constraints. Nigeria has a very weak linkage with the international capital markets. This weak linkage can be gauged by the small size of the current account, the amount of capital flows and what Fanelli defines as fresh money from abroad.[8] The capital inflows into the country were very low compared to the magnitude of trade shocks that the country experienced. This limited the ability of the country to mitigate the impacts of terms of trade shocks on the economy. Over the study period, capital inflow-GDP ratio was below 10 per cent. Most of the capital inflows were in the form of foreign direct investment (FDI) rather than portfolio investment, and usually flowed to the oil sector of the economy. The business environment and poor perceptions among international investors about the Nigerian economy have ensured that it is not an attractive destination for foreign portfolio investment.

The current account balance, which is a reflection of the difference between domestic output and absorption, swung between deficit and surplus over the years. As a percentage of GDP, the current account balance was low. We can also discern a close relationship between the price of crude oil and the current account balance. The mostly positive balance recorded in Nigeria's current account in recent years was due to the rising trend in the price of oil (see Figure 13.4).

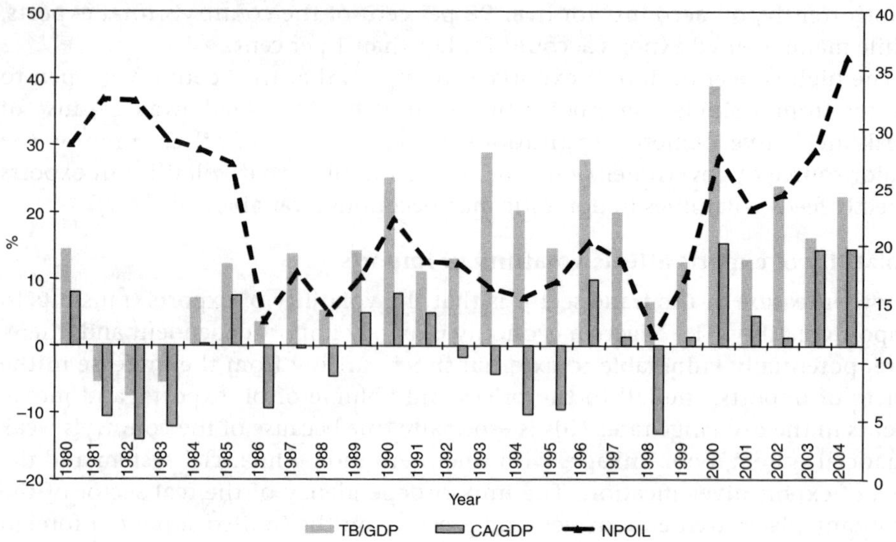

Figure 13.4 Current balance, trade account balance, and the price of oil
Source: Central Bank of Nigeria (2004), Statistical Bulletin.

The country could not build up substantial foreign reserves because of the significant volatility in foreign exchange earnings and the absence of any stabilization account. Hence, any excess foreign exchange earnings during boom years were easily wiped out during the years of lower trends in oil prices. Foreign reserves have been deliberately built up in recent years with a more effective management of oil revenues.

The persistent deficit in the current account balance led to a rapid accumulation of external debt. Nigeria collected her first external jumbo loan of US$1 billion in 1979. However, while Nigeria did not incur much in direct loans on the international capital market after 1985, the high interest rates on existing loans and penalties on loan default resulted in a significant increase in the debt volume over the years. A developing country with an economic and political structure like that of Nigeria tends to be penalized by the market for inability to service the debt and creditors' perception about the country's risk level. Table 13.6 shows that the market perceives Nigeria to be riskier than other emerging markets. Batini (2004) attributes this partly to the 'absence of financial buffer to cushion them against a decline in oil prices, of the weak tax system and of the poor quality and effectiveness of public spending programs. All these imply that government possibility of defaulting on its debt is very high.'

Thus, Nigeria cannot easily access the international credit market for urgent financial needs. This credit constraint in the international credit market means that the bulk of the necessary adjustments in TOT fluctuations falls on current absorption rather than allowing it to be distributed over time.

Table 13.6 Emerging Markets Bond Index (EMBI+) (based on monthly averages 1997:01–2002:12)

Country	Average	Standard deviation	Coefficient of variation
Brazil	879.35	389.07	0.44
Colombia	651.18	118.48	0.18
Mexico	443.4	150.03	0.34
Nigeria	1634.52	129.83	0.08
Peru	601.75	120.64	0.2
Poland	233.03	38.17	0.16
South Korea	236.37	145.39	0.62

Source: IMF (2004).

Poor-quality fiscal institutions

The impact of volatility on the economy has been amplified by the difficulty of managing Nigeria's complex federal system. There are disagreements between the federal and state governments on the revenue allocation formula, treatment of oil-producing states and on the sterilization of excess earnings from crude oil exports. The existing political arrangements and fiscal relationships across the three tiers of government complicate the federal government's capability to manage volatility in Nigeria. Under the current revenue-sharing arrangements, the budgets of state and local governments are heavily influenced by oil revenue uncertainty and indeed exhibit substantial procyclical postures. The inability to effectively manage the fiscal arrangement between the tiers of government, especially under the current democratic government, has been a major constraint on the ability of the federal government to effectively manage volatility. Ordinarily, fiscal federalism should not be a problem if it is properly managed and more resources are devoted to developmental objectives at the lower tiers of government. However, an allocation system that permits a strong center and the pooling of resources for sharing, without much consideration for the macroeconomic consequences of fiscal operations, causes distortions in macroeconomic variables.[9]

The Nigerian federal system is made up of a central government, 36 states and 774 local governments. In 2004, for example, federal government expenditures amounted to N1377 billion, while the states and the local governments expended N1125 billion and N462 billion, respectively. Thus, state and local government finances combined exceeded that of the central government. This implies that for fiscal stabilization to succeed, there must be a consensus across the three tiers of governments. This has been extremely difficult to achieve.

Another problem that complicates the practice of fiscal policy in Nigeria is the dependency of all three tiers of government on oil revenues. Over 80 per cent of federal government revenue comes from oil revenues (see Figure 13.5). The situation is even worse at the lower levels of government – the state and local government dependency ratios are about 88 and 95 per cent, respectively. This high dependence leaves little room for maneuver during the period of oil price shocks

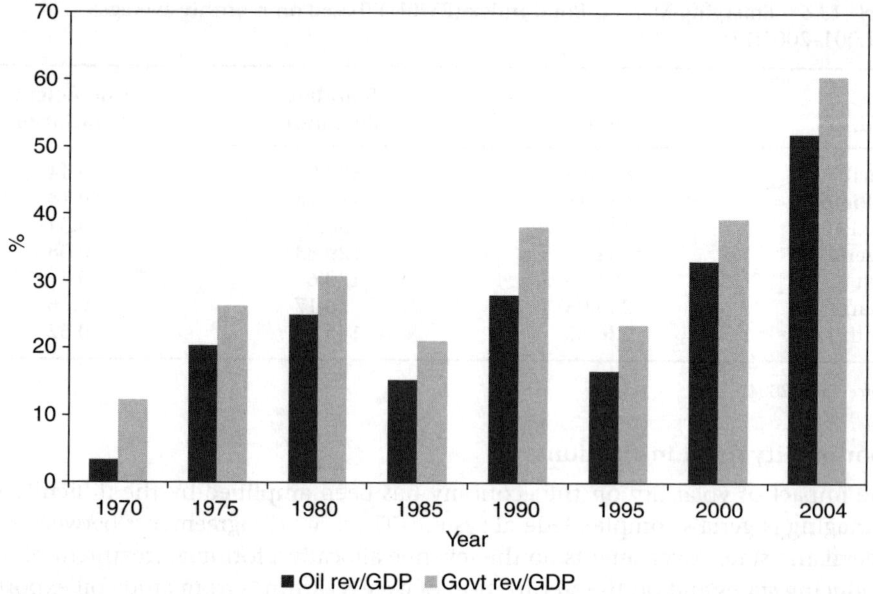

Figure 13.5 Government revenue versus oil revenue as proportions of GDP, selected years (%)
Source: Derived from Central Bank of Nigeria (2004), Statistical Bulletin.

and has made agreement for stabilization across the three tiers of government very difficult to achieve. This contributes to the procyclical nature of government expenditures in Nigeria.

Finally, there is also tension arising from the unequal distribution of oil wealth. The country's oil resources are located in the southern part of the country. The distribution of oil revenues among the states and between the federal and state governments has not adequately reflected the issue of derivation, leading to claims of neglect by the oil-producing states.

Government expenditure in Nigeria is procyclical. The oil crisis, which began in 1981, led to a sharp drop in government revenues and expenditures. Although the drop in government expenditures was lower than the fall in government revenues, the decrease was sufficient to have major impacts on the economy because the government is the largest investor as well as non-agricultural employer of labor in the economy. In addition, the near collapse of government revenue imposed pressure on the domestic credit market as the government increasingly financed its revenue shortfall through borrowing from the domestic credit market and the printing of new money.

Persistent high fiscal imbalances invariably translate into high public debt. Rising international interest rates and the inability of the country to meet its debt repayment commitments have led to significant increases in debt servicing. Total public debt by the end of 2003 amounted to N5.6 trillion which was equivalent to 74 per cent of GDP and 138 per cent of non-oil GDP. External debt at the end of 2003 was US$32.8 billion (57 per cent of GDP) owed mainly to Paris

Club creditors. This has, however, dropped to US$5 billion after a successful debt cancellation agreement with the members of the Paris Club of Creditors.

In conclusion, this section has shown the various ways in which the structural features of the Nigerian economy have contributed to generating excess volatility in Nigeria. The external dependence of the country on monocultural exports and the procyclical nature of a fiscal structure coupled with very weak access to international capital markets provided the country with few opportunities to mitigate the impact of external shocks before they became a major source of economic crisis.

13.4 Reforming the DFA: structural reforms and financial liberalization

Financial sector reforms in Nigeria

Financial liberalization was one important component of the IMF-World Bank supervised structural adjustment program implemented in 1986. In this section we outline the key components of the financial reforms. The process of financial liberalization in Nigeria commenced in 1986 with the establishment of two foreign exchange markets. This was followed in 1987 by the liberalization of interest rates and bank licensing. The foreign exchange markets were subsequently unified. In 1988, foreign exchange bureaus were established, bank portfolio restrictions were relaxed and the Nigerian Deposit Insurance Corporation was established.

Four major initiatives were introduced in 1989. First, banks were permitted to pay interests on demand deposits. Second, auction markets for government securities were introduced. Third, capital adequacy standards were reviewed upwards, and fourth, the extension of credit based on foreign exchange deposits was banned. A risk-weighted capital standard was introduced in 1990 and banks' required paid-up capital was increased. The Central Bank of Nigeria (CBN) also introduced uniform accounting standards for Nigerian banks. Stabilization securities to absorb excess liquidity were introduced the same year. In 1991, bank licensing was embargoed following signs of distress in the banking system. The Bank and Other Financial Institutions Decree (BOFID) was enacted the same year. The decree empowered the CBN to regulate and supervise all financial institutions. However, following a rapid increase in interest rates, the government intervened once again to control interest rates charged by the bank.

In 1992, interest rate controls were removed once again. Government also commenced the privatization of government-owned banks. Other measures introduced in 1992 included the deregulation of the capital market, the reorganization of the foreign exchange market, and the dismantling of credit controls. A change in the orientation of monetary policy in Nigeria started with the introduction of indirect monetary instruments in 1993. The seeds of a banking crisis, which had begun to manifest itself in the country, led to the takeover of five banks for restructuring by the Nigeria Deposit Insurance Corporation (NDIC). In 1994, interest and exchange rate controls were reimposed.

Table 13.7 Minimum required paid-up capital for Nigerian banks, 1989–2005

	Minimum capital requirement		Remarks
Year	**Naira**	**US$**	
1989	20 million	4.4 million	Commercial banks
	10 million	2.2 million	Merchant banks
1991	50 million	5.0 million	Commercial banks
	40 million	4.0 million	Merchant banks
2000	1 billion	10.8 million	All banks (universal banking started)
2003	2 billion	15.4 million	All banks
2004	25 billion	185.2 million	All banks (December 2005 was the deadline to meet capital requirement)

Source: Compiled from Central Bank of Nigeria, Annual Reports.

The Universal Banking Scheme was introduced in 2001, in order to create 'a more level-playing field for the financial sector operators, encourage greater efficiency through economies of scale and foster competition by opening up various areas of entry by banks' (Sanusi, 2004).

In July 2004, the CBN announced the increment of bank capitalization from N2 billion to N25 billion within 18 months.[10] This was designed, among other things, to encourage mergers and consolidation among the banks and to strengthen their performance. This new capitalization is important because of the role that poor capitalization has played in banking crises in the past. Table 13.7 shows the trends in minimum capitalization requirement for Nigerian banks between 1989 and 2005.

In order to improve the corporate governance environment, a Code of Corporate Governance was approved in 2001 and revised in 2006. The Banks and Other Financial Institutions Act (BOFIA) was amended in 2001 to provide additional safeguards against insider abuse and promote good corporate governance by defining the functions and responsibilities of a director and stipulating the procedures for lending and other related practices. The CBN has also adopted codes of good practice both in monetary and financial policies, as well as in the international standards on auditing, and is moving to adopt international accounting standards.

In line with international best practice, the CBN adopted the principles of the Basel Committee on Banking Supervision, including the Prudential Guidelines for licensed banks to promote banking soundness and financial sector stability. The CBN is also making progress in implementing the recommendation of the Financial Action Task Force (FATF) to combat money laundering and advance-fee fraud. In late 1999, IMF staff assessed Nigeria's prudential norms to be largely compliant with the intent of the principle, but noted that, in practice, supervising and enforcement gaps existed, allowing many requirements to be circumvented.

The CBN is already making preparations for the adoption of some of the components of the new Basel Accord. One of the important pillars of Basel II, pillar 3 focuses on market discipline and disclosure requirements that aim to improve the market's ability to assess a bank's risk and values. The CBN hopes that the implementation of Basel II will further strengthen the Nigerian banking sector.

However, problems identified with the implementation of the new Accord in Nigeria include the limited capacity of the regulatory agency to understand and adapt the provision of the new capital accord to suit the Nigerian banking environment. Further, risk agencies are almost nonexistent. There is the need for development of the capital market to allow for the development of risk mitigation techniques, such as asset securitization and the increased issuance of rated bonds. Furthermore, Nigerian banks may find it too expensive to develop, verify, and implement their own risk control models. The inability to do this may make it difficult to achieve the most favorable capital treatment possible and this may affect access to international capital markets. The IFA could therefore assist developing countries like Nigeria to develop the capacity to implement some of the new international standards before they are enforced internationally. Otherwise, developing countries may be put at serious disadvantage in the international capital markets.

There are other ongoing reforms designed to strengthen the DFA and facilitate its capacity to cope with crisis, including opening up the capital market to greater foreign participation. The Nigeria Securities and Exchange Commission (SEC) has signed a Memorandum of Understanding with the Chinese Securities Regulatory Authority, and other MOUs have been signed with South Africa, Ghana, and Uganda. The commission is also in the process of signing the IOSCO's Multilateral Memoranda of Understanding, which will assist in information exchange and full disclosure among member countries.

Most of these reforms were undertaken under the direct supervision or in line with the policy guidelines of the IMF, the World Bank and other international financial institutions. One immediate outcome of the financial sector liberalization was the proliferation of financial institutions in Nigeria. Low entry requirements and high potential rents from the arbitrage exchange market encouraged the creation of new banks. By the end of 1997, the financial system of Nigeria consisted of the central bank, the National Deposit Insurance Company (NDIC), 66 commercial banks, 54 merchant banks and some development banks. In addition, there were 1050 community banks, 275 branches of peoples' banks, more than 600 finance companies, 132 bureaus de change, 200 mortgage and insurance companies, the stock exchange, stock brokers, and discount houses. However, many of these institutions did not survive the ensuing financial crisis in the economy. By the end of 2002, the Nigerian financial sector was made up of 90 commercial banks,[11] 769 community banks, 80 primary mortgage institutions, 102 finance companies, and 83 bureaus de change.

A criticism of the financial liberalization program supervised by the IMF and World Bank in Nigeria has been that of poor sequencing. Ikhide and Alawode (1995) observe that financial liberalization was started without first restoring macroeconomic and financial stability in the economy. Weak financial institutions were neither restructured nor liquidated. The liberalization of bank licensing took place before strengthening the regulatory environment and bank supervision capacity of the central bank. Direct controls were abolished before establishing indirect control instruments. In the light of these policy errors, there was a loss of control over the money supply, and the growth rate in narrow money for 1993 (71.1 per cent) was unprecedented in the record of the previous decade and a half (Ikhide and Alawode, 1995).

Furthermore, the bank reforms were carried out at a time when the entire economy was going through major economic reforms. The financial sector grew more rapidly than the capacity of the regulatory agencies for monitoring and effective supervision. Neither were the appropriate institutions established to guide their operations. However, as Caballero (1999) reported for Mexico, the years of dependence on public sector lending hardly prepared the banks for the risk of lending to the private sector. Most of the newly established banks were owned privately and not necessarily subject to external audit. Their accounts were not rigorously scrutinized and therefore the account statements they prepared were of questionable reliability.

It was not until much later that the financial liberalization addressed the issue of corporate governance among Nigerian banks. The weak corporate governance contributed significantly to the collapse of many banks between 1992 and 2001.[12] There are two features of bank ownership in Nigeria that have adverse impacts on bank soundness. The first relates to government ownership and the second relates to a banking ownership policy that allows an individual 100 per cent ownership of a banking institution. Both types of ownership led to compromise in terms of loans and quality of investment decisions. Apart from ownerships, the banking industry lacked the requisite skills and capacity to assess risks at the point of embarking on financial liberalization. Bank boards and staff were constituted by people without the requisite skills to hold such positions.

One major result of the Nigerian reform experience was the high frequency of changes in regulation and unstable DFA. Because there was no proper footing for the reforms and they were inadequately carried out, they were unable to prevent the crisis. Moreover, there was little progress in the legal and judicial infrastructure to complement the reforms and enforce compliance.

Monetary policy problems

The weakness of the DFA has been complicated by monetary policy problems. The conduct of monetary policy in emerging economies is very difficult (Caballero, 1999). This is because of political interference, the weak financial system, and in the case of Nigeria because of the existence of a large informal credit market that has very weak linkages with the relatively smaller, modern and formal financial sector (Adenikinju and Oyeranti, 1999). The latter characteristic has in particular limited the efficacy of the monetary policy.

The weakness of monetary policy prevented the economy from implementing countercyclical policies. In the first two-and-a-half decades after independence,

Nigeria pursued direct monetary policy that was characterized by credit and interest rate control. The urge to facilitate industrialization and economic development led to an attempt by policymakers to deliberately control interest rates. Through credit guidelines, the government set interest rates and the sectoral allocation of credit. The exchange rate was also administratively determined during this period and was largely stable except for a few instances of limited devaluation of the naira. The CBN was placed under the direct supervision of the Federal Ministry of Finance and was later transferred to the presidency. Over this period, the central bank lacked the autonomy to implement an independent and credible monetary policy.

The weak monetary policy and the lack of independence of the CBN affected the capacity of monetary authorities to contain inflationary pressures in the economy. When the external crisis exerted pressure on the government budget, the CBN was compelled to accommodate the resultant deficit in the government budget. Accommodating monetary policies coupled with a consistent decline in the exchange rate placed pressure on prices. Persistent inflation resulted in currency substitution from naira to international currency and a flight of savings out of the country.[13]

However, following the liberalization of the economy, monetary policy moved in the direction of indirect policy targeting. Both the exchange rate and interest rates were liberalized. This led to a rapid increase in nominal interest rates. Incidentally, interest spreads have increased since the liberalization, which reflects the low efficiency of the financial market. The switch to indirect monetary policy imposes a challenge to the technical capacity of the CBN and to the provision of accurate and timely information. Reliance on indirect instruments such as OMO requires the generation of data on CBN balance sheets and on the banking system as a whole, as well as other information generated by data agencies in the economy.

Insufficient operational autonomy of the central bank and fiscal dominance have made it difficult for the central bank to control the money supply and to achieve its other monetary objectives (IMF, 2004). With the exception of 2004, monetary objectives have not been met, owing to shortcomings in the conduct of monetary policy, which also undermined the development of financial systems. The extensive reliance on reserve requirements and the high liquid asset ratio (at 40 per cent) serves as a tax on financial intermediation and has hampered money market development.

Financing fiscal deficits through ways and means has worsened the problem of inflation over the years. Persistent fiscal deficits financed through borrowing from the central bank have led to expectations about inflation culminating in increased interest rates, as well as the appreciation of exchange rates. Currently, the CBN targets monetary aggregates M2 rather than inflation. The CBN has been granted instrumental autonomy that allows it full discretion on instruments to meet monetary objectives in the economy. Presently, the monetary authority is committed to a stable exchange rate regime and effective liquidity management.

Fiscal policy problems

The structure of public finance in Nigeria also makes it difficult to implement a countercyclical fiscal policy. The public sector is very prominent, and is the largest employer of non-agricultural labor. The operation of fiscal policy depends heavily on volatile oil revenue. Because international oil prices are volatile, the government revenue from oil and gas is also volatile, leading to boom–bust cycles. In addition, steep falls in government revenues impose pressure on domestic credit markets as the government increasingly finances revenue shortfalls through borrowing from the domestic credit market and by ways and means. This keeps the nominal and expected inflation rate high, further worsening distress in the economy.

The government's participation in the capital market is very low. The bonds market is very weak and therefore the money market and the banks continue to meet the credit needs of the government. This crowds out private sector access to credit as well as pushing up interest rates in the domestic economy. The increases in interest rates also put enormous pressures on fiscal targets that again increase the deficit and pressure exchange rates. As the government turns inwards for debt to finance its deficit, there are pressures on interest rates that further amplify the effects of volatility on the economy.

In addition, the banking system is heavily dependent on government accounts and government credit, which contributes to the procyclical impact of government finances. For instance, in 1996, the federal government issued a directive that all commercial and merchant banks, as well as other financial institutions, transfer all public sector deposits at their disposal to the central bank. This directive exposed the overdependence of the banks on public funds. About N8.3 billion or 15 per cent of banking system credit was involved in the exercise. Although the primary purpose of the policy was to shore up the sliding value of the naira, the directive had far-reaching impacts on the liquidity positions of the banks and exposed the problem of mismatched assets and liabilities in some banks that were over-reliant on volatile deposits for long-term lending (Odusola, 2002).

While the CBN remains the main source of funding of government fiscal deficit, the commercial banks also play a very important role (see Figure 13.6). Banks have a very high liquid asset ratio (40 per cent) and hold government papers to meet this requirement. Banks also have, at times, held more government paper than necessary by regulatory standards. This reflects not only the weak macroeconomic environment but also institutional factors, such as inefficiency within the legal system and operations of the courts (delays and backlogs) and difficulties in foreclosing and collecting non-performing loans, all of which discourage banks from lending to the private sector (IMF 2004).

The non-banking financial sector – insurance companies, public and private pension funds, typically the natural investors in government securities in most advanced economies – are not large buyers and holders of government securities. They invest primarily in equity and real estate in Nigeria but have recently become more active buyers of longer-dated state bonds, though there have been

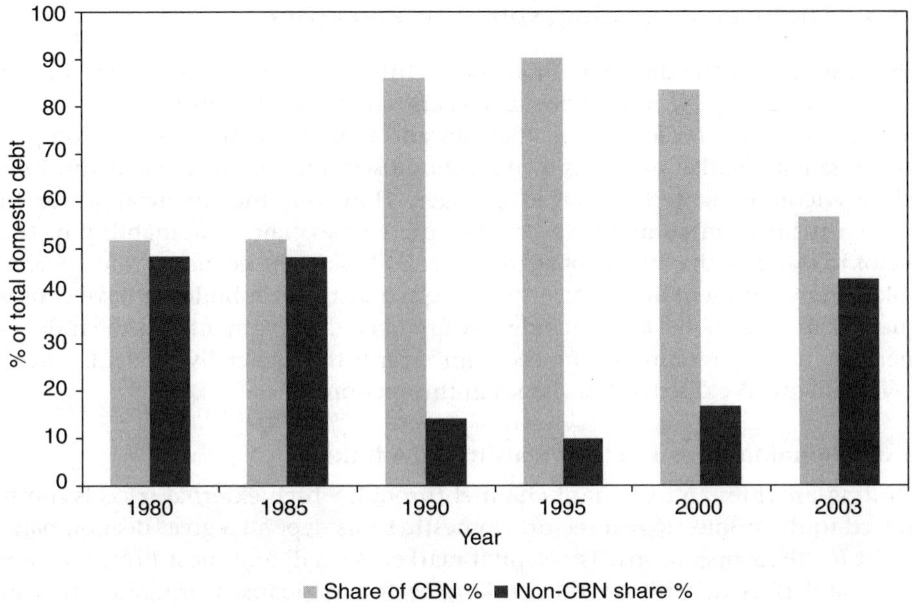

Figure 13.6 CBN versus non-CBN domestic debt as proportion of total domestic debt
Source: CBN (2004), Statistical Bulletin.

very few of such bonds (IMF, 2004). All these mutual dependencies between the government and the monetary and financial institutions affect the ability of the government to pursue countercyclical policies effectively.

A positive development in recent years was the establishment of the Stabilization Fund in 2003. The literature on oil-dependent countries points out that delinking spending from revenue is important in promoting macro stability and creating an enabling environment for growth. The adoption of an oil-based fiscal rule in the 2004 and 2005 budgets has been an important step in improving management of the oil windfall and demonstrates a major departure from the past. Since 2004, the government has adopted a fiscal policy rule determined by a moving average of all prices over the past 3–5 years to insure the economy against a necessary adjustment. Thus, the Stabilization Fund holds excess income from oil exports once the export price rises above a predetermined (budget) price. The establishment of the fund has led to a significant increase in foreign reserves, which by the end of June 2005 reached nearly US$30 billion. In addition, the eventual passage of the Fiscal Responsibility Bill, currently with the National Assembly, will allow for a more coordinated fiscal policy among the three tiers of government.

This section shows that the DFA has become highly unstable under macroeconomic volatility. The frequent changes in the 'rules of the game' fuel the crisis created by macro volatility. In the case of Nigeria, the structure of the economy makes it difficult for the government and monetary authorities to design and effectively implement countercyclical fiscal and monetary policies.

13.5 Financial deepening, volatility, and crises

The structure of the domestic financial architecture (DFA) plays an important role in mitigating or amplifying aggregate volatility. A competitive banking system is essential for long-term efficiency and soundness. An open and competitive financial market exerts its own form of discipline against weak institutions while encouraging well-managed changes. However, the financial sector in Nigeria is far from competitive or efficient. This explains the inability of the sector to mitigate the impact of aggregate volatility on the economy. Moreover, a volatile environment and deficiently-designed institution-building have consequences for the DFA. These include low financial development and the inducement of adaptive responses from economic agents that generally hinder financial development. We discuss these issues in this section.

Institutional failures and the volatility–DFA linkage

Lending provides an important channel through which external crisis is transmitted to the domestic real sector. Domestic firms depend a great deal on bank credit for their operations. The capital market is small and most firms are very small and thus depend on the banking sector for loans. Corporate linkages between firms, especially between foreign-owned firms with better access to international finance and domestic firms are very low, further accentuating the dependence of local firms on available domestic credit channels. The banking system is the dominant financier of the real sector. This makes the banking system vulnerable to adverse macroeconomic influences on the real sector and explains the poor quality of the risk assets of most banks at the moment.

Nigerian-quoted companies are heavily dependent on external finance. In 1985–87, on average, internal funds constituted about 20 per cent of total funds employed by the Nigerian corporate sector, while over 80 per cent of total funds employed were obtained from external funds. Debt constituted the dominant source of external finance, providing almost three-fifths of total funds employed. The importance of debt in the corporate finance portfolio in Nigeria is a function of two major factors – tax advantages that interest payments on debt offer firms and low bankruptcy costs. The slow pace of judicial processes does not favor instituting bankruptcy proceedings against any defaulting firm (Adenikinju, 2002)

The importance of both capital market imperfection and firm dependence on banking finance limits the ability of bank-dependent firms to mitigate the shortfall in bank lending with other sources of finance when policy-induced increases in interest rates (which are both real and nominal) cause a deterioration in the firm's net worth.

At the height of the oil crisis, loans to the private sector declined, limiting the ability of the financial sector to leverage the impact of the volatility. Moreover, the increase in the number of banks did not directly translate into higher credit to the private sector, as many banks prefer to arbitrage on the exchange rate or deal in government papers.

Table 13.8 Nigerian bank system indicators

S/N	Description	1990	1991	1992	1993	1994	1995	1996	1997	1998	1999	2000	2001
1	Number of banks	107	119	120	120	116	115	115	115	89	90	89	90
2	Ratio of deposits of distressed banks to total deposits (%)	9	8	16	33	55	60	50	47	15	13	12	9
3	Ratio of deposits of distressed banks to total deposits (%)	14.6	4.4	18.1	19.2	29.4	14.1	14.7	9	3.5	1.6	2.5	2
4	Ratio of distressed banks to total assets of all banks (%)	23.7	16.4	20.9	16.1	18.6	19.8	11	7.6	3.9	1.5	2	3
5	Amount required for recapitalization of distressed banks (N billion)	2	2.4	5.5	13.6	23.4	30.5	43.9	42.8	15.5	15.3	10.3	12.1

Source: NDIC, Annual Reports.

The adoption of the Prudential Guidelines in line with the 1988 Basel Capital Accord exposed the very weak state of Nigerian banks. As can be seen in Table 13.8, the number of distressed banks fluctuated from 9 in 1990 to a peak of 60 in 1995, falling back to 50 and 47 in 1996 and 1997, respectively. The ratio of deposits of banks in crisis to total deposits of the banking system peaked at 29.4 per cent in 1994 from where it fluctuated to 2 per cent in 2001. Also, the ratio of total assets of distressed banks to total assets of all banks stood at a high of 23.7 per cent in 1990 and fluctuated to 3 per cent in 2001.

The weak state of the banks makes them incapable of providing effective leverage to the volatility from the external sources that became rampant during the period of economic crisis. Rather, the weak state of the banks amplified the volatility crisis and, inadvertently, the banking crisis itself became a major source of volatility in the economy.

The Nigerian experience shows that there is a bi-directional causality between the banking crisis and volatility. Volatility weakens the macroeconomic environment. Demirguc-Kunt and Detragiache (1998) in a study of 65 countries between 1980 and 1994 find that a banking crisis erupts when the macroeconomic environment is weak, particularly when growth is low and inflation is high. 'Macroeconomic shocks deteriorate the financial position of domestic agents and performances of loan portfolios and structural weaknesses of the financial system impair the financial systems resilience to these shocks' (le Fort, 1989, cited in Odusola, 2002). Wide swings in relative prices, which increased the proportion of non-performing bank loans, also had a negative impact on the health of the financial system. Moreover, external volatility that impacts on fiscal deficit, foreign exchange instability, and oscillating inflation have devastating effects on the income flow and the financial structure of economic agents, enterprises, and financial institutions (Odusola, 2002). This was the exact experience of Nigeria.

Odusola (2002) finds that the deterioration in the banking system's health contributes very significantly to the price increases in the economy. In fact, the period when the banking crisis was most pronounced (1992–96) coincided with the worst period of price movements over the past three decades in Nigeria.

On the other hand, the banking crisis also contributed to volatility in Nigeria. A banking crisis weakens the economy's institutional capacity to reduce the impact of volatility on the growth process. This stems from various channels. First, a reduction in the quality of certain financial services, especially credit intermediation, results in an increase in the real cost of credit intermediation and impairs the flow of credit to the real sector. Second, a weak and vulnerable banking system may impede recovery and jeopardize macroeconomic instability (Bernanke, 1983). Evidently in Nigeria, the period of banking crisis was characterized by very high inflation rates, high lending rates and low capacity utilization of industrial enterprises. As we have seen, the leverage of Nigerian firms is high. High leverage aggravates the impact of volatility, as the interest rate, the inflation rate, and slow economic growth increase the rate of non-performing loans and worsen the bank crisis. Finally, a banking crisis raises the demand for real money balances as depositors take flight to higher quality owing to a rise in uncertainty in payment systems and credit market conditions.[14]

Another consequence of the volatile macroeconomic environment is the short-term nature of contracts. Economic agents are unwilling to enter into long-term contractual relationships. Banks prefer to lend short term and firms commit to short-term investments. The absence of opportunities to insure away risks associated with long-term contracts and the weakness of the judicial and legal system play an important role in this development in the economy. In addition to the incentives provided by the foreign exchange markets, bouts of macroeconomic instability also make lending (other than short-term) less attractive, and the level of private credit in Nigeria drifted from about 20 per cent of GDP in 1986 to nearly 10 per cent in the early 1990s (IMF, 2004).

Figure 13.7 is illustrative of the points being raised here. We see a clear illustration of the preference of deposit banks for short-term lending.

Therefore, for the long-term development of interest in the economy, there is a need for deposit banks to attract a reasonably stable deposit base as opposed to volatile short-term deposits. The lack of secondary market liquidity is a key structural obstacle to long-term finance in Nigeria. The absence of a secondary market for government and corporate bonds creates substantial liquidity risk for investors as they are less willing to invest in long-term securities without liquid exit options.

Financial underdevelopment problem

The weak financial development of the Nigerian economy contributes to the inability of economic agents to diversify risk. According to Caballero (1999), 'The development of domestic financial markets is instrumental not only to foster investment and growth, but also to aggregate resources during distress.' The Nigerian financial market is very shallow, limiting its capacity to diversify risks

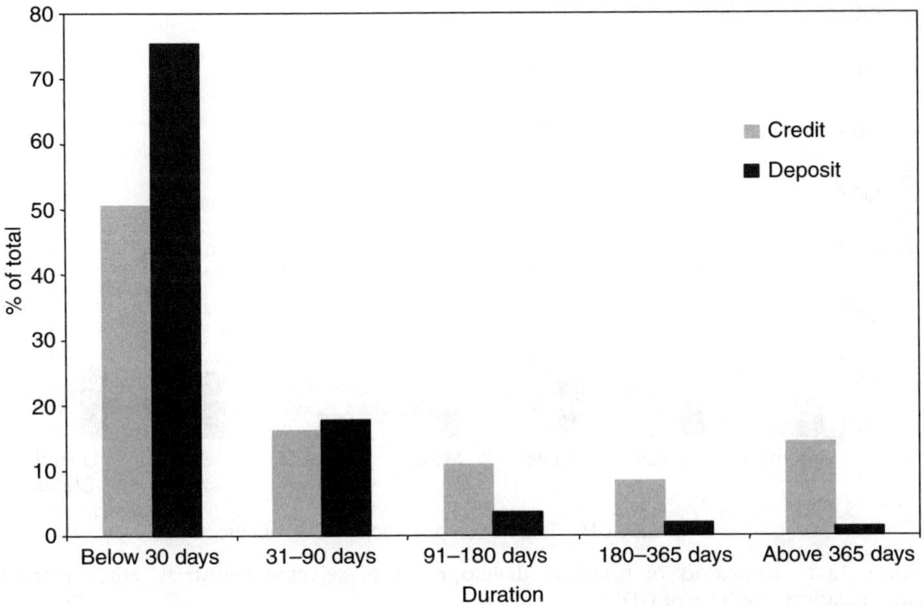

Figure 13.7 Deposit and credit structure of deposit banks in Nigeria, 2005 (%)
Source: World Bank (2006).

arising from external volatility. The financial system is underdeveloped and the level of financial intermediation – narrow M2/GDP ratio, low private sector credit/GDP ratio and large share of cash transactions – is low. The use of credit cards and leasing arrangements is limited. Moveables, such as equipment, inventory or receivables, cannot be pledged as security. Mortgage loans in Nigeria are less than 0.5 per cent of GDP compared to about 18 per cent in South Africa, and the markets for debentures and bonds are largely nonexistent.

There are several ways of measuring the size and efficiency of the financial sector. These include M2/GDP, market capitalization and interest rate spread. The shallowness of the domestic financial market is reflected in the low M2/GDP ratio (26 per cent at end of 2003), high domestic debt/M2 ratio and narrow investor base, with the banking sector being the main holder of government securities. The low financial deepening created by weak institutions and volatility makes risk management very difficult. The shallow financial market adversely influences interest rates and risks, in addition to crowding out private sector credit in the face of the government's large borrowing requirements (IMF, 2004). The low share of capital markets in the Nigerian economy further attests to the low risk diversification outlet for the private sector to mitigate the impact of aggregate volatility on consumption.

Figure 13.8 provides a cross-country comparison of some indicators of financial development between Nigeria and selected countries. The figure confirms the relatively low level of financial development in the emerging countries and, in particular, Nigeria.

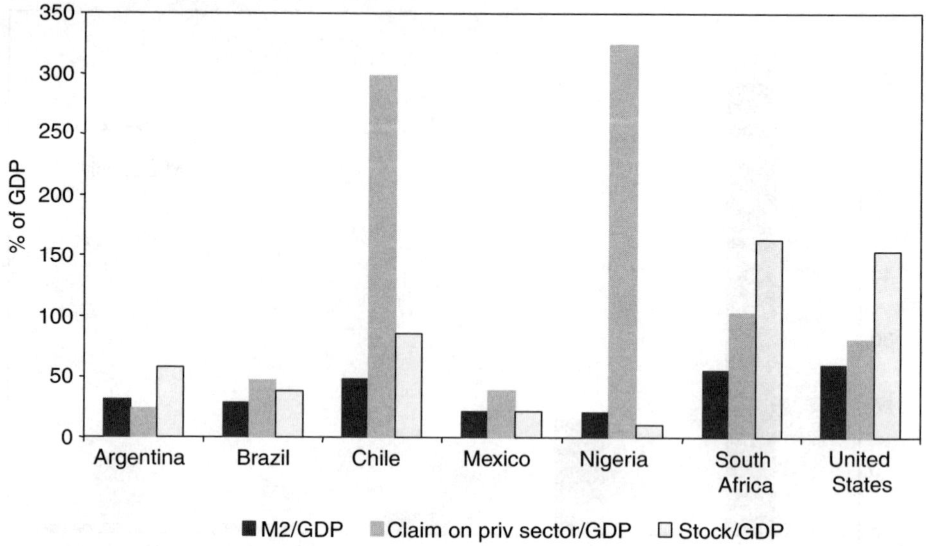

Figure 13.8 Indicators of financial development of selected countries' stock market capitalization, 2000 (% of GDP)
Source: World Bank (2004), World Development Indicators.

Another indicator of the shallowness of the financial sector is the high interest rate spread between lending and deposit rates. Cross-country studies have shown that high interest spreads limit the breath and depth of banking sectors. In particular, countries with higher spreads have substantially lower levels of credit to the private sector (as a share of GDP). The high interest rate premium is suggestive of an inefficient financial sector. Incidentally, the interest rate spread increased during the period of liberalization relative to the pre-liberalization period, reflecting the oligopolistic structure of the Nigerian banking sector.

Senbet (2001) notes that a symptom of a weak financial sector is a higher cost of funds than would prevail with better functioning financial markets since creditors are likely to demand higher interest rates relative to an environment where bankruptcy, effective enforcement of debt contracts, covenant and/or collaterized, are effective. The high cost of intermediation is also a reflection of the high cost environment where banks have to provide their own infrastructure such as electricity, satellite communication with branches, and security for transporting cash. In addition, high staff cost, high provision for loan losses, and insider fraud were common reflections of the problems of managerial agencies which constrained the efficient functioning of the system.

In sum, macro volatility worsens the weak state of financial institutions in the country. This, in turn, affects their capacity to provide domestic agents with options to mitigate the impact of externally induced macro volatility. The preference of economic agents for short-term contracts, capital flight, and other non-optimal decisions actually block growth and amplify the impact of macroeconomic volatility.

13.6 Conclusion

The main hypothesis which the Nigerian study has confirmed is that there is a bi-directional causal relationship between volatility and financial institutions that constrains DFA reforms and weakens the linkage between the DFA and the IFA. The key findings of our study are consistent with the hypotheses of the project. First, we find that the structural features of Nigeria, including the high concentration of exports, weak integration with the international financial market, and poor-quality fiscal policy, plus the failures of domestic financial institutions contributed to generating excess volatility and crisis in the Nigerian economy during the period under study.

Second, we find that macro-instability leads to financial crisis which induces endogenous modification in regulations, as was experienced during the period of financial liberalization in Nigeria. However, as the country experience has shown, the prevalence of weak institutions makes it difficult to have a strong DFA that can enforce banking regulations, prudential guidelines and corporate governance that can protect all shareholders. We find that during the period of crisis, the DFA became very unstable and changes in regulations became frequent.

Third, we show that the weak state of financial institutions and imperfect financial markets have prevented economic agents from diversifying away from the sources of shocks and have thus amplified rather than mitigated the impact of these shocks on the economy. The response of economic agents to the weak DFA and macro volatility include shortening of contracts, capital flight, and the procyclical generation of deficit, all of which further deteriorate the DFA and worsen volatility.

Finally we find that there were limited options available for domestic economic agents to manage risk efficiently. This leads to inefficient means of risk management as agents resort to 'real' rather than 'financial' means to manage risk. In Nigeria, economic agents insure themselves against the impact of volatility by shifting from financial assets to real estate, in particular.

The Nigerian experience with financial liberalization, which was designed to manage the impact of volatility and crisis in the economy, shows a number of issues that are important for the DFA-IFA linkage. First, it is important to pay attention to the sequencing and pace of reforms, as well as to the state of the DFA. This implies that reforms must be tailored to particular country experiences, as well as the state of financial development rather than fostering 'one-size-fits-all' sets of policies on all developing countries. The capacity of the country to implement the various international statutes and codes to which it is a signatory is also very important. Although Nigeria is a signatory to a number of international codes and protocols, many of these have not yet been enacted domestically; nor is the country in a position to implement all of them. The international financial institutions could play a visible role in helping to establish and build domestic capacity to implement many of the international codes and protocols.

In addition, given the structural features of the Nigerian economy and the state of financial development, the IFA could be valuable to the extent that it allows a smoothing of volatility in financial conditions, and assists in the diversification of national risk. There is an evident need to strengthen the country's link with international financial markets. International trade must also be made more favorable. The country's efforts to diversify its economy from reliance on exports of primary product are being frustrated by, among other things, trade barriers in the OECD countries and other domestic supply capacity constraints. In spite of WTO agreements, developed countries use significant tariff and non-tariff barriers to restrict developing country exports, in particular manufactures. There is a tariff escalation on processed products and high tariffs on imports that are of interest to Nigeria. The indiscriminate use of standards, sanitary and phytosanitary (SPS), are among the significant challenges facing attempts by Nigeria to diversify its export base. The country also needs assistance in addressing its domestic supply-side capacity constraints.

The IFA could also assist developing countries like Nigeria to reduce commodity fluctuations, strengthen their capacities to cope with commodity fluctuations and improve their response capacities to short-term volatilities. One way to do this is by creating stabilization funds that developing countries can tap into without the present tough conditionality imposed by the IMF and the World Bank. The existing IFA has not been very relevant in preventing or managing economic crisis in Nigeria. It is perceived within the economy that the current IFA structure and conditionality are more focused on ensuring that the country meets its commitments to creditors.

Finally, IFA policies must be designed to assist in deepening the financial sector. In particular, the issues of legal and judicial reforms and corporate governance are critical and must catch up with the other financial liberation policies taking place in the economy.

Notes

1. Members of the Paris Club to which Nigeria owes the bulk of the debt recently cancelled Nigeria's external debt after the country agreed to pay US$12 billion out of the US$30 billion debt. Nigeria's external debt now stands at US$5 billion owed mainly to members of the London Club of Creditors.
2. This was primarily due to pressures from strong interest groups and to the slow pace of the benefits of reforms.
3. Most of our analyses are done using annual data because of the absence of quarterly data series for most of the variables of interests.
4. We are grateful to José María Fanelli for pointing this out to us. We will refer to these below.
5. The correlation coefficient between the growth rates of output and consumption was 0.31 compared to 0.07 between growth rates of output and savings.
6. See Fanelli (2005b) for formal proof of this.
7. We use US consumption growth as a proxy. All variables are from World Bank Economic Indicators from 1965 to 2000.
8. This is measured as reserve accumulation minus trade balance.

9. One major development that may have a significant impact on fiscal relations between the tiers of government is the Fiscal Responsibility Bill, which is still under discussion in the National Assembly. It prescribes among other things how excess revenue from oil exports will be treated instead of just sharing the proceeds between all the tiers of government, as is now the practice.
10. Although there was initial resistance to the consolidation efforts, a relatively successful outcome was achieved within the time frame originally stipulated by the CBN.
11. Including the former merchant banks.
12. Even with the release of the new corporate governance guidelines by the CBN, enforcement remains an important issue. However, the fact that all the new 26 banks are quoted on the Nigerian Stock Exchange will allow the market to exercise some control and discipline on the operations of the banks.
13. See Ajayi (1992) for a detailed discussion on capital flight in Nigeria.
14. Sobodu (2000) reports that depositors shift funds into real estate that does not depreciate during periods of inflation.

References

Acemoglu D., S. Johnson, J. Robinson and Y. Thaicharoen (2003), 'Institutional Causes, Macroeconomic Syndrome: Volatility, Crisis, and Growth', *Journal of Monetary Economics*, 50: 49–123.

Acemoglu D., S. Johnson and J. Robinson (2004), 'Institutions as the Fundamental Cause of Long-run Growth', NBER Working Paper 10481.

ACFB (Editorial Committee of Almanac of China's Finance and Banking) (1995).

Adenikinju, O.O. (2002), 'Capital Structure and the risk of Corporate Failure: the case of Nigeria', unpublished PhD thesis submitted to the Department of Economics, University of Ibadan, Ibadan.

Adenikinju, A. (2003), 'African Imperatives in the New World Trade Order: Country Case Study of the Manufacturing Sector: Nigeria', Final Report Submitted to the AERC, Nairobi, Kenya.

Adenikinju, A.F. and O.A. Oyeranti (1999), 'Characteristics and Behaviour of African Factor Markets and Market Institutions and their Consequences for Economic Growth', CID Working Paper 31, Harvard University.

Aghion, Ph., G.-M. Angeletos, A. Banerjee and K. Manova (2004), 'Volatility and Growth: Financial Development and the Cyclical Composition of Investment', mimeo, http://elsa.berkeley.edu/users/webtac/auerbach/e231_f04/aghion.pdf.

Aghion, Ph., Ph. Baccheta, R. Ranciere and K. Rogoff (2006), 'Exchange Rate Volatility and Productivity Growth: the Role of Financial Development', NBER Working Paper, 12117.

Agosin, M. (2001), 'Strengthening Regional Financial Cooperation', *CEPAL Review*, 73 (April); Santiago, Chile: Economic Commission of Latin America and the Caribbean (ECLAC).

Ahmed, S., A. Levin and B.A. Wilson (2004), 'Recent US Macroeconomic Stability: Good Policies, Good Practices, or Good Luck?', *Review of Economics and Statistics*, 86(3): 824–32.

Aizenman, J. and N. Marion (1999), 'Volatility and Investment: Interpreting Evidence from Developing Countries', *Economica*, 66(262): 157–79.

Aizenman, J. and B. Pinto (2004), *Managing Volatility and Crisis: a Practitioner's Guide*, New York: Cambridge University Press.

Ajayi, S.I. (1992), 'An Economic Analysis of Capital Flight from Nigeria', World Bank Policy Research Working Paper, 993.

Ajayi, S.I. and A. Adenikinju (2006), 'Domestic Financial Architecture, Macro Volatility and Institutions: the Nigerian Case', paper prepared for the CEDES-IDRC project 'International Financial Architecture, Macro Volatility, and Institutions: the Developing World Experience'.

Athanasoulis, S., R. Shiller and E. van Wincoop (1999), 'Macro Markets and Financial Security', *FRNBY Economic Policy Review*, April: 21–39.

Ayogu, M. and H. Dezhbakhsh (2006), 'International Financial Architecture, Macroeconomic Volatility and Institutions: South Africa Experience', paper prepared for the CEDES-IDRC project 'International Financial Architecture, Macro Volatility, and Institutions: the Developing World Experience'.

Bank for International Settlements (BIS) (2001), '71st Annual Report', June, Basel.

Bank for International Settlements (BIS) (2005), '75th Annual Report', June, Basel.

Basel Committee on Banking Supervision (1997), 'Core Principles for Effective Banking Supervision', Basel, September.

Basu, S. and A. Taylor (1999), 'Business Cycles in International Historical Perspective', NBER Working Paper, 7090, http://www.nber.org/papers/w7090.pdf.

Batini, N. (2004), 'Achieving and Maintaining Price Stability in Nigeria', IMF Working Paper, WP/04/97.
Bayoumi, T. and B. Eichengreen (1992), 'Shocking Aspects of European Monetary Unification', NBER Working Paper, 3949.
Bebczuk, R., J.M. Fanelli and J. Pradelli (2003), 'Determinants and Consequences of Financial Constraints Facing Firms in Argentina', in A. Galindo and F. Schiantarelli (eds), *Credit Constraints and Investment in Latin America*, Washington: Inter-American Development Bank.
Beck, T., R. Levine and N. Loayza (2000), 'Finance and the Sources of Growth', *Journal of Financial Economics*, 58: 261–300
Beck, T., A. Demirguc-Kunt and R. Levine (2001), 'Law, Politics, and Finance', World Bank Policy Research Working Paper Series, 2585, The World Bank, Washington, DC, July.
Beck, T., A. Demirguc-Kunt and V. Maksimovic (2003), 'Bank Competition, Financing Obstacles and Access to Credit', World Bank Working Paper, 2996,
Bergsten, C.F. (2000), 'A Shanghai Asia Pacific Financial Institute', unpublished manuscript, Institute for International Economics, Washington, DC.
Bergsten, C.F. and Y.C. Park (2002), 'Toward Creating a Regional Monetary Arrangement in East Asia', ADB Institute Research Paper, No. 50, Tokyo.
Bernanke, B.S. (1983), 'Non-monetary Effects of the Financial Crises in the Propagation of the Great Depression', *American Economic Review*, 73: 257–76.
Berkowitz, D., K. Pistor and J.F. Richard (2003), 'Economic Development, Legality, and the Transplant Effect', *European Economic Review*, 47(1): 165–95.
Berry, A. (2006), 'Improving Measurement of Latin American Inequality and Poverty with an Eye to Equitable Growth Policy', mimeo, University of Toronto.
Bhagwati, J. (2004), *In Defense of Globalization*, New York: Oxford University Press.
Blanchard, O. (2004), 'Fiscal Dominance and Inflation Targeting: Lessons from Brazil', NBER Working Paper, 10389.
Blanchard, O. and J. Simon (2001), 'The Long and Large Decline in US Output Volatility', *Brookings Papers on Economic Activity*, 1: 135–64.
Blanchard, O., F. Giavazzi and F. Sa (2005), 'International Investors, the US Current Account, and the Dollar', *Brookings Papers on Economic Activity*, 1: 1–66.
Bolton, P. and X. Freixas (2000), 'Equity, Bonds and Bank Debt: Capital Structure and Financial Market Equilibrium under Asymmetric Information', *Journal of Political Economy*, 108(2): 324–51.
Booth L., V. Aivazian, A. Demirguc-Kunt and V. Maksimovic (2001), 'Capital Structures in Developing Countries', *Journal of Finance*, 56(1): 87–130.
Bordo, M., B. Eichengreen, D. Klingebiel and M. Martínez-Peria (2001), 'Is the Crisis Problem Growing More Severe?', *Economic Policy*, 32(April): 51–82.
Borensztein, E. and P. Mauro (2004), 'The Case for GDP-indexed Bonds', *Economic Policy* (April): 165–216.
Brandt, L. and X. Zhu (2000), 'Redistribution in a Decentralized Economy: Growth and Inflation in China under Reform', *Journal of Political Economy*, 108(2): 422–39.
Bresser Pereira, L.C., J.M. Maravall and A. Przeworski (1993), *Economic Reforms in New Democracies: a Social-democratic Approach*, New York: Cambridge University Press.
Brown, G. (1998), 'The New International Financial Architecture: Codes and Standards and the Developing Countries', Speech to the Annual Meeting of the International Monetary Fund and the World Bank, Washington, DC, 6 October.
Buch, C.M., J. Dopke and C. Pierdxioch (2005), 'Financial Openness and Business Cycle Volatility', *Journal of International Money and Finance*, 24(5) (September): 744–65.
Buira, A. (2005), 'Financial Crises and International Cooperation: Briefing Note Prepared for the Orderly Resolution of Financial Crises: a G20-led Initiative', 29 and 30 January 2005, Mexico, www.globalcentres.org.
Caballero, R. (1999), 'Structural Volatility in Mexico: a Policy Report', unpublished manuscript, MIT.

Caballero, R. (2000a), 'Aggregate Volatility in Modern Latin America: Causes and Cures', *Economia*, 1(1) (Fall): 31–108, reprinted in *Estudios de Economia*, 28(1) (June 2001) 5–52.

Caballero, R. (2000b), 'Macroeconomic Volatility in Latin America: a View and Three Case Studies', NBER Working Paper, 7782.

Caballero, R. (2002), 'Coping with Chile's External Vulnerability: a Financial Problem', in N. Loayza and R. Soto (eds), *Economic Growth: Sources, Trends, and Cycles*, Banco Central de Chile.

Caballero, R. (2003), 'On the International Financial Architecture: Insuring Emerging Markets', NBER Working Paper, 9570.

Caballero. R., K. Cowan and J. Kearns (2005a), 'Fear of Sudden Stops: Lessons from Australia and Chile', NBER Working Paper, 10519.

Caballero, R., E. Farhi and P.O. Gourinchas (2005b), 'An Equilibrium Model of "Global Imbalances" and Low Interest Rates', unpublished manuscript, MIT and University of California, Berkeley.

Calomiris, C. W. and A. Powell (2000), 'Can Emerging Market Bank Regulators Establish Credible Discipline? The Case of Argentina, 1992–1999', NBER Working Paper Series, 7715.

Calvo, G. and E. Mendoza (2000), 'Rational Contagion and the Globalization of Securitized Markets', *Journal of International Economics*, 51: 79–113.

Calvo, G. and C.M. Reinhart (1999), 'Capital Flow Reversals, the Exchange Rate Rebate, and Dollarization', *Finance and Development*, 36(3): 13–15.

Calvo, G. and C.M. Reinhart (2000), 'Fixing for Your Life,' *Brookings Trade Forum 2000*: 1–38, Washington DC: Brookings Institution Press.

Calvo, G. and C.M. Reinhart (2002), 'Fear of Floating', *Quarterly Journal of Economics*, 117(2): 379–408.

Calvo, G. and E. Talvi (2004), 'Sudden Stop, Financial Factors and Economic Collapse: a View from the Latin American Frontlines', paper presented in the Universal Forum for Cultures, Barcelona, September.

Calvo, G., L. Leiderman and C. Reinhart (1993), 'Capital Inflows and Real Exchange Rate Appreciation in Latin America: the Role of External Factors', *IMF Staff Papers*, 40(March): 108–51.

Campbell J., M. Lettau, B. Malkiel and Y. Xu (2000), 'Have Individual Stocks Become More Volatile? An Empirical Exploration of Idiosyncratic Risk', NBER Working Paper, 7590.

Caprio, G. and D. Klingebiel (1996), 'Bank Insolvencies: Cross-country Experience', World Bank Policy Research Working Paper, 1620, Washington, DC, July.

Carvalho, F.J.C. (1991), 'A Post Keynesian Approach to Inflation, High Inflation and Hyperinflation', in P. Davidson and J. Kregel (eds), *Economic Problems of the 1990s*, Cheltenham: Edward Elgar.

Carvalho, F.J.C. (1993), 'Strato-inflation and High Inflation: the Brazilian Experience', *Cambridge Journal of Economics*, 17 (1) (March): 63–78.

Carvalho, F.J.C. (1998), 'The Real Stabilization Plan and the Banking Sector in Brazil', *Banca Nazionale Del Lavoro Quarterly Review*, 51 (206) (September): 291–326.

Cassim, R., D. Onyango, Z. Skosana and D.E. van Seventer (2003), 'A Review of the Changing Composition of the South African Economy', unpublished paper prepared for the Presidency's Ten Year Cabinet Review (at http://www.sarpn.org.za).

Castro, A. (1994), 'Renegade Development: Rise and Demise of State-led Development in Brazil', in W.C. Smith, C.H. Acuña and E.A. Gamarra (eds), *Democracy, Market and Structural Reform in Latin America*, Miami: Transaction Publishers.

Cavallo, M. and G. Majnoni (2001), 'Do Banks Provision for Bad Loans in Good Times: Empirical Evidence and Policy Implications', mimeo, World Bank, Washington, DC, June.

Chen, S. and M. Ravallion (2004), 'How Have the World's Poorest Fared since the Early 1980s?' Development Research Group, World Bank, Washington, DC.

Cifuentes, R., J. Desoemeaux and C. Gonzáles (2002), 'Capital Markets in Chile: From Financial Repression to Financial Deepening', Economic Policy Paper, Central Bank of Chile, 4.

Claessens, S. (2004), 'Finance and Volatility', in J. Aizenman and B. Pinto (eds), *Managing Volatility and Crisis. A Practitioner's Guide*, New York: Cambridge University Press.

Clements M. and D. Hendry (1998), *Forecasting Economic Time Series*, Cambridge: Cambridge University Press.

Cline, W.R. (2005), 'The Case for a New Plaza Agreement', Policy Briefs in International Economics, 05–4, Institute for International Economics, December.

Cogley, T. (1990), 'International Evidence on the Size of the Random Walk in Output', *Journal of Political Economy*, 98: 501–18.

Collier, P. and J. Dehn (2001), 'Aid, Shocks and Growth', Policy Research Working Paper, No. 2688, World Bank

Confederação Nacional da Indústria, Financiamento no Brasil (2003), *Desafio ao Crescimento*, Brasília: CNI.

Conlisk, J. (1996), 'Why Bounded Rationality?', *Journal of Economic Literature*, 34: 669–700.

Corsetti, G., P. Pesenti and N. Roubini (1998), 'What Caused the Asian Currency and Financial Crisis? Part I: A Macroeconomic Overview', NBER Working Paper, No. 6833, Cambridge, MA.

Culpeper, R. (2006), 'Reforming the Global Financial Architecture: the Potential of Regional Institutions', in J.A. Ocampo (ed.), *Regional Financial Cooperation*, Washington, DC: Brookings Institution Press and ECLAC.

Cunha, P. (2003), 'Viabilizando a Transformação: O Financiamento do Desenvolvimento', UFRJ mimeo, Rio de Janiero.

Cyert, R.M. and J.G. March (1963), *A Behavioral Theory of the Firm*, Englewood Cliffs, NJ: Prentice-Hall.

De Brouwer, G. and Y. Wang (2004), *Financial Governance in East Asia: Policy Dialogue, Surveillance and Cooperation*, London: Routledge Curzon Studies in the Growth Economies of Asia.

De Gregorio, J., S. Edwards and R. Valdes (2000), 'Controls on Capital Inflows: Do they Work?' *Journal of Development Economics*, 63: 59–83.

De Nicoló, G., P. Honohan and A. Ize (2003), 'Dollarization of the Banking System: Good or Bad', IMF Working Paper, WP/03/146, Washington, DC, July.

Dehn, J. (2000), 'The Effects on Growth of Commodity Price Uncertainty and Shocks', Policy Research Working Paper, 2455, World Bank, Washington, DC.

Demirguc-Kunt, A. and E. Detragiache (1998), 'The Determinants of Banking Crises in Developing and Developed Countries', *IMF Staff Papers*, 45 (1) (March): 81–109.

Denizer, C., M.F. Iyigun and A.L. Owen (2000), 'Finance and Macroeconomic Volatility', World Bank Policy Research Working Paper, 2487, Washington DC.

Dmitriyev M., M. Matovnikov, L. Mikhailov, L. Sycheva, Y. Timofeev and A. Warner (1996), *Rossiyskiye Banky Nakanune Finansovoy Stabilizatsii*, St Petersburg: Norma.

DNA (Department of National Accounts, National Bureau of Statistics of China) (2004), *Data of Gross Domestic Product of China*, 1996–2002, Beijing: China Statistical Press.

DNEA (Department of National Economic Accounts, National Bureau of Statistics of China) (1997), *Historical Data of Gross Domestic Product of China, 1952–1995*, Shenyang: Northeast University of Finance and Economics Press

Dodd, R. and S. Spiegel (2005), 'Up from Sin: a Portfolio Approach to Financial Salvation', in Ariel Buira (ed.), *The IMF and the World Bank at Sixty*, London: Anthem Press, pp. 85–115.

Doyle, O. and J. Fidrmuc (2003), 'Anatomy of Voting Behaviour and Attitudes during Post-Communist Transition: Czech Republic 1990–98', CEPR Discussion Paper, DP3801, London.

Easterly, W. (2001), *The Elusive Quest for Growth*, Cambridge, Massachusetts: MIT Press.

Easterly W., R. Islam and J. Stiglitz (2000), 'Shaken and Stirred: Explaining Growth Volatility', Annual World Bank Conference on Development Economics.

Edwards, S. (1991), 'El Monetarismo en Chile, 1973–1983: algunos enigmas de la economía', in S. Edwards and S. Teitel (eds), *Crecimiento, Reforma y Ajuste: las políticas comerciales y macroeconómicas de América Latina en los decenios e 1970 y 1980*, Fondo de Cultura Económica – BID, México/Argentina.

Edwards, S. (1999), 'How Effective are Capital Controls', *Journal of Economic Perspectives*, 13 (4): 65–84.

Edwards, S. and I. Magendzo (2003), 'A Currency of One's Own? An Empirical Investigation on Dollarization and Independent Currency Unions', NBER Working Paper, 9514.

Edwards, S. and R. Rigobon (2005), 'Capital Controls, Exchange Rate Volatility and External Vulnerability', NBER Working Paper, 11434.

Eichengreen, B. (2003), 'What to Do with the Chiang Mai Initiative', *Asian Economic Papers*, 2: 1–49.

Eichengreen, B. (2004), 'Global Imbalances and the Lessons of Bretton Woods', NBER Working Paper, 10497, May.

Eichengreen, B. and T. Bayoumi (1999), 'Is Asia an Optimum Currency Area? Can It Become One? Regional, Global and Historical Perspectives on Asian Monetary Relations', in S. Collignon, J. Pisani-Ferry and Y.C. Park (eds), *Exchange Rate Policies in Emerging Asian Countries*, Routledge Studies in the Growth Economies of Asia, London and New York: Routledge.

Eichengreen, B. and P. Luengnaruemitchai (2004), 'Why Doesn't Asia Have Bigger Bond Markets?', NBER Working Paper, 10576.

Eichengreen, B., R. Hausmann and U. Panizza (2003), 'Currency Mismatches, Debt Intolerance and Original Sin: Why They Are Not the Same and Why They Matter', NBER Working Paper, 10036, October.

Eichengreen, B., K. Kletzer and A. Mody (2005), 'The IMF in a World of Private Capital Markets', NBER Working Paper, 11198.

Erikson, R.S. (1989), 'Economic Conditions and the Presidential Vote', *American Political Science Review*, 83(2): 567–73.

Fair, R.C. (2004), 'A Vote Equation and the 2004 Election', New Haven, Yale University, http://fairmodel.econ.yale.edu.

Fan Q., U. Lee and M. Schaffer (1996), 'Firms, Banks and Credit in Russia', in S. Commander, Q. Fan and M. Schaffer (eds), *Enterprise Restructuring and Economic Policy in Russia*, EDI, World Bank, pp. 140–65.

Fanelli, J.M. (2002), 'Growth, Instability and the Convertibility Crisis in Argentina', *ECLAC Review*, 77.

Fanelli, J.M. (2004), 'Methodological Background Paper for the Project: International Financial Architecture, Macro Volatility, and Institutions: the Developing World Experience', CEDES, September 2004.

Fanelli, J.M. (2005a), 'Notes on International Volatility for the Country Studies', mimeo, CEDES.

Fanelli, J.M. (2005b), 'Domestic Financial Architecture, Macro Volatility and Institutions: the Argentine Case', mimeo, CEDES.

Fanelli, J.M (2006), 'Macro Volatility and Financial Institutions', CEDES, Argentina, May.

Fanelli, J.M. and M. Gonzalez Rozada (2003), 'Business Cycle and Macroeconomic Policy Coordination in Mercosur', mimeo, CEDES.

Fanelli, J.M. and S. Keifman (2002), 'Finance and Changing Trade Patterns in Developing Countries: the Argentine Case', in J.M. Fanelli and R. Medhora (eds), *Finance and Competitiveness in Developing Countries*, London and New York: Routledge, pp. 21–44.

Fanelli, J.M. and R. Medhora (2001), 'The Emerging International Financial Architecture and its Implications for Domestic Financial Architecture', Latin America Research Group, Federal Reserve Bank of Atlanta. Proceedings of the conference 'Domestic

Capital and Global Finance in Latin America', Miami, Florida, November 1–2, www.frbatlanta.org/econ_rd/larg/larg_index.cfm.

Fanelli, J.M. and G. McMahon (2006), 'Introduction to the Regional Syntheses and Country Case Studies', in J. Fanelli and G. McMahon (eds), *Understanding Market Reforms vol. II*, Basingstoke: Palgrave Macmillan.

Fanelli, J.M., M. Gonzalez Rozada and S. Keifman (2001), 'Comercio, régimen cambiario y Volatilidad: Una visión desde la Argentina de la Coordinación Macroeconómica en el Mercosur', in J.M. Fanelli (ed.), *Coordinación de políticas macroeconómicas en el Mercosur*, Madrid: Siglo XXI, pp. 25–70.

Feldstein, M. and C. Horioka (1980), 'Domestic Saving and International Capital Flows', *Economic Journal*, 90 (358): 314–29.

Feltenstein, A. and S. Iwata (2005), *Journal of Development Economics*, 76 (2): pp. 481–501.

Fernández de Lis, S., J. Martínez and J. Saurina (2001), 'Credit Growth, Problem Loans and Credit Risk Provisioning in Spain', *BIS Papers*, 1: 310–30.

Ferranti D., G. Perry, S. Indermit and L. Servén (2000), 'Securing our Future in Global Economy', World Bank – Latin American and Caribbean Studies.

Ffrench-Davis, R. (2003), *Economic Reforms in Chile*, Ann Arbor: University of Michigan Press.

Ffrench-Davis, R. (2001), *Financial Crises in 'Successful' Emerging Economies*, Washington DC: Brookings Institution Press and ECLAC.

Fidrmuc, J. (2000), 'Economics of Voting in Post-communist Countries', *Electoral Studies*, 19 (2): 199–217.

Filatochev, I. (1997), 'Privatisation and Corporate Governance in Transitional Economies', *The World Economy*, 20 (4) (July): 497–510.

Frankel, J. (1999), 'No Single Currency Regime is Right for All Countries or at All Times', NBER Working Paper, 7338.

Frenkel, R. (1979), 'Decisiones de precio en alta inflación', *Revista Desarrollo Económico*, 19 (75).

Frenkel, R. (2005), 'External Debt, Growth and Sustainability', in J. A. Ocampo (ed.), *Beyond Reforms: Structural Dynamics and Macroeconomic Vulnerability*, Palo Alto: Stanford University Press and ECLAC, pp. 189–209.

Frey, B. S. and A. Stutzer (2000), 'Happiness, Economy and Institutions', *Economic Journal*, 110: 918–38.

Friedman, M. (1957), *A Theory of the Consumption Function*, Princeton, NJ: Princeton University Press.

Fritsche, U. and V. Kuzin (2004), 'Declining Output Volatility in Germany: Impulse, Propagation and the Role of Monetary Policy', University of Missouri-Columbia, http://www.missouri.edu/~econwww/Conferences/PDF/Ulrich%20Fritsche.pdf

Frye, T. (1997), 'Governing the Russian Equities Market', *Post Soviet Affairs*, 13 (4): 366–95.

García, M., P. García and B. Piedrabuena (2005), 'Fiscal and Monetary Policy Rules: the Recent Chilean Experience', Central Bank of Chile Working Papers, 340.

Giambiagi, F. and A. Alem (1999), *Finanças Públicas. Teoria e Prática no Brasil*, Rio de Janeiro: Campus.

Goldfajn, I. and G. Olivares (2001), 'Can Flexible Exchange Rates still "Work" in Financially Open Economies?' G-24 Discussion Paper, No. 8, January.

Goodhart, C., P. Hartmann, D. Llewellyn, L. Rojas-Suarez and S. Weisbrod (1998), *Financial Regulation: Why, How and Where Now?* Bank of England, London and New York: Routledge.

Griffith-Jones, S. and A.T. Fuzzo de Lima (2006), 'Mitigating the Risks of Investing in Developing Countries; Currency-related Guarantee Instruments for Infrastructure', in K. Inge and P. Conceicao (eds), *The New Public Finance: Responding to Global Challenges*, New York: Oxford University Press.

Griffith-Jones, S. and J.A. Ocampo (2003), 'What Progress on International Financial Reform? Why so Limited?' Stockholm: Expert Group on Development Issues (EGDI).

Griffith-Jones, S. and K. Sharma (2006), 'GDP-Indexed Bonds: Making it Happen', DESA Working Paper, No. 21

Griffith-Jones, S. and S. Spratt (2001), 'Will the Proposed New Basel Capital Accord Have a Net Negative Effect on Developing Countries?' mimeo, Institute of Development Studies, University of Sussex.

Griffith-Jones, S., M.F. Montes and A. Nasution (2001), *Short-term Capital Flows and Economic Crises,* New York: Oxford University Press.

Griffith-Jones, S., M.A. Segoviano and S. Spratt (2004), 'CPE and Developing Countries: the Potential Impact of Diversification Effects on International Lending Patterns and Pro-cyclicality', http://www.ids.ac.uk/ids/global.

Group of 24 (2005), 'Communiqué', September 23.

Guo, R., K. Yang, R. Zhao and E-G. Hwang (2004), 'How to Reform a Centrally Planned Economy: the Case of China', paper for the GDN project 'Understanding Reforms'.

Hausmann, R. and A. Velasco (2004), 'The Causes of Financial Crises: Moral Failure versus Market Failure', December, http://ksghome.harvard.edu.

Hausmann, R. and U. Panizza (2003), 'On the Determinants of Original Sin: an Empirical Investigation', *Journal of International Money and Finance,* 22: 957–90.

Hausmann, R., U. Panizza and E. Stein (2000), 'Why do Countries Float the Way They Float?', Inter-American Development Bank Working Paper, No. 418.

Hayashi, F. (1997), 'The Main Bank System and Corporate Investment: an Empirical Reassessment', NBER Working Paper, 6172, Cambridge, MA.

Held, G. and L.F. Jiménez (1999), 'Liberalización financiera, Crisis y Reforma del Sistema Bancario Chileno: 1974–1999', Serie Financiamiento del Desarrollo, CEPAL.

Helmke, G. and S. Levitsky (2003), 'Informal Institutions and Comparative Politics: a Research Agenda', Working Paper, 307, Notre Dame: Helen Kellog Institute for International Studies.

Herrera, L.O. and R.O. Valdés (2004), 'Dedollarization, Indexation and Nominalization: the Chilean Experience', Central Bank of Chile Working Paper, 261.

Hirschman, A.O. (1963), *Journeys Towards Progress,* New York: The Twentieth Century Fund.

Hirschman, A.O. (1975), 'Policy Making and Policy Analysis in Latin America: a Return Journey', *Policy Sciences,* 6 (4): 385–402.

Hnatkovska, V. and N. Loayza (2004), 'Volatility and Growth', in J. Aizenman and B. Pinto (eds), *Managing Volatility and Crises: a Practitioner's Guide,* http://www1.worldbank.org/economcipolicy/documents/mv/pgchapter01.pdf.

Hodrick, R.J. and E.C. Prescott (1997), 'Postwar US Business Cycles: an Empirical Investigation', *Journal of Money, Credit, and Banking,* 29: 1–16, http://www1.worldbank.org/economicpolicy/mv/mvcguide.html.

Hubbard, G. (1998), 'Capital-market Imperfections and Investment', *Journal of Economic Literature,* 36 (1): 193–225.

Hutchison, M. and I. Neuberger (2002), 'How Bad Are Twins? Output Costs of Currency and Banking Crises', Pacific Basin Working Papers Series, No. PB02–02, Federal Reserve Board of San Francisco.

IBGE/Andima (1997), *Sistema Financeiro. Uma Análise a Partir das Contas Nacionais, 1990–1995,* Rio de Janeiro: IBGE e Andima.

Ikhide, S.I. and A.A. Alawode (1995), 'Financial Sector Reform, Macroeconomic Instability and the Order of Economic Liberalization: Evidence from Nigeria', AERC Research Paper, 112, Nairobi, Kenya.

Imbs, J. (2002), 'Volatility, Growth and Aggregation', London Business School and CEPR.

Inter-American Development Bank (2004), *Economic and Social Progress Report: Unlocking Credit in Latin America: The Quest for Deep and Stable Bank Lending,* Washington, DC.

International Monetary Fund (1998), *World Economic Outlook, 1998 – Financial Crises: Characteristics and Indicators of Vulnerability,* Washington, DC, May.

International Monetary Fund (2000), *Report of the Acting Managing Director to the International Monetary and Financial Committee on Progress in Reforming the IMF and*

Strengthening the Architecture of the International Financial System, Washington DC: International Monetary Fund.

International Monetary Fund (2004a), 'Assessing Sustainability', document presented to the Executive Board, May 28.

International Monetary Fund (2004b), 'Nigeria: Selected Issues and Statistical Appendix', IMF Country Reports, No. 04/242, August.

International Monetary Fund (2005a), 'The Managing Director's Report on the Fund's Medium-term Strategy', Document Presented to the International Monetary and Financial Committee, Washington, DC, September 15.

International Monetary Fund (2005b), 'Contingent Financing', IMF Survey, April.

International Monetary Fund (2005c), 'Evaluation of PRGF', document presented to the Executive Board, July

International Monetary Fund (2005d), 'Asia-Pacific Regional Outlook', September, Asia and Pacific Department, Washington DC: International Monetary Fund.

International Monetary Fund (2006), 'Consideration of a New Liquidity Instrument for Market Access Countries' Washington, DC, 3 August.

Ito, T. (2003), 'Construction of Infrastructure for the Development of Regional Bond Market,' in C. Ahn, T. Ito, M. Kawai and Y. C. Park (eds), *Financial Development and Integration in East Asia*, Korea Institute for International Economic Policy.

Ito, T. (2004), 'Promoting Asian Basket Currency Bonds', in T. Ito and Y.C. Park (eds), *Developing Asian Bond Markets*, Asia Pacific Press: The Australian National University.

Ito, T. and Y.C. Park (2004), *Developing Asian Bond Markets*, Asia Pacific Press: The Australian National University.

Ito, T., E. Ogawa and Y. Sasaki (1999), 'Establishment of the East Asian Fund', Chapter 3 in *Stabilization of Currencies and Financial Systems in East Asia and International Financial Cooperation*, Institute for International Monetary Affairs.

Jadresic, E. and J. Selaive (2005), 'Is the FX Derivatives Market Effective and Efficient in Reducing Currency Risk?', Central Bank of Chile Working Paper, 325.

Jeanneau, S. and C.E. Tovar (2006), 'Domestic Bond Markets in Latin America: Achievements and Challenges', *BIS Quarterly Review*, June: 51–64.

Jones, S. and A. Müller (1992a), 'External Trade and the Balance of Payments since 1961', *The South African Economy, 1910–90*, London: Macmillan, pp. 341–57.

Jones, S. and A. Müller (1992b), 'The Diversification of Mining since 1961', *The South African Economy, 1910–90*, London: Macmillan, pp. 257–77.

Jorion, P. (1997), *Value at Risk: the New Benchmark for Controlling Market Risk*, Chicago: Irwin.

Kahn, B. (1991), 'The Crisis and South Africa's Balance of Payments', in Stephen Gelb (ed.), *South Africa's Economic Crisis*, Cape Town: David Philip, pp. 59–87.

Kaminsky, G.L. and C.M. Reinhart (1999), 'The Twin Crises: The Causes of Banking and Balance-of-Payments Problems', *American Economic Review*, 89(3): 473–500.

Kaminsky, G.L., C.M. Reinhart and C.A. Végh (2004), 'When it Rains, it Pours: Pro-cyclical Capital Flows and Macroeconomic Policies', NBER Working Paper, No. 10780, September.

Kandel, E. and E. Lazear (1992), 'Peer Pressure and Partnerships', *Journal of Political Economy*, 100: 801–17.

Kaufmann, D., A. Kraay and M. Mastruzzi (2005), *Governance Matters IV: Governance Indicators for 1996–2004*, Washington DC: World Bank.

Kelkar, V.L., P.K. Chaudhry and Ma. Vanduzer-Snow (2005), 'Time for change at the IMF', *Finance & Development*, 42 (1) (March): 46–8.

Kimbal, R. (2000), 'Failures in Risk Management', *New England Economic Review*, January/February: 3–12.

Kingdon, J.W. (1984), *Agendas, Alternatives, and Public Policies*, Boston: Little, Brown.

Knight, F. (1921), *Risk, Uncertainty and Profit*, Boston: Houghton and Mifflin.

Kosacoff, B. (2005), 'El desarrollo económico argentino: Una perspectiva desde los sectores productivos', Corrientes, December (presentation, www.deyccorrientes.gov.ar/PresCorrientes.ppt).

Kose, M.A., E.S. Prasad and E.M. Terrores (2003), 'Financial Integration and Macroeconomic Volatility', IMF Working Paper, 50, Washington DC.

Kose, M., E.S. Prasad and E.M. Terrones (2006), 'How Do Trade and Financial Integration Affect the Relationship between Growth and Volatility?', *Journal of International Economics*, 69(1): 176–202.

Kouparitsas, M.A. (2002), 'Understanding US Regional Cyclical Comovement: How Important are Spillovers and Common Shocks?', *Economic Perspectives*, Fourth Quarter, Federal Reserve Bank of Chicago, Chicago.

Krueger, A. (2003), 'Detecting and Preventing Financial Crises – Recent IMF Approaches', speech at the Bretton Woods Committee Annual Meeting, June 12, http://www.imf.org/external/np/speeches/2003/061203.htm.

Krugman, P. (1995), 'Growing World Trade: Causes and Consequences', *Brooking Papers on Economic Activity*, 1: 327–77.

Kwan, Simon H. (2001), 'Impact of Deposit Rate Deregulation in Hong Kong on the Market Value of Commercial Banks', Working Papers in Applied Economic Theory 2001–11, Federal Reserve Bank of San Francisco.

Latin American Shadow Financial Regulatory Committee (2001), *The New Basel Capital Accord and Financial Stability in Latin America*, Statement No. 2, Caracas, April 2001.

Leijonhufvud, A. (2003), 'Macroeconomic Crises and the Social Order', mimeo, University of Trento.

Levine, R. (2005), 'Law, Endowments and Property Rights', *Journal of Economic Perspectives*, 19 (3): 61–88.

Levy, D. and H. Dezhbakhsh (2003), 'International Evidence on Output Fluctuation and Shock Persistence', *Journal of Monetary Economics*, 50: 1531–53.

Liew, L.H. (1997), *The Chinese Economy in Transition: From Plan to Market*, Cheltenham, UK and Brookfield, US: Edward Elgar.

Liew, L.H. and H. Wu (2007 forthcoming), *The Making of China's Exchange Rate Policy*, Cheltenham, UK and Northampton, MA, USA: Edward Elgar.

Liew, L.H., L. Bruszt and L. He (2005), 'Causes, National Costs and Timing of Reforms', in J.M. Fanelli and G. McMahon (eds), *Understanding Market Reforms Vol. 1: Philosophy, Politics and Stakeholders*, Basingstoke and New York: Palgrave Macmillan.

Lindblom, C.E. (1959), 'The Science of "Muddling Through"', *Public Administration Review*, 19: 79–88.

Lindblom, C.E. and E.J. Woodhouse (1993), *The Policy-making Process*, Upper Saddle River, NJ: Prentice Hall.

Lou, J. (1997), 'Macroeconomic Reform in China: Laying the Foundation for a Socialist Market Economy', World Bank Discussion Paper, No. 374, Washington: The World Bank.

Lucas, R. (1990), 'Why Doesn't Capital Flow from Rich to Poor Countries,' *American Economic Review*, 80: 92–6.

Ma, G. (2006), 'Who Pays China's Bank Restructuring Bill?', CEPII Working Paper, No. 2006–04.

Machinea, J.M. and G. Rozenwurcel (2005), 'Macroeconomic Coordination in Latin America: Does it Have a Future?' in J.A. Ocampo (ed.), *Regional Financial Cooperation*, Washington, DC: Brookings Institution Press and ECLAC.

MacKuen, M.B., R.S. Erikson and J.A. Stimson (1992), 'Peasants or Bankers? The American Electorate and the US Economy', *American Political Science Review*, 86(3): 597–611.

Mackuen, M.B., R.S. Erikson and J.A. Stimson (2002), *The Macro Polity*, Cambridge: Cambridge University Press.

Maddison, A. (1998), *Chinese Economic Performance in the Long Run*, Paris: OECD.

Maddison, A. (2001), *The World Economy: a Millennial Perspective*, Paris: OECD.

Maddison, A. (2003), *The World Economy: Historical Statistics*, Paris: OECD.

Magendzo, I.I. and D. Titelman (2006), 'Domestic Financial Architecture, Macro Volatility and Institutions: Chile, From Financial Deepening to Financial Development', paper prepared for the CEDES-IDRC project 'International Financial Architecture, Macro Volatility, and Institutions: the Developing World Experience'.

Manzano, G. (2001), 'Is There Any Value-added in the ASEAN Surveillance Process?', *ASEAN Economic Bulletin*, 18: 94–102.

Marcel, M., M. Tokman, R. Valdés and P. Benavides (2001), 'Balance Estructural del Gobierno Central: Metodología y Estimaciones para Chile: 1987–2000', Estudios de Finanzas Públicas, Dirección de Presupuestos, Ministerio de Hacienda.

Marfán, M. (1998), 'El Financiamiento Fiscal en los Años 90', in R. Cortázar and J. Vial (eds), *Construyendo Opciones, Propuestas Económicas y Sociales para el Cambio de Siglo*, Santiago: CIEPLAN-Dolmen Ediciones.

Marfán, M. (2005), 'Fiscal Policy, Efficacy and Private Deficits: a Macroeconomic Approach', in J.A. Ocampo (ed.), *Beyond Reforms: Structural Dynamics and Macroeconomic Vulnerability*, Palo Alto: Stanford University Press and ECLAC, pp. 161–88.

McConnell, M. and G. Perez-Quiros (2000), 'Output Fluctuations in the United States: What Has Changed since the 1980s?', *American Economic Review*, 90(5): 1464–76.

Medeiros, E.S. and M. Taylor Fravel (2003), 'China's New Diplomacy', *Foreign Affairs*, 82(6): 22–35.

Meier, G.M. (1990), 'Trade Policy, Development, and the New Political Economy', in R. Jones and A.O. Krueger (eds), *The Political Economy of International Trade: Essays in Honor of Robert E. Baldwin*, Oxford: Basil Blackwell.

Meller, P. (1991), 'Adjustment and Social Costs in Chile during the 1980s', *World Development*, 19(11): 1545–61.

Mendonça de Barros, J.R., M. Baer, T.M. Fernandez Dias da Silva and M.A.M. Macedo (2002), *Negociações internacionais em serviços financeiros*, São Paulo: MB Associados.

Mendoza, E. (2001), 'Credit, Prices and Crashes: Business Cycles with a Sudden Stop', NBER Working Paper, No. 8338.

Merton, R.C. and Z. Bodie (2004), 'The Design of Financial Systems: Towards a Synthesis of Function and Structure', NBER Working Paper, 10620.

Ministry of Finance, Secretariat of Economic Policy (1996), *A Reestruturação do Sistema Financeiro no Brasil*, www.fazenda.gov.br/spe/artigos/1996/art0701c.htm.

Minsky, H.P. (1982), *Can 'It' Happen Again? Essays on Instability and Finance*. Armonk, NY: M.E. Sharpe.

Mistry, P.S. (1999), 'Coping with Financial Crises: Are Regional Arrangements the Missing Link?' *International Monetary and Financial Issues for the 1990s*, Vol. 10, Geneva: United Nations Conference on Trade and Development (UNCTAD).

Mobarak, A.M. (2005), 'Democracy, Volatility and Development', *Review of Economics and Statistics*, 87 (2): 348–61.

Modigliani, F. and R. Brumberg (1954), 'Utility Analysis and the Consumption Function: an Interpretation of Cross-section Data', in K.K. Kurihara (ed.), *Post Keynesian Economics*, New Brunswick, NJ: Rutgers University Press.

Montes, M. and V. Popov (1999), 'The Asian Crisis Turns Global', Institute of Southeast Asian Studies, Singapore.

Mosley, P. (1976), 'Towards a "Satisficing" Theory of Economic Policy', *Economic Journal*, 86: 59–72.

Mosley, P. (1984), *The Making of Economic Policy*, Basingstoke: Macmillan.

Murase, T. (2004), 'The East Asian Monetary Zone and the Roles of Japan, China and Korea', mimeo, Kyoto University.

Nannestad, P. and M. Paldam (1994), 'The VP-function. A Survey of the Literature on Vote and Popularity Functions after 25 Years', *Public Choice*, 79: 213–45.

NBS (National Bureau of Statistics) (various issues), *Statistical Yearbook of China*, Beijing: Zhongguo Tongji Chubanshe.

Nelson, J.M. (1990), 'Introduction: the Politics of Economic Adjustment in Developing Nations', in J.M. Nelson (ed.), *Economic Crisis and Policy Choice*, Princeton, NJ: Princeton University Press.

Norpoth, H. (1996), 'Presidents and the Prospective Voter', *Journal of Politics*, 58(3): 776–92.

North, D.C. (1995), 'Institutions', *Journal of Economic Perspectives*, 5: 97–112.

Obstfeld, M. (2004), 'Globalization, Macroeconomic Performance, and the Exchange Rates of Emerging Economies', NBER Working Paper, 10849.

Obstfeld, M. and K. Rogoff (1996), *Foundations of International Macroeconomics,* Cambridge, Massachusetts: MIT Press.

Obstfeld, M. and K. Rogoff (2005), 'Global Exchange Rate Adjustments and Global Current Account Balances', *Brookings Papers on Economic Activity*, 1: 67–123.

Obstfeld, M. and A.M. Taylor (2004), *Global Capital Markets: Integration, Crisis and Growth*, Cambridge: Cambridge University Press.

Ocampo, J.A. (2003), 'Capital Account and Counter-cyclical Prudential Regulations in Developing Countries', in R. Ffrench-Davis and S. Griffith-Jones (eds), *From Capital Surges to Drought: Seeking Stability for Emerging Markets*, Basingstoke: Palgrave Macmillan.

Ocampo, J.A. (2005), 'A Broad View of Macroeconomic Stability', DESA Working Paper, No. 1, October.

Ocampo, J.A. (2006), 'Regional Financial Cooperation: Experiences and Challenges', in J.A. Ocampo (ed.), *Regional Financial Cooperation*, Washington, DC: Brookings Institution Press and ECLAC.

Ocampo, J.A. and J. Martin (2003), *Globalization and Development*, Palo Alto: Stanford University Press and ECLAC.

Ocampo, J.A., J. Kregel and S. Griffith-Jones (2006), *International Finance and Development*, New York: United Nations.

O'Donnell, G. (1994), 'Delegative Democracy', *Journal of Democracy*, 5(1): 55–69.

O'Donnell, G. (1995), 'Do Economists Know Best?', *Journal of Democracy*, 6(1): 23–8.

Odusola, A.F. (2002), 'Banking Crisis and Macroeconomic Performance in Nigeria', unpublished PhD thesis submitted to the Department of Economics, University of Ibadan, Ibadan.

OECD (2002), *China in the World Economy: the Domestic Policy Challenges*, Paris: OECD.

Olivei, G.P. (2000), 'Consumption Risk-sharing across G-7 Countries', *New England Economic Review*, March/April 2000: 3–14.

Pacek, A. and B. Radcliff (1995), 'The Political Economy of Competitive Elections in the Developing World', *American Journal of Political Science*, 39(3): 745–59.

Padayachee, V. (1991), 'The Politics of South Africa's International Financial Relations, 1970–1990', in Stephen Gelb (ed.), *South Africa's Economic Crisis*, Cape Town: David Philip, pp. 88–109.

Park, Y.C. (2006), 'Regional Financial Integration in East Asia: Challenges and Prospects', in J.A. Ocampo (ed.), *Regional Financial Cooperation*, Washington, DC: Brookings Institution Press and ECLAC.

Park, Y.C. and D. Park (2004), 'Creating Regional Bond Markets in East Asia', in T. Ito and Y.C. Park (eds), *Developing Asian Bond Markets*, The Australian National University: Asia Pacific Press.

Park, Y.C. and Y. Wang (2002), 'What Kind of International Financial Architecture for an Integrated World Economy?' *Asian Economic Papers*, 1 (1): 91–128.

Park, Y.C. and Y. Wang (2005), 'The Chiang Mai Initiative and Beyond', *The World Economy*, 28(1): 91–101.

Pastore, A. and M.C. Pinotti (2000), 'One Year of Inflation Targeting in Brazil: What Have We Learned about the Channels of Monetary Transmission? Um ano de metas de inflação' (Seminário), Rio de Janeiro: Banco Central do Brasil.

Peng, Z. (2003), *The Study of Advanced Problems of China's Finance* [zhongguo jinrong qianxian wenti yanjiu 2003], Beijing: China Finance Publishing House.

Peresetsky, A., A. Karminsky and S. Golovan (2004), 'Probability of Default Models of Russian Banks', BOFIT Discussion Paper, 21/2004, http://www.bof.fi/bofit/fin/6dp/04abs/pdf/dp2104.pdf.

Persaud, A. (2000), *Sending the Herd off the Cliff Edge: the Disturbing Interaction between Herding and Market-sensitive Risk Management Practices*, London: State Street Bank.

Pholphirul, P. (2007) 'Trade Creation and Trade Diversion of ASEAN and ASEAN+China: a Thai Perspective', *NIDA Economic Review*, 2: 97–130.

Pires de Souza, F.E. and C. Hoff (2003), 'O regime cambial brasileiro: flutuação genuína ou medo da flutuação?' *Anais do XXXI Encontro da Anpec*, Porto Seguro, BA, December 9–12.

Pires de Souza, F.E., G. Borges da Silveira and F.J. Cardim de Carvalho (2006), Country Study of Brazil for the IDRC/CEDES Project on 'International Financial Architecture, Macro Volatility and Institutions: the Developing Country Experience'.

Pistor, K. (2002), 'The Standardization of Law and its Effect on Developing Economies', *American Journal of Comparative Law*, 50(1): 97–130.

Pistor, K., M. Raiser and S. Gelfer (2000), 'Law and Finance in Transition Economies', *Economics of Transition*, 8(2): 325–68.

Popov, V. (1999), 'The Financial System in Russia as Compared to Other Transition Economies: the Anglo-American versus the German-Japanese Model', *Comparative Economic Studies*, 41(1): 1–42, http://www.cbs.dk/centres/cees/network/pdf/Popov.pdf.

Popov, V. (2000), 'Shock Therapy versus Gradualism: the End of the Debate (Explaining the Magnitude of the Transformational Recession)', *Comparative Economic Studies*, 42 (1) (Spring): 1–57.

Popov, V. (2003a), 'Currency Crises in Russia and other Transition Economies', in G.R.D. Underhill and X. Zhang (eds), *International Financial Governance under Stress. Global Structures versus National Imperatives*, Cambridge and New York: Cambridge University Press.

Popov, V. (2003b), 'Does Russia Need to Strengthen the Ruble? Accumulation of Foreign Exchange Reserves and Economic Growth', PONARS Policy Memo, No. 306, November, http://www.csis.org/ruseura/ponars/policymemos/pm_0306.pdf.

Popov, V. (2005), 'The Exchange Rate in a Resource-based Economy: the Case of Russia', PONARS Policy Memo, No. 386. December 2005.

Popov, V. and A. Peresetsky (2006), 'Country Study: Russia', paper prepared for the CEDES-IDRC project 'International Financial Architecture, Macro Volatility, and Institutions: the Developing World Experience'.

Posner, D. and D. Simon (2002), 'Economic Conditions and Incumbent Support in Africa's New Democracies: Evidence from Zambia', *Comparative Political Studies*, 35: 313–36.

Prasad, E. and S.-J. Wei (2005), 'The Chinese Approach to Capital Inflows: Patterns and Possible Explanations', NBER Working Paper, 11306.

Prasad, E., T. Rumbaugh and Q. Wang (2005), 'Putting the Cart before the Horse? Capital Account Liberalization and Exchange Rate Flexibility in China', IMF Policy Discussion Paper, PDP/05/1, International Monetary Fund.

Przeworski, A. (1991), *Democracy and the Market. Political and Economic Reforms in Eastern Europe and Latin America*, Cambridge: Cambridge University Press.

Puga, F.P. (1999), 'Sistema Financeiro Brasileiro: Reestruturação Recente, Comparações Internacionais e Vulnerabilidade à Crise Cambial', in F. Giambiagi and M. Moreira (eds), *A Economia Brasileira nos Anos 90*, M.M., BNDES.

Qian, Y. and G. Roland (1998), 'Federalism and the Soft Budget Constraint', *American Economic Review*, 88(5): 1143–62.

Rajan, R.G. and L. Zingales (1998), 'Financial Dependence and Growth', *American Economic Review*, 88: 559–87

Rajan, R.G. and L. Zingales (2003), *Saving Capitalism from the Capitalists*, New York: Crown Business.

Ramey, G. and V. Ramey (1995), 'Cross-country Evidence on the Link between Volatility and Growth', *American Economic Review*, 85: 1138–51.

Rana, P.B. (2005), 'Economic Integration in East Asia: Trends, Prospects, and a Possible Roadmap', paper presented at the third high-level conference on Building a New Asia: Towards an Asian Economic Community, Taiyuan, China, September 15–16.

Razin, A. and A. Rose (1994), 'Business Cycle Volatility and Openness: an Exploratory Analysis', in L. Leiderman and A. Razin (eds), *Capital Mobility: the Impact on Consumption, Investment and Growth*, Cambridge and New York: Cambridge University Press.

Reinhart, C.M. (2000), 'The Mirage of Floating Exchange Rates', *American Economic Review*, May: 65–70.

Reinhart, C.M., K.S. Rogoff and M.A. Savastano (2003), 'Debt Intolerance', *Brookings Papers on Economic Activity*, 1: 1–74.

Reisen, H. (2001), 'Will Basel II Contribute to Convergence in International Capital Flows?', in *Osterreichische Nationalbank, Proceedings 29*, Volkswirtschaftliche Tagung 2001 Vienna: Austrian National Bank, pp. 49–69.

Remmer, K.L. (1991), 'The Political Impact of Economic Crises in Latin America', *American Political Science Review*, 85: 777–800.

Remmer, K.L. (1993), 'The Political Economy of Elections in Latin America, 1980–1991', *American Political Science Review*, 87(2): 393–407.

Renaud, B. (2000), 'How Real Estate Contributed to Thailand's Financial Crisis', in K. Mera and B. Renaud (eds), *Asia's Financial Crisis and the Role of Real Estate*, Armonk, NY: M.E. Sharpe.

Rius, A. and N. van de Walle (2005), 'Political Institutions and Economic Policy Reform', in J.M. Fanelli and G. McMahon (eds), *Understanding Market Reforms, Vol I*, Basingstoke: Palgrave Macmillan.

Rodrik, D. (1996), 'Understanding Economic Policy Reform', *Journal of Economic Literature*, 34 (March): 9–41.

Rodrik, D. (1999), 'Governing the Global Economy: Does One Architectural Style Fit All?', paper prepared for the Brookings Institution Trade Policy Forum Conference, Governing in a Global Economy, 15–16 April.

Rodrik, D. and A. Velasco (2000), 'Short-term Capital Flows', in *Proceedings of the Annual World Bank Conference on Development Economics 1999*, Washington DC: World Bank, pp. 59–90.

Rojas-Suarez, L. (2001), 'Rating Banks in Emerging Markets: What Credit Rating Agencies Should Learn from Financial Indicators', Institute for International Economics, Working Paper WP01–6, May.

Rojas-Suarez, L. (2004), 'International Standards for Strengthening Financial Systems: Can Regional Development Banks Address Developing Countries Concerns?', in N. Birdsall and L. Rojas-Suarez (eds), *Financing Development: the Power of Regionalism*, Washington, DC: Center for Global Development.

Rojas-Suarez, L. (2005), 'Financial Regulations in Developing Countries: Can They Effectively Limit the Impact of Capital Account Volatility?' CGD Working Paper 59, Washington, DC, May.

Rojas-Suarez, L. and S. Weisbrod (1997), 'Toward an Effective Financial Regulatory and Supervisory Framework in Latin America: Dealing with the Transition', in L. Rojas Suarez (ed.), *Safe and Sound Financial Systems – What Works for Latin America*, Washington, DC: IADB.

Sabatier, P.A. and H.C. Jenkins-Smith (1999), 'The Advocacy Coalition Framework: an Assessment', in P.A. Sabatier (ed.), *Theories of the Policy Process*, Boulder, Colorado: Westview Press.

Sakakibara, E. (2003), 'Asian Cooperation and the End of Pax Americana', in J.J. Teunissen and M. Teunissen (eds), *Financial Stability and Growth in Emerging Economies: the Role of the Financial Sector*, The Hague: FONDAD, pp. 227–40.

Sanusi, J.O. (2004), 'Keynote Address: Nigeria's Financial Sector Stability: Issues and Challenges', *CBN Bulletin*, 28(1): 3–5.

Schneider, B. (2003), *The Road to International Financial Stability: Are Key Financial Standards the Answer?*, Basingstoke: Palgrave Macmillan in association with the Overseas Development Institute.

Schneider, B. and S. Silva (2002), 'Conference Report on International Standards and Codes: the Developing Country Perspective', Overseas Development Institute, London

Senbet, L.W. (2001), 'Global Financial Crisis: Implications for Africa', *Journal of African Economies*, 10 (1) (February).

Servén, L. (1998), 'Macroeconomic Uncertainty and Private Investment in LDCs: an Empirical Investigation', World Bank Policy Research Working Paper, No. 2035.

Shih, V. (2004), 'Dealing with Non-performing Loans: Political Constraints and Financial Policies in China', *The China Quarterly*, No. 180.

Shiller, R.J. (1981), 'Do Stock Prices Move Too Much to be Justified by Subsequent Changes in Dividends?' *American Economic Review*, 71(3): 421–36.

Shleifer A. and R. Vishny (1995), 'The Limits of Arbitrage', NBER Working Paper 5167.

Simon, H.A. (1952), 'A Behavioral Model of Rational Choice', *Quarterly Journal of Economics*, 69: 99–118.

Simon, H.A. (1976), 'From Substantive to Procedural Rationality', in S. Latsias (ed.), *Method and Appraisal in Economics*, Cambridge: Cambridge University Press.

Simon, H.A. (1987), 'Bounded Rationality', in J. Eatwell, M. Milgate and P. Newman (eds), *The New Palgrave: a Dictionary of Economics*, New York: Stockton Press.

Singh, A. (2003), 'Capital Account Liberalization, Free Long Term Capital Flows, Financial Crises and Economic Development', *Eastern Economic Journal* (Spring): 1–23.

Sirivedhin, T. (1997), 'Financial Reform and the Monetary Transmission Mechanism: Case of Thailand', *Quarterly Bulletin, Bank of Thailand*, 37 (June): 33–54.

Sobodu, O.O. (2000), 'The Determinants of Capital Structure Choice under Banking Reform: an Empirical Investigation', Draft Final Report Submitted to the AERC, Nairobi.

Sosunov, K. and O. Zamulin (2005), 'Monetary Policy in a Resource-based Economy: the Case of Russia', manuscript.

Stallings, B. (1990), 'Politics and Economic Crisis: a Comparative Study of Chile, Peru and Colombia', in J.M. Nelson (ed.), *Economic Crisis and Policy Choice*, Princeton, NJ: Princeton University Press, pp. 113–67.

Stiglitz, J.E. (2000), 'Capital Market Liberalization, Economic Growth, and Instability', *World Development*, 28 (6): 1075–86.

Stiglitz, J.E. (2003), 'Whither Reform? Toward a New Agenda for Latin America', *ECLAC Review*, 80: 7–38.

Stock J. H. and M.W. Watson (2003), 'Has the Business Cycle Changed? Evidence and Explanations', prepared for the Federal Reserve Bank of Kansas City symposium, 'Monetary Policy and Uncertainty'.

Stulz, R. (2000), 'Financial Structure, Corporate Finance, and Economic Growth', *International Review of Finance*, 1: 11–38.

Sturzenegger, F. and M. Tommasi (eds) (1998), *The Political Economy of Reform*, Cambridge, Massachusetts: MIT Press.

Sussangkarn, C. and P. Vichyanond (2006), 'Directions of East Asian Regional Financial Cooperation', presented at Asian Economic Panel held in Seoul, Korea, 20–21 March.

Tao, S. (1998), 'Wuaihui chongxiao zhengce de xiaoying fenxi yu duice sikao' [The efficacy of foreign exchange sterilization and policy implications], *Guoji Maoyi Wenti* [International Trade Journal], 2: 26–32.

Tavares, M.C. (1997), *Da Substitutição de Importações ao Capitalismo Financiero*, 6th edn, Rio de Janeiro: Zahar.

Titelman, D. (2006), 'Subregional Financial Cooperation: the Experiences of Latin America and the Caribbean', in J.A. Ocampo (ed.), *Regional Financial Cooperation*, Washington, DC: Brookings Institution Press and ECLAC.

Tommasi, M. (2002), 'Crisis, Political Institutions and Policy Reform: It is not the Policy, it is the Polity, Stupid', Buenos Aires, Argentina, Universidad de San Andrés and Center of Studies for Institutional Development, paper prepared for the Annual World Bank Conference on Development Economics, June, http://wbln0018.worldbank.org/eurvp/web.nsf/Pages/Paper+by+Mariano+Tommasi/$File/MARIANO+TOMMASI.PDF.

Tommasi, M. and A. Forteza (2006), 'On the Political Economy of Market Reform in Latin America', in J.M. Fanelli and G. McMahon (eds), *Understanding Market Reform: Motivation, Implementation, and Sustainability*, Basingstoke and New York: Palgrave Macmillan pp. 193–228.

Ueda, K. (1998), 'The East Asian Economic Crisis: a Japanese Perspective', *International Finance*, 1(2): 327–38.

United Nations (1999), *Towards a New International Financial Architecture*, Santiago: ECLAC.

United Nations (2006), *World Economic and Social Survey 2006: Diverging Growth and Development*, New York: United Nations.

UNDP (2004), *MDGs report 2004 Nigeria*, Abuja: UNDP.

Valdés-Prieto, S. and M. Soto (1998), 'The Effectiveness of Capital Controls: Theory and Evidence from Chile', *Empirica*, 25(2): 133–64.

Vdovichenko, A. and V. Voronina (2004), 'Monetary Policy Rules and their Applications in Russia', Working Paper, 04/09, EERC.

Velasco, A. (1991), 'Liberalization, Crisis, Intervention: the Chilean Financial System, 1975–85', in T. Balino and V. Sundarajan (eds), *Banking Crises*, Washington, DC: International Monetary Fund.

Vichyanond, P. and P. Pholphirul (2006), 'International Financial Architecture, Macroeconomic Volatility, and Institutions: Perspective on the Thai Experience', paper prepared for the CEDES-IDRC project 'International Financial Architecture, Macro Volatility and Institutions: the Developing World Experience'.

Villarreal, A. (1999), 'Public Opinion of the Economy and the President among Mexico City Residents: the Salinas Sexenio', *Latin American Research Review*, 34(2): 132–51.

Wang, Y. and W.T. Woo (2004), 'A Timely Information Exchange Mechanism, an Effective Surveillance System, and an Improved Financial Architecture for East Asia', Chapter 11 in *Monetary and Financial Integration in East Asia: the Way Ahead*, Vol. 2, Basingstoke: Palgrave Macmillan and the Asian Development Bank.

Warr, P. (1993), 'The Thai Economy', in *Thai Economy in Transition*, Cambridge: Cambridge University Press.

West, K. and W. Newey (1987), 'A Simple Positive Semi-definite Heteroskedasticity and Autocorrelation-consistent Covariance Matrix', *Econometrica*, 55(3): 703–8.

White, W. (2006), 'Procyclicality in the Financial System; Do We Need a New Macrofinancial Stabilization Framework?', BIS Working Paper, 193, June.

Williamson, J. (2005), 'The Economics of Governance', *American Economic Review*, 95(1): 1–18.

Wolf, H. (2004a), 'Volatility: Definitions and Consequences', in J. Aizenman and B. Pinto (eds), *Managing Volatility and Crisis: a Practitioner's Guide*, New York: Cambridge University Press; World Bank, http://www1.worldbank.org/economicpolicy/mv/mvcguide.html.

Wolf, H. (2004b), 'Accounting for Consumption Volatility Differences', *IMF Staff Papers*, 51 (Special Issue), http://www.imf.org/external/pubs/ft/staffp/2003/00–00/w.pdf.

World Bank (1993), *The East Asian Miracle: Economic Growth and Public Policy*', New York: Oxford University Press.

Wu, H.X. and E.Y.P. Shea (2006), 'Institutions, Domestic Financial Architecture and Macro Volatility in China', presented at the seminar 'International Financial Architecture, Macroeconomic Volatility and Institutions: the Developing World Experience', organized

by CEDES and the Department of the Economic and Social Affairs (DESA) of the United Nations, the UN Headquarters, New York, 17–18 April.
Wu, H.X. (2000), 'Measuring China's GDP level and growth performance: Alternative Estimates and the Implications', *Review of Income and Wealth*, 46 (4): 475–99.
Wu, H.X. (2002), 'How Fast has Chinese Industry Grown? Measuring the Real Output of Chinese Industry', *Review of Income and Wealth*, 48 (2): 179–204.
Wu, J. (2005), *Understanding and Interpreting Chinese Economic Reform*, Ohio: Thomson.
Wyplosz, Ch. (2006), 'Regional Exchange Rate Arrangements: the European Experience', in J.A. Ocampo (ed.), *Regional Financial Cooperation*, Washington, DC: Brookings Institution Press and ECLAC.
Yi, G. and F. Min (1997), 'Renminbi huilü de jueding yinsu ji zoushi fenxi' [The determinants of RMB exchange rate and its trend], *Jinji Yanjiu* [Economic Research Journal], 10: 26–35.
Yi, Q. (2004), *Zhongguo de fei junheng rinrong* [Chinese Disequilibrium Finance], Beijing: Economy & Management Publishing House.
Yu, Q. (1997), 'Economic Fluctuation, Macro Control, and Monetary Policy in the Transitional Chinese Economy', *Journal of Comparative Economics*, 25: 180–95.
Zahler, R. (2005), 'Estabilidad Macroeconómica e Inversiones de los Fondos de Pensiones: El Caso de Chile', in R. Ffrench-Davis (ed.), *Crecimiento Esquivo y volatilidad Financiera*, CEPAL
Zhang, W. (1999), *Qiye lilun yu zhongguo qiye gaige* [Theory of firm and China's enterprise reform], Beijing: Beijing University Press.

Index